Contemporary Readings in
Curriculum

The reader is dedicated to the students we have taught who constantly challenged us as teachers to keep exploring ideas and sharing our knowledge. We also dedicate this reader to those who have taught us, specifically, Dr. O. L. Davis, Jr., Professor Emeritus, The University of Texas at Austin. O. L. made the curriculum field a fascinating scholarly pursuit for both of us, and we are truly grateful to him for his guidance, leadership, and most of all for his continual friendship.

—Barbara Slater Stern, Associate Professor, James Madison University

—Marcella L. Kysilka, Professor Emerita, University of Central Florida

Contemporary Readings in
Curriculum

Barbara Slater Stern
James Madison University

Marcella L. Kysilka
University of Central Florida

Editors

Contemporary

CRS

Readings Series

SAGE Publications

Los Angeles • London • New Delhi • Singapore

For information:

SAGE Publications, Inc.
2455 Teller Road
Thousand Oaks, California 91320
E-mail: order@sagepub.com

SAGE Publications Ltd.
1 Oliver's Yard
55 City Road
London EC1Y 1SP
United Kingdom

SAGE Publications India Pvt. Ltd.
B 1/I 1 Mohan Cooperative Industrial Area
Mathura Road, New Delhi 110 044
India

SAGE Publications Asia-Pacific Pte. Ltd.
33 Pekin Street #02-01
Far East Square
Singapore 048763

Printed in the United States of America

Library of Congress Cataloging-in-Publication Data

Contemporary readings in curriculum / Barbara Slater Stern, Marcella L. Kysilka.
    p. cm.
Includes bibliographical references and index.
ISBN 978-1-4129-4472-4 (pbk.)

  1. Education—Curricula—United States. 2. Curriculum change—United States. 3. Curriculum planning—Social aspects—United States. I. Stern, Barbara Slater, 1949- II. Kysilka, Marcella L.

LB1570.C8135 2008
375.000973—dc22   2007049060

This book is printed on acid-free paper.

08 09 10 11 12 11 10 9 8 7 6 5 4 3 2 1

Acquisitions Editor:	Diane McDaniel
Editorial Assistant:	Lea Mori
Production Editor:	Diane S. Foster
Copy Editor:	Tony Moore
Typesetter:	C&M Digitals (P) Ltd.
Proofreader:	Penny Sippel
Indexer:	John Roy
Marketing Manager:	Nichole M. Angress
Cover Designer:	Candice Harman

CONTENTS

Article Abstracts ix

Topic Guide xvi

Preface xvii
    Acknowledgments xviii

Advisory Board xix

SECTION I: WHERE DO WE BEGIN? 1

    1. Why Education Is So Difficult and Contentious 3
        Kieran Egan

    2. Questionable Assumptions About Schooling 11
        Elliot W. Eisner

SECTION II: WHAT IS CURRICULUM? 21

    3. What Is Really Important in the Curriculum World? 23
        Judith Dziuban and Marcella Kysilka

    4. Curriculum Alignment Revisited 27
        Allan A. Glatthorn

    5. Knowledge Alive 33
        David Perkins

SECTION III: HOW DO WE THINK ABOUT CURRICULUM? 39

    6. The Curriculum-Curriculum: Experiences in Teaching Curriculum 41
        William H. Schubert

    7. Human Agency and the Curriculum 49
        Hanan A. Alexander

8. Adolescent Needs, Curriculum, and the Eight-Year Study 59
Robert V. Bullough, Jr. and Craig Kridel

9. Toward a Renaissance in Curriculum Theory and Development in the USA 69
William G. Wraga and Peter S. Hlebowitsh

10. The Information Age: A Blessing or a Curse? 75
Neil Postman

SECTION IV: HOW CAN CURRICULUM BE ORGANIZED? **81**

11. The Memories of an All-Black Northern Urban School: Good
Memories of Leadership, Teachers, and the Curriculum 83
Adah Ward Randolph

12. Integrating High School and the Community College: Previous
Efforts and Current Possibilities 91
Carrie B. Kisker

13. Building a Plane While Flying It: Early Lessons
From Developing Charter Schools 101
Noelle C. Griffin and Priscilla Wohlstetter

SECTION V: WHAT IS THE STATUS OF THE ACADEMIC CURRICULUM? **113**

14. Learning to Read in Kindergarten: Has Curriculum
Development Bypassed the Controversies? 115
Bruce Joyce, Marilyn Hrycauk, and Emily Calhoun

15. Literacy Education and Reading Programs in the Secondary School:
Status, Problems, and Solutions 123
Freya M. J. Zipperer, M. Thomas Worley, Michelle W. Sisson, and Rhonda W. Said

16. A Deeper Sense of Literacy: Curriculum-Driven Approaches to
Media Literacy in the K–12 Classroom 129
Cynthia L. Scheibe

17. War, Critical Thinking, and Self-Understanding 135
Nel Noddings

18. The Math Wars 143
Alan H. Schoenfeld

19. Chemistry, the Central Science? The History of the
High School Science Sequence 155
Keith Sheppard and Dennis M. Robbins

20. School Days (Hail, Hail Rock 'n' Roll!) 163
Rick Mitchell

SECTION VI: WHAT IS THE EXTRA- OR CO-CURRICULUM?   169

21. Extracurricular Activities and Adolescent Development   171
    Jacquelynne S. Eccles, Bonnie L. Barber, Margaret Stone, and James Hunt

22. After-School Programs Are Making a Difference   183
    Marianne Russell Kugler

23. The Effect of Interscholastic Sports Participation
    on Academic Achievement of Middle Level School Students   189
    Larry J. Stephens and Laura A. Schaben

24. Hearts and Minds: Military Recruitment and the
    High School Battlefield   195
    William Ayers

SECTION VII: ARE THERE POLITICAL ASPECTS TO CURRICULUM?   201

25. Curriculum Matters   203
    W. James Popham

26. Cashing In on the Classroom   209
    Alex Molnar

27. Politics of Character Education   215
    Robert W. Howard, Marvin W. Berkowitz, and Esther F. Schaeffer

28. No Pot of Gold at the End of the Rainbow   225
    Murry R. Nelson

29. A Contemporary Controversy in American Education: Including
    Intelligent Design in the Science Curriculum   235
    Vicki D. Johnson

**SECTION VIII: HOW DOES THE CURRICULUM
MEET THE NEEDS OF DIVERSE POPULATIONS?**   243

30. The Plains City Story   245
    *Marcela van Olphen, Francisco Rios, William Berube,
    Robin Dexter, and Robert McCarthy*

31. How Global Is the Curriculum?   251
    Andrew F. Smith

32. Designing Appropriate Curriculum for Special
    Education Students in Urban Schools   255
    Timothy E. Morse

33. Urban Public High School Teachers' Beliefs About
    Science Learner Characteristics: Implications for Curriculum   263
    Glenda M. Prime and Rommel J. Miranda

34. Tried and True: The Rural School Curriculum
in the Age of Accountability   273
Aimee Howley

**SECTION IX: WHAT ARE CURRENT HOT-BUTTON
ISSUES IN CURRICULUM?**   **281**

35. Curriculum, Instruction, and Assessment:
Amiable Allies or Phony Friends?   283
W. James Popham

36. It's the Curriculum, Stupid! There's Something Wrong With It   291
Dave F. Brown

37. Teaching for Social Justice, Diversity, and Citizenship in a Global World   299
James A. Banks

38. Beyond Zero Tolerance: Restoring Justice in Secondary Schools   305
Jeanne B. Stinchcomb, Gordon Bazemore, and Nancy Riestenberg

SECTION X: WHERE ARE WE NOW?   **319**

39. It's Time to Start the Slow School Movement   321
Maurice Holt

40. The Lure of Learning in Teaching   329
Daniel P. Liston

References and Endnotes   **341**
Internet Resources   **375**
Index   **381**
About the Editors   **395**

ARTICLE ABSTRACTS

Article 1

Egan, K. (2001). Why education is so difficult and contentious. *Teachers College Record, 103*(6), 923.

This article explains why education is so difficult and contentious by arguing that educational thinking draws on only three fundamental ideas—those of socializing the young, shaping the mind by a disciplined academic curriculum, and facilitating the development of students' potential. The problems we face in education stem from the fact that each of these ideas is significantly flawed and also that each is incompatible in basic ways with the other two.

Article 2

Eisner, E. W. (2003). Questionable assumptions about schooling. *Phi Delta Kappan, 84*(9), 648–657.

Eisner discusses 12 mistaken assumptions about the aims, content, and structure of schooling that have long been taken for granted and argues that examining those issues is a vital first step toward true school reform.

Article 3

Dziuban, J., & Kysilka, M. (1996). What is really important in the curriculum world? *Journal of Curriculum & Supervision, 11*(2) 188–193.

The authors believe that curriculum should not be restricted to considerations only of subject matter or a series of planned activities. The greater relevance is of curriculum as cultural reproduction and curriculum as experience; the irrelevance regards academic debates over curriculum to children in dire need.

Article 4

Glatthorn, Allan A. (1999). Curriculum alignment revisited. *Journal of Curriculum & Supervision, 15*(1), 26–35.

This article focuses on a study that explains how educators can use curriculum alignment constructively and expands the concept. It includes analysis of the written curriculum and the development of mastery units, types of curriculums, and interactions of the curricula.

Article 5

Perkins, D. (2004). Knowledge alive. *Educational Leadership, 62*(1), 14–18.

Perkins offers observation on the knowledge arts, including information on how people create knowledge, an explanation on thinking routines, reflections on teaching for understanding, and the importance of knowledge arts for teachers.

Article 6

Schubert, W. H. (2003). The curriculum-curriculum: Experiences in teaching curriculum. *Curriculum & Teaching Dialogue, 5*(1), 9–21.

The experiences of several educators in teaching curriculum studies in the United States provides background on the development of a perspective on teaching curriculum studies with a focus on recurrent curriculum orientations or ideologies that emerged in each decade of the 20th century. Why this is important to understanding the knowledge base is explored.

Article 7

Alexander, H. A. (2005). Human agency and the curriculum. *Theory and Research in Education, 3*(3), 343–369.

It is generally supposed that a curriculum should engage students with worthwhile knowledge, which requires an understanding of what it means for something to be worthwhile: a substantive conception of the good. In this article Alexander explores the meeting between curriculum and human agency in four seminal curriculum theories and offers a framework to engage the curriculum with this key concept of substantive ethics.

Article 8

Bullough, R. V., Jr., & Kridel, C. (2003). Adolescent needs, curriculum, and the eight-year study. *Journal of Curriculum Studies, 35*(2), 151.

This article explores the concept of needs as a basis for curriculum development through the deliberations of the U.S. educators associated with the Progressive Education Association's Commission on the Secondary School Curriculum of the Eight-Year Study (1933–1941). Noting how divergent views of "needs" influenced American educational thought from the 1930s to the life-adjustment movement of the late 1940s and 1950s, the importance of social philosophy is underscored as a prerequisite for curriculum development. The authors close with criticism of the current standards-based reform movement in U.S. education for the lack of concern with both student needs and social theory.

Article 9

Wraga, W. G., & Hlebowitsh, P. S. (2003). Toward a renaissance in curriculum theory and development in the USA. *Journal of Curriculum Studies, 35*(4), 425–437.

The curriculum field in the United States has existed in a chronic state of disarray, even crisis, for many years. It concludes by suggesting that four issues should be examined in order to establish a vital sense of community among curriculum scholars and to create favorable conditions for a renaissance in the U.S. scholarly field of curriculum theory and development.

Article 10

Postman, N. (2004). The information age: A blessing or a curse? *Harvard International Journal of Press/Politics, 9*(2), 3–10.

This article was excerpted from a talk given at the Shorenstein Center on February 7, 1995. Postman contends that humankind has created a new problem—information overload—and that in doing so people have lost the sense of narrative in their lives, which is what helps them know what to do with information.

Article 11

Randolph, A. W. (2004). The memories of an all-Black northern urban school: Good memories of leadership, teachers, and the curriculum. *Urban Education, 39*(6), 596–620.

A case study examined the history of an all-black de facto segregated school in Columbus, Ohio, before *Brown v. Board*. The findings may help educational scholars in implementing factors important to the success of Black youth.

Article 12

Kisker, C. B. (2006). Integrating high school and the community college: Previous efforts and current possibilities. *Community College Review, 34*(1), 68–86.

This article explores three incarnations of the idea of integrating high school and the community college. The author discusses rationales for integrating high school and the first 2 years of college. The article concludes with a look to the future in terms of integration of high school and college.

Article 13

Griffin, N. C., & Wohlstetter, P. (2001). Building a plane while flying it: Early lessons from developing charter schools. *Teachers College Record, 103*(2), 336.

There has been a rapid increase in past years in both the number of charter schools in the United States and the enthusiasm for the concept among legislators, educators, and the general public. The authors discuss three major categories of issues that charter schools deal with: developing curricular and instructional programs, developing a meaningful accountability system, and developing management/leadership systems.

Article 14

Joyce, B., Hrycauk, M., & Calhoun, E. (2003). Learning to read in kindergarten: Has curriculum development bypassed the controversies? *Phi Delta Kappan, 85*(2), 126–132.

This article reports on a reading curriculum project geared toward kindergarten students. It covers conceptualization of the project, background on the school district, categories of studies on developments in literacy processes, components of the action research inquiry, and interpretation of the outcomes.

Article 15

Zipperer, F. M. J., Worley, M. T., Sisson, M. W., &. Said, R. W. (2002). Literacy education and reading programs in the secondary school: Status, problems, and solutions. *NASSP Bulletin, 86*(9), 3–17.

The status of literacy education and the reading program at the secondary school level is examined. Current problems and possible solutions for those problems are discussed.

Article 16

Scheibe, C. L. (2004). A deeper sense of literacy: Curriculum-driven approaches to media literacy in the K–12 classroom. *American Behavioral Scientist, 48*(1), 60–68.

The writer discusses how media literacy can be used effectively as a pedagogical approach for teaching core content across the K–12 curriculum that meets the needs of both teachers and students by promoting critical thinking, communication, and technology skills. She describes the basic principles and best practices for using a curriculum-driven approach and presents specific examples from social studies, English/language arts, math, science, health, and art, along with methods of assessment employed to address effectiveness in the classroom.

Article 17

Noddings, N. (2004). War, critical thinking, and self-understanding. *Phi Delta Kappan, 85*(7), 489–495.

Can students learn to think critically if they are not asked to engage with critical issues? Fostering critical thinking is frequently stated as a fundamental aim of education, and yet many teachers report that they have been forbidden to discuss such critical issues as current wars, religion, and cultural differences in parenting styles. War is already a major strand in the social studies curriculum, but the discussion is usually confined to political causes, leaders, battles, and the resulting rearrangement of national boundaries. Psychological issues related to war that should concern all citizens, especially the young who might join the military right out of high school, are addressed.

Article 18

Schoenfeld, A. H. (2004). The math wars. *Educational Policy, 18*(1), 253–286.

During the 1990s, the teaching of mathematics became the subject of heated controversies known as the math wars. Traditionalists fear that reform-oriented, "standards-based" curricula are superficial and undermine classical mathematical values; reformers claim that such curricula reflect a deeper, richer view of mathematics than the traditional curriculum. A historical perspective reveals that the underlying issues being contested—Is mathematics for the elite or for the masses? Are there tensions between "excellence" and "equity"? Should mathematics be seen as a democratizing force or as a vehicle for maintaining the status quo?—are more than a century old.

Article 19

Sheppard, K., & Robbins, D. M. (2005). Chemistry, the central science? The history of the high school science sequence. *Journal of Chemical Education, 82*(4), 561–566.

The historical development of the traditional U.S. high school biology/chemistry/physics sequence is detailed from the early 19th century to the present time. The recommendations of several important historical committees are described along with the sequencing practices adopted by the schools to illustrate how chemistry came to be the "central science"—i.e., the science taught in the middle of the high school sequence. It is shown that the present high school science sequence is more a product of historical accident than of educational design.

Article 20

Mitchell , R. (2005–2006). School days (Hail, hail rock 'n' roll!) *Rethinking Schools, 20*(2), 56–59; *20*(3), 234–256.

Mitchell focuses on the integral role music plays in the curriculum in his ninth-grade U.S. history class. While major military and political events serve as natural landmarks in any history syllabus, the true and oft-untold history of our world consists of what societies were doing both during and between these cataclysmic chapters. Curricula integrating musical recordings offer vivid evidence of what was taking place in previous decades and centuries and can bring history alive in ways that books, photos, and even films cannot.

Article 21

Eccles, J. S., Barber, B. L., Stone, M., & Hunt, J. (2003). Extracurricular activities and adolescent development. *Journal of Social Issues, 59*(4), 865–889.

This article summarizes: (a) participation in structured leisure activities to promote positive youth development, (b) the association of extracurricular activity involvement with both educational and risky behavior, and (c) possible mediating mechanisms of these associations. Participants in most extracurricular activities achieved better educational outcomes than non-participants even after controlling for social class, gender, and intellectual aptitude. Participation in service and religious activities predicted lower rates of drinking and drug use. Participation on school sports teams predicted both better educational outcomes and higher rates of drinking.

Article 22

Kugler, M. R. (2001). After-school programs are making a difference. *NASSP Bulletin, 85*(9), 3–11.

The author explores some of the societal issues addressed by after-school programs and describes examples of programs found in secondary schools that have been effective in addressing these issues. Among the examples are those that provide support to academic achievement as well as those that address other areas of learning.

Article 23

Stephens, L. J., & Schaben L. A. (2002). The effect of interscholastic sports participation on academic achievement of middle level school students. *NASSP Bulletin, 86*(3), 34–41.

Eighth graders were divided into two groups: students who had participated in at least one interscholastic sport and were classified as athletes, and students who had not participated in interscholastic sports and were classified as non-athletes. The mean grade point average (GPA) for each group and subgroup was computed and compared by group, subgroup, and sex. As interscholastic sports participation increased, GPAs improved.

Article 24

Ayers, W. (2006). Hearts and minds: Military recruitment and the high school battlefield. *Phi Delta Kappan, 87*(8), 594–599.

The article discusses the controversial issue of recruiting by the U.S. military in high schools. The author states that adolescents are susceptible to recruiters because they are at an age when being part of a group with a mission and a shared spirit is of exaggerated importance. One of the most effective recruiting programs is the Junior Reserve Officers' Training Corps (JROTC), established by an act of Congress in 1916. Today, 40% of JROTC recruits join the military.

Article 25

Popham, W. J. (2004). Curriculum matters. *American School Board Journal, 191*(11), 30–33.

Popham explains that there is a need to develop effective state-approved curricular aims to improve instructional practices in U.S. public schools. The discussion centers on the impact of a state-approved curriculum syllabus on a teacher's instructional practices, the influence of the No Child Left Behind (NCLB) Act of 2002 on the relationship between curriculum and instruction, the measures to address the curriculum crisis, and the importance of deriving a state's NCLB assessment targets based on the existing curricular aims.

Article 26

Molnar, A. (2003). Cashing in on the classroom. *Educational Leadership, 61*(4), 79–84.

This article reports that U.S. schools are turning to private sources for funding owing to budgetary concerns. It discusses the amount of money received by schools every year from business relationships with corporations, the role of the Commercialism in Education Research Unit of the Education Policy Studies at Arizona State University, the categories of school commercialism, and the states whose education interest groups have lobbied against company deals and marketing activities in schools.

Article 27

Howard, R. W., Berkowitz, M. W., & Schaeffer, E. F. (2004). Politics of character education. *Educational Policy, 18*(1), 188–215.

The writers consider the politics of character education in K–12 public schools. They define character and character education and discuss historical issues in the politics of character education. They then address current issues, specifically character education and democratic citizenship, the relationship of families to schools, the relationship of church and state, the politics of federal character education pilot programs, politics and character education research, and the politics of state funding and support of character education.

Article 28

Nelson, M. R. (2001). No pot of gold at the end of the rainbow. *Journal of Curriculum & Supervision, 16*(3), 206–227.

Nelson presents a study that examined the development, implementation, and controversies that arose over the curriculum guide "Children of the Rainbow," published in New York City in 1990. Reasons for the development of the curriculum, content of the curriculum guide, and creation of a Grade 1 guide are reviewed.

Article 29

Johnson, V. D. (2006). A contemporary controversy in American education: Including intelligent design in the science curriculum. *Educational Forum, 70*(3), 222–236.

The battle between creationists and evolutionists has waxed and waned in American culture and education for decades. This conflict is evident in the contemporary debate between the proponents of intelligent design and its opponents. This article illuminates the intelligent design movement by describing major proponents' beliefs, goals, and tactics.

Article 30

Van Olphen, M., Rios, F., Berube, W., Dexter, R., & McCarthy, R. (2006). The Plains City story. *Journal of Cases in Educational Leadership, 6*(9), 23–32.

This case study portrays a contemporary phenomenon that affects many U.S. school districts. The gradual development of the pig farming industry in Plains City generated an increasing demand for workers, resulting in the number of Mexican students enrolled the Plains City school district to increase significantly. The authors present an account of some of the actions taken to promote dialogue and to decrease the tension that was generated as a result of the social changes in the community.

Article 31

Smith, A. F. (2002). How global is the curriculum? *Educational Leadership, 60*(2), 38–41.

There have been four major curriculum shifts in K–12 global education since 1979. These shifts have seen an expansion in foreign language instruction, the promotion of geography teaching, the development of world history as a subject, and the creation of public magnet schools with an international focus. Furthermore, students' understanding of global matters has been strengthened by various extracurricular activities and by technological advances that provide opportunities for direct communication with students and teachers in other countries. Some of the challenges that remain in relation to developing a global curriculum are also discussed.

Article 32

Morse, T. E. (2001). Designing appropriate curriculum for special education students in urban schools. *Education & Urban Society, 34*(1), 4.

Morse discusses the design of an appropriate curriculum for special education students in urban schools in the United States including circumstances of urban special education students, provisions of the Individuals With Disabilities Education Act Amendments of 1997, and challenges faced by special education programs in inner cities.

Article 33

Prime, G. M., & Miranda, R. J. (2006). Urban public high school teachers' beliefs about science learner characteristics: Implications for curriculum. *Urban Education, 41*(5), 506–532.

This article addresses the link between urban high school teachers' beliefs about their students' preparedness to achieve success in science and the teachers' reported curricular responses to those beliefs. The research suggests that teachers view science as a special subject that requires special qualities. Teachers saw their own students as largely lacking in those qualities needed for success in science and reported such modifications to the curriculum as "slowing down," deemphasizing some topics, and reducing the depth of coverage.

Article 34

Howley, A. (2003). Tried and true: The rural school curriculum in the age of accountability. *Educational Forum, 68*(1), 14–23.

The writer discusses the traditional curriculum currently being used in most rural schools. She considers the origins of the rural school curriculum, the present state of the rural school curriculum, the benefits and inadequacies of the traditional rural curriculum, and two progressive alternatives. She then provides suggestions on how to respond to the curriculum needs of rural schools.

Article 35

Popham, W. J. (2004). Curriculum, instruction, and assessment: Amiable allies or phony friends? *Teachers College Record, 106*(3), 417–428.

Specialists in curriculum, instruction, and assessment typically work with colleagues in their own field. It is argued that such isolationism is educationally harmful, especially during today's era of heightened accountability for educators.

Article 36

Brown, D. F. (2006). It's the curriculum, stupid! There's something wrong with it. *Phi Delta Kappan, 87*(10), 777–783.

This article discusses teaching curricula and gives advice for curricular design. The author advises teachers to choose meaningful outcomes by creating a priority list for student needs. The author also examines problems with current curricular design and instills the idea that curricular design belongs to students.

Article 37

Banks, J. A. (2004). Teaching for social justice, diversity, and citizenship in a global world. *Educational Forum, 68*(4), 296–305.

Racial, ethnic, cultural, and language diversity is increasing in nation-states throughout the world owing to worldwide immigration. The deepening ethnic diversity within nation-states and the quest by different groups for cultural recognition and rights are challenging assimilationist notions of citizenship and forcing nation-states to construct new conceptions of citizenship and citizenship education. Citizenship education should help students to develop thoughtful and clarified identifications with their cultural communities, nation-states, and the global community.

Article 38

Stinchcomb, J., Bazemore, G., & Riestenberg, N. (2006). Beyond zero tolerance: Restoring justice in secondary schools. *Youth Violence and Juvenile Justice, 4*(4), 123–147.

Zero tolerance policies in secondary schools now embrace an array of misbehaviors varying widely in seriousness. Their utility has therefore come into question, especially because they do not address causal factors and generally maintain an emphasis on suspension and expulsion. In contrast, responses based on a restorative justice philosophy embrace stakeholders in an interactive process to repair harm by addressing the nature of the misbehavior and resulting damages. Employing restorative justice principles in response to school-related misbehavior, which could be combined with traditional practices in a synergistic approach, might help in restoring order in our schools, responsibility in our students, and, ultimately, hope in our communities.

Article 39

Holt, M. (2002). It's time to start the slow school movement. *Phi Delta Kappan, 84*(4), 264–271.

Holt focuses on opposition to educational techniques that emphasize uniformity, predictability, and the measurability of processes and results. He discusses the effects of the pressure for students to proceed quickly in school; the status of standards-based tests in the United States; the educational changes begun by the administration of President George W. Bush; the tendencies for tests to reflect culturally embedded concepts of student quality; and the comparisons between education and fast-food and suggests the consideration of slow schools by the public sector.

Article 40

Liston, D. P. (2004). The lure of learning in teaching. *Teachers College Record, 106*(3), 459–486

Teaching entails the creation of connections among teacher, student, and content so that educational experiences can be had. To explore the love of learning, and its place in teaching, Liston evokes a bit of what this attraction feels and looks like. He then highlights features of what this love of learning looks like in teaching. It is the teacher who invites us beyond the boundaries of ourselves, to another territory—an invitation to join and take part in the human inheritance, the human conversation.

TOPIC GUIDE

1. Foundations of Curriculum
2. Philosophical Foundations
3. Educational Philosophies
4. Historical Foundations
5. Progressive Education
6. Curriculum Committees and Reports
7. Social Foundations
8. Definition of Curriculum
9. Principles of Curriculum
10. Curriculum Approaches/Camps
11. Curriculum Development
12. Curriculum Design
13. Curriculum Implementation
14. Curriculum Organization
15. Curriculum Integration
16. Arts Education
17. Curriculum Alignment
18. Curriculum Evaluation/Assessment
19. National Curriculum Standards
20. High-Stakes Testing
21. Theory and Practice
22. Social Justice
23. Multicultural Curriculum
24. Moral Education
25. Character Education
26. Ethics and Curriculum
27. Values Education
28. Humanistic Education
29. Schools as Conservers of Society
30. Schools as Agents of Change
31. Literacy and the Curriculum
32. Curriculum Reform
33. Urban Schools
34. Rural Schools
35. Academic Freedom and the Curriculum
36. Academic Curriculum
37. Extra-Curriculum
38. Co-Curriculum
39. Global Curriculum
40. Citizenship Curriculum

PREFACE

T his book was written to provide beginning teachers and other educational leaders with a series of articles that can help them build their curriculum knowledge base. Essential to understanding the current field of curriculum studies, it is imperative for the novice curriculum scholar to understand the historical past to see how the schools have gotten themselves into some of the curricular dilemmas they now face. While looking historically at the curriculum field, it is also necessary to understand some of the chaos that was imbedded in the study of curriculum.

Many people interested in education have tried to make sense out of the K–12 school curriculum. Questions abound: What should be taught at the various grade levels? How should content be taught so that students read better? What will students need to know in order to go to college? What will the non-college-bound student need to know? Do different students need different curricula to be successful in school? Thus, curriculum (the "what" that is taught in schools) has typically been examined by "curricularists," psychologists, sociologists, assessment specialists, philosophers, and politicians.

However, how is curriculum taught to different students? What is the appropriate sequence of courses or content? Why have the individuals most affected by what is taught in schools, the students and the teachers, had very little input into the curriculum debates that have permeated the study of curriculum? And, the parents of the children who attend the schools often don't ask questions about the "what" until their children are not successful in school, or someone raises issues about a particular book the children are assigned, or a type of science they are learning, or mathematics the parents don't understand.

For teachers and educational leaders to effectively grapple with the "what" of public and private school education, it is essential that they become familiar with the ongoing and often contentious issues that inevitably become focus points of debates in curriculum discussions. These discussions frequently get sidelined by another aspect of education: the instruction . . . the "how" to teach. Way too often people unfamiliar with curriculum studies often confuse the how to teach with the what to teach. Obviously, both the what and the how are important aspects of a teacher's work. Certain teaching strategies can be more effective with certain types of knowledge, while other strategies can work with different types of students. The what and how go together. And, in our current accountability environment, the what and the how together better produce a successful "score" on some pre-established test of achievement.

The readings in this book attempt to provide the reader with some historical context for the curriculum field, how curriculum might be organized, what is happening in the academic curriculum of schools as well as the extra- or co-curriculum of the schools, an understanding of the political nature of curriculum, and how we must be attentive to the increasingly diverse populations found in our schools. We also included some issues that currently are front and center in discussions of what we teach in our schools. We end the reader with some ideas to ponder, hopefully to provide you with some hope that all might be well in our schools in spite of the pressures currently placed on the teachers and students to excel.

The readings in this book are organized into ten sections—each of which is formulated as a question and containing possible approaches toward an answer. Each section is framed by a short discussion of the issues explored and a key idea to ponder while reading the articles included. Each article is concluded by a few questions to help the reader consider the specific issues that are raised therein. We close the text with a list of Internet Resources to help readers more fully explore the curriculum issues introduced in these pages.

ACKNOWLEDGMENTS

The authors wish to acknowledge the persons who have helped us to complete this project. Specifically, Dr. Mark Stern, whose understanding and encouragement made this project possible; friends and colleagues who believed this was a worthwhile project; and importantly, students who used, read, and critiqued articles being considered for inclusion in this reader. The authors wish to thank James Madison University for providing professional development time to Dr. Barbara Stern in order to help her meet the publication deadlines.

ADVISORY BOARD

Section I

WHERE DO WE BEGIN?

Before one can engage in good curriculum dialogue, there is some basic background information that is important in order to form the context of any exchange of ideas. In the curriculum field, that means that the curriculum scholar must have a broad understanding of what schooling and education are all about.

Both articles in this section of the reader focus on the assumptions upon which educational decisions are made. Egan claims that the premises we use to build the foundations of our educational programs are fundamentally flawed. Eisner looks specifically at the assumptions used to explain the aims, content, and structure of schooling.

As you read these two articles, think about the following:

- The experiences you had in K–12 education and evaluate them with respect to your current goals

- How the schools are structured in your community and whether or not they are meeting the needs of your community

- The changes you would make to the basic premises of education given the current environment in our schools

- Eisner's assumptions and whether or not you agree with his analysis

- What criteria you would use to "reform" our schools

Article 1

WHY EDUCATION IS SO DIFFICULT AND CONTENTIOUS

KIERAN EGAN

SOCIALIZATION IS A GREAT IDEA FOR HUNTER–GATHERERS

For the educationalist today, this first great educational idea we inherit comes as a good news, bad news, worse news, and really bad news scenario.

I suppose our educational troubles began around a quarter of a million years ago when our hominid ancestors ran into an evolutionary snag. Around that time, it seems, hominid brains were increasing in size quite rapidly. The snag was the limits to which the architecture of the female pelvis could be stretched to enable the women to give birth to these larger-brained babies while also allowing the women to walk efficiently. The remarkable evolutionary solution was to give birth to the babies while their brains were immature and let them do most of their growing outside the womb.

This peculiarity of human brains and human childhood created the need for that extended care and instruction that has become a part of what we mean by education. Along with the larger brains came language and language was used prominently to tell stories (Donald, 1991, Ch. 7). The most important stories were designed to create for their hearers a conceptual image of what we may call the meaning of life. They gave to the young, and reinforced for the older, images of who "we" are and what we are doing here.

The good news is that the techniques invented in hunter–gatherer society to create a homogeneous image of "our" society, of "our" individual roles within it, and of the cosmos in which the drama of our lives is played out have worked with great success for countless generations. The continuing good news is that the procedures we have inherited from ancient oral cultures remain today wonderfully effective in socializing our young.

The bad news is that our evolution equipped us to live in small, stable, hunter–gatherer societies. We are Pleistocene people, but our languaged

SOURCE: Excerpted from Egan, K. (2001). Why education is so difficult and contentious. *Teachers College Record, 103*(6), 923. Reprinted by permission.

brains have created massive, multicultural, technologically sophisticated, and rapidly changing societies for us to live in. Now that's not so bad in itself, as our brains also can adapt to a huge range of social conditions. The bad news is tied into that ingenious evolutionary adaptation that led to the extended growth of our brains outside the womb. One result—wonderfully efficient for hunter–gatherer tribes—was to enable us to learn effortlessly in our early years a language, an image of our society and its norms and values, and images of the meaning of life, the universe, and everything. We are equipped, that is, very early and quickly, to orient ourselves conceptually. Whatever children learn from the stories they are first told becomes quickly fixed and serves as a template for future learning. This rapid and deeply etched early learning served hunter–gatherer societies well because their stability and solidarity was sustained by their members all sharing an unquestioned and homogeneous worldview or ideology.

If one were to try to model human conceptual development, it would be tempting to say that evolution equipped us with two kinds of learning. There is, first, that largely effortless learning of our early years, which we use to pick up a language and those images of our society and the cosmos. It seems to work a bit like cement or plaster of paris: At first it is enormously flexible, able to adapt to widely varied external constraints, and then gradually it sets and becomes rigid. It also seems to be focused on very specific objects—like language social behavior, and so forth. The second kind of learning remains flexible throughout our lives and is a kind of all-purpose utility, but it is more laborious and slow. The difference between the two is often said to be evident in the efficiency with which we learn a language and adapt to social customs in our early years, in contrast with the relative difficulty and inefficiency with which we learn a new language and adapt to new social customs later in life.

Jerry Fodor (1983) suggests that we might see the mind as having a set of input systems and a somewhat distinct central processor. The input systems are relatively specific to particular parts of the normal brain; they are focused on such things as touch, hearing, seeing, and language; and they are fast and "stupid"—we can't *not* hear or *not* learn a language in normal conditions. The central processor is "smart" and is slow and general in both brain location and operations. This allows very fast responses to some things by the "stupid" brain systems and contemplation and analysis by the other. Fodor (1985) notes that, "it is, no doubt, important to attend to the eternally beautiful and true. But it is more important not to be eaten" (p. 4).

We might wisely be cautious in inferring such a sharp distinction in kinds of learning as we are still unsure about the underlying cognitive reality such distinctions refer to (Bruer, 1997). But for now it helps to clarify the bad news that comes along with inheriting the idea of socialization *as a part of education.*

Socialization relies heavily on the early "stupid" kind of learning and the commitments it forms. If told that the earth is a flat disk that rests on the back of a turtle, nearly everyone will believe this and see the earth in terms of this belief. (An earthquake? The turtle shifted.) If told that it is a huge ball that turns on its axis at high speed while also traveling unimaginably fast around the sun, people will believe this. The cement-like learning of our early years can accommodate almost anything; then it fixes and becomes almost immovable. The other, general purpose, learning capacity can, of course, accumulate knowledge that contradicts the first-formed beliefs; and we know that we can, as a result, change our earlier beliefs and commitments. We also know that this is rare and difficult for most people.

The bad news, then, is that we live in a world that requires flexibility in adapting to changing norms, beliefs, and values, and evolution has equipped us to be socialized in a manner that creates rigidity and unquestioning commitment to unchanging norms, beliefs, and values.

The worse news, which follows from the bad news, is that if we are really successful in socializing, we get someone who is indoctrinated. Now most people tend to be very acute at recognizing the ways in which "others" indoctrinate their children but are largely oblivious to the forms of indoctrination they deploy themselves—"they" indoctrinate, "we" educate.

This leads to a conundrum. "We" distinguish indoctrination from education on the openness of inquiry the educator encourages about the values taught, whereas the indoctrinators teach "their" values as unquestionable truths. But we do not typically encourage our children to question the value of our kind of "openness of inquiry"—we teach its value as an unquestionable truth.

Thinking in language leads us to recognize and name things as distinct from all other things—*x* is what not-*x* is not, goes the logic. Whether this results from the hardwiring of our brains or from the way language shapes our consciousness, we have a powerful tendency to construct our conceptual grasp on the world in terms of opposites. Our sense of "good" is tied to our sense of "bad"—big to little, brave to cowardly, safety to security, and so on.

Socialization today not only fits us to a particular social group but also identifies "us" to ourselves as distinct from other groups. Becoming American or Canadian or English still involves learning about the distinctive qualities that characterize the excellence of one's nation by contrast with other nations which lack those qualities. Even within the country, whichever "we" belong to, we will identify ourselves again in contrast with others; so we conservatives or liberals identify ourselves in some degree by contrast with those liberals or conservatives.

Our seemingly inescapable tendency to oppositional thinking produces a horrible result when it works in socializing. It sets people against each other in greater or lesser degrees.

Socialization as an educational ideal worked well in hunter–gatherer tribes. But today we can't easily avoid squirming a little about the dilemma it creates for us. On the one hand, for our children to become familiarly at home in our society, we have to allow considerable scope for socialization to occur unimpeded; and, on the other, our commitment to rationality in our everyday affairs is affronted by the indoctrinatory element in successful socialization. On the third hand, to fail to socialize adequately produces alienation. Our general solution to the dilemma has been to recognize that single-minded

socialization—à la Hitler Youth—is unacceptable and that we need double-mindedly to give rational reflection a large role in the process.

The difficulty of building flexibility into socialization creates a discarding of generations, as the conditions they were conditioned to deal with change under their feet. The flexibility was to come from being able rationally to reflect on events and adapt to them where appropriate. And that's where we try to plug Plato in.

THE ACADEMIC IDEAL AND ASSES LOADED WITH BOOKS

The next really big development in human intellectual culture after the development of language was the invention of literacy. Clearly literacy has been in general a good news scenario, but it also carries for the educator some bad news, some worse news, and some really bad news.

The good news is easy to see. Literacy has allowed generations of people to record their knowledge and experience. Further generations can compare that recorded knowledge with what they can see or discover and leave a more accurate record; and they can compare others' experience with their own, enlarging and enriching their experience in consequence. Today we have stored vast amounts of knowledge in written records, and we have access to a vast array of varied human experience. These enable our minds to transcend our own time, place, and circumstances.

Eric Havelock (1963, 1982, 1986) argued that Plato's great achievement was to work out how to think once alphabetic literacy became common. The result is both described and, if you'll excuse the term, paradigmatically exemplified in Plato's dialogues. When the best accumulated knowledge coded in writing is learned, Plato taught, it transforms the mind of the learners and enables them to understand the world more accurately and truly.

The bad news in this for today's educators is that they have to work out what, among the vast accumulation available, is the best knowledge for children to learn. Herbert Spencer (1966, Ch. 3) was confident that his answer to the question "What knowledge is of most worth?" was unassailable. But, of course, everyone assailed it. Is the best knowledge that of the "timeless classics . . . , the best that has been taught and said," as Matthew Arnold (1986, p. 458) argued, or of urgent knowledge about current social conditions, or of economically productive skills, or should children's own interests determine their curricula, or should our school curricula be a smorgasbord of all the above laid out by committees of "stakeholders," or should we have different curricula for different people, or a common or core curriculum for all, or what? The bad news is not so much that we don't know the answer in any generally agreed way, but we don't seem able to agree on how we might go about reaching an agreed upon answer. In the absence of any convincing theoretical grasp on the question, it is left to political power—to the committees of "stakeholders" laying out the smorgasbord. This might be a good solution if we think of education simply as socializing, but it is a lousy solution if we think education has something to do with that ideal Plato articulated for enabling us to understand the world and transcend the (socialized) conventions of our time and place.

The worse news is that, whatever the knowledge some group decides is worthiest for inclusion in our curricula, most students find literacy a sufficient barrier that they will be unable to access it anyway.

For most children, school disrupts and significantly destroys the orality of their early years by insistently trying to teach literacy and the knowledge coded in literate forms. For most children, school fails to provide the glories of literacy and to provide the access to literacy's transcendent culture.

The really bad news is that there isn't any knowledge stored in our libraries and databases. What we can store are symbols that are a cue to knowledge. People can read the symbols and not understand the knowledge, or partially understand it, or have a vague sense of what it means. This happens in schools to such an

extent that we expect it and grade children by the degree of understanding we think they have achieved.

The problem here is that knowledge exists only in living human tissue, and the literacy codes we use for storage are cues that need to go through a complex transformation before they can be brought to life again in another mind.

Many educationalists, and even more non-educationalists, confuse the codes with knowledge. They assume that if the students internalize the codes they will have the knowledge. Alas, this is not so. We can relatively easily compel or persuade or seduce people into internalizing literate codes—so they can pass exams and seem knowledgeable. This kind of learning has been the bane of insightful educators down the centuries. What it produces is not knowledgeable people but, as Michel de Montaigne put it, asses loaded with books.

This well-schooled, exam-passing, information-loaded person has always exasperated the major educational thinkers. That bookish man who described how his own early reading set his mind afire—J. J. Rousseau (1762/1979)—in a characteristic outburst famously wrote, "I hate books: they only teach one to talk about what one does not know" (p. 184).

We all recognize the difference between genuine knowledge and accumulated codes—we talk of education as against training, wisdom as against "book learning," insight as against literal thinking, and so on. But our schools are not good either at recognizing the difference or, consequently, promoting the genuine article rather than the counterfeit.

The really bad news, then, is that some kind of magic (or technique we don't understand) is required to bring back to new life in a new mind the desiccated written codes in which knowledge was stored by some other, perhaps long-dead, human mind. But even if we can manage the magic, I'm afraid there is even worse news than the really bad news. That is, even at its best, Plato's academic ideal can't deliver on its promises.

Plato describes an educational program that will carry the mind from the confusions and illusions of the folk physics, folk psychology, folk sociology learned effortlessly in our early years through a curriculum of disciplined knowledge to an understanding of the true nature of things. It is a program that requires the sacrifice of easy pleasures and the deployment of our laborious general learning capacity to remake all our early false knowledge, converting our minds always toward rationality and truth and away from the seductions of beliefs, myths, and superstitions. Plato's idea is probably a better educational idea than anyone before or since has had, but it is not adequate. The worst news, then, is that the academic ideal of education is designed to achieve a kind of understanding it simply can't deliver—its justification is an ideal that is unrealizable.

THE IDEAL OF DEVELOPMENT

I linked the two previous educational ideas/ideals with, first, the development of language and, second, the invention of literacy. For the sake of symmetry, it would be nice to link this third educational ideal with the invention of printing and the new learning and "Enlightenment" it seemed to many in Europe to promise. Even if the causal connection is not quite so easily made, the printing press was certainly importantly complicit in those intellectual changes, which included the radical rethinking of the nature of education in the work of John Locke (1632–1704), Etienne Bannot de Condillac (1715–1780), and, crucially, Jean-Jacques Rousseau (1712–1778).

Rousseau argued that human beings also have a nature and a natural process of development that could be disclosed by careful observation aided by reason. As we can observe the body's regular pattern of development from birth to senescence, so we can, with more difficulty perhaps, observe the mind's regular pattern of development. Education was reconceived as the activity of supporting the fullest achievement of the natural process of mental development. This idea came as good news for educationalists.

The good news was that it promised to solve a problem that Plato's idea left us with. Rousseau (1762/1979) acknowledged that Plato (hitherto) had been the greatest educational thinker. He had recognized how knowledge shaped the mind and how particular kinds of abstract knowledge and the disciplines they required shaped the mind to understand the world in more adequate and effective ways. But it had become clear that this wasn't enough. The common product of a Platonic education was asses loaded with books—informed pedantry without imagination, originality, or vigor. Rousseau proposed that the missing element was the knowledge that we could deduce from careful observation of the natural course of development.

So Plato, Rousseau (1762/1979) suggests, was right about the importance of knowledge in education, but his insight was of limited value without recognition of the stages at which the young can best learn the various kinds of knowledge. Plato failed to recognize the mind's autonomous growth, and so his conception of mental development was just a mirror-image of his conception of the logic whereby knowledge was elaborated. By understanding the autonomous growth of the mind, one could coordinate the logic of knowledge elaboration with the psycho-logic of mental development.

The continuing good news is that educationalists more or less universally now believe that it is important to attend to the nature of the child's learning at particular developmental stages, to different learning styles, and to that range of sensitivities to learners that became a hallmark of progressivism. Once attention to the distinctive psychological development of the child was made central to educationalists' understanding of their task, a number of considerable benefits followed. The first and perhaps still the most important was the recognition that failures to learn the curriculum might be due to faults other than the child's recalcitrance. It might, for example, be due to the method of teaching, or the stage at which a topic was being taught. This recognition led to relieving children's school lives of the constant fear of violence for failures to learn.

The combination of Plato's idea about knowledge and Rousseau's (1762/1979) idea about the mind was launched by Rousseau with the promise of a revolution in learning. Through the 20th century, each claim to have more adequately exposed the developmental process—most notably in the work of Jean Piaget—has led to renewal of the promise of a revolution in learning.

The bad news is that the revolution in learning has stubbornly refused to occur. It seemed and still seems to many that research, which discloses increasing knowledge about children's development and learning must lead to at least evident improvements in general education. The trouble with promising a revolution in learning is that people expect to see some evidence of it in the learners.

What did become evident was that the commitment to freedom for natural development didn't take one very far. As an educational idea, it makes it difficult to determine a curriculum and tends to leave the selection open to local prejudice, charismatic enthusiasts, or blind chance. To keen progressivists, this doesn't matter that much because the curriculum isn't the point. We have had a century of fairly intensive experiments in implementing varied forms of the idea we have inherited from Rousseau, of progressivism's interpretations of it, and of educational psychology's attempts to flesh it out scientifically. It seems fair to observe at this point that something is still missing. Plato's and Rousseau's ideas together are not able to bring about for most children the kind of learning we see in some and the kind of learning that it doesn't seem unreasonable to expect from hugely expensive schools. The promise of Rousseau's idea has not been delivered. Alas, it hasn't worked.

The worse news . . . What? There is worse news than that it hasn't worked? Yes—that it can't work. The worse news follows the observation that human beings don't have a nature. Well, that overstates it—to underline a point. There are obviously regularities in human mental development, but they are so tied up with our social experience, our culture, and the kinds of intellectual tools we pick up that we can't tell whether the regularities are due to our nature, to our society, to our culture, to our intellectual tools, or what. We can't simply measure the regularities, which turn out to be pretty irregular from person to person, and see through them to our nature or to some autonomous developmental process.

The really bad news is that Rousseau (1762/1979) put in place for the modern educational world a binary distinction between an autonomously developing mind and an "external" body of knowledge. Once education became thought of in terms of knowledge and mind (content and method, curriculum and instruction), the problem became how to get them back together again. The history of educational thinking in the 20th century prominently involved a bizarre war between these two—between those who were "child centered" and those who were "subject centered," between progressivists and traditionalists.

Tatters of the old classical curriculum hang around, partly out of an intuition that there might be something in Plato's idea and partly to satisfy the minority who still want that old-style "ornamental" education. For the core of the new progressive curricula, however, utility trumps transcendence every time—Career and Personal Planning or Drug Education or Economics for Everyday Living or Computers 101 trump Latin hands down in the competition for limited curriculum time.

Rousseau's (1762/1979) dichotomy has given us a century of polemical battles between supporters of "child centeredness" against "subject centeredness."

INSTITUTIONS BASED ON INCOMPATIBLE IDEAS

We obviously haven't inherited these three great educational ideas in the more or less discrete packages described above. We don't, of course, think of our conception of education as a composite but rather as a unitary idea. But those three ideas have become entangled with each other through the centuries and have produced our contemporary schools and curricula and teaching practices.

When we do note differences between the competing demands of these three ideas—when, for example, politicians or businesspeople demand from the schools more relevant social knowledge or work skills or when some neoconservatives demand we concentrate on developing academic knowledge—we say that there are "tensions" among the requirements of the various "stakeholders." The job of the good educational administrator is to balance these tensions so that the requirements of all the major stakeholders are met to an adequate degree.

Schools provide an exposure to academic material to all students and clearly allow some to excel in academic work, they socialize all students in a basic way while avoiding fanatical extremes, and they attend to the general development of all children and provide special help to some who clearly need it. Of course there are tensions among the three general educational ideas that drive our schools—successful education is achieved by finding the right community-supported balance.

I think this complacent view is mistaken and that the three ideas undermine each other rather than complement each other.

Consider this scenario: Let us say you are a movie fan and enjoy going out to a cinema once each week. The government imposes a new requirement on cinemas. As you come out of the cinema, you will be required to take a test on the movie you have just seen. You will be asked the color of the villain's car in the chase scene, or the adequacy of the motivation of the leading woman's sister, or the gist of the alien's speech before it transmogrified, or the name of the brother-in-law's pet dog, and so on. Your score on the test will determine your salary for the next week, when you will face another test and another salary adjustment. Consider for a moment how such tests and their consequence would likely influence your watching movies. At the very least, they would change what was carefree entertainment into anxiety. You would also spend a lot of effort watching movies trying to second-guess the kinds of questions you are likely to be asked, and the focus of your attention would be shifted to fit your expectations of the test.

What does this remind you of? Right. School. The above absurd scenario creates a social institution—with, no doubt, huge testing services and solemn officials and entrepreneurs setting up test-coaching companies—which confuses two conflicting aims. There is no problem with having two aims for an institution except if the aims conflict with each other. If one of our aims for an educational institution is the pursuit of academic knowledge, we will interfere with that in all kinds of destructive ways if we then impose a social sorting role on the institution and use academically inappropriate testing to do that social sorting. Also the social sorting role would be confused because academic prowess—which we are only marginally testing for anyway—is hardly the most important determiner of social value. That is, this kind of undermining of separate and conflicting aims is precisely what we get if we try to make the school an institution that tries both to socialize and implement the academic ideal at the same time. The result is that neither is adequately or sensibly achieved, as, in the cinema scenario, neither carefree entertainment nor an appropriate manner of determining salaries is achieved.

Yet we have created such an institution and keep trying to make it work to realize conflicting ideals. Adequate socialization requires successfully inculcating a set of beliefs, values, and norms of behavior in the growing child. The academic program is specifically designed to enable the growing child to question the basis for any beliefs, values, and norms of behavior. The two aims pull against each other: The more successfully one socializes, the less one achieves the academic ideal; the more successfully one inculcates disciplined academic thinking, the less easy it is to socialize successfully.

The academic commitment to shaping the mind by teaching disciplined forms of understanding isn't compatible with the belief that the minds of different people can be optimally developed by knowledge chosen to suit their particular style of learning, kind of intelligence, needs, and interests. One cannot have two masters, especially when both mandate different things. We can't construct a coherent educational institution using radically different criteria.

But, of course, that's precisely what we require of our schools today. We require that they acknowledge, and accommodate as far as possible, different styles of learning and different ends of the process for different people. "Education" for one child may have a quite different character from that attained by another; quite different "potentials" might be developed and each be an example of successful education. We require also that the academic ideal be acknowledged, which recognizes education only in the degree to which minds are shaped by progress in understanding the range of disciplines. The result, of course, is not a coherent curriculum but one that tries to accommodate both conflicting principles. The result, also, is perpetual strife by adherents of the conflicting principles fighting about which should have greater influence over children's education.

Conclusion

We have inherited three foundational ideas about education. Each one of them has flaws, at least one flaw in each being fatal to its ambition to represent an educational ideal we might reasonably sign on to. And the worse news is that each of the ideas is incompatible with the other two. These warring ideas hovered around the cradle of the state schools, proffering their gifts. The schools eagerly took them all, and so education remains difficult and not anti contentious.

Well, having thought about the ideas we usually think with, where are we? A plausible answer is, in something of a mess. The commonest response to inspecting the foundations of our ideas and finding them inadequate is to turn and carry on with everything much as before. I mean, think of the trouble we would have to go to if we were to conclude that indeed our conception of education is flawed in the way this article has argued and that we should do something about it. In general, most people seem to be sustained by institutions not ideas. That the institutions are as they are because of particular ideas seems not to be a matter that concerns most people in the education business. Practical folk just get on with doing the best they can within the institutions that exist. And, of course, without this pragmatic commonsense approach, we would be in a bigger mess.

But what would we have to do if we take ideas seriously, understand how they shape institutions, and conclude that the above argument is right? First off, we need a better idea of education than the fractious confusion we currently stumble along with. And where will we find such things? Well, we just have to make them up. If you want an example of a new conception of education that avoids the problems of our current tripartite incompatibilities, may I recommend *The Educated Mind* (Egan, 1997). In that book, I show how we can, drawing somewhat on Vygotsky's ideas (Reiber & Carton, 1987), reconceive education as a process of stimulating and developing a set of kinds of understanding. From such foundations we can then derive new forms of curricula, teaching practices, and appreciation of varied forms of student learning. The result is not so strange that it will seem entirely alien to our current traditions, because it grows out of them.

If we want to improve our schools, it is with the abstract and awkward realm of ideas that we must first deal.

Discussion Questions

Why does Egan believe that modern schools fail to educate children sufficiently?

What do you see as solutions for the problems Egan describes?

Kieran Egan is a professor at Simon Fraser University, Edmonton, Canada.

Article 2

QUESTIONABLE ASSUMPTIONS ABOUT SCHOOLING

ELLIOT W. EISNER

The aims, content, and organization of schools are so embedded in our culture that the assumptions on which they rest are seldom examined. Schools are a part of the furniture of our communities, historically rooted institutions that we take as much for granted as the streets upon which we walk, the stores from which we purchase goods, and the houses in which we grow up and raise our families. Yet the fundamental features of schooling—its dominant practices, its mode of organization, its reward system, its aims, its *culture*—have an extraordinary impact on how the young come to think about knowledge, how they regard success, what they consider intelligent, and how they see their place in the world. In short, the institution we know as "school" teaches by its very nature.

And the nature of schools is rooted in the historical traditions, values, and assumptions into which we have been socialized. Although we act on these values and assumptions, we seldom examine them, even as we try to influence schools.

Schools have a special difficulty in changing their nature. Part of this difficulty stems from the fact that all of us have served an apprenticeship in them—and from an early age. Indeed, teaching is the only profession I know in which professional socialization begins at age 5 or 6. Students, even those of so tender an age, learn early what it takes to "do school."[1] They learn early what a teacher does in a classroom. They learn early how they must behave in order to get on. In fact, aside from their sleeping hours, most children spend more time in the presence of their teachers than they spend in the presence of their parents. In short, students and parents, like the rest of us, know what to expect of schools. Those expectations, rooted as they are in our past, also shape our present.

SOURCE: Excerpted from Eisner, E. W. (2003). Questionable assumptions about schooling. *Phi Delta Kappan, 84*(9), 648–657. Reprinted by permission of Elliott Eisner.

Given the impact that schools have on the young, it seems useful to examine some of the assumptions, indeed some of the questionable assumptions that give direction to our schools.

1. The aim of schooling is to get all students to the same place at about the same time. Schools are sometimes likened to railroads. Students are to get aboard as 5- or 6-year-olds and, when teaching and learning go well, to arrive at a relatively common destination by the time they're 18. The basic assumption is that the goals of schools should be common; the differentiation of destinations is problematic since it is believed that to differentiate aims is to condemn the less able to positions in society that are neither as lucrative nor as personally rewarding as those destinations available to the more able. Thus a common set of goals is, some believe, a mark of educational equity.

As we all know, the destinations that so well suit the children of the educationally savvy often have the very effects that those who worry about the differentiation of goals want to avoid. Those talented in ways the school does not reward—or even recognize—continue to fall short when they compete in a race that they must struggle to win. Rather than conceive of educational progress as a race whose garlands go to the swiftest, running on a track for which their life experiences have advantaged them, we would do well to recognize both the array of talents that all youngsters possess and our need to honor and foster competence in a considerably wider range of abilities than we now acknowledge.

Given this perspective, the good school, in my view, does not expect all students to arrive at the same destination at the same time. Indeed, it provides conditions in which variability among students can be increased. What we ought to be doing in schools is increasing the variance in student performance while escalating the mean. In an ideal approach to curriculum and instruction— an approach in which every aspect of teaching is ideally suited to each student, and each aspect of curriculum is appropriate for the abilities students possess—variability among students will increase, not decrease.

The virtue of such an outcome for society is that it promotes self-actualization by enabling students to play to their strengths and so to give to one another and to society precisely those gifts that others cannot give.

2. A teacher should work with 30 youngsters for an academic year and then students should move on to another teacher. The way we have organized schools in the United States, with few exceptions, is to have youngsters at the elementary level work with a particular teacher for 9 or 10 months and then move on. What is especially ironic about this arrangement is that, at about the time the teacher gets to know the child, the child leaves the teacher and heads elsewhere. What is doubly ironic is that the test data that are usually secured from tests given near the end of the academic year are unavailable to the teacher in whose class the students were tested, since by the time the teacher receives the scores, the students have moved to another teacher.

It is not unusual for teachers to resist working with the same group of students for a 2- or 3-year period. Elementary school teachers, like professors, develop a repertoire of skills and acquire a body of content knowledge that they bank on using in their teaching. Their closets are filled with materials that are quite familiar to them, and the prospect of assuming responsibility for students at a grade level higher or lower than the one they know requires them to become competent in new material. For many teachers, this is daunting. In describing this state of affairs, I am not defending it, only explaining that since efficiency and effort are issues for teachers, as they are for all of us, it is understandable that some teachers balk at the prospect of staying with the same class for more than a year.

Not all schools organize themselves along these lines or build their programs on the assumption of a 9-month contract. Many Waldorf schools, for example, have students remain with the same teacher for 6 to 8 years. They also operate in many locales without a principal. Both can be done.

3. The best form of school organization is age grading. In many ways, this assumption is related to the previous two. The graded school system was invented in America in Quincy, Massachusetts, in 1847.[2] The idea is very simple. Children of the same age should be grouped together, and that grouping should be enumerated by grade level. Thus, 6-year-olds should be in the first grade, 7-year-olds in the second grade, 8-year-olds in the third grade, and so on.

The age-graded school system is an administrative and organizational convenience, but it has very little to do with what we know about child development. For example, consider the range of reading ability in an average elementary school classroom. It turns out that the range of reading ability approximates the grade level.[3] This means that in the second grade, when children are approximately 7 years old, the range of reading ability is about 2 years. In the third grade, the range is about 3 years; in the fourth grade, about 4 years. Thus in a typical fourth grade, some students will be reading at the sixth-grade level, and some will be reading at the second-grade level. By the time students reach the sixth grade, some will be reading at the third-grade level, and some will be reading at the ninth-grade level.

As children mature, their personalities become increasingly distinctive. Their aptitudes develop, their proclivities emerge, and they develop distinctive interests, traits, and ways of working. The idea that all children who are 10 are or should be at the same level is a bogus expectation. In fact, a teacher who taught only a body of content defined by a single grade level would be providing a level of teaching inappropriate for most of the class.

4. The real outcomes of schooling can be measured by tests employed within the school. In the United States, we have developed a sophisticated technology of testing. This technology was given a major push during the First World War when tests were first used to select men suitable as candidates for officers' training. American schools give more tests to students each year than schools in any other country in the world. The testing industry in the United States is large and highly profitable. One argument for using tests is that teacher judgment cannot be trusted, while tests, which are standardized and therefore yield comparable data, have a degree of precision that teachers cannot match. Moreover, tests are statistically reliable instruments, and equivalent forms yield scores that are highly correlated. Thus, tests possess a scientific aura and are used extensively as the primary data source for making judgments about the quality of education students are receiving.

One important educational purpose of testing is to provide information that has some relationship to tasks that go beyond the particular items to which students are asked to respond. However, getting a high score on a test that has little predictive or concurrent validity is no educational virtue. Yet this is precisely the problem that pervades testing practice. What test scores predict best are other test scores. Their status as proxies for other forms of performance is dubious.

In any case, the function of schools is surely not primarily to enable students to do well on tests—or even to do well in school itself. What one wants, it seems to me, is to provide a curriculum and a school environment that enable students to develop the dispositions, the appetites, the skills, and the ideas that will allow them to live personally satisfying and socially productive lives. In other words, the really important dependent variables in education are not test scores or even skills performed in the context of schools; they are the tasks students are able to complete successfully in the lives they lead outside of schools. There is a huge difference between knowing how to read and having an interest in doing so. And interest shows up in out-of-school contexts.

I would argue that the major aim of schooling is to enable students to become the architects of their own education so that they can invent themselves during the course of their lives.

5. Knowledge consists of true assertions about empirical states of affairs. Therefore, what students cannot say, they do not know. This belief is rooted in classical Greek epistemology and silently permeates modern schools and, even more broadly, modern culture. *Logos* was the term the Greeks used not only for words but also for knowledge—more specifically, for reason. Reason, the Greeks believed, required the use of language, since it depended upon logic, and logic deals with relationships between the meanings of words that are used to form propositions. Indeed, to have scientific knowledge one must provide warrants for one's assertions. What is not assertable is not testable. And what is not testable cannot be warranted.

In schools, we place a premium on the use of words and on the use of numbers. Literacy and numeracy, as they are referred to, are regarded as not only the primary processes we wish to promote, but also the most sophisticated manifestations of human intelligence. As a result, this view—often unarticulated, but expressed in the choices we make about what to teach and about how much time to devote to doing so—has substantial implications for the breadth of our curriculum and for the equity of our treatment of students whose aptitudes are irrelevant to the school's priorities.

The limits of our cognitive life are not defined by the limits of our language. As [Michael] Polanyi points out, "We know more than we can tell."[4]

To take such an acknowledgment into serious consideration we would need to provide opportunities for students to work in areas in which reasoning is employed, but such reasoning would have to pertain to forms of problem solving that depend not on the uses of logic but on the organization of qualities, including, but not limited to, linguistic qualities. This kind of work is best exemplified by artists who make sophisticated judgments about the ways qualities are composed. Such qualities emerge in the visual arts in the context of visual imagery, in music in the context of sound, in movement in the context of dance, in poetry and fiction in the context of language chosen for its expressive and evocative potential. I speak also of those who work in the universe of practical activity, where the application of algorithm, rule, and even logic is often irrelevant or inappropriate to the successful execution of a task.

Clearly, considerable thought must be devoted to the place of such matters in our curriculum, the amount of time to be devoted to them, the manner in which they are to be employed in classrooms, and the like. But as long as the nonlinguistic expression of human intelligence is marginalized in school programs, our programs will fail to develop the rich varieties of human potential that our students possess. We will also continue to emphasize curricular content and aims that create educational inequities for students whose areas of greatest potential are either marginalized or absent from school programs.

6. Teaching at its best is the application of scientific knowledge to practical states of affairs emerging in the classroom. One of the dominant assumptions in universities is that the scientific work that researchers do will yield the theories and generalizations that will provide the procedures that can then be disseminated to those who function in particular contexts. For example, research in agronomy is designed to produce knowledge that will enable farmers to increase yield per acre. The dissemination process is from the university researcher, to the field extension officer, to the farmer, and ultimately to the society. It is a top-down, scientifically based approach to improvement. The same model has dominated our assumptions about the dissemination of research in the field of education.

What is discounted, however, are the limitations of generalizations and theories when practitioners need to apply them to the particular situations in which they work. First, most theories and generalizations in the social sciences are inadequate for addressing the problems within their own discipline, let alone the particular circumstances in which individual teachers and students work. As Joseph Schwab has pointed out, theory addresses ideal states of affairs.[5]

Teachers, however, deal with what is particular or idiosyncratic. Second, theories used to understand phenomena reveal only one side of the issue, the side theory addresses. All problems in education are multifaceted, and no single theory can encompass the variety of factors that must be considered. Third, while the aim of the researcher is to know, the aim of the practitioner is to act and to make good decisions in the process. Practitioners are not primarily concerned with the production of scientific knowledge; they are concerned with the conduct of efficient, effective, and, at its best, satisfying and morally right action.

What the dominant assumption about the connection between research and practice neglects is the kind of practical knowledge that Aristotle alluded to when he contrasted productive and theoretical knowledge. Practical knowledge aimed at the achievement of moral ends is what the Greeks referred to as *phronesis*.[6] Practical knowledge is concerned with moral decision making. But even more than Aristotle's characterization of practical knowledge, teachers are not only engaged in practical activity; they are also engaged in artistic activity. They are engaged in the act of creating something—an explanation, a relationship between themselves and their students, an activity that will effectively introduce students to an issue, problem, or dilemma. In short, teachers are makers of things, and to the extent that things well made constitute an art, a theory of teaching predicated on the assumption that teachers simply or mainly implement what researchers discover is naive and ill founded.

The conception of teaching that I have discussed implies that we need to address the conditions through which artistry in teaching and in other forms of practical action can be promoted, improved, and developed. It also implies that there should be a much greater parity between those who work in the university and those who teach in our schools. Practitioners have a kind of knowledge that might be referred to as "insider knowledge," a kind of knowledge that can be secured only in the context of practice itself.[7]

This is a context to which teachers have access, and it is one that can inform the views of theoreticians. And even beyond this characterization of the conditions of improved teaching, we need to recognize that teachers can also inform one another if they have opportunities in the course of their day to discuss with their peers common problems and individual achievements. We need to think about the ways in which such arrangements can be created, for in the end such arrangements will have much to do with the improvement of teaching.

7. The best way to organize the curriculum is to identify its constituent disciplines and then to create a series of small steps within each so that the discipline can be learned. A disciplinary orientation to curriculum is especially attractive to professors and other academics who themselves work within a disciplinary structure. The tacit view is that a solid education prepares students to think like those in the academic disciplines. This view curriculum was salient in the United States in the 1960s.[8] It was the view that Jerome Bruner advanced at a time when America was concerned with its position in the race for space. People who were anxious about the quality of education and who believed that curricula had softened under the onslaught of progressive education saw in a return to the disciplines a return to intellectual rigor.[9]

What we learned was that, although a disciplinary orientation to curriculum was conceptually appealing, it also tended to lack relevance for many students.[10] Academic hurdles were set up that resulted in a reduction of high school enrollments in physics, chemistry, and other fields believed to be intellectually rigorous. Thus the push toward a curriculum that was discipline-oriented had just the opposite effect from the one we wanted to achieve.

The kinds of problems that the average citizen addresses are, as I suggested above, transdisciplinary or multidisciplinary. They are seldom adequately addressed through a single discipline. In fact, they often require modes of thought that are not defined within a specific discipline.

Trying to understand the social conditions of young people requires much more than the application of economic theory or sociology or history; it requires something that might be called firsthand contact with the young themselves. Furthermore, designing an educational program that is almost exclusively mediated through disciplinary language denies youngsters the opportunity to think with and within forms of representation that are nonlinguistic.

The development of mind is related to the modes of thought that schools enable and encourage students to use. The curriculum that is provided in schools is essentially a mind-altering device, and our choices about what students will attend to and the forms in which that material is presented and responded to are of critical importance.

8. School reform is most effective when competition among schools is promoted and when supervisors can mandate goals, manage teachers, monitor students, and measure outcomes. Public anxiety over the quality of schools typically leads to pressures that, in turn, lead to higher levels of prescription for schools. These include the articulation of standards and milestones to be met and the use of an assessment program to measure student performance. In the United States, test data on student performance are arrayed for schools within school districts and from state to state. Test scores are then produced and published in local newspapers in what are the equivalent of league tables that identify the position or rank of each school or district. School reform is being driven by a competitive model in which student scores constitute the data to be rank-ordered. That competition should be seen as motivating is, of course, entirely consistent with the values of a capitalist economy. The tacit belief is that, if competition is good for business, it's good for schools because schools, when you get down to it, are businesses, and the business of schools is producing measurable student performance.

This argument seems impeccable, but it has a number of troubling consequences. First, knowing someone's position in a distribution tells you nothing about what needs to be done to improve it.

Second, the belief that education reform is likely to endure if a top-down approach to school improvement is employed is another dubious assumption. Top-down approaches often begin and end with changed education policies, while schools continue on their merry way, largely oblivious to policy changes. Or when schools are not wholly oblivious to policy changes, they engage in forms of adaptation that give the illusion of change but do not constitute its reality. Indeed, unless teachers and school administrators buy into reform efforts, unless they are a part of the group that participates in designing the reforms, little is likely to happen. After all, the only place where education reform makes an educational difference is where the rubber meets the road: in classrooms. And in classrooms, teachers are kings and queens. Thus, the idea that policy can be prescribed from on high, issued ex cathedra, is a comforting one for policy makers, but it is a problematic one as far as school improvement is concerned.

9. Artistry in teaching, when it occurs, is basically the result of the absence of scientifically grounded knowledge of teaching practices. This questionable assumption is, again, rooted in the belief that science is the only dependable source of knowledge and that artistry is neither a realistic aspiration nor a dependable resource for the conduct of practice. I would argue that any practice at its best is an artistically crafted affair. In the practice of surgery, when decisions about a course of action must be made, artistry is present, since scientific knowledge is never entirely adequate for the treatment of a particular patient with any particular disease. Indeed, one of the important criticisms of modern-day medicine is that individuals are reduced to generalized cases—he's a tonsillectomy, she's an appendectomy, he's a fractured femur, and the like. Somehow, the individuality and personal particulars of the patient get lost. The loss of individuality is not simply a psychological liability; it has consequences for the success of medical practice, since to miss the distinctive features of the individual case is to hamper diagnosis and treatment.

Artistry in teaching represents high levels of pedagogical performance. Artistry depends on sensibility, it uses imagination, it employs technique, it takes pride in its craft. Teachers as artists are sensitive to the tempo of the classroom, to matters of timing, and to the quality of their own performance and the ways in which it can be shaped to be appropriate for the occasion. Such considerations are in no way prescribable from scientific research.[11]

I wish to make it clear that, as I speak about the limits of scientific theory in education, I have no intention of dismissing research by consigning it to the junk heap. Science gives us one very useful approach to the comprehension of action and its improvement, but it is only one approach. The arts and artistic forms of thinking have generally been neglected as ways of knowing and as qualities of performing. My aim here is not to dismiss science, but to call attention to additional ways of thinking about thinking in the context of practice.

10. The best way to identify schools that work well is to examine their students' test scores. Ironically, we encounter tests in just a few places outside of the context of schools. Thus, we have designed a system that employs culturally rare events to make significant judgments about the quality of education students receive.

This system has several important consequences for schools. First, the curriculum typically gets narrowed so that it reflects a relatively narrow array of what tests are capable of measuring. Second, the tests themselves have very little predictive validity on most of the tasks and forms of action that students engage in outside the context of schools. Third, the use of tests leads students to focus their attention on grades or scores and thereby diverts attention away from engagement in the task itself. Extrinsic rewards gradually displace intrinsic satisfaction.

The quality of education students receive is determined by much more complex and subtle forms of attention. To know about the quality of education students receive, one must be in a position to appraise the significance of the ideas, skills, and attitudes that a school is developing. This typically requires attention to the culture of schooling and not only to the behavior of students. One needs to know something about the kinds of questions that are being raised by both students and teachers; about the sorts of opportunities students have to formulate their own purposes and to design ways of achieving them; about the degree to which multiple forms of representation are promoted, not only through the literal use of language and correct computation, but also through such poetic means as the visual arts, music, and dance. The forms of consciousness and understanding of which humans are capable are not exhausted by what is measurable or by what can be articulated in the literal use of language.[12]

To call for this wider agenda for education and to identify its features as criteria for appraising the quality of educational practice is not to reject the need to promote literacy and numeracy in their conventional forms. It is a plea to recognize a wider educational mission and to use a vision of that mission as a basis for judging and improving schools. Raising test scores on narrow measures of educational achievement is no significant educational victory.

11. The primary content that students learn in school is what their teachers intend to teach them. John Dewey once remarked that the greatest fallacy in education is the assumption that students learn only what they are being taught at the time.[13] In fact, what students learn is both more and less than what teachers intend to teach. They learn less because students seldom achieve the lofty aims that teachers hold for them; our ambitions, educationally speaking, virtually always exceed our capacity. Indeed, if all students achieved what we hoped they would, we would probably regard our aims as being too low.

At the same time, students learn more than we intend to teach. They learn more because what they learn is not simply a function of what teachers intend to teach, but of what students themselves bring to the table. The concept of interaction is key here. The meanings that are made by students are a function of their intentions and the conceptual material they bring to the situation that teachers create. And since for each student that background is in some degree different, meanings always differ. These meanings are related to the interaction between the individual and the situation that is created. Teachers may think they are teaching one thing, but what students learn may be quite another. A teacher might intend to help students understand quadratic equations, while the student may intend to get a passing grade in the course or to use the math class to do homework for a history class.

These observations imply that schools need to create situations that engender aims for the student that are congruent with those of the teacher. To say that they ought to be congruent is not to say that they must overlap completely. Indeed, they cannot. Yet, when the student's aims are educationally marginal—or worse, miseducational—teaching cannot have educational value. Students learn quickly to make the kind of moves that enable them to get by without being touched by the material they study.

12. Some subjects are primarily affective while others are primarily cognitive. It is unfortunate that our general conception of cognition is that it requires linguistic forms of mediation. As I indicated above, we associate knowing with linguistically mediated thought. But cognition as a term is not limited to what can be linguistically mediated.[14] Cognition refers to the process of becoming aware.[15] Cognition depends on human sensibility, and the more differentiated the sensibilities, the greater the degree of awareness. Indeed, it is the content of such sensibility that serves as the material to which language refers. The best way to ensure that students will engage in meaningless verbal learning is to make sure they have no experience of that to which their language refers.

Concept formation, therefore, is embodied in experience with qualities, and qualities are pervaded by human affect. Thus, the mathematician and the logician, two individuals whose work seems to be unrelated to qualitative matters, are in fact dealing with relationships that, at their best, are themselves qualitative and from which feeling is evoked. When it comes to the arts, we have a paradigmatic case of affect-laden qualities being composed to serve human experience. Education in the arts is the education of feelingful thought at its most acute level.[16]

But even those arenas of activity that seemingly are without affect are, in fact, freighted with affect. To be kissed without feeling is to know that one has been kissed without feeling because of the feeling that unfeeling kisses reveal. Experience always has an affective aspect, and the so-called absence of affect is itself an affect. The development of intelligence in all areas of human action is never complete without attention to the affective part of the materials with which we compose, regardless of the domain in which we function. The practice of a science at its best is an art that depends upon the affective experience of the scientist in the context of doing his or her research. The absence of attention to such matters in our own teaching is a form of fundamental neglect, for it robs our students of the opportunity to secure the satisfactions of genuine work.

DIMENSIONS OF SCHOOL REFORM

What are we to make of this formidable list of questionable assumptions upon which our schools operate? Is it to be merely a taxonomy of erroneous beliefs, or is there some way to think about these assumptions in relation to dimensions of school reform? I believe there is a way to connect this analysis to school reform. Consider the following five dimensions.

First, I believe it would be well for us to think about school reform in relation to the aims of our schools. What really matters? Do we harbor contradictory aspirations? What are our priorities?

Why do we have them? Such questions provide a beginning for deep examination.

Second, we can examine our assumptions about the conduct of schools in relation to the structure of schooling. By structure I mean the ways in which time and space are parsed, how roles are defined within the school, how, for example, we organize classes and what it does to the way we treat time. Such questions can be grouped under structural features that need attention.

A third dimension pertains to the curriculum itself. We make assumptions about the centrality of the disciplines, about the autonomy of subjects, and about the emphasis on language as the virtually exclusive carrier of meaning. These assumptions may interfere with more creative views of how curricula can be selected and organized and, most important, how they are encountered by students.

A fourth dimension pertains to pedagogy. We appear to work with the assumptions that teachers should work alone, that 30 or more children should be assigned to a teacher, and that students should remain with a teacher for a year and then move on to another teacher. Assumptions about pedagogy need to be examined critically, for it is their practical translation in the classroom that determines significantly what students will or will not have an opportunity to learn. At the same time, though, the context in which the teacher functions—both in the classroom and as a part of the school organization—also influences pedagogical practice. We need to think about the environment as a whole.

Fifth, we need to examine our assumptions about evaluation practices. All too often we tend to equate evaluation with testing. But tests are only a mechanism, a procedure, a way through which information about how students are doing can be secured. But it is not necessary either to test or to measure in order to evaluate. Assumptions about evaluation need to be examined because evaluation practices influence the priorities of schools and affect the kinds of incentives that both teachers and students come

to believe are important in "doing school." Thus we have a scheme in which aims, structure, curriculum, pedagogy, and evaluation become five major dimensions for thinking about school reform. The dozen questionable assumptions that I have addressed here are all candidates for attention within one or more of these dimensions.

Given the questionable assumptions I have identified and the conceptual structure I have described, how shall we think about the practice of reform? There are two salient models of reform, one systemic and the other incremental. Systemic approaches to reform emphasize the need to pay attention to virtually everything, since everything affects everything else. Incremental approaches recognize that we can't pay attention to everything and that, even if we could, it is unlikely that everything could be addressed at the same time. To the extent that factors that one cannot change influence what is to be changed, the problem of reform is enormous.

Schools have demonstrated themselves to be robust institutions, something like giant gyroscopes that, when pushed to the side, accommodate the push and then come back to their upright position. Although "tinkering toward utopia," as my colleagues have put it, may not be ideal, it may be the most realistic approach.[17] What can we actually do? I believe it is possible to think big but start small. I believe that a comprehensive plan can be drafted and that undertakings incremental efforts toward the realization of such a plan are the most realistic option.

With a plan that addresses the problematic assumptions that I have described and with procedures developed for dealing with them, progress toward creating schools that genuinely educate is a real possibility. In so many efforts at school reform, superficial factors are addressed. As a result, the "reforms" are short-lived and lead to no real reform at all. This is not the picture I have tried to paint. I am trying to penetrate the surface and identify our deep-seated assumptions. By problematizing questionable assumptions, we may put ourselves in a position to create a better vision of what schools might become.

Discussion Questions

Based on your experiences, which of Eisner's assumptions about schools seem most valid? Which least?

Looking at the five dimensions of school reform suggested, how would you change school curriculum?

———————— ∽ ————————

———————

Elliot W. Eisner is a professor emeritus at Stanford University.

Section II

WHAT IS CURRICULUM?

Important to the study of curriculum is the understanding of what curriculum is and should be. The articles in this section were selected because they raise questions about the curriculum of schools, what it is, how it works, and what it could be. These particular articles were selected because they provide four perspectives that educators ought to be aware of when they engage in the study of curriculum.

All too often in the pressure cooker of schooling, educators do not take, nor do they have, the time to seriously think about what is happening to the curriculum in their school. Schooling is often overwhelmed with minutia that is required by local, state, or federal mandates, to the exclusion of the bigger issues, and perhaps more important issues, of what is happening to the students in the classrooms: What are they really learning? Is what they are learning the most important things they should be learning? What should they be learning?

Dziuban and Kysilka pose the question, What is really important in the curriculum world? They attempt to show how the building of the curriculum must take into account the children for whom the curriculum is being built. Without this essential ingredient in curriculum though, the purpose of the curriculum for students may be irrelevant.

Curriculum alignment addresses the relationship between what is taught, how it is taught, and how what is taught is assessed. How well the curriculum aligns with national and state standards is extremely important in today's accountability movement. Glatthorn suggests ways in which curriculum alignment can be controlled by the teachers as they confront the various forms of curricula present in their classrooms.

Education is not just about acquiring a myriad of knowledge; more important, education is about how to do something significant with that knowledge. Perkins calls the doing something with knowledge the "second curriculum," the knowledge arts curriculum. He points out how important this aspect of curriculum thinking is and how it may get shortchanged in the current "high stakes" testing environment of our schools.

The world of schooling is changing rapidly in the United States because of several factors, including advances in technology, immigration, increasing diversity, and a growing gap between the haves and have-nots. How will these factors influence the curriculum of the future? How can we build community, preserve all the voices of humanity, and find a curriculum that will work?

As you read this section of the reader think about the following:

- The meaning of curriculum
- The control of the curriculum
- The challenges of providing an appropriate curriculum for all students
- The importance of what is taught and why it is taught
- The role teachers can play in defining the curriculum

Article 3

WHAT IS REALLY IMPORTANT IN THE CURRICULUM WORLD?

JUDITH DZIUBAN

MARCELLA KYSILKA

Many events not directly related to education nonetheless affect it. Curriculum workers continue to ask questions like Herbert Spencer's "What knowledge is of most worth?" They also pose other questions—for example, "Should curriculum center on subject matter issues, student needs, or societal demands?" Teachers vigorously participate in the public debate about the most appropriate textbooks to use in their classrooms, and some states, such as Florida, have established elaborate statewide textbook-selection processes to ensure that a list is developed from which schools and/or districts must choose the books or materials that they will use for instruction. Questions related to student needs, societal concerns, and use of textbooks, to be sure, merit consideration and debate. However, many far-reaching issues affecting education, schools, and curriculum have little to do with such questions.

Daily newspapers, radio and television news programs bring Americans face-to-face with the desperate conditions under which some children live. At one extreme is the cruel war in Bosnia-Herzegovina. A fairly recent *Orlando Sentinel* news report was accompanied by a photograph of a boy waiting in the streets of Sarajevo for his school to begin. There he sat with his books amid the rubble of war. The report noted that children not only lived in the midst of tragic conditions but also continued to try to attend school.[1] Sarajevo's children sit three to a chair in the basements of apartment buildings because their schools have been destroyed. Notebooks have become a black market item. Teachers urge students to begin class sessions even if they, the teachers, are not there; they may be late because of being caught in shelling or sniper fire. In at least one school, a teacher and some students were killed when

SOURCE: Excerpted from Dziuban, J., & Kysilka, M. (1996). What is really important in the curriculum world? *Journal of Curriculum & Supervision, 11*(2), 188–193. Reprinted by permission of ASCD.

a mortar bomb struck their classroom. In all, nearly 15,000 children have been killed and 600,000 children are refugees.[2]

On April 21, 1994, Judy Collins appeared on *Good Morning America* to promote a new UNICEF book, *I Dream of Peace*. The book is a collection of drawings and compositions produced by children from the former Yugoslavia. According to James P. Grant, executive director of UNICEF, "In dozens of schools and refugee camps throughout the region, children have been encouraged to draw and write as a way to unlock the doors to their inner emotions."[3]

The book dramatically spotlights the plight of these children. Their concerns for family, friends, and each other are evident. Their messages burn into readers' minds and tug at their hearts.[4]

As you suffer, I suffer, and my nights are sleepless too. I swear to you, I do not kick the football like before, I do not sing the way I did. I have locked up my bicycle, and I have locked up my smile.

—Nemanja, 11, Sutomore

My father is a Croat, my mother is a Serb, but I dont [sic] know who I am.

—Lepa, 11, Belgrade

So many people have been killed fighting for justice. But what justice? Do they know what they are fighting for, who they are fighting? . . . We are children without a country and without hope.

—Dunja, 14, Belgrade

Our teacher has told us about Anne Frank, and we have read her diary. After fifty years, history is repeating itself right here with this war, with the hate and the killing, and with having to hide to save your life.

We are only twelve years old. We can't influence politics and the war, but we want to live! And we want to stop this madness. Like Anne Frank fifty years ago, we wait for peace. She didn't live to see it. Will we?

—Students from a 5th-grade class in Zenica

The former Yugoslavia is not the world's only area of unrest. Somalia, Haiti, Rwanda, and El Salvador are among the others. In each, children seek "normalcy" in their lives. In Cambodia, Lebanon, Kuwait, and Iraq, children have been traumatized by war. Still, in all these war-weakened countries, children and teachers have continued with the institution of school even under monstrously adverse conditions. School seems to be the one constant factor in the children's lives. School represents stability in the midst of instability. For most children, school is the one part of their world that has not been emotionally or psychologically torn apart.

A September 1994 article in the *Orlando Sentinel* reported that schools in war-ravaged Ruhengeri, Rwanda, had recently opened. The new government and UN agencies believe "opening the schools is key to normalizing daily life . . ."[5] As Nemanja, age 11, writes, "We will enjoy the singing of the birds and do our homework together."[6]

Although daily news reports heighten our concerns about the plight of children in war-ravaged countries, Americans need not look only to these countries to find children living under traumatic conditions. Consider the inner-city children described in Jonathan Kozol's *Savage Inequalities*.[7] These children live in the United States of America. They do not have textbooks, learning materials, writing paper, or enough teachers willing to teach them. These children live in a different kind of war—one of poverty and hunger.

Children in American communities suffer physical and emotional abuse every day, frequently without teachers' knowledge. And even if we can identify them, teachers and school leaders are not always able to provide the necessary services quickly to free them from the abuse. Many educators know something of the impact of war on society and children. On the other hand, children of hunger, poverty, and abuse often suffer silently. Their distress remains distant; they give few hints of their need for a lifeline. These children's schools may be the only safe haven for them. For these children, like the children of war, school offers stability and security, even if only for a short time each day. The extreme conditions of political war in other countries spotlight the plight of children caught in its midst and wrenchingly remind us of the hidden plight of so many American children caught in their own war of hunger, poverty, and abuse and the role school plays and does not play in their daily struggles to survive.

Against the backdrop of these calamities, curriculum simply cannot be restricted to considerations only of subject matter or a series of planned activities. How can war, poverty, hunger, and abuse be pigeonholed into a planned activity? In these situations, curriculum as cultural reproduction and curriculum as experience appear to be more relevant, offering more power and hope than simple conventions. Certainly children in destructive environments will develop very different images of school and learning than will children who live in less extreme situations. The children of the former Yugoslavia share an intense and common experience. Children caught up in disasters such as the recent earthquakes in California and Japan have also shared an intense common experience. Children in inner cities who dodge bullets on their way to school and witness classmates killed on school grounds share intense common experiences.

The definition of "curriculum as experience" originally did not include attention to these extreme types of experiences. However, war, poverty, hunger, and abuse must not be neglected in deliberations about what should be taught in school. Curriculum as *currere*, on the other hand, may be an appropriate image to use as teachers help these children, in the midst of turmoil, gain increased perspective and personal control of their lives.

No single image of curriculum is ideal or appropriate for deciding what should be taught in school. Before engaging in the public and often acrimonious debate over the selection of textbooks, appropriate reading lists, or which curriculum frameworks to adopt and which tests to administer, the curriculum community simply must stop and think: What do we really know about our students? We must develop a better understanding of the circumstances in which our children live before we can decide what to teach them.

Teachers and administrators are responsible for their own actions in schools. They can and must nurture children in schools and provide them with safe environments, even for just a few hours of the day. Teachers and fellow educators offer the only chance some of these children have; these adults—we—are their security, their "touchstone."

More important, we must understand that all the people's children, wherever or however they may live—in war-torn countries, in poverty, in hunger, and in abuse—are *our* children. They constitute *our* future—as extensions of ourselves and our society. In our work, we must insist that the school, its curriculum, and its influence in their lives are known rightly. Questions of which curriculum and which textbook to use are trivial unless posed within the framework of the lives of children. If children in their routinely difficult circumstances are lost, they are lost no matter what curriculum decisions have been made or what curriculum has been planned. In today's complex society, awareness of our children's life conditions, needs, hopes, and desires is essential *before we begin* to deliberate about what they should be taught.

American schooling can be devoured by its academic debates—evolution versus creationism, whole language versus phonics, traditional testing versus authentic assessment, the rightful and appropriate place of technology in the curriculum, and which books to keep on the library shelves, to name a few. Such debates can consume schooling without touching the lives of children.

Reality is raw: Much of the inflamed rhetoric loses its power in the face of real-world conditions that confront our children.

We educators must ask a simple question of ourselves and our society: How can we make a difference? Can we teach these children *anything* to help them—and us—break the devastating patterns of war, poverty, hunger, and abuse? How can a curriculum be developed that responds to the pleas of 10-year-old Sandra from Vukovar? "Don't ever hurt the children. They're not guilty of anything."[8]

Discussion Questions

How is curriculum defined in this article?

What issues facing children in your classroom concern you the most?

Judith Dziuban is an elementary teacher in the Seminole County Schools, Florida.

Marcella Kysilka is a professor emerita at the University of Central Florida.

Article 4

CURRICULUM ALIGNMENT REVISITED

ALLAN A. GLATTHORN

Curriculum alignment is one of those issues about which individual scholars and practitioners express seemingly irreconcilable differences.[1] Whereas many come out strongly in favor of curriculum alignment, others present forceful views in opposition. This article intends to explain how educators can use alignment constructively and expand it beyond its present narrowness.

At the outset, an understanding of teachers perceptions of curriculum alignment as they know it and use it is helpful. To see through teachers' eyes, for example, assume that you are a sixth grade teacher in one of the 40 or more states with "strong" accountability programs. The state department of education has issued curriculum guides for every subject—guides based on state-developed content standards and their related benchmarks. This state agency has also decreed that examinations will be administered to all sixth graders. Moreover, students' results on those examinations will be used for several purposes: to evaluate your teaching, to judge your school, to reward or punish you and the school, and to determine if students will be retained or promoted. To assist you, state department staff has published "testlets," practice tests that you can use to develop test-wiseness in your students and to prepare them for these high-stakes tests.

The prudent response that most teachers make in such situations is a commonsense one. They check the content of the state tests by using nonconfidential materials, examine the curriculum guide to remind themselves about what else should be taught, develop plans to accommodate the guide and the test, and teach as best as they can. This process, in essence, is curriculum alignment as most teachers know and understand it.

One step toward the reconciliation of advocacy and dissent about curriculum alignment is

SOURCE: Excerpted from Glatthorn, A. A. (1999). Curriculum alignment revisited. *Journal of Curriculum & Supervision, 15*(1), 26–35. Reprinted by permission of ASCD.

the realization that the process is only a tool, one that can be used foolishly or wisely. Used foolishly, curriculum alignment diminishes the art of teaching, sterilizes the curriculum, and makes the classroom a boring place.[2] Used wisely, it offers teachers a practical method by which they may ensure that their students are well prepared for the mandated test. This wise and practical use of alignment was advocated by several experienced teachers. In writing personal essays on how they respond to standards, accountability, and high-stake tests, most replied, "We cope creatively."[3]

In a time of mandated standards and high-stakes tests, ignoring the need for alignment is foolish at best. The issue is not "Should we align?" Rather, it is "How can we align so that alignment is teacher directed and teacher friendly?"

CREATIVE COPING

Curriculum alignment can be used wisely and constructively in several ways. The process explained below is one that teachers in workshops have found useful, but the process has not been rigorously evaluated.

Analysis of the Written Curriculum

The first step is to analyze the school districts' written curriculum in terms of three types of outcomes—mastery, organic, and enrichment. The mastery curriculum has several features that distinguish it from the other two types of outcomes. The mastery curriculum is essential for all students, it is best learned when carefully organized and structured, it is based on state standards and benchmarks, it should be emphasized in one specific grade, and it likely is tested. Here is an example of a mastery benchmark from a compilation of content standards by Kendall and Marzano (1997) (although they do not use the term *mastery benchmark*): "Understands the similarities and differences in colonial concepts of community (e.g., Puritans covenant community, Chesapeake colonial emphasis on individualism)" (p. 139).[4]

The organic curriculum also is essential for all students. However, rather than being assigned to one grade level, it is emphasized at every appropriate occasion. (Some districts have preferred to use the term *objectives for continuing development.*) The organic curriculum usually is not tested. Here is a benchmark from the Kendall and Marzano compilation that may be classified as organic: "Knows how to perceive past events with historical empathy" (p. 114).[5]

The enrichment curriculum is not essential for all students; it is simply "nice to know." Obviously such a classification is a matter of judgment. This benchmark from the same compilation would be classified as enrichment, although others might classify it differently: "Understands the differences among several state constitutions" (p. 145).[6]

In general, the mastery curriculum should require only from 60 to 80 percent of class time to teach, leaving the remainder of the time for the organic and enrichment curriculums—and any remediation that becomes necessary. Obviously, this reasonable allocation should vary with the subject, the grade level, and the nature of the students.

This classification system has several practical advantages. It gives the classroom teacher some room for "slippage." It helps curriculum developers make a critical distinction between mastery benchmarks, which should be emphasized at a given grade level, and organic benchmarks, which should be emphasized whenever appropriate. Finally, it enables teams of teachers to design enrichment units for all students, not just for the gifted, who perhaps need enrichment least of all.

Development of Mastery Units

With the foregoing analysis conducted, teachers then can align the written, tested, and taught curriculums. They review their identification of the mastery benchmarks by checking the curriculum guide, the nonconfidential information about the test, and their textbooks. By clustering related mastery benchmarks and using their own creativity, they develop units that they know will interest their students. For example, the mastery benchmark noted above can provide the foundation for a unit entitled "Whose Community?" which can begin with students' present understanding of their community, briefly examine current concepts of an ideal community, and then emphasize the similarities and differences between some of the colonial communities. In this sense, teachers will have developed their own written curriculum, all within the limits of prescribed state standards and state tests.

Teachers then can implement the unit flexibly, modifying it to respond to the needs and abilities of their students. In this manner, they align the tested curriculum with their written curriculum and their written with their taught. As they implement the unit, they try to build students' empathy for the early settlers, thus nurturing the organic curriculum. If time is available, they can teach a brief enrichment unit on utopian societies.

In summary, this process of aligning the written, tested, and taught curriculums can achieve seemingly contradictory goals: to enable students to do well on high-stakes tests and to provide students with in-depth units of study that are likely to engage their interests.

Expansion of the Concept of Alignment

In addition to its susceptibility to abuse, the prevalent model of curriculum alignment can be faulted for its narrowness. Rather than focusing solely on the written, the tested, and the taught, alignment should be expanded so that it goes well beyond this restrictive focus. To achieve this goal, I have found useful a concept of eight types of curriculums.

EIGHT TYPES OF CURRICULUMS

The *hidden curriculum* (a term coined by Jackson[7]) is the unintended curriculum—what students learn from the schools culture and climate and related policies and practices. It includes such elements as use of time, allocation of space, funding for programs and activities, and disciplinary policies and practices. One example of the hidden curriculum follows: An elementary school allocates each week 450 minutes to reading and 45 minutes to art. The unintended message of this plan to students is "Art doesn't matter."

The *excluded curriculum* is what has been left out of the curriculum, either intentionally or unintentionally. Eisner calls this type the "null curriculum" because it has no effect.[8] Several issues typically omitted from the U.S. history curriculum include the labor movement in the United States, the importance of religion in American life, and the internment of Japanese-Americans during World War II. Gehrke, Knapp, and Sirotnik point out that the excluded curriculum is "powerful by virtue of its absence" (p. 53).[9]

The *recommended curriculum* is the curriculum advocated by experts in the subject fields. Almost every discipline-based professional group has promulgated curriculum standards for its field. An excellent compilation of these standards appears in the Kendall and Marzano book referenced earlier.

The *written curriculum* is the document(s) produced by the state education agency, the school system, the school, and/or the classroom teacher. It specifies what is to be taught. Most states issue their own standards; some identify benchmarks as well. District-level documents usually include a curriculum guide and a scope and sequence chart. The written curriculum, to be sure, also includes materials developed by classroom teachers. The written curriculum is the one usually meant by educators who say, "We're going to develop a mathematics curriculum."

The *supported curriculum* is the curriculum that appears in textbooks, software, and multimedia materials. Some state authorities designate which textbooks are approved for school use; in other states, school district committees make these choices.

The *tested curriculum* is the curriculum that is embodied in state tests, school system tests, and teacher-made tests. The term test is used broadly here to include standardized tests, competency tests, and performance assessments.

The *taught curriculum* is the curriculum that teachers actually deliver; it is the curriculum that is enacted or put into operation. Researchers have pointed out the enormous variation in the nature of what is actually taught, despite the superficial appearance of uniformity.[10]

The *learned curriculum* is the "bottom-line" curriculum—what students learn. Clearly, it is the most important curriculum of all.

INTERACTIONS OF THE CURRICULUMS

How do these several curriculums interact? Based on my personal experience and research, I propose several answers.

The hidden curriculum has a powerful influence on students. Every day, students are exposed to its elements and internalize the messages sent. Thus, if the school system leaders speak about the importance of physical education in elementary school but allocate it to only 45 minutes each week, the message of that aspect of the hidden curriculum is that physical education does not matter.

The recommended curriculum in general has little impact on the written curriculum and perhaps less on classroom teachers. A notable exception was the recommendations advanced by the National Council of Teachers of Mathematics.[11] They seem to have influenced the written mathematics curriculums of many school systems and have been received positively by most mathematics teachers.

The written curriculum has only a moderate influence on the taught curriculum. Most experienced teachers review the guide at the beginning of the year and then put it aside as they weigh other factors in deciding what to teach. They tend to give greater attention to factors such as student interests, their assessment of what has worked in the past, and their inferences about what types of items will be on the state and district tests.

At present the tested curriculum seems to be having the strongest influence on teachers and students. In an era of accountability, teachers understandably are concerned about how their students perform on the test. Much classroom time is spent on developing test-wiseness and practicing on test like items. In almost every class, students ask the perennial question, "Will this be on the test?" A positive side to this emphasis on tests exists, especially when it takes the form of classroom assessment. Black and Wiliam conclude from their experience and the accumulated research that formative classroom assessment is the best way to raise standards.[12] Note, however, that a major research study concluded that high-stakes testing rewards harmful instructional practices and has no effect on school improvement.[13]

The supported curriculum continues to exert a strong influence on the taught curriculum, especially for elementary teachers who teach four or five subjects. The textbook, consequently, becomes their major source of content knowledge.

A significant gap exists between the taught and the learned. Students do not always learn what they are taught. Several factors account for the gap: teachers' failure to make the curriculum meaningful and challenging, teachers' failure to monitor student learning, students' low level of motivation, students' cognitive abilities, and students' short attention span.

ALIGNING THE MOST IMPORTANT TYPES OF CURRICULUMS

If, as noted above, eight types of curriculums exist, each of which may be aligned with each other, then at least 36 alignment possibilities exist. Of this number, however, only a limited number seem to be worth the effort to align. Based on my experience and knowledge of the research, I propose that the following are ones that best might be added to the written/taught/tested triad.

Hidden/taught. In this alignment, the faculty would work together to uncover their hidden curriculum. They would then identify those elements of the hidden curriculum that are conveying lessons that are discrepant with the intent of the taught curriculum. Subsequently they would modify the hidden curriculum to ensure that it conveys the messages intended. Suppose, for example, that the teachers strongly support a multicultural curriculum. However, their analysis of the hidden curriculum might reveal that currently only the interests of the majority culture are advanced. Then, the teachers would change the hidden curriculum so that it reflected a multicultural orientation.

Written/recommended. In this process, developers would compare the state standards and benchmarks for a given subject with those recommended by the professional organizations. The intent here is the improvement of the state standards through the addition of the best standards suggested by professional groups. The need to improve the state standards is borne out by Saxe's evaluation: Of 38 state social studies standards examined, only 13 received a grade of C or better.[14] Nineteen were rated "useless" (p. 10).

Excluded/written. The purpose of this alignment is to recapture content from the excluded curriculum that should be added to the written curriculum. Consider this example from the English language arts curriculum. Very few of the English curriculum guides I have evaluated make any mention of dialect studies. In this diverse society, such content would seem to be essential. The written curriculum should include such knowledge as the following: the nature of dialect, the extent of dialects ("we all speak a dialect"), changes in dialect, dialect as a barrier to increased social status, dialect as a bonding mechanism, the influence of television on dialects, and the types of dialect.

Supported/written. In an informal study I conducted a few years ago, I compared one of the textbooks on a state-approved list with the state-mandated course of study. Only 25 percent of the content of the state curriculum guide appeared in the state-adopted textbook. In one sense, school districts that adopted this book were wasting 75

percent of their textbook budget. Such an alignment is relatively simple, although practitioners should not rely on the publisher's own analysis.

Tested/learned. This alignment is a reminder for teachers to use the results of both the states mandated tests and the teacher's tests to diagnose teaching/learning problems. In too many instances, test results are simply recorded and then forgotten until grading time arrives.

Aligning the Taught/Learned Curriculums

The discrepancy between the taught and the learned curriculums is so significant that it deserves special analysis.

What is the taught/learned gap? The *taught/learned gap* is the difference between what the teacher teaches, as seen by a trained observer, and what the students learn, as determined by a valid assessment.

How much of a gap exists? Although no conclusive evidence exists with respect to a quantitative difference, the available research indicates that the gap is considerable. Based on my observations of classrooms and analysis of 40 taped segments, my informed guess is that the typical student in a given class period learns 50 percent of what the teacher teaches. Viewing one particular ASCD (Association for Supervision and Curriculum Development) videotape, I estimated that the students learned about 10 percent of what the teacher was teaching.

What causes the gap? Several causative factors are at work here. Consider first the environmental factors, starting with classroom climate. If the climate is conflict ridden, students will be inclined to deal with the conflict, thus taking their minds off what the teacher is teaching. If the climate is too "hot," in the sense of extreme closeness of teacher and students, then too much time will be spent on interpersonal issues. A second factor is external noise. Although internal noise does not seem to be a factor, external noise (e.g., trains, construction, trucks, fire engines, airplanes) seems to distract students from learning tasks.

Several teacher factors also contribute. Teacher behaviors that would result in a large gap include poor organization of lessons; unclear explanations of concepts with insufficient examples; speech without sufficient volume or clarity; provision of misinformation to students; insufficient monitoring and assessment; interruption of explanations with disciplinary concepts and actions; no provision of corrective feedback to students; possession of insufficient content knowledge; and choice of lesson content that is not developmentally appropriate.

To be sure, several student factors are easily noted. These include inattentiveness; lack of prior knowledge or incorrect prior knowledge; learning, auditory, or visual disability; emotional problems; absorption with a personal agenda; influence of peers who disparage school learning; disconnectedness with lesson content; fatigue or illness; interference because of cultural differences; and a preference for avoiding failure rather than being embarrassed by participating.

What can be done to narrow the gap? In my work with teachers, I have found that teachers are receptive to the use of peer collaboration in diagnosing and remediating the problem. They begin by discussing their experience as it relates to the particular issue. For example, Teacher A volunteers to have a videotape made of his or her teaching. After viewing the tape alone, Teacher A can scrap the tape if it is felt that the tape is not representative, or Teacher A and the peer associate—Teacher B—can view the tape together, with Teacher A leading the analysis and discussion. Then Teacher B takes a turn in the same manner. In all of this viewing and analyzing, teachers focus on student learning.

A Concluding Note

Curriculum alignment is a tool that can be used to damage or to strengthen the curriculum. The processes explained above can contribute to the construction of a learning-centered curriculum.

Discussion Questions

How do the eight types of curriculum that are defined in the article differ from one another?

After reading this article, what is your understanding of the concept of curriculum alignment?

Allan A. Glatthorn was a Distinguished Research Professor, East Carolina University, Greenville, NC.

Article 5

KNOWLEDGE ALIVE

DAVID PERKINS

Perhaps the broadest and most basic question for educators—before matters of method, testing, or grading—is "What should we teach?" And perhaps the most basic answer is "knowledge." Knowledge in the broad sense—facts, ideas, and skills—provides the mainstay of the school curriculum from kindergarten through college.

Fine for knowledge. But then there's the question of what you do with it. Education has always been more generous about exposing learners to large volumes of knowledge than about teaching them the diverse skills involved in handling knowledge well—the *knowledge arts.*

The knowledge arts include communicating strategically, insightfully, and effectively; thinking critically and creatively; and putting school knowledge to work out in what educators sometimes humbly call the "real world." The knowledge arts bundle together deep reading, compelling writing, strong problem solving and decision making, and strategic and spirited self-management of learning itself within and across the disciplines.

We need to put the knowledge arts on the table—to celebrate them for the depth and power they provide and for the ways they make knowledge meaningful. And we need to worry about their neglect.

THE KNOWLEDGE ARTS IN SOCIETY

To get a picture of how the knowledge arts work in schools, let's start with the bigger picture of how they work in society. We can tell the broad story of knowledge in four chapters, starting with creating it and moving on to communicating it, organizing it, and acting on it.

People create knowledge in various ways. Scientists examine the sky or the sea or quarks or viruses, historians puzzle over ancient documents and artifacts, pollsters survey public opinion, engineers design and test prototypes, newspaper reporters investigate political dogfights, police officers comb for evidence about crimes. Then we communicate that knowledge in

SOURCE: Excerpted from Perkins, D. (2004). Knowledge alive. *Educational Leadership, 62*(1), 14–18. Reprinted by permission of ASCD.

various ways through writing and reading mathematical equations, maps and diagrams, news broadcasts, electronic mailing lists, and works of art. We organize knowledge in various ways for ready access (notes, concept maps, Web sites) or for particular purposes, judgments, plans, and decisions (the court's verdict, the advertising campaign, the blueprints for a new building). And eventually, we act on all this knowledge. We carry out the judgment, erect the building, or launch the mission.

Of course, the story of knowledge in the form of these four chapters is far too linear. Creating, communicating, organizing, and acting on knowledge mix with one another in complex and generative ways. However, the four chapters provide a rough and ready overview.

THE KNOWLEDGE ARTS IN SCHOOL: A REPORT CARD

Keeping the four chapters in mind, how well does schooling develop the knowledge arts of learners? The report card for business-as-usual schooling would look like this:

Creating knowledge: D

Communicating knowledge: B

Organizing knowledge: C

Acting on knowledge: D

The first D reflects the fact that in typical schools, investigative, inquiry-oriented activities in which learners create knowledge are sparse. Of course such activities occur here and there—for instance, in some kinds of science learning—but even then they often entail simply going through the motions of a laboratory experiment rather than genuinely wrestling with ideas.

Acting on knowledge also earns a D. We rarely ask students to do much with their learning outside school—except homework, of course. As a result, knowledge tends to become passive or inert. In both academic and practical

contexts, learners fail to connect what they have learned to new situations or to act effectively on that knowledge (Bransford, Franks, Vye, & Sherwood, 1989). Students may memorize key information about biology for the science test but never ponder what that knowledge says about personal health care or public health issues.

Problems of transfer of learning have long plagued education (Bransford & Schwartz, 1999; Detterman & Sternberg, 1992; Perkins & Salomon, 1988). Typical schooling does not even encourage students to carry their knowledge from one classroom to another. Science instructors often complain that the math from math class somehow evaporates in the science room. History instructors grumble that some cognitive Bermuda Triangle in the corridor between the English and history classrooms has sucked away students' knowledge of writing.

Conventional education probably does best at communicating knowledge, so why does it rate only a B in this area? On the receptive side of communication, although learners spend a great deal of time loading up on knowledge, schools do not typically teach them to do so strategically. Many young readers can decode competently but have never learned to ask themselves what they are reading for, to monitor their reading as they go, to assess themselves afterward, and to fill in what they missed. The productive side of communication includes not only writing but also artistic expression, presentations, multimedia work, and so on. These areas typically receive little time or guidance, except for the mechanics of writing.

Further, some schools direct dogged attention to skill and content learning in a narrow sense, with the unsettling consequence that skills become ritualized into mere recipes to follow (Perkins, 1992). For instance, students who know how to add, subtract, multiply, and divide can become quite confused about how to apply these operations to story problems, and they often fall back on limited keyword strategies, such as "*all together* means *add*." Students learn what they are supposed to say in class without really understanding it. Science educator Marcia

Linn (2002) amusingly noted what one student made of a Newtonian principle of motion: "Objects in motion remain in motion in the classroom, but come to rest on the playground."

Organizing knowledge also receives little attention in typical schools—thus, the grade of C. In most school settings, strategic guidance in this skill appears only during review sessions or around such products as essays. Yet learning logs, concept mapping, debates, group presentations, and many other activities can dramatically expand students' skills in organizing knowledge.

At this point, dedicated educators will object: "My kids are deeply engaged in inquiry-oriented science learning!" "My students keep learning journals and review their learning every week!" "We stage a debate after every unit!" "Teams of youngsters are out there in the community investigating local history!" Good. These undertakings certainly cultivate the knowledge arts and deserve kudos when and where they occur. But we need to ask, How often is this kind of teaching and learning happening, and how well? Between the oases of glory, stretch deserts of neglect.

BRINGING KNOWLEDGE TO LIFE

What does it look like to enliven teaching and learning through the knowledge arts? The following examples come from the work of my colleagues at Project Zero of the Harvard Graduate School of Education (www.pz.harvard.edu).

Making Thinking Visible

One way to advance the knowledge arts is to use *thinking routines* (Ritchhart, 2002) to make students' thinking visible, increasing their awareness of what goes into creating, communicating, organizing, and acting on knowledge.

For instance, Shari Tishman (2002) and her colleagues have explored a simple way to make certain kinds of thinking visible by asking two key questions: What's going on here? and What do you see that makes you say so? They adapted this approach from a procedure for examining works of visual art thoughtfully (Housen, Yenawine, & Arenas, 1991), but learners can apply these questions to many different objects—for example, a short poem or a satellite photograph of a hurricane. Or a history instructor might show a historical artifact like a crossbow, accompanied by the slightly tweaked questions, How does this work? and What do you see that makes you think so?

Tina Grotzer and her colleagues have developed inquiry-oriented activities that engage students in communicating about the complex causal models that can often make science concepts difficult to understand—models that involve such invisible features as electrons, causal loops, and simultaneous cause and effect (Grotzer, 2003; Perkins & Grotzer, 2000). For instance, fourth graders studying electrical circuits compare different ideas about what the current does. Does it start at the battery and fill the circuit, like turning on a hot-water radiator system for the first time, and then continue to cycle? Or does the current of electrons move all at once, like a bicycle chain? Young learners lean toward the first idea, but the second is more scientifically accurate. The following discussion shows how the teacher can help students make visible their thinking about the scientific explanation of electrical flow (Grotzer, 2000):

Teacher:	Let's compare how cause and effect works in these two different kinds of cyclic models. In the cyclic sequential model [as in the radiator system analogy], what makes the electrons move?
Student 1:	They want to get out of the battery because of all the electrons so they go onto the wire.
Teacher:	And then what happens?
Student 2:	They go along the wire till they get to the bulb and that makes the bulb light up.
Teacher:	Why do the electrons move in the cyclic simultaneous model [as in the bicycle chain analogy]?

Student 1:	The electrons push the one in front but at the same time they are pushed by the one behind them. So everything moves at the same time.
Teacher:	Yes, each electron repels the next one but is repelled by the one behind it. It's both a cause and an effect at the same time. The whole thing turns like the chain on a bicycle. What causes the bulb to light?
Student 3:	When the electrons start to flow.

Grotzer's research shows that conversations like this one, along with simple experiments and activities, can make causal thinking visible and lead to higher levels of understanding.

Teaching for Understanding

Understanding is one of the most cherished goals of education. Teaching for understanding can bring knowledge to life by requiring students to manipulate knowledge in various ways. For instance, understanding a historical event means going beyond the facts to explain them, explore the remote causes, discuss the incident as different people might see it from their own perspectives, and skeptically critique what various sources say.

A number of years ago, several colleagues and I developed the Teaching for Understanding framework, which centers on the idea of performances of understanding (Blythe & Associates, 1998; Gardner, 1999; Perkins & Blythe, 1994). Here are two examples of classrooms using this framework, drawn from Wiske (1998).

Joan Soble employed the Teaching for Understanding framework to organize and deliver an introductory writing course for at-risk ninth graders—students whom she described as "perpetually overwhelmed." The students engaged in a wide range of understanding performances, including working with collages as preparation for writing: keeping and critically reviewing portfolios and setting and pursuing goals individually, using a form that listed writing skills they wanted to improve, from sentence structure to revision practices to aspects of self-management. Thus, these students worked directly on the knowledge art of writing, learning how to practice it with more skill, confidence, and flair. Soble's approach also helped students with another knowledge art: the thoughtful management of their own learning.

Lois Hetland's seventh-grade class examined fundamental questions about colonial America throughout the year. Some questions concerned the land: How does land shape human culture? How do people think about the land? How do people change the land? Another line of questioning concerned historical truth: How do we find out the truth about things that happened long ago or far away? How do we see through bias in sources? These *throughlines,* as Hetland called them, provided abiding points of reference for the learners. Discussing the same throughlines in connection with topic after topic helped students to develop not only a deeper understanding of colonial America but also important knowledge arts: the ins and outs of historical inquiry and the management of their own learning through sustained questioning.

Such practices engage students in various mixes of the four broad activities identified earlier—creating, communicating, organizing, and acting on knowledge—in ways linked to the disciplines. Moreover, research has revealed something quite striking: Students who participate in Teaching for Understanding classrooms display shifts in their attitudes toward understanding. Compared with other students, they think of understanding in a more dynamic and exploratory way, rather than as a collection of facts and skills (Wiske, 1998). This stance toward understanding amounts to a knowledge art that equips students for deeper learning.

Creating a Culture of Learning

The knowledge arts—like any art—are more than skills: They involve passion, energy, and commitment (Tishman, Perkins, & Jay, 1995). Teachers promote the knowledge arts when they strive to establish a classroom culture of inquiry and excitement.

Ritchhart (2002) describes an algebra teacher who began the first day of school by displaying a mathematical puzzle problem from the newspaper, noting that a student had brought it in, saying that he loved little problems, and encouraging students to provide other puzzle problems throughout the year. Then he wrote on the chalkboard an elaborate arithmetic computation drawn from an episode in *The Phantom Tollbooth*, asking students to work out the answer and commenting that he had better figure it out himself. Inevitably, students came up with a variety of answers. The teacher gave his own answer but warned that he didn't think it was correct. He challenged students to find the right answer.

Through these actions and others like them—informal, welcoming, and inquiring—this teacher signaled that the coming school year would bring knowledge alive.

THE SECOND CURRICULUM

One natural reaction to these examples—and others from ingenious teachers across the world—is that they simply illustrate good teaching methods. They show ways of teaching content that enhance student engagement and make knowledge more meaningful.

True enough, but the knowledge arts are more than just tools for teachers to teach with; they encompass ideas, skills, and attitudes for learners to learn—a second curriculum. Thinking of the knowledge arts in this way creates new responsibilities for educators. As teachers teach science, history, or literature, they should be able to specify what *skills of inquiry*, strategies of communication, methods of organization, and ranges of application they are striving to develop in students; how they are spending time on it; and how they are exciting students' interest and providing serious guidance. Without such an account, the second curriculum does not exist in any substantive sense.

The bad news: All this amounts to one more agenda in an era in which educators must prepare students for high-stakes tests that often emphasize *having* knowledge far more than *doing* something with it. The good news: The second curriculum is not just an add-on to the first. Instead, it's a meld, a fusion, an infiltration designed to bring knowledge to life and keep it alive. Taking the second curriculum seriously will not only equip students with knowledge-handling skills they need but also deepen and broaden their mastery of the first curriculum.

Behind the second curriculum is a simple idea: Education is not just about acquiring knowledge but about learning how to do significant things with what you know. It's not about dead knowledge but about bringing knowledge alive. To educate for today and tomorrow, every school and every classroom should teach the knowledge arts seriously and well.

Discussion Questions

What are the knowledge arts?

How do you teach for curricular meaning and understanding?

David Perkins is a professor in the Harvard Graduate School of Education.

Section III

HOW DO WE THINK
ABOUT CURRICULUM?

To understand today's current curriculum concerns about what should be taught in schools, it is helpful for those who are affected by the curricular decisions made by government legislation or administrative mandate to know how past curriculum thinking has influenced (positively, negatively, or not at all) those decisions. If we can't learn from out past, what hope do we have for our future? The series of articles in this section provides historical perspective to curriculum theorizing and draws conclusions about what might happen in the future if we do not heed lessons previously learned.

William Schubert, a well-respected curricularist shares his thoughts in "The Curriculum-Curriculum," on how he teaches curriculum theory to teachers so that theory becomes meaningful and useful to the practitioner.

Hanan Alexander revisits four seminal curriculum theories. She examines how they relate to human beings through the concept of human agency. By human agency she means the need for humans to form their own beliefs and actions and to understand their mistakes. Her concern is how curricular thinking can help develop human agency.

Progressive education was a major curricular event in the history of American education. Bullough and Kridel focus their article on the debates of individual needs and social philosophy as foundations for curriculum building. These debates contributed to the demise of the progressive movement. Although progressive education as a movement died, the influence of the movement continues today in curriculum thinking.

Professors Wraga and Hlebowitsh provide a succinct historical perspective of 20th-century curriculum thought. They suggest ways to exit the curriculum chaos that interferes with contemporary curriculum decision making.

Neil Postman closes this section with a humorous look at the glut of information confronting us and how dealing with that information poses interesting challenges to the schools. He offers a suggestion on how schools can organize all this information around five narratives that could build a sense of purpose to learning.

As you read through this collection of articles, you need to think about the following:

- How knowledge of past curriculum theory informs present thought

- How curriculum deliberations can be useful activities for teachers to participate in to provide appropriate educational opportunities for students

- How teaching can influence what is learned within the curriculum

- Why progressive education failed—or did it?

- The role schools need to play in coping with the enormous increase of information provided through technological advancements

Article 6

THE CURRICULUM-CURRICULUM

Experiences in Teaching Curriculum

WILLIAM H. SCHUBERT

To share my teaching of curriculum studies raises the question of where to begin. I am convinced that my curriculum discourse was born in childhood play as an only child on a farm where I generated a host of imaginary playmates. Coupled with travels I was fortunate to have in a family of educators, I lived the journey metaphor that is a founding archetype of curriculum studies. As a young child, I reveled in planning where we would drive each summer, what we would see, and why it would be worth experiencing.

I continued this process of talking to myself throughout my life, although it would be more accurate to say talking with *my selves.* I am increasingly convinced that *I am several.* Perhaps, *I am a conversation.* I submit that over the years my real and imagined companions, journeys, and ponderings of the worthwhile have helped my

selves thrive. These *selves* [like the cells that L. Thomas Hopkins (1954) analogized to self-development] expand, differentiate, and integrate as the curriculum of my life unfolds in a panoply of conscious effort and untold surprise.

Before doctoral study, as an elementary school teacher for eight years, I recall that my most important *in-service education* was the continuous conversation among the conflicting selves that emerged within me—sometimes collaborating, often conflicting, but almost always bringing a rich diversity of expansion, differentiation, and integration of my emerging self. During those years, reading philosophy or talking about ideas with friends (including students) provided much greater stimulation for my teaching than did the drudgery of writing lesson plans or behavioral objectives. I began to find curriculum literature that augmented my conversation

SOURCE: Excerpted from Schubert, W. H. (2003). The curriculum-curriculum: Experiences in teaching curriculum. *Curriculum & Teaching Dialogue*, 5(1), 9–21. Reprinted by permission of Information Age Publishing.

about what is worth knowing, doing, needing, being, becoming, overcoming, sharing, and contributing. This *multilogue* helped me see that few important issues were settled and that a productive uncertainty was the best place to be on the toughest issues.

My experience with family, friendship, journey, hope, and imagination doubtless is a seedbed for the way I teach curriculum studies. Imaginative playmates came in handy as I role-played my way through eight years of elementary school teaching and later made their way into my professing of curriculum studies.

One of my enduring methods grew from my elementary teaching, wherein I would *be* a person from history, rather than simply tell about that person; for instance, I might transform myself to become a prehistoric man, a Buddhist, or a serf in the Middle Ages. Later, as I worked on my first book, *Curriculum Books: The First Eighty Years* (Schubert & Lopez, 1980), I saw recurrent curriculum orientations or ideologies emerge in each decade of the 20th century, so I named them: *social behaviorist, intellectual traditionalist, experientialist,* and *critical reconstructionist.* I saw some of each of them in myself, and so it was not too difficult to summon up the pure form of each to teach in my classes. These mysterious visitors became known to my students as Schubert's *guest speakers.* Soon, I took them on consulting ventures, as well.

What I want to convey in this article is an interpretation of the story of strategies I used to teach curriculum studies and the internal reflection that accompanied their development. I do so in the spirit of *dialogue.* My thoughts on teaching curriculum studies, and on generating dialogue about teaching and curriculum, have evolved under the title *Curriculum-Curriculum.* The point (although not realized by my spell and grammar check, which sees the term *curriculum-curriculum* as a redundancy) is that if I am teaching about curriculum studies, I am trying to influence the curriculum that helps students understand and engage with the field of curriculum studies. So, I encourage them to think about the curriculum (or personal journey) of their

current exploration of curriculum and, as well, the explorations they hope to carry out as they continue their career in curriculum studies.

When I began to teach curriculum studies, I realized this purpose only on a superficial level. I somehow wanted my students to realize the whole panorama of the curriculum studies field in one or two courses. Perhaps due to my own indoctrination through school and college experiences that saw coverage as a possibility, I dished out curriculum *knowledge* fast and furiously, wanting instant expertise. I was well meaning, and clearly naïve. After all, it had taken me several years of study to learn what I wanted graduate students to comprehend in a quarter. I wanted students to know what I knew, so we could have discussions from that mutual stance. To determine if they knew what I had presented via lecture and reading, I gave tests.

I began questioning what *understanding the knowledge base* meant. I began to question whether (or how much) the meaning or essence of curriculum studies really pertained to amassing details on such matters as the Committee of Ten and Fifteen reports, the Eight Year Study, life adjustment curriculum, post-Sputnik curriculum reform, or the comprehensive high school. I wondered how much everyone should be able to recite about John Dewey, Edward L. Thorndike, Harold Rugg, George Counts, Franklin Bobbitt, W. W. Charters, William Kilpatrick, Wilford Aikin, L. Thomas Hopkins, Alice Miel, Theodore Brameld, Ralph Tyler, Hollis Caswell, Florence Stratemeyer, Max Corey, Edward Krug, Virgil Herrick, Hilda Taba, B. Othanel Smith, or J. Harlan Shores, among others. With faith in the possibility of the synoptic, we claim to *cover* world history and biology in a year, or economics or psychology in a semester. Incredible! I recall a story (perhaps apocryphal) that Einstein agreed to give a graduation address, and the high school valedictorian sitting next to him asked what Einstein did. He replied, "I study physics." The student looked at his white hair and aged features and said incredulously, "Well, I studied physics last year!" Her implication was that she completed the study in a year, so why is this Einstein fellow taking so long to study it!

So, I thought about my expectations, noting how the students struggled to be able to give cursory identification of characters and events in the curriculum field that came so easily for me. I listed 100 sets of four or five items about curriculum. All but one fit a category of curriculum studies, and students had to identify which item did not fit with other members of the set. If they thought more than one could be excluded, they were asked to include written justification. Few did. They had been programmed by years of "giving the right answers" to try to *psych out* the teacher or professor to give what they wanted. While I thought the activity made the necessary drudgery of amassing information fun, anxiety continued (although students acted as if the exercise were fun because this attitude was part of "the right answer," too).

Why is it so difficult to break away from the diabolical identification of information acquisition with learning and growth? Is it merely that the former is easier to request and measure than insight and understanding, which are much more defensible outcomes of study? I pondered such matters and realized that the curriculum field, for me, was like family and friends, because I lived it. I knew the people. I saw a connection between my own personal wonderings about life's meaning and what curriculum scholars ask. As I thought about why I was so drawn to curriculum literature, it came to me that amid all of the emphasis on planning, surveillance, and control, there exists in that literature a persistent voice that asks, "What is worthwhile?" As I pondered this observation, I concluded that if I could somehow get students to ask this question, and keep it alive in their educational endeavors, the rest would follow. They would come to appreciate the legacy of curriculum dialogue and discourse, characters and events, and even contextual details. So I concluded that the *what is worthwhile* question is the essence of the curriculum field. I thought that maybe I could somehow connect whatever students considered worthwhile in life generally with this *what's worthwhile* heart of the curriculum field.

So, I began to develop alternative approaches.

I began a curriculum theory class as usual with students telling something of who they are. Expanding a bit beyond asking about each student as an educator, I inquired about his or her outside interests. Each was asked to identify a topic about which he/she knew well. Choices included restaurants, cars, shopping, chess, cards, golf, pets, musical instruments, sports, travel, and much more. I then asked students to note several (say, 5–10) subcategories of their interest. So, for television, someone might list cartoons, family shows, news, movies, dramas, commercials, soap operas, specials, game shows, and sports. Then they spent a few weeks reading short pieces by a wide variety of curriculum authors. Finally, they were asked to categorize the theorists using the subcategorical scheme of their interest area. Since their interest area was something they knew a good deal about, it was not difficult for them to explicate in detail a rationale for placing curricularists into their subtopics. By connecting their interests with the purport of curriculum essays, curriculum meanings came closer to students' life concerns. This activity confirmed my contention that we learn best when we make analogies that connect the novel with the familiar in our lives. It occurred to me that doing so puts one rather close to John Dewey's (1916) connecting of the *psychological* (interests and concerns of learners) with the *logical* (extant knowledge in disciplines or personal experience).

I also tried individual conferences, thinking that focus on personalized concerns in light of curriculum questions would highlight the question of worth. It also helped those who could express ideas better orally than via writing. So, I constructed six questions built around central themes in readings and class sessions, stating them in ways that enabled discussion to move to application in each student's realm of experience. To avoid an emphasis on role memorization, I gave the questions to students in advance and said they could bring notes to help center discussion on ideas that students deemed relevant to their lives as educators. Students had to do considerable study in preparation for the conference. Nonetheless, anxiety was not much relieved, as compared with the test situation. Shortly, I dropped this highly charged conference. My surveillance quotient was still too high, and my uneasy feelings persisted.

Knowing how I have benefited from talking with curriculum theorists at conferences and through corresponding with them, I thought of another tack to simulate similar experiences in the classroom. I asked students to identify two or three of the theorists whose work spoke significantly to them and to pose questions that they would like to ask these theorists. I often followed this activity by having the students construct responses that they thought the theorist in question would be likely to make. Sometimes I would role-play as the theorist responding, and a conversation would ensue. An alternative activity, perhaps more connected to lived experience, was to have students write letters to theorists after reading an article or book. While only an exercise for theorists no longer alive, I actually mailed the letters to living authors. Both students and authors expressed enjoyment and personal benefit from the transactions that occurred.

As a variation on this theme of communicating with authors, I instigated a simulated conference or seminar among authors read, with each student role-playing as an author, sketching out his or her major points, and engaging in dialogue that I moderated. As moderator, I attempted to provide additional background on the authors and ideas found in other works they had written. I began to invite scholars to visit with my students, even offering a stipend to have a colleague from another university visit in the rare instance that the financial wherewithal existed. Moreover, the following idea struck me about 20 years ago: If I could attend conferences, so might my students.

Influenced by the corpus of Elliot Eisner's work, I decided that assignments should not be so unidimensionally discursive. So, sometimes I have asked students to make a nonverbal, artistic rendition of the impact of an article or book.

I have also asked students to keep elaborate card files (in a recipe box) of different categories of curriculum-related artifacts. This works especially well with students of teacher education. Nevertheless, it could be a basis for analysis and discussion of the *worthwhile* question for experienced educators who are already doctoral students. I usually ask that the cards include book cards (with brief summary and commentary on major ideas or perspectives), methods or approach cards (with practical ideas for curriculum and teaching, noting underlying assumptions), materials cards (actual notes on resources and materials and their rationale for use), frequent thought cards (any ideas that enhance perspective or reflection on curriculum matters), and salient quotation cards (exact words from pieces read, for future incorporation in dissertations or other writings that students might do).

Since it is next to impossible to read and write comments on the voluminous selections of cards that often emerge, I have also asked students simply to provide one-page, single-spaced, 10–12 font, written commentaries that are merely a slice of the continuous reflection that each normally carries out; strangely and *quantitatively*, this is a kind of *sample* of the stream of consciousness that any serious budding scholar experiences all of the time! I ask that students leave marginal space for my comments, which is not difficult to provide for one-page per student, a few times per semester.

Most recently, along with these one-page renditions, my larger assignment is for students to present what I call their *curriculum-curriculum.* Rather than teach and then test (trying to see if what students recall is what I want them to recall), I simply ask them to imagine ways to express how they are growing through their encounters with curriculum literature. Expressions of the *curriculum-curriculum* take many forms: journals, video, audiotapes, personal conferences, relevant stories, and varied commentaries (e.g., mini reviews of books, projections of next readings, imagined projects, discussions of the meanings of work encountered, and related experiences in education and life). Oral presentations on key dimensions of each student's *curriculum-curriculum* serve as culminating experiences for the course. A course, I have increasingly come to believe, is not a completion of study; rather, if worth its salt, it is a beginning of lifelong pursuit that will move in yet uncharted directions.

By my *curriculum-curriculum* assignment, I therefore mean to ask students, How is this journey of learning (journey as a root of curriculum, derived from the course of a chariot race) into curriculum studies providing you with insight into the curriculum of your own life? How does this course influence your ongoing journey toward images of the worthwhile? How is your journey toward educational worth also a journey toward personal, societal, and environmental worth? How does it provide meaning and sense of direction or purpose in your life as an educator?

How do I as each of my guest speakers (social behaviorist, intellectual traditionalist, critical reconstructionist, and experientialist) encourage this curriculum-curriculum journey? Let me give a few examples of each. As a social behaviorist, I often return to Franklin Bobbitt (1918 and 1924), well known for his notion of activity analysis. Unwilling to take a stand on what is worthwhile, I (as social behaviorist) claim to be a curricular engineer, who seeks to find and facilitate the voice of the majority, while also protecting minority opinion. Almost forgotten, activity analysis is shown to be a prerequisite that gives defensibility to the commonly assumed starting point of curriculum development—namely, needs assessment. From a Bobbitt-esque posture, I ask students (usually practicing educators) if they want their own students to be successful. Seldom does anyone oppose success as a marker to strive for, although a few want me to define success. With Bobbitt, I claim that we can discover it empirically. Imagining Bobbitt's practice of observing successful persons in an effort to delineate their frequent activities, we recall persons we consider to be successful in an admirable sense (famous and not, past and present). I call for an analysis of key qualities or characteristics that

define successful practices of these persons. Personages commonly named include Oprah Winfrey, Michael Jordan, President [Whomever], Bill Gates, Mother Theresa, Martin Luther King, Jr., Ralph Nader, Bono, Jesus, Gandhi, Buddha, a good friend, an admirable relative. In any case, we then launch into what must these individuals know, value, and be able to do in order to make the good contributions they make. Hence, addressing the basic curriculum question: What is worthwhile? Once identified and carefully defined and defended, these qualities of knowing and being become a baseline from which to do a needs assessment. Herein is the basis for curriculum development, and the social behaviorist shows how to convert needs into purposes and objectives (behavioral whenever possible). Continuing with the Tyler rationale (see Tyler, 1949), purposes are conveyed through a delivery system known as content, learning activities, or experiences; they are engineered via organizational patterns of scope, sequence, and learning environment and are enacted through instructional strategies and materials; they are evaluated (measured whenever possible), and the results are used as feedback for curricular improvement (see Schubert 1986/97, Chapters 8–11). Extant scientific research is sought as a valid and reliable basis for carrying out each phase of this process of curriculum design.

My *intellectual traditionalist* visitor answers the basic curricular question of worth by saying that the great works should be the basis for curriculum. After all, they embody the best that humans have created—the best wisdom and knowledge in philosophy, history, the arts, literature, science, mathematics, and social science. I ask students each to identify a great work or genre of work that has moved them deeply and influenced their journey toward that which is worthwhile. Once identified, I challenge students to figure out how the creator of the work(s) reached them. It is noteworthy that the author or artist did not know them personally. I argue that the great work in question is, in fact, *a curriculum* that has influenced them greatly. How has the creator of that *curriculum* known what to do to extend such influence? How is he or she a great teacher? Has this teacher–curricularist–artist implicitly employed what Gilbert Highet (1950) called *the art of teaching*, based on knowing the subject, loving the subject, knowing the students, caring about the students? Isn't great teaching and curriculum making from an intellectual traditionalist stance more of an art than the science of the social behaviorist? How can the qualities of the greatest teachers (creators of our great works) be identified and utilized as models of curriculum and teaching in schools and other places of education? Although they do not know us personally, do great authors and artists reach us because they know that we are all concerned with [Adler's] great ideas or [Ulich's] mysteries and events of life, since these are common human qualities or interests? How can we make better use of great works and their creators as a basis for understanding curriculum and teaching?

When my *critical reconstructionist* emerges, I focus on social justice as a worthy object of curricular discourse. Saturating students with the literature of inequity (vis-à-vis race, socioeconomic class, gender, sexual orientation, appearance, health, ableness, age, membership, place, ethnicity, religion, language, belief or unbelief, cultural practices, nationality, and more), I [as the critical reconstructionist] encourage students to tell stories from their own experience about discrimination (for or against) that they have known personally and learned from others. From these stories, they sense what it means to name their experience (see Freire, 1970) without the imposition of hegemonic master narrative. Drawing from Jean Anyon's provocative analyses (1980), how is it that some groups must learn that the route to success (if there is one at all) is to learn and play the rules, while slightly more privileged groups learn to find success by *psyching out* the persons in charge and giving them *the right answers*? How is it that even more privileged groups (those considered potentially dangerous by rulers—governmental, corporate, or military) are given a special *deal* that allows them to be creative and rather well-to-do, if they promise not to challenge ruling class supremacy? How is it

that *rulers* are kept in power through success that derives from large amounts of money and power-wielding connections? To this duo, obedient educators can add high-quality (e.g., Ivy League) certificates.

Teachers often tell students that they have to leave their problems [of a toxic waste dump near their homes, pressure to buy or sell drugs, or threat to join a gang] at the doorstep of the school and come in to *circle the verbs* (see Rehak, 1996), seldom addressing the meaning of such activities. The surreptitious meaning—could it be to prevent questioning of inequities? Instead, what if we enabled students to see that their oppressions (repressions, suppressions, and depressions) could be addressed by *carefully* integrating subject matters and personal experience to pose and act on real life problems and concerns, as *named* by students themselves.

The *experientialist*, less strident than the critical reconstructionist, suggests that curriculum should come from a full range of experience and the wonders therein, oppression being one of many. I often ask students to make a list of six things they hate to do, with extra credit given for items on their list that they cannot do well. I ask them to imagine that the next Monday they have to arise early, go off to a factory-like building, and have an hour of each. This is their schedule. They groan. I assure them it is only five days a week, 200 days a year, and for merely 13 years. Somehow, this does not make them feel better. When there, they will be compared with others, some of whom can pursue these topics rather well, others very well, and a few [like themselves] do poorly. They will be tested and graded and their marks will determine opportunities for the future. So will their conduct. Would they ever feel like dropping out, causing trouble, being destructive to property, others, or themselves? They would, of course. Who wouldn't? Only a few say it would be good for them to be forced to improve through suffering. Then we reflect on the fact that there are many students who look at their schedules (math, science, reading, English, foreign language, social studies, and more) and feel as these educators do when they look at the list of things they hate to do and can't do well. Herein, we consider the deficit model and its prominence in schools, as we too often see played out in reality (see Ayers, 2001, 29–32, for critique of the deficit model).

What of the possibility of defining students in terms of their strengths, instead of their deficits? As an exercise, I ask students to think of one of their strengths—perhaps a skill, an area of knowledge, an interest, a value or belief that guides their lives. I ask them to draw a pathway, a meandering circuitous journey, with *birth* at one end and *now* at the other. I have them draw some milestones on the pathway to represent significant influences that inspired development of one or more of the strengths they identify. In pairs or small groups, students tell stories about those milestone experiences. They become enthralled in memories of experience—their own and those of others. I ask them to interview someone outside of class [e.g., a friend, relative, or significant other] and to reflect on what they have heard. What builds strength and capacity? What conditions, kinds of interactions, inspirations, exemplars? They reflect on how to bring more such capacity builders to their situations as educators.

All of the attempts to inspire reflection, with the help of my guest speakers, often merge with lived experience. Sometimes this takes the form of direct applications by students in educational situations outside of the university. Sometimes students (teachers and administrators) take these activities to their work and share them with colleagues for in service education or professional development. They might build curriculum from studying meanings of success, as the social behaviorist admonished them to do. Or, from an intellectual traditionalist standpoint, they might relate educational experience to great ideas or life's mysteries and events. Alternatively, they might struggle to integrate curricula around student experience of oppression, responding to the critical reconstructionist call to remake society. Or, from the experientialist, they might begin by learning about their own students' milestones on their journeys of experience and ask together how they can create meaning, growth, and beneficial contributions in the world.

For me, the essence of any project, dissertation, article, or book is *to consider what is worth doing and being, experiencing and knowing, needing, sharing, overcoming, imagining, and contributing.* I think that this is the essence of education itself.

Discussion Questions

How is your educational journey reflected in your teaching philosophy?

How would you define each of the curriculum approaches delineated by Schubert: the social behaviorist, the intellectual traditionalist, the critical reconstructionist, and the experientialist?

William H. Schubert is a professor at the University of Illinois, Chicago Center.

Article 7

HUMAN AGENCY AND THE CURRICULUM

HANAN A. ALEXANDER

Philosophers since Plato have held that education in the fullest sense entails initiation into communities in pursuit of worthwhile knowledge (Plato, 1987). This means, as Richard Peters (1965) put it, that education involves two conditions, one concerning knowledge and the other desirability. Regardless of how one conceives the nature of knowledge, however, addressing the question of what is *worth* knowing requires a conception of what it means for something to be worthwhile (Bode, 1927; Spencer, 1945). Yet, recent curriculum thought has tended to deny or undermine one or another aspect of the key assumption upon which a meaningful account of desirability depends—that people are the agents of their own beliefs, desires, and actions. This renders a significant encounter between the curriculum and substantive ethics highly problematic.

ETHICS AND HUMAN AGENCY

Crucial to any ethical stance is the assumption that human beings possess agency. This means that they have the freedom within reasonable limits to choose their beliefs, desires, and actions, the intelligence to distinguish between better and worse according to some conception of these notions, and the capacity to make mistakes in what they believe, feel, and do. Elsewhere I have called these the conditions of moral or ethical discourse: freedom, moral intelligence, and fallibility (Alexander, 2001, pp. 44–48).

These conditions can be clarified by reference to three concepts that emerge in the thought of Charles Taylor (1964): self-determination, self-expression, and strong evaluation. Free will is related to self-determination. Taylor followed Kant in believing that personal autonomy is a

SOURCE: Excerpted from Alexander, H. A. (2005). Human agency and the curriculum. *Theory and Research in Education*, 3(3), 343–369. Reprinted by permission of Sage.

"transcendental condition" of ethics, an assumption we must make for any conception of normative discourse to make sense. Ethics is concerned with persuading a person to discipline her will to act or arrange her life in a certain way. If it is not in fact within a person's sphere of influence to direct her will, because it is controlled by some other agent such as society or history or chemistry or the gods, if she is not in this sense autonomous, then it is futile to endeavor to persuade her to desire this rather than that or to behave in this way rather than that, since she is not the agent in charge of her desires or behavior.

Moral intelligence is connected to what Taylor calls self-expression. He follows Hegel in recognizing that for a person to be able to exercise autonomy she must be able to ground her choices in some sort of reasoning or understanding; otherwise her choices would not actually be hers, but rather a product of caprice. This requires "horizons of significance" or "transcendental ideals" embedded in moral traditions sufficiently "thick" to sustain meaningful moral choice, not mere reflections of arbitrary taste, personal whim, or momentary feeling, to which competing conceptions of the good give expression, even if we cannot agree on their content (Alexander, 2001, pp. 145–50; Smith, 2002, pp. 65–66; Taylor, 1991; Walzer, 1994, p. xi).

For self-expression to be meaningful, moreover, we must suppose that people have the capacity to engage in a particular kind of self-evaluation. This is connected to what I have called fallibility, or the capacity to err. Unlike animals that possess only first-order desires concerning such needs as food, procreation, and survival, humans also possess second-order desires—desires about desires—in which they evaluate their primary preferences (Frankfurt, 1971). I can choose, in the first instance, between two flavors of ice cream, say. Taylor calls this "weak evaluation," because the decisive factor in choosing one flavor over another is how I feel at that moment. Today I feel like vanilla, but tomorrow, I might prefer chocolate. I can also choose, however, between risking my life to save a friend in battle or running away to save myself. The crucial factor in this instance is not how I feel at a given moment, but how I assess the worth of a particular feeling. I might consider the desire to save a friend courageous or generous, for example, and the motivation to run cowardly or selfish. Or, I might think it foolish to risk my life for another and eminently sensible to look out for myself first. It is this sort of assessment, which Taylor calls "strong evaluation," that we must express in making autonomous ethical decisions if they are be meaningful in other than a weak sense.

Curriculum thought must assume that teachers and students possess agency, that they are capable of self-determination, self-expression, and strong evaluation.

THE TYLER RATIONALE

Ralph Tyler (1949) is often associated with the technological movement in curriculum thought. He responded to the so-called scientific curriculum making of Franklin Bobbitt and W. W. Charters, according to which the curriculum should prepare students for adult life (Bobbitt, 1924). The tasks to be mastered to that end are to be determined by means of a statistical survey of daily adult behaviors (Charters, 1923). Unfortunately, this assumes that current adult behaviors are those that ought to be taught to children, which, as Boyd Bode pointed out, is not always the case (Bode, 1927). Additionally, it assumes that we can conclude from the way things are how they ought to be, and as David Hume (1953) long ago pointed out, this is logically problematic. This problem is commonly associated with what G. E. Moore called the "naturalistic fallacy," although Moore's formulation differed in significant ways from Hume's (Moore, 1993).

Tyler addressed this among other concerns by suggesting that three sources be consulted to determine curriculum objectives: the learners themselves, the social environment, and the subject matter. By comparing an assessment of what students know in a given field to what the society and subject matter require them to learn, we can establish the proper objectives in each discipline. Since there are likely to be many more objectives than can be attained, the results of this process should be sifted through two screens; the philosophy of the school and the psychology of learning. The first establishes the normative priorities of the school and the latter the appropriate developmental stages at which each priority should be addressed.

To establish the objectives of a language or mathematics curriculum, for instance, we should first assess what the students already know and compare this to what the social environment and subject matter require. French or American schools will demand different levels of language proficiency at home than they do abroad, and a math program in a science magnet will have different expectations from that of an arts-centered school. Whatever the environment, the subject matter will require much more than can be accomplished in any given academic year. So the school philosophy should be consulted to establish priorities and educational psychology to determine developmental appropriateness. The school philosophy can help to allocate resources such as instructional time, money for textbooks, language laboratories, and other instructional aids. Educational psychology will assist in deciding what students of a given age can be expected to achieve.

Once the objectives have been determined, Tyler then asked the curriculum planner to consider the experiences that might ensure that they are achieved, the ways in which those experiences should be organized, and how they ought to be evaluated. Tyler was among the first curriculum theorists to conceive the curriculum process in terms of student learning and social conditions rather than subject matter alone.

In a well-known critique, curriculum historian Hebert Kliebard (1975) pointed out that to assess students' knowledge or the demands of any given subject matter we must first know what subjects are to be taught. However, this is the whole point of curriculum development: to determine what those subjects ought to be. In other words, according to Kliebard's critique, to determine what subjects should be taught we

must already know what they are. The sources of objectives may help to refine the desired behaviors the curriculum should seek to attain, but at the end of the day the real work of curriculum development comes down to the normative philosophy of the school, which is predetermined by the adult society. Yet, Tyler offers no guidance as to how to evaluate competing claims among normative philosophies of education. Similar to his predecessors Bobbitt and Charters, he uncritically assumes that the way things are is the way they ought to be.

However, Tyler's difficulties with the normative side of the curriculum run deeper than this. Kliebard also questioned the morality of manipulating educational environments to achieve predetermined behavioral objectives. Does not the very idea of stating curriculum aims in terms of predetermined measurable objectives presume that the outcomes of learning can be controlled by the educational experiences in which the learner is required to participate? Where is the will, or desire, or interest of students in this scheme? To be sure, Tyler calls upon the curriculum planner to measure the interests of students in assessing the needs of the learners, and even asks that student interest be taken into account when planners select educational experiences for learners. Yet in the final analysis, the interests of society—expressed in the philosophical screen and translated into experiences designed to ensure outcomes—will always trump student desires. It would appear that interest is to be consulted in Tyler's curriculum primarily for the purpose of packaging predetermined social objectives to make them appealing to students, rather than to actively engage their genuine aspirations and concerns.

Tyler might respond, of course, that aspirations are socially determined, and that one purpose of the curriculum is to shape student desires according to social needs, or at least to provide a basis upon which autonomous decisions might later be founded. Communities of all sorts—political, cultural, religious, linguistic, or ethnic—have legitimate interests in inculcating their particular concerns in their children (see Counts, 1978). But this response misses the key point: Kliebard questioned not only the adequacy of Tyler's approach to competing social needs and rival educational philosophies but also the morality of his assumption that learning should be defined primarily in terms of experiences designed to produce predetermined outcomes.

The only way for students to embrace desired outcomes according to the Tyler rationale would be through experiences that are prearranged to produce those outcomes whether or not a student might at some point be so convinced or inclined. Yet, the very idea that social or any other sort of interests are *morally* legitimate only makes sense when we recognize that people, including students, are agents endowed with the capacity for self-determination. We flatten the ethical significance of social or other concerns, therefore, to the extent that we suppress or subvert this essential human capacity.

There is a deep tension within a curriculum that offers an account of what is most worth knowing, which is what the Tyler rationale proposed to do, but that flattens the self-determination of students; for the very idea of something being worthwhile requires the assumption that within reasonable limits students are agents of their own desires, beliefs, and actions.

SCHWAB AND THE STRUCTURE OF THE DISCIPLINES

An especially influential approach to the academic curriculum during the past half century was launched in the 1960s as "the structure of the disciplines" movement. Joseph Schwab (1982), Tyler's colleague at the University of Chicago, was a towering figure in this tradition.

Schwab and his structuralist colleagues responded to the rapid growth of knowledge by arguing that the curriculum could no longer provide students with a comprehensive knowledge of any given subject matter, since scientific discovery is moving so rapidly that what is believed to be true today may turn out to be false tomorrow. Instead of focusing solely on the *substance* of a

discipline, its basic concepts and findings, the curriculum should also teach the *syntax* of a discipline, its methods of discovery and justification. Such an inquiry-based curriculum would teach students not only the matter of a discipline as Richard Peters (1965) called it, but, more important, its epistemological form, the tools of investigation and critical assessment used by scholars to discover new knowledge (Hirst, 1974; Hirst & Peters, 1970; Schwab, 1982). For this reason, the structuralist approach to curriculum has sometimes been associated with what came to be known as the "discovery method" (Shulman & Keisler, 1968).

How are we to devise such a curriculum? Schwab had a unique and ingenious answer. Following Aristotle's distinction between theoretical knowledge (*sophia*) and practical wisdom (*phronesis*), he held that curriculum is a practical not a theoretical discipline (Aristotle, 2001). Its aim is not to discover laws of nature, society, behavior, or education but to translate those discoveries into practical strategies for teaching the structure of disciplines. The products of curriculum development are alternative lesson plans that anticipate instructional challenges in teaching a particular subject matter, not experiences designed to meet objectives measurable by the tools of social or behavioral science.

Arriving at such plans is a complex process because the disciplines to be taught, and the research that provides guidance for how to teach them, are not static doctrines to be memorized and applied but dynamic disciplines rich with scholarly discussion and debate. The challenge is to create an ongoing conversation between those working to discover new disciplinary and pedagogic knowledge and those endeavoring to teach students in school. This process, which Schwab called "curriculum deliberation," engages representatives of the essential ingredients of curriculum in dynamic discussions about how best to translate theory into practice. He called these ingredients "commonplaces"—teaching, students, subject matter, and milieu. Since there is no one right way to teach a discipline, the creation of practical pedagogic wisdom requires the "arts of eclectic," an integrated application of the most compelling and relevant theories from both the subject matter itself and the study of how best to teach it (Schwab, 1982, pp. 322–383).

Schwab and his structuralist colleagues were not ambivalent about normative discourse in curriculum thought; but they were ambiguous. A normative educational philosophy is implied in the communal requirements of what Schwab called milieu. However, Schwab is unclear about whether normative philosophy should provide the conceptual and ethical frame that guides curriculum deliberation. If so, how is it to be determined given Schwab's complex, plural, and evolving conception of theory? If normative visions of education are to be considered as one of a number of types of theories to be taken into account during the process of deliberation, how can it be said that the curriculum subscribes to a normative vision?

This ambiguity is related to an epistemological problem with curriculum structuralism that raises questions about the second condition of human agency—moral intelligence and self-expression. Schwab was among the pioneers of what later became known as postempiricist and postpositivist philosophy of knowledge that argued that scientific theories are more tentative and partial than was previously supposed (Bernstein, 1983; Phillips & Burbules, 2000). Since the findings of inquiry are underdetermined by data according to this view, theoretical expectations and conceptual frameworks play a significant role in the formulation of explanations. These frameworks are organized into disciplines or forms of knowledge each with its own assumptions, concepts, and methods of inquiry. This leads to a strong form of cognitive relativism, which holds that truth is a function of conceptual framework.

Although it does not follow logically from his epistemological position, Schwab appears to treat moral traditions like structures of knowledge. Since all moral positions are underdetermined by reasoning, and no argument exists that can sustain the superiority of one over another, normative positions must be evaluated within the context of the conceptual frameworks within which they are formulated, and a variety of competing (even contradictory) positions should be considered in making curriculum decisions.

His intention was to create an eclectic basis for educational practice in which a rich variety of normative as well as empirical traditions, from Plato and Aristotle to Freud and Skinner, could play equally challenging roles in making curriculum decisions.

In throwing out arbitrary and overly simplistic empirical standards, however, Schwab may have gone too far by blurring important epistemological distinctions between truth and falsehood. And in adopting a parallel stance toward moral traditions, Schwab may have embraced an overly eclectic attitude toward normative visions of education that weakens our capacity to identify value differences between better and worse. This threatens the possibility of moral intelligence and self-expression. If every moral tradition is as good as every other, it becomes impossible in principle to distinguish between good and bad or right and wrong according to any theory.

EISNER'S ESTHETIC HUMANISM

If Tyler's technological curriculum focuses on producing desired behaviors and Schwab's academic structuralism focuses on cognitive processes, the humanistic curriculum turns our attention to emotional dimensions of education. One important theorist in this tradition is Elliot Eisner (2001).

To conceive education as an art requires an esthetic theory. For this Eisner turned to Suzanne Langer's analysis of art as the symbolic expression of feeling. Langer (1957) grounded art in two important distinctions, between discursive and nondiscursive expression, and between logical and dynamic form. Discursive expression is abstract, conceptual, and theoretical. We use it to communicate about our world in daily and academic life, from shopping lists and travel directions to scholarly discoveries and scientific theories. Nondiscursive expression, on the other hand, is concrete, particular, and experiential. We use it to communicate about dimensions of experience where words and concepts fail us— for instance, in expressing intense emotions such as love or anger. This sort of expression often relies on religious rituals, artistic symbols, or metaphoric language to create immediate, virtual, or vicarious experience.

Logical form, according to Langer, is rigorous, structured, and fixed. It is concerned with the precise measurements and conceptual contours of reality. For instance, two lampshades that share precisely the same profile but for size can be said to have the same logical form. Dynamic form, on the other hand, speaks to the shape of experiences that are fleeting and in flux. A dry riverbed, for example, can be said to capture the dynamic form of flowing water at the moment the water ceased flowing. The description of an automobile accident by a police officer, to take another example, will strive to express the logical form of the events in discursive language: when the accident happened, the direction of each car before they collided, where they ended up immediately afterward, and so on. But the stories told by the drivers to their families and friends will be filled with emotion. They will seek to capture the emotional shape of the accident through expressive language that involves the listener in a vicarious experience of it.

The academic curriculum prefers discursive expression of logical form. It aims to convey concepts, methods of inquiry, and truths in the precise theoretical language associated with scholarship. The fine arts, on the other hand, aim to capture the dynamic form of human feeling in nondiscursive expression such as symbols and metaphors (Goodman, 1978). To take seriously the image of teaching and education as fine arts, then, we must understand how they use nondiscursive expression to capture and communicate the shape of human feeling. Eisner offers such an understanding by rethinking curriculum content and evaluation, rather than in a new approach to its design and construction.

Eisner conceives curriculum subject matter in terms of what he calls "forms of representation."

In contrast to the structure of a discipline that emphasizes its mode of inquiry, the notion of a form of representation stresses a mode of expression. "People don't paint what they see," Eisner is fond of musing, "they see what they can paint." The shape of consciousness is determined by the ways we represent experience, not by how we study it. Art and science are both forms in which we represent what we experience. Excluding forms of representation such as the fine arts from the curriculum, as so often occurs in state schools, denies students the opportunity to appreciate the sort of experience that they capture, indeed to enjoy those experiences altogether.

If the curriculum initiates students into a collection of artistic forms, the evaluation of curriculum entails appreciating and critiquing the ways in which those forms have been represented. To view teaching and education as fine arts requires that assessment be conceived as artistic connoisseurship and criticism. Connoisseurship refers to the refined taste for a particular art form that is acquired through extensive personal experience as either a creator or student of that art. It involves the capacity for judging quality, for assessing the artistic merit of a particular work of art. Educational connoisseurship, then, is a form of understanding what goes on in classrooms based on personal experience. Educational criticism, on the other hand, is a form of representing that knowledge. It involves commenting on pedagogic activities in rich, metaphoric terms in order to transform how we perceive and do our educational work (Eisner, 1997).

This conception of curriculum and evaluation expands our thinking about the tasks of education by placing the affective domain and subjective experience at its core. It recognizes that the curriculum needs to influence feeling and creative self-expression as well as thinking, to foster love of learning, mold commitment and dedication, and shape the student's deepest appreciation of what it means to be devoted to people and ideals. Following Plato, Schwab called this the education of "eros" (Garrison, 1997; Schwab, 1982, pp. 105–132).

Nevertheless, although Eisner is acutely sensitive to the impact of what we choose not to teach (see Eisner, 2001, pp. 97–107), he offers little guidance concerning how to make those choices. If every form of representation is as suitable for inclusion in the curriculum as any other, how are we to distinguish between those that are more or less worthwhile? Under these circumstances, it is difficult to assess whether or to what degree particular curriculum alternatives are more or less desirable. This undermines the third assumption of moral agency mentioned above, fallibility, or the possibility of being wrong (Alexander, 1989). The very self-expression Eisner seeks to promote would appear to require what Taylor calls strong values that enable the assessment of the quality of an experience (Taylor, 1991). Yet, Eisner shies away from such strong evaluation when he fails to offer an account of how to distinguish the relative worth of forms of representation that compete for time and resources in the curriculum. In short, Eisner's esthetic approach to self-expression appears to rely on too "weak" or "thin" or "merely" personal an account of the values needed to make curriculum decisions and assess classroom experience (Walzer, 1994).

This point is driven home it seems to me by Eisner's tendency to posit a personal conception of connoisseurship as the primary source for assessing the merit of education experiences. This weakens the meaning of the term *merit*. It is not enough for educational criticism to re-educate our perception of educational events according to the connoisseurship of an experienced educator alone. For this sort of personal assessment to be meaningful, it must carry weight because the connoisseur has acquired an appreciation for a standard of excellence; and for such standards to have meaning they must appeal to strong values that transcend self and society (Alexander, 1986; Phenix, 1971). Yet it is the very possibility of this kind of strong evaluation that Eisner appears to avoid in stressing the role of personal understanding in the assessment of school programs.

CRITICAL PEDAGOGY AND THE RADICAL CURRICULUM

Eisner wrote of the three curricula that all schools teach: the explicit curriculum that is announced in brochures, course syllabi, and textbooks; the implicit curriculum, which is embedded in classroom norms and student–teacher relations; and the null curriculum, which refers to what we do not teach (Eisner, 2001). Practitioners and policymakers often ignore the latter two curricula. For radical curriculum theorists such as Michael Apple (1979), however, the implicit and null curricula are not merely ignored; they are hidden by those in power.

Neo-Marxist critical theorists hold that beneath the surface of social life lies conflict between the powerful and the powerless (Horkheimer & Adorno, 1972). Those who have power, based on wealth, lineage, or majority-rule, use culture to impose an ideology on others that sustains their power. This ideology—expressed in language, media, religion, knowledge, morality, and education—obscures the fact of oppression from those who are enslaved to the degree that some even prefer subjugation to liberation. Marx called this "false consciousness" (Marx & Engels, 1947). Epistemological ideas such as truth and knowledge and moral ideas such as right and wrong have no "objective" basis outside of the power interests they serve. At the end of the day, all beliefs and behaviors are ideological save those dedicated to liberating the oppressed (Watt, 1994, pp. 1–26). The task of critical pedagogy, an educational orientation influenced by critical theory, is to expose the hidden tools of oppression utilized by those in power so that students can embrace more authentic ideologies that reflect their own cultural, social, and political interests (Gur-Zeev, 2003; McLaren, 1989).

Neo-Marxist analysis assumes that all education is ideological. The question is not whether but which ideology to inculcate (Counts, 1978). It might appear that this is entirely consistent with my call for a return to substantive ethics in curriculum thought, but this is not so, because radical curriculum theory uses the term *ideology* in what I have called an amoral (or nonethical) rather than a moral (or ethical) sense. Moral ideologies embrace the conditions of human agency. They are not moral in the sense that they embrace a particular substantive ethic, although the conditions of moral agency are by no means value free, but in that they accept the transcendental conditions that make it possible to have meaningful ethical discourse. Amoral ideologies, on the other hand, deny these conditions. They assume that beliefs and behaviors are not chosen but determined by family or socioeconomic class or culture (Alexander, 2001).

By advocating that children ought to be liberated from hegemonic culture to serve ideological interests they may not necessarily embrace, radical curriculum theory employs the term *ideology* in an amoral sense; and since all truths and values that do not reflect the necessity of liberating the oppressed are relative to class, or culture or gender, there is no way to assess whether the interests of a particular child, however they might be interpreted, are in fact being served by this new ideology of liberation (Watt, 1994, pp. 1–26). This undermines all three assumptions of human agency. The child does not make choices that give expression to her own strong values, either now or upon reaching maturity. Values are not chosen at all but determined by ideology, culture, and class. It is assumed, therefore, that the child will express the values of her culture or social class and embrace liberation as defined by others, whether or not she would choose such a form of liberty for herself. Positions of this kind do not engage substantive ethics; they render such an engagement deeply problematic (Alexander, 2001, pp. 94–107).

My point is not that radical curriculum theory is illiberal because it fails to embrace autonomy, but rather that in diminishing the significance of human agency, it tends to undermine the *moral* bite of the claim that one group or another has suffered oppression, because it undercuts the conditions necessary for ethical concepts to be meaningful altogether. Instead, its antidote—"liberation" or "positive liberty"—runs the risk of replacing one form of subjugation with another. In an amoral universe, power not ethics is the primary court of appeals; and force of one kind or another too often appears to be the only recourse to resolve differences or redress perceived injustice (Alexander, 2003).

HUMAN AGENCY IN THE CURRICULUM

To speak of ethics in the curriculum does not require an alternative account of instructional content, design, or evaluation. Rather, to engage ethics in the curriculum requires a conception of what it means for an educational program to be better or worse, and this can be articulated only within the context of a conception of the good. Although there is no single ethical vision that all curricula are bound to promote, they must embrace the formal criteria without which the very idea of an ethical stance is meaningless in other than a weak sense, that people have the capacity for agency. Let us conclude then by considering how each of the conditions of agency—(a) free will or self-determination, (b) moral intelligence or self-expression, and (c) fallibility or self-evaluation—might be incorporated into the curriculum.

Free Will

To foster free will and self-determination, the primary concern of any curriculum must be the ultimate independence of children, their ability upon reaching maturity to understand within reasonable limits the options they face and the consequences of choosing one direction over another, and their ability to make intelligent choices based on this understanding.

To live meaningfully in and contribute productively to a liberal democracy requires the ability to assess not only the strength of an argument but also the quality (according to some conception) of a piece of art or literature, the significance of a historical or a sociological development, or the contribution of a scientific or technological innovation as well as the capacity to understand or reproduce them (McPeck, 1990). Education for self-determination implies fostering a critical stance toward subject matter, not only in the sense of the ability to employ and assess reasons (Siegel, 1988; Norris, 1992; Paul, 1994; Ennis, 1996) but also—and perhaps more importantly—in terms of the capacity to appraise quality or significance, to evaluate not only the amount of happiness one may achieve by making one choice rather than another, or the strength of the reasoning that favors that choice, but also the relative worth of the satisfaction that may be realized from making it.

Moral Intelligence

However, qualitative judgments of this kind only make sense within the context of ethical orientations that enable one to say that this is more important than that. And to make such judgments possible, a tradition must meet at least two conditions: (a) to serve as a basis for a person's self-determined choices—what Taylor (1989) calls a "source of the self"—a moral tradition must be an expression of one's identity, integral to how one conceives who one aspires to be. And (b) to achieve this level of ownership and investment, a tradition needs to be sufficiently robust and emotionally compelling to inspire affiliation and identification.

Fallibility

Finally, to assume that students are fallible and to promote strong evaluation means among other things that the moral understanding necessary to acquire or construct worthwhile knowledge is not innate but learned, that it is not in a person's very nature to grasp the wisdom of an ethical tradition, or to behave well or poorly. Students might just as readily misunderstand as understand that tradition, or choose poorly as wisely. Whether or not they do so is a contingent matter, which implies that if they in fact comprehend the tradition's conception of what counts as

worthwhile, or learn to desire or appreciate something of particular value, or choose to follow a virtuous course of action, they are to be credited with a meritorious intellectual, emotional, or practical accomplishment. And if they fail to achieve this understanding or appreciation, or to exercise this choice, they are in some measure responsible for the failure.

This is not to say that there are no factors beyond the student's control. All students are disadvantaged in some way or another, and some are obviously more advantaged than others, economically, intellectually, emotionally, artistically, and physically. Surely curriculum theory and educational policy should consider whether, when, and how to address these imbalances. However, insofar as we are unwilling to hold students accountable for any portion of their learning, or to see them as responsible in some way when they miss the mark, they will face grave difficulty in acquiring or constructing or doing whatever a tradition deems appropriate with the knowledge that it considers to be worthwhile. An equally, if not more, important curricular and educational task, therefore, is to cultivate within students this sense of responsibility and accountability. This requires that students be encouraged to experience the exhilaration of genuine accomplishment when they succeed and to examine their own beliefs, desires, and actions when they have not achieved all that they had hoped. What might I have done differently? Where have I missed the mark? The strong evaluation required of future life choices begins with an assessment of the quality of personal investment a student has made in the learning process.

Although this may sometimes mean that students will need to face uncomfortable aspects of their own personalities, and this can result in fear or stress, the up side is that they will come to recognize that they have the capacity to change course, to make a difference. What they do, feel, and think does in fact matter; and their inherent worth is to be discovered not in the feeling that they will get it right no matter what but rather in the realization that they matter even when they get it wrong, indeed because they have the capacity to get it wrong, since were this not the case, it would literally make no sense to speak of anything mattering at all. Students can thus learn to accept themselves as imperfect but nonetheless worthwhile beings, even as they strive to improve where they can.

A meaningful account of curriculum must begin with what can count as desirable, with what it means for knowledge on any account to be considered worthwhile, with the conditions of human agency: attempts to conceive the curriculum in terms of establishing, realizing, and evaluating behavioral objectives, or the structure of disciplines or knowledge or rationality, or forms of esthetic representation and evaluation, or the liberation of the oppressed have tended to undermine one or more of these conditions. To engage worthwhile knowledge requires that the curriculum not only presuppose these conditions as human capabilities, but also that it actively promote them. This requires that students learn to make independent choices grounded in assessments not only of the reasoning entailed but also the relative worth of various human activities, that these choices express their personal identification with thick ethical traditions within which strong evaluation makes sense. It also requires students to recognize that in the context of those traditions they have the capacity to err in what they think, feel, and do but that they can also change course and make a difference. This is a source of fear and trepidation but also of great joy. Cultivating this sort of existential joy is, to my mind, the highest aspiration of any curriculum.

Discussion Questions

Like Schubert, Alexander examines different schools of curricular thought, and she finds each lacking for different reasons. How do you assess her critique?

What, according to the author, is the relationship between curriculum and ethics?

Hanan A. Alexander is an associate professor at the University of Haifa in Israel.

Article 8

ADOLESCENT NEEDS, CURRICULUM, AND THE EIGHT-YEAR STUDY

ROBERT V. BULLOUGH, JR.

CRAIG KRIDEL

The concept of "needs" has played a central role in U.S. curriculum decision making since the early years of the 20th century. The word is frequently used uncritically, as if its meaning were understood and its value obvious. In this article, we explore the concept of needs in the deliberations of the educators associated with the Eight-Year Study (1933–1941) of secondary schools and consider the implications for current educational theory and practice, particularly the movement toward a standards-based curriculum.

FRAMING THE DEBATE

In his history of U.S. curriculum ideologies, Kliebard (1986, p. 219) demonstrated that by the middle of the 20th century the notions of "needs" or the "needs curriculum" provided a "convenient meeting ground" for developmentalists and educators committed to efficiency and functionalism. That these two apparently contending groups could find a comfortable place beneath the same conceptual umbrella ought to give pause. However, the way in which the debate around "needs" and the "needs curriculum" was initially and commonly framed—with the individual and the society placed in juxtaposition with one another—permitted such reconciliations.

Such thinking still exists, although one now rarely hears talk about individual needs in the sense argued by the "developmentalists." Rather, in the spirit of efficiency and functionalism, contemporary debate in the U.S. centers on identifying "student lacks," those gaps in knowledge, skill, and character that likely will interfere with success—namely the ability to be economically

SOURCE: Excerpted from Bullough, R. V., & Kridel, C. (2003). Adolescent needs, curriculum, and the eight-year study. *Journal of Curriculum Studies*, 35(2), 151. Reprinted by permission.

self-sufficient. Certainly, this perspective under-pins the standards movement sweeping across the United States.

In his well-known rationale for curriculum work, the *Basic Principles of Curriculum and Instruction,* Tyler (1950) recognized this social-deficit-driven way of framing the issue as mis-guided, and in his "rationale" placed the two orientations—individual needs and social needs (as well as a third orientation, subject areas)—alongside one another, thereby asserting that each had legitimate claims on the curriculum. In this way, he attempted to sidestep the contro-versy that, according to Taba (1962, p. 285), "split the Progressive Education Association in 1942" and led to its demise.

THE EIGHT-YEAR STUDY

Tanner and Tanner (1975, p. 319) have described the Eight-Year Study as "the most important and comprehensive curriculum experiment ever car-ried on in the US." Yet, misconceptions abound (Kridel & Bullough, 2002).

The study originated from the concern that curriculum experimentation in secondary edu-cation was made impossible by college and university admissions requirements. Under the leadership of Wilford Aikin, then headmaster of the John Burroughs School of St. Louis, Missouri, the Commission on Relation of School and College was formed by the Progressive Education Association (PEA) in the fall of 1930:

1. To establish a relationship between school and college that would permit and encourage recon-struction in the secondary school.

2. To find, through exploration and experimenta-tion, how the high school in the US can serve youth more effectively. (Aikin, 1942, p. 116)

The view was that secondary schools needed to be freed from the domination of college and university admissions requirements. Stimulated by the effects of the deepening Depression and

with the promise that rich data useful for making admissions decisions would be provided in due time, over 300 college and university administra-tions agreed to suspend their established admis-sions policies for a time to enable curricular experimentation in a few select secondary schools.

Sides were taken and camps formed in the debate over the meaning and proper place of needs in educational decision making. Sharp dif-ferences emerged, even within the progressive camp itself, including a disagreement between Boyd H. Bode, a professor of education at Ohio State University, whom, in 1938, *Time* magazine had dubbed "Progressive Education's No. 1 present-day philosopher," and V. T. Thayer (Zepper, 1970), chair of the PEA Commission on the Secondary School Curriculum (CSSC) (the curriculum arm of the Eight-Year Study) and educational director of the Fieldston School in New York City, one of the 30 participating schools. To make sense of the argument, we must situate the Eight-Year Study within a conceptual and social context, beginning with a brief consideration of the emergence of the idea of adolescence as a way of thinking about human development. This is important because psychology became the great champion of individual needs in contrast to social demands.

ADOLESCENCE AND SOCIAL DEVELOPMENT

The concept of adolescence, as a particular stage of human development, emerged in the late-19th and early-20th centuries. Gillis (1974, p. 138) con-tends that the concept, a "discovery" of the middle classes and a product of "elite secondary schools," spread outward to the laboring population.

Hollingworth recognized adolescence as a period of "transition" that brought with it unique biological and social challenges from "learning to shave" to "getting away from the family" and find-ing a place within the larger society (1928, p. 36).

While Hollingworth and others were explor-ing human development, the social setting within which that development took place was in great turmoil. The Depression had a profound effect on schools and on young people who found themselves unable to obtain employment and increasingly dependent on parents for longer periods of time. Following a 3-month cross-country trip to survey the condition of U.S. youth, Davis (1936) concluded they were a "lost generation."

Lacking employment opportunities, young people stayed longer in school where they encountered a curriculum out of touch with their experience.

RESPONDING TO THE CHALLENGE

The PEA maintained that one of the reasons for the disconnection between adolescents and the high school and the unresponsiveness of the curriculum was the dominance of the college over the high school curriculum. A call was made for curriculum reform. However, as the Eight-Year Study began, its directing committee quickly realized that the participating schools needed help in rethinking the curriculum. The grip of traditional practices on educational thought was tight, and simply declaring a faculty free to experiment did not guarantee innovation would follow. Thus, in May 1932, the PEA Executive Board organized the CSSC under the direction of V. T. Thayer. From the beginning of its work, the CSSC was concerned with determining needs and the problem of creating responsive school programs.

SCIENCE IN GENERAL EDUCATION AND THE DEBATE OVER NEEDS

The CSSC committee charged with exploring the implications of science for general education was chaired by Harold Alberty, a former student of Bode's and his colleague at Ohio State University, and co-author with Thayer of a book on democratic supervision. In addition to Thayer, other members included Robert Havighurst,

director for general education of the General Education Board, and Caroline Zachry. Ultimately, this committee set the definition of needs that shaped much of CSSC's discussion and all of its publications, including *Science in General Education* (CSSC, 1938). This volume's influence was profound.

The view of needs presented in *Science in General Education* (CSSC, 1938) emerged over a period of 3 to 4 years of intense discussion. Teachers provided pointed feedback on an early draft that was shared at the first workshop sponsored jointly by the Commission on the Relation of School and College and CSSC in 1936. [Psychologist] Caroline Zachry became a key figure in the debate. Under Zachry's leadership, CSSC established the Committee on Adolescents. The committee was given a broad charge: "gain increased understanding of young people for the purposes of education" (Zachry, 1940, p. v).

Observation and written case studies in various settings of 650 adolescents from participating and nonparticipating Eight-Year Study schools were the central methods of study.

In May 1935, CSSC members met to discuss the early work of Zachry's committee as it related to the subject committees' charge. A report was presented that included a section on "social maturity." Alberty found the approach taken to social maturity in the report somewhat troubling. Notes from the meeting report that "Dr Alberty . . . said he always shies away from the word 'adjustment,' for to him it denotes a passive attitude of acceptance of a condition, rather than attempts to improve it" (CSSC, 1935, p. 12). Zachry responded to Alberty, saying that:

> adjustment is a dynamic thing. . . . That [the individual] must adjust to society as it is now in order to be able to change it. If he is maladjusted he will go to pieces, be powerless to change. (p. 12)

Alberty asked, "Will he be competent to react to change if he is always lagging behind, adjusting to present conditions?" To this comment,

Zachry said, "Adjusting to society does not mean [being] satisfied with it. . . . A person who is satisfied with his own present adjustment is a turtle." Alberty retorted, "I'm wondering what in this description keeps us from being turtles." Then Thayer commented, "But the goal is not, certainly, passive adjustment to the present conditions; nor is it being radical to the point where you are not living in the present at all."

PSYCHOLOGICAL PREJUDICES AND CURRICULAR UNDERSTANDINGS

In the Study of Adolescents, Zachry engaged educators, psychologists, psychiatrists, physicians, anthropologists, sociologists, and psychiatric social workers. Her bias was obviously a psychological one. The minutes from this meeting report that Zachry thought:

> The philosophy of progressive education is based to a large extent upon the belief that the individual learns best when he is conscious of a purpose. One of its main objectives has been to help the individual work out, become conscious of his purpose. The mental hygiene group is likewise concerned with purpose but maintains that *all* behaviour has a purpose, whether it be conscious or otherwise. (CSSC, 1935, p. 12)

Yet, her view was decidedly not philosophical but more concerned with identifying patterns of normal individual development within an established social context.

Adolescent needs were a topic of additional seminars. Making links between the CSSC subject committees and the emerging results of the Study of Adolescents became urgent, and discussion intensified as data accumulated and publishing deadlines approached. Following a far-ranging and sometimes heated discussion of "needs," Zachry pressed her view in a later seminar: "teachers will have to be as much concerned with [the student's] total needs and the total environment in which he is functioning as they are with the specific subject matter, and

those two things have to go hand in hand" (Zachry, 1937, n.p.).

There were, she said, both conscious and unconscious needs, and to meet unconscious needs required a curriculum that anticipated the emergence of a need but not too far in advance of its development:

> We have to train teachers to . . . sense these problems, understand the psychology of the child well enough to see when he is about ready for it [i.e., a curricular topic or activity designed to address a need], instead of organizing it ahead and giving it when he isn't ready.

This discussion continued and, perhaps in frustration, Harold Alberty remarked:

> It seems to me that one of our difficulties in these discussions is the very broad way in which we use the word "needs." We start in by using needs as a very definite drive on the part of the individual and then later use needs to mean those things which we, as adults in our present culture, anticipate that young people need. I am wondering whether or not before we can really get very far with our discussions, we don't have to settle upon some meaning of this word "need." (Zachry, 1937, section II, p. 2)

To decide what a need is, and whether or not once identified, it should be honored within the curriculum, presented a philosophical and a sociological problem. Psychology could not answer questions of this kind.

Zachry did not see the issue. To her, the philosophy guiding the study was straightforward and simple, an extension of her view of the PEA and its purpose.

The view she supported was that "fundamental needs are the same as those of an adolescent anywhere. . . ." Fundamental needs were first biological, but how they were expressed or satisfied depended on the wider environment. The challenge then became one of generating, in Thayer's words, an "inventory of needs," a "specific statement of needs" (Zachry, 1937, section III, n.p.).

Dissension emerged. Some participants thought it unwise, if not impossible, to generate such a list, fearing that in so doing, the emphasis in the curriculum would shift away from concern for the individual adolescent's development and toward responding to a predetermined list of needs. Yet again, the question of philosophy was raised.

Thayer disagreed: "I think the difficulty is not so much philosophical as verbal." Later, Thayer pressed a more sociological position than that of Zachry's, a view that influenced the way in which the list of needs that eventually emerged was framed and presented in the various subject publications, including *Science in General Education* (CSSC, 1938): "I think that if we recognize needs as something that arise out of the interaction of the individual and the environment, defined by both, then we must have an analysis of both" (Zachry, 1937, section VIII, n.p.).

SUBJECT COMMITTEES AND THE CLASSIFICATION OF NEEDS

Each of the five volumes produced by the subject committees of CSSC (1938, 1940a, b, c, d) is organized around the classification of adolescent needs first presented in *Science in General Education* (CSSC, 1938, p. 24).

The committee is not, of course, proposing a curriculum based on the notion that the adolescent is always conscious of his needs or of his range of interests, or that he be permitted to do as he pleases. Neither is it proposing a curriculum based solely upon an adult conception of what is valuable as a preparation for adult living.

The committee asserted that needs evolve in response to the environment and develop through experience, a view consistent with Thayer's. In contrast to a curriculum imposed from the outside, the committee proposed that "needs serve as a point of departure in curriculum construction" (p. 24).

Following an acknowledgment and brief discussion that the word *need* has various meanings, the authors claimed they sought a middle ground, one that unites the individual and the social context: needs are "personal-social in character" (p. 25). Thayer's view, which he earlier presented in the Zachry seminar, is clearly evidenced:

> A need will have always a personal or individual aspect which may best be understood as a biological or somatic tension. . . . Needs do not exist "under the skin" of the individual or in a vacuum. They arise and work themselves out in living, dynamic events which can only be described as *interactions between the individual and the social situation.* Thus when we speak of "the need of the student to select and use goods and services wisely," we refer to a want (biological tension) or a desire on the one hand, and the requirements, demands, standards of social living on the other. (p. 25)

Yet, the values of adjustment are also present: "a need—the tension in the already organized personality of the adolescent as he interacts with the demands of the environment and the standards or ideals which it sets—is truly unique with the individual" (p. 26).

Four categories of need were presented: needs in "Personal Living," "Immediate Personal-Social Relationships," "Social–Civic Relationships," and "Economic Relationships." The framework was to be used by teachers heuristically, as "convenient centres of reference for identifying worthy interests and needs and for selecting and organizing appropriate learning experiences." Chapter 2 of *Science in General Education* (CSSC, 1938, 23–57) points to a serious issue: Adolescents live within a democracy and have civic obligations; but the connection between democracy and the aim of meeting adolescent needs is unclear and surprisingly undeveloped. The apparent presumption was that the listed personal characteristics associated with democracy are somehow needs, yet they fall outside the social–civic category that is concerned with two needs: "the need for responsible participation in socially significant activities" and "the need for social recognition" (p. 188). Rather than operate as a social philosophy and social agency, as Bode contended, democracy appeared as an addendum to rather than as an integral part of the committee's argument.

BODE AND AN OPPOSING CONCEPT OF NEEDS

As Zachry's seminar group debated the meaning of needs, Bode was busily at work clarifying his own views. Earlier, Bode had resigned from CSSC, reportedly because it was "far too sentimentally child-centred" and dominated by the attitude of "the psychiatrist" (Lagemann, 2000, p. 146).

Bode (1938a) maintained that a standard is needed not only to determine which desires are educationally legitimate but also to serve as a means for resolving conflicts between desires. This requires a "long-range programme" that attends to "remote aims" (p. 64). He then takes a swing at "guidance," a role and position highly favored by progressive educators, including Zachry: "Guidance work often has to do with the discovery of needs which are not recognized as such by the persons concerned" (p. 66). Bode asserted that the "only way to discover a need is in terms of a 'pattern' or scheme of values or an inclusive philosophy of some kind" (p. 66). Later, Bode (1940) would argue that "it is just as true to say that needs must grow out of the curriculum as to say that the curriculum must grow out of needs" (p. 536).

It was toward a philosophy of democracy as a way of life that Bode (1937) had looked for a solution to the problem: "What is needed is a moratorium on needs, so that we can get down to serious business and bring to fruition the splendid promise that is contained in the philosophy of progressive education" (p. 67).

THAYER RESPONDS: THE BATTLE BEGINS

Bode (1940) wrote a negative review of *Reorganizing Secondary Education* (Thayer, Zachry, & Kotinsky, 1939) within which Thayer and Zachry again presented CSSC's conception of needs. Among Bode's charges was that the book lacked an adequate social philosophy. Thayer (1940, p. 538) reacted with "shock and . . . disappointment," but his response was carefully measured.

Thayer insisted that Bode had misread the book. Thayer had a point. However, so did Bode. Bode found no value in the concept of needs as an organizing principle for education. In his view, in one form or another a need is a lack, and the best means for gaining insight into what students ought to learn, be able to do, feel, appreciate, and experience arises from clarity in social vision and not from a predefined conception that displays students' deficiencies. To be sure, student development and student interest have a place in determining how one goes about organizing the environment to encourage the desired growth. However, the concept of needs as a determining factor for curriculum development was beyond redemption in Bode's view. Bode failed to appreciate Thayer's defense of the concept: The division of needs into four categories helped to orient educators to aspects of human experience too often ignored by a school system bent on serving the college-bound student. Bode suspected that what would follow in the wake of an education driven by needs so conceived would be a wholesale dismissal of intellectual content with the result that young people would fail to develop the qualities required to make sense of the cultural complexity and confusion that surrounded them.

Thayer and his colleagues (Thayer, Zachry, & Kotinsky, 1939, p. 15) acknowledged cultural dislocation. The challenge on one hand was to avoid indoctrination, the inculcation of a fixed social vision; and on the other, relativism born of an open-ended and generous pursuit of student desires of the sort Bode found so troubling.

They (Thayer et al.) thought their concept of democracy avoided both difficulties:

> Defining desirable directions of growth in terms of the democratic tradition is not indoctrination in the derogatory sense of the word. It does not mean that the school must serve the interests of the *status quo*. Change is an axiom in American society, and democracy by its very nature implies change and the reimplementation of its own values under the changing conditions of life. (p. 75)

But, further, they thought, "democratic tradition embodies values that all men seek, and its principles must guide social arrangements if these values are to be realized" (p. 75). However, their argument is not self-evident. If, as Thayer thought, the environment of the school is anchored in the essential principles of democracy noted earlier, then needs will be met in ways that are consistent with an evolving understanding of democracy, an understanding and practice that will enable adolescents to sort out the confusion in their culture and strengthen their allegiance to those principles. In this way, Thayer believed the personal and social aspects of needs would be brought together and resolved.

BODE'S WORST FEARS REALIZED

Bode (1938a, pp. 43–44) concluded his discussion of the concept of needs in *Progressive Education at the Crossroads* with a warning. Lacking an adequate social philosophy, the future was bleak for progressive education.

In the later stages of the war, educators began to look ahead and consider the future. Stimulated by the G.I. Bill, which supported university education for war veterans, college and university enrolments would soon explode and college administrators would no longer need to experiment with admission policies or practices. The domination of the college over the high school curriculum, the issue that initially lead to formation of the Eight-Year Study, would continue unchallenged. Yet, questions over the appropriateness and value of the high school curriculum remained. Dropout rates were high and a perception again grew that change was necessary. It was within this context that the life-adjustment movement was born (Kliebard, 1986, pp. 240–270), a well-intentioned reform effort that proved Bode's prescience: Lacking a democratic social philosophy, a curriculum driven by student needs would fail.

Douglass (1950, p. v), one of the most articulate champions of life adjustment as an educational aim and program, had high hopes for the movement:

Various movements, reports, statements, commission activities, and investigations such as the Eight-Year Study of the 30 schools by the Progressive Education Association have come and gone, with no great effect upon the practice of the great mass of secondary schools. Only in the past few years has there seemed to be a real possibility of thoroughly reviewing the educational program of our high schools with a view to developing markedly improved opportunities for becoming adjusted to, and developing a capacity for adjusting to, life as we find it today.

With U.S. Office of Education (USOE) support, the intention of life adjustment, in the words of J. Dan Hull, assistant director of the USOE Division of Elementary and Secondary Education, was straightforward: "As developed in regional and national conferences, life adjustment education means organizing and reorganizing schools to achieve useful living purposes" (Douglass, p. 9). Harkening to an important reform document of an earlier era in the United States, *The Cardinal Principles of Secondary Education* (National Education Association, Commission on the Reorganization of Secondary Education, 1918), the intention was to make the high school curriculum directly "functional," and the language of students needs was prominently called upon as justification: "there is obvious and material acceleration in revamping the entire high school curriculum in order better to meet the needs of young people and of modern life" (Douglass, p. 27). Furthermore:

> It is obvious that a study of many of the subjects in the high school will reveal their potentialities for conditioning young people so that they may make more effective and happy adjustments to life problems and situations than has been the case in the past, when objectives have been in terms of preparation for college, training of the mind, or objectives stated in terms of the subject itself. (p. 41)

Douglass's use of the word *conditioning* is revealing. Alberty's concern, expressed in the Zachry seminar, that students would become "turtles" proved to be closer to the mark than he likely imagined.

Even as the movement began to gather energy, criticism grew. Bestor (1953) led the attack and charged that students were not learning the disciplines as they should; the schools were anti-intellectual. Despite gross exaggerations, Bestor's characterization of the movement played to national fears and garnered support. Soon the movement faded and the last remnants of educational progressivism slipped into memory as the USA became preoccupied with the Cold War.

The intellectual roots of life adjustment sit squarely in the psychological traditions of progressivism as exemplified by Zachry and the mental hygienists. A "human relations standpoint" (Meek, 1943, p. 123) that elevated group work, social acceptance, and guidance as educational aims is prominent within the membership of the commissions and committees associated with the Eight-Year Study. A biological and evolutionary model of human development emerges within which needs reveal themselves as the child ages and to which teachers are urged to respond. The human relations challenge was to focus on present needs and extend them:

> The teacher will meet the individual where he is and will provide *first,* rich opportunities for the satisfaction of present needs and interests and *second,* experiences which will continually extend the individual's horizon so that new needs and interests will emerge which in turn must find satisfaction. This process continues throughout the life of an individual and is essential to a democratic way of life. (p. 165)

While democracy served as a rallying cry for the PEA in the 1930s, Meek linked it to extracurricular activities, clubs, and student government. Democracy was reduced merely to learning how to get along with others, a matter of human relations.

Thayer sought to forge a dynamic bond between the individual and the social aspects of needs, and "democracy" was to be the conceptual glue. As Bode argued and Thayer agreed, democracy required young people who have knowledge of democratic traditions and who have consistent experience in school working with these principles. Students need to consider consequences of their actions in terms of their likely long-term effects, not only on their own lives but on those of others far-removed from them in time and place. This is what is meant by "social sensitivity." And they require an experimental attitude and knowledge of the disciplines because they form the basis of informed decision making and intelligent action.

Working beneath the umbrella of the Eight-Year Study, educators who sought to elevate the importance of social philosophy in educational decision making resisted the temptation presented by the challenge to democracy from the right and the left to prescribe a specific program.

School faculties wanted assistance and it was given, but only in order to facilitate the effort to produce clarity in aims and not to prescribe outcomes. To this end, the following criteria were proposed in 1937 and further developed as guides to developing and articulating an educationally useful democratic social philosophy:

- Is the announced social philosophy of the school the product of group thinking on the part of the entire teaching staff, the pupils, and the parents?

- Is the social philosophy of the school in the process of continuous reconstruction and revision in the light of changing conditions?

- Does the social philosophy of the school provide a sense of direction in all areas of school life?

- Does the social philosophy of the school serve as a basis for integrating school–community attitudes and practices?

- Does the social philosophy of the school aid the pupil in developing standards for determining beliefs, attitudes, and plans of action concerning personal problems of school and community life?

- Is the effectiveness of the school's social philosophy being systematically tested by available means of evaluation? (Alberty, 1937)

Clearly, a school's social philosophy was expected to further the cause of democracy and, like democracy itself, evolve in response to changing conditions and aspirations.

NEEDS AND SOCIAL PHILOSOPHY IN OUR OWN TIME

As we write, a "standards" movement is sweeping across the United States. Scores on standardized tests are taken as proof of educational accomplishment. Soon, such tests may determine who graduates from high school, just as increasingly they determine what gets taught. Nowhere in the current discourse about education does one hear talk about individual student needs other than in the sense that all children need to be able to read fluently, write with a degree of skill, and understand mathematics and science at some basic level because these abilities are understood as necessary to employment. This certainly is not the kind of moratorium Bode had in mind. The principles of democracy Thayer and Bode took so seriously have been replaced by a single principle: the individual's right to choose. Nothing is said about wise choice, nor how choices reverberate outward and shape a shared social and natural world. Education is accepted as the primary means for maintaining international competitiveness, but with the deterioration of the Japanese economy, even this aim is now seldom discussed. It is merely understood. Such is the current condition of the United States.

The central educational and curricular challenge for the United States in our time is to rekindle and invigorate debate over the purposes of education and the place of schools in a democracy. A focus on democracy will bring with it concern for the individual and his or her development.

Discussion Questions

What kind of curriculum do you believe would best meet the needs of adolescents?

How do the authors examine the concept of the social needs of children?

Robert V. Bullough, Jr., is a professor at Brigham Young University.

Craig Kridel is a professor at the University of South Carolina.

Article 9

Toward a Renaissance in Curriculum Theory and Development in the USA

William G. Wraga

Peter S. Hlebowitsh

The "Stubborn Disarray" of the Curriculum Field

The U.S. curriculum field has long existed in a state of "conceptual disarray." During its formative years in the early 20th century, conceptual disagreement fell along the lines of the preferred source of educational purposes, with camps rallying around varied subject-centered, child-centered, and activity-analysis approaches to curriculum development (Whipple, 1926). During the Great Depression of the 1930s, sharp disputes erupted between progressive curricularists and educational philosophers, social reconstructionists, and academic "traditionalists" (Hlebowitsh & Wraga, 1995). During the decade following World War II, attacks on progressive education from the political and educational right aggravated divisions within progressive

education at large and the curriculum field in particular (Cremin, 1961; Foshay, 1975). With the launch of *Sputnik* in 1957 and the dominance of the U.S. National Science Foundation's (NSF) discipline-centered curriculum projects of the 1960s, all of these traditions of curriculum theory, questions, and work were firmly ushered to the sidelines of educational work (Tanner & Tanner, 1990).

Beginning in the 1970s, a new generation of curriculum scholars pronounced the historic curriculum field "dead" and launched a self-styled "reconceptualization" of curriculum studies (Marshall, Sears, & Schubert, 2000; Pinar, Reynolds, Slattery, & Taubman, 1995). However, by the 1990s, even as "reconceptualized" perspectives dominated the academic curriculum field, internal ideological feuding and external critique fractured even the reconceptualist camp. Presently, with the appearance of several new

SOURCE: Excerpted from Wraga, W. G., & Hlebowitsh, P. S. (2003). Toward a renaissance in curriculum theory and development in the USA. *Journal of Curriculum Studies, 35*(4), 425–437. Reprinted by permission of Taylor & Francis.

curriculum associations and conferences, and with little evidence of interest in communication among the various factions often represented by these affiliations, Cuban's (1995, p. vii) recognition of "the stubborn disarray that marks the academic field of curriculum" in the United States continues as an apt characterization of the field.

The reconceptualization of the U.S. curriculum field that began in the 1970s was premised partly on the assumption that this new project would extract the field from the crisis that Schwab, himself a newcomer to the field, had diagnosed (Marshall et al., 2000; Pinar et al., 1995).

SCHWAB'S SIGNS OF CRISIS REVISITED

As early as 1988, Pinar (1988) confidently declared the reconceptualization complete; recent retrospectives (see Marshall et al., 2000; Pinar et al., 1995) depict the triumph of the reconceptualization as a self-evident fact. Wright (2000, p. 8) considers the consequences of the reconceptualization so pervasive that use of the term when discussing curriculum scholarship is unnecessary. An assumption of the reconceptualization of that field was that it would arrest the continual decline of the field into a moribund state as Schwab had discerned.

However, has reconceptualized curriculum theorizing rescued the curriculum field from the troubles that distressed Schwab? Let us explore this question by testing Schwab's six signs of crisis against contemporary circumstances, particularly against curriculum work engendered by the reconceptualization.

Schwab's (1969, p. 3) first sign of crisis in the curriculum field involved "a translocation of its problems and the solving of them from the nominal practitioners of the field to other men." Current reforms in the United States, notably the standards movement, have been driven largely by politicians and corporate leaders. Moreover, the reconceptualist priority of pursuing curriculum theory to the neglect of curriculum practice represents a clear and conscious flight from the practical curriculum development work of the historic field (Pinar, 1992). That is, while the exclusion of curriculum professors from the post-*Sputnik* reforms was involuntary, the reconceptualist distancing of theory from practice has been intentional. Schwab's first sign of crisis in the curriculum field, that persons other than curricularists bear primary responsibility for solving curriculum problems, remains apparent.

Schwab's second sign involved a flight "from *use* of principles and methods to *talk* about them" (pp. 3–4, emphasis in original). The reconceptualist commitment to seeking new ways of understanding curriculum at the expense of developing curricula seems to be the most obvious manifestation of this crisis in the contemporary field. Varied forms of enquiry, including structuralism, poststructuralism, deconstructionism, and postmodernism (to name a few) have been introduced to the field, manifesting a greater commitment to talk about rather than to engage with curriculum endeavors.

Schwab's third sign of crisis involved "an attempt by practitioners to return to the subject matter in a state of innocence, shorn not only of current principles but of all principles" (p. 4). Although Schwab characterized this sign as a "missing symptom in the case of curriculum," in the contemporary field it may partly exist as a consequence of the reconceptualist repudiation of the historic field. By dismissing principles and practices that emerged from the historic U.S. field, reconceptualists are able to return to curriculum matters innocent of earlier work. New theories displace established principles. The frequent result of this repudiation, however, is a reinvention of ideas and practices, but with no acknowledgement of preceding work. Indeed, reconceptualist theorists have been known to identify ideas and practices that the historic U.S. field in fact was invented as emerging from reconceptualist theorizing. Slattery (1995), for example, identifies practices such as interdisciplinary curriculum, thematic units, authentic assessment, team teaching, nongraded schooling, laboratory work, and field trips with "postmodern" curriculum theory rather than with the "modern" curriculum field. Each one of these practices, of course, was advocated, if not invented, by the historic U.S. curriculum field.

Schwab's (1969) fourth sign of crisis in the U.S. curriculum field involved retreat of the curriculum professor "to the role of observer, commentator, historian, and critic of the contributions of others to the field" (p. 4).

This is not to say, however, that the theorists around the reconceptualization completely ignore practical curriculum matters. Schwab's fifth sign of crisis in the curriculum field involved "a repetition of old and familiar knowledge in new languages which add little or nothing to the old meanings as embodied in the older and familiar language" (p. 4). This sign is an effect of the presence of Schwab's fourth sign.

Finally, Schwab's sixth sign of crisis in the curriculum field involved "a marked increase in eristic, contentious, and *ad hominem* debate" (p. 4). Milburn's (2000) characterization of the 1999 exchange between Pinar (1999) and Wraga (1999a, b) as "heated" probably provides sufficient evidence to suggest that this sign remains apparent. In addition, the inclination to label academic analyses of reconceptualized curriculum theory as "harsh," "uncivil," "passé," or "naïve" without substantiating such claims, while characterizing reconceptualized work as self-evidently "diverse," "emancipatory," and "eloquent," can foster a contentious, divisive climate that is not conducive to intellectual exchange.

A comparison of the current conceptual disarray in the curriculum field to previous manifestations of disarray reveals other problems. During the 1950s, for example, the sources of the crisis in thc U.S. curriculum field were largely external: first the conservative assaults on progressivism in education, then the political surrender of curriculum reform to arts and sciences professors by federal legislators. The current "crisis" in the field has both external and internal sources, the former stemming from the sheer irrelevance of the curriculum field in educational reform and the latter from conceptual and theoretical disputes within the field. During the first half of the 20th century, "conceptual disarray" in the U.S. curriculum field resulted largely from internal disputes among differing theoretical perspectives. During the 1920s, however, and to a lesser extent during the following decade, not only did disagreement not suppress dialogue, but a concerted commitment to conversation produced some consensus that was inclusive of a diversity of perspectives. Taking a cue from our predecessors, we think that continual debate and dialogue is the only way to establish a universe of curriculum discourse that is animated by both consensus and diversity.

A WAY OUT OF CURRICULUM CONFUSION

What, then, should curriculum professors discuss? We think that for the U.S. curriculum field to extract itself from its state of chronic crisis, curriculum scholars would do well to confront frankly at least four fundamental issues.

Curriculum Boundaries

The U.S. curriculum field in general, and reconceptualist theory in particular, needs to mark the boundaries of the field. The demarcation of the field defines the field. The curriculum field needs to identify those phenomena considered in the domain of curriculum inquiry. We think that these phenomena should be limited largely to matters pertaining to the life and program of the school. Cultural studies, writ large, and personal psychosocial therapy, writ small, for example, are worthy pursuits but lie beyond the bounds of curriculum enquiry. We need to heed Reid's (1992, p. 166) caution that "research that is about everything is about nothing." His suggestion that "At some point, a certain humility is in order—a willingness to render unto curriculum the things that belong to it, rather than strive to expand it to the whole of life" (p. 168), warrants serious, candid deliberation. Or, using Kuhn's (1970) language, curriculum scholars should fix their gaze on the "constellation of objects" that are curricular, rather than casting their gaze toward the whole vast heavens. Distinguishing curriculum phenomena from noncurriculum phenomena will impinge little on "diversity" in the field, because the range of perspectives to bear on those phenomena will remain appropriately wide.

History Is With All of Us

The U.S. curriculum field in general, and reconceptualist theory in particular, needs to come to terms with curriculum history. Pronouncements of the death of curriculum development and the consequent repudiation of the historic field appear more as rhetorical tactics than as considered scholarship. The rejection of the historic field contradicts the reconceptualist commitments to understanding curriculum as historic text (Pinar et al., 1995) and to affirming and validating diverse perspectives. In addition, the reconceptualist interpretation of the historic field suffers from an inherent historical presentism that enlists history largely for the purpose of rationalizing the reconceptualist movement (Lincoln, 1992; Milburn, 2000; Wraga, 1998). The reconceptualist interpretation of the historic field is also based on claims that are contradicted by the historic record (Hlebowitsh, 1992, 1993; Wraga, 1998). Moreover, the fact that practices ostensibly engendered by reconceptualized curriculum theorizing often bear a striking resemblance to practices invented by the repudiated historic U.S. field not only points to internal inconsistencies in reconceptualized scholarship but also raises questions about the extent to which reconceptualized curriculum theorizing has reinvented the curriculum wheel (Wraga, 1996). (Perhaps Faulkner's [1966] epigrammatic admonition from *Requiem for a Nun* applies here: "The past is never dead. It's not even past" [p. 96].)

The conscious building upon past accomplishments makes creative advances possible. In virtually all fields of human endeavor—except, perhaps, education—established conventions form the foundation for subsequent invention. The great creative achievements of the Italian Renaissance, for example, were enabled in part by a rediscovery of knowledge and methods of Roman architecture and sculpture that had been forgotten for centuries during Europe's so-called Dark Ages (Csikszentmihalyi, 1996). Similarly, in a more recent U.S. example, John Coltrane's extraordinary inventiveness in the jazz arena was the outgrowth of his near obsessive mastery of a range of historic musical material (Porter, 1998). Such examples are legion (Csikszentmihalyi, 1996). The reality is that creative contributions are almost invariably predicated upon mastery of the particular domain of human endeavor. Reconceptualized curriculum theorizing, however, has been based upon a repudiation of the very domain it claims to recreate.

As Hargreaves and Moore (2000) demonstrated, some of the benefits new curricularists seek for children and youth are obtainable through curriculum forms developed and advocated by the historic U.S. field. Apple and Beane (1995), too, have endorsed the democratic forms of curriculum developed by that field. In short, reconceptualist curriculum theory must be situated in the context of the entire U.S. curriculum field, historically and contemporaneously; we also need to move beyond presumptuous claims that reconceptualized work embodies the whole of the field. To propel the field progressively and inventively into the future, we must build upon past accomplishments and develop a constructive synthesis of historic principles and practices and new ideas.

From Ideology to Ideas

We think that the lack of sustained deliberation and dialogue about these and other issues perhaps is attributable in part to an exaltation of ideology over ideas in reconceptualized curriculum theorizing. Positions such as the repudiation of the historic field, the separation of theory from practice, and the redefinition of curriculum from the course of study to the course of one's life experience originated as planks in the platform of "reconceptualized" thought. Over time, however, as these positions were operationalized in reconceptualized curriculum scholarship, they became reified into doctrine. These positions now seem to function more as articles of faith than as ideas to be tested. The lack of substantive response to criticism of these positions perhaps can be explained by recognizing that, typically, ideological tenets prove intellectually indefensible.

Moreover, not only is the rationale for the reconceptualization based on academic ideologies, but as well reconceptualized scholarship is often driven by and devoted to advancing particular political ideologies. From our perspective, advancing any political ideology or doctrine is incompatible with sound scholarship.

The argument that all scholarship is inherently ideological and, therefore, the propagation of ideology through scholarship is both inevitable and acceptable hinges on equivocation of the meaning of the term *ideology*: *Ideology* as signifying a set of ideas gives way to *ideology* as signifying political doctrine. If personal biases are largely inescapable, however, political ideologies are largely a matter of choice. Is not the argument for promoting ideology through scholarship tantamount to imploring that, because prejudice and stereotyping will likely always exist, researchers not only should cease working to mitigate prejudice and stereotyping, but that they even should embrace and foster them? Clearly, both of these positions are unacceptable. Social scientists (e.g., Myrdal, 1944) have long recognized the fact that personal bias does, and that political ideology can, influence research. They also called for methods to mitigate the effects of both personal bias and political doctrine because of the obvious distortions in the record of evidence and fallacious conclusions that usually result.

Every person, including curriculum scholars, is obviously entitled to his or her personal beliefs, political or otherwise. However, ideology as political doctrine, by definition, ignores mitigating evidence and rejects contradictory arguments. Ideology as doctrine privileges personal preference over proof and results, ironically, in positivistic positions. Ideology as doctrine compromises accuracy and constrains perspectives. And ideology as doctrine militates against free and open communication; dogma displaces debate.

Our concerns about ideology may be interpreted by some readers as a manifestation of a positivist epistemology; we think our position is better characterized as pragmatic. Constructive conversation and communication are virtually impossible if academic or political doctrine governs the representation of evidence and the evocation of arguments.

Finally, the resurgence of interest on the part of U.S. academics in ideological social-reconstructionist curriculum theory is both problematic and symptomatic of some of the issues just mentioned. For all of its commitment to "critical" analysis of social structures and cultural values, this renewed interest in social reconstructionism has been remarkably ahistorical and un-self-critical. Cautions against the antidemocratic nature of curricula imbued with ideology and committed to indoctrination were something of a fixture of the historic U.S. curriculum field, at least among progressives. The Committee on Curriculum-Making (Whipple, 1926), for example, contended that when school curricula include investigation of social problems, as they should:

> the curriculum maker must take care that the material presented and the treatment given shall be fair to all sides. The chief aim will not be to reach final solutions for such problems—still less to establish any prior chosen position—but to build in the children methods of attacking controversial issues and increasingly to develop attitudes of open-mindedness and sympathetic tolerance. (pp. 15–16)

When Counts and others ignored this principle and advocated open indoctrination through the instrument of the school curriculum, criticism of their position was incisive. Dewey (1987), for example, objected to curriculum designed "to impress upon the minds of pupils a particular set of political and economic views to the exclusion of every other" (p. 415). Bode (1935) accepted indoctrination in education only in the sense of "indoctrination in the belief or attitude that the individual has the right to a choice of beliefs." Bode continued, "Stated negatively and in terms of paradox, it is indoctrination in the belief that the indoctrination of beliefs is wrong." For Bode, the failure to allow students to think reflectively and independently amounted to an admission "that our belief in democracy was a mistake." The progressive critique of social reconstructionism largely has been lost on contemporary educators who advocate a critical pedagogy that accommodates, and even encourages, indoctrination (Hlebowitsh and Wraga, 1995). Our position is that such approaches to curriculum theory and practice will likely thwart democratic forms of living and learning.

The Interplay of Theory and Practice

The U.S. curriculum field in general and reconceptualist theory in particular, needs to confront frankly the relationship between theory and practice. As an academic field with a professional–practitioner constituency, curriculum theory and development cannot neglect practice and reasonably expect to thrive. The curriculum field must serve as an "agent," not merely as a "spectator" (Rorty, 1998).

The express commitment to distancing, even divorcing, theory from practice as a variable in the calculus of reconceptualized curriculum studies has surprised and troubled even some reconceptualists. Perhaps this reaction indicates that favorable conditions already exist for refocusing curriculum studies on practical matters (Milburn, 2000). The potential for fostering a vital interplay between curriculum theory and curriculum practice is a key to advancing the field.

A Renaissance in Curriculum Theory and Development

The reconceptualization [of the U.S. curriculum field], which involved a conscious and calculated repudiation of historic forms of curriculum development, cannot in any historically accurate sense of the word be considered a "renaissance."

When U.S. curriculum scholars shed ideological blinders, clearly delineate the boundaries of the field, consciously build upon the field's constructive legacies, and foster a robust interplay between curriculum theory and curriculum practice, then a renaissance in curriculum theory and development will be at hand.

Discussion Questions

This article focuses on deep disagreements in the field of curriculum. What are the basic disagreements discussed?

Given your readings to this point, how do you understand the field of curriculum studies?

William G. Wraga is a professor at the University of Georgia.

Peter S. Hlebowitsh is a professor at the University of Iowa.

Article 10

THE INFORMATION AGE

A Blessing or a Curse?

NEIL POSTMAN

The following is an abbreviated transcript of Neil Postman's Brown Bag Luncheon talk given at the Shorenstein Center at Harvard University on February 7, 1995. Postman was the Shorenstein Center's Visiting Lombard Professor in the spring of 1991.

The title of this session is "The Information Age: A Blessing or a Curse?" Or maybe it says a curse or a blessing, I don't know. But, when we get to talking about it, many of you, I would guess, will want to talk about the blessings of the information age. So let me begin with the curse. And the curse was spoken of in a prophetic poem by Edna St. Vincent Millay, and this poem is from her book *Huntsman What Quarry*. Wonderful book. This is a fragment of this poem in which Miss Millay describes precisely the problem that bothers me so much. This is the fragment: "Upon this gifted age, in its dark hour, rains from the sky a meteoric shower of facts. They lie unquestioned, uncombined. Wisdom enough to leech us of our ill is daily spun. But there exists no loom to weave it into fabric."

I like that—no loom. Now what the poet speaks of here is a great paradox. Beginning in the 19th century, humanity creatively addressed the problem of how to eliminate information scarcity, how to overcome the limitations of space, time, and form. And we did this in spectacular fashion, especially in the 19th century. For those of you who are unfamiliar with the 19th century, here are some of the inventions that contributed to the solution: telegraphy, photography, the rotary press, the transatlantic cable, the electric light, radio waves, movies, the computer, the x-ray, the penny press, the modern magazine, and the advertising agency. By the way, we also invented the safety pin in the 19th century. Of course, in the first half of the 20th century, we added some important inventions, so that the

SOURCE: Excerpted from Postman, N. (2004). The information age: A blessing or a curse? *Harvard International Journal of Press/Politics*, *9*(2) 3–10. Reprinted by permission of Sage.

burdens of information scarcity were removed once and for all.

But in doing so we've created a new problem, never experienced before—information glut, information incoherence, and information meaninglessness. To put it far less eloquently than Miss Millay, we have transformed information into a form of garbage and ourselves into garbage collectors. Like the sorcerer's apprentice, we are awash in information without even a broom to help us get rid of it. Information comes indiscriminately, directed at no one in particular, in enormous volume, at high speeds, severed from import and meaning. And there is no loom to weave it all into fabric. No transcendent narratives to provide us with moral guidance, social purpose, intellectual economy. No stories to tell us what we need to know and what we do not need to know.

So this is the problem we have to confront. This is the curse I was referring to. We have to confront this with as much intelligence and imagination as we can muster. So, how should we begin? Well, we have to stop consulting our engineers, our computer gurus, and our corporation visionaries, who though they claim to speak for the future are strangely occupied in solving a 19th-century problem that was already solved. Instead, I think we need to consult our poets, playwrights, artists, humorists, journalists, theologians, and philosophers, who alone are capable of creating or restoring those metaphors or stories that give point to our labors, give meaning to our history, elucidate the present, and give direction to the future. These people are our weavers, and I have no doubt that there are men and women among us who have the looms to weave us a pattern for our lives. And the prospect of their doing so is for me the gleam of light on the horizon.

We have this special problem, created by our own ingenuity, on one hand that our amazing technologies permit the constant flow of unedited, as Millay says, unquestioned, and uncombined facts; on the other hand, we have lost our sense of narrative in our lives, which is always what helps people know what to do with information.

And these narratives come from many different sources. When I grew up there were some great American national narratives, which I don't think my students at NYU, it may be different here at Harvard, believe in anymore. One of them was that the great revolution that took place here at the end of the 18th century was not just an experiment in government but part of God's own plan, and because of that it gave a moral authority to our believing that we could be a light unto other nations. I can tell you don't believe that anymore.

There was the great narrative of the melting pot, which is now being challenged in a return to tribalism. By the way, the return to tribalism that we see around now is a kind of response to the decline of great national transcendent narratives; that is, people not believing in some of these stories return to the stories of their own group, their own tribe, in order to find a sense of identity and a sense of meaning. I want to add to all of this notion of the increase of information with a decline in narrative that some of the authority of important social institutions has also declined. Religion, the family, school, even political parties—institutions of that kind have acted as filters to immunize people against unwanted information.

If you look at the Harvard or NYU catalog, what you have there is a statement of what sort of information the faculty believes is important, and what is not there is a statement of what the faculty thinks you can do without, astrology for example. Now there's a lot of information about astrology. Is there a course at Harvard in astrology? Probably not, because the faculty has determined this is information that educated people can do without. But there would be a course, let's say, in American history, because the faculty thinks you should let this information in. So, every social institution has a kind of theory about what sort of information is worthwhile and what is irrelevant.

The decline of political parties, by the way, is almost a catastrophe on this issue. I will give you an example. I grew up in New York in a standard Democratic, with a large D, household. And we had a theory that helped us manage information, helped us know what information we needed to pay attention to and what information we could ignore. The theory went like this. Anything a Republican says, you could ignore. [Laughter] Now that helps enormously, right there. Now then, the theory went on. Anything a Democrat says you should pay attention to, except if the Democrat is from the South, because they are racist and you don't have to pay attention to them. So, this made one's political education simplified. All theories tend to simplify. That's the purpose of theories—to help people manage information.

With the decline of the authority of religious systems and political parties, and the authority of education and families, what you have is people without information-immune systems. I have used this metaphor before, which some people find offensive, but I hope you won't. We are suffering from a kind of cultural AIDS in this sense. AIDS is a breakdown in the immune system. What does the immune system do biologically? It protects the organism from unwanted cells. If the immune system breaks down so that it cannot destroy unwanted cells, we basically get cancer. Now to use that metaphor here I would say narratives and the theories of social institutions are somewhat like information immune systems in that they help you manage information by discarding information you do not need in order to function. But if you lose those filters, then you do not know what is relevant, you do not know what is irrelevant, and therefore there is a general breakdown down in your, our, grasp of what is meaningful. And that's what I think is the curse of this information age.

Think of any serious problem in the world today and I think you'll have to conclude it has nothing to do with insufficient information. The problem lies elsewhere, and I think it is a loss of meaning. People don't know what to do with the information. They have no organizing principle—what I would call a transcendent narrative.

Now there are a couple that the media have promoted. One of them is technology *uber alles.*

We have this other theology which says the pathway to Heaven is through technological innovation. Technological innovation is the same thing, according to this narrative, as human progress, and therefore anyone who would stand in the way of technological innovation is a reactionary neo-Luddite. Should we say a word about the Luddites? You all know about the Luddites and it's something of an insult today to call someone a Luddite. But, when you look at the Luddites, I think you would see them in a favorable light.

This was a group of people in England who between 1811 and 1818 tried to resist the factory system and the machine system.

These are people who wanted their children to have a childhood, who wanted a community life, and they saw this machinery crushing that, so they resisted it. Of course, eventually they were put down, and in our own time the word Luddite has come to mean someone who is reactionary and is not with it and is not in touch with the future. Well, I'm not a Luddite. It would be pointless to be a Luddite, although I secretly like it [Laughter] when something happens, as it occasionally does, where a group of people in political concert say no to a machine.

Well, suppose it were 1946 and we knew in '46 what television would do and we made our list of possible advantages and disadvantages. Destroy the idea of childhood, that's part of it, and many other things, corrupt political discourse and so on. On the other hand, there'd be a lot of wonderful things. Well in 1946, we say, should we go ahead with this? And people would probably say, "Yes, it's great." But then someone pipes up and says, "What can we do to minimize the negative consequences?" So here's how dumb I am. I thought that television was going to be the last technology that Americans would go into with their eyes totally shut. And of course I'm completely wrong about this, because the same stuff is happening with computers now. Everyone wants to talk about what they will do for us, and it is not so easy to find someone who'll say what it will undo. What I'm interested in is not destroying any machines but changing the way our citizens view technology.

I went in to buy, about eight months ago, a Honda Accord. Do you know this car? So the salesman tells me it has cruise control. I said to the salesman, what is the problem to which cruise control is the solution? [Laughter] He says, "Well, first of all—" He's a little taken aback [Laughter] so then he thinks and he says it's the problem of keeping your foot on the gas. I said I'd been driving for thirty-five years and I never really found that to be a problem. [Laughter] Then he says, well, you know, this car has electric windows. You know what I asked him. What's the problem to which electric windows is the solution? So he was ready for me this time—he says it's the problem of going like this, up and down with the windows.

I said, well, I never really found that to be a problem. As a matter of fact I'm an academic and I live a sort of sedate life and I kinda like the exercise. [Laughter] Well, I bought the Honda with cruise control, with the electric windows, because you cannot get this car without electric windows and cruise control, which is a very interesting point to keep in mind because lots of people think that new technologies, information technologies as well as any other kind, increase people's options. And sometimes they do, but just as often they decrease their options.

So, we have to face up to the issues that technological change brings, especially in relation to this issue of information. What are we going to do with all this information? And in the end, I think that the great contribution of the computer is not going to be that it gives us access to more information but that it can be used to eliminate unwanted information. And in the end that may be how we will discover the blessing of the computer—that it simply functions like an immune system does biologically in the realm of information.

Now these transcendent stories are not always "good" stories. When I talk about "good," I mean a story that gives meaning to your life, but it may not ensure your survival. Hitler's story of the Aryan race is a transcendent narrative and it gave point to the labors of Germans, it gave them a way to interpret their past, to understand their present, and it predicted the future—the Third Reich was to last for a thousand years. It lasted for exactly eleven years. It was a flawed story in many ways, and we could study that now.

Of course, one of the most interesting things that's happening in the world, we are talking now about transcendent narratives, not the O. J. Simpson story, is what Vaclav Havel has been talking about. The great story that Karl Marx, and then Lenin, provided is that their revolution was not part of God's plan but part of history's plan. That history is moving inexorably toward the triumph of the proletariat. We can join in the movement of history or we can oppose it, but inexorably it is moving in this direction. This is a great story, and a billion people in the world believed that story, or so we were led to think. It's sort of strange that almost overnight they said, "Ah, to hell with that story." [Laughter]

What happened: Havel has been saying that if you take a story like that away from people, all of a sudden, they'd better find another story fast. Without one, it means living without meaning. It's worse than death in a way. So, they're going to find stories that could be very dangerous to others and themselves. Havel asks what are we going to do in Eastern Europe, what are these people going to believe in?

The kinds of transcendent narratives that we're talking about here cannot be manufactured by the carload. There are a limited number of themes that mean something to people and are powerful enough to allow them to organize their lives around them. Now, you mention science fiction. In a movie like *E.T.*, Steven Spielberg is trying to amplify an interesting new narrative that young people do respond to—that we are crew members on the spaceship Earth and we must be stewards of the Earth. We're Earthlings not Bulgarians and not Somalians and not Chileans, but we're Earth people and the loss of the rainforest is not a Brazilian problem it's an Earth problem and the toxicity of the ocean is not a Miami problem it's an Earth problem.

By the way, I'm quite sure that this is the essential problem in education in America. I've just done a book that'll be out in the fall, which I call *No Gods to Serve*, and what the book is about is this issue: What makes public education possible is not that all schools have the same goals but that all the children have the same gods. By god I mean a small *g*. That there's some story that connects them and gives meaning to learning. Now the problem I see in education now is there is no god, there is no transcendent. Why should you stay in school— to get a better job?

I propose five narratives around which school might be organized. I don't know if they would work because a school or an education system cannot in itself create a narrative. Schools amplify narratives that are in the culture, make them more articulated and visible, but teachers especially in the public schools have no authority really to create narratives on their own. So, I tried to find stories that I think have some resonance in the culture and around which schools could build a sense of purpose in learning. One of them I mentioned already, my Spielberg narrative, the stewards of the Earth, and I think young people respond to that idea.

Another one is human beings as fallen angels. Meaning that what we should do in education is study human error that the most human thing about us is that we make mistakes all the time. There isn't an hour that goes by that any one of us doesn't make a mistake. So, I've proposed a curriculum where whatever subjects we study— philosophy, biology, physics, linguistics, history— we're studying the history of human error and our attempts to overcome error. Now that's the "fallen" part of my metaphor, the fallen angel, that we make mistakes all the time. The "angel" part is that we can overcome our error if we accept our status as the error-prone species. But in overcoming error, what do you think happens? We make more errors.

I mean, Aristotle was a genius—he believed that women had more teeth than men. The guy was married twice. You would think it would have occurred to him to ask one of his wives if he could count her teeth. [Laughter] He believed that if you dropped a 10-pound weight from a height it would fall to the ground ten times faster

than a 1-pound weight. He never took the trouble to try it out.

But, it took almost 2,000 years for someone to correct Aristotle's error on that. Galileo finally said no, things don't work that way. Ptolemy was a genius, but he had it a little mixed up, so Copernicus corrected him. But Copernicus would have been amazed to see how Newton had corrected him. And if Newton could have read any of Einstein's papers, I think he would have said some version of "whoops." [Laughter] Now, this doesn't mean that Einstein is better than Newton or Copernicus is better than Ptolemy. It doesn't mean that at all. It means that people address the work of their predecessors by finding the limitations and the mistakes they've made and then they give us what they have and then the next come along and do the same. I mean, Ibsen is not better than Shakespeare, but Shakespeare couldn't write about ordinary people and their problems. That was the limitation that he had, and Ibsen could. And Freud is not better than John Locke, but Freud looked in places that Locke dared not to look.

One theme is what I call diversity, because I think the principle of diversity is extraordinarily rich, but this is not the same thing as what most people are calling multiculturalism, which Jacques Barzun called multiprovincialism. As a matter of fact, it's the opposite of ethnicity. A lot of people think diversity and the promotion of ethnicity are sort of the same thing, but ethnicity wants one to feel pride in being a member of a specific group, whereas diversity, I think, celebrates the contributions of many different groups, and there's a principle, that we even get from physics, that promotes the idea of diversity, that strength and power and excellence come when you introduce new perspectives, new energies from outside the system. When people are just interested in cloning themselves, as it were, and building walls around themselves they lose energy and power. A country like America is a wonderful place to build a strong education around the principle of diversity.

Do we offer in America, in education or any other place, something to live by? That's what we're talking about. I don't think to live by technological innovation is going to be the answer.

Discussion Questions

How do you deal with information overload for yourself and your students?

Explain Postman's five narratives for school organization and discuss which might be most practical for your classroom situation.

———————— ∞ ————————

Neil Postman was a professor at New York University.

Section IV

HOW CAN CURRICULUM BE ORGANIZED?

Throughout the history of American education, there has been a struggle over how to organize schools to benefit the children they serve. As more and more students attend school and school populations become more diverse, the organizational questions continue. Not only do public schools in the United States serve pre-K–12 populations, but they serve nearly all children regardless of their mental or physical attributes or deficits, religious beliefs, economic status, gender, or language(s) spoken. The challenge to meet the needs and deficits of all these children requires constant rethinking about the structure of schools and the curriculum.

The articles in this section of the reader provide a multitude of organizational ideas that might work to assure a variety of educational opportunities for all of America's youth.

In contemporary times, we often read about how many of our Black inner city schools do not serve their population well. Yet history tells us that many of these schools were, at one time, institutions of quality and pride within the Black community. Randolph's article provides insight into what worked in an all-Black inner city school.

There has been growing support for restructuring American high schools. This section includes three proposals for restructuring. Carrie Kisker explores the options of integrating the last 2 years of high school with the first 2 years of community college. Precedent already exists with programs such as dual enrollment. A plan for integrating high school and community colleges is viewed as means of accelerating learning, reducing high school dropouts, and cost saving for higher education.

Another alternative to the typical public school is the charter school. Charter schools are financed with public funds but focus their programs to meet the special needs of selected populations. Charter schools have, by law, more flexibility in terms of what and how they deliver the curriculum and are free from many of the constraints placed upon typical public schools. For example, charter schools do not have to administer many of the tests required by traditional schools, but they must have in place an accountability plan that can document the progress of their students. Griffin and Wohlstetter provide an extensive review of the charter school movement in the United States, focusing on 17 schools in Boston, Los Angeles, and Minneapolis.

As you read this collection of articles, think about the following:

■ The different schools in your community. What do you know about them?

■ What school structure might best serve the students in your community

■ What impact restructuring of high schools would have in your community

■ How the public would think about various restructuring plans for high schools

■ How charter schools can enhance educational opportunities for children and how they might detract from quality educational opportunities for children

Article 11

THE MEMORIES OF AN ALL-BLACK NORTHERN URBAN SCHOOL

Good Memories of Leadership, Teachers, and the Curriculum

ADAH WARD RANDOLPH

Before the 1954 *Brown* decision, little was known about the actual schooling practices of all-Black educational institutions (Butchart, 1988; Pitts, 2003). Since *Brown,* however, the American public, students of history, and even educational historians and policy analysts have generally assumed that all-Black segregated education was inferior. "*Brown*'s basic premise [was] that in American society, separate schools are inherently unequal" (Orfield & Eaton, 1996, p. xvii). However, educational scholars have not fully examined the actual schooling practices in all-Black educational institutions to determine the breadth or depth of their effectiveness before desegregation, particularly in the urban North.

There is a need for analysis of an all-Black school that not only addresses the history of an actual school but also assesses the effectiveness of the school within the pre-desegregation context of de facto, northern, urban education.

METHOD

In this research, the author used historical analysis to examine an urban, northern, de facto segregated school and elucidated factors associated with educational effectiveness or goodness. The examination is based on history, context, and the memory of what "good" meant in this all-Black school. This inquiry also addresses the actual schooling

SOURCE: Excerpted from Randolph, A. W. (2004). The memories of an all-Black northern urban school: Good memories of leadership, teachers, and the curriculum. *Urban Education, 39*(6), 596–620. Reprinted by permission of Sage.

practices and the specific variables of historical goodness related to the effective school literature.

The community nominated Champion [Avenue School] as an example of a good school that represented the values, strengths, and weaknesses of the Black community.

This inquiry will focus on four historical factors related to the memory of goodness associated with Champion Avenue School, the first de facto segregated all-Black school in Columbus, Ohio. These factors—historical leadership, teachers, community memories of the school, and the school's curriculum and activities—are significant in the success of effective schools (Lightfoot, 1983; Siddle Walker, 1996).

LEADERSHIP

Even though segregated education had been illegal since 1887, Columbus's Board of Education (BOE), led by William Oxley Thompson, president of The Ohio State University, sought through extralegal means such as gerrymandering to construct and maintain a segregated school system. Despite the confinement of Black teachers and the majority of Black students at Champion, good things did occur at Champion because of its leadership. Champion's first leader was an African American woman.

MAUD C. BAKER: AND A WOMAN SHALL LEAD THEM

Maud C. Baker exemplified the educated Black woman of the era whose primary occupation was teaching. As principal of the first all-Black, de facto segregated school, she "understood that her fate was bound with that of the masses" (Giddings, 1984, p. 97). In her belief in her responsibility to lift the African American race through educational means, Baker resembled her contemporary, educated, middle-class, Black women (Futrell, 1985; Giddings, 1984; Laney, 1899; Perkins, 1987). Baker was one of the few

Black women recognized for her role in building Columbus (White, 1936). As principal of a northern, urban, all-Black school, Baker, like Fannie Jackson Coppin, "found herself in the presence of responsibilities which ramify through the profoundest and most varied interest of her country and race" (Guy-Sheftall, 1990, p. 91).

The BOE believed she was competent to educate and to control Black students at Champion. Yet, in September of 1920, with increased migration of southern Blacks and subsequent enrollment at Champion, the BOE altered the organization of the school. Under the direction of Superintendent Francis, Champion changed from an elementary school to an intermediate school made up of grades K–8. Because Baker lacked the qualifications to head an intermediate school and because she was disinclined to contend with older male students, she retired after 34 years of service in Columbus public schools. Baker was the first Black woman principal of Champion, but people would remember John Arnett Mitchell's indelible print on the school.

JOHN ARNETT MITCHELL: A "GOOD" SCHOOL BUILDER

Dr. J. A. Mitchell became the principal of Champion Avenue School (Cook, 1934). Mitchell believed that education would quell racist deprecations of the intellectual abilities of Black youth. As the principal of Champion, he would erase racist notions about Black people, particularly doubts of the educability of Black youth.

In 1924, in the *Educational Research Bulletin,* Mitchell published an article entitled, "The Problems of the Negro Child of School Age in the Light of Mental Tests." Mitchell argued against "the general hazy impression that the Negro is intellectually inferior" (p. 322). He attested to the "tremendous influence of good schools in stimulating the growth of intelligence" (p. 329). Mitchell contended that African American youth did better educationally "in states where educational opportunity was better" (p. 322). Ohio was one such state. Mitchell argued against the current educational research. He challenged the current educational curricular ideology, intellectual tests, and faculty psychology, all of which deemed Blacks as possessing little intellectual ability. As a principal and scholar, Mitchell set out to prove that Blacks could learn as well as Whites given the proper environment.

By 1934, Mitchell had attained his master's degree from The Ohio State University and earned recognition in *Who's Who in Colored America* and in *Who's Who in American Education* (Boris, 1928; Cook, 1934). Mitchell worked to create a school recognized as effective by both Blacks and Whites. In his 38 years as leader at Champion, he created pride in Champion within the Black community, the students, and the teachers. Mitchell, like his Sigma Pi Phi contemporaries, distinguished himself within and outside of his race (Franklin, 1990; Gatewood, 1990). Mitchell's contributions, educational philosophy, and practices were remembered by Champion's parents, student, and teachers.

Memories of John Arnett Mitchell: Building Community and Parent Relations

As a member of Phi Beta Kappa and of Sigma Pi Phi, the oldest Black Greek fraternity that inducted men who had "demonstrated outstanding ability to compete successfully with whites" (Gatewood, 1990, p. 234), Mitchell stressed educational excellence. To serve as a role model, he always wore his Phi Beta Kappa key at Champion. However, he was more than just a role model (Franklin, 1979; Gatewood, 1990; Irvine, 1989; Ward Randolph, 1996). Mitchell did not believe in discussing the race problem in the school. His emphasis was "on preparing students to accept the challenge of a fast changing world. Equip them with the necessary tools to solve the many problems they will encounter in life, not as Negroes, but as citizens." Consequently, Mitchell "always eliminated the stress of race and the

obstacles of color" (*Ohio Sentinel*, May 1959). Mitchell's stance on the race question placed him in a precarious position with some members of the Black community. However, the majority understood that because of his job in an urban, northern, de facto segregated system, Mitchell could not take a stand on the issue.

Mr. Lucien Wright, principal of the all-Black Felton Avenue elementary school in 1943, stated, "Mitchell had to walk a fine line. Otherwise, they would have thrown him out of there." Wright explained, "Mitchell could have done more in the community. He couldn't. He was more active in the Boule'. It was rare for a Black man to have run both an elementary and a junior high. Not many had that" (Saunders, 1996; Wright, 1992). Mitchell was a member of the Urban League, a charter member of Frontiers of America (1954), and a member of other service organizations that developed leadership among Black youth in the city. Mitchell's position required him to walk a tightrope and straddle the fence between the Black and White communities, but his students viewed him in other ways.

Some Blacks were convinced that Mitchell was an Uncle Tom. However, Eugene Walker, a former student at Champion, author, and adjunct professor of music at The Ohio State University, contends that students did not. Walker's remarks support Mitchell's belief in his purpose at Champion: to create a good school. Walker (1996) [said],

> Because of his qualifications, the whole community, I mean the White community looked to him for insight. They would come see Mitchell and find out his views like Martin Luther King. He was like the Superintendent of the Black schools. He had this Black school and he said what was what. . . . He commanded respect. He was not a real tall man, but you got the idea that you did not want to go up against him. So, you toed the line.

Mr. William Hayes, a student at Champion and its principal in 1996, also attested to Mitchell's power in the school. "Mr. Mitchell was good. When I was at the school, he had such a sense of power even though he walked with a limp and a cane. You still felt fearful of the man" (Walker, 1996).

Former students of Champion remember Mitchell as stern but approachable. He was determined to make the best of the students at Champion despite segregation and poverty. The context of the urban North circumscribed Mitchell's behavior but not his belief that education could be a means to solve the race problem for his students. He hoped that education would be their panacea.

Mitchell's philosophy rested on educational excellence, discipline, parental support, community service and citizenship, athletic excellence, and the establishment of an exemplary school through the work of excellent, all-Black teachers. He created a good school, but he could not have established the historical memory or legacy of Champion's goodness without the support of an exemplary teaching staff.

TEACHERS

Johnetta Cole (1993) contends, "In those 'colored schools' more often than not there were African American teachers who believed in our children and their capacity to learn" (p. 165). Champion was one of those schools. Mitchell and his cadre of hand-picked teachers expected respect, order, and success. The teachers at Champion were disciplined, competent, and highly educated. They embodied another measure of goodness (Lightfoot, 1983; Lomotey, 1989; Smith & Chunn, 1989; Sowell, 1976).

Historically, Black teachers and principals were leaders in the Black community (Franklin, 1990; McCluskey, 1989; Perkins, 1987). As principal, Mitchell lived around the corner from the school. The teachers of Champion were leaders in their community. They lived in the community, attended church in the community, and often visited the homes of students. The teachers were builders of community with parents and students— another indicator of goodness. Champion's all-Black teachers believed that in the all-Black setting, excellence could be achieved. Champion's

educators, according to Mrs. Brooks, a former student and the librarian in 1996,

> we're just like family. There was no difference between what they expected from you and what your parents expected from you. Our parents respected the teachers. When we had activities, it would be full because not just your parents went. Your aunts, uncles, and even neighbors went to see how you were doing at school. There was no need for a difference in curriculum. Culture was embedded in the context. It was always there.

A significant component of Champion's success was that its teachers shared expectations with parents. As principal, Mitchell recruited Black teachers who surpassed the qualifications for employment. Unlike principals today, Mitchell decided who would teach at Champion. Eventually, Mitchell also decided who would be hired in the developing de facto segregated system of all-Black elementary schools.

Mitchell's first recruit for Champion was Mr. Charles E. Pieters, who graduated cum laude from Lincoln University, a historic Black institution in Chester, Pennsylvania. Both men had also taught at Tuskegee. Pieters was recognized in *Who's Who in Colored America* in 1930 (Yenser, 1932). Mrs. Barbara Dorsey-Sanford, a 1938 graduate of Champion, remembered that "Mr. Pieters was a brilliant man. He should have been a Professor at Ohio State. The only thing that stopped him, was the color of his skin."

Mitchell set extremely high standards for his teachers. Within 1 year of his appointment as principal, Superintendent J. G. Collicott noted in his report that Mitchell's teachers were primarily college graduates or normal school graduates taking additional classes toward the baccalaureate. Mitchell demanded that his teachers possess more education than was required for teaching credentials (BOE Minutes, 1922). Mrs. Octavia Martin, who taught at Champion from the 1930s to the 1960s, had taught at Bennett College and Clark Atlanta. She held a master's degree in English from The Ohio State University, but Mitchell constantly encouraged her to earn another degree. She recalled, "Mitchell was after me to earn a master's degree. I told him I did not need another one. But, then he wanted me to get a Ph.D. I refused. What would I need it for?" By 1959, when Mitchell retired, Champion's teachers had more master's degrees than any other school faculty, including high schools, in the city (BOE Minutes, 1936).

From its inception until 1966, Champion had been designed by the BOE, under the leadership of William Oxley Thompson, as a school that would maintain an all-Black teaching staff. Parents, teachers, and administrators ensured that the lack of equitable equipment, proper facilities, and books did not hinder the educational development of the students. One could argue that this is why Mitchell sought out exemplary teachers who believed in the educability of the students. Moreover, Champion's teachers represented models of what Black people could accomplish through education. Their lived experience countered the general underestimation of African American educational ability (Philipsen, 1994). Another factor in the good memory of Champion was that the curriculum and activities at the school made educational choices possible for its students.

CURRICULUM AND ACTIVITIES: BUILDING CHOICES AND COMMUNITY SUPPORT

Mitchell designed the curriculum in accordance with the Committee of Ten's Cardinal Principles (Kliebard, 1987). Along with his motto that sought to develop citizenship, the curriculum provided students with choices of educational paths or careers. William Watkins (1993) notes that Black educational curriculum includes six different orientations. Mitchell's curriculum design crossed boundaries and possessed characteristics of functional, accommodational, and liberal education orientations. Mitchell's curriculum modeled possibilities rather than limitations. As noted earlier, Champion contained grades K–8 when Mitchell became the principal. However, in 1937, it became a junior high school of only grades 7–9.

At best, curriculum represents for students an opportunity to learn through integrated subject areas and through varied pedagogical methods. A curriculum implicitly contains what knowledge educators believe is worth knowing. As an all-Black, northern, urban school, Champion's curriculum coincided with the differentiated curriculum instituted at the turn of the century. With the development of the junior high school, curriculum orientations, particularly in city school districts, sought to provide classical and vocational options. Champion was not just a vocational school as believed by curriculum historians; its curriculum did not differ from other Columbus schools. This all-Black, northern, urban school provided better possibilities for Black youth just as Mitchell had asserted in his 1924 article. Mitchell (1924) was a pragmatic intellectual. Moreover, his curriculum supported the "tremendous influence of good schools in stimulating growth of intelligence" (p. 325). Champion's curriculum and activities stimulated educational opportunity and advancement.

In the 1947 *Champion Guide,* Mitchell wrote,

The purpose of the Champion School is to develop the use of the school plant for its greatest possible use. To stimulate pupils in line with their individual interests. To encourage democratic living. To train pupils to solve their problems through reflective thinking. To create an active learning situation. To seek to have every recitation and every activity conduce to physical health and wellbeing. To develop a rich offering through club periods, to provide guidance. To create an ever-widening circle of interests beginning with the school and community and broadening so as to include the state, the nation and the world. (p. 3)

To this end, Champion equipped students with varied and continual opportunities to learn. The subjects taught at Champion were music, physical education, English, commercial, social sciences, mathematics, science, French, home economics, biology, instrumental music, manual arts, and industrial arts. It was important for the students to be prepared to enter high school and to be productive. Mrs. Octavia Martin and her former student, Mrs. Ruthene Pearson, concurred that the role of the teachers and the curriculum was "to prepare them for senior high school and life" (Martin, 1998; Pearson, 1998). Mrs. Pearson was so well prepared that she became the first African American secretary for the BOE.

Activities were a major part of the school's program and were all student- and teacher-supported activities endorsed by the community. These opportunities stimulated student intelligence and interests and made students feel competent in their ability to succeed academically and socially within and outside of their community. Mr. Larry Clark, a former student of the school, remembered that the activities and the club period "made students feel like they were a part of the school. *And they could be good at something.* They had choices" (Clark, 1997). Mitchell supported teachers who identified the interests and aptitudes of students and directed them toward clubs and activities that would foster their development.

Through the curriculum and activities, parents and teachers instilled in their children their collective values, provided sufficient role models, and demonstrated alternative as well as traditional measures of success. Champion's curriculum was another of its characteristics of a good school.

In 1974, Albert Stone, a teacher at Champion, developed and instituted the "Hall of Champions." The goal was to recognize the many achievements of Champion's graduates. Mr. Stone hoped that "current and future students can now be inspired to achieve just as the honorees who began in similar backgrounds have achieved" (*Champion Middle School: Hall of Champions,* 1977, p. 3). In the first induction, 16 former students of Champion were initiated. The following disciplines and careers were represented by the achievements of the honorees: fine arts (1), architecture (1), mechanical engineering (1), athletics (5), performing arts (1), medicine (1), social work (2), business (4), media (1), and education (1). Some of the graduates were successful in more than one area of influence. The graduates had been students of Champion during the 1930s through the 1960s. They represented the memory of a successful past.

The effective school literature forecasts characteristics of effective schools and frames success in terms of quantitative measures such as the numbers of graduates. Little is known about what graduates have done once they leave the institutions (Jones, 1981; Moody & Moody, 1988; Sowell, 1976). Faustine C. Jones, in *A Traditional Model of Educational Excellence: Dunbar High School of Little Rock, Arkansas* (1981), surveys the professions of Dunbar graduates. Her text, however, focuses on the graduates of a Black high school. From its inception until 1977, Champion served the Black community as an elementary, intermediate, and junior high school. Consequently, the graduates of Champion would continue their education in the high schools of Columbus, most notably East High School. The success of Champion's graduates speaks to their ability to leave a nurturing environment and still succeed in a hostile environment. Champion's graduates exemplified the standards of their former all-Black teaching staff, the Black community, and the Black leadership that demanded standards of excellence. Rev. N. Jeanne Woodward graduated from Champion in the 1940s, as did Mrs. Ruthene Pearson. Both women contributed their success to the foundation laid at Champion and not the context of East High School, which possessed a desegregated student body.

By 1977, the last year of induction into the Hall of Champions, the number of inductees totaled 56. In 1976, Dr. Janice Hale was inducted into the Hall of Champions. Dr. Hale is the author of *Black Children: Their Roots, Culture and Learning Styles* (1986), *Unbank the Fire: Visions for the Education of African American Children* (1994), and *Learning While Black: Creating Educational Excellence for African-American Children* (2001). Clearly, Hale has sought to affect the educational access and quality of education of Black youth. This was learned at Champion through the teachers, the leadership, and the community. Other inductees included Bernie Casey, NFL football player and actor; James G. Jackson, Columbus's first Black police chief; Geoff Tyus, jazz musician; William "Bill" Willis, original member of the Cleveland Browns; William Thomas, Jr., actor; Walter Smith, the first Black certified public accountant in Columbus; Leslie N. Shaw, Los Angeles's first Black postmaster; Howard Spiller, recipient of *Black Enterprise* magazine's Business Award; and Earl S. Sherard, M.D., Purple Heart recipient and former professor of pediatrics and neurology at The Ohio State University. Champion's hall of fame assisted students in understanding the school's history of achievement, thereby assisting them in constructing or connecting to historic "beliefs and values concerning education" (Philipsen, 1994, p. 265) held by the Black community, Black teachers, and Black principals.

Conclusion

The memory of Champion is bound by place: the urban North. In *Dark Ghetto*, Kenneth Clark (1965) wrote,

> In the North, segregation has been supported by community custom and indifference. . . . Segregation and inferior reinforce each other. . . . The cycle of systematic neglect of Negro children must be broken, but the powerlessness of the Negro communities and the fear and indifference of the white community have combined so far to keep the cycle intact. (pp. 109–111)

In the case of Champion, segregation and inferior education did not reinforce each other. Does Clark's analysis work for Champion? Had the community had a generally hazy memory of Champion? Champion had problems like all schools. Good does not mean perfect (Lightfoot, 1983; Moody & Moody, 1988). Proponents of desegregation, such as Gary Orfield, contend that "what happens inside these desegregated schools—their curricula, teacher training, and other policies and programs—will determine whether desegregation's potential is harnessed" (Orfield & Eaton, 1966, p. xix). Champion's

historical memory affirms that effective teaching and learning were part of the Black educational experience in the urban North before desegregation (Sowell, 1976). In desegregated or, now, second-generation segregated contexts, Black youth are still struggling to achieve educational success (Dawson, 1984; Dempsey & Noblit, 1993; Dilworth, 1988; Hale, 2001; Perkins, 1989; Siddle Walker, 1996; Stewart, Meier, & England, 1989; Stringfield, 1997; Trent, 1997a).

The memory of Champion challenges us to accept that *all-Black* can be synonymous with *good*. Memory and standard empirical measures support the community nomination of Champion as a good school. As Frederick Douglass stated in 1895, "There is nothing the matter with the Negro, whatever, he is all right. Learned or ignorant, he is all right" (Gaines, 1996, p. 67). Black schools such as Champion were all right. Champion was not perfect, but it met the needs of the students and the community. The community's memory and nomination of Champion as a good school is valid. If education "history is to have a value beyond a literary form of collecting antiques, it must provide a guide to action . . . history must appraise the past to suggest political, social and economic strategies for the present and the future" (Butchart, 1988, p. 363). This analysis of the memory of Champion represents our past, but it also provides insight into how to measure goodness in predominately Black or minority northern urban schools today. Whereas Champion superseded and surpassed the *Brown* decision, its memory, its history, and its effectiveness question the ideology behind *Brown*.

With the 50th anniversary of the *Brown* decision approaching, Black children still have not achieved equal educational access and success despite desegregated settings (Hale, 2001; Trent, 1997b). Maike Philipsen (1994) argued that there were two promises related to the *Brown* legacy: "the promise of overcoming legally enforced separation in school on the basis of race and the promise of providing equal educational opportunity for all students irrespective of racial background" (p. 259). Philipsen argues that the second promise has yet to be fulfilled. In the case of Champion, the second promise of equal educational opportunity had been partially fulfilled despite the de facto segregated context. Champion, however, provides other lessons.

In examining all-Black schools, it is the understanding garnered from an analysis of the "roles, factors, and functions that schools represent for their respective community that have to be unearthed, understood, and taken into account if we are to attempt an evaluation" (Philipsen, 1994, p. 261). Champion, as a de facto segregated school, alters the perception of inferior all-Black schools prior to *Brown*. Champion teaches us about the successful education of Black youth. This may shed light on how to educate Black youth in desegregated contexts (Hale, 1994; Orfield & Eaton, 1996).

Educators of African American youth must provide a quality educational experience bound by an understanding of the political function often served by historic Black schools (Philipsen, 1994). Teachers of African American youth must have a vision, because without it, the children will perish. The vision of the teachers, principals, and community that surrounded Champion was of success for their youth despite the lack of equal access and opportunity for Black youth. They prepared youth so they would be ready when opportunities would be open to them.

Discussion Questions

What factors described in this article might help teachers working with inner city youths with a high percentage of at-risk students?

How did the curriculum designed in this school meet the requirements outlined in curriculum reports we studied in the previous sections of this text?

Adah Ward Randolph is a professor at Ohio University, Athens, OH.

Article 12

INTEGRATING HIGH SCHOOL AND THE COMMUNITY COLLEGE

Previous Efforts and Current Possibilities

CARRIE B. KISKER

Early-college high schools are small, autonomous institutions that combine high school and the first 2 years of college into a coherent educational program. By minimizing the physical transition between high school and college, and allowing students to move ahead in subjects as they demonstrate success, early colleges enable students to earn a high school diploma and complete 2 years of college credit (or an associate's degree) within 4 to 5 years of entering ninth grade (Jobs for the Future, 2004). Most early-college high schools are located on or near community college campuses, as these institutions have the most experience with dual enrollment initiatives and committed to serving low-income, minority, and at-risk students (Webb, 2004).

The idea to integrate the last few years of public secondary school with the first 2 years of college is not new. In the 1930s and 1940s, Leonard Koos, an influential scholar at the universities of Minnesota and Chicago, promoted the 6-4-4 plan of public education then in place in the Pasadena and Compton school districts in California as well as districts in Kansas, Missouri, Oklahoma, and Mississippi. According to Koos (1946), the 6-4-4 plan, which places grades 7 through 10 in junior high school and grades 11 through 14 in junior college, "is at once the most effective and the most economical means of bringing the full advantage of the junior high school and the junior college to the community" (p. 187). And in the early 1970s, educators in the Bronx section of New York City created the Middle College High School (MCHS) at LaGuardia Community College for disadvantaged 9th through 12th graders who might benefit from a nontraditional setting in

SOURCE: Excerpted from Kisker, C. B. (2006). Integrating high school and the community college: Previous efforts and current possibilities. *Community College Review, 34*(1), 68–86. Reprinted by permission of Sage.

which they could learn with and from community college students.

RATIONALES FOR INTEGRATING HIGH SCHOOL AND COMMUNITY COLLEGE

Throughout the past century, many scholars and educators have advocated integrating high school and community college education, arguing that it enhances curricular unity, allows for accelerated and flexible coursework, provides students with a liberal education before—or in case they do not attend—the university, keeps students in one institution throughout their adolescence, creates cost savings for states and institutions, and reduces the number of students who drop out or otherwise fail to move successfully through the secondary and postsecondary education systems.

Enhances Curricular Unity

As Wechsler (2001) noted, many early advocates of integrating high school and the community college believed that combining grades 11 through 14 would produce greater curricular and administrative unity. They argued that the division between grades 12 and 13 was artificial, at once denying many students an opportunity to participate in postsecondary education and permitting unnecessary duplication in high school and college coursework (Koos, 1946). As the Educational Policies Commission of the National Educational Association and American Association of School Administrators wrote in 1938, "The first two years of college work as commonly offered in American institutions of higher education are more certainly related to the secondary school than to the higher education offered in the last two years of college" (as quoted in Koos, 1946, p. 5). Integrating grades 11 through 14 would help to eliminate these curricular gaps and overlaps and allow for a more natural transition from general to specialized coursework.

According to the President's Commission on Higher Education, inadequate planning for students who left college after grade 14 resulted in curricular waste. In contrast, Koos's 6-4-4 plan allowed for more curricular flexibility, greater enrollment in appropriate course sequences, and reduced duplication of coursework.

Many of these same arguments are echoed today. As a white paper about the early college initiative (Jobs for the Future, n.d.) pointed out, many high school students take nonchallenging, repetitive classes that, although they may meet high school exit standards, do not prepare students to succeed in credit-generating college courses. As a result, students must take one or more remedial sequences before they can proceed to college-level work. By integrating high school and the first 2 years of college and allowing students to move through disciplinary sequences as they demonstrate mastery, educators can eliminate the curricular gaps and overlaps between high school and college coursework.

Allows for Accelerated and Flexible Coursework

Integrating high school and community college can also result in significant time savings. As Wechsler (2001) noted, many of the idea's early advocates believed that eliminating curricular duplication would allow students to earn a college degree in fewer years and would provide them with more time to enroll in additional courses, thereby enriching their educational experience. This argument is echoed today in white papers and issue briefs supporting the early-college high school initiative. In addition, by integrating high school and community college education, students who would not otherwise receive the academic preparation necessary to meet high school and college standards can move through course sequences at their own pace and enroll in college-level classes as soon as they demonstrate subject mastery and competence. By changing the structure of the nation's secondary and postsecondary education systems, students can experience a more flexible and individually tailored program of study (Jobs for the Future, n.d.).

Provides Students With a
Liberal Education Before—or in Case
They Do Not Attend—the University

Some of the idea's early advocates supported the 6-4-4 plan because it would allow students to obtain a liberal arts education before proceeding to graduate or professional schools (Wechsler, 2001). In other words, the 6-4-4 arrangement would help separate general from "scholarly" education (Goodwin, 1976). David Starr Jordan, Stanford University's first president, once wrote that he looked forward "to the time when the large high schools of the state in conjunction with the small colleges will relieve the two great universities from the expense and from the necessity of giving instruction of the first two university years," as that instruction is "of the same general nature as the work of the high school itself" (as quoted in Wechsler, 2001, p. 7). In addition, as Robert M. Hutchins, president of the University of Chicago in the 1930s, argued, this curricular arrangement would expose all students—not just the university bound—to a liberal education and provide them with the skills necessary to participate in society (Wechsler, 2001).

Keeps Students in the Same
Institution Through Adolescence

Advocates of integrating high school and community college also note developmental justifications. Many look to G. Stanley Hall, a late-19th-century psychologist, for evidence that the gap between grades 12 and 13 is artificial. Hall asserted that there is

> a real and not a merely theoretical break or transition in the intellectual development of a youth and in his appropriate studies at about the time which is marked in the United States by the completion of the second or sophomore year of college work. (as cited in Wechsler, 2001, p. 9)

Janet Lieberman (2004), one of the founders of MCHS, echoed Hall's sentiments a century later:

Intellectual maturation is a continuous process: there is little or no difference between a student at the conclusion of twelfth grade and the beginning of college enrollment. Therefore, learning should be a continuous process; the transitions should be smooth; and the curriculum between high school and college should be coordinated. (p. 3)

Other advocates of integrating high school and college have cited psychological theories that suggest students between the ages of 16 and 20 are in "middle adolescence," a period in which "the life-long habits of thought and action are determined" (Eby, 1929, as cited in Wechsler, 2001, p. 9). Students would benefit, U.S. Commissioner of Education William J. Cooper argued in 1929, "if a single school unit with a trained staff could deal with this period in life" (p. 340). Similarly, Ralph W. Tyler, former chairman of the Department of Education at the University of Chicago, wrote in 1944 that between the ages of 14 and 16, students gain the biological and mental maturity that makes successful college work possible. He argued that although 15-year-olds have 90% of the mental abilities characteristic of adults, unless they are provided with "continuous intellectual stimulation during the period from age 15 though adulthood, mental growth will largely stop" (as quoted in Koos, 1946, p. 83).

Creates Cost Savings

According to Koos (1946), combining grades 11 through 14 would also permit savings in capital construction, housing, maintenance, and operation.

Reduces Dropouts and Equalizes
Educational Opportunity

In addition to the preceding rationales for integrating high school and community college education, many proponents have cited social justifications. For example, Janet Lieberman and Joseph Shenker, founders of MCHS at LaGuardia Community College, believed that this model might increase the aspirations and abilities of students who might not otherwise attend college or who were at risk of dropping out of high school (Wechsler, 2001). Similarly, Jobs for the Future (n.d.), the organization coordinating the early college initiative, cited low high school graduation and college enrollment and persistence rates among African American, Latino, and Native American youth as a rationale for integrating high school and college education. By targeting low-income and first-generation college students, as well as English-language learners and students from races and ethnicities traditionally underrepresented in higher education, early college proponents believe they can remove major barriers to postsecondary access and success for underprivileged students.

PREVIOUS EFFORTS—KOOS'S 6-4-4 PLAN AND MIDDLE-COLLEGE HIGH SCHOOL

Throughout the past century, many educators have attempted to connect or integrate the last few years of high school and the first few years of college. This section describes two of these efforts: Leonard V. Koos's 6-4-4 plan of public school organization and MCHS and LaGuardia Community College.

Koos's 6-4-4 Plan

The idea to integrate high school and community college education did not originate with Leonard V. Koos, although he is considered the greatest proponent of the 6-4-4 plan of public school organization. Rather, the idea is inextricably intertwined with the emergence of community colleges themselves. As Eby (1928) noted,

> The originators of [the junior college], President William Rainey Harper of the University of Chicago and Dean Alexis F. Lange of the University of California, fully expected that these two years of work would be organized directly with the regular four-year high school. (p. 536)

The junior college movement began in the late 19th century when secondary schools and districts across the country began to experiment with postgraduate and collegiate-grade courses. Most 2-year colleges were established as upper extensions of secondary schools and, in many states, were operated as departments within high schools until 1960 (Pedersen, 2000). As a result, some of the earliest literature about the idea to integrate high school and community college coursework can be found in the writings of the 2-year college's earliest advocates and historians, including Leonard Koos and Walter Crosby Eells.

Leonard Koos was one of the first community college scholars and in 1925 published *The Junior College Movement*, in which he outlined the purposes and curricular offerings of the 2-year college. Much of this book was dedicated to an evaluation of the amount and scope of overlap in high school and community college coursework.

In 1946, after many years of promoting his 6-4-4 plan at national conferences and meetings of educational associations (Pedersen, 2000), Koos published a book summarizing his arguments, titled *Integrating High School and College: The Six-Four-Four Plan at Work.*

The Six-Four-Four Plan at Work. Including a chapter titled "The Superiority of the Four-Year Junior High School," Koos's book cited the preferences and opinions of high school and community college administrators, the overlap between coursework in grades 11 through 12 and 13 through 14, and administrative and cost savings as reasons to restructure public education along the lines of his 6-4-4 plan. Koos also briefly discussed some of the obstacles to 6-4-4 reorganization but noted that "they should in few instances be permanent obstruction" (p. 201).

Walter Crosby Eells, a professor of education at Stanford University, was another of the 2-year college's earliest scholars. In 1931 he published a hefty treatise on the junior college, noting that since Koos's book appeared in 1925, "the number of junior colleges has more than doubled,

widespread public interest has greatly intensified, and the literature in the field has increased
at an astonishing rate" (p. xiii). Unlike Koos,
Eells favored a 6–3–3–2 model of public school
organization in which junior colleges are administered and funded separately from high schools.
Disputing each of Koos's rationales for the 6-4-4
plan and noting that many of the arguments put
forth in support of a 4-year junior college were
just as applicable to a separate 2-year college,
Eells asked if advocates of the 6-4-4 plan
were "really thinking in terms of the *four-year
unit in particular* or of the *junior college in general*" (p. 688).

Building on this question, Eells outlined
the merits of a separate, 2-year junior college,
emphasizing, in particular, that a 4-year junior
college went against the "psychology of the
American people" (p. 720). This argument may
be a significant reason why the 6-4-4 plan was
not as widely implemented as Koos and other
advocates envisioned. As Eells noted,

> Going to college has been the great American
> ambition, and it is rapidly becoming the great
> American habit. . . . It is difficult enough to get the
> notion into the public consciousness that the two-
> year junior college is real college; it will be far
> more difficult for it to feel that "college" is a
> centaur-like hybrid, half high school and half col-
> lege. (pp. 726–727)

Indeed, a question at the heart of this article—
why the 6-4-4 plan and other programs to integrate high school and community college have
fallen short of widespread implementation—also
seemed to weigh on Eells. As he wrote,

> In reviewing the literature on the six-four-four plan,
> one is reminded of the classic remark of Mark Twain
> with reference to the weather that a great deal has
> been said about it, but very little seems to have been
> done about it! Much has been said and written about
> the six-four-four plan . . . but only a few such insti-
> tutions have been established. (p. 683)

Spurred in large part by Koos's active lobbying, the idea to integrate high school and college

coursework was a common topic in educational
journal articles and association meetings during
the 1920s and 1930s (Kisker, n.d.). Nonetheless,
Koos's 4-year junior colleges had few takers at
the local level (Pedersen, 2000). By 1941, only
10 public school systems were operating under a
6-4-4 model (4 of them in California), although
a few private 4-year junior colleges also existed
(Stoel, 1988). And by 1955, even Pasadena
Junior College—the shining star of the 6-4-4
movement—had relegated grades 11 and 12 to
Pasadena High (Pasadena City College, 2003).
The idea to integrate high school and community
college virtually disappeared for the next 30
years, reemerging with the establishment of
MCHS in the early 1970s.

MIDDLE COLLEGE HIGH SCHOOL

In 1971, City University of New York's acting
chancellor, Timothy Healy, asked Janet Lieberman
at LaGuardia Community College to design a
program that would increase the college's enrollments and help stem the large numbers of
students dropping out of New York City high
schools. Drawing on the works of Leonard Koos,
G. Stanley Hall, and a report issued by the head-
masters of four elite residential preparatory
schools advocating the education of "late adolescents" in a single institution that offered a multidisciplinary, liberal arts curriculum (Four School
Study Commission, 1970), Lieberman proposed
that LaGuardia sponsor an educational program
targeted at students aged 16 to 20 who were identified by their middle schools as potential
dropouts (Carter, 2004). Supported by a grant
from the Carnegie Corporation, Lieberman and
MCHS cofounder Joseph Shenker, president of
LaGuardia Community College, spent 3 years
planning and attaining approval of the school's
design. Key features of the MCHS proposal
included a flexible curriculum through which
students could move at their own pace; a collaborative relationship with LaGuardia that allowed
students to enroll in college courses after

demonstrating subject mastery; a cooperative "prejob" educational program that included field-trips, internships, and apprenticeships; and a counseling-heavy "house" structure that would encourage student–faculty relationships, cooperative learning, and student visibility and individuality (Lieberman, 1988; Wechsler, 2001). Although MCHS successfully incorporated the majority of these features when it opened its doors in 1974, it struggled to fully integrate high school and college education. As Wechsler noted,

> LaGuardia's Middle College High School became neither a grades 10–14 school for at-risk students nor a high school-level department preparing at-risk students exclusively for one community college. Novelty was limited when the state compelled high school attendance but left postsecondary education volitional, when the need for revenue tempered collaboration, and when the age gap between community college and high school students widened. (p. 167)

Although it fell short of its goal to truly integrate high school and community college coursework, MCHS demonstrated much success in educating and graduating at-risk students. As a result, in 1985 the New York State Legislature allocated funds to create other middle colleges in the region. A year later Lieberman received the first of several Ford Foundation grants to create seven new middle colleges across the nation. By 2000, 30 replications, including 5 of the original 7 Ford-sponsored sites, were in operation (Wechsler, 2001). To this day, MCHS is heralded as one of the most promising approaches to high school-community college collaboration. Roughly 90% of MCHS students graduate high school, and more than 75% go on to college (New York Department of Education, 2003). And although there are fewer middle colleges today than Lieberman and other advocates may have hoped, MCHS replications across the country have been featured in the U.S. Department of Education's (1998) profile of the nation's leading-edge schools and have been cited as promising pathways to college access and success (Hughes, Karp, Fermin, & Bailey, 2005). Nonetheless, by 2002, few if any middle

colleges had truly integrated high school and community college education.

WHY DID THE 6-4-4 PLAN AND MIDDLE-COLLEGE HIGH SCHOOL FALL SHORT?

A few scholars have speculated about why the idea to integrate high school and community college has not yet become part of the educational mainstream. As noted earlier, Eells (1931) felt that the 6-4-4 plan of school organization went against the psychology of the American public and would never give students the sense that they were attending a true undergraduate college, complete with school spirit. Wechsler (2001) also speculated as to why Koos's 6-4-4 plan was never fully adopted. He noted that despite the President's Commission on Higher Education's (1947) endorsement of the 6-4-4 plan, it did not recommend restructuring grades 11 through 14, and as a result the states chose not to disturb the organization of local high schools. Also, advocates of the traditional junior high school opposed the 6-4-4 model and were successful in convincing members of educational associations, including the North Central Association, which had previously supported Koos's 6-4-4 plan, that "the preservation of the junior high school [was] more important than the saving of two years in the student's program" (Krugg, 1972, as cited in Wechsler, 2001, p. 13). As a result of pressures to maintain traditional junior high and high school structures, the only high school–college collaborations that gained significant ground after 1950 were those such as Advanced Placement that did not require organizational change (Wechsler, 2001).

Furthermore, by the 1970s most states had established separate governance and funding structures for secondary and postsecondary education, and this formalization of distinct educational sectors may have precluded the substantial integration of grades 11 through 14 envisioned by founders and advocates of middle-college high schools. As Wechsler noted, significant collaboration between MCHS and LaGuardia Community College was initially inhibited by the disparate and often conflicting requirements of New York's Board of Education and Board of Higher Education. Also, the fact that New York high school teachers and college faculty faced different credentialing requirements and had separate union representation may have hindered integration of high school and college coursework. MCHS was able to move past these potential barriers by gaining autonomy from both LaGuardia and the school district, but this autonomy came at the cost of integration. Carter (2004) echoed this sentiment, noting that until the early college initiative offered MCHS at LaGuardia private funding, it was beholden to both New York's secondary and postsecondary systems and thus not able to substantially alter the way students move through high schools and community colleges.

Riesman's (1956) theory of institutional isomorphism may also help to explain why efforts to integrate high school and the community college have not yet gained a significant foothold in American education. Since their establishment in the early 20th century, many community colleges have aspired to award the baccalaureate degree and earn the prestige and respect traditionally reserved for their 4-year counterparts (Cohen & Brawer, 2003; Eells, 1931). As Eby observed in 1932, "Many communities are nursing the secret yearning that their junior colleges will burgeon into senior colleges. . . . The number of institutions throughout the country which have taken this step and become senior institutions is fairly large" (p. 473). As he correctly assessed, "No junior college which has such aspirations is likely to link itself with the high school grades" (p. 473). The isomorphic tendency may thus help to explain why, throughout the past century, "direct relations between schools and colleges have been problematic and short-lived rather than purposeful and productive" (Orrill, n.d., p. 1).

A final explanation—one that I explored more fully in other work (Kisker, n.d.)—is that state policies and governance and funding structures precluded widespread integration of high school and the community college. Within individual states, high schools and community colleges are most often governed, funded, and accredited by separate bodies, which makes significant cross-sector collaboration—let alone integration—difficult.

CURRENT POSSIBILITIES—EARLY-COLLEGE HIGH SCHOOLS

The early college initiative is perhaps the most ambitious attempt yet to integrate high school and community college, as it allows students to complete their high school coursework and earn an associate's degree or 2 years of college credit within 4 to 5 years. Early colleges are designed for students traditionally underrepresented in higher education as well as those who have not had access to the academic preparation necessary to succeed in college. Early college academies, each which serve an average of 400 students when fully enrolled, eliminate the physical transition between high school and college and provide students with a personalized learning environment where mastery of subject matter, rather than matriculation through grade levels, is supported and rewarded (Jobs for the Future, 2004).

Sponsored by the Bill and Melinda Gates Foundation, the Carnegie Corporation of New York, the Ford Foundation, and the W. K. Kellogg Foundation, and coordinated by Jobs for the Future, a nonprofit educational foundation, the first four early-college high schools opened in 2002. Today, 67 early college academies are in operation in 24 states (Jobs for the Future, 2005). Most are located on or near a community college campus, although a few allow students to take lower division college coursework at a 4-year institution. To date, the early college initiative has received more than $120 million in philanthropic funding (Jobs for the Future, 2004). Jobs for the Future anticipates that 166 early college high schools will have opened by 2011, serving more than 62,000 students.

Although outcome data are not yet available for the vast majority of early-college high schools, a few publications provide preliminary information about the initiative's potential for educating at-risk and disadvantaged youth. According to the Gates Foundation, early-college high schools report an average attendance and promotion rate (students passing a grade or assessment gateway and moving on to the next) greater than 90%. Also, most early college students earn at least a C or better in their college courses (Jacobson, 2005, p. A36). A few outcomes are available from individual early college academies as well. For example, Goldberger and Haynes (2005) reported that students at the California Academy of Liberal Studies earn math and English test scores that are significantly higher than both state and district averages. Similarly, in a report on five innovative models for high school student success published by the Bill and Melinda Gates Foundation, Huebner and Corbett (2004) noted that ninth graders at the Dayton Early College Academy (DECA) outperformed their Dayton public school counterparts in all five components (reading, language, math, science, and social studies) of the mandatory Ohio achievement exam. Furthermore, in surveys and interviews conducted by researchers at Harvard University, DECA students have shown more interest in higher education—or in careers that require higher education—than their peers at local public schools. According to Harvard's Michael Nakkula, this finding suggests that DECA and other early-college high schools are "off to a good start" (as quoted in Jacobson, 2005, p. A36).

Leaders of the early college initiative have also attempted to gather qualitative data about how students experience early college high schools. In a study commissioned by the Jobs for the Future foundation, a group of Harvard researchers analyzed students' perspectives at two early college academies and recently published a summary of results from the first year of the study. Although the researchers noted that their findings are preliminary and much remains to be learned, they found that students in early college academies valued the chance to create an educational identity, appreciated continuous support and commitment from faculty and staff, and benefited from a challenging learning environment and opportunities to construct knowledge (Wolk, 2005).

Despite these early positive outcomes, whether early-college high schools will be able to integrate high school and community college education on a national scale remains unclear. It is possible that state policies created around educational initiatives such as dual enrollment and Tech Prep—which support or accelerate students' paths through high school and the first 2 years of college—may have paved the way for early colleges and other reform efforts that seek to integrate or connect the K–12 and higher education systems. Yet as Hoffman and Vargas (2005) pointed out, no state has in place all the policies necessary to support early college high schools. If early colleges are to be truly effective in integrating grades 10 through 14, states must reexamine (and in many instances, redesign) their policies governing dual enrollment and dual credit, high school students' eligibility for college courses, transfer and articulation, teacher certification, school funding, and institutional autonomy.

Furthermore, although early colleges can and do operate in states that govern and fund their secondary and postsecondary sectors as discrete entities, the early college initiative and similar educational reforms would benefit greatly if states created formal decision-making vehicles—such as joint K–12 and higher education governing boards and legislative committees—that view the path from kindergarten through the baccalaureate as a seamless system. As Venezia, Callan, Finney, Kirst, and Usdan (2005) wrote,

> Governors and legislative committees must move beyond the traditional divide between K–12 and postsecondary education and address public education as a continuum of related issues and needs. At a minimum, states must have staff and funds that are dedicated to K–16 reform efforts. (p. 24)

America's schools have many outstanding features, but they are clearly failing to provide all students with a challenging and engaging high school curriculum that adequately prepares them for success in higher education. Furthermore, there is increasing evidence that simply pushing a larger number of students through a pipeline that only works for a portion of them will not solve the problem (Cohen, 2001). Institutions of higher education must become active players in high school reform (Adelman, 2006), and educators from all sectors must work together to create a high-performing system of multiple pathways that takes advantage of different institutional arrangements, pedagogical approaches, and ways of measuring educational progress (Pennington, 2002). Integrating high school and the community college is not the only way to reform and improve secondary and postsecondary education in the United States, but it is a potentially important idea and one that can build

on several disparate reform agendas, such as creating smaller, more autonomous high schools and expanding Tech Prep, International Baccalaureate, Advanced Placement, and dual enrollment programs that allow students to complete some college work while in high school. So rather than asking whether the early-college high school initiative and similar reform efforts will succeed, perhaps we should be asking what we—as educators and policy makers—should be doing to ensure that they do.

Discussion Questions

The idea of restructuring high school and the need for all students to have at least a K–14 education are currently very popular educational reform items. What is your belief about the programs described in this article?

Is it possible that students will receive equal educational depth when collapsing 6 years of education (4 high school and the first 2 of college) into 4 years? Is that much time really wasted in high school and college?

Carrie B. Kisker is a professor at the University of California–Los Angeles.

Article 13

BUILDING A PLANE WHILE FLYING IT

Early Lessons From Developing Charter Schools

NOELLE C. GRIFFIN

PRISCILLA WOHLSTETTER

There has been a rapid revolution. In the years since Minnesota passed the first charter school law, over 40 states and the District of Columbia have passed some form of charter school legislation. As of the 1999–2000 school year, there were almost 1,700 charter schools in operation (Center for Educational Reform, 2000).

This exploratory study of charter schools investigated instructional and organizational issues faced in the start-up years of 17 charter schools, located in three areas across the United States—Boston, Los Angeles, and Minneapolis/St. Paul.

CHARTER SCHOOLS: A NEW APPROACH TO SCHOOLING

Charter schools are publicly funded schools that may be developed by individuals or a group of individuals including teachers, administrators, and other school staff, parents, or other members of the local community in which the charter school is located. Developers of charter schools are given flexibility to decide their own educational objectives and how to organize and manage the school. The extent of the flexibility these

SOURCE: Excerpted from Griffin, N. C., & Wohlstetter, P. (2001). Building a plane while flying it: Early lessons from developing charter schools. *Teachers College Record, 103*(2), 336. Reprinted by permission.

schools are given varies from state to state based on the strength of the state's charter school law (Center for Educational Reform, 2000). Strong laws facilitate the opening of charter schools. The charter school concept is intended to free schools from most of the administrative constraints that other public schools face in exchange for accountability for results: Charter schools must have their charters renewed, typically every 5 years.

In addition to offering a new governance structure within the public education system, charter school advocates argue that the innovation has the potential to improve student performance through the development of high-quality teaching and learning. As autonomous entities, charter schools not only serve the function of increasing consumer choice in public education but also aim to implement effective teaching and learning practices in classrooms. Specifically, advocates posit that the increased autonomy granted to charter schools will both draw those with cutting-edge, innovative educational ideas into starting charter schools and allow such innovators to fully and effectively implement their ideas (Nathan, 1996). The intended result is an expanded variety of educational communities within the public school system with one common characteristic: high-quality teaching and learning. The freedom of parents and students—the education consumers—to choose is thought to further buttress the quality of charter schools, as high-quality schools will be in demand and flourish, while poorly functioning schools will be rejected by consumers and fail.

What we learned from our research is what those working in charter schools already know: It is very hard work to both design and operate a charter school and keep the focus on teaching and learning.

Study Methods

To begin to understand the strategies that charter schools utilize and the problems they face in their start-up process, we held three focus groups with a combination of charter school founders/directors, administrators, and teachers—one each in Boston, Los Angeles, and Minneapolis. Although some schools in our sample had been open previously as traditional public schools, all of them had only recently begun operating as charter schools.

The focus group methodology allowed us to explore in a broad way issues that previous researchers had not. However, focus groups present some limitations in terms of generalizing results. That is, the charter schools and participants in this study were not randomly sampled, and thus the information gathered cannot be assumed to be representative of charter schools in the three states or nationally. A further limitation of the focus group methodology in this study is that it relies on the point of view of one or two individuals from each school site to gain a picture of the school. Any information gathered is thus influenced by that individual's subjective interpretation.

The schools in our sample were all part of the "first generation" of charter schools, developed in the earliest states to have charter school laws. We invited only schools that had been operating as charter schools for at least a year (and were within driving distance of each city), so that participants had been through some building and learning experiences. Nearly all of the invited schools sent representatives. Most of the schools had been open for at least 2 years.

The schools were sampled based on diversity—we wanted to get a sample including schools of various sizes serving a variety of grades. The schools were a mix of conversion sites (schools that had been previously managed by school districts) and new start-ups (newly created schools). In Los Angeles, nearly all the participating schools were 3 years old and had converted to charter status from district-run, site-based managed schools. The charter schools in the Minneapolis/St. Paul area were a mix of conversions and new start-ups. The charter school that had been open the longest—5 years—was in Minnesota, the first state to enact charter school legislation. Likewise, the participating schools in the Boston area tended to be the youngest and all but one were new start-ups.

Charter schools participating in this study spanned different levels of schooling and reflected a broad spectrum of sizes and student body compositions. The majority of charter schools in the United States are elementary schools (Buechler, 1996; RPP International, 1998), and this was reflected in the high percentage of participants from elementary schools in our focus groups. In terms of size, elementary schools tended to be the largest, with student populations over 1,000; at the other extreme, many of the new start-ups were smaller than traditional schools and had 200 or fewer students.

Most participating charter schools had ethnically diverse student populations; however, some schools in Boston and Minneapolis/St. Paul served predominantly white student populations.

Student populations also were varied in terms of their educational backgrounds. Some charter schools focused on students who had not been successful in traditional schools (for example, a prep school for dropouts) while some others catered to parents and students looking for more rigorous academic programs (for example, an elementary school that offered "a classically based, challenging curriculum for motivated students"). The Minneapolis/St. Paul charter schools that participated in our focus group tended to serve "high risk" students more than charter schools from the other two cities, which served more varied student populations. Based on a national study of charter schools, this appears to be characteristic of Minnesota charter schools as a whole (RPP International, 1998).

COMMON ISSUES
FACED BY CHARTER SCHOOLS

In our analysis, several common issues emerged in the participants' discussions of the charter school experiences. These are issues that participants felt that their schools had to address in some fashion in the start-up and development of their educational programs. These issues centered on three general areas: developing an instructional/curricular program, developing a meaningful accountability system, and developing school management/leadership processes.

Developing an Instructional/Curricular Program

In a best-case scenario, a school's instructional program should include both clear curricula and pedagogy, detailing how teachers will get all students to achieve at high levels. Similar to district-operated schools, charter schools in our study found it difficult to develop coherent instructional programs. Other research (Gusky & Peterson, 1996; Slavin et al., 1996) has highlighted the challenges of developing instructional programs. With the charter schools in our sample, the difficulty was exacerbated by rather vague school missions and the press to create something quickly within a short timeframe.

Initial Program Design

As charter schools went about developing their instructional programs, educators were often faced with the challenge of developing curriculum and instructional strategies within a short timeframe. This was a particular problem for new start-up schools, as the conversion sites often already had many instructional components in place prior to attaining charter status. The search for a "quick fix" sometimes led to tension between those who wanted to create their own instructional program and those who advocated buying an instructional package that could be implemented quickly. The "make versus buy" dilemma, although not endemic only to charter schools, was frequently present in the sample schools, and particularly among start-up schools. Charter school participants in our three focus groups tended to have a "pioneer" ethos, and this feeling often led to a strong desire to create their own instructional program—a time-consuming task that flew in the face of getting the charter school up and running quickly.

Given these conflicting demands, what we observed were instructional programs that often featured curricula developed by educators outside the school. Some charter schools adopted whole design packages and connected the school with experts and resources to help them implement their designs. Within our sample of charter schools, slightly less than one-third of the schools (5/17) were connected with national reform efforts and had instructional programs, or at least guides, that were developed outside the school by education reformers (half of the charter schools participating in the Boston focus group fell into this category). Two of the participating schools were members of the Coalition of Essential Schools. Another school was run by the Edison Project, another was part of the Accelerated Schools Network, and another followed E. D. Hirsch's core classical education curriculum.

Other charter schools developed their instructional programs by putting together pieces from different sources—some bought and some made. The Los Angeles schools tended to fall into this category. They assembled different pieces of their instructional programs from published curricula (for example, at one school "Writing to Read" [an early literacy program], a program for bilingual education, and several math packages ["Math Land" and "Math Their Way"]) and also designed their own unique approach to, for example, integrating technology across the curriculum.

In the many cases where at least some part of the instructional program was bought, educators faced the challenge of how to integrate their unique educational missions and ideas about education with already-existing materials. For example, one middle school, whose mission emphasized an integrated, holistic curriculum and real-world applicability, adopted "University of Chicago Math" and "Montana Math" early on when the school felt the pressure to have a program in place, in spite of the fact that the curricula collided with the school's philosophy not to teach math formally as a separate subject.

A third group of charter schools created their instructional programs from scratch, often "doing it as we go," a process another participant likened to "building a plane while we're flying it." This approach was most characteristic of the charter schools in the Minneapolis/St. Paul area. Where the schools tended to be smaller and served student populations, the public schools have traditionally not been successful in educating at-risk students and students who have dropped out.

Similarities Across Instructional Programs

Although our sample included a diverse group of schools, we observed some commonalities in their approaches to instruction. Regardless of the educational level or the size of the charter school (our sample ranged from 80 students to 1,300 students), instruction generally was characterized by low student–faculty ratios, small class size, and personalized learning.

There also was a major push in many of our sample charter schools to emphasize personalized learning. Several of the schools featured individualized learning plans for all students. Computer technology, both as an instructional tool and as an instructional goal, was also a common theme across the schools' instructional programs. In Los Angeles, this was at least partially due to the California charter school legislation, which requires that charter schools address preparing students for the 21st century.

Instructional programs within charter schools tended to be interdisciplinary and focused on integrating the school with the community, often through applied "real world" projects. Curricular requirements in one K–12 charter school included math and science "action projects" that involved students in developing and implementing projects that solved real-world practical problems. At one charter middle school, the entire afternoon was devoted to research projects in all curricular areas. Other charter schools had students use their math skills to plan field trips, design family vacations, and manage household finances.

Across our sample of charter schools, there was a strong push to integrate teaching and learning with the school's surrounding community. Many charter high schools created partnerships with community businesses and educational institutions, and students participated in internships and training activities focused on preparing them for college or careers. In addition, some of the charter high schools had community service requirements for graduation. Other links with the community brought community members into the instructional program at the school. An elementary school, for example, implemented a tutoring program for at-risk students that brought parents and other community members (mostly retirees) into the school to tutor students.

Decision-Making
Structure Around Curriculum

There were different levels of involvement of stakeholders in curricular decisions reported among the charter schools in our focus groups. However, across most schools there was a push for broader involvement in the decision-making process, and there appeared to be tension between various factions of the school community when this did not occur. In one K–12 charter school that started about two years ago, curricular decisions were made by the six core staff who founded the school. Parents and other teachers often complained about curricular issues at various staff and board meetings, but there was no formal structure for their involvement in or feedback about the curricular decisions made by the core group.

Decision-making structures in many other charter schools tended to be more decentralized with committees, families, task forces, or teams usually organized by subject areas or grade levels taking on decision-making responsibility related to the curriculum. What was surprising was that several schools opened their doors with no formal decision-making structure in place, in spite of the research findings suggesting the importance of formal structure (David, 1996; Elmore, 1995; Wohlstetter, Mohrman, & Robertson, 1997). In our sample, smaller schools were particularly unlikely to have a well-developed structure. As an administrator at one new charter elementary school explained:

> We limped through the first year in our approach to math—we had no textbook, no formal curriculum, and no one in charge of making those decisions. In the second year, we set up a formal math task force that included teachers, parents, and board members

to address the issue of a math curriculum for the school. This group looked around and identified several different math approaches, and this year we're piloting several of them.

Within our sample of charter schools, the Los Angeles schools were far more likely at the outset to have formal structures in place for involving various groups in decisions related to teaching and learning. The schools' experience with school-based management (SBM)—all Los Angeles conversion schools converted from SBM to charter—may help explain why the Los Angeles schools in our study created formal decision-making structures, while many new start-up charter schools did not.

> A noteworthy distinction between district-run SBM schools and charter schools was the involvement of parents in decisions about teaching and learning. Charter schools in our sample tended to formally include parents in such decisions; by contrast, district-run SBM schools typically leave such decisions to professional educators, involving parents in more oversight or advisory roles with respect to curriculum and instruction decisions. (Newmann & Wehlange, 1995; Wohlstetter, Mohrman, & Robertson, 1997)

Teacher Professional Development

Professional development—the process by which teachers acquire new knowledge and skills—was not described as being present at levels typically observed in high-performing schools (Louis, Marks, & Kruse, 1996; Newmann & Wehlange, 1995; Wohlstetter et al., 1997). Several focus group participants described how their schools seemed to assume that teachers had the expertise to implement the instructional program and made decisions "on faith." This was often without the presence of ongoing, integrated professional development to ensure effective implementation. Underlying these decisions is the assumption of expertise: Teachers have the expertise; all they need is a good curriculum.

The counterpoint to this was reported for some of the charter schools that had converted from existing schools. The conversion schools, particularly the ones that had been SBM schools, were described by participants as making more attempts to consider or integrate the professional knowledge base into their curriculum decisions. One charter elementary school created a specific curriculum committee that researches and investigates curricular changes. At another charter elementary school, a "standards consultant" was hired to keep teachers informed of national and district-level standards so that professional standards/expertise could be used to develop their own curriculum. Indeed, the only charter school among our sample described as having a formalized school-wide professional development program was a school that converted from an SBM school. This charter elementary school had a highly structured, focused professional development program. All staff members were required to attend professional development retreats each semester that were organized around specific curricular changes scheduled for implementation. The professional development program also featured follow-up evaluations with teachers to determine the extent to which changes were implemented in classrooms. The charter school's fiscal and decision-making autonomy, in concert with the educators' prior experience, seemed to facilitate the adoption of this program—there was control over how much money would be spent on professional development, and what professional development requirements would be implemented at the school, as well as an understanding of what was needed to effectively implement a professional development program.

At many other charter schools where collective time was set aside for professional development, focus group participants reported that the time was used more for planning and school culture building than for helping teachers master new skills related to curriculum and instruction. Consequently, we heard about forums that facilitated ongoing dialogue among teachers but surprisingly little formal, topic-focused professional development. Another characteristic common across several of the charter schools was a reported emphasis in professional development on personal mastery rather than whole-school learning.

Developing a Meaningful Accountability System

In policy talk about charter schools, an integral part of the conversation is about high-stakes accountability with significant consequences for charter schools—renewing charters or closing schools. But, as the reform was being implemented, we found that accountability requirements from authorizing agencies, including the state, district, university, and other groups, tended to be weak or unstable, and charter schools in all three cities generally were charged with creating their own accountability systems. We found, moreover, that for our sample of "first generation" charter schools, the myth of greater accountability for charter schools exceeded the reality. While some charter schools received intense scrutiny through authorizer-sponsored evaluations, accountability in terms of consequences for underperformance generally was not present.

Defining and Assessing Accountability

Consistent with the research on accountability (Abelmann, Elmore, Even, Kenyon, & Marshall, 1999; Kirst, 1990; Newmann, King, & Rigdon, 1997; Wohlstetter, Smyer, & Mohrman, 1994), we defined accountability as the process by which authorizers of charter schools and other stakeholders, such as parents and students, ensure that charter schools meet their goals. Accordingly, accountability systems for charter schools require:

1. *Performance standards* for judging whether or not charter schools are meeting their goals

2. *Assessment information* for evaluating student performance at charter schools

3. *Rewards/sanctions* for the success or failure of charter schools in meeting their goals

In general, we found that authorizing agencies in our sample states required assessment information on performance from charter schools (sometimes via standardized tests and sometimes via internally generated assessments) but often failed to specify any clear performance standards or consequences. Typically, state charter school laws prescribe three general criteria:

1. Reasonable progress on meeting each school's own goals for its students

2. Standards of fiscal management concerning the proper use of funds

3. General probity and avoidance of scandal (Finn, Manno, & Bierlein, 1996, p. 64)

Judging from early implementation experience, the focus of authorizing agencies has been on the second criterion and, to a lesser extent, the third. At the time this research was conducted, there had been school closures mostly due to fiscal, administrative, or ethical violations, and a few charter schools had been sanctioned due to underperformance.

Given the unique missions of charter schools, it is not surprising that state legislatures vested the schools themselves with the authority to set their own performance goals. State charter school laws generally require that schools discuss goals, performance standards, and assessment measures in their charter school applications, but most offer little guidance to schools. Many focus group participants reported feeling that the external accountability system was weak in that the state did not provide solid performance standards or goals for the schools to work toward. It is important to note that among the three states in our sample—California, Massachusetts, and Minnesota—none had statewide assessments in place at the time the charter school law was enacted, although the three states' laws required charter school students to take the tests that other public school students take. What has emerged is a continuing dispute over standards for student performance—should the performance of charter schools be judged by the relative improvement of their students based on the unique goals and mission of the charter school, or by state performance standards, like other public schools?

Current practice in charter schools tended to be a combination of both.

Aside from standardized tests, charter schools also were encouraged by authorizers to develop their own evaluation measures to document progress in their own terms (for example, a charter high school preparing students who formerly had been dropouts for college or a career adopted "testing out of college entrance exams" as one of their outcome measures). The "make-versus-buy" dilemma, discussed earlier with respect to instructional programs, also surfaced with assessment. Many charter schools in our study elected to buy standardized testing materials mainly because staff members did not have the experience, the expertise, or the time to develop their own performance-based assessment systems. At the same time, focus group participants expressed strong concern about the accuracy of the results, since the "bought" assessments were not tailored to the charter school's instructional program— "Can the tests adequately measure changes in student achievement stemming from our instructional focus on the real world?"—nor were the assessments integrated into the charter school's curriculum. But, for the reasons listed above— lack of experience, expertise, and time— standardized tests continued to be used in many of the charter schools.

Some state charter school laws allow schools to submit applications that leave open the specific standards and measures schools plan to use, deferring to some future time when the charter school would actually develop or decide on what it would use.

Although none of the charter schools participating in this study were described as having a strong formal internal accountability system in place, many of the schools appreciated the need for such a system and were working toward developing one. However, a major problem facing the schools was the scope of student outcomes— content based, rather than strictly academic. Many of the charter schools in our sample emphasized in their applications a focus on outcomes related to students' social and emotional development: "the ability to function as a citizen," "to demonstrate the appropriate control and release of emotions," "identify and implement ways to develop better self," and "having an ethic of giving." Such learning processes, moreover, were often difficult to define and measure, even by those with specific expertise in the area. Beyond the application itself many focus group participants personally defined success based on vague, social/emotional criteria, such as "not letting kids fall through the cracks" or "making a place where kids feel they belong." In sum, with the charter schools in our sample, performance standards—both in terms of academic achievement and emotional development— were unclear. There also was a general lack of understanding about how to assess results—"we know there is change; we just don't know how to show it."

Although difficulties regarding outcome accountability were prominent in each of our three focus groups, we also heard about the importance of professional accountability at the charter schools—that is, feelings of collective responsibility among administrators and teachers for school performance. A complex of charter schools that form a feeder system set aside time every Friday for cross-campus dialogue and coordination. As one of the principals reported, "There is a feeling of teacher-to-teacher accountability in all our schools and across the complex. We all know that the kids from one teacher at one school will eventually end up in another teacher's class at one of the other schools in the complex, and that teacher will know who was responsible for the child's prior instruction."

Market/Client Accountability

Across all charter schools in our study, the strongest feelings of accountability were to the local school community, especially to parents and students. "We know we are being watched and evaluated by the parents on an ongoing basis, and there is the pressure to live up to the standards and goals of the parents." An elementary charter school created a three-page contract that parents were asked to sign, requiring them to volunteer 30 hours each year at the school. Called the "Home-School Contract," one page of the document outlines the school's responsibilities to each child and another details what is expected of parents. The school will provide

a safe environment, monthly reports to parents regarding their children's performance, and translators for parent–teacher conferences; and parents are bound to return all necessary forms and documents to the school on time, obtain a library card for their children, and ensure that homework is done daily and reviewed. On a more basic level, the clearest measure of accountability for some participants was student enrollment; if the charter school did not attract enough "customers," it would close.

There also were strong feelings of accountability to students reported by teachers, administrators, and founders. One of the charter high schools in our study held daily discussion groups with students to get feedback about students' experiences and evaluations of the school.

In sum, self-generated accountability systems in the charter schools we studied tended to emphasize internal accountability to the local school community—both parents and students. The systems also tended to rely more on informal reports of progress, rather than formal documentation through standardized test scores.

Performance Rewards

Consistent with recent studies of restructuring schools (Newmann et al., 1997; Wohlstetter et al., 1997), we found that neither the charter schools nor their teachers received significant monetary rewards based on the performance of their students. Thus, although most charter schools, through their control over budgets, had the autonomy to create an incentive system, almost none of the schools did. The one exception was a charter elementary school that designed a performance-based reward system, based on best ideas from research in schools and private-sector organizations (Kelley 1997; Kelley & Odden, 1995). Pioneered by strong leadership from the principal (who learned about the ideas from one of her professional network connections), the charter school rewarded all teachers with bonuses if test scores across the school were raised to a pre-set level. Additional bonuses were given to individual teachers if they set and met performance standards for their own classrooms that used standardized test scores.

Some focus group participants also mentioned "soft" extrinsic rewards, including parent-sponsored faculty appreciation luncheons, recognition in school newsletters, thank-you assemblies, staff appreciation days, and showcase displays on campus. More often, however, administrators and teachers talked about the intrinsic rewards of working at the charter school—collaboration among professionals, advanced technology resources, additional staff development, and control over what went on in the school, from hiring colleagues to shaping classroom practices. Thus, educators in charter schools viewed their working conditions as high quality and professional, and such conditions clearly offered powerful rewards to the people working in the schools (for similar findings, see Newmann et al., 1997; Wohlstetter et al., 1997).

Developing School Management/Leadership Processes

Effective school leadership and management plays a critical role in fostering effective teaching and learning (Lindle, 1996; Murphy & Beck, 1995; Robertson, Wohlstetter, & Mohrman, 1995). The charter schools in our study varied in their approaches to leadership and management. We also heard from many charter schools about their struggles to design an organizational structure that distributed leadership responsibilities in ways that worked best for the individual school community. The varying levels of experience of the staff in leadership positions further complicated this process.

Characteristics of School Leadership

Although the experience of the leaders in our sample of charter schools varied, several common traits emerged. Many charter school leaders exhibited an "outlaw mentality." They usually came from outside of the public school system or had worked within that system but had a history of challenging the "status quo." These "outlaws"

saw themselves as fighting what they perceived as wrong with American public education by starting a charter school.

A second common characteristic among charter school leaders reported in the focus groups was a sense of entrepreneurship.

Charter school leaders also worked with municipalities to secure school buildings, teacher training opportunities, support for curriculum development, and social and health services for students.

Finally, members of the focus groups characterized school leadership in charter schools by a sense of collaboration between administrators and teachers. Sometimes collaboration occurred through formal structures (teacher committees or "families" working with the principal); oftentimes collaboration was more informal (discussion groups, posting problems in the main office for teachers to write in solutions). Regardless of the forum, charter school participants at the three focus groups talked frequently about teams of people working toward a common goal. An administrator from one of the elementary charter schools summed it up this way: "We're all here for a purpose . . . we're all here together because we chose to be."

Tensions Between Centralized and Decentralized Management

An ongoing tension mentioned by many of the charter schools in our study was, on the one hand, a desire for total inclusiveness among staff in decision making and, on the other, a concern for more efficiency, which often led to demands for a centralized organizational structure. In general, we found that individuals involved in the initial design and development of charter schools tended to reject hierarchical structures typical of the public school system and to value a more even distribution of power within the school community. Such an approach sought equal contributions from all participants in school decision making, with the goal of building consensus. However, once charter schools opened and continued to add faculty and staff, participants began to feel the pressure for a more centralized system of decision making that could help lessen the time teachers spent on issues not related to teaching and learning. In addition, focus group participants reported that radically decentralized decision making made it difficult for decisions and follow-up actions to be made in a timely manner. As one participant noted, "When push comes to shove, someone has to make a decision." Thus, at many charter schools, designing an organizational structure was an evolving, dynamic process that focused on balancing a desire for inclusiveness with the more practical needs for some centralized structures. However, the ability of charter school leaders to create an effective balance oftentimes appeared to be hampered by their lack of professional knowledge and experience in the management area.

The process of balancing pulls for centralized and decentralized management appeared to be an endemic issue for nearly all charter schools. The evidence that we heard also suggested that a balance was more easily reached earlier in the life of a charter school, before structures became routinized or unwieldy. Furthermore, the autonomy over school governance, granted by the three state charter school laws, both created the need to address the issue of how to self-govern and helped the schools address and successfully work through the process.

Types of Leadership: Managerial and Instructional

Regardless of how charter schools were organized, two distinct areas of leadership were evident—managerial leadership and instructional leadership. Further, we found that charter schools that had greater autonomy from their districts were also more consumed by managerial decisions. These day-to-day issues of running charter schools included the budget, insurance, meals, security, custodians, substitutes, psychological services, bus companies, and relevant district, state, and federal policies. As one charter school administrator commented: "The logistics can kill you. The smallest part of my time goes to teaching and learning issues." This is consistent with other research on self-managed schools (for example, Caldwell, 1996; Levacic, 1995; Odden & Odden, 1994).

The demands on school managers were often compounded by weak management experience: Although a few charter school administrators had experience in running schools as principals in private, public, or alternative schools, many charter school leaders had teaching experience only. Across the three focus groups, a number of charter school teachers specifically noted that expertise in managerial and fiscal issues was a major deficit at their schools. However, even for administrators with prior management experience, charter schools presented difficult, new demands. As one charter school administrator who had previously run an alternative school commented, "We are building a ship that is heading out to sea and winter is approaching and we're in the North Atlantic."

The division of responsibility across the two types of leadership varied among charter schools in our study. In some schools, managerial and instructional leadership were integrated in that the same individual or groups of individuals held responsibilities in both leadership areas. However, when this occurred, charter school leaders were often overwhelmed with demands. As an administrator from a K–12 charter school described the situation: "The old principal left because of the overwhelming responsibilities of running the school. It was a crushing weight for the guy to carry."

In other charter schools, managerial and instructional leadership responsibilities were divided so that there was a clear distinction between those involved in each type of activity. "I do 'out-house,'" remarked one charter elementary school principal, "and my staff does 'in-house.' I'm responsible for management and money issues, and my staff is responsible for day-to-day instructional issues." In several other charter schools, management responsibilities were contracted out to experts, so that staff was not distracted from instructional concerns. Finance consultants were often used to handle fiscal matters.

In our focus groups we did riot probe whether dividing leadership responsibilities produced communication difficulties. However, in studies of leadership in SBM schools (see, for example, Louis & Kruse, 1995; Murphy & Louis, 1994; Wohlstetter & Briggs, 1994) some principals have been accused of being too preoccupied with "out-house" responsibilities. It is thus possible that, consistent with the research on SBM schools, even charter school leaders with an "out-house" focus need to have in place mechanisms for staying in touch with the "in-house" needs of the school.

CONCLUSIONS AND FUTURE DIRECTIONS

Since this study was completed, both state departments of education and independent technical assistance centers have taken steps to further support charter schools in the start-up process of developing instructional programs and organizational practices. This is similar to the support that was undertaken earlier with grant-maintained schools in England (Wohlstetter & Anderson, 1994). This support may assist subsequent generations of charter schools in addressing some of the problems that emerged in our sample. Some of the steps to support charter schools have included

- Increased financial support for charter school start-ups at both the federal and state levels

- The development of strong state accountability systems including clearer standards and assessment strategies (*Education Week*, 1999)

- Charter school authorizers demanding increased specificity from schools in their charter applications.

The focus group methodology used in this study limits the generalization of the findings. As noted earlier, the charter schools we studied are not representative of the charter school population generally. The focus groups also included only one or two participants from each charter school we studied. Finally, our study design did not include a comparison group of noncharter public schools, so we relied on previous research with site-based managed public schools.

Given the exploratory nature of this study and the limited number of schools involved, we offer these findings mainly to guide further in-depth research with charter schools throughout the United States. Previous research has not directly dealt with the instructional and governance issues that can be key to a charter school's success or failure. Although this article is a first step toward identifying some of these issues, clearly research with a broader sample is needed to draw implications for practitioners involved in the development of charter schools. Furthermore, as noted previously, the experiences of "second generation" charter schools may differ from charter schools at the outset of the charter school revolution.

In theory, charter schools accept increased accountability in exchange for decreased regulation and independence. Findings from this exploratory study suggest that individual charter schools are operating in environments that afford various mixes of autonomy, assistance, and accountability and that the mix likely is a strong influence on charter schools' abilities to create and sustain themselves. The challenge for future research is to enhance our understanding about connections between charter school policies in states and school districts and existing practices in charter schools.

Discussion Questions

After reading about these charter schools, which might you want to work in and why?

Do you believe that charter schools will improve education in substantive ways? Why or why not?

Noelle C. Griffin and Priscilla Wohlstetter are professors in the Rossier School of Education, University of Southern California.

Section V

WHAT IS THE STATUS OF THE ACADEMIC CURRICULUM?

The primary focus of school curriculum has always been what is to be taught in the core subject areas: English/language arts, mathematics, science, and social studies as well as supportive subjects like foreign language, art, music, and physical education. Depending on priorities set by the federal government, different core subjects become the focus of curriculum reform. For example, after Russia launched *Sputnik* in 1957, mathematics and science were the hot curriculum topics for reform—after all, we had to catch up with the Russian technology. When the curriculum movement was the "back to basics," courses in art and music disappeared from many school programs. Today, the push in public schools is about reading, literacy, and mathematics because these subjects are the prime target for "high stakes" testing. Science has been added at the elementary level, and social studies is currently under consideration.

However, concern for what should be taught in our schools should not be a function of the newest priority of government. Rather, curriculum reform should be driven by what is most important for today's students to learn in order to survive in a rapidly changing society.

The articles in this section of the reader examine curriculum issues in K–12 settings. The specific topics are reading, literacy, media literacy, social studies, mathematics, science, the arts, and music.

Children are typically taught to read in first grade. However, more and more schools are thinking about introducing reading in kindergarten to help the schools get a jump start on the reading problems of today's children. Bruce Joyce and his colleagues describe a kindergarten reading program that was implemented in Alberta, Canada. They followed these children through second grade and reported the results of their findings, which should be of interest to any teacher.

Technology has had an impact on what and how we teach in the schools. Some schools have developed special courses in technology to help students become efficient learners using the new technologies. But most schools do not have the luxury of offering separate technology courses. Thus, integrating technology into the core curriculum of their schools is their goal. Scheibe explores how media literacy and core curriculum can be mutually beneficial.

There are many "topics" taught in the existing curriculum of a school, and most teachers are faced with how to teach some of these topics, which could be controversial. Too often, teachers will teach "just the facts" when dealing with these topics rather than engaging students in deeper discussions to promote better understanding of them. Noddings suggests the use of critical thinking skills to help students understand the complexity of war.

Mathematics is a field of study that has been constantly scrutinized and reformed since 1957. Young children are fascinated by mathematical content until grades 3 and 4, when they begin to study more about the rules of mathematics than the concepts. By the time students reach high school, most either have an intense dislike for mathematics or believe they cannot learn mathematics. Thus, teachers face a major motivational problem as they try to get students through the required mathematics courses in high school. To add to the misery of both students and teachers, there is a conflict in mathematics referred to as the "math wars"—the argument about the purpose and goals of mathematics. Alan Schoenfeld presents an excellent review of the math wars, including issues of standards, national curriculum, balanced curriculum, and democratic equality.

The science curriculum, much as the mathematics curriculum, has had its debates about which sciences ought to be taught to students and when they should be taught. Sheppard and Robbins look at the placement of science courses in the curriculum from the time of the Committee of Ten to present day.

As schools face curriculum reform demanded by legislation such as No Child Left Behind, the arts (drama, art, music, etc.) are frequently lost in the overall academic curriculum of the schools. "School Days" illustrate how the arts can be integrated in elementary and secondary curricula to the benefit of all students.

As you read this section think about the following:

■ How you can build reading and literacy skills into your curriculum

■ How you can enhance the "what" of your teaching through the use of technology

■ How you can reach the visual or auditory learner through the use of art or music in your curriculum

■ Your attitudes toward mathematics in school and what influenced those attitudes

■ The sequence of science and mathematics courses you took in high school—did it make sense?

Article 14

LEARNING TO READ IN KINDERGARTEN

Has Curriculum Development Bypassed the Controversies?

BRUCE JOYCE

MARILYN HRYCAUK

EMILY CALHOUN

We'll begin with a simple proposition: Let's teach our kindergarten students to read. We already know how to do it, so why don't we?

Within schools and school districts, decisions about curriculum and instruction in literacy have to be made on the basis of present knowledge and judgment. Such decisions can't wait until all controversies have been resolved and all the evidence is in with regard to available options. In the case of kindergarten, decisions about curriculum are complicated by debates about whether there *should be* a formal curriculum in reading or whether the components of the kindergarten program should be designed to develop the dimensions of emergent literacy only. But research on how to teach beginning readers grows apace, and we believe that we should take advantage of it.

In the Northern Lights School Division in Alberta, Canada—a district of 20 schools and about 6,500 students—we decided to design a formal reading curriculum for kindergarten,

SOURCE: Excerpted from Joyce, B., Hrycauk, M., & Calhoun, E. (2003). Learning to read in kindergarten: Has curriculum development bypassed the controversies? *Phi Delta Kappan, 85*(2), 126–132. Reprinted by permission.

prepare the teachers to implement it, and conduct an action research study of student learning. Our decision stemmed from the judgment that research on beginning reading had reached the point where an effective, engaging, and multidimensional curriculum could be designed and implemented without placing our students at risk in the process. And if such a curriculum proved successful, it seemed likely that the much-publicized "learning gap" would be reduced.

Over the past five years in Northern Lights, we ("we" includes the superintendent, Ed Wittchen; the trustees; and representative teachers and administrators) had concentrated on the development of "safety nets" for low-achieving students at the second-grade level and in Grades 4 through 12.[1] We based the two curriculum designs on strands of research on beginning literacy for young children and for older struggling readers and writers.[2] Currently, in both safety net curricula, about three-fourths of the students are progressing well and narrowing the distance between themselves and the district's average students. The others are holding their own.

The need for the safety net programs and our observation of the frustration and hopelessness experienced by students who needed help caused us to consider the K–3 literacy curricula and to explore whether we could strengthen them and so reduce the need for the later safety nets. We take seriously the statement by Connie Juel, who, in reacting to the National Research Council report *Preventing Reading Difficulties in Young Children*, wrote that "children who struggle in vain with reading in the first grade soon decide that they neither like nor want to read."[3] Our teachers who work in the safety net programs confirm that their job is half instruction and half therapy.

For some decades, because of the concerns about not generating demands beyond the capabilities of the students or introducing students to reading in unpleasant ways, there has been a dearth of studies on formal reading programs for kindergarten. A few studies did suggest that formal reading programs in kindergarten could have positive effects that lasted throughout schooling.

For kindergarten interventions as such, though, we had to go back to Delores Durkin's work of 30 years ago. In building a kindergarten curriculum, we were not able to draw on a body of recent research on, say, alternative kindergarten reading programs or dimensions of learning to read at age 5. We drew on the literature relevant to learning to read in Grades 1 through 3 and above. Building greater literacy is a matter of considerable importance, and not damaging our students is of even greater importance. But it may be that the concerns about hurting students are based on images of brutal and primitive curricula rather than on humane and sophisticated approaches. Certainly those concerns are not based on reports of failed attempts.[4]

We made the decision that there would be no danger to the students if we proceeded deliberately and, particularly, if the teachers tracked the responses of the children carefully and were prepared to back off or change their approach if a student appeared to be stressed. Not to challenge students cognitively might be an even larger mistake than challenging them. In addition, we wanted the early experience to be not only effective but joyful—learning to read should be a delightful experience.

Our view of a nurturant curriculum appears to differ widely from the image that many people have of a reading curriculum for young children, and we believe it is that image that causes them to shy away from formal literacy instruction for kindergartners. We did *not* imagine students with workbooks, alphabet flash cards, or letter-by-letter phonics drills. Instead, we imagined an environment in which students would progress from their developed listening/speaking vocabularies to the reading of words, sentences, and longer text that they had created, where they would examine simple books in a relaxed atmosphere, where they would begin to write with scribbling and simple illustrations, where they would be read to regularly, and where comprehension strategies would be modeled for them through the reading and study of charming fiction and nonfiction books. If the work of childhood is play, we imagined the students playfully working their way into literacy.

PATHWAYS TO LITERACY:
DESIGNING THE CURRICULUM

Our idea for a nurturing curriculum came from developments in the field of curriculum having to do with several of the emergent literacy processes. Most of the literature in this area presents ideas about and studies of students in Grades 1 through 6. We saw this literature as defining dimensions for early literacy that could be incorporated into components of a kindergarten curriculum. Essentially, we categorized dozens of studies around the several dimensions:

- *The development of sight vocabulary from the students' listening/speaking vocabulary and the study of words encountered through wide reading.*[5] Words are recognized in terms of their spelling, and, once a hundred or so are learned, the phonetic and structural categories are available to the students.

- *The need for wide reading at the developed level.* At the beginning, students can engage at the picture level and, gradually, can deal with books at the caption level as they learn how meaning is conveyed by the authors.[6]

- *The regular study of word patterns, including spelling.*[7] The students need to learn to classify words, seeking the phonetic and structural characteristics of words and seeing the language as comprehensible. For example, as the students study the beginnings and endings of words ("onsets" and "rimes"), they build concepts, such as "Words that begin with xxxx sounds often begin with xxxx letters," and they apply those concepts when they encounter unfamiliar words: "If it begins with xxxx letter(s), then it might sound like xxxx usually does."

- *The need for regular (several times daily) writing and the study of writing.*[8] Writing involves expressing ideas through the learned words and patterns—the essential connection between reading and writing. The attempt to write consolidates what is being learned through reading.

- *The study of comprehension strategies.*[9] Although most of the research on comprehension has been done with older students, the search for meaning begins early, and the modeling of comprehension strategies is important from the beginning.

- *The study, by both teacher and students, of weekly and monthly progress, including the levels of books the students can read, sight words learned, phonetic and structural analysis skills, information learned, and fluency in writing.*[10] For example, students can build their own files of words and can see what they are learning. Or students can record their classifications of words, can see that they have developed categories of words (e.g., these begin with . . .), and can add to them. Knowing what you know enables you to assess progress and to celebrate growth.

For our early literacy curriculum, we found that the Picture Word Inductive Model—derived from the tradition of "language experience" with the addition of concept formation and attainment models of teaching—was very important. The core of the language experience approach is the use of the students' developed listening/speaking vocabulary.[11] The students study topics and discuss them and dictate to the teacher. The dictated material becomes the source of their first sight words, and their first efforts to master the alphabetic principle come from their study of the structures of those words.

The Picture Word Inductive Model, as the name suggests, begins with photographs of scenes whose content is within the ability of the students to describe. For example, the photographs might show aspects of the local community. The students take turns identifying objects and actions in the picture. The teacher spells the words, drawing lines from the words to the elements in the picture to which they refer and so creates a picture dictionary. The students are given copies of the words, and they identify them using the picture dictionary. They proceed to classify the words, noting their similarities and differences. The teacher then selects some of the categories for extended study. Both phonetic features and structural characteristics are studied. The teacher models the creation of titles and sentences, and the students create some of their own by dictating them and learning to read the dictations. In the same fashion, the teacher creates paragraphs, and the students gradually learn to assemble titles and sentences into paragraphs about the content of the picture. The picture word cycles (inquiries into the pictures) generally take from 3 to 5 weeks.

A major assumption underpinning this view of the curriculum is that students need to become inquirers into language, seeking to build their sight vocabularies and studying the characteristics of those words as they build generalizations about phonetic and structural characteristics.

The curriculum was designed to facilitate growth through each of its strands—building vocabulary, classifying, creating sentences and paragraphs, and reading—in an integrated fashion so that each strand will support the others. As indicated above, as sight words are learned, phonetic and structural concepts will be developed through the analysis of those words. Similarly, the construction of sentences and paragraphs will be related to the sight vocabularies that are being developed. As the children read, they will identify known words and attack new ones through the phonetic, structural, and comprehension skills they are developing.

Providing Staff Development to Support Implementation

Once we decided that such a curriculum was feasible, designing staff development was the next step. We needed a program that was oriented to help the teachers both implement the curriculum and become a positive learning community that would study student learning and take pleasure in colleagueship and inquiry. Eight teachers in three schools in the Grand Centre/Cold Lake area were involved in the initial effort. The school faculties had agreed formally to participate, and all eight kindergarten teachers had agreed as well. Two had taught reading in the primary grades in the past, but none had attempted a formal literacy curriculum in the kindergarten. Two were first-year teachers. The superintendent, cabinet, and board of trustees were supportive, and meetings explaining the curriculum was held with parents in the spring and early fall.

The staff development included demonstrations, the study of early literacy, the analysis of practice, and the study of student learning, following the format developed by Bruce Joyce and Beverly Showers.[12] Peer coaching was embedded in the workplaces of the teachers.

The Action Research Inquiry

For the action research component of the initiative, the eight teachers and the district staff members were asked to focus on two questions: Did the multidimensional curriculum work? Did the students learn to read and to what degree, including the extent of their comfort with the process and their feelings about reading?

Informal observation was important, but the teachers were also provided with tools for the formal study of the students' learning of the alphabet, acquisition of vocabulary, general language development (including phonemic awareness), books studied or read, and development of the competence to manage unfamiliar books, including extended text, using the procedure developed by Thomas Gunning.[13] A team made up of district staff members and consultants administered the Gunning procedure in June in order to ensure standardization of the tricky process of measuring the reading competence of very young children.

To what extent is the variance in achievement explained by gender, by developed language competence as students entered kindergarten, and by class group—variables that occur repeatedly in the literature and are reported as factors in many studies? In the first year, all 141 kindergarten-age students in the three schools were enrolled and were included in the study. In all three schools, students came from a considerable variety of socioeconomic levels, and some 15 students came from First Nations reservations. Teacher judgment indicated that just one of the children entered kindergarten reading at any level. Just one student could recognize all the letters of the alphabet (tested outside the context of words).

Throughout the year the data were collected, summarized, and interpreted with respect to the response of the students. Here we concentrate on the most salient aspects of the students' learning. All eight kindergarten classes followed similar patterns. Differences between the classes were small by comparison to the general effects. For us, this was very important. Had it been that only half of the teachers had been able to implement the curriculum successfully, we would have had to do some heavy thinking.

Recognition of letters of the alphabet. In early October, the mean number of letters recognized (out of 52 upper- and lower-case letters) was 31. In January, the mean was 46. In March, it reached 52. That is, all the students could recognize all the letters out of context. Letter recognition was associated with the acquisition of sight vocabulary, but one was not necessarily a function of the other. The learning of sight vocabulary appeared to pull letter recognition as much as the learning of the letters facilitated the acquisition of sight vocabulary.

Acquisition of sight vocabulary. Our inquiry focused both on how many words were being learned and on the students' ability to learn new words. The learning of words was studied in terms of the Picture Word cycles, which ranged from about 4 to 6 weeks in length. Both the number of words learned in the cycles and the increased efficiency developed by the students were of interest here. The data below are taken from one of the classes.

Cycle 1. Twenty-two words were "shaken out" of the picture. At the end of the first week, the average number of words identified in an out-of-context assessment was five. By the end of the fourth week, the average was 16, and one student knew all 22.

Cycle 2. Twenty-two words were shaken out. At the end of the first week, the average number that the students could identify out of context was 12, and by the end of the third week, the average number identified was 20.

Cycle 3. Twenty-eight words were shaken out. At the end of the first week, the mean number of words recognized out of context was 20, and at the end of the second week, the mean was 26, with just three students recognizing 24 and *none* recognizing fewer than 24.

All the students appeared to increase in efficiency so that, by the end of January, they were able to add to their sight vocabularies, within the first week or two, just about all the words shaken out of the picture. For all sections, the mean percentage of words recognized after 2 weeks of the first cycle was 30%. By the third cycle, the mean for 2 weeks had risen to 90%.

Retention of words. In May, random samples of six students in each class were tested with respect to out-of-context recognition of the words that had been shaken out through the year—for example, about 120 words in the class cited above. Mean retention was 110. In addition, words added through the generation of titles, sentences, and paragraphs were learned, many of them in the high-frequency "useful little words" category In the class used as an example, those additional words added up to over 100.

Had the students had difficulty developing a sight vocabulary or retaining it, we would have had a serious warning signal. But such a signal did not develop, and, more important, the increase in capability was a positive signal. By midwinter, the students were mastering words within 2 weeks that had taken them 4 or 5 weeks in the first cycle.

Classification of words. Once the words were shaken out, they were entered into the computer, and sets of words were given to each student. (The students could examine them and, if they did not recognize one, could use the picture dictionary to identify it.) Classifying the words was an important activity. The students were asked to sort their word cards according to the characteristics of the words. The teachers modeled classifications of various types throughout the year. In the first cycles, most students built categories on the presence of one or more letters. Later, more complex categories emerged. The teachers selected categories for instructional emphasis and led the students to develop new words and unlock unfamiliar words by using the categories. For example, having dealt with *work, works, worked, worker*, and *working*, the students could hunt for other words from which derivatives could be made. Or, knowing *work* and encountering *working* in their reading, they could try to unlock it as they learned how the *-ing* suffix operates.

The teachers studied the categories that students were developing, keeping an eye on the phonetic and structural principles that were emerging. The results are too complex to summarize briefly, but, on the whole, about 30 phonetic and about 20 structural concepts were explored intensively.

Transition to reading books. Throughout the year, a profusion of books were available to the students. Books were carried home for "reading to and with," and little books generated from the Picture Word activities went home to be read to parents. As the students began to learn to read independently, books at their levels accompanied them home. Our records show that 80% of the students encountered 50 or more books in this fashion, in addition to any books from home or libraries.

The assessment of independent reading levels was built around the Gunning framework, in which the students attempted to read unfamiliar books at the following levels:

- Picture Level: single words on a page are illustrated

- Caption Level: phrases or sentences, most but not all illustrated

- Easy Sight Level: longer and more complex, mostly high-frequency words

- Beginning Reading: four levels, progressively longer passages, and less repetition and predictability

- Grade 2A: requires good-sized sight vocabulary and well-developed word-attack skills

When an assessment is administered, students read aloud books at each level, beginning with the simplest, and their deviations from print are noted. They are asked comprehension questions after the book has been read. Reaching fluency with total comprehension places a student at a particular level.

In the December assessment, all the students were able to deal with books at the Picture Level, and about one-fourth could manage Caption Level books comfortably. By February, about one-fourth had progressed to the Easy Sight Level, and a handful could manage books at a higher level.

In June, the independent test team administered the assessment using a specially assembled set of books from United Kingdom publishers to reduce the likelihood that the books would be familiar to the students. The aggregated results for the eight classes were indeed encouraging.

All eight classes apparently succeeded in bringing all the students to some level of print literacy. About 40% of the students appeared to be able to read extended text, and another 30% manifested emergent ability to read extended text. Indeed, 20% reached the Grade 2A level, which includes long and complex passages and requires the exercise of complex skills both to decode and to infer word meanings. All the students could manage at least the simplest level of books.

We felt it was very important that there were *no students* who had experienced abject failure. Even the student who enters first grade reading independently at the picture level is armed with skills in alphabet recognition, possesses a substantial storehouse of sight words, and owns an array of phonetic and structural concepts. However, a half dozen students will need to be watched closely because, even if they were able to handle books at the caption level, they labored at the task, manifesting difficulty either in recognizing relationships between text and graphics or in using their phonetic or structural generalizations to attack unfamiliar words.

We studied the data to determine whether gender or socioeconomic status influenced levels of success, and they did not. The distributions of levels for boys and girls were almost identical, as were the distributions for students having or not having subsidized lunches.

Typically, in our district, about 20 kindergarten students would have been referred as having special needs in those eight schools. At the end of this year, just two students were referred, both for speech problems.

Comfort and satisfaction. During the year, parents voiced their opinions regularly, and in May, we prepared simple questionnaires for both the parents and the children. We asked the parents a series of questions about the progress of their children and whether they and the children believed they were developing satisfactorily. The children were asked only whether they were learning to read and how they felt about their progress. We were trying to determine whether there was any discomfort that we were not detecting. But in response to our survey, no student or parent manifested discomfort or dissatisfaction related to the curriculum. However, some parents were anxious at the beginning and remained worried at the end of the year. Some were concerned that we had not taken a "letter by letter" synthetic phonics approach and worried that future problems might develop as a consequence. But even these parents appeared to believe that their children were progressing well "so far."

A YEAR LATER: LEAVING FIRST GRADE

Throughout first grade, we followed the students, and, at the end of the year, we gave them the Gray Oral Reading Test,[14] administered by a team of external testers. The mean Grade Level Equivalent (GLE) was 3.5 (the average for students at the end of Grade 1 is 2.0). Five percent of the students were below 2.0, which is quite a distance from the 50% typical in our district in previous years.

In June 2003, 47 students, a randomly selected half of the 94 students still enrolled in the district,

were administered the Gray Oral as they exited Grade 2. Their average GLE was 5.0 (the national average of exiting Grade 4 students). The distributions of male and female scores were almost identical. Five students (10%) scored below the average of exiting second-grade students. Typically, 30% of the students in this district or nationally in the United States and Canada do so.

In subsequent years, we will continue to monitor the progress of the students from each year, and we will follow the lowest-achieving students most intensively.

INTERPRETATION

The problem that faced us was whether research on beginning literacy had reached the point that we could design multidimensional curricula to introduce young children to reading with comfort and satisfaction. In our efforts to learn how much an initiative in kindergarten curriculum might improve literacy learning, reduce the likelihood of failure by students thought to be at risk, and also benefit students not thought to be at risk, our first experience must be described as positive. We will follow the students through the grades, and we will continue to scrutinize the curriculum.

The teachers were all new to a formal kindergarten reading curriculum. In the first year, they were scrambling to master a considerable number of unfamiliar instructional models, particularly the Picture Word Inductive Model, and they spent considerable energy tracking the progress of the students and trying to figure out whether they were proceeding optimally and whether the tasks were well matched to them. With greater experience, they will no doubt provide many ideas for improvement.

The issues of "developmental readiness" become moot if the knowledge base permits us to design effective and humane kindergarten curricula in reading. The progress of the students in these eight classes equals the progress of students in average first-grade classrooms and surpasses it in one very important way: No children failed, whereas one-third of the students in average first grades usually do. The half-dozen students who gained the least nonetheless arrived at first grade with substantial knowledge and skill.

In the next few years, we'll learn how these students do in the upper elementary grades, where similar efforts to change the curriculum are underway. Thus far, our results have been encouraging, but there are 400 students to follow now. We certainly want to continue the outstanding achievement we have seen so far, but we also hope to close the door on poor achievement and eliminate the need for the safety net programs. We'll see. Right now, our hypothesis is that a strong, multidimensional, formal reading program for kindergarten students can change the picture of achievement in the primary grades. Moreover, 5-year-old children, given a strong and humane curriculum, can learn to read at least as well as first-graders usually do, but without the high failure rates of so many first-grade classrooms.

We hope that our Northern Lights teachers, and all others in every venue, will set high standards and also treat their students affirmatively. We are bothered when states, provinces, and districts set goals at such a low level that they expect that 2% or 3% of the students will creep up to the next level of achievement any given year. Ninety-five percent is a better goal. Nearly all of our little second-grade graduates can now read with the best of upper-elementary-grade students. So could nearly all of the students in all school systems.

Discussion Questions

What do you think is an appropriate formal kindergarten curriculum?

If you are not a kindergarten teacher, what literacy skills did you read about that might assist you with the students you do teach?

Bruce Joyce is the director of Booksend Laboratories, St. Simon's Island, GA.

Marily Hrycauk, is the director of instruction, Northern Lights School Division #69, Alberta, Canada.

Emily Calhoun is director of Phoenix Alliance, St. Simon's Island, GA.

Article 15

LITERACY EDUCATION AND READING PROGRAMS IN THE SECONDARY SCHOOL

Status, Problems, and Solutions

FREYA M. J. ZIPPERER

M. THOMAS WORLEY

MICHELLE W. SISSON

RHONDA W. SAID

The ability of students to read, write, and communicate (a set of skills that by tradition are collectively referred to as "literacy") stands among the most current concerns pertaining to academic achievement in public education. Because literacy is seen as crucial to scholastic success, a school district's choice of a reading program takes on paramount importance. In many cases, the success or failure of the reading program in a school hangs upon the principal's understanding of and support for the program. According to Bauman (1984), the presence of a strong instructional leader (i.e., the principal) is crucial to an effective reading

SOURCE: Excerpted from Zipperer, F. M. J., Worley, M. T., Sisson, M. W., & Said, R. W. (2002). Literacy education and reading programs in the secondary school: Status, problems, and solutions. *NASSP Bulletin, 86*. Reprinted by permission of Sage.

program. Principals are responsible for scheduling and staffing their schools' reading programs and placing them in context with all of the other programs in their schools. They must decide on the qualifications of the teachers who will be given primary responsibility for reading. Should the school employ a "reading specialist," or should all teachers be required to include literacy skills in their courses? Will the school provide time in the schedule for reading, or will teachers be required to make time in their own class schedules to include reading practice? These and other administrative decisions will significantly affect a school's reading program. Although many secondary-school principals have little or no training in the teaching of reading, they are held accountable for the development, implementation, and evaluation of reading programs in their schools.

And those programs are in trouble. According to many critical observers, U.S. secondary schools have been failing in a number of areas, especially reading and literacy. Farr and Tone (1998) indicated that students experience a declining interest in reading through the secondary school years. According to the National Assessment of Educational Progress reading report card (Donahue, Voelkl, Campbell, & Mazzeo, 1999), only 40% of high school seniors in the United States were proficient or better in reading skills (where proficiency is defined as demonstrated competency over challenging subject matter). Binkley and Williams (1996) concurred with this negative outlook, indicating that nearly 30% of high school graduates failed to demonstrate basic literacy skills.

Survey Method

To determine the views of principals concerning the reading programs in their schools, we surveyed 46 principals from the Savannah–Chatham County School District. The principals attended an administrative staff meeting at which a reading workshop was presented. As part of this workshop, the principals were surveyed about their perceptions of the school system's reading program. Respondents included 7 secondary school principals, 11 middle school principals, and 28 elementary principals. The data presented in this article focus on the responses provided by the secondary school principals.

Regional Demographics

The Savannah–Chatham County School District is located in a mixed urban and suburban setting on the northeastern coast of Georgia. Although the 2000 U.S. Census (U.S. Census Bureau, 2002) indicated that the community is 40.5% Black and 55.3% White, 64% of the public schools' students are Black and 31.3% are White. According to the National Center for Education Statistics, White students nationwide averaged higher reading scores than Black, Hispanic, and American Indian students (Donahue et al., 1999). Therefore, the disproportionately large Black student population in the Savannah–Chatham County schools is a critical consideration for their reading programs. Socioeconomic status also plays a role in how well students develop literacy skills. Donahue et al. found that students eligible for the free or reduced-price lunch program had lower average reading scores than students who were not eligible for such programs. Savannah–Chatham County schools reported that 50.3% of their students were eligible for free or reduced-price lunches in the 1999–2000 school year (Georgia Department of Education, 2001).

According to the 1999–2000 Georgia Public Education Report Card, only 62% of Grade 11 students in Chatham County passed all components on the Georgia High School Graduation Test on the first administration (Georgia Department of Education, 2001). The statistic for the 1999–2000 cohort was revised the following year to 59%, and in 2000–2001 the number of Grade 11 students passing the test fell to 54% (Georgia Department of Education, 2002); it appears that the Savannah–Chatham County schools need to take action to address their deficiencies.

SURVEY FINDINGS

Among survey participants, the average length of service as a principal was 4.8 years; the range was from 1 year to 14 years. The survey population had an average of 25.5 years of overall experience in education. None of the principals surveyed had an undergraduate degree in reading.

When asked where they received their training in reading education, principals had various responses, including "from recent workshops," "a personal desire to read and learn," "an undergraduate class," or "graduate class in reading." Although the principals reported varying degrees of knowledge about reading instruction, they universally agreed as to its importance. One principal stated, "Reading is a basic element for all learning. It is a foundation which must be secure before advanced concepts can be attained."

The perception of the secondary principals polled in this survey concurred with critical assessments of literacy among U.S. secondary-school students. Fifty-seven percent of the respondents indicated that they believed that students today are poorer readers than students were in past years. More troubling yet is that only half of the principals surveyed believed the teachers in their buildings were prepared to address reading problems or plan instruction to foster reading development.

PROBLEMS IDENTIFIED IN LITERATURE AND SURVEY

If literacy skills in secondary schools are in fact poorer today than they once were, what has caused this decline? Goodlad (1984) suggested that part of the problem might be the lack of time devoted to reading instruction. He maintained that reading occupies only about 2% of class time in high school. This view was shared by Donahue et al. (1999), who reported that one-third of Grade 12 students read fewer than five pages each day for both school and homework. Horkay (1999) pointed out that students who

read for fun daily scored higher on national reading tests than their peers who read for fun less frequently. Horkay also stated that there was no significant change between 1992 and 2000 in the percentage of students reading for fun on a daily basis. Students appear to have insufficient time in school to do independent reading, which adversely affects poor readers who may not read independently outside of school. The amount of time watching television may be one factor involved in the amount of reading students accomplish. Donahue et al. related that 69% of high school seniors report watching 2 or more hours of television each day. And Pfordresher (1991) suggested that as students get older their interest in reading declines and they spend less of their free time reading.

In addition, Bean (1997) pointed out that poor readers use a narrower range of strategies to guide their own reading than good readers. More specifically, many students have difficulty with tasks that require interpretations of what they have read. These problems exist in conjunction with the lack of direct reading instruction and discussion within high school level classrooms.

It is possible that many teachers in other areas see themselves as specialists in their disciplines and assume that teaching reading, writing, and communication is the responsibilities of the English teacher. In high schools, reading is often limited to text materials, and students rarely read aloud in class. In many classrooms, reading is assigned as homework, and little or no class time is spent on this task. Apparently, many high school teachers assume—falsely—that students learned to read in elementary school and come to their classes with sufficient literacy skills to get the information they need from their textbooks. When content area teachers become aware of their students' lack of literacy skills, however, they feel unprepared to teach these skills in their classrooms. To better prepare secondary teachers to address this issue, Bean indicated that preservice teachers need to learn specific teaching strategies that will enable them to teach vocabulary development and reading comprehension skills.

One reason high school teachers might wish to avoid teaching reading is a belief that it would require them to teach phonics and other skills not related to their subject areas. The principals in our survey tended to concur with this false assumption, as 80% of them responded that they thought phonics instruction should be used in their schools' reading programs. The principals also indicated that they thought their teachers believed that phonics instruction was necessary at the high school level. Shannon (1991) suggested that false assumptions like these result from narrow definitions of literacy that reduce reading to phonics, writing to spelling and grammar, and language skills to English.

Ironically, the increasing emphasis in education on accountability—with its dependence on standardized testing by state boards and by NAEP—is having a damaging effect on the teaching of reading (Pfordresher, 1991). The time required to prepare students to take these standardized tests cuts down on the valuable time allowed for reading instruction and independent reading by students. Although all of the principals in the survey indicated that the daily schedule should include time for independent reading, teachers find themselves focusing on a narrow list of skills and the mechanics of reading that are typically covered on the tests. This discourages students from reading and may even decrease the pleasure good readers find in the pursuit.

This pressure to require "high stakes" testing in all realms of education has now reached kindergarten classes, where students generally receive their first pencil and paper test to gauge their "reading readiness." The results of this test can determine if a child is promoted or retained. However, according to Shepard (1987), there is little evidence that reading readiness scores correlate with reading success. The stress associated with reading tests appears to demoralize both students and teachers. With new educational standards based on test scores, control of reading programs has been shifted from schools to the state level, where decision makers are far removed from actual students. This makes it more difficult for teachers and principals to address the specific needs of their schools and students (Hoffman, Assaf, & Paris, 2001).

Although all of the principals in our survey agreed that reading is an issue that should be addressed by educators from pre-K through Grade 12, none of them felt that reading development is an issue that should be the sole responsibility of the school. Jensen, Strauser, and Worley (2001) asserted that reading is a common responsibility and that teachers and administrators should join forces with parents, staff, and the surrounding community to promote reading literacy among students and adults. Schools should demonstrate that reading is viewed as an important aspect of the curriculum as well as the nonacademic program.

It would be difficult to overstate the importance of reading that students do at home in the development of their literacy skills. Horkay (1999) reported that students who had more types of reading materials in their homes (including books, magazines, newspapers, and encyclopedias) tended to score higher on reading tests than those with fewer types of such materials. Horkay also observed that while the scores of higher-performing students have improved over time, those of lower-performing students have declined. The concept that "the rich get richer, and the poor get poorer" appears to apply to literacy education.

SUGGESTED SOLUTIONS

Administrators and teachers need to recognize that reading is an ongoing developmental process. All of the principals surveyed indicated that they considered themselves lifelong readers. They tried to model their belief in the importance of reading by reading for pleasure on a daily basis in addition to their professional reading. Seventy percent of the principals believed that their teachers also demonstrated that they valued reading in the same manner. We tend to make time for skills that we value; if teachers and administrators truly value reading as an important skill, it must be practiced in all classes.

To improve reading instruction in non-English/language arts courses, teachers in those subjects should be provided with inservice opportunities to acquire skills in reading instruction. Of the principals surveyed, 65% indicated that they had found this an effective way to learn about reading instruction. Another effective strategy, according to Beane (1993), is to encourage integration of the school curriculum. Reading becomes more meaningful to students when it is seen as a critical part of all courses rather than as an isolated skill in one. It is also important for educators to model reading for pleasure; all the principals surveyed indicated that this was something that they and their teachers tried to do. Students watch what instructors do more than they listen to what they say.

Process skills, especially reading and writing, can be taught concurrently with content. By providing instruction in the processes necessary to acquire content, teachers help students learn how to acquire knowledge effectively rather than just accumulate bits and pieces of information (Stevenson & Carr, 1993). Teachers need to provide guidance in all aspects of the instructional process rather than be one dimensional.

All language processes, not just reading, need to be used to help students learn from texts. Writing, listening, and speaking are interrelated and become additional tools to teach more content. Donahue et al. (1999) reported that students who read more pages daily in school and for homework tended to score higher on reading tests. Students who were required more frequently to write long answers on tests or assignments involving reading had higher test scores, as well.

The use of small groups enhances learning. When students are encouraged to work collaboratively with peers, productivity and achievement are increased. This is a result of what Ormrod (1999) calls the "zone of proximal development." This zone is a range of tasks that students cannot perform independently but can accomplish with the help and guidance of others. In addition to encouraging social development, this maximizes cognitive growth. Students also learn from knowledge and strategies used by others.

Integrating technology into the instructional process promotes an increase in learning from texts. A person must be able to use computers and other multimedia tools to be considered literate in the 21st century. Teachers who fail to use available technology in their instruction shortchange their students. Teachers must assist students by providing instructional and technical support to facilitate success (Curran, 1997).

All modes of learning need to be addressed. Teachers should use the multiple-intelligences approach in reading instruction. In addition, Whitin (1996) promoted the strategy of using symbols, pictures, and other nonlinguistic signs to represent ideas from reading.

Content teachers must become catalysts for learning by helping students in their efforts to read and learn from texts. Educators' focus must change from "learning to read" to "reading to learn." Principals can make literacy skills a priority by creating a climate that says to teachers (in professional ways) and students (in practical ways) that "We value reading in this school!"

Discussion Questions

How do you feel about the idea that secondary teachers will need to teach literacy skill across all subject areas?

How do accountability and high-stakes testing affect literacy concerns in secondary schools?

Freya M. J. Zipperer, M. Thomas Worsley, and Michelle W. Sisson are associate professors in the College of Education at Armstrong Atlantic University, GA.

Rhonda W. Said is the supervisor of Psychological Services, Duval County Public Schools, Florida.

Article 16

A DEEPER SENSE OF LITERACY

Curriculum-Driven Approaches to Media Literacy in the K–12 Classroom

CYNTHIA L. SCHEIBE

One hundred elementary school students are chattering loudly as they walk back up the snowy hill to their school, coming from the local movie theater, where they have just been treated to a special holiday showing of the movie *Antz*. The children are not just excited about seeing the movie; they have spent the past 2 weeks in their science class learning about ants and other insects, and now they are calling out examples of ways in which the movie misrepresented true ants. "Ants don't have teeth!" calls one boy. "Who were all those boy ants?" a girl asks. "I thought almost all ants were girls!" Her teacher nods and confirms that nearly all soldier and worker ants are sterile females.

Back in their classrooms, the students and teachers list the ways in which the ants were portrayed correctly (with six legs, three body segments, living in tunneled communities, carrying large loads) and incorrectly (talking, wearing clothes, with white eyes, etc.). The teachers take time to correct any misperceptions and to reinforce accurate information and then lead a discussion about why the moviemakers showed ants in ways that were not true. "Because they didn't know any better?" proposes one girl. "Because they wanted them to look like people!" suggests another. "It would be boring if they couldn't talk and just ran around like ants!"

This type of curriculum-driven approach to media literacy is at the heart of our work with K–12 teachers at Project Look Sharp, a collaborative initiative of the teacher education, psychology, and communications programs at Ithaca College. As many theorists have noted (e.g., Hobbs, 1997), media literacy is a logical extension of traditional literacy: learning to "read" visual and audiovisual messages as well as text-based

SOURCE: Excerpted from Scheibe, C. L. (2004). A deeper sense of literacy: Curriculum-driven approaches to media literacy in the K–12 classroom. *American Behavioral Scientist, 48*(1), 60–68. Reprinted by permission of Sage.

ones, recognizing the basic "language" used in each media form, being able to judge the credibility and accuracy of information presented in different formats, evaluating the "author's" intent and meaning, appreciating the techniques used to persuade and convey emotion, and being able to communicate effectively through different media forms. Media literacy, then, incorporates many elements from multiple literacies that are already central to today's education, including information literacy, computer literacy, scientific literacy, and cultural literacy. In addition, media literacy builds critical-thinking, communication, and technology skills and is an effective way to address different learning styles and an appreciation for multiple perspectives.

Before building media literacy into a curriculum unit, it is essential for teachers to have some basic training in media literacy theory and analysis (through staff development workshops and trainings). Project Look Sharp encourages teachers to weave the core elements of media literacy into their teaching practice early in the school year (see Best Practices below). We then work directly with individual teachers (or teams of teachers) to develop unique media literacy lessons that will help teach core content required by their districts and the state. We always start with core content (rather than the media literacy aspects), keeping in mind the teachers' own goals and needs, with a focus on basic learning standards for their grade and curriculum area.

Sometimes we are asked by school administrators to develop a series of lessons or resources to address a particular issue or need. For example, the second-grade social studies curriculum in New York State includes teaching about rural, urban, and suburban communities, and teachers were having a hard time conveying those concepts to 7- and 8-year-old children. Working with the teachers, we developed a series of lessons based on collective reading of historical pictures and short clips from television shows reflecting the three types of communities. Students from rural, urban, and suburban elementary schools then produced digital videos about their own communities and shared them with classes from the other schools. Students were surprised to find that there were many similarities in their videos (they all included fire stations, for example), and that some of the stereotypes they held about different types of communities were not true. Although this was a great deal of work, the unit went far beyond simply teaching the desired social studies and media literacy lessons by building (or reinforcing) a host of other social and organizational skills.

This approach has been surprisingly effective, not just in increasing the students' interest in a particular topic but also in deepening their understanding of the information itself. Teachers who gave a test about insects following the *Antz* movie found that students performed best on questions that related to the discussion of accuracy in the movie (e.g., the physical characteristics of insects), and that even 6 months later—at the end of the school year—most students remembered that information accurately.

By emphasizing media literacy as a pedagogical approach rather than a separate content or skill area, we have been able to help teachers multitask. We have also found that once teachers have developed an awareness themselves of the basic concepts and practices of media literacy, they begin to see opportunities for incorporating media literacy into their classrooms on an ongoing basis. For example, teachers whose classes were going to see *Antz* took a few minutes to explain the concept of "product placements" and told the students that they would be seeing some product placements in the film. When the first bottle of Pepsi appeared in the scene of Insectopia, there was a shout from the children in the audience—"Product placement!"—and students continued to identify product placements in videos and other media for the remainder of the school year.

In using a curriculum-driven approach, teachers sometimes take a narrow focus for a particular topic or lesson (e.g., linking current advertising appeals to a sixth-grade unit on Greek myths) or weave media literacy into ongoing activities in their classrooms (e.g., in a weekly discussion of current events). Sometimes media literacy is used to link several different parts of the curriculum together (e.g., investigating local history and literature through examining original documents at a local museum). And sometimes the production aspect of media literacy is used creatively to convey information to parents and administrators (e.g., fourth-grade students' producing a video to illustrate a typical school day for their parents to watch at open house).

This, of course, is not the only way to approach media literacy education. Students benefit greatly from specific lessons or courses focusing solely on media literacy, media production, and other media-related issues. But our experience has shown that this is rarely possible in the public school system, especially with the increasing focus on tests and a "back to basics" approach. For many teachers, finding even a few days to devote to media literacy is problematic; they are already swamped with core-content requirements they must teach. Even with a growing emphasis on technology skills and critical thinking, there are still only seven states that mandate media literacy as a separate strand in their states (Baker, 2004), and even those states have had difficulty grappling with how to assess media literacy as part of standardized state testing.

Kubey and Baker (2000) have noted, however, that nearly all states do refer to aspects of media literacy education as part of the mandated state standards, although they do not typically use the phrase *media literacy*. In New York, for example, media literacy is clearly reflected in requirements that students "evaluate importance, reliability and credibility of evidence" (Social Studies Standard 1, No. 4) and "comprehend, interpret and critique texts in every medium" (English Standard 2, No. 1). In California, social studies standards for Grades 9 through 12 specifically refer to evaluating "the role of electronic, broadcast, print media, and the Internet as means of communication in American politics" and "how public officials use the media to communicate with the citizenry and to shape public opinion" (Kubey & Baker, 2000, p. 9). Many states include specific references to media issues in

their health standards, especially related to tobacco and alcohol use, nutrition, and body image.

In taking a curriculum-driven approach to media literacy integration, it is crucial to explicitly lay out these connections between media literacy and state or district learning standards. Teachers then feel more comfortable about taking class time to teach the basics of media literacy and to weave a media literacy approach into their overall teaching practice. Media literacy can also be used to develop "parallel tasks" for students to build and practice their skills in analyzing information from different sources, listening and taking notes, and supporting their opinions with evidence in written essays—all of which are key components in standardized testing.

BEST PRACTICES FOR USING MEDIA LITERACY IN THE K–12 CLASSROOM

Various writers have described key concepts of media literacy (e.g., Hobbs, 1997) and basic questions to ask about any media message (e.g., Thoman, 1999). We have found the following set of questions to work well with students from elementary school through college:

1. Who made—and who sponsored—this message, and what is their purpose?

2. Who is the target audience, and how is the message specifically tailored to that audience?

3. What are the different techniques used to inform, persuade, entertain, and attract attention?

4. What messages are communicated (and/or implied) about certain people, places, events, behaviors, lifestyles, and so forth?

5. How current, accurate, and credible is the information in this message?

6. What is left out of this message that might be important to know?

Introducing these questions at the beginning of the school year as standard practice for evaluating any information or image that is part of the classroom experience promotes general critical-thinking and analysis skills. Other best practices include the following:

- Beginning the school year or the exploration of a new unit by developing an *information plan* in consultation with the students. What types of media and other information sources will the class be using? Where could students go for information on a particular topic, and what might be the strengths and weaknesses of each source? This overlays media literacy questions on the typical K-W-L pedagogical approach to teaching a new topic: What do you already *know* about this topic and where did you learn about it? What do you *want* to know, and where could you find out about it? Reflecting back at the end of the unit, what did you *learn*, and what sources were most (and least) useful?

- Encouraging students to pay attention to both print and visual elements in media sources, noting information that can be learned from the images themselves. This includes, of course, attending to the images in their textbooks.

- For any media source (including textbooks, videos, and Web sites), making sure the students know who wrote or produced it and when it was produced or published. If appropriate, discuss the implications for its usefulness in your current exploration. (What perspectives might be included or left out? What information might be out of date?)

- Training students to learn from videos (and other traditionally entertaining forms of media) in the same way that they learn from teachers, books, and other sources. When showing videos or films in the classroom, show only short segments at a time rather than the full film without interruption, leaving the lights on—if possible—to facilitate active viewing and discussion. Before showing a video, let the students know what things they should be looking and listening for. If appropriate, encourage students to take notes and to raise their hands during a video if they do not understand something they saw or heard.

- Building elements of media production into the classroom experience by

  encouraging students to scan or download images into reports and term papers, making sure that they use images as part of the research process by including captions and citing the appropriate sources

  providing options for individual or small group presentations such as using PowerPoint, audio- or videotape, or desktop publishing

  emphasizing an awareness of the six media literacy questions as part of the production process (e.g., What is *your* purpose? Who is *your* target audience? What information will *you* leave out, and how will that bias *your* message?)

BASIC PRINCIPLES FOR CURRICULUM INTEGRATION

In working with a range of teachers and curriculum areas, we have also developed 12 basic principles for integrating media literacy and critical thinking into the K–12 curriculum (Scheibe & Rogow, 2004). Discussions of four of these principles follow.

Identify erroneous beliefs about a topic fostered by media content. This is particularly relevant to curricular areas that emphasize "facts," such as science and social studies. Even young students bring existing assumptions and expectations to the classroom situation, and it is critical to examine those assumptions with the students to correct misperceptions and identify the media sources involved. Many adults, for example, believe that tarantulas are deadly or that lemmings follow each other blindly and commit mass suicide by jumping off cliffs into the sea. Both of these erroneous beliefs have been reinforced by the media, such as the 1957 Disney movie *White Wilderness,* which showed lemmings falling off cliffs into the sea (they were actually herded off the cliffs by the production crew off camera; see www.snopes.com/disney/films/lemmings.htm).

Develop an awareness of issues of credibility and bias in the media. This is critical in evaluating how any information is presented and has increased in importance with the rise of the

Internet as the dominant source of information students now use in preparing papers and reports. It also applies to math, especially with respect to media reports of statistics (particularly in misleading graphs in advertisements). Although math teachers already emphasize the importance of having both the *x*-axis and *y*-axis correctly labeled, for example, a media literacy approach would go beyond that to ask why those producing the graph (or reporting the statistics) would leave out such important information.

Compare the ways different media present information about a topic. Many English/language arts teachers have students compare the same story or play when presented in different media formats or by different directors. Approaching this from a media literacy perspective, the teacher might ask the basic six questions about each presentation, comparing the purposes and target audiences of each and identifying what is left out—and what is added—in each case and why. The same principle can be applied easily to the study of current events at nearly any grade level. Instead of having students cut out newspaper articles reporting three different events, for example, a teacher could have students identify *one* event that is reported in three different sources (e.g., English language versions of newspapers from different countries). The resulting report about the event would then draw from all three sources and could include an analysis of how the three sources differed and why.

Use media as an assessment tool. There are a number of ways to use media as part of authentic assessment at the end of a curriculum unit. For example, students can be shown an advertisement, a news article, or a short video clip and asked to identify information that is accurate (or inaccurate) in what they see (e.g., showing a clip from the movie *Twister* following a unit on tornadoes or a news report on the results of a political poll following a unit on statistics). Students can also work in small groups to produce their own media messages (e.g., a newspaper article, an advertisement, a digital video) illustrating their knowledge and/or opinion on a topic.

RESOURCES AND CURRICULUM MATERIALS

There are many excellent media literacy resources and materials that can be used within the context of teaching core content in K–12 education. Some media literacy curricula are designed with clear links to many subject areas, such as *Assignment: Media Literacy,* which was developed in line with Maryland state learning standards and features connections to language arts, social studies, math, health, and the arts (Hobbs, 2000). Other materials are excellent resources when using a media literacy approach to a specific subject area, such as *Past Imperfect: History According to the Movies* (Carnes, 1995). There are several good Web analysis resources. The two we have found most useful for teachers and librarians are both online: Canada's Web-awareness site (http://www.mediaawareness.ca/englishl/special_initiatives/webawareness/) and Alan November's site (http://www.anovember.com/infolit/index.html). One outstanding resource for curriculum-driven media literacy lesson plans and ideas is Frank Baker's *Media Literacy Clearinghouse* Web site (http://www.med.sc.edu:1081/).

Project Look Sharp has recently begun developing a series of media literacy kits that take a curriculum-driven approach. The first of these kits, *Media Construction of War: A Critical Reading of History* (Sperry, 2003), uses slides, print, and video materials to teach core historical information about the Vietnam War, the Gulf War of 1991, and the War in Afghanistan following Sept. 11, 2001. After students read short histories of each war, teachers lead collective readings of each image, discussing the overt and implied messages in each and relating the images back to core content that is part of their history curriculum.

EVALUATION AND ASSESSMENT

Project Look Sharp has begun conducting empirical studies of the effectiveness of media literacy integration using this type of curriculum-driven approach (reported elsewhere). Some of these studies involve pretest/posttest designs collecting data directly from the students, and some involve assessments of student-produced work. From a program evaluation standpoint, however, we have found it most useful to solicit qualitative feedback from the teachers themselves. They repeatedly say that media literacy lessons evoke active participation on the part of students, especially students who are nontraditional learners or disenfranchised for other reasons. Teachers also report that after adopting a media literacy approach to teach specific core content, they gradually find themselves weaving media literacy into other aspects of their pedagogy. As one teacher put it, "Oh, I see. You're trying to get us to change teaching practice!"

We also sometimes send home questionnaires to parents of students who have participated in a media literacy lesson or unit to assess what we call the "trickle up" effect—when students come home and talk about what they have learned and even change their behaviors related to media issues. Some parents have said that the "media literacy stuff" is the only thing their child has talked about related to school all year; many say their children raise media literacy questions when they are watching television or reading newspapers at home.

We believe that it is this ability for media literacy to empower students in so many ways that, in the end, will lead to its growth and stability in K–12 education. By meeting the needs of teachers and administrators, of parents, and of the students themselves, we can indeed foster a deeper sense of literacy in our children.

Discussion Questions

How do you define media literacy?

How do you integrate media literacy into your curriculum?

Cynthia Scheibe is a professor at Ithaca College.

Article 17

War, Critical Thinking, and Self-Understanding

Nel Noddings

C an students learn to think critically if they are not asked to engage with critical issues? Fostering critical thinking is frequently stated as a fundamental aim of education,[1] and yet many teachers report that they have been forbidden to discuss such critical issues as current wars, religion, and cultural differences in styles of parenting.

Critical thinkers raise questions about claims and about the motives of those who make them, they identify logical flaws in arguments, they evaluate the premises from which arguments are launched, they search for evidence to support claims, and they explore the likely consequences of proposed actions. Critical thinkers are also reflective in the important sense that they regularly turn their analyses and questions on their own thinking and practices. Thus critical thinking, as I am using the term here, addresses issues that are significant in the lives of those who

engage in the practice. Moreover, teachers may need to help students come to understand that certain issues they have not yet considered are indeed significant in their lives.

The study of formal and informal logic, reflection on past events, and simulation of conflicts all contribute to the development of critical thinking.[2] But the failure to confront issues critical to the present lives of students when we seek to teach critical thought sends a contradictory message: *Think critically—but not about really controversial issues! Or do it on your own time! School is not the place for analysis and discussion of critical issues.* As a result, students who end their formal schooling with high school may never encounter important and fascinating debates on war, religion, or parenting. And they may or may not learn to think critically.

Here I wish to present possible topics for a critical exploration of just one of these issues:

SOURCE: Excerpted from Noddings, N. (2004). War, critical thinking, and self-understanding. *Phi Delta Kappan, 85*(7), 489–495. Reprinted by permission of Ned Noddings, author of *Critical lessons: What our schools should teach.*

war. War is already a major strand in the social studies curriculum, but the discussion is usually confined to political causes, leaders, battles, and the resulting rearrangement of national boundaries. I wish to address psychological issues related to war that should concern all citizens, especially the young who might join the military right out of high school. The main question I address is this: How can critical thinking help us to understand ourselves better and come to terms with our attitudes toward war?

THE ATTRACTIONS OF WAR

"No one wants war" was a claim heard repeatedly as the U.S. and Great Britain prepared to invade Iraq. Were the political leaders who said this lying, or were they trying to reassure their citizens that *they* did not want war and would avoid it if at all possible? This question seems to be unanswerable, so I'll set it aside. Let's also set aside the obvious fact that some people make a great deal of money from war and its aftermath, and, although they deny it, they do want war. The questions that we must help young people to explore are these: Are there people, other than the greedy, who want war? Why? Are you such a person?

Anthony Swofford, a young marine, has written about the desperate attractions of war. He notes that stories and films that disgust "Mr. and Mrs. Johnson in Omaha or San Francisco or Manhattan"—films that threaten to convert many of us to pacifism—have a very different effect on military men. Swofford writes:

> [They] watch the same films and are excited by them, because the magic brutality of the films celebrates the terrible and despicable beauty of their fighting skills. Fight, rape, war, pillage, burn. Filmic images of death and carnage are pornography for the military man.[3]

The rest of Swofford's paragraph is too obscene to reprint here, but his story is a familiar one. Many men are attracted to war and mayhem.[4]

As students are confronted with some of these stories, they should be asked to consider whether the young men described by Swofford, Lawrence Le Shan, and many other writers are really attracted to war or are simply too insecure in their manhood to admit that they are not. This is not a question that can be answered definitively. It should lead to research and introspection. Surely, there are men who have loved war, and there are many who have feared it but feared dishonor and the accusation of cowardice even more. But there are also those who have hated war and have fought both bravely and reluctantly.[5] And there are those who have had the courage to refuse to participate in war against their own convictions.[6]

The question that needs closest examination is the one usually avoided: What makes war so attractive? It is not honest to cover this over with layers of propaganda extolling the virtues of "our heroes" who sacrifice willingly for "our freedom." Such sacrifice is indeed part of the story, and it should not be denied or mocked. But simply acknowledging sacrifice does not face up to the fact that many people—both soldiers and civilians—are excited by war. Chris Hedges has described war as a force that gives us meaning: "Even with its destruction and carnage it gives us what we all long for in life. It gives us purpose, meaning, a reason for living."[7] William James, too, noted that war calls forth sacrifice, that "war is a school of strenuous life and heroism." Deploring war as a "wholesale organization of irrationality and crime," James asks us to seek "the moral equivalent of war: something heroic that will speak to men as universally as war does, and yet will be as compatible with their spiritual selves as war has proved itself to be incompatible."[8] Can such an equivalent be found? Must each of us find his or her own "something heroic" to make life meaningful? Is it credible that ordinary lives are so empty and boring that war represents the only path to meaning?

A discussion of what makes war attractive should lead to a critical examination of gender and violence. Many peace activists argue that peace is not simply the absence of war but, more significantly, a condition of life in which no one suffers from violence or the threat of violence.[9] Rape and brutality seem to be part of a faulty vision of masculinity, one that supports both war and a "rape culture."[10]

THE GENDER CONNECTION

The relation of gender to violence is a broad and fascinating topic that should include at least three large subtopics: masculinity and war, rape and brutality, and violence as a way of expressing anger. On this last, educators should be aware that unhealthy visions of masculinity motivate much school violence. Almost all of the multiple killings committed in schools in recent years have been the acts of angry boys. Jessie Klein and Lynn Chancer, completing a study of these boys, remark, "When boys feel weak, sad, scared, anxious, lonely, or depressed, the negative experience is unnecessarily magnified when they feel this also indicates a lapse in the 'tough disposition' manhood demands."[11] Surely, critical thinking brought to bear on questions of masculinity is something schools should encourage.

Women, perhaps more often than men, have been outspoken opponents of war. Several women writers have traced this opposition to motherhood and women's bodily understanding of the "cost of human flesh."[12] Women organized peace campaigns during and after WWI, and the Women's International League for Peace and Freedom has worked steadily for peace since 1915. Indeed, if the suggestions made by the WILPF in 1919 had been heeded by the Paris Peace Conference, WWII and other conflicts might have been avoided.[13]

For present purposes, because we are interested primarily in the psychological causes and effects of war, it is worth noting that the women's recommendations in 1919 were rejected—at least in part—because they were made *by women*. This observation underscores the need for attention to matters of gender. To what degree are women's opinions on war and peace ignored even today?

Teachers must be careful, however, not to convey the idea that all men are pro-war and all women antiwar. Many, perhaps most, women have supported war. Sara Ruddick notes: "War is exciting; women, like men, are prey to the excitements of violence and community sacrifice it promises."[14] If men sometimes welcome war as a means of escaping the boredom of everyday life, it is reasonable to assume that women—long held to even more constrained and boring lives—would often find war attractive. Thus women are attracted to men in uniform, with whom they share the excitement. Both masculinity and femininity, as traditionally defined, are at fault. As Virginia Woolf put it, "No, I don't see what's to be done about war. It's manliness; and manliness breeds womanliness—both so hateful."[15] What Woolf alludes to, of course, is "manliness" that is defined by the warrior and patriarch and "womanliness" that admires and supports "strong" men—even when that strength is used to dominate women.

Where should these matters be discussed? Surely, they are relevant topics for study in social studies, literature, and science. But with a curriculum already groaning under the demands of high-stakes testing, how can we add still more? My answer is to get rid of the trivia and spend time on topics that really matter.

ART AND SOCIALIZATION

Woolf and, after her, Susan Sontag both name gender as an important contributor to the continuance of war. Both, however, explore the possibility that art—especially visual art—might make war so repugnant to viewers that many would actively oppose war.[16] Perhaps something like this is already happening, for the world has never seen so many participants in antiwar activities as in the case of the recent war in Iraq. Still, this impressive opposition had little effect, and it was strongly influenced on the domestic scene by the deeply socialized admonition to "support our troops." This admonition is enormously powerful, and students should be encouraged to analyze its effects on patriotism, on conformity, and on the preservation of traditional attitudes toward war and warriors. Can one be against a war and still support the troops? Must patriots provide such support? What else is supported when we give way to this pressure?

The idea (or hope) that vivid images of horrible events might make war less attractive has been shared by both women and men. Sontag cites the work of Ernst Friedrich in *Krieg dem Kriege!* (*War Against War!*) as an early (published in 1924) and dramatic example.[17] Despite government and patriotic opposition to the publication of this book, it eventually sold widely. Still, even more destructive wars lay ahead. Sontag notes: "It seems that the appetite for pictures showing bodies in pain is as keen, almost, as the desire for ones that show bodies naked."[18] As we have already noted, Swofford and his companions agree. The brutality of war has its own erotic magic. Critical thinkers should ask, "Am I the sort of person who looks forward to war? What justifies my attitude? How did I get this way?"

To ask the question "Am I this sort of person?" is to invite a study of how we are socialized. Indeed, a critical study of how we are socialized may be the single most important function of education. The task is not simply to encourage people to resist socialization but rather to help them understand the process—and then to decide (as nearly as anyone can) what to affirm, what to resist, and what to accept without wasting further energy.[19] Some socialized behaviors can be safely accepted with a shrug of indifference. Young people—with their first whiff of the possibilities of resistance—often resist rules and customs that are relatively innocuous. One job of the critical thinker is to make these distinctions and to engage in what Neil Postman and Charles Weingartner called "crap detecting"—uncovering "misconceptions, faulty assumptions, superstitions, and even outright lies."[20] This is hard intellectual work that should be applied to critical issues.

A full treatment of socialization is much too large a task to undertake here, but one aspect of it must he addressed. How do we come to the attitudes we take toward war? Our aim should be to increase self-understanding, not to convert students to a particular view. I think it would be

wrong, for example, to overemphasize the wrongdoing of our own nation, but it would be equally wrong to neglect it entirely. It is the job of teachers to confront students with the strongest (not the most extreme) arguments on all sides of an issue and to help them to arrive at and defend a view to which they can commit themselves.[21]

Students should certainly be made aware of how attitudes are manipulated by slogans and propaganda of all sorts. How does it happen, for example, that members of the military are often scorned and ignored during peace time and are suddenly transformed into "heroes" when war occurs?[22] Often, it is the students who are least academically inclined who fill the enlisted ranks of the military, and the public assumes that these kids need to "shape up" and "find themselves." Then war breaks out, and these same kids are suddenly credited with the virtues of warriors; they are now "our boys" who deserve our support. What accounts for the dramatic change in public attitude toward the military?

What forces shape the attitudes of the warrior and of the anti-warrior? How is it that some young men are drawn to the brutality of warfare, some so hate it that they become pacifists, and others accept it reluctantly as necessary? Do art, music, and literature influence our attitudes? Why do people disagree even on this? If literature is not powerful in shaping attitudes, why are some works banned from schools? Why were governments so outraged by Friedrich's *Krieg dem Kriege!*?

An important question for young people to consider is whether events can be so powerful that the people swept up in them lose all sense of themselves as moral agents. How is it that good people, brought up reasonably well, do horrible things in war?

ATROCITIES

Almost everyone has heard of the systematic murder and cruelty organized by Hitler, Stalin, Pol Pot, Idi Amin, and Saddam Hussein. But few Americans are as aware that cruel and disgusting acts have been committed by individual soldiers of all nations. Jonathan Glover has presented a comprehensive summary of the dreadful atrocities of the 20th century. His purpose is to encourage a psychological study of war and cruelty. He writes, "We need to look hard and clearly at some monsters inside us. But this is part of the project of caging and taming them."[23]

Students should read the words Glover quotes from a Soviet soldier who served in Afghanistan: "We're invited to speak in schools, but what can we tell them? Not what war is really like, that's for sure. . . . I can't very well tell the school kids about collections of dried ears and other trophies of war, can I?"[24] Yet this is exactly what students should hear, and they should know that identical stories—right down to the collections of human ears—could be told by American veterans of Vietnam. But they should also hear that some soldiers kept their moral resources intact and rejected the temptation to engage in vicious practices. How did they manage it?

Journalists have documented their own practice of withholding unwelcome news from their audiences. Glover writes, "People committed to a war do not want to hear things which call into question its justification, its success, or its methods."[25] They want the world sorted into "good guys and bad guys."

But even WWII—the so-called good war—produced atrocities on the part of the "good guys." Hatred for the Japanese was a strong motivating factor in the war in the Pacific.

American soldiers in WWII rarely knew much about the enemy they so despised. Would it have made a difference if they had heard the words of the Japanese philosopher Kitaro Nishida? "Love is the deepest knowledge of things. Analytical, inferential knowledge is a superficial knowledge, and it cannot grasp reality. We can reach reality only through love. Love is the culmination of knowledge."[26] Critical thinking must be applied even to love, lest it be misplaced or distorted. And we need to read many stories if we are to cultivate love and commitment. Critical thinking alone may not induce commitment and may even encourage a "spectator" attitude toward the world's problems.[27]

One work that high school students often read, *The Iliad*,[28] can be used to launch critical thinking about the ways in which warriors can lose their moral anchors. The pages retelling Achilles' merciless killing of Priam's son, Lykaon, are both dramatic and horrendous. Even though the young man was helpless and begged for his life, Achilles mocked and slew him. Then he threw his body into a stream.

Nor was this incident unusual. The volume is filled with such scenes and with comrades taunting one another with the shame of cowardice. In Achilles, we see a warrior enraged by grief, the desire for vengeance, and guilt. Similar stories have been told again and again over the centuries.

When students read *The Iliad*, they should also read at least part of Simone Weil's essay on it.[29] A powerful indictment of what war does to men, it starts this way: "The true hero, the real subject, the core of *The Iliad*, is might [or "force"]. That might which is wielded by men rules over them, and before it man's flesh cringes."[30] War (i.e., "might") changes human beings into *things*. Some, Weil notes, recover; others "become things for the rest of their lives."[31] "These men," she says, "are another species, a compromise between a man and a corpse."[32] At the end of her essay, Weil expresses the hope that, from the genius of *The Iliad*, people will "learn how to accept the fact that nothing is sheltered from fate, how never to admire might, or hate the enemy, or to despise sufferers. It is doubtful if this will happen soon."[33] Her essay was published in 1940.

Questions for students to ask themselves: Would I kill mercilessly if I had seen my dearest comrade slain in battle? Or if I saw my home city destroyed? Or if my comrades were engaged in such behavior? Or if I were ordered to do so?

UNDERSTANDING AND COMPASSION

How should we feel toward those who commit horrible crimes against human beings? It is not only natural to feel outrage but morally right to condemn such acts. But students should consider the possibility that responsibility for wartime atrocities is shared. Erich Maria Remarque's description of a guard at a Nazi concentration camp provides a dramatic introduction:

> Schulte was . . . twenty-three. . . . He had been a member of the Hitler youth group even before the seizure of power and that was where he had been educated. He learned that there were superhumans and subhumans, and he firmly believed it. . . . Killing [subhumans] was like killing vermin. Schulte had a completely calm conscience. . . . He was a reliable friend, loved music and poetry and considered torture an indispensable method of extracting information from prisoners, since all enemies of the Party were liars. . . . He was in love with the daughter of a provincial court councilor and wrote her charming, rather romantic letters. In his free time he liked to sing. He had a pleasant tenor voice.[34]

The point of juxtaposing descriptions of atrocious acts with those of pleasant personal characteristics is to remind readers that ordinary people, in the heat of battle or through faulty education, can come to believe ridiculous things, some of which can lead them to perform terrible and immoral acts. Understanding what contributed to their evil acts does not mean excusing the perpetrators. Our purpose in trying to understand is to prevent future horrors. Notice how we recoil with horror at the Nazi idea of subhumans, but we cover over or excuse the attitude of our own soldiers toward the Japanese in WWII.

An attitude that is at once realistic and challenging for educators is expressed by Primo Levi, himself a survivor of a Nazi camp:

> [We] are asked by the young who our "torturers" were, of what cloth were they made. The term *torturers* allude to our ex-guardians, the SS, and is in my opinion inappropriate: it brings to mind twisted individuals, ill-born, sadists, afflicted by an original flaw. Instead, they were made of the same cloth as we, they were average human beings, averagely intelligent, averagely wicked: save the exceptions, they were not monsters, they had our faces, but they were reared badly. . . . All of them had been subjected to the terrifying miseducation provided for and imposed by the schools created in accordance with the wishes of Hitler and his collaborators.[35]

This is a complex topic and presents a difficult challenge for educators. Many writers today put great emphasis on remembering the victims of 20th-century atrocities. Whole museums are dedicated to the effort. Quite naturally, some of these writers object strenuously to any attempt to understand the perpetrators of such crimes.[36] They fear that understanding may lead to sympathy, which can lead, in turn, to forgiving the unforgivable. Others of us think that understanding is essential if our purpose is prevention. Precisely because we care deeply for all children, we want them to be neither victims nor perpetrators. They must not become the victims of miseducation.

The study of atrocities and the psychological factors involved in committing them might include discussion of opposing philosophical/psychological theories of human nature. Are we completely shaped by our environments? What follows from such a belief? Or are we always—inevitably and tragically—psychologically free to choose and thus responsible for our choices? Or does the truth lie somewhere in between?

A topic such as this one demands critical thinking, and one product of that thinking might be a greater tolerance for ambiguity. Can we, without moral loss, commit ourselves to both the remembrance of victims and the understanding of perpetrators? Perhaps remembrance should be disconnected from hatred and hooked more reliably to a vigorous commitment to a better future.

Just recently writers have begun to describe and analyze the suffering of Germans during and after WWII. It took 50 years for this discussion to achieve legitimacy, and even now there are those who object—as though compassion were a zero-sum game.

Students should know that innocent Germans were killed by Soviet troops whose hatred demanded vengeance for the destruction of Russian cities and civilians. Germans were also the victims of ethnic cleansing after the war.[37] W. G. Sebald has speculated on the lack of genuine first-person accounts of such incidents as the fire-bombing of Dresden.[38] He notes that existing reports use such conventional wording that their authenticity should be doubted. He doesn't mean by this that the accounts are dishonest—simply that the narrators were so traumatized by both national guilt and the events themselves that they could find no language adequate to the experience. The true nature of the horror has yet to be depicted. Günter Grass, whose anti-Nazism cannot be doubted, has also begun to speak out on the suffering of the German people. How many Americans have heard of the sinking of the *Wilhelm Gustloff* by a Soviet submarine? With the loss of some 9,000 lives, many of them children, it is probably the worst sea disaster of all time.[39]

The great worry in inviting this discussion (or any others of this nature) is that the long-suppressed memory of suffering, once aroused, might induce a new round of hatred. But it may be, as Grass strongly suggests, that the suppression of discussion is far more dangerous than its encouragement. Grass's *Crabwalk* is the story of such suppressed memory bursting forth in violence and miseducated hero worship. It is one function of critical thinking to get things out in the open, connected to feeling and moral commitment. The object is to avoid the polarization, anger, hatred, repression, and resultant youthful search for a great leader to rescue us. The alternative to open discussion is a world in which patriotic fervor and hatred arise again and again.

In the words with which Grass ends *Crabwalk*: "It doesn't end. Never will it end."[40] It is the job of education to make it more likely that such cycles will end.

A FINAL WORD

Educators today are besieged by a movement that demands higher and higher scores on standardized tests. Anyone who has looked carefully at these tests knows that they are loaded with trivia—questions that most successful adults cannot answer and would indeed scorn to answer. Our children are being fed intellectual junk food, and we would do well to insist on a healthier educational diet.

The material I've suggested here represents a genuine raising of the bar. Although it is challenging, I think high school juniors and seniors are capable of reading and discussing it. Indeed, I think they are eager to do so.

But perhaps political leaders everywhere would prefer that the majority of our young people not engage in critical thinking and remain ignorant of these matters. This preference is one that seems to have endured for centuries. Like the fanatical search for a great leader, it seems never to end. But perhaps we can change that.

Discussion Questions

Looking at the subject areas you teach, what are the most controversial issues in your curriculum?

How do you handle the teaching of these controversial issues in your classroom?

Nel Noddings is a professor at Stanford University.

Article 18

THE MATH WARS

ALAN H. SCHOENFELD

HISTORICAL BACKGROUND AND CONTEXT

The counterpoint to the mathematics-is-independent-of-culture perspective is that knowledge of any type, but specifically mathematical knowledge, is a powerful vehicle for social access and social mobility. Hence, lack of access to mathematics is a barrier—a barrier that leaves people socially and economically disenfranchised.

Who gets to learn mathematics, and the nature of the mathematics that is learned, are matters of consequence. This fact is one of the underpinnings of the math wars. It has been true for more than a century.

The 20th century can be viewed as the century of democratization of schooling in the United States. In 1890, fewer than 7% of the 14-year-olds in the United States were enrolled in high school, with roughly half of those going on to graduate (Stanic, 1987, p. 150). High school and beyond were reserved for the elite, with fewer students graduating from high school back then than earn master's and Ph.D. degrees today. In short, "education for the masses" meant elementary school. In line with the ideas of the social efficiency educators, an elementary school education often meant instruction in the very, very basics. For example, one set of instructions from a school district in the 1890s instructed teachers that their students were to learn no more mathematics than would enable them to serve as clerks in local shops (Resnick, L. B., personal communication, January 10, 1987). In contrast, the high school curriculum was quite rigorous.

By the beginning of World War II, almost three-fourths of the children aged 14 to 17 attended high school, and 49% of the 17-year-olds graduated (Stanic 1987, p. 150). This expanding population put pressure on the system. Broadly speaking, the curriculum remained unchanged, whereas the student body facing it was much more diverse and ill prepared than heretofore.

In the 1940s it became something of a public scandal that army recruits knew so little math that the army itself had to provide training in the arithmetic needed for basic bookkeeping and gunnery. Admiral Nimitz complained of mathematical deficiencies of would-be officer candidates and navy

SOURCE: Excerpted from Schoenfeld, A. H. (2004). The math wars. *Educational Policy, 18*(1), 253–286. Reprinted by permission of Sage.

volunteers. The basic skills of these military personnel should have been learned in the public schools but were not. (Klein, 2003, Historical Outline: 1920 to 1980, para. 14)

The truth be told, however, there was not a huge amount of change in the actual curriculum, before or after these complaints.

The next major crisis did affect curricula, at least temporarily. In October 1957, the Soviet Union caught the United States off guard with its successful launch of the satellite *Sputnik*. That event came amidst the cold war and Soviet threats of world domination. *Sputnik* spurred the American scientific community into action. With support from the National Science Foundation (NSF), a range of curricula with "modern" content was developed in mathematics and the sciences. Collectively, the mathematics curricula became known as the new math. For the first time, some of the content really was new: Aspects of set theory, modular arithmetic, and symbolic logic were embedded in the curriculum.

The full story of the new math should be told (though not here); it shows clearly how curricular issues can become social issues. Specifically, it provides a cautionary tale for reform. One of the morals of the experience with the new math is that for a curriculum to succeed, it needs to be made accessible to various constituencies and stakeholders. If teachers feel uncomfortable with the curriculum they have not been prepared to implement, they will either shy away from it or bastardize it. If parents feel disenfranchised because they do not feel competent to help their children and they do not recognize what is in the curriculum as being of significant value, they will ultimately demand change.

In a reaction to what were seen as the excesses of the new math, the nation's mathematics classrooms went "back to basics"—the theme of the 1970s. There are various opinions about the level of standards and rigor demanded of students—some will argue that less was being asked of students than before, and some will disagree—but in broad outline, the curricula of the 1970s resembled those of the pre-*Sputnik*

years. In compensation for the "excesses" of the 1960s, however, the back-to-basics curricula focused largely on skills and procedures.

By 1980, the results of a decade of such instruction were in. Not surprisingly, students showed little ability at problem solving—after all, curricula had not emphasized aspects of mathematics beyond mastery of core mathematical procedures. But performance on the "basics" had not improved either. Whether this was due to back-to-basics curricula being watered-down versions of their pre-*Sputnik* counterparts, to a different social climate after the 1960s where schooling (and discipline) were deemphasized, or because it is difficult for students to remember and implement abstract symbolic manipulations in the absence of conceptual understanding, was (and is) hotly debated. What was not debated, however, is that the mathematical performance of U.S. students was not what it should have been.

In response, the NCTM [National Council of Teachers of Mathematics] (1980) published *An Agenda for Action*. NCTM proposed that an exclusive focus on basics was wrongheaded and that a primary goal of mathematics curricula should be to have students develop problem-solving skills. Back to basics was to be replaced by "problem solving."

From the jaundiced perspective of a researcher in mathematical thinking and problem solving, what passed for problem solving in the 1980s was a travesty. Although research on problem solving had begun to flow, the deeper findings about the nature of thinking and problem solving were not generally known or understood. As a result, the problem-solving "movement" was superficial. In the early 1980s, problem solving was typically taken to mean having students solve simple word problems instead of (or in addition to) performing computation. Thus a sheet of exercises that looked like this:

$$7 - 4 = ?$$

might be replaced by a sheet of exercises that looked like this:

John had 7 apples. He gave 4 apples to Mary. How many apples does John have left?

But otherwise, things remained much the same.

CONDITIONS IN THE 1980S— THE BACKDROP FOR THE *STANDARDS*

It is important to understand the context that made the *Curriculum and Evaluation Standards for School Mathematics* (the *Standards*) (and their impact) possible.

Yet Another Crisis

In the 1980s, the crisis was economic rather than military, but major nonetheless. Japanese and other Asian economies waxed as the American economy waned. The national deficit soared, and the nation felt besieged and vulnerable. In 1981, U.S. Secretary of Education T. H. Bell appointed the National Commission on Excellence in Education, which produced the very influential report *A Nation at Risk*. The National Commission on Excellence in Education (1983) report began as follows:

> Our Nation is at risk. Our once unchallenged preeminence in commerce, industry, science, and technological innovation is being overtaken by competitors throughout the world. . . . The educational foundations of our society are presently being eroded by a rising tide of mediocrity that threatens our very future as a Nation and a people. . . .
>
> If an unfriendly foreign power had attempted to impose on America the mediocre educational performance that exists today, we might well have viewed it as an act of war. As it stands, we have allowed this to happen to ourselves. We have even squandered the gains in student achievement made in the wake of the Sputnik challenge. Moreover, we have dismantled essential support systems which helped make those gains possible. We have, in effect, been committing an act of unthinking, unilateral educational disarmament. (p. 1)

In mathematics specifically, the very poor showing of U.S. students on the Second International Mathematics Study (McKnight et al., 1987; McKnight, Travers, Crosswhite, & Swafford, 1985; McKnight, Travers, & Dossey, 1985) gave license for change—although what direction that change might take was anybody's guess.

The (Non)role of the NSF

The NSF had played a significant role in supporting postcurricula in mathematics and other fields, but it could not play such a role in direct response to *A Nation at Risk* and the sentiments it reflected. The tide regarding federal funding of innovative education efforts had turned, thanks to a political controversy over an NSF-supported elementary school science and social science curriculum called Man: A Course of Study (MACOS). MACOS met with initial success, and then a strong political backlash:

> The first sign of impending trouble appeared in Lake City, a small market town in northern Florida (population 10,000), in the fall of 1970. Shortly after school opened in September, Reverend Don Glenn, a Baptist minister who had recently moved to Lake City visited his daughter's sixth-grade class. . . . The school was under a court ordered integration plan. The teachers had chosen the materials because they felt they might help ease racial tensions. However, when Reverend Glenn saw the materials he formed a study group to examine MACOS in detail. Glenn claimed that the materials advocated sex education, evolution, a "hippie-yippee philosophy," pornography, gun control, and Communism. With support of a local radio station he broadcast four hour-long programs criticizing MACOS. He read excerpts from the student and teacher materials and warned that MACOS was a threat to democracy. This set off a growing series of attacks on MACOS over several years that led to a full scale Congressional debate of MACOS in both houses in 1975. NSF launched an internal review of its Education Directorate activities including an audit of the fiscal management of the project at EDC. While the audit revealed little to complain about, the damage in a sense was done. Dow quotes the former acting assistant director for

science education, Harvey Averch, "It was the worst political crisis in NSF history." (Lappan, 1997, The MACOS Materials: How Success Can Go Awry section, para. 3)

In the 1980s, the NSF did not dare to engage in the support of what might be seen as a potential national curriculum. To do so would risk the wrath of Congress.

This story is important for at least two reasons. First, it establishes the context for private action by the NCTM. Had there been a federal presence in the reform arena, NCTM might or might not have gotten involved. But there was a clear perception of crisis in mathematics education and an absence of leadership in dealing with it. Thus the stage was set. Second, the MACOS affair shows how strongly politics can intervene in matters of curriculum. A well-organized group with no curricular expertise can get members of Congress to take up its cause, resulting in "the worst political crisis in NSF history."

The National Curriculum Context and the Role of Publishers

One of the American myths (in the anthropological sense of master narrative) related to "states rights" is that every one of the 50 states is educationally autonomous and can do as it sees fit with regard to educational goals and standards.

The reality was otherwise. There was indeed a free market, but market forces and the fact that teaching tended to be textbook driven constrained district choices to the point where the United States had a de facto national curriculum in mathematics, and one that changed slowly at that. Three states—California, Texas, and New York—were "textbook adoption states" in which mathematics curricula were specified and books meeting the curricular goals were identified. In California, for example, it is true that any school district could buy any books it wanted to. However, the district was reimbursed by the state for its textbook purchases only if the books purchased were listed on the state-approved textbook adoption list. Thus, although independence was theoretically available, the price was steep.

Relatively few districts were willing to bear the cost.

As a result, the major publishers' textbook series were all designed to meet California, Texas, and New York's textbook adoption criteria.

Cognitive and Epistemological Revolutions

The naïve view is that mathematical competence is directly related to what one "knows" (facts, procedures, conceptual understandings) and that knowledge accumulates with study and practice. This is hard to argue with, as far as it goes. It is, however, dramatically incomplete. Studies of expert mathematicians show that there are other, equally critical aspects of mathematical competence. The mark of powerful learning is the ability to solve problems in new contexts or to solve problems that differ from the ones one has been trained to solve. Competent mathematicians have access to a wide range of problem-solving strategies. They use these strategies to make sense of new problem contexts or to make progress toward the solution of problems when they do not have ready access to solution methods for them. Research shows that students often fail to solve problems because they use the resources at their disposal (including time and what they do know) inefficiently.

Mathematical competence was shown to depend on a number of factors:

- Having a strong knowledge base

- Having access to productive problem-solving strategies

- Making effective use of the knowledge one has (this is known as *metacognition*)

- Having a set of productive beliefs about oneself and the mathematical enterprise (which position in the individual to act in mathematically appropriate ways)

Research indicates that classroom instruction, which tends to focus almost exclusively on the knowledge base, deprives students of problem-solving knowledge. It gives them little experience grappling with tough challenges and fosters the development of numerous unproductive beliefs.

Demographics and National Context

In 1985, the National Research Council (NRC) established the Mathematical Sciences Education Board as a mechanism for devoting sustained attention to issues of mathematics instruction. The NRC produced a series of reports, including *Everybody Counts* (NRC, 1989) and *A Challenge of Numbers* (Madison & Hart, 1990), which documented some of the more troubling demographics surrounding the traditional curriculum and set the stage for something new (although not specifying what it might be).

A Challenge of Numbers shows that the attrition rate from mathematics, from ninth grade on, was roughly 50% per year; worse still, the attrition rate for Latinos and African Americans was significantly larger. For example, African Americans composed 12% of the populations of 8th graders, 11% of 12th graders, and 5% of those earning a bachelor's degree in mathematics, and 2% of those earning master's and Ph.D. degrees in mathematics. Madison & Hart (1990) also noted that "in the new-doctoral-degree populations . . . the fraction of U.S. citizens had tumbled from four-fifths to less than one-half" (p. 36). A major point of the volume was that the nation's preeminence in mathematics and science was in jeopardy because of declining numbers and interest.

The NRC's *Everybody Counts* took a broader perspective, also pressing the urgency of the situation.

Released in the spring of 1989, *Everybody Counts* set the stage for the release of the NCTM *Standards* that fall.

THE STANDARDS

In 1986, the NCTM's board of directors established the Commission on Standards for School Mathematics, chaired by Thomas Romberg. The following year, NCTM president John Dossey appointed a team of 24 writers to produce *Standards.*

The goal of the writers (including in commission) was to "create a coherent vision of what it means to be mathematically literate" in a rapidly changing world and to "create a set of standards to guide the revision of the school mathematics curriculum" (NCTM, 1989, p. 1). The definition of *standard* given by the authors was as follows: "*Standard.* A standard is a statement that can be used to judge the quality of mathematics curriculum or methods of evaluation. Thus, standards are statements about what is valued" (NCTM, 1989, p. 2). That is, the *Standards* were intended to be a "scope-and-sequence" document (a blueprint for curriculum development); nor were they intended to be a set of specifications for examinations that would say whether students "met the standard."

The NCTM's *Standards* focused on new goals for society at large and for students in particular: "New social goals for education include (1) mathematically literate workers, (2) lifelong learning, (3) opportunity for all, and (4) an informed electorate" (p. 3). The *Standards* were oriented toward

> Five general goals for all students: (1) that they learn to value mathematics, (2) that they become confident in their ability to do mathematics, (3) that they become mathematical problem solvers, (4) that they learn to communicate mathematically, and (5) that they learn to reason mathematically. (NCTM, 1989, p. 5)

They were grounded in assumptions about learning being an active process rather than one of memorization and practice:

> This constructive, active view of the learning process must be reflected in the way much of mathematics is taught. Thus, instruction should vary and include opportunities for:
>
> —appropriate project work;
>
> —group and individual assignments;
>
> —discussion between teacher and students and among students;
>
> —practice on mathematical methods;
>
> —exposition by the teacher. (p. 10)

The document was divided into four sections, three devoted to defining content and process standards for three grade bands (kindergarten through grade 4; grades 5 through 8; grades 9 through 12) and a fourth for defining standards for student and program evaluation. Much of the controversy has focused on content and process standards.

In many ways, the *Standards* was both a radical and a conservative document. On the conservative side, the document was written for the broad NCTM constituency: mathematics teachers across the nation. It represented a consensus among the writers as to what was possible—and thus fell far short (as it should have) of what some visionaries might have thought possible. The cost of consensus was precision: Michael Apple (1992) called the *Standards* a "slogan system" encompassing "a penumbra of vagueness so that powerful groups or individuals who would otherwise disagree can fit under the umbrella" (p. 413). Indeed, some years later, one state assessment system would assess students' mathematical competency via portfolios containing the students' work on extended projects, whereas another state would employ multiple-choice tests that focused on basic skills. Both did so in the name of the *Standards*.

On the radical side, the *Standards* challenged (or was seen as challenging) many of the assumptions underlying the traditional curriculum. As noted above, the traditional curriculum bore the recognizable traces of its elitist ancestry: The high school curriculum was designed for those who intended to pursue higher education. Yes, it is true that half the students dropped out of the mathematics pipeline each year after Grade 9—but as some see it, this is because honest-to-goodness mathematics is hard. The 50% annual attrition rate was taken by some as confirmation of the difficulty of mathematics. For them, there was the suspicion that the curriculum would have to be dumbed down for more students to succeed. That is, only a bastardized curriculum (a lowering of real standards) could result in greater success rates. These fears were exacerbated by, among other things, the "increased attention/decreased attention" charts in the *Standards*. Topics to receive decreased attention included the following: complex paper-and-pencil computations, long division, rote practice, rote memorization of rules, teaching by telling, relying on outside authority (teacher or an answer key), memorizing rules and algorithms, manipulating symbols, memorizing facts and relationships, the use of factoring to solve equations, geometry from a synthetic viewpoint, two-column proofs, the verification of complex trigonometric identities, and the graphing of functions by hand using tables of values. These can be seen as the meat and potatoes of the traditional curriculum.

The *Standards*, buttressed by NCTM's call for "mathematics for all" and the equity agenda in *Everybody Counts*, clearly sat in the education-for-democratic-equality and education-for-social-mobility camps. In contrast, whatever the intention may have been, the reality was that the traditional curriculum was a vehicle for social efficiency and the perpetuation of privilege. Statistically speaking, the rich stayed rich and the poor got disenfranchised. There is a long history of data indicating that race and socioeconomic status correlate with mathematics performance, with dropout rates, and with economic opportunity (Kozol, 1992; National Action Committee for Minorities in Engineering, 1997; NSF, 2000). Thus the *Standards* could be seen as a threat to the current social order.

Epistemologically, with its focus on process, the *Standards* could be seen as a challenge to the "content-oriented" view of mathematics that predominated for more than a century. Each of the three grade bands began with the following four standards: mathematics as problem solving, mathematics as communication, mathematics as reasoning, and mathematical connections. Only after these four process standards were described did the *Standards* turn to what has traditionally been called mathematical content.

In short, the seeds for battle were sown—not that anyone at the time could predict that the *Standards* would have much impact or that the battle would rage. The *Standards* were vague.

This was part of their genius and part of what caused so much trouble. Because of their vagueness, they served as a Rorschach test of sorts—people tended to read much more into them than was there. (For many years, people would claim this or that was in the *Standards,* when a close examination showed it was not.) The genius is that the *Standards* set in motion a highly creative design process during the following decade, far transcending what the authors of the *Standards* could have produced in 1989. Because it was in essence a vision statement rather than a set of design specs, it proved remarkably enfranchising: During the coming years, different groups produced very different sets of materials "in the spirit of the *Standards.*" And there is the rub. Some of the materials produced would be considered pretty flaky. Some of the classroom practices employed in the name of the *Standards* would appear pretty dubious. And the *Standards* would be blamed for all of them.

THE REACTION, PART 1:
THE FIRST FEW POST-*STANDARDS* YEARS

We are now about to turn to the origins of the math wars themselves, in California. One thing that must be understood as we do is that a decade of battle was conducted in the absence of any real data. Here is the chronology. The *Standards* were published in 1989 by the NCTM, and the California Department of Education (1992) published the *Mathematical Framework for California Public Schools, Kindergarten Through Grade 12* (the *Frameworks*, which took the *Standards* somewhat further along the lines of reform). In the early 1990s, NSF released its curriculum requests for proposals. Spurred on by the *Frameworks*, some mainstream textbook publishers made reform texts available for textbook adoptions in 1993 and 1994. No large-scale data were gathered on the effectiveness of these curricula. Many of the NSF-supported reform curricula were in either alpha or beta testing at that point; it was not until the mid-1990s that they

became widely available, and testing data on those curricula tended to use "home-grown" measures. It was not until the late 1990s that full cohorts of students had worked their way through the entire reform curricula. Only at the turn of the 21st century did large-scale data evaluating the impact of those curricula begin to become available. As it happens, the evidence at this point is unambiguously in favor of reform (see, e.g., ARC Center, 2003; Senk & Thompson, 2003). But such data turn out to be largely irrelevant to the story of math wars. When things turn political, data really do not matter.

WAR(S)!

Before the math wars in California, there were reading wars (see Pearson, 2004, for substance and details).

As noted above, the *Standards* and the *Frameworks* were "vision statements" (or "slogan systems" if you prefer the pejorative) regarding the substance and character of instruction rather than the blueprints for it. The up side of such documents is that they permit significant creativity, allowing designers to create innovative materials beyond the imagination of the *Standards'* and the *Frameworks'* authors themselves. But there is a significant down side as well. As Rosen (2000) noted,

> the new textbooks were radically different from the traditional texts' orderly, sequential presentation of formulas and pages of practice problems familiar to parents. New texts featured colorful illustrations, assignments with lively, fun names and sidebars discussing topics from the environment to Yoruba mathematics (prompting critics to dub new programs with names such as "Rainforest Algebra" and "MTV Math"). (p. 61)

In their alien appearance and inaccessibility to parents, the texts repeated some of the mistakes of the new math. Once the rhetorical battle heated up, they were easily caricatured as the "new-new math."

Moreover, reform called for new teaching practices. Teachers who had themselves been taught in traditional ways were now being asked to teach in new ways and not given much support in doing it.

To cut to the chase, new materials and new practices raised concerns among some parents, some of whom enlisted outside help (from mathematicians, legislators, etc.) in combating the new practices and materials.

Amid all this, advocates of reform committed some mistakes that were the public relations equivalent of handing the traditionalists a gun and saying "shoot me." For example, the California Learning Assessment System released a sample mathematics test item in 1994 in which students were asked to arrive at an answer and then write a memo justifying it. The sample response from a student who got the right answer but failed to write a coherent memo was given a low score, whereas a sample student response that contained a computation error but a coherent explanation was given a high score. Editorial comments raked the California Learning Assessment System (and reform in general) over the coals, saying that in the new, "fuzzy" math, being able to write baloney counted more than getting the right answer.

With some speed, what started out as a collection of local oppositional movements became a statewide movement—with the support of conservatives such as Governor Pete Wilson and California assemblyman Steve Baldwin, who, as chairman of the Assembly Education Committee, held public hearings on the *Frameworks* in 1995 and 1996. Ultimately the conservatives prevailed: State Board of Education president Yvonne Larson and state superintendent of Public Instruction Delaine Eastin agreed to convene a new mathematics *Frameworks* writing team ahead of schedule. The state legislature enacted Assembly Bill 170, which according to the official legislative summary,

> requires the State Board of Education to ensure that the basic instructional materials it adopts for reading and mathematics in grades 1 to 8, inclusive, are based on the fundamental skills required by these subjects, including, but not limited to, systematic, explicit phonics, spelling, and basic computational skills. (see http://www.cde.ca.gov/board/readingfirst/exhibit-i.pdf)

As a step toward a new framework, the state appointed a committee to produce mathematics content standards, which were ultimately adopted in December 1997 and which served as the content foundation for the framework. This process by which the document was adopted was unprecedented. Here is how it was described by David Klein (1998), an antireform activist:

> Question: What would happen if California adopted the best grade-by-grade mathematics achievement standards in the nation for its public schools?
>
> Answer: The education establishment would do everything in its power to make them disappear.
>
> In December 1997, the State Board of Education surprised the world by not accepting extremely bad "fuzzy" math standards written by one of its advisory committees, the Academic Standards Commission. Instead, in a few short weeks and with the help of four Stanford University math professors, the state board developed and adopted a set to world-class mathematics standards of unprecedented quality for California's public schools. (p. 15)

Note the rhetoric, both in tone and language: The draft standards submitted to the board were "extremely bad" and "fuzzy," and truly high standards would be challenged by "the education establishment." This kind of rhetoric had become common. *San Francisco Chronicle* columnist Debra Saunders (1995a, 1995b), for example, titled some of her columns "New-New Math: Boot Licking 101" and "Creatures From the New-New Math Lagoon." Maureen DiMarco, California state secretary of child development and education, and one-time candidate for superintendent of public instruction, referred to the new curricula as "fuzzy crap."

To return to Klein's 2003 discussion of the rewriting of the California Mathematics Standards: The truth is, shall we say, more complex than Klein made it out to be. The draft standards had been a year and a half in development and although far from perfect had undergone significant public review and comment. They reflected current research—but not the perspective of the conservative majority of the state board. The board summarily rejected the draft, rewrote much of the elementary grades section itself, and commissioned mathematics faculty from Stanford (who had negligible experience with K–12 classrooms or curricula) to rewrite comments from notables such as Hyman Bass, research mathematician and director of the NRC's Mathematical Sciences Education Board, and William Schmidt, who had conducted curriculum content analyses for the Third International Mathematics and Science Study, to the effect that the draft standards were of high caliber and that the alternative was not. In his letter to the board, Bass also commented on the tone of the debate:

> The tragedy of the current debate in California is that political forces and agendas, and the belligerent and scoffing rhetoric they employ, have usurped the stage for the kind of honest, probing, and multidisciplinary discourse which is now so desperately needed. (personal communication, November 13, 1997)

For examples of extremism in public discourse, readers may wish to look at the thesaurus of derogatory terms for reform curricula and texts on the Mathematically Correct Web site: http://www.mathematicallycorrect.com/glossary .htm. For examples of extreme and intemperate dialogue from both sides of the math wars, follow the threads of math-wars or standards discussions in the amte, math-learn, and math-teach discussion groups at the Mathematics Forum, http://mathforum.org/discussions/.

The gloves were off, and those who held power did not hesitate to use them. The revision of the *Standards* was one example; the late-1996 composition of the curriculum framework and criteria committee another. Appointments are made by the state board. The established process for creating such committees is for the board to solicit recommendations for membership from its curriculum commission—in this case the

commission that had earlier recommended the approval of reform-oriented texts.

> However, newly appointed board member Janet Nicholas led a successful campaign to overturn the Commission's recommendations for the Framework Committee and replace them with a new group containing leaders of the tradition campaign. . . . The California Mathematics Council and several allied groups loudly protested this move, decrying the Board's disregard for an established process and the expertise of its own commissioners. (Rosen, 2000, pp. 64–65)

Not only did the complaints fail, but Governor Wilson also went on to appoint another arch-traditionalist, Marion Joseph, to the board (Joseph had been a leader of the anti–whole language campaign).

By all reports, the discussion within the Curriculum Framework and Criteria Committee, and its interactions with the state board, were highly contentious. A series of "minority reports" by Bill Jacob (Becker & Jacob, 2000; Jacob, 1999, 2001; Jacob & Akers, 2003), a reform-oriented member of the committee, provide the gory details. I shall skip over most of those details, which make interesting reading but focus on one highly public and controversial set of actions by the state board.

California law requires that state-adopted instructional materials "incorporate principles of instruction reflective of current and confirmed research" (CA Education Code 60200c-3). But even in such an apparently noncontroversial area, California has opened new categories of dispute. For example, the state board invited E. D. Hirsch, Jr., to speak on this issue in April 1997. In the written version of his comments, Hirsch ridiculed "mainstream educational research," as found in "journals such as the *Educational Researcher*," explicitly stating, "This is a situation that is reminiscent of what happened to biology in the Soviet Union under the domination of Lysenkoism, which is a theory that bears similarities to constructivism. . . ."

Citing math education experts John Anderson, David Geary, and Robert Siegler on the matter of what research shows that math students need, he goes on,

> "They would tell you that only through intelligently directed and repeated practice, leading to fast automatic recall of math facts, and facility in computation and algebraic manipulation, can one do well at real-world problem solving." Hirsch received a standing ovation from the state board, and then the board moved forward in line with his recommendations. (Becker & Jacob, 2000, p. 535)

With all due respect, Hirsch's claim about Lysenkoism is unmitigated nonsense, indicating his total misunderstanding of and disregard for serious educational research. His claim about real-world problem solving is a dubious extrapolation from work that is not at all central to the problem-solving literature (my own area of expertise).

The math wars had grown to national scale by 1998. Diane Ravitch, Chester Finn, and Lynne Cheney among others had weighed in against fuzzy, new-new math in the national media. The dispute was so vitriolic that Secretary of Education Richard Riley pleaded for civility in his 1998 address to the joint mathematics societies. Klein (2003) wrote about the events that followed:

> In October 1999, the U.S. Department of Education recommended to the nation's 15,000 school districts a list of math books, including several that had been sharply criticized my mathematicians and parents of school children across the country for much of the preceding decade. Within a month of that release, 200 university mathematicians added their names to an open letter to Secretary Riley calling upon his department to withdraw those recommendations. The list of signatories included seven Nobel laureates and winners of the Fields Medal, the highest international award in mathematics, as well as math department chairs of many of the top universities in the country, and several state and national education leaders. By the end of the year 1999, the U.S. Secretary of Education had himself become embroiled in the nation's math wars. (Introduction, para. 1)

What Klein neglects to mention is that his was the first signature on the letter and that the powerful antireform network in which he plays a central role had orchestrated the signature gathering. The signature gathering was a highly political act.

By the late 1990s, the antireform movement had reached a level of organization and efficiency that enabled it to quickly mount high-profile, large-scale efforts as the one described above. Antireform Web sites promise quick help for those who find their own school districts "threatened" by reform.

As noted above, tactics employed in the math wars can be rather nasty. Robert Megginson has noted a strong similarity between the tactics used by some antireformers and the antievolution tactics used by "creations scientists." Referring to Michael Shermer's (2002) discussion of what might be called the "creation wars," Megginson asked:

> Has anyone noticed that the more extreme members of Mathematically Correct have taken their strategy and tactics, almost line for line, straight out of the creation scientists' playbook? In particular—
>
> 1. Number one tactic—Go after the boards in the big states, particularly California and Texas, that evaluate and approve textbooks. If you can get the books with your point of view at the top of the playlists, you are in great shape.
>
> 2. Number two tactic—Plant fear in the minds of well-meaning parents, who genuinely and understandably want the best for their children, that the schools are subjecting their children to unproven theories that may result in their not getting into heaven or Berkeley.
>
> 3. Number three tactic—Constantly demand proof of their positions (which you never intend to accept) from those who disagree with you, attempting to create the impression that they do not really have much. When they offer any evidence, poke and prod hard at every facet and in every crevice of it until something is found that seems not fully justified or a bit controversial or counterintuitive, and use that to discard the entire piece of evidence.
>
> 4. Above all, treat any disagreement among your opponents, or modification in position due to new evidence ("even so-and-so doesn't believe in her former position on this

anymore") as an indication that your opponents have it wrong, and therefore (!) that you have it right. (personal communications, July 5, 2003)

Generally speaking, those on the reform side of the wars have been slow to develop effective techniques to counter the most extreme attacks of the antireformers. Some (e.g., Jacob, 1999, 2001) have tried to provide public documentation of abuses of process. Some (e.g., Susan Ohanian; see http://www.susanohanian.org/) raise loud voices of protest. Some (e.g., Mathematically Sane; see http://mathematicallysane.com/home .asp) seek to provide both evidence and counterterrorist tools. Major reform organizations have gotten smarter about dotting their i's and crossing their t's in public documents. The most significant reform document since the 1989 *Standards* is its successor, NCTM's (2000) *Principles and Standards for School Mathematics*. It was clear from the beginning that this document would be controversial and that the only hope for it to get a fair reception was to involve all the relevant constituencies from the very beginning—asking for their input and then taking it seriously. NCTM created a series of association review groups that were asked for ongoing input and commentary. NCTM distributed thousands of copies of a draft version of the document (roughly 30,000 hardcopy versions of the draft were distributed, and roughly 50,000 copies were downloaded from NCTM's Web site). It commissioned the NRC to review the process by which it responded to the thousands upon thousands of comments it received. A result was a commendation by the NRC for the integrity of its process and an unprecedented "Letter of Appreciation" from the chief officers of 15 major mathematical societies.

Will it work? Will civil, disciplined, and probing discourse prevail, and will there be a return to balance? That remains to be seen.

REFLECTIONS

To a disinterested outsider, aspects of the reading wars and the math wars just make no sense.

Consider the controversy of phonics versus whole language, for example. Of course children need to learn to sound out words—a healthy dose of phonics at the right time is salutary. Of course children need to make sense of what they are reading—learning to use context is an essential skill and motivational as well. Any sensible person would realize that children need both phonics and reading for understanding. Either of the two perspectives, taken to extremes, is nonsensical. The polarization that resulted in a "winner take all" battle between the two extremes is equally nonsensical. The same is the case in mathematics. An exclusive focus on basics leaves students without the understandings that enable them to use mathematics effectively. A focus on "process" without attention to skills deprives students of the tools they need for fluid, competent performance. The extremes are untenable. So, why have so many people taken extreme positions, and why are things as polarized as they are? More important, what might be done about it?

Even though the wars rage, partly because there are some true believers on both sides and partly because some stand to profit from the conflict, I remain convinced that there is a large middle ground. I believe that the vocal extremes, partly by screaming for attention and partly by claiming the middle ground ("it's the other camp that is extreme"), have exerted far more influence than their numbers should dictate.

One way to reclaim the middle ground, suggested by Phil Daro (2003), is to define it clearly—to specify a set of propositions that will call from some degree of compromise from reformers and traditionalists alike. That middle ground would be broadly encompassing, containing propositions that most people would find reasonable (or at least livable). Daro offered a draft, "Math Wars Peace Treaty" (or perhaps "Math Wars Disarmament Treaty"), that includes the following stipulations:

We have among ourselves various agreements and disagreements. But about these things we agree:

- The status quo is unacceptable. Its defenders are wrong, mathematics instruction must improve.

- Teachers, especially K–8 teachers, should learn more mathematics throughout their careers.

- No students should be denied a fair chance to learn mathematics because they have been assigned unqualified mathematics teachers.

- All students should have a copy of the basic instructional materials (textbooks, handouts, etc.) to take home.

- Research and evidence should be used whenever it is available to inform decisions.

We also agree that students should learn to:

add, subtract, multiply, and divide single-digit numbers automatically and accurately;

add, subtract, multiply, and divide integers, decimals, and fractions accurately, efficiently, and flexibly without calculators;

understand the mathematics they study and use;

use the mathematics they know to solve problems with calculators and computers;

be fluent with the symbolic language of algebra and understand how to use the basic laws of algebra when solving mathematics problems;

explain and justify their reasoning and understand the reasoning of others;

reason with increasing rigor and mathematical maturity as they advance through the curriculum; [and much more]. (pp. 1–2)

The hope is that if such a list is put together well, most people will feel comfortable with most of it and be willing to part with a few things they would rather keep in the interests of making peace and working together in the interest of our children. If so, those who refuse to sign on will reveal themselves for the extremists they are.

It is not clear how optimistic one should be. There already exist documents that appear to have some consensus behind them (e.g., Conference Board of the Mathematical Sciences, 2001; NCTM, 2000; NRC, 2001). The tactic of the extremists has been to ignore such volumes and to attack what they can attack. To date, they have been fairly successful. Not only have some of the major state boards (Texas and California, for example) made the traditional choice, but current federal legislation (e.g., the No Child Left Behind Act of 2001) puts substantial force behind rather narrow and traditional assessments as well. Moreover, much of the public, ill served by media that seek to profit from conflict, sees curriculum choice as dichotomous—it is either traditional or reform. At the same time, there are grounds for some optimism. At the college level, "calculus reform" stimulated a great deal of controversy but then settled in as part of the mainstream. The same may well happen with regard to standards-based mathematics. One cannot simply turn the clock back; too much is known about mathematical thinking and learning. Despite extremist proposals (and mandates), there is a rational middle ground, and many teachers seek it. The short-term goal, however, must be to capture the middle ground for the majority. Efforts must be made publicly to identify the extremists for what they are and to marginalize them. The math wars have casualties—our children, who do not receive the kind of robust mathematics education they should.

Discussion Questions

What are the curricular issues discussed in the "math wars"?

How does this article serve as a case study for disagreements over curriculum in the subject area(s) you teach?

Alan H. Schoenfeld is the Edward Conner Professor of Education, Graduate School, at the University of California–Berkeley.

Article 19

CHEMISTRY, THE CENTRAL SCIENCE?

The History of the High School Science Sequence

KEITH SHEPPARD

DENNIS M. ROBBINS

A trademark of U.S. science education is the teaching of high school science in the fixed order: biology, then chemistry, and finally physics (B-C-P).[1] Somewhat baffling to non-Americans, this B-C-P sequence is found in more than 99% of high schools and is unique to the United States. Much recent debate, particularly in the physics-education community has questioned the educational wisdom of the B-C-P order, and many are calling for physics to be taught earlier in the sequence—the "Physics First" movement,[2] which notes that while chemistry was considered to be the *central science*,

physics was considered to be the *foundational science*. The relative merits of the Physics First or the traditional "Biology First" notwithstanding, an important first step in understanding these issues is to determine how the present B-C-P course order was established. Specifically, how and why did chemistry become the central high school science—that is, the course taught between biology and physics—and in general what impact did this placement have on the development of high school chemistry? Some answers to these questions can be found by considering educational decisions made between 1890 and 1930.

SOURCE: Excerpted from Sheppard, K., & Robbins, D. M. (2005). *Journal of Chemical Education*, 82(4), 561–566. Used with permission of Chemical Education, Inc.

CHEMISTRY EDUCATION IN SECONDARY SCHOOLS BEFORE 1890

Chemistry as a subject was introduced into American secondary schools in the first quarter of the 19th century,[3] and it soon became firmly established in the curricula of many schools.[4,5] The subject at the time was taught exclusively by lecturing, with the textbook as the principal resource. It was not until the last quarter of that century that demonstrations and laboratory work were added.[6,7] Despite the inroads chemistry made into a classics-dominated course of studies, it was generally viewed as having only limited educational value. Even by 1870, chemistry was not necessary for admission to any college,[8] and students who had taken chemistry in high school were often required to repeat the subject.[9] The quality of chemistry taught in high schools was understandably varied. Many science teachers had limited chemistry backgrounds—it was the normal practice for chemistry teachers to have taken only one general chemistry class in college.[6]

Before 1890, there was no specific high school science sequence, and chemistry could be taught in any grade. The only discernible pattern was that in schools that offered both physics and chemistry, the physics class usually preceded the chemistry class.[10] A lack of standardization was not confined to chemistry but was common for all other subjects and led to the creation of a national committee to address the issue. This committee, commissioned by the National Educational Association, the premier educational association of the time, became popularly known as the Committee of Ten (CoT). The CoT is often credited with establishing the B-C-P sequence, but this is an oversimplification.

THE COMMITTEE OF TEN

In 1892, the National Educational Association organized a committee of ten individuals who were charged with determining what should be taught in high school so students from different schools would have a more uniform preparation for college. The CoT organized nine subcommittees, each devoted to a different academic subject area and included Latin, Greek, English, modern languages, mathematics, and history. There were three science subcommittees: one for physical science (physics, chemistry, and astronomy), another for natural history (botany, zoology, and physiology), and a third for geography (physical geography, geology, and meteorology). All of the subcommittees were given the same questions to answer: How much time should be devoted to each subject? When and how should they be taught and assessed? What were the best methods for teaching each subject? What content should be included? Should the subject be different for college-bound students?

The physical science subcommittee included distinguished scientists and educators of the day. This subcommittee in answering the questions made 22 recommendations to the full committee. The recommendations that were pertinent to chemistry included the following:

- That the study of chemistry should precede that of physics in high school work

- That the study of physics be pursued the last year of the high school course

- That the study of chemistry be introduced into the secondary schools in the year preceding that in which physics is taken up

- That at least 200 hours be given to the study of chemistry in the high school

- That both physics and chemistry be required for admission to college

- That there should be no difference in the treatment of physics, chemistry, and astronomy for those going to college or scientific school and those going to neither

- That in secondary schools physics and chemistry be taught by a combination of laboratory work, textbook, and thorough didactic instruction carried on conjointly and that at least one-half of the time devoted to these subjects be given to laboratory work

- That in the instruction in physics and chemistry it should not be the aim of the students to make a so-called rediscovery of the laws of these sciences

In justifying their position on the relative placement of physics and chemistry, the majority of the subcommittee wrote:

The order recommended for the study of chemistry and physics is *plainly not the logical one* [italics added], but all members with one exception . . . felt that the pupils should have as much mathematical knowledge as possible to enable them to deal satisfactorily with physics, while they could profitably rake up elementary chemistry at an earlier stage.[11a]

While agreeing to the placement of chemistry before physics, they did not articulate why they considered a chemistry–physics sequence to be illogical, nor did they state any evidence to support their recommendation. In dissenting, Waggener, a professor at the University of Colorado, gave the minority opinion and argued that chemistry, being more abstract, should follow physics.

The subcommittees of all the subjects presented their recommendations to the full CoT, who then combined and coordinated them into plans for high school education. In the first stage, the CoT simply compiled the various subcommittee recommendations and included the majority recommendation that chemistry be placed in the 11th grade and physics in the 12th grade. In the second stage, the CoT "slightly modified" the offerings for the sciences. As none of the science subcommittees had recommended a science for the 9th grade, the CoT placed geography in the 9th grade and physiography and meteorology in the 12th grade. They also swapped the positions of physics and chemistry so that "the subject of physics may precede meteorology and physiography."[11b] In the third and final stage, further amendments were made and the CoT outlined what a high school curriculum might look like and suggested four "specific programs." The science classes and the order they proposed are shown in Table 1.

At first glance, Table 1 appears confusing for its unfamiliar pattern of course offerings. The

Table 19.1   Science Classes Proposed for High Schools by the Committee of Ten

	Type of High School Program[a]			
Year	*Classical*	*Latin-Scientific*	*Modern Languages*	*English*
1	**Physical Geography**	Physical Geography	Physical Geography	Physical Geography
2	**Physics**	**Physics** (Botany or Zoology)[b]	**Physics** (Botany or Zoology)	**Physics** (Botany or Zoology)
3	_____	(Astronomy, Meteorology)	(Astronomy, Meteorology)	(Astronomy, Meteorology)
4	**Chemistry**	**Chemistry** (Geology or Physiography and Anatomy, Physiology and Hygiene)	**Chemistry** (Geology or Physiography and Anatomy, Physiology and Hygiene)	**Chemistry** (Geology or Physiography and Anatomy, Physiology and Hygiene)

[a]High school programs were organized by language requirements: Classical—three foreign languages, one modern; Latin-Scientific—two foreign languages, one modern; Modern Languages—two foreign languages, both modern; English—one foreign language, ancient or modern.

[b]Parentheses indicate courses with half-year sequences.

classics dominated the high school programs at the time. The organizing principle for the proposed courses of study was the number of languages that students would take. Although course offerings were mostly uniform in science, according to these recommendations students might take more than one science in a school year. Parentheses show that students could take half-year sequences—for instance, in the junior year students would take a half-year course in astronomy and a half-year of meteorology in the Latin-Scientific, Modern Languages, and English programs. The CoT finally recommended that physics be taught in the 10th grade and chemistry in the senior year, a P-C sequence. They rationalized this choice of science sequence by noting that, because many students did not complete high school at this time:

> The Committee thought it important to select the study of the first two years in such a way that . . . scientific subjects should all be properly represented. Natural history being represented by physical geography, the Committee wished physics to represent the inorganic sciences of precision.[11c]

While the CoT is often cited as being the originator of the B-C-P sequence, it can be seen in each of the suggested courses of study that chemistry was placed after physics. Note also that a course in biology was absent from the table as it did not exist as a distinct subject at the time, although there were separate courses in botany, zoology, anatomy, and physiology.

Interestingly, the CoT and its subcommittees offered three different rationales for the suggested placement of physics and chemistry. First, physics should be in the 12th grade and chemistry in 11th grade because of the mathematical maturity needed to study physics. Second, physics should be in 11th grade and chemistry in 12th grade, due to physics being a prerequisite for studying other sciences. Third, physics should be in 10th grade and chemistry in 12th grade so that all students might be exposed to physics before leaving school.

AFTER THE COMMITTEE OF TEN

The Committee on College Entrance Requirements (CCER) was convened by the National Educational Association in 1896 to discuss how to implement the findings of the CoT. The committee followed the CoT proposals about sequencing and recommended that chemistry be taught after physics.[12] For college admission they proposed that students complete 16 units of study: 4 in languages, 2 in English, 2 in math, 1 in history, *1 in science,* and 6 units of electives. These units of study would later come to be known as Carnegie Units. An assumption made by the CCER was that several of the electives taken would be in the sciences. The CoT had recommended that both physics and chemistry be required for college admission; however, the CCER with its proposal of *only 1 year* of science for graduation, coupled with the subjects' late appearance in the sequence, essentially made chemistry and physics electives in high school.

Many states eventually followed the CCER recommendations, and so for high school students only one year of science became required for graduation. This would remain true in most states throughout most of the 20th century. Furthermore, the CoT and CCER recommendations led to another effect, unique to U.S. science education— that is, individual sciences became 1-year courses, not taught over multiple years. There was some debate about offering chemistry continuously through high school, but lack of suitably qualified chemistry teachers and appropriate laboratory facilities made such proposals untenable.[13] In contrast, high school chemistry in virtually all other countries in the world historically came to he taught over several years.[13,14]

In the late 1800s and early 1900s, major demographic changes were occurring in the United States. Most notably in high schools the number of students was increasing rapidly. In 1890 approximately 200,000 students were enrolled in high schools, by 1900 this population had more than doubled to over 500,000, and by 1920 there were more than 2 million students in high school.[15] Woodhull, in an address to the New York Chemistry Teachers' Club in 1917, illustrated the phenomenal growth: "we have several high schools in New York City now that have more pupils than all the United States had when I began to teach."[16]

The courses of study endorsed by the CoT had targeted college-bound students, but with the burgeoning high school population a smaller percentage of students were going on to college. Consequently, the courses proposed started to be viewed as unsuitable for the majority of students. This led to several important curricular developments, which would affect the science sequence.

Between 1900 and 1920 two new courses were created. General science was introduced and rapidly became the most frequently taken science subject, as it met the needs of students for whom it would be a terminal science course, and it was seen as a necessary introduction to another new course—general biology.[17,18] The separate courses in botany, zoology, anatomy, and physiology were amalgamated into a general biology course. Given the more descriptive natures of both general science and general biology, they were universally placed in the early years of high school before chemistry or physics.[19]

In 1920, The Committee on Reorganization of Science in Secondary Schools, commissioned by the National Education Association as part of the Commission on the Reorganization of Secondary Education, included general science and general biology in their proposed 4-year science sequence. The committee recommended that every high school should provide biology, chemistry, and physics courses. With regard to the sequence, they recommended that general science and biology should he offered in 9th and 10th grades respectively, with chemistry and physics either in the 11th or 12th grade. The committee approved the practice in small high schools of alternating physics and chemistry in successive years.[20] The general practice in the majority of schools at this time was still to offer physics before chemistry.[21]

By 1930 there was still no established order for physics and chemistry,[22] though biology had become firmly established as first in the sequence. Over the next few decades, recommendations were made by other committees[23] about the sequence of the sciences in high school. With the exception of the majority of the physical science section of the CoT, by World War II no committee had actually recommended that chemistry be placed before physics. But in the schools between 1890 and 1945, chemistry would find a definite position before physics.

Science Courses Offered in High Schools

Surprisingly, the recommendations of the various committees seemed to have little effect on the practice in schools.

Over the next few decades, Hunter conducted a series of surveys across the country, investigating the order in which the sciences were being taught in the high schools.[21,22,24,25] Over these decades, physics and chemistry swapped positions in the course order. At the beginning of the century, fewer chemistry courses were offered in the junior year than in the senior year. Physics had the opposite pattern. By the early 1930s physics became more frequently offered in the 12th grade and chemistry more frequently offered as an 11th-grade course. Unlike biology, which was recommended as the first course in the science order by virtually all committees, the relative placement of chemistry and physics was left unspecified. The swapping of the order of chemistry and physics was not the result of any specific educational, scientific, or historical decision. No committee proposed placing chemistry before physics, nor was there any discussion of the relative merits of various sequences by these committees, though, according to the Hunter studies it was the practice that evolved in the schools over this time period. Indeed, the changeover was slow and erratic and different states adopted different practices, as Hunter noted in 1931:

> In Pennsylvania, Michigan, Indiana, Massachusetts, Ohio, California, Wisconsin, Washington, and Oregon there is a definite tendency toward chemistry in 11th and physics in the 12th year. In Connecticut, New Jersey, New York, Illinois, Iowa, Missouri, Colorado, and Montana there seems to be fairly well established the reverse sequence of physics in the 11th and chemistry in the 12th year.[22a]

To confirm the results of his survey, Hunter visited "important schools" in 22 states and reported that "there is no agreement among supervisors as well as among teachers as to the proper sequence of high school chemistry and physics."[22b]

Some insight into the thinking of the time can be gleaned from the writings of the American Chemical Society's Committee on Chemical Education. Chemists were mindful of the issue of the placement of chemistry in high school and its significance for the status and development of chemistry as a subject. In 1924, the ACS Committee on Chemical Education met to discuss the content of the high school chemistry curriculum.[26] They advised chemistry teachers, "to encourage chemistry being placed in the fourth year of high school after the students have had a year of general science, and a year of biological science or physics, or preferably both." This represented the prevalent attitude of the day that seniors were more mature than juniors and so more material could be covered by them. The argument was similar to that made by the majority of the physical science subcommittee of the CoT in recommending that physics be placed in the final year. Clearly, in the 1920s, the science class closest to college held the most prestige. Despite this advice, the B-C-P sequence slowly gained ground so that by the late 1940s it had become the status quo.

Not unsurprisingly, given the seemingly arbitrary sequencing of physics and chemistry, the logic of the B-C-P order has been continuously challenged.[2,27–31] The primary criticisms being that the sequence fails to represent the structure of modern science and that it is pedagogically inappropriate. The development of the sequence did have a major impact on the student enrollment in these high school courses.

ENROLLMENT IN THE SCIENCES

The CoT had recommended that all students take chemistry and physics. The changing nature of the population in high schools, the setting up of an elective system, and a credit system as well as the development of biology and general science as subjects were potential factors affecting science enrollment. Enrollments in biology, physics, and chemistry changed from the 1890s to the 1980s.

An enrollment of 25% approximates to complete enrollment; that is, all students would take the subject at some point in their high school career. While the percentage of students enrolled in physics showed a dramatic decline, the percentage enrolled in chemistry remained approximately constant at slightly less than 10% of the population. For most of the 20th century less than 40% of U.S. students graduated high school with a credit in chemistry. Biology after its formation rapidly became the most taken science. By the 1930s more students took biology than physics and chemistry combined, clearly an outcome of its placement in the science sequence. After 1930 the relative enrollments of the subjects changed only slightly: Biology continued to grow, physics continued to decline, and chemistry stayed approximately constant.

After the publication of A Nation at Risk[32] in 1983, enrollment in the sciences started to rise. The report had called for an increase in the graduation requirement to 3 years of science. At the time of A Nation at Risk, 36 states still only required 1 year of science for graduation, as the CCER had recommended. By 1992 more than 40 states were requiring at least 2 years of science with some states in the process of moving to a 3-year requirement.[33] At present, biology is approaching universal enrollment in U.S. high schools, and the percentage of students completing chemistry has almost doubled in the last

20 years. While it is possible to take other sciences (e.g., earth science, physical science) to meet high school graduation requirements, these classes are predominantly organized around the B-C-P sequence. Due to chemistry's central position in the sequence, further increases in state science requirements will inevitably raise enrollment in chemistry.

DISCUSSION

Chemistry became the "central science" in U.S. high schools by accident, not by design. There were three important historical factors that influenced how high school science came to be sequenced, and these factors had a major impact on the development of U.S. science education.

First, decisions made before 1900 established individual sciences as 1-year courses. Inevitably, the sciences would have to be taught in a specific order. Chemistry, however, is not a static subject. The stunning growth of chemical knowledge in the 20th century with the development of atomic theory, bonding, acid–base theories, and so forth has naturally led to an increase in the quantity of material in introductory chemistry. This increase in material has not been accompanied by an increase in time allocation for chemistry but instead has been fitted into the preexisting timeframe. Chemistry has remained a single-year course with the same curricular time allocation; consequently, the introductory chemistry course has become overpacked with content. The CoT recommendation of 200 hours of study for each high school science was made before much of present day chemistry had been developed. Today, U.S. high school chemistry attempts to cover in one short year, as evidenced by the encyclopedic texts, what students in most other countries take several years to cover. It should be hardly surprising that chemistry developed an "obsession with content"[34] and is still on "the killer course list."[35] High school chemistry teachers need more curricular time, not to cover more material, but to do what they are actually being asked to do.

Secondly, the science courses became sequenced. By the 1920s, due largely to its descriptive nature at the time, biology had consolidated its position as the first specialized science taught in high school, with most schools offering physics next and finally chemistry. By the 1930s the relative positions of chemistry and physics had changed and the B-C-P order had been established. No committee made this decision; it was simply the practice that was adopted in the schools. Both the physics and chemistry communities were vying for their subjects to be taught last in the sequence. By the late 1940s the B-C-P sequence had become the status quo. The sciences were taught as distinct, unrelated courses in this specific order. Robinson has argued that the B-C-P sequence is strictly not a sequence, as biology is not a prerequisite for chemistry, nor chemistry a prerequisite for physics.[36] Haber-Schaim[37] supported this view by analyzing the concepts included in high school science texts and showed that from a conceptual point of view a physics-chemistry-biology order was more logical. A cursory glance at any introductory biology text or curriculum shows that it contains a wealth of chemistry, and consequently much elementary chemistry is understandably being taught by biology teachers. While physicists are calling for Physics First,[38] biologists could convincingly argue for Biology Last, if high school science is to be taught in a fixed order. More than 200 schools, including whole school districts (e.g., San Diego), have already moved to a physics-first order.[39] It seems likely that this number will continue to grow, even though such a change faces significant hurdles. In other countries, a B-C-P sequence did not develop, and chemistry is usually taught over multiple years and is more coordinated with the other sciences.

The third factor relates to the implications of changing state science graduation requirements. As science is taught in a specific order, any increase in overall requirements significantly increases enrollment of the later offered sciences. This has had a major impact on chemistry education. With most states initially having only a 1-year science graduation requirement, chemistry was an elective, taken by a fraction of the students. When the majority of states moved to a 2-year requirement in the 1980s, enrollment for all sciences increased, biology essentially became a requirement, and the percentage of students taking high school chemistry doubled. Today, most high school students graduate with a chemistry credit.[40] With a significant number of states moving to a 3-year requirement, chemistry will become a requirement in these states. It would appear that the belief that all students should take chemistry is being achieved through legislation.

The impact of having a fixed high school science sequence on the U.S. science education system has largely been overlooked. If the United States is to develop a world-class science education system for the 21st century, then it is time to reconsider not only what chemistry is taught but also when it is taught and how much time should be devoted to it. We would suggest that re-answering the questions set by the CoT in 1892 would be a good place to start.

Discussion Questions

Why is the scope and sequence in your subject area designed in its current format?

Do you believe that your students would learn more effectively if the curriculum scope and sequence were redesigned for the subject you teach? Why or why not, and what suggestions would you make for restructuring?

Keith Sheppard is an assistant professor at Columbia University, Teachers College.

Dennis M. Robbins is an instructor at Columbia University, Teachers College.

Article 20

SCHOOL DAYS (HAIL, HAIL ROCK 'N' ROLL!)

RICK MITCHELL

I am usually impressed when teachers tell me that they've always known they wanted to be teachers, and that they've never had another job. I am one of those who took a more circuitous route to this profession. In fact, I might have been voted "least likely to become a teacher" among the class of 1970 by the administration of Katella High School in Orange County, Calif., which suggested that I unceremoniously depart midway through my senior year.

In college, I thought I found my calling as a journalist. Instead, I became a professional rock critic, which is sort of like being a journalist except that you never have to grow up. Perhaps no career besides that of professional athlete or musician affords such an opportunity for supposedly mature individuals to extend their adolescent passions so deep into adulthood. For 20-odd years, through countless mainstream newspapers and alternative magazines, seedy dives and concert halls, I soldiered on with my appointed duty,

until I finally outgrew the mysterious joy and pride I once had found in telling people that the music they enjoyed actually sucked. Only then, in a desperate epiphany cleverly disguised as altruism, did I decide that education was my true calling. I now teach English, history, and philosophy at a private international school in Houston.

So how does my past life as an opinionated and erudite pop-culture snob influence what I do in the present as a kind and caring adult who is routinely interrupted and ignored by teenagers?

Well, I still listen to a lot of music, new and old, for my own enjoyment. The fact that I am far more conversant in hip-hop than the average middle-aged white guy gives me a semi-secret code for relating to certain students who otherwise might be difficult to reach. I also try to stay current with trends in rock, R&B, jazz, various regional styles, and music from around the world. As a result, a few of my more musically astute students seem to think I'm pretty cool for

SOURCE: Excerpted from Mitchell, R. Winter 2005/2006. School days: Hail, hail rock 'n' roll. *Rethinking Schools*, 20(2), 56–59, www.rethinkingschools.org.

an old fart and ask to borrow obscure stuff from my collection or want to know my opinion of their favorite new CDs.

Most of my students, on the other hand, couldn't care less what music I listen to on my own time. What is relevant to them, and to the purposes of this article, is the music we listen to together in class. I regularly incorporate music into lesson plans for all three of the subjects I teach, from thematic connections between song lyrics and poetry in English, to the epistemological implications of aesthetics as a philosophical area of knowledge. I also give an 8-week series of guest lectures on the history of jazz for the advanced music classes.

What I want to focus on here, however, is the integral role music plays in the curriculum for my ninth-grade U.S. history class. Although I sometimes have to remind students that listening to music in class is not an invitation to start the party before the bell rings, the music lessons are treated as special events by most students, and, like historically based films, they serve to augment and enliven the lecture/discussion cycle that necessarily takes up the bulk of the class periods.

RACE IN AMERICAN MUSIC

One of the central themes of my history course is that America is a nation of great contradictions. The history of American music provides an excellent means for illuminating perhaps the most basic contradiction of all in U.S. society, that of race. How could the author of the Declaration of Independence, which declares that "all men are created equal" and possess an "inalienable right to life, liberty, and the pursuit of happiness," have been a slave owner? How could the founding fathers be inspired by the example of limited government set by the Iroquois nations yet engage in a policy of genocide when indigenous tribes interfered with westward expansion?

American music—jazz, rock, rap, R&B, gospel, country—has been the most alive and innovative musical tradition in the world for at least the last century. All these forms come out of the gumbo pot of African, European, and Native American sources that characterizes the musical heritage of both North and South America. Yet, in the United States, Black artists typically have done the lion's share of the innovating, while White artists (and White-owned record labels) have reaped the lion's share of the financial rewards. Furthermore, our cultural elites still overwhelmingly look to Europe to validate American "high" culture, when what makes us unique is the unprecedented cultural crossbreeding that has taken place here. Compare the corporate and government support for "classical" forms such as the symphony, opera, and ballet to what's afforded to jazz, which should be considered the classical expression of American vernacular music. It is impossible to seriously study the history of 20th-century American music, from ragtime to rap, without also studying the history of racism.

Yet American music is also the story of gradual and sometimes spectacular triumphs over racism and class discrimination, of self-taught geniuses and bootstrap capitalists who neither asked for nor received public subsidies, and whose musical creations, for better and worse, have captured the imagination of the world for the past half-century. As trumpeter/educator Wynton Marsalis frequently has commented, jazz music can be seen as the ultimate artistic expression of American democracy, in its emphasis on individual expression within a cohesive group context.

My ninth-grade U.S. history course syllabus begins with the European conquest of the Americas and the disastrous consequences that followed for the Native American population and enslaved Africans. During the first week of class, as the class is doing homework assignments from the text about European conquest and colonization, I devote the better part of two 50-minute periods to demonstrating how Native American, African, and European elements came together and evolved into all the myriad forms of American music. I use recordings that reflect the traditional roots of the music, while explaining that all musical forms evolve over time and that

20th-century recordings inevitably have introduced modernizing influences.

Because of time constraints, I generally explain what elements I want students to listen for in a given piece and then play an excerpt that illustrates the point I am trying to make. I often fade the music down to talk over it, then fade it back up to let the music reinforce what I've just said. The DJ in me would, of course, prefer to play each track in its entirety—and sometimes students will implore me to let the music play—but excerpts are usually better suited to 50-minute periods and short adolescent attention spans. (See www.rethinkingschools.org for a listing of albums and individual tracks used in this lesson.)

I begin in South America with an example of Inca music from Peru, pointing out the distinctive handmade instrumentation and piping melodies. I next play some West and Central African drumming, focusing on the complex polyrhythms not commonly found in European or Native American music. This is followed by examples of Spanish and Portuguese guitar music, during which I refer to the earlier North African influence on Spanish flamenco. I then show how these distinct elements were fused to create Afro-Cuban salsa, Colombian cumbia, and Brazilian samba.

For example, the music of Toto la Momposina, a wonderfully folkloric female singer from Colombia, consciously combines Native American flutes with Afro-Latin percussion and Spanish guitar. When her full band brings in the horns, it becomes a contemporary cumbia orchestra. As I point out to students, this sort of pervasive intercultural exchange characterizes not only the music of the Americas but virtually all aspects of our culture—our food, language, religion, and social customs. It is, effectively, what defines us as Americans.

I launch the North American segment of the lesson by explaining some of the ways in which the practices of British slave owners in North America differed from the Spanish, French, and Portuguese in Latin America and the Caribbean. Most notably, the British banned hand drums and other African instruments, so that slaves were forced to invent their own instruments or adapt those of the Europeans to their purposes. The polyrhythmic hand clapping in Black churches and the bottleneck slide guitar favored by Delta blues singers are examples of such improvised African retentions. (The exception to this was New Orleans, essentially a Caribbean city until the early 1800s, which is why New Orleans plays such an important role in the birth of blues and jazz.)

I first play recordings of West African griot music, in which singer-songwriter historians travel from village to village, singing praises to the various clans. I then play examples of traditional Celtic music from Ireland and Scotland, noting the similarities between West African griots and Celtic bards. Both functioned as oral historians as well as musicians, and both made their livings by bestowing praise upon wealthy clan chieftains. (Rappers who give "shout outs" to fellow rappers and their record label execs are thus perpetuating an old African tradition.) Next, I show how the West African griot tradition survived in North America in the archetype of the itinerant Delta bluesman, and how Irish and Scottish music mated with African American blues in the backhills of the Appalachians to produce country and bluegrass music. Then I briefly fast-forward to the mating of "Black" blues, gospel, and R&B with "White" country and bluegrass that gave birth to rock 'n' roll. The first rockers, I tell my students, were the slave musicians who took the master's instruments back to the slave quarters and put them to their own purposes, whether praising the Lord or getting the party started. Elvis Presley's first record featured a bluegrass cover on one side and a blues tune on the other. Both sides came out sounding like what we now call rockabilly.

Students are invited to ponder the ironic contradiction. Because of slavery, African and European musical concepts met and made love on unfamiliar ground. The heritage spawned by this act of cultural miscegenation is contemporary American music, in all of its artistic glory and commercial crassness.

It has conquered the world in a way that U.S. military and political might never will. That such a terrible and dehumanizing institution as slavery could create the conditions that allowed the brilliance and beauty of great Black artists such as Louis Armstrong, Duke Ellington, Otis Redding, and Aretha Franklin to flourish is one of the tragic ironies of modern Western civilization. U.S. history is full of such contradictions. As historians, and as citizens in a nominally democratic society, we must study these contradictions so that we will not be fooled by those who would insist that Americans have always been the good guys. Or, for that matter, the bad guys.

There are, of course, no recordings to document how American music evolved from the 17th century through the 19th century. But from the invention of the phonograph in the early 20th century, popular musical recordings have charted what average Americans were thinking and feeling, how they talked, how they sang, and how they danced. For history teachers not to take advantage of these historical artifacts, especially in light of the technological advancements that have vastly improved the sound quality of old recordings, is comparable to leaving the photographs out of a textbook.

From Harlem Renaissance to "Hippie Day"

I come back to music throughout our study of 20th-century America. When we read about the Harlem Renaissance in the 1920s, I play classic recordings by blues and jazz greats such as Bessie Smith, Fletcher Henderson, Armstrong, and Ellington to demonstrate the cultural sensibility that produced the poetry of Langston Hughes and Zora Neale Hurston. In 2000, Rhino Records released an excellent four-disc set called *Rhapsodies in Black: Music and Words From the Harlem Renaissance,* featuring poetry readings by well-known African American actors, musicians, and celebrities spliced with original recordings from the era by the artists mentioned

above and many others. For students to hear rappers such as Ice T and Chuck D, and actors such as Debbie Allen and the late Gregory Hines, reading African American poetry helps to make the connection between the historical context and their own lives. It also helps make the music—which was, of course, the funkiest party music of its time—come more fully alive.

When we discuss the Great Depression and the New Deal, the class watches the movie *The Grapes of Wrath* (one of the few films I show in its entirety) over two and a half class periods. This is followed by a half-period lesson on the tradition of White, working-class protest music, from Woody Guthrie's Dustbowl Ballads through Bob Dylan's early political-protest songs, Bruce Springsteen's *The Ghost of Tom Joad* and Rage Against the Machine's rock/rap cover of Springsteen's title track, which echoes Tom Joad's last lines from the movie: "Wherever there's somebody fighting for a place to stand/Or a decent job or a helpin' hand/Wherever somebody's struggling to be free/Look in their eyes, Ma, you'll see me."

In this case, I don't announce what I am about to play before I play it. I'd rather have students make the connection on their own.

When we come to the 1950s I devote two class periods to retracing the musical and cultural conditions that gave rise to rock 'n' roll. In the first, I cover the parallel development of Black music (gospel, blues, swing, rhythm and blues) and White hillbilly music (country, western-swing, bluegrass) from the 1920s through the 1940s. I then show how these styles were crossbred in the early 1950s by Black artists such as Fats Domino and Chuck Berry and White artists such as Bill Haley. For example, Chuck Berry's "Mabellene," an early rock classic, has the same beat as Bob Wills and the Texas Playboys' "Ida Red," a traditional western-swing tune from two decades earlier. Yes, Chuck Berry, like many Black artists of his generation, was influenced by country music as well as blues. On the other hand, Bill Haley's "Rock Around the Clock," one of the first rock 'n' roll records by a White artist, takes its musical cues from Joe

Turner's "Shake, Rattle and Roll," a jump-blues tune sung by a much-older Black artist with roots in the swing era.

Rock 'n' roll existed in form before Elvis Presley, but the moment of pop-culture conception arrived with Presley's first single for Sun Records in Memphis, which, as I alluded to earlier, covered Bill Monroe's "Blue Moon of Kentucky," a bluegrass tune, on one side and Arthur "Big Boy" Crudup's "That's Alright, Mama," a blues tune, on the other. It's no coincidence that Presley's next single was a cover of Roy Brown's "Good Rockin' Tonight," one of the first R&B hits to use the term *rock* (a frequent euphemism for sex) in the title.

In the next day's lesson, we examine the relationship between rock 'n' roll and the postwar emergence of a popular mass culture focused on youth. We watch excerpts from Presley's movies—the big dance number from *Jailhouse Rock* is always a winner—and listen to his huge hits from the late 1950s, as well as those of other teen idols from the period including Jerry Lee Lewis, Little Richard, Buddy Holly, and Frankie Lyman. We also listen to Otis Blackwell, an obscure Black musician whose original recordings of "Don't Be Cruel" and "All Shook Up" were "borrowed" by Presley, almost note for note. (Hear for yourself on Blackwell's only CD release, *All Shook Up,* reissued on the Shanachie label in 1995.)

The music lesson should naturally lead to a discussion of the impact popular youth culture has had on American life in the past 50 years, and how musical integration opened the door to legal integration. Once large numbers of average White kids started listening to popular Black music and attending concerts featuring White and Black acts sharing the same stage, it became increasingly difficult for local authorities to keep audiences racially separated.

Rock 'n' roll promoters such as Cleveland disc jockey Alan Freed began to insist that their concerts be integrated. It is widely assumed by rock historians that Freed's conviction in the payola scandal of the late 1950s was due, at least in part, to his courageous stand against segregation.

Undoubtedly, the most anticipated music lesson I give all year is Hippie Day, which has become a spring tradition at my school. On the day after the big essay exam that covers the civil rights movement and Vietnam, the principal gives the entire freshman class permission to come to school dressed in 1960s fashions instead of the usual uniforms. At lunch, we hold a "sit-in" on the quad, featuring performances by student and faculty musicians.

During my history class periods, I play classic rock and R&B records while explaining the evolution of 1960s protest music from the folk-music revival through folk-rock and into acid-rock, and from civil rights–era soul to Black Power funk.

Explaining the drug references in some songs is always a bit dicey, since I do not want to be accused of promoting drug use, and that's exactly what these songs do. But my students seem to be sophisticated enough to appreciate that while much of the music was great, and much of the politics admirable, the 1960s counterculture bequeathed a mixed legacy to subsequent generations.

It's too simple to blame today's crack babies on the Beatles' use of LSD and to blame the AIDS epidemic on "free love." But it's also too simple to say there is no connection at all. It's another of those contradictions that serve to make the United States the complex society that it is, and another reason why we should be suspicious of those who try to make complex issues seem simpler than they really are, like those who thought drugs would be a shortcut to nirvana and those who now brandish the slogan "zero tolerance" as a weapon of righteousness.

CULTURAL HISTORY IS REAL HISTORY

For culture-war conservatives, I suppose my music lessons could be considered at best fluff, at worst a subversive challenge to the notion of a classical eurocentric education. I would agree that they might very well be subversive, but they are not fluff. They are instead the stuff of real history.

Too often, history is taught as a timeline of wars and famous leaders, in which average people are little more than pawns and cannon fodder. Just as thousands of anonymous soldiers died when Napoleon met his Waterloo, from which he emerged unscathed, so too will the war in Iraq be remembered as Bush's war, though he is likely to survive no matter how many historically nameless Iraqis and Americans do not.

While major military and political events serve as natural landmarks in any history syllabus, the true and often untold history of our world consists of what societies were doing both during and between these cataclysmic chapters. Musical recordings offer vivid evidence of what was taking place in previous decades and centuries and can bring history alive in ways that books, photos, and even films cannot. Of course, it is important to examine how culture reflects and influences political events. But cultural history should not be considered merely a sidebar to military and political history. It is important in its own right, perhaps more important than memorizing the names of past presidents and generals.

In "School Day," his ebullient mid-1950s ode to the newborn child called rock 'n' roll, schoolboy Chuck Berry can't wait for the bell to ring so he can head down to the corner juke joint and rock out. Why wait for the bell, Chuck, when we can learn so much about who we are as a society from listening to your records? Hail, hail rock 'n' roll!

Discussion Questions

How open are you to using "nontraditional" approaches to teaching your curriculum?

How might you deal with individuals who might not understand nontraditional approaches to curriculum mastery?

Rick Mitchell is a former music critic for the Houston Chronicle *and the* Portland Oregonian *and is currently a freelance writer.*

Section VI

What Is the Extra- or Co-Curriculum?

Not everything we learn in school is accomplished in the core curriculum classes or the elective classes we may take. Much of our learning is developed by our participation in the extracurricular or co-curricular activities. These activities are voluntary, and most offer no academic credit to students. Yet they are a major part of school life, particularly at the secondary level. Participation builds other skills that can benefit the students' success in school.

The four articles in this section of the reader provide a background of how extra- and co-curricular activities enhance student learning.

Eccles and her colleagues provide us with an excellent analysis of how participants in extracurricular activities achieve better academic outcomes than nonparticipants. Their analysis was based on surveys administered to 1,259 10th graders.

Marianne Kugler explores the growth of and participation in after-school programs for teens. The programs examined were related to academic, social, emotional, physical, and safety needs of teens.

Sports are a huge part of American life. Billions of dollars are spent annually promoting sports events—NASCAR, the Super Bowl, the College National Football Championships (BCS), the NBA playoffs, the Final Four in college basketball, cheerleading competitions, gymnastics, golf tournaments, tennis matches, swimming, dancing, skating competitions, and, of course, the Olympics and Special Olympics. The issue of sports in schools is important as there is much contention about the role of sports as an integral part of the curriculum of the schools.

Interest in school sports is spawned in the middle schools and continues through high school, college, and adulthood. Stephens and Schaben investigate the relationship between student participation in sports and academic achievement of middle school students.

William Ayers examines the Junior Reserve Officers' Training Corps (JROTC) program that is offered at many high schools as a recruiting tool for the military. He points out that

NCLB legislation mandates that military recruiters have access to high school students and that schools are obligated to turn over to military recruiters students' names, addresses, and home phone numbers. He raises concern that JROTC programs target poor, Black, and Latino students.

As you read these articles think about the following:

- How your participation in extracurricular activities affected your achievement in school

- The role sports played in your life as a teenager and, consequently, as an adult

- How after-school programs may provide a safe haven for children or an escape from parenting

- Whether military recruitment should be a part of the high school curriculum

- How your personal reading interests educate you as compared to required reading in school

Article 21

Extracurricular Activities and Adolescent Development

Jacquelynne S. Eccles

Bonnie L. Barber

Margaret Stone

James Hunt

There is growing interest in the developmental consequences of extracurricular and after-school programs for youth, fueled, in part, by (a) concerns about the role such activities might play in promoting school achievement and preventing school disengagement and other problems, (b) the continuing social class and ethnic group disparities in school achievement, (c) concerns about the preparation of American youth for an increasingly demanding and technical labor market, and (d) the amount of unsupervised time experienced by so many youth (e.g., Eccles & Gootman, 2002; Eccles & Templeton, 2002; Pittman, Tolman, & Yohalem, 2005; Scales, 1999). Children and adolescents in the United States spend more than half of their waking hours in leisure activities (Larson & Verma, 1999). For many, much of this time is spent in either unstructured peer-focused activities or in front of the television set. Both developmental scientists and youth policy advocates have suggested that this leisure time could be better spent in ways (such as participating in high-quality out-of-school and after-school

SOURCE: Excerpted from Eccles, J. S., Barber, B. L., Stone, M., & Hunt, J. (2003). Extracurricular activities and adolescent development. *Journal of Social Issues, 59*(4), 865–889. Reprinted by permission of Blackwell Publishing Ltd.

programs) that would both facilitate positive development and prevent the emergence of developmental problems (see Eccles & Gootman, 2002). These scholars and advocates have noted also that the availability of such programs is inequitably distributed across communities in the United States—with much lower availability in precisely those communities where the adolescents are at highest risk for poor developmental outcomes (Mahoney, Larson, & Eccles, 2005; Pedersen & Seidman, 2005). Interest in the developmental consequences of extracurricular and after-school programs has been stimulated also by the growing interest in positive psychology and positive youth development. Advocates for positive youth development, in particular, argue that such programs are needed to fully prepare our youth for the transition into adulthood (e.g., Pittman, Tolman, & Yohalem, in press). Again the need for such programs is especially acute for youth living in poor communities.

Developmentalists and youth advocates argue that constructive, organized activities are a good use of the adolescents' time because such activities provide opportunities (a) to acquire and practice specific social, physical, and intellectual skills that may be useful in a wide variety of settings including school; (b) to contribute to the well-being of one's community and to develop a sense of agency as a member of one's community; (c) to belong to a socially recognized and valued group; (d) to establish supportive social networks of peers and adults that can help in both the present and the future; and (e) to experience and deal with challenges. In turn, these assets are predicted to facilitate both current levels of school engagement and achievement and subsequent educational and occupational attainment and to prevent the emergence of risky behavior patterns that can mortgage young people's future.

Recently, research in both leisure studies and adolescent development provides support for the benefits of participating in the kinds of constructive leisure activities associated with extracurricular activities and service learning (see Larson, 2000; Larson & Kleiber, 1993;

Mahoney et al., in press; Youniss, McLellan, & Yates, 1999). For example, Mahoney and his colleagues have documented the link between extended participation in extracurricular activities during high school and reduced rates of school dropout and criminal offending, particularly during the early high school years and for high-risk youth (Mahoney, 2000; Mahoney & Cairns, 1997). Participation in extracurricular and service learning activities has also been linked to increases in interpersonal competence, self-concept, high school grade point average (GPA), school engagement, and educational aspirations (Elder & Conger, 2000; Marsh & Kleitman, 2002; Youniss, McLellan, & Yates, 1999), as well as to higher educational achievement, better job quality, more active participation in the political process and other types of volunteer activities, continued sport engagement, and better mental health during young adulthood (Barber, Eccles, & Stone, 2001; Glancy, Willits, & Farrell, 1986; Marsh, 1992; Youniss, McLellan, Su, & Yates, 1999). Finally, sports participation has been linked to lower school dropout and higher rates of college attendance, particularly for low-achieving and blue-collar male athletes (Gould & Weiss, 1987; Marsh & Kleitman, 2003; McNeal, 1995).

Together, these studies provide good evidence that participating in extracurricular activities is associated with both short- and long-term indicators of positive development, including school achievement and educational attainment. Some of these relations hold even after the other obvious predictors of such outcomes are controlled—giving us some confidence that these effects do not just reflect the selection factors that lead to participation in the first place. These predictive findings, however, tell us less about the reasons for these associations. For the most part, the studies use either cross-sectional or longitudinal survey methods. These provide good evidence of an association but weak evidence for an actual causal inference and even weaker evidence regarding the actual features of the experience that might matter. We are now at a point where we need more longitudinal studies that include appropriate controls for selection factors and are designed to evaluate specific theoretically based hypotheses about the mechanisms likely to mediate the association between activity participation and development. In addition, we need randomized, trial experimental studies that actually test our hypotheses about the mediating mechanisms.

Some of this more rigorous work is beginning to emerge in the fields of developmental and prevention science and sport psychology. For example, Mahoney has suggested that participation in voluntary, school-based, extracurricular activities increases school participation and achievement because it facilitates (a) the acquisition of interpersonal skills and positive social norms, (b) membership in prosocial peer groups, and (c) stronger emotional and social connections to one's school. In turn, these assets should increase mental health, school engagement, school achievement, and long-term educational outcomes and should decrease participation in problem behaviors, provided that problem behaviors are not endorsed by the peer cultures that emerge in these activities (Mahoney et al., 2005).

THE MICHIGAN STUDY OF ADOLESCENT LIFE TRANSITIONS

The Michigan Study of Adolescent Life Transitions (MSALT) is a longitudinal study that began with a cohort of sixth graders drawn from 10 school districts in southeastern Michigan in 1983. The vast majority of the sample is White and comes from working- and middle-class families living in primarily middle-class and working-class communities based in small industrial cities around Detroit. We have followed approximately 1,800 of these youth through eight waves of data collection: two while they were in the 6th grade (1983–1984), two while they were in the 7th grade (1984–1985), one while they were in 10th grade (spring, 1988), one while they were in 12th grade (spring, 1990), one in 1992–1993 when most were 21–22 years old, and one in 1996–1997 when most were 25–26 years

old. The analyses presented here focus on the 1,259 respondents who completed the 10th-grade survey items about activity involvement. At each wave, the adolescents were administered an extensive interview with items tapping a wide range of constructs. The specific constructs used for this article are summarized below. All results summarized are significant at the $p < .05$ level or better.

Activity Involvement

In the 10th grade, we collected detailed information on the adolescents' involvement in a wide variety of activities in and out of school. Adolescents were provided with a list of 16 sports and 30 school and community clubs and organizations. They checked off all of their activities. We aggregated the extracurricular activities into five categories: prosocial activities—church attendance and/or volunteer and community service type activities; performance activities—school band, drama, and/or dance; team sports—one or more school teams; school involvement—student government, pep club, and/or cheerleading; and academic clubs—debate, foreign language, math, or chess clubs, science fair, or tutoring in academic subjects.

On average, the adolescents in the study participated in between one and two activities and/or clubs—with girls participating in more total activities and in a wider range of activities than boys. In fact, girls participated more than boys in all types of activities except sports, where boys participated more than girls. Finally, 31% of the sample did not participate in any activities or clubs, and 45% did not participate in any school athletic team (Eccles & Barber, 1999).

Risk Behaviors

During Grades 10 and 12, age 21–22, and age 25–26, we asked our participants how often in the last 6 months they had drunk alcohol, gotten drunk, or used drugs. During grade 12, we asked them, also, how often they had skipped school.

Educational Outcomes

During both Grades 10 and 12, we asked participants how much they liked school, and we collected information on academic performance and assessment test scores from each participant's school files. We used participants' cumulative GPA at Grade 12. Also, we used their ninth-grade verbal and numerical ability subscores on the Differential Aptitude Test (DAT) (Psychological Corporation, 1981) as control variables in most of our regression analyses in order to control for intellectual aptitude. During ages 21–22 and 25–26, we assessed college enrollment and total number of years of tertiary education.

Job Characteristics

We measured job characteristics at ages 25–26. The job with a future scale assessed the extent to which the participants considered themselves in a career path job; the job autonomy scale assessed the degree to which participants could make important decisions about what they did at work, had the opportunity to use their ideas and imagination in their job, and were their own boss.

Family Characteristics

We included mother's education as a measure of family social economic status as a control variable in all of our multiple regression analyses. Forty-six percent of the mothers had no more than high school diploma, 38% had some college, and 16% had a bachelor's degree or more.

ASSOCIATION OF PARTICIPATION WITH OTHER INDICATORS OF DEVELOPMENT

Prosocial Activities

Adolescents involved in prosocial activities in 10th grade reported less involvement in risky behaviors at all three subsequent waves of data collection: During 12th grade, youth involved in prosocial activities reported lower rates of drinking alcohol, getting drunk, using drugs, and of skipping school than non-participants. At ages 21–22, they reported lower rates of drinking alcohol, getting drunk, using drugs, and of both driving while alcohol impaired and riding with an alcohol-impaired driver. Interestingly, although rates of drinking were no longer lower at age 25–26, differences in drug use, driving while impaired, and driving with an impaired driver were still lower than those of nonparticipants.

We next ran a series of longitudinal regression analyses on the 12th-grade outcome data. In each equation, we entered the 10th-grade level of the risky behavior in order to get an estimate of the extent to which each of the other predictors predicted change in frequency of engaging in the particular risky behaviors. Using this strategy also controls for those selection characteristics that predict involvement in risky behavior at 10th grade, thus reducing substantially the possible confounding role of unmeasured variables in accounting for our findings. We also entered gender, mother's educational level, and two intellectual aptitude variables (performance on the differential aptitude tests for verbal and mathematical abilities) as controls because these constructs have emerged in other studies as predictors of both academic achievement and involvement in risky behaviors. Finally, we entered 10th-grade prosocial activity involvement. As one would expect, the strongest predictor was the 10th-grade level of involvement in the risky behavior—suggesting considerable stability in the individual differences in these behaviors over the high school years. Nonetheless, involvement in prosocial activities predicted change in this engagement in a protective direction—that is, the students who were involved in activities like attending church and doing volunteer work showed less of an increase in these risky behaviors over the high school years than their noninvolved peers. Involvement in prosocial activities at 10th grade also predicted greater enjoyment of school at 10th grade, a higher GPA at 12th grade, greater likelihood of attending college full-time at age 21, graduating from college by age

25–26, and more total years of tertiary education at age 25–26. However, only the relation to 12th-grade GPA remained significant in the multiple regression analyses.

Team Sports

On the one hand, unlike prosocial activities, participation in team sports predicted greater involvement in risky behaviors: At grade 12, both male and female athletes drank and got drunk more often than non-athletes. In addition, being involved with team sports predicted significant increases in alcohol use and getting drunk over the high school years after controlling for mother's education, student gender, and intellectual aptitude. These differences were less marked at ages 21–22 and 25–26 because of the increase in drinking during the college years for all youth. On the other hand, involvement in team sports was a promotive factor for academic outcomes. Sport participants liked school better than non-participants at both the 10th- and 12th-grade levels. They were also more likely to attend college full-time at age 21 and to have graduated from college by age 25–26. In addition, team sports participation predicted an increase in liking school between the 10th and 12th grades, a higher than expected 12th-grade GPA, and more total years of tertiary education by age 25–26 even after gender, maternal education, and 9th-grade DAT scores were controlled. Finally, team sports participation predicted having a job with a future and a job with autonomy at age 24.

Performing Arts

Those adolescents who were involved in performing arts at Grade 10 were less frequently engaged in risky behaviors at both Grades 10 and 12 than those who were not involved in performing arts. This was particularly true for alcohol-related behaviors. However, when we controlled for prior levels of drinking in the longitudinal regression analyses, there was no evidence that 10th-grade involvement in performing arts predicted the magnitude of change or direction in drinking behavior over the high school years. In addition, participation in performing arts was not related to drinking behavior in either of the two young adult waves of data. Participation in performing arts was related also to greater enjoyment of school at both 10th- and 12th-grade levels, higher 12th-grade GPA, greater likelihood of attending college full-time at age 21–22, and greater likelihood of graduating from college by age 25–26. In the longitudinal regression analyses, however, this promotive role was significant for only 12th-grade GPA. Finally, we found it interesting that performing arts was the only activity domain with consistent evidence of a gender by activity involvement interaction: Both the protective and promotive roles of being involved were more significant for boys than for girls. This was particularly true for total years of education by age 25–26. Participating in performing arts at 10th grade predicted more total education for males but not for females.

School-Involvement Activities

Participation in student government and school-spirit types of activities was not related consistently to engagement in risky behaviors. In contrast, it was positively related to enjoying school at Grade 10 and to both 12th-grade GPA and the likelihood of attending college full-time at age 21. By and large, these patterns were confirmed in the longitudinal regression analyses. Participating in these kinds of school-related activities predicted better than expected 12th-grade GPA, greater likelihood of attending college full-time at age 21, and more total years of tertiary education by age 25–26 even when the set of family and DAT controls were included.

Academic Clubs

Participation in academic clubs was related only to educational and occupational outcomes. According to both the bivariate and longitudinal, multivariate analyses, adolescents who participated in academic clubs enjoyed school more in 10th grade, had higher than expected high school GPAs, and were more likely to be enrolled in college at 21 than their noninvolved peers.

Summary

Consistent with other studies, we found clear evidence that participation in extracurricular activities during the high school years provides a protective context in terms of involvement in risky behaviors and a promotive context in terms of academic performance. Participation in all five types of extracurricular activities predicted better than expected educational outcomes, including high school GPA, college attendance, and college graduation. Participation in sports, school-based leadership and spirit activities, and academic clubs predicted increased likelihood of being enrolled full-time in college at age 21. Also, involvement in sports predicted increases in school attachment over the high school years. Participation in prosocial activities predicted lower rates of increase in alcohol and drug use, as well as lower levels at both Grades 10 and 12; participation in performing arts served this same function for boys. Furthermore, each of these results held true when social class, gender, and academic aptitude were controlled. The patterns for sport participation were more mixed. On the one hand, participation in sports was linked to increases in use of alcohol. On the other hand, participation in sports was strongly linked to positive educational and occupational outcomes.

What can we conclude? Our findings are mostly consistent with the conclusion reached in recent reviews. However, the patterns were not as simple as one might expect. Both the magnitude and the direction of the relations depended on the outcome being considered and, to some extent, on the gender of the adolescent. For example, although participation in team sports was related to increased GPA and increased probability of attending and completing college, it was related also to such risky behaviors as drinking alcohol and getting drunk. Similarly, although being involved in school spirit and leadership clubs neither increased nor reduced the frequency of such risky behaviors as using drugs, drinking alcohol, or skipping school, it was related in a positive direction to academic success. Only involvement in prosocial activities (in this case primarily church attendance) was protective against increases in alcohol and drug use and increases in skipping school.

Other investigators also report mixed patterns for the correlates of activity participation. For example, both Stattin and his colleagues and Dishion and his colleagues have suggested that the negative effects of participating in some activities result in the fact that participation in some types of less structured leisure activities increases the likelihood of being recruited into a risky peer group (Dishion, McCord, & Poulin, 1999; Stattin, Kerr, Mahoney, Persson, & Magnusson, in press). Finally, intervention programs do not always produce any significant effects (Eccles & Gootman, 2002). Clearly, both program and individual characteristics influence the nature of the impact of participation on individuals' development.

Several investigators have suggested specific characteristics as key mediators of both the positive and negative effects of program participation. For example, in 1969 Rehberg suggested five possible mediators for the positive effects of sports participation: association with academically oriented peers, exposure to academic values, enhanced self-esteem, generalization of a high sense of personal efficacy, and superior career guidance and encouragement. More recently, investigators have focused on the links between peer group formation, identity formation, and activity involvement. For example, Fine (1987) stressed how participation in something like Little League shapes both the child's definition of himself as a "jock" and the child's most salient peer group. In turn, these characteristics (one's identity and one's peer group) influence subsequent activity choices—creating a synergistic system that marks out a clear pathway into a particular kind of adolescence. Similarly, Eckert (1989) has explored the link between the peer group identity formation and activity involvement. As individuals move into and through adolescence, they become identified with particular groups of friends or crowds (see also Brown, Mory, & Kinney, 1994). Being a member of one of these crowds helps structure both what one does with one's time and the kinds of values and norms to which one is exposed. The coalescence of one's personal identity, one's peer group, and the kinds of activities one participates in as a consequence of both one's identity and one's peer group should shape the nature of one's pathway through adolescence (Erikson, 1968; Youniss & Yates, 1997).

ACTIVITIES AS PEER CONTEXTS

Activities link adolescents to certain types of peers. To the extent that one spends a lot of time in these activity settings with the other participants, it is likely that one's friends will be drawn from among the other participants. It is likely, also, that the collective behaviors of this peer group will influence the behaviors of each member. To the extent that this is true, some of the behavioral differences associated with activity participation may be a consequence of the behavioral differences of the peer groups and of the peer cultures associated with these different activity clusters. For example, adolescents who play on the same teams or work together on projects or performances are likely to spend considerable amounts of downtime together, developing new friendships; sharing experiences; discussing values, goals, and aspirations; and co-constructing activity-based peer cultures and identities. Adolescent friends are likely, also, to "go out for" activities together.

To test these ideas [using MSALT data], we examined the link between activity participation and the characteristics of one's high school friends. In the 10th and 12th grades, participants were asked what proportion of their friends regularly drank alcohol, used drugs, and skipped school and what proportion of their friends planned to go to college and were doing well in school. Response options ranged from 1, "none," to 5, "all."

At 10th and, particularly, 12th grades, the peer group characteristics were consistent with the outcomes reported earlier: Consistent with the positive association of activity group membership with academic outcomes, the peer groups for participants in each of the activities except team sports were characterized by a higher proportion of friends who planned to attend college and were doing well in school than the peer groups of nonparticipants. Consistent with the protective association of prosocial activities with drug and alcohol use, adolescents involved in prosocial activities had fewer friends who used alcohol and drugs and who skipped school than their peers. Finally, consistent with the association of team sports with increased drinking, adolescents who participated in team sports had a higher proportion of friends who drank than their peers.

We next classified participants as being in a relatively more risky or less risky peer context for each grade compared to mean proportion for that grade and then assessed the differential distribution of these peer context categories across our five activity types. Because the same adolescent can participate in more than one activity type, we ran separate chi-square analyses for each activity type. We then assessed the relation of peer contexts to our indicators of adolescent functioning in order to determine whether the characteristics of peer contexts were consistent with the types of outcomes associated with activity participation and activity-based social identities. Because these are new analyses, we provide more detailed statistical information along with the findings. We follow this procedure whenever we are reporting new findings.

Risky Peers

The distribution of having a relatively risky high school peer context differed significantly in ways consistent with the patterns reported earlier for activity group differences in risky behaviors in two activity types for everyone (prosocial activities [χ^2 = 19.86 ($p < .001$)] and performing arts [χ^2 = 10.69 ($p < .01$)]) and in one for girls (academic clubs [χ^2 = 4.05 ($p < .05$)]). In each case, the activity participants reported fewer risky peers than would be expected by chance.

Academic Peers

Having a relatively more academically oriented group of friends was predicted, also, by activity participation: Participants in prosocial activities (χ^2 = 13.97 [$p < .01$]), team sports (χ^2 = 28.02 [$p < .001$]), performing arts (χ^2 = 4.97 [$p < .05$]), school promotion activities (χ^2 = 14.43 [$p < .001$]), and academic clubs (χ^2 10.674 [$p < .01$]) had a higher proportion of academic friends than expected by chance. In contrast, nonparticipants in each of these activities had fewer academic friends than expected by chance. These patterns were true for both females and males with one exception: sports. Although female athletes were more likely than expected to have high proportions of academically oriented friends (χ^2 = 49.997 [$p < .001$]), male athletes were not (χ^2 = 1.15). Thus, as predicted, the nature of one's friends did vary in the predicted directions across the five activity types. These findings are consistent with the work being done by others reported earlier (e.g., Eckert, 1989). Similar to these other studies, we find that activity settings can be linked to both risky and academic peer groups in ways that map nicely onto the association of activity involvement with both risky and positive behavioral outcomes. In the future, we will assess the extent to which the characteristics of one's peer group are one of the mediators of the relation between activity participation and other developmental outcomes.

ACTIVITIES AS IDENTITY FORMATION CONTEXTS

Like Erikson (1963) and Youniss & Yates (1997), we believe that voluntary participation in discretionary activities stimulates assessment of one's talents, values, interests, and place in the social structure. To the extent that more rigidly structured arenas of participation such as school and work provide less freedom to explore and express identity options than discretionary activities, adolescents should find more personal development opportunities, including experiences related to reflection and exploration, in youth activities than in academic settings. In support of this suggestion, Hansen and colleagues found that adolescents were more likely to say that the youth development activities (particularly faith-based, service-related, and sports) "got me thinking about who I am" or "doing new things" than academic classes did, and that those experiences differed, depending on the type of activity (Hansen, Larson, & Dworkin, 2003).

Also, activities provide a forum in which to express and refine one's identity (Eccles, 1987; Eccles & Barber, 1999). We refer to this aspect of activities as attainment value—the value of an activity to demonstrate to oneself and to others that one is the kind of person one most hopes to be. Eccles (1987), for example, argued that gender-role identity influences activity participation because activities vary in the extent to which they provide the opportunity to explore one's masculine or feminine self. Participating in team sports provides a very good example of these processes. Engaging in sports allows one to demonstrate that one is an athlete or a "jock" and to explore whether being an athlete or a jock is a comfortable identity. The decision to engage in sports should be influenced by the extent to which one places high value on being athletic or being a jock. Engaging in sports should also facilitate the internalization of an identity as an athlete or a jock. To the extent that one both develops a jock identity and engages in sports, one is likely to pick up other characteristics associated with the athletic peer culture in one's social world. We explored these hypotheses with data from MSALT.

At the 10th-grade level, we asked the participants to make a prototype judgment regarding their identity. Because the movie *The Breakfast Club* was quite popular at the time, we asked the participants to indicate which of the five characters (*princess, jock, brain, basket-case,* or *criminal*) they were most like, after ignoring the sex of the character. Less than 5% left the question blank. Nine percent selected the *criminal*; 11% the *basket-case*; 12% the *brain*; 28% the *jock*; and 40% the *princess.* Although there was a gender stereotypic distribution, there were sufficient numbers of each sex in each of the five identity groups to allow for analyses.

In summary, in Eccles and Barber (1999), we found that the patterns of developmental outcomes differed depending on the type of activity adolescents were involved in and their social identity group. Both involvement in prosocial activities and having a *brain* identity were associated with low alcohol and drug use and more positive academic outcomes. Also, these adolescents had the most academically oriented peer group and the fewest friends who drank or used drugs. The *jocks* were most involved in sports; the *princesses* reported the highest rates of involvement in school spirit and governance activities. Both involvements in sports and school spirit activities and having a *jock* or a *princess* social identity were associated with a mixed pattern of outcomes: positive academic outcomes and higher alcohol use. Not surprisingly, a relatively high proportion of these adolescents' friends was both academically oriented and regularly drank alcohol. The *criminals* were not generally engaged in organized extracurricular activities, were involved in risky behaviors such as alcohol and drug use, and had the highest proportion of friends who both drank and used drugs. The *criminals'* most common activity was sports.

Negative Consequences of Dropping Out of Sports for the Jocks

What are the consequences of dropping out of a highly valued activity such as sports that is also central to one's identity? Among our 10th-grade athletes, those who discontinued sport participation by 12th grade started lower and declined in their sports ability self-concepts, while those who continued to play had higher sports ability self-concepts at 10th grade, which got even higher by the 12th grade (Hunt, 2002). These results suggest there is an identity-affirming role of continued sports play in the domain of sports competence.

To further examine the value of sports to one's identity, we tested the convergence of sports play, activity participation, and jock identity: The three-way interaction was significant for depressed mood. As one would expect within our framework, those youth who saw themselves as *jocks* in the 10th grade and were no longer playing sports at 12th grade reported among the highest levels of depressed mood. Interestingly, the other group that showed relatively high levels of depressed mood was the group of students who did not consider themselves to be *jocks* in Grade 10 and were involved only in sports at Grade 12. These two groups share a poor identity activity fit: They are either not doing what is most consistent with their prior activity identity or they are doing something that is not consistent with their prior activity-based identity. Equally interestingly, the group of students who had considered themselves as *jocks* at Grade 10 and who were involved in other activities but not sports at Grade 12 looked quite good on this aspect of mental health. Perhaps these youth had found an alternative to sports once participating in competitive high school sports was no longer an option.

Dropping out of sports may also undermine attachment to school. Though a sense of belonging at school can result from a number of personal and social contextual factors, extracurricular activities are an especially likely path to school attachment, particularly for those youth who do not excel academically. Participating in extracurricular activities should predict better academic achievement, higher educational aspirations, and reduced likelihood of dropping out of school.

Several researchers, including us, have documented this relation (e.g., Barber et al., 2001; Eccles & Barber, 1999; Mahoney and Cairns, 1997; Marsh, 1993; Marsh & Kleitman, 2002). Furthermore, some studies suggest that the relation is especially true for sports and for youth who are at risk. For example, in the nationally representative National Education Longitudinal Study (NELS) data set, athletic participation was related to numerous positive academic indicators, including educational aspirations, time on homework, and level of postsecondary education (Marsh & Kleitman, 2003). These effects were particularly pronounced for extramural sports compared to intramural, and for team sports compared to individual sports. Additionally, in MSALT, the relation of high school sport participation to educational attainment at age 24 was particularly strong for those males who reported having the highest proportion of friends who engaged in risky behavior.

But what are the consequences of dropping out of team sports in the MSALT population? Consistent with our theoretical perspective, the association of discontinuing team sports participation was most negative for those athletes who highly valued sports (Barber, Jacobson, Horn, & Jacobs, 1997).

Taken together, these findings on activities as identity contexts suggest that one mechanism through which organized activities have a positive influence is through their validation of identity. When activities confirm or support one's self concept, they are also likely to promote psychological well-being and attachment to the institutional settings that provide the participation opportunities. When opportunities are withdrawn, or are unavailable to those who desire them, or are a bad match to the interests of the adolescents, such support for identity exploration and affirmation is likely to be lacking.

ACTIVITY PARTICIPATION AND CONNECTIONS WITH NONFAMILIAL ADULTS

Another mechanism through which activities can influence positive development is through the social networks created through participation. Structured out-of-school and extracurricular activities provide adolescents with access to caring nonfamilial adults. Coaches, club advisors, and other involved adults often invest a great deal of time and attention in these young people—acting as teachers, mentors, friends, gate keepers, and problem solvers (e.g., Cooper, Denner, & Lopez, 1999; Elder & Conger, 2000; Youniss & Yates, 1997). With the right adults, such contact is likely to have positive effects on development particularly during adolescence.

But, like peers, adults can have both positive and negative effects. Work in sports psychology provides some of the most compelling evidence of the importance of the characteristics of the adult supervisors in structured youth activities. In general, these studies show that youth develop better mental health, motivation, and values in sports programs that emphasize skill acquisition and mastery motivation rather than social comparison and winning (e.g., Roberts & Treasure, 1992) and that stress the importance of coaches providing strong emotional support (e.g., Smoll, Smith, Barnett, & Everett, 1993). Furthermore, using an experimental design, Smoll and colleagues demonstrated that youth who work with a coach who has had a 3-hour training program focused on emotional support show greater increases in their self-esteem than youth working with coaches who have not had this training.

We investigated participation in team sports and school involvement activities and connection to nonfamilial adults. In addition to the simple yes/no participation dichotomy for team sport participation, we examined which students had continued with sports and which ones had dropped out by the time of the 12th-grade data collection and created a second sports variable with three categories: nonparticipants, participants who discontinued play, and participants who continued their affiliation with teams through 12th grade.

Both sport and school involvement participants had a broader range of adults to talk with at school than their noninvolved peers. In addition, the participants in both team sports and school involvement reported more frequent educational and occupational advice from teachers and counselors. Again, the greatest amount of advice was reported by those still competing in sports in 12th grade. Thus, although many students reported talking to teachers or counselors about their educational or occupational futures, many fewer had school-based adult support for personal problems or a diverse network of adults to consult for advice. Those athletes who participated in team sports throughout high school were especially privileged on these dimensions. Such adult investment, at a critical developmental time for future job and education decision making, may be a partial explanation for the advantages in educational attainment and job quality evidenced in young adulthood by these athletes (Barber et al., 2001).

DISCUSSION OF NEXT STEPS AND POLICY IMPLICATIONS

More work is needed on identifying the specific mechanisms through which participation in structured activities influence children's and adolescents' development. Such work is particularly important if we hope to use such activity settings as positive socialization contexts for our children. As noted at the beginning of this article, many people are interested in the potential of such contexts for facilitating positive youth development and preventing problematic youth development. Both governmental agencies and private foundations are investing substantial amounts of money on such programs in the hope that they will promote positive youth development particularly for youth living in poor communities (Eccles & Gootman, 2002). It is critical that these investments be directed toward programs that work. Do we know enough to help policymakers and financial supporters pick the right programs to support? Yes and no. In a recent committee report from the National Research Council and Institute of Medicine, the committee concluded that we do know quite a bit and that many excellent programs have been designed and evaluated (see Eccless & Gootman, 2002).

However, although general characteristics of effective programs have been identified, we still know very little about the specific mechanisms through which these programs work. The existence of such programs and the increasing call for more programs provide social scientists with a unique opportunity to work with program developers and program evaluators to design evaluations that will let us study these mechanisms (Lerner & Galambos, 1998). The research reviewed in the article provides examples of what can be done using longitudinal designs guided by strong theory. We are at a point in the field of positive youth development to do more such longitudinal studies as well as to do experimental studies designed to test specific theoretical hypotheses about the mediating mechanisms.

Much more research is needed also on the role of participant characteristics.

In conclusion, we now know enough about the kinds of programs likely to have positive effects on children's and adolescents' development. We need to know more about the specific mechanism that explain these effects and we need to know more about which programs work for which youth—that is, we need to know more about the interaction between the participants' and the programs' characteristics in determining the effectiveness of specific program characteristics for specific individuals. We believe that this type of work will contribute to our fundamental understanding of the impact of social experiences on human development. The growing interest in designing effective structured activity-based programs for youth provides a unique opportunity to do high-quality, theoretically driven naturalistic studies. We hope that psychologists, social scientists, and developmental scientists will take advantage of this opportunity.

Discussion Questions

What was your experience with extra- and co-curricular activities as a student? Did it mirror the research results? How or how not?

What are the positives and negatives of extra- and co-curricular experiences?

———————— ⌘ ————————

Jacquelynne S. Eccles is a professor at the University of Michigan.

Bonnie L. Barber is a professor at the University of Arizona.

Margaret Stone is a professor at the University of Arizona.

James Hunt is a professor at the University of Arizona.

Article 22

AFTER-SCHOOL PROGRAMS ARE MAKING A DIFFERENCE

MARIANNE RUSSELL KUGLER

A young woman recently came up to me after I had given a speech. She introduced herself and said she was a college student in a family of five older children and one much younger child. Her little sister had been home alone nearly every school day for at least 3 and often 4 hours from the age of 8. As the girl entered middle school the family had begun to worry because she spent more and more time in her room sleeping or just daydreaming, even when the family was home. Her grades were dropping and her teachers said she was definitely not working up to her potential. Then the college student, with tears in her eyes, said, "This year K's in eighth grade and one of her teachers talked her into joining the computer club after school. Within two weeks she was a totally different person. Now she stays at school every day after school. She is not only a member of the computer club; she tutors younger students and

is a member of the chess club as well. Last night at dinner we couldn't shut her up. She had been on a field trip and she wanted to tell us all about it. I just want to thank you and the Mott Foundation from our whole family." What magic power do co-curricular, extended-day, after-school programs have? Why do I hear this story, and many others like it, over and over again as I travel across the United States?

The sudden growth of after-school programs is the result of three major societal concerns. The first, a dramatic shift in employment patterns, has resulted in many, many young people like K who are home alone for long periods of time in the late afternoon. The estimate is that between 8 and 15 million young people (including secondary students) and 35% of 12-year-olds have the same experience every day (U.S. Department of Education, 2000b). They come home to an empty house in an empty neighborhood. They tend not to

SOURCE: Excerpted from Kugler, M. R. (2001). After-school programs are making a difference. *NASSP Bulletin, 85*(9), 3–11. Reprinted by permission of Sage.

be allowed out of the house. They tend to be afraid to answer the door and to have limited phone access, but they often have unlimited television access. This pattern translates to 15 to 20 waking hours weekly without live human contact for as many as 28% of the nation's young people during a time that they should be learning to develop relationships and experience their community. In addition, teachers complain that students home alone are less likely to get their homework done and more likely to have classroom behavior problems (National Commission on Time and Learning, 1994). After-school programs provide these students with safe places to be, positive relationships with other students and adults, and opportunities for active learning beyond the classroom. As published in a *Chicago Tribune* article (March 4, 2001), Chicago Public Schools chief Paul Vallas is reported to have said, "Our philosophy is that schools should be open all day, year-round." In the same article, a Chicago professor, referring to women entering the workplace, said, "We no longer have extended families in the neighborhoods, and schools are picking up the slack." A recent New York study reported the results of a parent survey in which more than half of surveyed parents indicated that their children's participation in the studied program helped parents miss less work than before, hold onto their jobs more easily, and work more hours (After-School Corporation, 2000b).

The second societal concern results from the realization, for some people an astonishing discovery, is that all children can learn. Although some students need more time or different approaches to learning, most voters are now convinced that the achievement gap is an artifact of students' limited experiences, poorly funded schools, and struggling families, not the inevitable result of low potential. Given this realization, the obligation to close the achievement gap has become a critical issue. Extended-day programs, with homework help, poetry and chess clubs, drama programs, field trips, and reading tutors, provide the extra learning opportunities needed to help close the achievement gap. More than 80% of the programs receiving federal

funds through the 21st Century Community Learning Centers initiative for after-school programs include a reading component as one of the activities. Mathematics activities or clubs (91%) and science clubs (76%) are also well represented in after-school programs (U.S. Department of Education, 2001). A recent 12-district California study indicated achievement gains for after-school students in reading that were almost twice as large as the statewide increase and nearly as high in mathematics (University of California at Irvine, 2001). A significant finding in this study indicated that those students who participated more in after-school programs improved their scores even more.

The *St. Petersburg Times* reported on an after-school experiment in 8 middle schools and 11 high schools designed to answer the question, "Is it better to help struggling students while they are struggling or months later in summer school?" (March 12, 2001). One student participating in the extended-day program indicated that he was getting extra help with algebra after school and had moved his grade from a C to an A because of the help. The article also quoted a parent who said her daughter was "going to school more." The federally funded 21st Century Community Learning Centers programs report a consistent pattern of improved school attendance when after-school programs are implemented (U.S. Department of Education, 2001). In several programs the average number of days absent was reduced by as much as 15%. The reduction in student absences was nearly 25% in one program. Improved grades often result from improved attendance. The California study found that students who had patterns of frequent absence demonstrated greater improvement in attendance after entering an after-school program (University of California at Irvine, 2001).

The third societal concern that has contributed to the growth in after-school programs involves the patterns of youth crime and youth victimization. Teen crime is highest between tile hours of 3:00 and 6:00 P.M. A 1997 FBI report indicated that juvenile crime peaks between 3:00 and 8:00 P.M., tripling during these hours

(Newman, Fox, Flynn, & Christeson, 2000). The Office of Juvenile Justice and Delinquency Prevention reported in 1996 that children are most likely to be the victims of violent crime by nonfamily members between 2:00 and 6:00 P.M. (Newman et al., 2000). Others are simply bored, and their remedies for boredom are intentional risks to themselves and others. In one Michigan community, the rate of teen crime dropped by 40% when after-school programs were instituted (U.S. Department of Education, 2000a). A Police Athletic League after-school program in Baltimore reduced crime by 42% in the first year, and many other communities are experiencing similarly improved safety patterns (After-School Corporation, 2000a).

After-school programs have existed for the youngest members of some communities for many years. These three important societal issues—changing employment patterns, achievement challenges, and community safety—have led to the conviction that extended-day programs are now necessary for many secondary students as well (Lake Snell Perry & Associates & The Tarrance Group, 2001). The public believes that, just as latchkey children need these programs, so do students who need help with homework or broader learning opportunities. Young people who need adult and peer relationships, who have special talents or interests, or who want to develop specific skills also need after-school programs. In fact, in a recent voter poll, more than 90% of the respondents indicated that all children and youth can benefit from such programs. Voters see these programs as necessary for their communities and for the nation as a whole.

BUILDING PROGRAMS

Although many after-school programs begin at the suggestion of principals and school staff members, a surprising number are created through the interest of community members. In some cases the school advisory council or parent–teacher association starts the process. In others, a group of interested community businesses gets the ball rolling. At the national level one of the principal forces behind the scaling up of after-school programs is the Partnership for Family Involvement in Education, a group of business leaders and citizens formed to support the work of education and to advise the U.S. Department of Education on family and education issues.

No matter how the idea begins, one of the first steps to building a strong program is creating an advisory committee. In some secondary schools the advisory committee is composed of parents, students, and staff members. In others, there are two committees—one composed of adults and one of students. In many programs the overall committee meets monthly and is responsible for the general development of the program, but the student committee meets weekly. The responsibilities of the student committee include surveying students, suggesting activities, monitoring student attendance, and planning field trips.

The middle school Bridges Program in Flint, Michigan, for example, includes a student committee that meets weekly and that pays close attention to the rhythm of interest and suggests when a unit has begun to lose momentum. The committee surveys the adult community to find special talents and interests that provide the basis for new units and activities. They survey the students and lead focus groups to identify the student interests and attitudes toward existing programs. One young leader from this program made a presentation to a congressional subcommittee in spring of 2000 and astonished the members with her depth of knowledge about the program and its management.

Almost every after-school program in the country includes some components designed to provide homework help. The Boys and Girls Clubs and the Virtual YMCAs have excellent homework help designs. Other programs use combinations of technology and tutoring to provide strong support for students. One mother in New York said, "The greatest part is the homework help. I'm not fighting with the kids to get their homework done but just looking it over and having them explain it now. As a single mother with teenagers, this is terrific!" A recent article in the *Omaha World-Herald* (February 3, 2001) described an after-school program in the Omaha School District that provides study skills training and homework assistance, weekly tutoring, regular mentoring, and parent training. According to the article, the program is designed to prevent school dropout, especially among American Indian students.

Few successful after-school programs run without a staff member dedicated to the coordination of the program. In most cases the staff member is assigned to work from late morning until the close of the program. In some cases program coordinators are also teachers or administrators in the school; in others, they are responsible only for the work of the after-school programs, and their school-day time is used in planning and in coordinating with the core day staff. Many coordinators are selected because they are community leaders and have the trust of the students and their families. In a large Sacramento, California, program, for example, the assistant principal for instruction serves as the director of the extended-day programs, but the program coordinator and assistant coordinator are leaders from the community.

After-school program staffing is a serious challenge. In less successful programs the staff turnover creates a constant need for programming changes and the danger of unprepared activity leaders and teachers. By contrast, successful programs are often staffed by people who have worked in them for many years, and the turnover in any given year is zero. Programs with low staff turnover tend to have a mix of staff members, some of whom come from the community and some who are already teachers in the school. These programs are responsive to the special needs and talents of the staff as well as to the interests of the students and are flexible in the scheduling of activities. College students make excellent staff members, often staying for their entire college career. Senior citizens may also make good staff members; in one exciting

program in the South the coordinator and all of the staff are senior citizens.

Many programs report an increase in parent participation in the school-day activities as a result of the after-school programs (After-School Corporation, 2000b). The use of community leaders as after-school staff members and the more informal setting found in most after-school programs seem to lead to a more open relationship between the home and the school and to an increase in trust.

Few secondary schools alone run extended-day programs. Most involve partnerships with Boys and Girls Clubs, YWCA and YMCA programs, Campfire Boys and Girls, the Extension Service, and many other community organizations. Libraries and museums are developing programs for secondary students in which either staff members visit the schools or students visit the sites on a regular basis. In one after-school program in Arizona, the zoo brings animals to the school weekly and science museum staff members run a daily science club. Faith-based groups often provide regular field trips and service opportunities. The key to the success of these partnerships seems to be an intentional, mutually accepted structure with written goals and benchmarks and regular meetings.

Balance in activity is one of the challenges of running after-school programs. Recently a high school principal told a large audience that their school had to start over in preparation for the second year of the after-school program. In the first year they had emphasized academics to such an extent, doing many of the same things the students did during the school day, that the students had all dropped out of the program. He said that the second year they formed a committee, did a survey, and were trained on the development of hands-on activities. In addition, they formed a partnership with a university and hired college students as mentors. In the third year the program grew to include nearly every student in the school at some time during the year, developed a large, popular summer program, and was now one of the jewels of the school.

The Community Oriented Policing (COP) program for students at risk at five Los Angeles high schools is a good example of this balance, providing students with 15 additional hours of library and computer lab time, a writing workshop, weight-training class, Scrabble club, hikes, cycling, nutrition programs, and community service opportunities. Primary partners in the program include the Los Angeles Unified School District and the Los Angeles Police Academy.

Last fall I had the privilege of visiting several small rural schools along the Mississippi. At one of the schools I attended a potluck in the gymnasium where I sat across from a young woman who had graduated two months earlier, a beautiful teen with a few teeth missing and a painfully clean but too large dress. She was clearly bright and shy. I searched for something to say that would start a real conversation, beginning with the usual adult query, "What are you going to do now?" She lit up! "Oh," she said. "I have a full scholarship to the University of Arkansas." "What are you thinking of studying?" I inquired. "Well," she said, "I've always been a good student and I tutored in the after-school program. I thought I wanted to be a doctor, so the after-school coordinator arranged for me to spend time in a clinic in the evenings during the last month of school. I discovered that I don't want the responsibility doctors have, but I still love the subjects, so the after-school coordinator and I searched the Net. I am going to go to Arkansas and become a forensic pathologist."

STRONG PROGRAM ELEMENTS

This story of the future forensic pathologist includes elements of four of the most popular and productive of the extended-day activities: tutoring, community service, technology, and career development. Recent research indicates that tutoring projects, including peer tutoring, are almost always productive for most students if the tutors are given adequate training (Owings & Kaplan, 2001). The most effective tutorial extended-day programs involve either community tutors or peer tutors who receive monthly training. The training sessions include preparation of materials and construction of academic games, discussion of child and youth development concepts, and planning of concrete approaches to grouping and time on task. Most frequently, the reading and mathematics specialists for the district or the master secondary teachers do this training. The keys to a successful tutoring project seem to be a positive relationship between the tutor and the student, the tutor's confident knowledge of the subject being taught, and the varied learning experiences provided for the student.

Community service, a popular second element of successful after-school programs, can be a particularly effective way of connecting secondary students with school and community and of connecting basic skills learning with the real world need for such skill (Superintendents' Task Force, 1999). Programs at the secondary level that have been especially successful with student service learning projects have tended to involve longer term experiences—for example, twice a week for a semester at one site, rather than a menu of projects where each student selects a different one each week. Although many schools grant graduation credit for student participation in service learning experiences, many do not. In some cases, participation fulfills a graduation requirement but does not lead to course credit. Effective programs include a regular schedule of training and debriefing for the participants. Many communities have clean parks and beautiful murals and better young readers because of these programs. Many secondary students have made their college selection and the choice of their future career on the basis of community service experiences.

Technology is a third element of effective extended-day programs. Even in schools where classroom computers are dusty with lack of use or where early Apples are the only technological tools available, the computer in the school library with Internet access or the office computer gets heavy after-school use for homework help. In schools with intentional extended-day programs involving technology, the outcomes have been exciting and surprising. In many middle schools the computer club is the most popular 3–6 P.M. activity. Two interesting examples of interactive after-school projects were created in the Midwest. In one case, first- and second-year students in a small urban high school are each assigned a university student mentor. The mentor and the high school student read and then discuss (via e-mail) a work of literature. During after-school time the mentor and the student work on essays and other take-home assignments required for the next day's English class. In most cases the mentor and the student never meet but develop productive online relationships that result in higher level analysis skills, a deeper understanding of the messages of the literature, and greater clarity and elegance in the written language. In another program each student creates and manages his or her own Web site. In several cases students from the after-school computer clubs stay into the evening to serve as teachers for the adults who arrive to learn about computers.

Several programs combine video work with computer technology, and the students create one presentation each quarter built around a student-selected theme. Although many extended-day programs in the early stages of development used technology to provide remedial opportunities, most programs have gone on to create experiences that combine the development of basic skills with problem-solving skills and opportunities for creativity.

The fourth component of productive after-school programs is career development. Many secondary schools use after-school time to create awareness of and interest in careers and provide hands-on experiences related to those careers. Activities in such programs include listening to speakers from a variety of careers, participating in field trips and short-term work placements, taking interest and skills assessments, and receiving training on résumé writing and interviewing. College campus visits are among the most frequent field trips in extended-day programs. Local businesses often support this work financially and by supplying volunteers.

Discussion Questions

What societal concerns are after-school programs targeting?

What elements are necessary for extracurricular programs to be effective in terms of achieving desired results?

Marianne Russell Kugler is a professor at the Université Laval in Canada.

Article 23

THE EFFECT OF INTERSCHOLASTIC SPORTS PARTICIPATION ON ACADEMIC ACHIEVEMENT OF MIDDLE LEVEL SCHOOL STUDENTS

LARRY J. STEPHENS

LAURA A. SCHABEN

Eighth graders ($n = 136$) were divided into two groups: students who had participated in at least one interscholastic sport and were classified as athletes ($n = 73$), and students who did not participate in interscholastic sports and were classified as non-athletes ($n = 63$). The mean grade point average (GPA) for each group and subgroup was computed and compared by group, subgroup, and sex. There were six categories of sports participation, ranging from no sports to five sports. As interscholastic sports participation increased, GPAs improved.

The relationship between academic achievement and participation in interscholastic sports at middle level schools, high schools, and colleges is of interest to principals and college administrators. The relationship, which may well differ at the three academic levels, plays a role in answering questions about the amount of money, time, and personnel that should be devoted to interscholastic sports programs at the middle level and high schools. At the college level, a successful football program, for example, can mean income for the college. However, this is not true for high school football programs.

SOURCE: Excerpted from Stephens, L. J., & Schaben L. A. (2002). The effect of interscholastic sports participation on academic achievement of middle level school students. *NASSP Bulletin*, *86*(3), 34–41. Reprinted by permission of Sage.

Considerable research (reviewed below) exists concerning the relationship between academic achievement and participation in inter-scholastic sports at the high school and the college levels, but little research exists about such a relationship at middle level schools. This research investigates some aspects of this relationship at the middle level school. In particular, students in Grade 8 who participated in sports were compared with students who did not with respect to academic achievement. Gender differences were also investigated in the study, as well as the interaction between the level of sports participation and academic achievement.

Previous Research

The importance of extracurricular activities (sometimes referred to as *student activities* or *co-curricular activities*) was discussed in two 1985 journal articles. Gholson (1985) stated that "there is a positive correlation between student involvement in cocurricular activities and success in nonacademic pursuits following high school and college" (p. 19). Joekel (1985) pointed out that achievement in co-curricular activities is a factor that can predict success in life beyond school.

Studies from the 1960s and earlier revealed that athletic participation had a negative effect on academics. One team of researchers reviewed 41 studies and concluded that non-athletes performed slightly better in schoolwork than athletes (Ballantine, 1981). The majority of studies from the past two decades, however, indicate that students involved in sports excel in the classroom. Ballantine cited six studies showing a positive relationship between academic achievement and athletic participation, and a study by the U.S. Department of Education revealed that students who participate in co-curricular activities are three times more likely to have a grade point average (GPA) of 3.0 or better (Mihoces, 1996).

High School Students

Soltz (1986) found statistical significance in the higher GPAs of athletes compared to non-athletes, whereas Durbin (1986) and Silliker and Quirk (1997) reported that athletes actually excel during their season of competition. A study by Stegman and Stephens (2000) revealed that high-participation athletes (at least one sport each year of high school) outperformed low-participant athletes in class rank, overall GPA, and math GPA. Both female and male athletes in the high-participant group outperformed their low-participant counterparts, but the differences were only statistically significant for the female athletes. Not only did the high-participant female athletes outperform the low-participant female athletes, but they also had higher GPAs and GPA-based class ranks when compared to low-participant and nonparticipant males and female. These results enhance Lederman's (1989) finding that 78% of female athletes competing in Division I basketball had a B or better average in high school.

Middle Level School Students

Buhrmann's (1972) findings for students in Grades 7, 8, and 9 were similar to Stegman and Stephens's (2000) findings for high school students. The athletes who participated in inter-scholastic sports for many seasons and many years had a higher level of scholarship than the athletes who competed in only a few seasons or for only one year. He found the same relationship to be true between athletes and non-athletes.

Two convincing studies of middle level school students used data from the National Educational Longitudinal Study of 1988 (NELS:88), a long-term project sponsored by the U.S. Department of Education's National Center for Educational Statistics (NCES). The NCES used questionnaires, cognitive achievement tests, and other sources to obtain data from 10,944 nationally represented students in Grade 8. Prior to NELS:88, several researchers questioned the validity of studies that did not include factors such as race, gender, and socioeconomic status (SES). Because NELS:88 incorporated these factors, the results of prior studies were validated. Gerber (1996) found that SES was significantly related to achievement for both African American and White students in Grade 8. She also found the relationship of achievement to gender was even more significant than the relationship to SES. Even after eliminating the effects of SES and gender, Gerber's analyses showed a significant relationship between co-curricular participation and academic achievement. Interestingly, the effect was strongest in mathematics. Furthermore, school co-curricular activities showed a stronger relationship to achievement than did outside co-curricular activities.

A second team of researchers who used data from NELS:88 was Braddock, Royster, Winfield, and Hawkins (1991). Their results were similar to those of Gerber. They contended that students involved in interscholastic sports are more likely to look forward to core curriculum classes and less likely to exhibit school-related social conduct problems such as fighting and misbehaving. This finding was unchanged when factors such as SES, age, standardized test scores, and family and school characteristics were statistically controlled.

PARTICIPANTS

Participants in this study were students in Grade 8 during the 1998–1999 academic year at an urban middle level school in Omaha, NE. Both athletes and non-athletes were asked to participate in the study to determine if any correlation exists between academic achievement and interscholastic sports participation. Each of the participants was classified as either an athlete or a non-athlete. For this study, an athlete is defined as any student who participated in one or more of the five interscholastic sports seasons during the 1998–1999 school year. A non-athlete is defined as a student who did not participate in interscholastic sports.

Of the 136 participants, 73 were athletes (42 male and 31 female) and 63 were non-athletes (26 male and 37 female). There were an equal number (68) of male and female students overall.

PROCEDURE

Data collection was initiated after securing permission from the school district to perform the study. School records and reports supplied semester math course and grade, cumulative GPA, national percentile on the math portion of the California Achievement Test (CAT), and the sex of each participant. During math class, a questionnaire was distributed describing the study and requesting that each student record his or her level of participation in interscholastic sports. Once the data file was complete, four comparisons were made: athletes versus non-athletes, male athletes versus male non-athletes, female athletes versus female non-athletes, and female athletes versus male athletes. MINITAB (version 13.30; www.minitab.com) was used to evaluate the differences in mean math grades, mean GPAs, and mean CAT scores between each group. Standard deviations and significance test data were also computed for each comparison.

RESULTS

Athletes had significantly higher GPAs than non-athletes. Within-sex comparisons produced similar results. Both male and female athletes had significantly higher GPAs than non-athletes of the same sex. In conjunction with the findings of Stegman and Stephens (2000), female athletes had significantly higher GPAs than male athletes.

Results for mean CAT scores and mean math grades for each comparison parallel the results for GPAs. Athletes had significantly higher math CAT scores (64% vs. 48%) and math grades than non-athletes, whereas male and female athletes performed significantly better than non-athletes of the same sex in both measures. Female athletes had slightly higher math CAT scores and math grades than male athletes, but these differences were not statistically significant.

Non-athletes account for nearly one-half of the participants, and their GPAs and CAT scores are well distributed in the zero column of each figure. As the number of sports increases along the horizontal axis, the number of participants in each column decreases. This is not unexpected, but the corresponding GPAs and CAT scores reveal an unexpected and remarkable trend. As interscholastic sports participation increases, GPAs and CAT scores improve considerably over the previous category before being evenly distributed in the column. In every case but one, the lowest GPA and CAT score in any category exceeded the lowest GPA and CAT score of the previous category. Most notably, the two students who participated in the five-sport category had GPAs near the top of their class. There is clearly a strong relationship between academic success and athletic participation.

DISCUSSION

The age-old question from teachers and parents, "Does participation in interscholastic sports harm the academic achievement of students?" appears to have been answered in the negative in this and numerous other studies. In fact, involvement in interscholastic sports seems to enhance the academic performance of students. The question now is why do athletes perform better academically than non-athletes? Do they get higher grades because they are athletes, or do they get higher grades because of something innate? Does the latter imply that an athlete would continue to do well academically in the absence of athletics? Consider a high school graduate who earned a 4.0 GPA and who was highly involved in interscholastic sports. Would that student have performed equally well if athletics had not been part of his or her experience?

This question is not easy to answer. Many non-athletes are outstanding students, but their successes cannot help investigators determine whether athletes would have performed differently under other circumstances.

Participation in athletics can help students build discipline, set goals, organize time, and develop self-confidence. Athletes who transfer these skills to their academics are greeted with success, yet the effects of athletic participation reach beyond classroom walls and gymnasium floors. Much can be said about the effect of sports on the social world of students. In a study by Goldberg and Chandler (1992), each of the 182 junior high school participants identified academic performance as the primary source of parental approval, but 68% of girls and 90% of boys agreed that boys gain peer recognition and popularity by being outstanding athletes. Athletics contribute, whether really or perceptually, to the identity and social status of students. For this reason, the role of athletics cannot be ignored when trying to comprehend the developmental and socialization processes of adolescents.

Limitations of the Study

Two limitations of the study are sample size and lack of control for SES. A larger sample size would have been more helpful. An analysis adjusted for SES would also be desirable.

SUMMARY

The reason athletes excel in the classroom, at this point, does not seem important. The fact remains that students involved in co-curricular activities, especially interscholastic sports, perform better than those who are not involved. All of the studies reviewed in this article reinforce this assertion. When budget cuts threaten the existence of interscholastic sports programs, administrators, counselors, teachers, parents, and students can negotiate or even diminish the effects of such proposed cuts with data indicating the academic benefits of such programs to underscore their necessity. Although not every student will be a stellar athlete, the numerous studies linking academic success to co-curricular participation indicate that educators should encourage students to be involved in interscholastic sports, intramurals, or other co-curricular activities.

Discussion Questions

Specifically, what is the relationship between sports participation and middle school student performance?

How do you feel about the allocation of resources, the pressure, and the competition generated by interscholastic athletics at the middle and high school levels.

Larry J. Stephens is a professor at the University of Nebraska, Omaha.

Laura A. Schaben is a science teacher in the Omaha Public Schools.

Article 24

HEARTS AND MINDS

Military Recruitment and the High School Battlefield

WILLIAM AYERS

In her book *Purple Hearts,* the documentary photographer Nina Berman presents 40 photographs—two each of 20 U.S. veterans of the American war in Iraq—plus a couple of accompanying paragraphs of commentary from each vet in his or her own words.[1] Their comments cohere around their service, their sacrifice, their suffering. The Purple Heart binds them together—this award is their common experience, this distinction is what they embrace and what embraces them. This is what they live with.

Their views on war, on their time in arms, on where they hope they are headed with their lives, are various; their ways of making sense about the U.S. military mission, wildly divergent.

Josh Olson, 24 years old, begins: "We bent over backwards for these people, but they ended up screwing us over, stabbing us in the back. A lot of them, I mean, they're going to have to be killed. . . . As Americans we've taken it upon ourselves to almost cure the world's problems I guess, give everybody else a chance. I guess that's how we're good-hearted. . . ." He's missing his right leg now and was presented with his Purple Heart at Walter Reed Military Hospital by President Bush himself. He feels it all—pride, anger, loss.

Jermaine Lewis, 23, describes growing up in a Chicago neighborhood where "death has always been around." He describes basic training as a place where "they break you down and then they try to build you up." To him, the "reasons for going to war were bogus, but we were right to go in there."

SOURCE: Excerpted from Ayers, W. (2006). Hearts and minds: Military recruitment and the high school battlefield. *Phi Delta Kappan, 87*(8), 594–599. Reprinted by permission of William Ayers.

The vets are all young, and several recall deciding to enlist when they were much younger still, more innocent, more vulnerable, but feeling somehow invincible. Jermaine Lewis says, "I've been dealing with the military since I was a sophomore in high school. They came to the school like six times a year, all military branches. They had a recruiting station like a block from our high school. It was just right there."

Tyson Johnson III, 22, wanted to get away from the poverty and death he saw all around him. His life was going nowhere, he thought, and so he signed on: "And here I am, back here . . . I don't know where it's going to end up."

Joseph Mosner enrolled when he was 19. "There was nothing out there," he writes. "There was no good jobs, so I figured this would have been a good thing."

Frederick Allen thought going to war would be "jumping out of planes." He joined up when recruiters came to his high school. "I thought it would be fun."

Adam Zaremba, 20, also enlisted while still in high school: "The recruiter called the house; he was actually looking for my brother and he happened to get me. I think it was because I didn't want to do homework for a while, and then I don't know, you get to wear a cool uniform. It just went on from there. I still don't even understand a lot about the Army." The Purple Heart seemed like a good thing from a distance, "but then when it happens you realize that you have to do something, or something has to happen to you in order to get it."

RECRUITING HIGH-SCHOOLERS

Military recruiting in high schools has been a mainstay of the so-called all-volunteer armed forces from the start. High school kids are at an age when being a member of an identifiable group with a grand mission and a shared spirit— and never underestimate a distinctive uniform— is of exaggerated importance, something gang recruiters in big cities also note with interest and exploit with skill. Kathy Dobie, quoting a military historian, notes that "basic training has been essentially the same in every army in every age, because it works with the same raw material that's always been there in teenage boys: a fair amount of aggression, a strong tendency to hang around in groups, and an absolute desperate desire to fit in."[2] Being cool and going along with the crowd are big things. Add the need to prove oneself to be a macho, strong, tough, capable person, combined with an unrealistic calculus of vulnerability and a constricted sense of options specifically in poor and working-class communities—all of this creates the toxic mix in a young person's head that can be a military recruiter's dream.

One of the most effective recruitment tools is Junior Reserve Officers' Training Corps (JROTC), the high school version of ROTC that was established by an act of Congress in 1916 "to develop citizenship and responsibility in young people."[3] JROTC is now experiencing the most rapid expansion in its history. Some credit the upsurge to Colin Powell's visit to South Central Los Angeles after the 1992 riots, when he was head of the Joint Chiefs of Staff. Powell stated that the solution to the problems of city youths was the kind of discipline and structure offered by the U.S. military. In the ensuing decade the number of JROTC programs doubled, with over half a million students enrolled at over 3,000 schools coast to coast and an annual Pentagon budget allocation in excess of $250 million. Today the evidence is clear: 40% of JROTC graduates eventually join the military, making the program a powerful recruiting device.

Chicago has the largest JROTC program in the country and the "most militarized school system in America,"[4] with more than 9,000 students enrolled in 45 JROTC programs, including one Navy and five Army JROTC academies that are run as "schools-within-a-school" and two full-time Army military academies, with another slated to open next year. That distinction is only the start: Chicago is also in the vanguard of the Middle School Cadet Corps (MSCC), with 26 programs in junior highs and middle schools involving 850 kids, some as young as 11.[5]

Defenders of the JROTC and MSCC claim that the goal is leadership and citizen development, dropout prevention, or simply the fun of dressing up and parading around. Skeptics point out that the Pentagon money for these programs provides needed resources for starving public schools and question why the military has become such an important route to adequate school funding. Chicago spends $2.8 million on JROTC and another $5 million on two military academies—"more than it spends on any other special or magnet program,"[6] and the Defense Department puts in an additional $600,000 for salaries and supplies.

There is no doubt that JROTC programs target poor, Black, and Latino kids who don't have the widest range of options to begin with. Recruiters know where to go: Whitney Young High School, a large, selective magnet school in Chicago, had seven military recruiter visits last year, compared to 150 visits from university recruiters; Schurz High School, which is 80% Hispanic, had 9 military and 10 university visits.[7] *New York Times* columnist Bob Herbert points out that all high schools are not equal in the eyes of the recruiters: "Schools with kids from wealthier families (and a high percentage of college-bound students) are not viewed as good prospects. . . . The kids in those schools are not the kids who fight America's wars."[8] Absent arts and sports programs or a generous array of clubs and activities, JROTC and its accompanying culture of war militarism, aggression, violence, repression, the demonization of others, and mindless obedience—becomes the default choice for poor kids attending low-income schools.

The military culture seeps in at all levels and has a more generally corrosive impact on education itself, narrowing curriculum choices and promoting a model of teaching as training and of learning as "just following orders." In reality, good teaching always involves thoughtful and complicated judgments, careful attention to relationships, and complex choices about how to challenge and nurture each student. Good teachers are not drill instructors. Authentic learning, too, is multidimensional and requires the constant construction and reconstruction of knowledge built on expanding experiences.

The educational model that employs teachers to simply pour imperial gallons of facts into empty vessels—ridiculed by Charles Dickens 150 years ago and discredited as a path to learning by modern psychologists and educational researchers—is making a roaring comeback. The rise of the military in schools adds energy to that malignant effort.

A vibrant democratic culture requires free people with minds of their own capable of making independent judgments. Education in a democracy resists obedience and conformity in favor of free inquiry and the widest possible exploration. Obedience training may have a place in instructing dogs, but not in educating citizens.

"MY RECRUITER LIED TO ME"

Today, 2 years into the invasion of Iraq, recruiters are consistently failing to meet monthly enlistment quotas, despite deep penetration into high schools, sponsorship of NASCAR and other sporting events, and a $3 billion Pentagon recruitment budget. Increasingly, recruiters are offering higher bonuses and shortened tours of duty; and violations of ethical guidelines and the military's own putative standards are becoming commonplace—in one highly publicized case, a recruiter was heard on tape coaching a high school kid about how to fake a mandatory drug test. "One of the most common lies told by recruiters," writes Kathy Dobie, "is that it's easy to get out of the military if you change your mind. But once they arrive at training, the recruits are told there's no exit, period."[9] Although recruiters are known to lie, the number of young people signing up is still plummeting.

The military manpower crisis includes escalating desertions: 4,739 Army deserters in 2001 compared to 1,509 in 1995. According to an Army study, deserters tend to be "younger when they enlist, less educated . . . come from 'broken homes,' and [have] 'engaged in delinquent behavior.'"[10] In times of war, rates of desertion tend to spike upward, and so after 9/11 the Army "issued a new policy regarding deserters, hoping to staunch the flow." The new rules required deserters to be returned to their units in the hope that they could be "integrated back into the ranks." This has not been a happy circumstance for either soldiers or officers: "I can't afford to babysit problem children every day," says one commander.

At the end of March 2005, the Pentagon announced that the active-duty Army achieved only about two-thirds of its March goal and was 3,973 recruits short for the year; the Army Reserve was 1,382 short of its year-to-date goal.[11] According to military statistics, 2005 was the toughest recruiting year since 1973, the first year of the all-volunteer Army. Americans don't want to fight this war, and a huge investment in high school recruiting is the military's latest desperate hope.

The high school itself has become a battlefield for hearts and minds. On one side: the power of the federal government; claims (often unsubstantiated) of financial benefits; humvees on school grounds; goody bags filled with donuts, key chains, video games, and T-shirts. Most ominous of all is No Child Left Behind, the controversial omnibus education bill passed in 2001. Section 9528 reverses policies in place in many cities that keep organizations that discriminate on the basis of race, gender, or sexual orientation—including the military—out of schools. It mandates that military recruiters have the same access to students as colleges. The bill also requires schools to turn over students' addresses and home phone numbers to the military unless parents expressly opt out.

On the other side of the recruitment battle: a mourning death toll in Iraq, a growing sense among the citizenry that politicians lied and manipulated us at every turn in order to wage an aggressive war outside any broad popular interest, and organized groups of parents mobilizing to oppose high school recruitment.

A front-page story in the *New York Times* reported a "Growing Problem for Military Recruiters: Parents." The resistance to recruiters, according to the *Times* report, is spreading coast to coast and "was provoked by the very law that was supposed to make it easier for recruiters to reach students more directly. 'No Child Left Behind' . . . is often the spark that ignites parental resistance."[12]

And parents, it turns out, can be a formidable obstacle to a volunteer Army. Unlike the universal draft, signing up requires an affirmative act, and parents can and often do exercise a strong negative drag on their kids' stepping forward. A Department of Defense survey from November 2004 found that "only 25 percent of parents would recommend military service to their children, down from 42 percent in August 2003."[13]

In a column called "Uncle Sam Really Wants You," Bob Herbert focuses attention on an Army publication called *School Recruiting Program Handbook*. The goal of the program is straightforward: "school ownership that can only lead to a greater number of Army enlistments." This means promoting military participation in every feasible dimension, from making classroom presentations to involvement in Hispanic Heritage and Black History months. The handbook recommends that recruiters contact athletic coaches and volunteer to lead calisthenics, get involved with the homecoming committee and organize a presence in the parade, donate coffee and donuts to the faculty on a regular basis, eat in the cafeteria, and target "influential students" who, while they may not enlist, can refer others who might.[14]

The military injunction—hierarchy, obedience, conformity, and aggression—stands in stark opposition to the democratic imperative of respect, cooperation, and equality.

THE REALITY OF WAR

A little truth telling, then. War is catastrophic for human beings and, indeed, for the continuation of life on Earth. With over 120 military bases around the globe and the second largest military force ever assembled, the U.S. government is engaged in a constant state of war, and American society is necessarily distorted and disfigured around the aims of war. Chris Hedges provides an annotated catalog—unadorned, uninflected—of the catastrophe:

- 108 million people were slaughtered in wars during the 20th century.

- During the last decade of that spectacular century, two million children were killed, 20 million displaced, six million disabled.

- From 1900 to 1990, 43 million soldiers died in wars and 62 million civilians were killed. In the wars of the 1990s the ratio was up: between 75% and 90% of all war deaths were civilian deaths.

- Today 21.3 million people are under arms—China has the largest military with 2.4 million people in service (from a population of 1.3 billion citizens), followed by the U.S. with 1.4 million (from a population of 300 million). About 1.3 million Americans are in Reserve and National Guard units.

- Vets suffer long-term health consequences including greater risk of depression, alcoholism, drug addiction, sleep disorders, and more. About one-third of Vietnam vets suffered full-blown post-traumatic stress disorder. Another 22% suffered partial post-traumatic stress disorder. This is the nature of the beast. Anyone who's been there knows. [15]

There are now more than 300,000 child soldiers worldwide. Why do children join? Here is Hedges's entire answer to that question: "They are often forced to. Some are given alcohol or drugs, or exposed to atrocities, to desensitize them to violence. Some join to help feed or protect their families. Some are offered up by their parents in exchange for protection. Children can be fearless because they lack a clear concept of death."[16]

The United States, which consistently refused to ratify the UN Convention on the Rights of the Child, agreed in 2002 to sign on to the "Optional Protocol" to the Convention, covering the involvement of children in armed conflicts. In its "Declarations and Reservations," the U.S. stipulated that signing the Protocol in no way carries any obligations under the Convention and that "nothing in the Protocol establishes a basis for jurisdiction by any international tribunal, including the International Criminal Court." It lists several other reservations, including an objection to Article I of the Protocol, which states, "Parties shall take all feasible measures to ensure that members of their armed forces who have not attained the age of 18 years do not take direct part in hostilities." The U.S. stipulates that the term "feasible measures" means what is "practical" when taking into account all circumstances, "including humanitarian and military considerations," and that the article does not apply to "indirect participation in hostilities, such as gathering and transmitting military information, transporting weapons, ammunition, or other supplies, for forward deployment."

Because recruiters do lie, because the United States steps back from international law and standards, and because the cost of an education for too many poor and working-class kids is constructed as a trip through a minefield and a pact with the devil, teachers should consider Bill Bigelow's advice to make a critical examination of the "Enlistment/Reenlistment Document—Armed Forces of the United States" that recruits sign when they join up. (Copies can be downloaded as a PDF at rethinkingschools.org.) There they will find a host of loopholes and disclaimers, like this one in section 9b: "Laws and regulations that govern military personnel may change without notice to me. Such changes may affect my status, pay, allowances, benefits, and responsibilities as a member of the armed forces regardless of the provisions of this enlistment/reenlistment document."

When Bigelow's students analyzed the entire contract, they concluded that it would be more honest to simply say something like, "Just sign up. . . . Now you belong to us." They offer sage advice to other students: "Read the contract thoroughly. . . . Don't sign unless you're 100% sure, 100% of the time." One of Bigelow's students, who had suffered through the war in Bosnia, recommended that students inclined to enlist might "shoot a bird, and then think about whether you can kill a human."[17]

Jermaine Lewis, the 23-year-old vet from Chicago who spoke about the war being "bogus" in the book *Purple Hearts,* always wanted to be a teacher but worried about the low pay. Now, with both legs gone, he calculates that a teacher's salary plus disability pay will earn him an adequate income: "So I want to go to college and study education—public school, primarily middle school, sixth to eighth grade." He went through the minefield to get what more privileged kids have access to without asking. It's something.

Discussion Questions

Schools receiving federal monies must allow military recruiters and in many cases JROTC and ROTC programs to operate on their campuses. How do you feel about this mandate?

Comparing this article with the Noddings et al. article in the last section, do you believe this is a political or a national security issue?

William Ayers is a professor at the University of Illinois at Chicago.

Section VII

ARE THERE POLITICAL ASPECTS TO CURRICULUM?

Curriculum and politics go hand in hand. The politics can be driven by government agencies or by professional groups. In recent years, government has created a greater political influence over what is taught in schools. This most recent influence was precipitated by the establishment of National Goals for education and the subsequent standards movement and then exacerbated by the renewal of the Elementary and Secondary Education Act, better known as No Child Left Behind. This legislation exerts more control than any previous federal legislation, and the failure of schools to meet mandates identified in the legislation means loss of both federal and state funding for schools.

Within the profession, there are many camps that believe their perceptions of what students should learn are the "right" ones. Consequently, specific curriculum content draws much attention, with professional groups, parents, and special interest groups taking sides. The articles in this section of the reader present examples of how government and private policymakers influence what is taught in the classroom.

Public schools never seem to have sufficient funds to provide all the resources they need to help teachers and students meet their goals of teaching and learning. Consequently, administrators often look toward outside funding to support various school programs. When such support is provided by private industry, the resulting collaboration is referred to as the commercialization of schools. Alex Molnar has written extensively in this area. His article describes commercialism in the schools and the impact it has on the lives of students.

Character education has always been part of the public school curriculum. Its explicit inclusion in schools is highly dependent on the political trends of the country. Howard and his colleagues provide a thorough discussion of the history of character education in the U.S. curriculum and its status in contemporary times.

Murry Nelson describes how a curriculum designed to meet the growing diversity of students in New York City's schools turned into a national debate about homosexuality. The story of the Rainbow Curriculum is the prime example of how politics, media, and irrational thinking can destroy a fundamentally good idea.

The science curriculum has had its share of controversy—namely, evolution vs. creationism. Intelligent Design is the new challenge to evolution, and Vicki Johnson tells the story of what happened when the writers of the Ohio Science Standards debated the inclusion of Intelligent Design in the 2002 science curriculum standards for Ohio.

As you read these articles, think about the following:

■ How politics in your state have affected what teachers can teach

■ How the standards movement in your state has changed the school curriculum from what you experienced in school

■ Why NCLB was so quickly supported by parents and politicians as a way to improve schools

■ How character education is currently taught in the schools

■ How government, special interest groups, and parents can control what is taught in schools

Article 25

CURRICULUM MATTERS

W. JAMES POPHAM

American educators use the word *curriculum* almost every day—and why not, since it describes the stuff we want our students to learn. What a curriculum contains, however, has historically had far less impact on instructional practice than is widely thought. But curriculum's modest influence on instruction has been dramatically transformed in the past few years, especially with respect to state-sanctioned curricula. These days, a state's curricular aims can have a decisive impact—either positive or negative—on the way students are taught.

Note that I am using the term *curriculum* in its traditional sense—namely, to describe the knowledge, skills, and (sometimes) feelings that educators want their students to acquire. In this time-honored definition, a curriculum represents educational *ends*. Educators hope, of course, that such ends will be attained as a consequence of instructional activities, which serve as the *means* of promoting the curricular ends.

In the past, the curricular things we wanted our students to learn were typically described as *goals* or *objectives*. These days, however, most educators tend to use the term *content standards* instead. But regardless of the label that's used, what's in a curriculum is supposed to describe the intended impact of an educational enterprise on the students being taught.

A PERSONAL PERSPECTIVE

My first serious brush with curriculum occurred some five decades ago, when I began teaching in eastern Oregon. Even way back then, Oregon had a state-approved curriculum syllabus, and I was given a copy of that thick text for my bookshelf. And that's where it stayed—right on that shelf. Other than glancing at the syllabus for an hour or so before the school year began to find out what goals the state decreed for the courses I was scheduled to teach, I never looked at it again.

What actually determined the content I taught in my classes was, almost totally, the textbooks I used. As a first-year teacher in a small high

SOURCE: Excerpted from Popham, W. J. (2004, November). Curriculum matters. *American School Board Journal*. Copyright © 2004 National School Boards Association. Reprinted with permission. All rights reserved.

school, I had five different preparations. Accordingly, my frantic instructional planning revolved completely around the textbooks I'd been told to use for those five courses. To illustrate, I was required, by a principal who had never heard of "highly qualified teachers," to teach a course in geography even though I had never in my entire life taken a course in geography. Given my lack of geographic expertise, I truly cherished the large red geography text without which I could not have survived a class of 30 sophomores, most of whom did not truly care about the location of Khartoum or the subtleties of a Mercator map projection.

But I was not alone. All of the other teachers in my school paid little, if any, attention to the state curriculum syllabus. My faculty colleagues, too, decided on what they should teach according to what was treated in their textbooks. In retrospect, "alignment" in those days might have referred to whether a teacher's lesson plan meshed suitably with the textbook's upcoming chapter.

No Clarity, No Consequences

The trifling impact that official curriculum documents have on teachers' instructional practices can probably be attributed, at least in part, to the documents' excessive generality. If, for example, social studies teachers discover that their students are supposed to acquire "a meaningful understanding of how our nation's government functions," there is obviously so much latitude in this curricular aim that a wide range of instructional activities legitimately could be regarded as germane. The mushiness of many curricular aims certainly plays a role in reducing the impact of those aims on classroom instruction.

However, a more fundamental reason that our nation's curricula have had so little influence on instructional practice is that what was in a curriculum, even a state-sanctioned or district-sanctioned curriculum, rarely made any sort of difference to anyone.

Oh, certainly, there have been occasional instances when a particular body of content was thought to be appropriate or inappropriate for a state curriculum. You might recall, for instance, the recent flap in Kansas about the inclusion of evolution content in the state's science curriculum. And, when a state's textbooks are under consideration for adoption, those doing the adopting surely pay some attention to what's in the state's curriculum when they review contending textbooks. But, considering the full-blown panorama of American public education, what has been identified in official curriculum documents has typically had only a slight impact on what actually goes on in classrooms.

Then Came NCLB

But that situation came to a screeching halt on January 8, 2002, when President Bush affixed his signature to the No Child Left Behind Act. This important reauthorization of a federal law, first enacted in 1965, substantially altered the relationship between curriculum and instruction in America.

That's because NCLB first tied *assessments* to a state's curriculum, then tied important decisions to students' performances on those curriculum-based assessments. If students failed to make sufficient progress in their *assessed* mastery of a state's curricular aims, then all sorts of sanctions and public embarrassment would follow for educators who were running the schools and districts where insufficient progress had been seen. Because NCLB required a state's annual assessments to be based on the state's official curriculum, and because those annual assessments could cause plenty of trouble, what was in the curriculum suddenly mattered.

Educators, of course, were eager to avoid NCLB sanctions (or NCLB-induced embarrassment) by having been identified as failing to make adequate yearly progress in students' test performances. Accordingly, educators became far more attentive to what would be covered in their state's NCLB tests. But a state's NCLB tests, as required by law, must be based on the state's official curriculum, as represented by a state's "challenging" content standards.

Let me quickly tie a ribbon around this logic chain:

1. A state's schools and districts can get battered by NCLB sanctions and/or public embarrassment if students don't score well enough on the state's annual NCLB tests;

2. But what's measured on those annual NCLB tests must be based on a state's official curriculum; and, therefore,

3. Teachers will be certain to try to boost NCLB test scores by devoting substantial instructional time to what's likely to be assessed by their state's curriculum-based NCLB tests.

So, for the first time in the history of American public schooling, a potent federal law has made curriculum truly count—big time.

The problem is that most state curricula, against a backdrop of these significant NCLB pressures to improve test scores, are actually *lowering* the quality of education in a state's schools. We need to understand why that is so. And we need to do something about it.

Too Many Targets

Here, in a nutshell, is what currently constitutes an NCLB-triggered, curriculum-caused calamity. The content standards now found in almost all of our states originally were devised by competent, well-intentioned individuals—but at a time when a state-approved curriculum was merely supposed to reflect worthwhile educational aspirations for a state's students.

Unfortunately, in most states' current collections of content standards, there are far too many curricular aims to teach or to test in the time available for teaching or testing. Almost all states' content standards reflect a "wish list" mentality; that is, the determiners of a state's content standards in, say, mathematics, have listed all the nifty mathematical skills and knowledge they *wish* the state's students would be able to master.

But the result of these cover-the-waterfront curriculum exercises—carried out before NCLB's arrival made curriculum a potent factor in a state's accountability game—was invariably to lay out way too many curricular targets.

A state's educators, therefore, have been forced to deal with—or try to deal with—an excessive number of curricular targets. Too many curricular aims must be assessed by a given year's NCLB tests, so teachers are obliged to guess which ones actually will be tested in a given year. On probability grounds alone, of course, many teachers guess wrong and end up teaching things that aren't on the NCLB tests or not teaching things that are on the tests.

A related problem arises because teachers are unable to learn from the results of NCLB tests which of their instructional activities have or haven't worked. Because there are so many curricular aims, the ones that actually are measured on a given year's test can't be assessed with enough test items to supply any sort of sensible estimate about which curricular aims were or weren't well taught. A collection of too-general score reports simply doesn't provide teachers with the information they need to improve their instruction, for those reports do not let teachers know *which* curricular aims have or haven't been mastered by their students. And, lurking as the culprit in this instructionally meaningless score reporting is a state curriculum containing too many curricular aims in the first place.

Given this regrettable situation, is it any wonder that some NCLB-pressured teachers engage in rampant curricular reductionism, excising any content—even important content—if it seems unlikely to be tested? Is it any wonder that some teachers oblige their students to take part in endless, mind-numbing test-preparation sessions? Is it any wonder that some engage in such dishonest practices as supplying their students with advance copies of covertly copied items from the actual tests?

All of these bad outcomes could be reduced or eliminated if only more sensible NCLB tests were employed. But, as you have now seen, first we must grapple with the inappropriate curricular targets found in so many states. Unless a state's decision makers figure out a way to have their state's NCLB tests function as a force for instructional improvement, not instructional decline, too many students will suffer. That suffering can be traced directly to curricular aims that, though perhaps serviceable in a former time, just don't work today.

These days, because of NCLB, curriculum *does* make a difference. And these days, because of NCLB, we need to rethink whether our state curricula are suitable.

THREE OPTIONS

The task before education policymakers is to reduce the number of eligible-to-be-assessed curricular aims so that (a) teachers are not overwhelmed by too many instructional targets and (b) a student's mastery of each curricular arm that's assessed can be determined with reasonable accuracy.

Teachers who can focus their instructional attention on a modest number of truly significant skills usually can get their students to master those skills—even if the skills are genuinely challenging. Accurate reports of students' mastery of each skill will let the students and their parents know which curricular aims have or haven't been mastered—and let teachers know which ones have or haven't been well taught.

Here are three potential ways of coping with this curricular crisis:

Brand-new content standards. The first option involves a start-from-scratch approach to identifying a state's curricular aims. Given a clean slate and the recognition that a subject matter's most important curricular aims must be assessed by NCLB tests, a state's curriculum makers could attempt to come up with a markedly winnowed, more instructionally beneficial set of unarguably significant curricular aims.

Coalesced content standards. A second alternative would be for a state's curriculum

officials to rework existing curricular aims so that the most important of them were subsumed under a smaller number of reconceptualized and measurable targets. Although, in many ways, this approach is similar to the first option, it might represent a modest repackaging of a state's extant curricular aims without a complete start-again approach to curriculum building.

Derivative assessment frameworks. The final option is to leave the state's current content standards untouched but derive from them a framework for NCLB assessment that focuses on a small number of reconceptualized, eligible-to-be-taught curricular targets. That way the state's curriculum-based NCLB tests would be likely to have a beneficial rather than a harmful impact on education. The skills and bodies of knowledge identified in an NCLB assessment framework would, of course, influence instructional practices and would need to be chosen with consummate care.

PROCEEDING SENSIBLY

Because the first two options are both likely to involve substantial time-consuming and resource-consuming activities, I believe option three is the most sensible way to proceed. Indeed, in many states the existing content standards have already been approved by a state school board or, sometimes, by the legislature itself—usually after substantial input from the state's educators and citizens. I prefer to leave those extant content standards as they are—untouched. If the content standards truly exert much of a positive influence on schooling (which I doubt), then that positive influence should continue. But if the content standards really aren't a positive factor (which I suspect), then letting them languish will be just fine.

However, because the law requires that a state's NCLB tests be clearly based on the state's content standards, it would be imperative to build a defensible case for federal officials that describe both the framework-derivation process and the relevant stakeholders involved. It is important that the state's NCLB assessment targets be *demonstrably* derivative from a state's existing curricular aims.

Let me illustrate, in the field of reading, how a defensible NCLB assessment framework might be derived from a state's existing curricular aims. Most states' content standards in reading contain a dozen or more specific reading skills, such as identifying a selection's main idea, isolating key details in a reading passage, and using context clues to infer the meaning of unfamiliar words. A markedly more comprehensive curricular aim in reading has recently been devised by Indiana University's Roger Farr. It is a sort of "super-skill" that effectively subsumes a great many more specific skills such as those just mentioned. Farr's super-skill requires students to be able to read different kinds of reading materials in order to accomplish any of the most common real-world purposes for which people read such materials.

Described as *purposeful reading,* this super-skill can be assessed via constructed-response items (for example, essay or short answer) or selected-response items (for example, multiple choice). From an instructional perspective, delightfully, a student's responses to such items are always evaluated by using a scoring guide whose key evaluative criteria can be taught directly to students. The criteria, always based on the reader's purpose as well as the type of material being read, focuses on the *relevance, accuracy*, and *sufficiency* of a student's response. Thus, a powerful and teachable curricular aim can be derived from a flock of more specific skills that therefore can be regarded as "en route" or "enabling" skills for the more comprehensive super-skill that would be assessed via a state's NCLB tests.

Farr's *purposeful reading* is clearly analogous to the kinds of composition skills we routinely assess when we measure students' ability to write via writing-sample tests. In these tests, which have been in widespread use for over two decades in the United States, we call on students to display a super-skill—namely, being able to write an original composition (for example, a persuasive or narrative essay). Based on the student's essay, we are then able to gauge the student's ability to organize content, to use appropriate mechanics, and to display a number of other more specific subskills relevant to composition.

To derive an appropriate assessment framework from a state's collection of numerous existing curricular aims requires more than modest instructional and assessment acumen. The trick is to isolate a small number of aims that can be described to teachers, are genuinely teachable, and coalesce the most important of the state's existing curricular aims. That sort of activity, of course, demands loads of curricular artistry from those who are deriving the assessment framework. But this approach seems to be the most sensible way of dealing with our current NCLB-induced curricular crisis.

A Final Plea

The need to deal with our current state-approved curricular aims is, in my view, imperative. The longer we delay in coming up with educationally sound, curriculum-derived NCLB tests, the more children there will be who receive a less-than-lustrous education because their teachers are being driven by ill-conceived, curriculum-based NCLB assessments into shabby instructional practices.

Sure, I know many states have invested dollars galore in the creation of customized state-based tests that are supposedly "aligned" to their states' official curriculum. And, of course, it would be costly to move toward different tests. But those existing tests were developed at a time when a state's curriculum exercised little or no impact on classroom instruction. Those times have changed. And that's because, unless NCLB is seriously altered or disappears altogether, today's state curricula do make a difference. It's time to fix them.

Discussion Questions

How should curriculum drive assessment?

As a teacher, do you feel that curriculum drives your assessment or do you feel that assessment drives your curriculum?

——————— ⌾ ———————

W. James Popham is a professor emeritus at the University of California, Los Angeles.

Article 26

CASHING IN ON THE CLASSROOM

ALEX MOLNAR

Andrea Boyes was trying to do things right. The 15-year-old student at West Salem High School in Oregon wanted to raise money for her cheerleading squad. She showed entrepreneurial savvy, devising a plan to resell bottled water for $1 per bottle and negotiating a deal that enabled the squad to net 55 cents per bottle sold. She designed her own label for the fund-raiser bottles that featured the school's logo. And she was socially responsible, privately hoping to harvest enough profits to create a scholarship program that would enable students who could not afford the cost of cheerleading uniforms to join the squad. In an era when adults often complain that teenagers lack initiative, it was the sort of moxie that might be expected to win the student praise from principals, teacher, or the PTA (Associated Press, 2002).

Instead, the school stopped the project dead in its tracks. A Pepsi-Cola exclusive contract blocked Andrea from selling the water on school grounds. In fact, it blocked anyone from selling any beverage not made by Pepsi. For Gary Boyes, Andrea's father, the incident was a wake-up call that raised questions about "the actual rights of the contracting parties to inhibit student rights and modify accepted uses of publicly owned properties" (G. Boyes, personal communication, November 22, 2002).

Andrea Boyes had run headfirst into the clout that giant corporations wield today in U.S. schools. It is pervasive and firmly entrenched, as the *Sixth Annual Report on Trends in Schoolhouse Commercialism, Year 2002–2003* shows.

The Commercialism in Education Research Unit (CERU) of the Education Policy Studies Laboratory at Arizona State University has monitored media references to commercialism in schools since 1990. CERU defines and tracks media references to eight categories of commercial activity in schools through searches on news archival services. In the July 2002–June 2003 study period, six of the eight categories monitored showed a marked increase in activity compared with the 2001–2002 study.

SOURCE: Excerpted from Molnar, A. (2003). Cashing in on the classroom. *Educational Leadership, 61*(4), 79–84. Reprinted by permission of Alex Molnar.

Hard numbers about the extent of corporate moneymaking activities in schools remain difficult to pin down. One industry group favoring corporate involvement in schools reported that schools receive $2.4 billion a year from what it calls "business relationships" with corporations (Council for Corporate and School Partnerships, 2002). How those number should be interpreted, however, is not entirely clear in the absence of a generally agreed-on set of definitions, the ability to assess the actual value of the funded school activities, or an understanding of how the corporations benefited.

Corporate links to schools usually carry the gloss of charity, which tends to obscure what corporations get out of those connections. According to a marketing executive quoted in the advertising and marketing magazine *Promo,* school leaders are becoming more open to commercialism as a means of reducing budgetary problems (Macmillan, 2002). And this commercialism is far more sophisticated than it was in the old days of book covers and posters. Brands are learning to create curriculum-based programs when possible or appropriate, bring mobile tours to schools, and infiltrate locker rooms and sports fields.

This year's review, however, finds evidence of a mounting backlash against corporation–school match-ups. Critics are threatening lawsuits, charging that certain sponsorship programs interfere with school operations, instruction, or students' health. Some school districts have banned corporate relationships, such as exclusive agreements with soft-drink bottlers. And parents are speaking out against the relentless marketing to their children, with public health advocates and legislators, in some instances, taking up the cause.

TRACKING THE CATEGORIES

The Commercialism in Education Research Unit's 2002–2003 annual report tracks media references to commercialism in schools in the following categories: sponsorship of programs and activities, exclusive agreements, incentive programs, appropriation of space, sponsored educational materials, electronic marketing, fund raising, and privatization. Recently, the media have heavily scrutinized privatization—the private management of public schools—in light of the Edison Schools and Philadelphia's privatization contracts. This category received the largest number of references of any of the eight categories—1,570—although the total number of references to privatization in 2002–2003 were down 15% from the previous year.

Research on the remaining seven categories, however, has been far less publicized and reveals some interesting trends in school commercialization.

Sponsorship of Programs and Activities

Although the number of citations in this category was up just 1% from last year, the category as a whole generated the second-largest number of media references in the 2002–2003 study periods—1,206 stories.

Grant programs from such companies as General Electric and Shell Oil Company are a traditional source of sponsorship references, and ExxonMobil Corporation offers ABCs for schools—awards, books, and computers. Corporate sponsors often fund academic competitions and special educational programs, such as national science bowls and honor rolls. As tight budgets increasingly threaten programs in art, music, and athletics, the search for corporate sponsorship intensifies.

According to football coach Tony Monken of Vernon Hills High School in Illinois, corporate sponsorship "is the wave of the future." Not surprisingly, Vernon Hills High sold naming rights to its stadium. "Everyone wants to reduce taxes," said Monken, "and it's hard to get referendums passed. . . . So anything you can do to raise funds for your school, you should do" (cited in McGraw, 2002).

Exclusive Agreements

Exclusive agreements give marketers rights to sell products or services on school or district grounds and to exclude competitors. References to exclusive agreements were up by 65%, from 153 hits in 2001–2002 to 252 hits in 2002–2003. These references were not necessarily favorable to such agreements. Although there were many reports of such contracts, a substantial number referred to criticism and opposition to the deals.

Coke, for one, has been frank about its goals: "The school system is where you build brand loyalty," said John Alm, president and chief operating officer of Coca-Cola Enterprises (Grannan, 2003). But exclusive soft-drink agreements prompted outcry as attention increasingly focused on problems of childhood obesity and fears that diets heavy in sugary snacks could contribute to type 2 diabetes (Bruce, 2002). Statewide bans or restrictions on junk food cropped up in Texas and California, and school districts in Los Angeles, San Francisco, Philadelphia, and New York banned or restricted soft-drink sales. As many as a dozen states were reported to be considering legislation to curb sweets and fatty snacks in schools, and George Washington University law professor John Banzhaf—who was among those leading the fray to sue tobacco companies—predicted lawsuits against soda makers and school boards (Auchmutey, 2002).

Yet despite what appears to be mounting opposition, exclusive agreements retain considerable support. Some districts sought an acceptable middle ground by negotiating exclusive agreements that provided equal space in schools for more healthful drinks.

Incentive Programs

Incentive programs provide some sort of reward in the form of a commercial product or service to students who achieve such goals as perfect attendance or reading a given number of books. Media references to incentive programs increased by 87%, from 189 hits in the 2001–2003 survey to 354 hits in 2002–2003.

Pizza Hut's national reading incentive program, Book It!, enrolled students from 875,000 classrooms in 50,000 public and private schools (Rawlings, 2002). In a corporate first, the company gave $50,000 to sponsor the Dallas Junior League's state literacy programs. The

pizza chain, noted the *Dallas Morning News,* "will thereby 'own' [the league's] education issue area" (Miller, 2002). Other incentive programs included an essay contest sponsored by Scholastic and a reading program sponsored by the National Basketball Association that featured its newest star, Chinese center Yao Ming.

Verizon Communications was also active with school incentive programs and grant competitions. Altruism isn't the sole motivator for such efforts. In an industry trade magazine, a telecommunications lobbyist wrote candidly about how telecommunications firms build their business by targeting students through the schools (Allardyce, 2002).

Appropriation of Space

Appropriation of space refers to using school property to promote individual corporations through such mechanisms as naming rights or general advertising. Discussions of naming rights—the practice of naming public facilities for corporate sponsors in return for a cash payment—continued in the 2002–2003 study period. The number of references in this category tripled, from 110 in 2001–2002 to 326 in 2002–2003.

The New York City Public Schools revived a program to sell sponsorships of schools' names and facilities. The Chicago suburb of Vernon Hills named its high school stadium for Rust-Oleum in return for $100,000. A computer company sponsored the scoreboard for another $80,000. Advertising signs or naming rights proposals involving schools, school property, and school buses surfaced in Massachusetts and Louisiana as well. And in February 2003, due to a shortfall amounting to one-fifth of the district's annual $20 million budget, the Belmont–Redwood Shores School District in suburban San Francisco proposed selling naming rights not only for school buildings and classrooms but for the entire district (Kim, 2003).

Sometimes commercial ventures appropriate not the physical space of the school but rather the relationship between schools and students' families. An Apple Computer store in Short

Hills, New Jersey, hosted school nights on its premises. Parents came to the store rather than the school to see their children's work, and the store provided discounts on Apple products for parents, teachers, and schools. These events were part of a national program launched by the computer company in January 2003. By early 2003, 176 schools had signed up.

Sponsored Educational Materials

Sponsored educational materials are curriculum materials produced largely by or for an outside corporate entity. Such materials may be thinly disguised advertising plugs for particular products, or they may be blatant or subtly disguised propaganda for particular policy positions that serve corporate interests. Of all the categories identified in the trends report, this may be the most difficult one to track because curriculum decisions often don't reach the public eye. Nevertheless, the 2002–2003 report showed a fourfold increase in references to such materials— from 75 references in the 2001–2002 report to 310 in 2002–2003.

When the New York *Daily News* reviewed high school textbooks in December 2002, it found books "infested with brand names and plugs for commercial products" (Gendar & Feiden, 2002). Procter & Gamble's history lesson for middle school students on the Civil War came complete with sleek visuals and a page titled "Did You Know?," which informs students that the company provided soap supplies to the Union army (Applebaum, 2003).

Field Trip Factory, an organization that arranges school field trips to commercial establishments, clearly promoted the destination businesses during the time period studied. Corporate partners include General Mills and Campbell Soup, whose participation ensures that their products are prominently pointed out to the touring students. A store's own employees act as tour guides and make a point of promoting its house brands as cheaper alternatives to national brands. Field Trip Factory president Susan Singer pointed out the importance of reaching students

in this way because of their influence on hundreds of millions of dollars in sales and their increasing tendency to do supermarket shopping on their own (Angrisani, 2003).

Electronic Marketing

Many of the electronic marketing references we found consist of reports about Channel One, the television service that provides schools with free television equipment on the condition that each day students watch a 12-minute news program that includes 2 minutes of commercials. Channel One references found during the study period included both attacks on and defenses of the program. Overall, electronic marketing references showed an 11% increase in the 2002–2003 study compared with the previous year, with the number of references rising from 248 to 276.

Cable in the Classroom, a cable television industry promotional program, seems to have undergone a facelift (Brady, 2002). Unlike Channel One, Cable in the Classroom airs no commercials but is arguably a running promotion for the various premium cable channels that furnish its programming, including CNN, Bravo, the National Geographic Channel, and Court TV, among others. Court TV, a commercial entity, provides curriculums to teachers covering various topics: bullying, drug use, and, most recently, forensic sciences for investigating crime scenes (Fromm, 2003).

Futures for Kids, a nonprofit organization in Raleigh, North Carolina, runs a Web portal that, according to the organization, "organizes a public high school student's options for the future into a user-friendly format" (LaScala, 2002). Corporate sponsors—such as IBM, GlaxoSmithKline, Cisco Systems, Monster.com, and Apple Computer—fund the program. The portal directs students searching for career information to relevant company Web sites.

Fund Raising

Fund raising showed a 17% increase in the study, from 827 references in 2001–2002 to 970 in 2002–2003. Two themes emerged from the coverage: the increased dependence on outside fund raising to cover not just extracurricular expenses but also operational costs (*Critics balk*, 2002) and the growing ambivalence—ranging to hostility—that some parents and even school officials expressed toward the necessity of fund raising (St. John, 2003).

Other citations relating to fund raising described campaigns through grocery chains and label programs for Tyson Foods, Campbell's, and Community Coffee. The merger of General Mills with Pillsbury resulted in the expansion of the cereal maker's Box Tops for Education program, which rewards schools for submitting coupons clipped from the company's products. A General Mills executive called the program "good merchandising" to boost sales (*Q1*, 2002). The Safeway supermarket chain and Target Corporation were among other companies involved in school fund-raising campaigns.

Some objections to fund raising arise from the practice of recruiting students to sell food products in many school-based fund-raisers. This has raised the same concerns about health that arise when schools enter into exclusive soft-drink contracts. According to the research, some campaigns responded to health concerns and increasingly included healthful foods or practical items as part of their fund-raising efforts (Karlin, 2003).

One sign of the pressure students feel as a result of incentive-driven fund-raising programs surfaced in Slidell, Louisiana, where a 10-year-old was charged with forgery for changing customers' checks so that she could win a prize for raising the most money in a school sales fund-raiser. Fund raising also appears to reinforce the disparities in socioeconomic status that continue to plague education (Dunnewind, 2002; Kelly, 2003).

VIABLE ALTERNATIVE OR OUTRAGE?

Although references turned up by the CERU searches indicated efforts to encourage various commercial practices, they also showed growing resistance to commercialism in its various forms from schools, parents, and policymakers. Much of the opposition to commercial activities focused on the health and impact of practices that promoted junk food or soft-drink consumption.

For example, Maryland's General Assembly considered a bill requiring schools to offer as many nutritional snacks as junk foods, and an Oregon state senator sponsored a bill to restrict the sale of junk foods in schools. Over the past 4 years, legislators have introduced at least 30 bills in the U.S. Congress and at the state level that would, in varying degrees, govern commercial activities in schools.

Despite increased opposition, commercialism in schools has become so pervasive that it is virtually invisible. It blends seamlessly with the marketing maelstrom that defines a contemporary U.S. culture in which parents work hard to pay for the possession they covet, arrive home late with a bag of fast food under the arm, spend leisure hours patrolling the malls, and maintain hefty-credit card balances.

It may be naïve to think that parents can recognize the dangers of commercialism in schools. Yet CERU's annual report suggests that parents and ordinary citizens are actually more concerned about the problem than educators are.

In Vermont, Maryland, and California, education interest groups have actually lobbied against banning soft-drink bottling company deals, limiting sales of soft drinks, and restricting corporate marketing activities in schools. Year after year, professional education journals remain silent on the moral and pedagogical implications of such practices.

This situation must change. It is indefensible to direct millions of dollars worth of sophisticated advertising at children to convince them to consume harmful products, nag their parents to buy specific brands, and define their worth in terms of their possessions. Yet people who should know better defend the practice. Too often, educators voice this simple-minded logic: Thousands of ads target children outside of school; a little advertising in school won't hurt.

Others express the outrageous view that children are so sophisticated and critically aware that ads won't influence them. A quick trip to the library to read James McNeal's *Kids as Customers: A Handbook of Marketing to Children* (1992) will prove the contrary.

The fact that marketing takes place *in school* compounds its immorality. Society requires children to attend school; children understand that the experience should benefit them and promote social goals. When teachers hand out "supplemental" instructional materials that market such items as candy, personal care products, sport shoes, and soft drinks, they manipulate children for the benefit of a special interest group and very likely encourage cynicism over the long haul.

Pedagogically, marketing in schools is destructive. Who should students take more seriously, a health and nutrition teacher who encourages them to eat a balanced diet low in fat, sugar, and salt, or a principal who promotes an exclusive agreement with a bottling company that includes bonuses if students meet certain consumption goals? The curriculum should represent the essence of a school's purpose. Nevertheless, it is easy to imagine the principal's real-world message overwhelming the "official" nutrition lesson.

In the real world, short-term financial gain trumps the long-term health and well-being of students. This is the lesson that students learn.

When they are not hawking their products and services, corporations labor mightily to tell students their own stories. Often, corporations or industries experiencing problems want to get their stories into classrooms. Not surprisingly, they have told students over the years that burning plastics constitutes recycling, that the Valdez oil spill "wasn't so bad," and that only a dunce would oppose the North American Free Trade Agreement. They lose sight of the idea that curriculum content should be based on a serious professional assessment of good teaching practices. Instead, they conceive of school curriculum as a sort of flea market in which anyone with enough money to buy a booth can present his or her story.

Commercialism in schools is a complex phenomenon that reflects powerful economic social, cultural, and political forces. Whether or not schools and their students become increasingly subordinated to the marketplace depends in large measure on how we understand childhood and the proper relationship between adults and the children for whom they are responsible.

Discussion Questions

What is the legitimate role of business in the schools?

What is the legitimate role of business in the curriculum? Is this different than your first answer? How?

Alex Molnar is a professor at Arizona State University–Tempe.

Article 27

POLITICS OF CHARACTER EDUCATION

ROBERT W. HOWARD

MARVIN W. BERKOWITZ

ESTHER F. SCHAEFFER

Today, character education continues—and by many measures is growing—in spite of various pressures, most notably the standards-based environment of contemporary public schooling. Character education, a vital tool for preparing our young people in our schools, has had to confront political issues and challenges of its own. What these issues are, why they surface, and what and how they have been addressed compose the focus of this article. Although advocating for character education, the approach here to the issues is descriptive and as impartial as possible, and the focus is on K–12 public schools.

WHAT IS CHARACTER AND CAN IT BE TAUGHT?

In this examination of the politics of character and moral education, let us start with defining *character* and *character education*. The field of character and moral education deals with questions of ethics and ethical behavior.

Over the years, educators have given this quest different names (e.g., *moral education, values education*). The most common term at present is *character education*. Terminology can be problematic, because *character education* can

SOURCE: Excerpted from Howard, R. W., Berkowitz, M. W., & Schaeffer, E. F. (2004). Politics of character education. *Educational Policy, 18*(1), 188–215. Reprinted by permission of Sage.

refer either to the entire field or to one of three major approaches (described in more detail in a subsequent section): caring, (traditional) character, and developmental. The caring and developmental approaches tend to use the term *moral education*. For clarity, we will use the term *traditional character education* in reference to the narrow approach and *character education* to refer to the entire field.

Thomas Lickona (1989) provided one definition of *character*:

> Character consists of . . . values in action. Character . . . has three interrelated parts: moral knowing, moral feeling, and moral behavior. Good character consists of knowing the good, desiring the good, and doing the good—habits of the mind, habits of the heart, and habits of action. We want our children . . . to judge what is right, care deeply about what is right, and then do what they believe to be right—even in the face of pressure from without and temptation from within. (p. 51)

In Lickona's definition, the major philosophical traditions—and tensions—are present. As will be detailed below, there are three major approaches to character education: the cognitive–developmental approach (often called moral education) gives primacy to "knowing the good," the caring approach emphasizes "desiring the good," and traditional character education, which sees "doing the good" as fundamental. In classroom practice and character education programs, the three approaches are frequently integrated. There is also a growing inclusion of social and emotional learning and academic service learning in character education initiatives (e.g., Berman, 1997; Elias, Zins, & Weissberg, 1997). For clarity, this article will focus on what might be called the pure types of the three approaches and distinguish between and among them. These differences are major and frequently contentious within the field; however, there are also many points of common ground. Perhaps the most fundamental is the general agreement that (at minimum) character involves making and acting on ethical judgments in a social context and that this is the aim of character education.

HISTORICAL ISSUES IN THE POLITICS OF CHARACTER EDUCATION

From the beginning and growth of the public school movement in the United States, character education has been a component—sometimes the primary mission—of schools, sometimes divisive, but ever present. Character education has typically been seen as synonymous with, compatible with, and/or a subset of citizenship education. With the development and expansion of free public schools in the United States in the 1830s and beyond came the concern that "values of the home" (or at least some of them) be reinforced in the classroom and that the children of others—particularly immigrants—learn and practice them as well. Women were to be teachers of good character, as they were considered to be better role models. After virtuous teachers, textbooks were the second major source of moral instruction (e.g., McGuffey's *Readers*).

As the Puritans' concern with a strict character education became less rigid and more informal, it evolved into a desire for dominance through a nonsectarian, albeit Protestant, character education. Changes in immigration brought large Catholic populations into the United States in the 1840s and 1850s. Catholics, seeing these Protestant beliefs as incompatible with their doctrine and hesitant to recognize any state authority in character education, established a system of parochial schools to foster their own version of traditional character education.

By the 1890s, two approaches were evident. The first, the traditional character education approach, sought to instill traditional values and virtue as a struggle against the perceived corrosive effects of modernity. Traditional character education with an emphasis on doing the good has its roots in the Aristotelian tradition that sees action and habit as fundamental, over knowing and desiring.

The Boy Scouts and their oath is a classic traditional character education approach of specifying a list of virtues, then creating a community environment that imbues youth with the virtues and reinforces them through formal instruction, visuals (e.g., posters), positive peer culture, and ceremonies. McClellan (1999) wrote of the opposition to this approach:

> The codes and clubs so cherished by these reformers sometimes did little more than reinforce the standards of middle-class respectability. The scheme showed little tolerance for cultural diversity, and there can be no doubt that reformers expected it to play an important role in eliminating the differences that set immigrants off from the mainstream American life. (pp. 54–55)

In contrast, the second approach had progressive change as the primary goal of schooling and a developmental—process-oriented—pedagogy for character education. The progressives saw the ethical world less in terms of absolutes and viewed ethical decisions and action as contingent on context (including cultural contexts). The terms used, *relativity* and *relativist,* sometimes were seen and attacked as ethical nihilism (and in some populations have only pejorative meaning and no neutral definition). It was not the absence of "right and wrong" but teaching children to engage in critical thinking and to have a process on which to call in making decisions and actions that was the core of the progressive approach. The progressive tradition is more Socratic, with its emphasis on reasoning captured in the phrase (albeit an oversimplification) "to know the good, is to do the good." Lawrence Kohlberg (1981, 1984) and Jean Piaget (1932/1965) are the best known figures in the developmental approach, which has its roots in the progressive movement of the early 20th century.

The progressives focused on development of the individual and a broader agenda: the betterment of society. Combined, as McClellan (1999) observed, progressives

> consistently gave more attention to great social and political issues than to matters of private conduct. Reversing the emphasis of earlier moral educators, they expressed little interest in the drinking habits or sexual conduct of individuals as long as such personal behavior did not impede the ability to operate as intelligent and productive citizens. (p. 57)

Given the interest in public behavior and political movements to better society, progressives emphasized democratic participation in social groups, not to instill and reinforce specific virtues but to engage in the skills of democratic citizenship: deliberation, problem solving, and participation in governance of the group.

In many ways, John Dewey embodied the major precepts of the Progressives (Scheffler, 1974; Westbrook, 1991). He lost his faith in the conservative religion of his youth and early adulthood. Dewey was born in Burlington, Vermont, but moved to larger urban settings (e.g., University of Chicago and Teachers College, Columbia). Dewey was actively involved with political movements (e.g., women's suffrage) and organizations promoting social justice. Dewey was a founding member of the NAACP and the American Association of University Professors. He also was a strong advocate for the role of education for democratic citizenship (e.g., see Dewey, 1916/1966).

Dewey (1909/1975) argued that the best way to prepare for full citizenship is to engage in it in educational environments. One of Dewey's anecdotes illustrates, by analogy, what he believed to be the futility of other approaches:

> I am told that there is a swimming school in a certain city where youth are taught to swim without going into the water, being repeatedly drilled in the various movements which are necessary for swimming. When one of the young men so trained was asked what he did when he got into the water, he laconically replied, "Sunk." The story happens to be true; were it not, it would seem to be a fable made expressly for the purpose of typifying the ethical relationship of school to society. The school cannot be a preparation for social life excepting as it reproduces, within itself, typical conditions of social life. . . . The only way to prepare for social life is to engage in social life. (pp. 13–14)

The progressives eschewed the list of desirable values and gave great weight to the findings of Hartshorne, May, and their colleagues that cast doubt on the efficacy of what was later derisively called the "bag of virtues" approach (Kohlberg, 1981). In measuring cheating in 10,000 children and adolescents in multiple experiments, Hartshorne and May found that they could not simply assign adolescents into "good character" and "bad character" categories based on behavior. Cheating in one situation was not a good predictor of cheating in another. Children and adolescents who reported that they valued honesty could not be distinguished, in their behavior, from those who did not (Hartshorne & May, 1928; Hartshorne, May, & Mailer, 1929; Hartshorne, May, & Shuttleworth, 1930).

Progressives were attacked for subjecting students to the tyranny of the majority, for substituting one form of conventional morality with one indistinguishable from it, for eroding both the moral authority of adults (e.g., in their roles of teachers) and the moral authority of the community through tolerance of other perspectives, and for emphasizing context (or relativity) as a legitimate factor in moral considerations.

In public schools, the traditional character education approach and the religious approach have largely become one and the same and embrace the traditional character education approach. The direct instruction of virtues and socialization of the young are a point of common ground between Protestants and Catholics. The historical tension between Protestant character education and Catholicism has largely vanished, as is evident in the large number of Catholic educators and philosophers who are prominent advocates of traditional character education, among them Bennett (1993), Kilpatrick (1992), Lickona (1989), and Ryan and Bohlin (1999). From this point forward, we will treat religion-based character education as a subset of traditional character education.

The mid-1940s to the mid-1960s was a nadir for character education in K–12 public schools. McClellan's (1999) analysis of the causes is compelling. He cited, first, the influence of positivism; second, the ubiquitous anticommunism in the United States; and third, a greater distinction between public and private behavior and a fear that character education was, or would be seen as, improperly invading the privacy of students and families. In the 1960s, there was a perceived erosion of moral authority based on opposition to U.S. policy in the war in Vietnam, support for the civil rights movement, challenges to traditional sexual norms and values, and a growing cultural pluralism across generations with an increasing diversity of the population. During this time, there was growing pressure for a greater separation of church and state, most notably with the *Engle v. Vitale* (1962) decision of the U.S. Supreme Court, which prohibited teacher-led prayers in public classrooms. For the many who see religion as the foundation of ethics, banning prayer was perceived as tantamount to banning character education.

In the late 1960s, there was a revival of interest in the school-based promotion of student moral growth. Given the growing focus on cultural pluralism and antipathy toward conventional authority, the newly arising approaches avoided the indoctrinative aspects of traditional character education. One of the influential initiatives was "values clarification" (e.g., Raths, Harmin, & Simon, 1966; Simon, Howe, & Kirschenbaum, 1972). The values clarification movement was an understandable attempt to address the increasing cultural pluralism, engaging students in a range of exercises designed to increase personal awareness of and/or make critical decisions about the values they held. The range of values is vast, ranging from personal likes in foods and aesthetic preferences in music to choices faced in ethical dilemmas (e.g., situations where one is forced to choose between telling the truth or loyalty to a friend). Being clear about which cuisine one prefers is rarely controversial. However, the notion of value clarity falls far short of ensuring ethical action. Theodore Kaczynski was clear about the values outlined in his "Manifesto," but that does not justify his actions as the so-called Unabomber. Because values clarification did not draw firm distinctions between ethical and other values, the movement drew criticism as being relativistic in the extreme. This relativism and the lack of empirical support of positive impact of values clarification (e.g., Berkowitz, 2002) resulted in decline of values clarification.

One indication of the nadir of values clarification is the fact that an author of one of the major values clarification books could in 1995 write a history of character education that never mentions *values clarification* by name (Kirschenbaum, 1995). In terms of influence, values clarification was eclipsed by the cognitive–developmental approach of Kohlberg (Kohlberg, 1981, 1984; Power, Higgins, & Kohlberg, 1989; Reed, 1997).

Seemingly ubiquitous in the 1970s and early 1980s, Kohlberg's approach to moral education grew out of his research focused on highlighting and discussing hypothetical ethical dilemmas in curricula. (Reed, 1997; Reimer, Paolitto, & Hersh, 1983/1990). Questions such as whether Heinz should steal a drug to save his dying wife (a parallel to Jean Valjean in *Les Miserables*) became a staple in courses in psychology and education. In a second, less widely known focus, Kohlberg attempted to create Just Communities in which students participated in governance through direct democracy and where real-life dilemmas received more emphasis than hypothetical ones (Power et al., 1989; Reed, 1997).

Kohlberg was criticized on several fronts, and during the late 1980s and 1990s, the dominance of the developmental approach waned. Shweder (1982) and Simpson (1974) challenged Kohlberg's claim of universal and invariant stages of development, and Sullivan (1977) presented a critique from a "critical" point of view (see Kohlberg, 1984, for a response to the critics).

The most influential critiques of Kohlberg—in terms of character education—were arguments from feminist theorists.

The caring approach to morality differs from the character and developmental approaches in significant ways: (a) a morality of care is relational rather than individual; (b) it gives primacy to moral emotions and sentiments, claiming these to be the stimulus to moral action and moral reasoning (not always in that order); and (c) care does not require that moral decisions need to be "universalized" to be justified. Creating and maintaining relationships and a restructuring of school curricula to include a broader range of content and a greater appreciation for the affective is at the core of the caring approach's prescriptions for schools.

It is ironic, given the historical power of the feminists' arguments against Kohlberg, that many of the prescriptions of caring character education are found in practicing Just Communities. Notably, they share constructivist approaches, an emphasis on relationships, and using, addressing, and resolving real ethical dilemmas that arise in community to promote character development.

CONTEMPORARY ISSUES IN THE POLITICS OF CHARACTER EDUCATION

The issues that surrounded character education from the outset of public schools in the United States continue today. Before detailing how these issues are framed, let us examine the range of character education programs that exist in today's schools.

Character Education and Democratic Citizenship

One of the points on which all approaches to character education in the United States agree is that there is a relationship between character education and preparing a student to become a democratic citizen. A well-functioning democracy is dependent on an enlightened citizenry and one that can engage in the "pursuit of happiness" while also considering the common good. Education for democracy is a central aim of education, and many scholars argue it is the central aim (e.g., Banks, 1997; Goodlad & McMannon, 1997; Parker, 2002; Soder, 2001).

As might be anticipated, however, citizenship education and developing democratic character (Berkowitz, 2000; Soder, 2001) are fraught with political issues and division. The definition of *responsible citizen* is also a critical matter of contention. Character Counts!, one of the high-profile programs, cites citizenship as one of the "six pillars" of character. The brief definition of *citizenship* gives imperatives to follow: "Do your share to make your school and community better, Cooperate, Stay informed, Vote, Be a good neighbor, Obey laws and rules, Respect authority, Protect the environment" (Josephson Institute, 2001, 2002). The orientation to transmit values of what is seen as a prima facie good society is evident in the charge to obey laws and rules and to respect authority. This raises questions of whether those, such as Rosa Parks for example, should be considered as good citizens or having good character. As Noddings (2002a) and Kahne and Westheimer (2003) argued, these traits are not unique to democracy; in fact, they would be viewed with approval by dictators and tyrants.

Whether education is primarily a matter of transmitting democratic values to the young or whether the focus is on fostering the capacities necessary for the process of democracy is the feature that distinguishes the major approaches in citizenship education. .

The terms for citizenship education, *traditional* and *progressive,* are consistent with how the terms are used in character education. Both the traditional and progressive approaches to citizenship emphasize (a) the obligation to vote, (b) deliberation of significant public issues, and (c) recognizing that democracy is always (to steal a phrase from existentialists) in "the process of becoming" and therefore requires constant vigilance.

Parker (1996, 2003) outlined and advocated a third concept and approach, "advanced democracy," which differs from traditional and progressive citizenship education by placing an explicit focus on diversity and what is frequently referred to as "identity politics" and/or "the politics of difference" (e.g., Grillo, 1998; Wilmsen & McAllister, 1996; Young, 1990). In identity politics, it is the smaller rather than the larger group to which the individual has allegiance. For example, in contemporary politics, identity politics is evident in debates and deliberations about issues of abortion with the competing pro-choice and pro-life identity groups. In the case of Northern Ireland, Protestant and Catholic and the differences between them are, for some, of greater importance than what they have in common.

Parker (1996) outlined the challenge of diversity and identity politics for advanced democracy:

> Liberal democracy's basic tenets of human dignity, individual liberty, equality, and popular sovereignty need to be preserved but extended and deepened within a new sense of citizenship that is not subtly or overtly hostile to diversity. This is a citizenship that embraces individual differences, multiple group identities, and a unifying political community all at once. The task ahead is to recognize individual and group differences and to unite them horizontally in democratic moral discourse. (p. 117)

As Parker noted, this required discourse is ethical in nature and, therefore, related to issues of character and character education (e.g., Habermas, 1990; Noddings, 2002a, 2002b).

The tension between the good of the individual or identity group and the commonweal is one that was noted by Alexis de Tocqueville (1835/2000) in his study of democracy in the United States. It is the "habits of the heart" by which individuals constrain their own self-interest and consider the good of the community. It has been dealt with in different ways by the three approaches to character education. Traditional character educators who rely on a finite list of virtues may differ in the number included in their lists but have few doubts that the virtues are universal and on reflection will supersede the narrow interests of any individual or identity group. The developmentalists have a tradition that emphasizes social justice. They see universality embodied in developmental stages rather than a set of virtues and see resolution through a careful examination of competing claims being judged in terms of rational ethical principles, most notably based on justice.

In contrast, the caring approach does not claim universality and questions both traditional character education and developmentalists in their shared liberal tradition. The liberal tradition is seen by proponents of caring as placing too much emphasis on individualism and rationality.

Citizenship education consists of knowledge, skills, and dispositions. Learning the history of concepts of the U.S. Constitution is an example of the first, developing an ability to engage in respectful political deliberation is an example of requisite skills, and dispositions refers to being engaged in the community (sometimes called "social capital"; e.g., Putnam, 2000). One of the strategies to foster democratic dispositions is "service learning." Service learning is a teaching strategy where students learn portions of a discipline's curriculum by providing community service (e.g., Bhaerman, Cordell, & Gomez, 1998; Billig & Waterman, 2002; Education Commission of the States, 2001; Eyler & Giles, 1999; Kielsmeier, 2000; Wade, 1997, 2000). Teaching immigrants the answers to the United States' test for citizenship is both a service and a way for students themselves to know the content. Providing a résumé service to unemployed homeless as a service and as a means of teaching one form of writing and vocational skills is another example. In many service-learning experiences, students confront ethical issues (e.g., what responsibilities individuals and government have toward the homeless, poor, or the abused).

That citizenship and character education have an unbreakable link and that service learning is a strategy to foster both are two points of common ground among the three approaches. They do not, however, have a shared definition or a broad set of educational prescriptions or strategies (Berkowitz, 2000).

Relationship of Families to Schools

It is shibboleth of the character approach, to quote George W. Bush (2002), that the family is the primary unit of traditional character education.

In our experience, many educators fear that character education will create major controversy, but the fear is exaggerated. That is not, however, to claim that such controversies do not exist. There are some parents and networks—formal and informal—who object to character education in public schools—frequently called "government schools" (e.g., see http://www.learnusa.com). The arguments offered often include that schools are teaching values counter to those held by the

families and that the focus of schools should be limited to "core knowledge disciplines."

Many of these parents are on the political right and, ironically, also use an argument often associated with the political left: that school is trying to produce workers, sacrificing the interests of the child and the family for those of corporations and the economy (e.g., Bowles & Gintis, 1976).

Relationship of Church and State

As noted earlier, there is a strong historical connection between religion and character education in the United States. The tension is evident also in the U.S. Constitution and the Bill of Rights, which simultaneously prohibit a state-sponsored religion and guarantee the right of any person to join and follow any faith community, but where communities remain separate from the state.

These issues continue today. There is a strong perceived connection between religion and character in the minds of the U.S. population.

However firm the connection between religion and character is in the public's perception, citizens demonstrate a tolerance for other religions and faiths and in the views on many religious issues, such as school prayer.

The administration of President George W. Bush supports federal funding to faith-based organizations for delivery of education, health, and human service programs. President Bush sees religion as providing the meta-ethical foundation for and as being the genesis of character as well as providing the foundation for character education.

Advocating character education, while simultaneously holding that character education starts with religion, is a restatement of the tension of the constitutional requirement for a separation of church and state.

Some parents see secular character education as incompatible with their beliefs; however, most schools implement character education without such controversies. The major distinction in character education, and all academic disciplines, is between teaching about religion rather than promoting or proselytizing a particular faith. (e.g., Haynes & Thomas, 1998; Nord, 1995; Nord & Haynes, 1998). Knowing about religion is essential to an understanding of the situation in the Middle East. In character education, understanding the religious faiths of Desmond Tutu, Martin Luther King, Jr., Mahatma Gandhi, and the Dali Lama are required for a full understanding and appreciation of their moral philosophies and actions.

Politics of Federal Character Education Pilot Programs

The U.S. Department of Education (2003) started funding character education programs during the Clinton administration with competitive grants.

In the presidential election of year 2000, character education was an issue supported by candidates George W. Bush and Al Gore. After taking office, the Bush administration in August 2001 unveiled its Communities of Character program. President Bush's recommendations for teaching strategies fall within the framework of the traditional conception of character education:

> There are schools in our country where children take pledges each morning to be respectful, responsible and ready to learn—it's an interesting idea—where virtues are taught by studying the great historical figures and characters in literature; and where consideration is encouraged and good manners are expected. (Bush, 2002, para. 18)

The administration's Communities of Character program was a major focus in late summer of 2001, and it was sufficiently high in profile that it drew the attention of political pundits, op-ed pages, and newspaper editorial boards (e.g., *Values, depoliticized,* 2001). Bush's plans to put character education at the center of the citizenry's attention evaporated in the events of September 11, 2001. However, the administration—working with bipartisan sponsors—tripled the amount of character education pilot grants available through the U.S. Department of Education.

There was a range in the quality of implementation of character education in the early years of the federal funding. The same was true of the efforts to evaluate the effects of these programs.

Politics and Character Education Research

What research does exist on character education is sketchy relative to the number of character education efforts extant. Nevertheless, it is appropriate to pose the question regarding the impact of character education, just as it is appropriate to examine the relationship of instructional strategies and/or curricula on character development.

The most recent major change in federal involvement in education is the reauthorization of what was previously the Elementary and Secondary Education Act, now titled the No Child Left Behind Act of 2001 (not to be confused with the policies of the Children's Defense Fund, which has used the phrase No Child Left Behind as its motto for many years). In 2003, The U.S. Department of Education issued contracts to assess the effectiveness of character education programs through "scientifically based research." The legislation requires that the research

- Involves the application of rigorous, systematic, and objective procedures to obtain reliable and valid knowledge relevant to education activities and programs;

- Includes research that employs systematic, empirical methods that provide reliable and valid data across evaluators and observers, across multiple measurements and observations, and across studies by the same or different investigators;

- Is evaluated using experimental or quasi-experimental designs in which individuals, entities, programs or activities are assigned to different conditions and with appropriate controls to evaluate the effects of the condition of interest, with a preference for random assignment experiments or other designs to the extent that those designs contain within-condition or across-condition controls;

- Ensures that experimental studies are presented in sufficient detail and clarity to allow for replication or, at a minimum, offer the opportunity to build systematically on their findings; and has been accepted by a peer-reviewed journal or approved by a panel of independent experts through a comparably rigorous, objective and scientific review. (American Psychological Association, 2002, p. 53)

This effort is in many ways admirable; however, the research contract opportunity ignores some of the political realities of schools and communities. It is often difficult to find, as required by the contract, 8 to 10 schools sufficiently interested in character education to implement a program. It is even more difficult to put them in a situation where, through the required random assignment, they have only a 50% chance of implementing the program. They would be forced not to implement for 2 years if random assignment makes them a control school ineligible for the "treatment category." This concern is more than hypothetical. Character Counts! experienced this problem in an evaluation in South Dakota, where control schools did not remain in the research project. The Community of Caring (a character education program of the Joseph P. Kennedy Jr. Foundation) had one control school implement the program in the second year of implementation in the experimental school.

Even if there are schools that have the character and discipline to delay educational gratification by being control schools and if data are gathered, based on the history of "evidence-based" research and policy implications in reading, one cannot be sanguine that the forthcoming results will be viewed as objective by all educators and policymakers (e.g., Zimmerman & Brown, 2003). The evidence demonstrating the ineffectiveness of the drug-abuse prevention education (DARE) program (e.g., Ennett, Tobler, Ringwalt, & Flewelling, 1994; U.S. General Accounting Office, 2003) has had only limited and delayed effects on convincing schools to drop the program in favor of programs with solid research evidence of effective prevention.

Politics of State Funding and Support of Character Education—States

Schooling is a responsibility of the states. The majority of school funds come from local and state coffers. In the 1999–2000 academic year, the average contribution of federal funds to the budgets of the 100 largest school districts was 8%. With the exception of the District of Columbia, the high was 15.3% and 2% the low (National Center for Education Statistics, 2003). The federal government is sometimes accused of creating unfunded mandates with regulations that accompany the funds (the annual testing required by the No Child Left Behind Act and special education are oft-cited examples). This is not the case with character education. In the first round of the "pilot" funding, state education agencies receiving federal grants were required to attempt to secure state funding to replace the federal dollars at the end of the 4-year period of the grants. Indiana, Missouri, and New Jersey were successful, whereas most others failed. The politically charged issue of mandating, but not funding, character education is more prevalent at the state level.

For clarity and simplicity, let us consider three differing types (of the many existing and potential permutations) of support for character education: (1) a state mandate without funding, (2) a state that encourages without providing funding, and (3) a state mandating or encouraging with funding.

In 2000, the bipartisan co-chairs of the House of Representatives introduced legislation supporting and funding character education. There were many parallels between Iowa in 2003 and Washington in 2000, including support from both Democrats and Republicans and a negative editorial from the state's largest newspaper, the *Seattle Times,* titled "Voting for Character Ed: So Light, Tasty and Flaky" (2000). The major difference between Iowa and the state of Washington was funding. Iowa's legislation supports character education without funding and was passed; the Washington State legislation that would have provided support and funding went down to defeat.

Based on its survey, the Education Commission of the States (2001) reported that

> one measure of how character education is growing is the number of states that have passed legislation; as of January 2001, nine states and Puerto Rico have mandated character education through legislation, and 11 more states plus the District of Columbia have policies that recommend some form of character education. (para. 6)

It is difficult to generalize about character education and state support because of the different types of policies and lack of a consistent definition of character across states (Education Commission of the States, 1999). Forty-nine states and the District of Columbia received and implemented character education pilot grants through the U.S. Department of Education during the first version of the Character Education Pilot Program in years 1995 through 2001 (U.S. Department of Education, n.d.-a, para. 3). In 2002, Nevada joined the list of state education agency grantees, and Texas received funds in awards to local education agencies (U.S. Department of Education, n.d.-b). Of the awardees in 2003, all were in states that had earlier character funding (U.S. Department of Education, 2003). A total of 47 states and Washington, D.C., have received federal character education funds through either state or local education agencies. Less than half that number of states were reported by the Education Commission of

the States (2001) to have formal state-level policy support. Although it is possible to quibble about the precision of the numbers, there is evidence to indicate that character education has a strong presence and support, even in a standards-based era.

CONCLUSION

Character education is inherently part of education. The emphasis on it has fluctuated throughout the history of public education in the United States. It is tempting to conclude with an emotional call for character education "now, more than ever" and provide a laundry list of pressing issues and dilemmas; we conclude, however, on a note of determination. As noted by many educators (e.g., Goodlad, Soder, & Sirotrik, 1990; Sizer & Sizer, 2000), character education comes with the territory of teaching and schooling. It is not a question of whether to do character education but rather questions of how consciously and by what methods. The political sands will shift and create different contexts. In spite of these changes, character education will continue and character educators will continue to grapple with questions of how to be our best ethical selves and how best to help students to know, care about, and do the right thing. Political pressures can support or thwart the effective implementation of character education.

Discussion Questions

Why do you think there is such a concern with character education today?

After analyzing the history of character education as discussed in this article, what do you believe is an appropriate program for character development in our schools?

Robert W. Howard is an assistant professor at the University of Washington, Tacoma

Marvin W. Berkowitz is a professor at the University of Missouri, St. Louis.

Esther F. Schaeffer is CEO of the Character Education Project.

Article 28

NO POT OF GOLD AT THE END OF THE RAINBOW

MURRY R. NELSON

The unfortunate political entanglement that has ensnared American education, particularly curriculum, reached its zenith in New York City in the 1990s when a local school board turned a diverse and thoughtfully developed curriculum into a narrow discussion of homosexuality. The story illustrates the powerful role of politics in forging the curriculum.

The task was straightforward—develop a curriculum more reflective of the polyglot of citizens populating New York City in order to promote tolerance and respect for this diversity. The immediate result was an enormous volume of background information, activities, bibliographic materials, and caveats for teachers. The long-term results, however, were much more dramatic, ultimately contributing to the ouster of the chancellor of the New York City Public Schools. Furthermore, rather than promoting tolerance, the effort abetted intolerance. Its story illustrates the potential

volatility of curriculum, how easily it can become politicized, and how multiculturalism may become marginalized in its goals and products.

This case also has inextricable ties to and with the media, mostly the local print media; but when the local area is New York City, coverage and concerns swiftly become national. With the ready availability of local media on the Internet, the curricular "model" described may well become a kind of template for local curricular issues in the future becoming, unavoidably, national issues.

THE CURRICULUM

In 1989, the Board of Education of the City of New York passed a resolution urging the schools to promote a greater appreciation of diversity by race, religion, sex, and sexual orientation.[1] The board's resolution recognized the increasing

SOURCE: Excerpted from Nelson, M. R. (2001). No pot of gold at the end of the rainbow. *Journal of Curriculum & Supervision, 16*(3), 206–227. Reprinted by permission of ASCD.

immigration to the United States and, most specifically, to and through New York City.

Along with cultural diversity came the language diversity that has always been the hallmark of New York City. Of persons aged 5 to 17—that is, school-age youngsters—471,000 spoke a language other than English at home, and nearly 60,000 of those spoke English not at all or very poorly. Most of these second-language or non-English speakers spoke Spanish, but the number of Italian speakers was still quite high, and the number of Chinese speakers was the third highest of those with languages identified. It was this that led to the establishment of Newcomers High School in 1995. This high school offers courses in a number of languages, including Bengali, Chinese, Korean, Polish, Romanian, and Spanish.[2]

The task of developing a curriculum to implement the Board of Education's resolution fell to the chancellor's staff. The chancellor, Joseph A. Fernandez, was a former mathematics teacher, but, despite prior expertise in curriculum, he had delegated responsibility in that area since taking on larger administrative roles. Indeed, he had made his greatest impact by advocating and practicing school-based management (SBM) in Dade County, and this experience was a great selling point to the board of education in New York City when it hired Mr. Fernandez.[3]

In her brief foreword to the new curriculum that was produced by the chancellor's staff, entitled *Children of the Rainbow,* Nilda Soto Ruiz, the chief executive for instruction of the New York City Public Schools, reiterated some of the statistical realities noted earlier in order to put into context the social and curricular climate in which *Children of the Rainbow* was created:

> It must be noted that over one hundred languages are spoken in the New York City Public Schools, and that almost half of the sixty thousand children attending kindergarten come from homes where a language other than English is spoken. As the research strongly supports the idea that children learn best when the home language is incorporated into the school environment, it is important that all kindergarten classrooms, not just ESL and bilingual

programs, reflect home cultures in their instructional strategies. When children value their own individuality and cultural identity, they learn to appreciate and respect others as well.[4]

These important words essentially framed the task as well as the strategy of the curriculum and curriculum makers. They were reflective of social development and social reconstructionist goals of schooling and the curriculum. Although content was hardly eschewed, it was to be taught within the parameters that framed the social process. The *Children of the Rainbow* curriculum would be developed in an accretive manner, beginning with kindergarten and expanding by at least one new grade level each year.

In 1990, the first volume, *Implementing a Multicultural Kindergarten Curriculum,* appeared.[5] In more than 350 pages, the guide presented 15 sections of strategies, activities, and materials for the city's kindergarten classes. It identified more than 25 district personnel as principal writers of the guide. Of those, five were specifically identified as being from a bilingual or second-language office in the district. Fifteen individuals were identified with early childhood duties or specific transitional home-to-kindergarten programs in New York City. Others represented special education, general staff development, or school improvement. Nearly 25 other individuals within and outside the district were identified as reviewers from the "educational community." Half of the reviewers were external, including three from outside the State of New York.

CONTENT OF THE GUIDE

The *Children of the Rainbow* guide for kindergarten was described as "a comprehensive guide to implementing a developmentally appropriate, multicultural kindergarten program."[6] Almost every section contained background information for the teacher, teaching strategies, suggestions for home/school partnership, and teaching activities. The first section, the introduction, outlined the program and its philosophy:

By acknowledging, respecting, and celebrating diversity, the teacher recognizes the whole child and can plan experiences, which extend multicultural awareness. By understanding the similarities and differences of cultural groups, children learn that all people have the same basic needs, though they may respond to them in different ways. Parents and community members are vital components in the process.[7]

The section, "Looking at Today's Children," was the most reflective of what appears to be a social reconstruction curriculum philosophy. After a discussion of the value and characteristics of play, the remainder of the section addressed societal concerns—preventing child abuse; alcohol, drug, and substance abuse; and homeless/shelter children. The focus on child abuse directly responded to the rising number of reported cases of such abuse in New York City and the nation. Indicators of child abuse were offered so that teachers would be alerted to symptoms. Strategies for talking with possibly abused children *privately* were offered. Lesson ideas for individuals or small groups regarding protective behaviors were offered. Presentation ideas for working with parents informally were given, as well as a final reference to the Chancellor's Memorandum No. 20, 1987–88, on the commitment of all schools to the safety, health, and welfare of the child.

The alcohol, drug, and substance abuse section was fairly standard, discussing healthy foods, dangerous household substances, and "common" illegal drugs. The danger of these items was emphasized continually. The final part on homeless/shelter children was presented because "families with young children are the fastest growing segment of homeless Americans."[8] These two pages provided information to assist the teacher. No activities or teaching ideas were included.

All in all, the kindergarten guide for *Children of the Rainbow* was well received and hardly controversial. The "societal concerns" section was well contextualized and strongly justified by the rising numbers of abused children and of children exposed to dangerous substances and the increase in the homeless. Though these topics were uncomfortable, their reality prompted a sad resignation, and their examination implied no acceptance of them as appropriate societal conditions. Possibly buoyed by this situation, the chancellor's staff writing the first grade guide may have considered that the public understood this difficult task that had been undertaken and was willing to accept more controversial issues as appropriate for curricular study. When the first grade guide was presented in 1991–1992, this situation would not be the case.[9]

THE GRADE 1 GUIDE

The generally positive response to the kindergarten curriculum of *Children of the Rainbow* may have emboldened the chancellor's staff that wrote the first grade guide. A number of changes were implemented in the production of this latter guide. The first difference was that the first grade guide was both smaller *and* larger. It was about 40 pages longer, but its actual content was divided into two parts. Both of these might not be used by the same teacher because they were in two languages (English and Spanish); teachers would have to be bilingual to use both parts. The sections were not simply the same content translated into the other language. Large sections overlapped, but the Spanish section was almost exclusively limited to the content enunciated in the "Chancellor's Learning Objectives" for Grade 1 presented on pages xiii–xxviii. The objectives were performance based and divided into the content areas of communication arts, mathematics, science, and social studies.

Much of the guide's content replicated the kindergarten guide and was acknowledged as such. Fewer credited writers prepared the first grade guide: 5 being credited for the Spanish section and 14 for the English section, compared with 27 who worked on the kindergarten guide. Five authors appeared on both guides' list of writers. Six of the reviewers for the kindergarten guide were credited as reviewers for the first grade guide. Thus, the first grade guide reflects both continuity and "freshness" in the choices of authors and reviewers.

As noted earlier, the Spanish portion focused almost exclusively on content, whereas the English language materials had two areas, "Societal Concerns" and "Assessment," that had a broader perspective. Controversy would focus on "Societal Concerns," Section 5.

In the Introduction, the program philosophy presented in the kindergarten guide was reiterated with a first grade emphasis:

> The widely differing needs, interests, and expectations of first grade children should be addressed through personalized, multicultural, developmentally appropriate learning experiences. Children should be continually encouraged to recognize and respect other groups and individuals while developing their own identity and sense of self-worth.[10]

This introduction failed to discuss any of the content of Section 5, "Societal Concerns— Children With Special Needs," except to note that it "looks at current societal pressures and concerns affecting young children. Health problems, responsibilities for 'latchkey' children, and alternative family structures are explored."[11]

Sections 1 through 4 were similar in scope to the kindergarten curriculum.

Section 5—Curricular Content

Ultimately, a small part of Section 5 proved to be most troublesome for this curriculum. Thus, that section requires further scrutiny. The first part of the section addressed "Children With Special Needs." "Desirable modes of behavior" for children were stressed. These included concerns for the feelings of others, acceptance of individual differences, and support for the insecure. Ways for the regular teacher to teach concepts to individual students with special needs were offered with a variety of teaching strategies, caveats, and suggested activities.

Following these nine pages came nine more on "Alcohol, Drug, and Substance Abuse." The general approach was similar to that provided in

the kindergarten guide, but it developed a concerted emphasis, not seen the previous year, for young children prenatally exposed (PED) to drugs/alcohol. Characteristics of PED children, facilitative processes for classrooms with PED children, and a philosophy of such educational programs were offered. Following that, teaching strategies for at-risk children were included. Despite the discomfort in acknowledging the existence of children in these situations, little or no criticism was ever directed to this part of the curriculum.

The next part of the section, three pages in length, was entitled "Understanding Family Structures to Meet Children's Needs." Here, the definition of a family was listed as "two or more people who share love, care, and responsibilities."[12] This definition, which failed to mention marriage, was only the beginning of what would arouse the ire of many critics of the curriculum. The guide offered a number of family structures, many of which might be considered unconventional, most notably, lesbian/gay parents.

The guide presented the teacher's role as one of determining the various family structures within the classroom and suggested how to meet the individual needs of children in relation to this knowledge. Also of concern in the guide was where or how children were cared for after school. It suggested that parent–teacher conferences were the best forum from which to obtain such information because of the need for discretion, compassion, and time for discussion.

The guide also offered caveats on activities that related to the family. For example, a child whose parent may have died recently might become distraught during discussions of family issues, or "a child being raised by a single mother or by lesbian co-parents may not have a male figure to relate to during Father's Day celebrations."[13] Teachers were urged to overcome their personal prejudices regarding cultural, social, or economic issues so that they might create a sense of respect for the diversity of families. The subhead of the next part was entitled "Fostering Positive Attitudes Toward Sexuality." Because this information proved to be so publicly volatile and easily could be mis-construed when taken out of context, all four paragraphs of the part are reprinted here:

Fostering Positive Attitudes Toward Sexuality

It is important for teachers of first graders to be aware of the changing concept of family in today's society. To help teachers work effectively with every child, it is important to know that:

- Children of lesbian/gay parents may have limited experience with male/female parental situations; if there is no representation of their lives in the classroom, they may suddenly be made to feel different.

- Children growing up in heterosexually headed families may be experiencing contact with lesbians/gays for the first time.

Many children have lesbian/gay relatives. According to statistics, at least 10 percent of each class will grow up to be homosexual. Because of pervasive homophobia (the irrational fear of homosexuals) in society, lesbian/gay teens are more likely to drop out of school, commit suicide, abuse drugs/alcohol, or get pregnant than the rest of their peers. Lesbian/gay students (or even those just perceived as gay) are frequently assaulted verbally and physically by other students and their parents. It is also common for them to be thrown out of their homes once their parents find out their child is gay.

Teachers of first graders have an opportunity to give children a healthy sense of identity at an early age. Classes should include references to lesbian/gay people in all curricular areas and should avoid exclusionary practices by presuming a person's sexual orientation, reinforcing stereotypes, or speaking of lesbians/gays as "they" or "other."

If teachers do not discuss lesbian/gay issues, they are not likely to come up. Children need actual experiences via creative play, books, visitors, etc., in order for them to view lesbians/gays as real people to be respected and appreciated. Educators have the potential to help increase the tolerance and acceptance of the lesbian/gay community and to decrease the staggering number of hate crimes perpetrated against them.[14]

The next short section dealt with overcoming sexism, which provided relatively commonplace information and attitudes. It noted that television, books, and family notions often perpetuate sexism and that confrontation of misconceptions "in order to show that men and women need not hold restricted work or family roles" was important.[15] Criteria were given for determining appropriateness of books in terms of sexist bias and attitudes.

The next two sections presented information about "Latchkey Children" and "Homeless/Shelter Children," followed by a section entitled "Preventing Child Abuse." These sections focused on recognition of signs of abuse in order to help children. This part was almost identical to the section in the kindergarten guide.

The next part of Section 5 was "Facts About HIV Infection." These four pages sought to alert teachers to the dangers of as well as to clarify misconceptions about the disease. The first two topics, "Description and Cause of AIDS" and "Clinical Manifestations," consisted of straightforward information for the teacher. The next topic, "Transmission," also was solely for teacher information, although some teachers may have found some of the information disquieting. The spread of the disease through unprotected sexual intercourse mentioned anal intercourse and cautioned, "Anal intercourse is most risky, since tissue tearing and bleeding frequently occur."[16]

The topics of "Incidence" and "Research and Treatment" were largely scientific in both scope and presentation. The last topic addressed, "Responding to a Young Person's Questions," listed seven questions that children frequently asked about HIV and AIDS, such as "What is AIDS?" Two questions—"How do people 'catch' HIV?" and "Will I get HIV?"—both mentioned sharing unclean needles with an infected person and unprotected sexual intercourse.

The remainder of the English section and the entire Spanish section were relatively pedestrian. Overall, very little attention in the curriculum was addressed to issues of homosexuality. The guide included a number of bibliographic materials, but, in its first printing, three children's books that would galvanize debate on the curriculum were not listed. By 1992, those books—*Heather Has Two Mommies, Daddy's Roommate,* and *Gloria Goes to Gay Pride*—had been added, as had a host of other books and articles.[17]

The curriculum guide was distributed to all school districts in the city during 1991–1992 with the expectation that each local board would accommodate the materials in their planning for the 1992–1993 school year. Before the 1991–1992 school year ended, however, the *Children of the Rainbow* curriculum guide was plunged into controversy.

THE CURRICULUM CONTROVERSY

Each of the local school boards has a certain degree of autonomy in New York City. Upon receiving a new curriculum guide, each local board is charged to examine the material and determine how best to implement it. This process is usually pro forma, but that was not the case in this instance. The New York City schools had been decentralized following a particularly bitter teachers strike in 1968. In April of the following year, then-Governor Nelson Rockefeller signed a bill providing for community control in New York City schools through 32 community school districts, beginning with the elections of 1970. The effects of community control were not without problems. Diane Ravitch notes, for example, in her extensive history of the New York City schools:

> The drive for community control was a direct assault on the idea of the common school, that is, a school which is supported by all, controlled by all, and which propagates no particular religious, ideological or political views. The advocates of community control wanted public schools supported by all, but controlled and ideologically directed by whomever won the local school board elections.[18]

This change in structure reflected what Larry Cuban saw as a change in public attitudes over a 50-year period.

What had changed more than anything were public attitudes. Belief in the legitimacy of the school board and staff as guardians of children's intellectual and moral development had eroded. During the post–World War II years, confidence diminished in the public schools to do what they were supposed to do.[19]

Thus, not surprisingly, "discourse," including dissent, arose from some local school boards at the issuance of almost any directive emanating from the central offices of the New York City schools. In April 1992, the District 24 school board in Queens announced that it would not use the new curriculum guide for first graders in its schools. Specifically, the board stated it would not allow use of a guide that told teachers to "be aware of valid family structures, including gay and lesbian parents." Mary Cummins, then president of the District 24 school board, was quoted in a *Newsday* article as saying, "We do not tell first graders about homosexuals."[20]

A district spokesperson, in defense of the guide, noted that it was about tolerance and appreciation of diversity, not the promotion of "gay and lesbian lifestyles." In a trice, the public outrage had shifted discussion from the overall purpose and content of the curriculum to a narrow discussion of homosexuality. A New York Civil Liberties Union representative claimed that the actions of the District 24 board raised issues of censorship and equality of education, whereas the superintendent of local District 20 questioned the age-appropriateness of the suggested texts, *Heather Has Two Mommies, Gloria Goes to Gay Pride,* and *Daddy's Roommate.* In another section of this April 1992 *Newsday* article, individuals were quoted as questioning the age-appropriateness of the disputed books (but not the curriculum itself) as well as defending the books (this latter action from a babysitter who had read the books to her young charges and found them useful and understood).

The District 24 school board had sent a letter in March to all the districts in the city to warn that the new curriculum was not consonant with local community standards. This board previously had passed a policy that forbade any discussion of homosexuality in schools. Board president Cummins noted, "We did not want to teach anything that would conflict with a moral code or religion at home."[21] Actually, the District 24 policy forbade the mention of four words—*abortion, contraception, homosexuality,* and *masturbation*—in classes in the district. Despite being a public board chosen in a community-wide election, the District 24 school board members were all white Roman Catholics and included one priest. This board represented a district in which more than 70% of the 27,000 students were members of minority groups. Moreover, the district had one of the fastest growing immigrant populations in the city, but only one of the school board members still had children enrolled in the schools.[22]

This region of Queens, particularly the Glendale and Ridgewood neighborhoods, was not new to controversy involving change. Its conservative ideological views had been established as early as 1958 when the New York City Board of Education attempted to integrate the city's schools. Queens parents demonstrated against integration as the superintendent of schools, John Theobald, "launched the first trial of permissive zoning; almost 400 black elementary pupils in Bedford-Stuyvesant were transferred to underutilized all-white schools in the Ridgewood and Glendale sections of Queens."[23]

The response of these Queens communities was racist, but was not surprising. These parents felt duped by the superintendent and feared for their neighborhoods and property values. They held community protest meetings and school boycotts, but ultimately they acquiesced. Members of the District 24 school board surely would have remembered these earlier frays because they had grown up mainly in these neighborhoods. The district also recently had sued the chancellor over a directive to permit parents and teachers to participate in the hiring of principals and assistant principals.[24]

Against this background, many parties then chose to enter this extensively politicized fray. The disputed curriculum seemed almost ancillary to the political and religious direction that

the District 24 school board had taken in pursuit of the issue.

In June, shortly before school dismissed for the summer, Chancellor Fernandez wrote a letter to all community school boards and superintendents in the city in which he emphasized that "all school districts must teach first grade students respect for gay families."[25] According to a spokesman, Fernandez ordered boards either to adopt the *Children of the Rainbow* curriculum or to develop an alternative curriculum plan by June 30 or "he would run the multicultural curriculum himself." *Newsday* coverage revealed that four other districts (other than District 24) had decided to delete the section on alternative families. Political positions seemed to be hardening, making any compromise more challenging. In his autobiography, Chancellor Fernandez reported that he was experiencing difficulties with the larger issue of school decentralization in the city and that this controversy merely accentuated all that he saw wrong with community school boards.

Decentralization created what was essentially a two-headed monster: one, the 32 districts where community boards were given almost total control of the elementary and middle schools (and in far too many cases took advantage of that autonomy to create, in the worst New York City tradition, their own corrupt little fiefdoms, complete with cronyism and nepotism and a depressing sense of mismanagement); and two, the more than 5,000-man central bureaucracy headquartered at 110 Livingston Street in Brooklyn where the seven-member Board of Education, made up of appointees from each of the five boroughs and two from the mayor's office, held policymaking sway over the system and its titular leader, the chancellor.[26]

At this point, journalists outside the New York City region first noticed the Rainbow Curriculum controversy. John Leo, a contributing editor for *U.S. News and World Report,* contributed an editorial to the *Seattle Times* that brought the issues to the attention of readers on the West Coast. Leo claimed to like the Rainbow Curriculum but felt that these books celebrated diversity rather than respected it. Most of his concern was directed to *Heather Has Two Mommies* and *Daddy's Roommate* and why the curriculum was *pushing* stories like those. He perceived the guide as honoring positive aspects of each type of household but felt that it crossed a line from tolerance to approval/endorsement. Leo claimed to seek a value-neutral curriculum. Such a position on this issue was almost certainly impossible, but Leo's writing, for many readers, had the ring of logical truth to it. Leo picked up on an article in a conservative New York City weekly that claimed that the chancellor's office was practicing "academic imperialism" and that 70% to 90% of Americans would disagree with the doctrines being advanced by the curriculum—that is, appreciation of the homosexual "lifestyle."

Within a week, Leo's guest editorial was republished, almost verbatim, in the August 17 edition of *U.S. News and World Report.*[27] The Rainbow Curriculum, as presented by John Leo, became a national issue, and that issue was the promotion of homosexuality in schools, particularly through the (mandated) use of two books of fiction for children.

The fall of 1992 seemed to be the time of a "showdown" between Chancellor Fernandez and several recalcitrant districts. In September, he extended the deadline to October 31 for individual districts to submit to him their plans to teach about gay families without bias.[28] Fernandez subsequently extended that deadline to November 13 because four of the dissenting districts were now talking with the chancellor's staff about their plans. The District 24 board did not budge.

Finally, on December 1, Chancellor Fernandez suspended the entire District 24 school board. On that same day, *Newsday* noted a variety of issues that were plaguing Fernandez and causing problems in the schools. These included the Rainbow Curriculum, budget problems, and the overall difficulties in dealing with Queens School District 24.[29] The District 24 school board stated, through its attorney, Hartigan, "we won't crawl" in defying the chancellor's orders to appear. Hartigan also noted that the *Children of the Rainbow*

curriculum needed to include more attention to the discouragement of religious intolerance and not to present "misinformation about sodomy."[30]

A few days later (December 6), George Will's column, carried in scores of newspapers (including the *Washington Post,* the *Chicago Sun-Times,* the *Cleveland Plain Dealer,* the *Atlanta Journal* and *Constitution*), focused attention on the *Children of the Rainbow* curriculum. Clearly following John Leo's lead and most likely not having read the materials in question, Will railed against Fernandez and "the homosexual aspects of the curriculum."

New York City's central board voted 6 to 0 to nullify Fernandez's suspension of the local board and urged another attempt at negotiation between the parties. Notwithstanding this action, the District 24 board refused to negotiate, even after making preliminary agreements with mediators for both sides.[31]

Shortly afterward, H. Carl McCall, president of the central board, criticized Fernandez for having weak aides in the area of multiculturalism. He also announced that Evelyn Kalibala had been replaced as director of multicultural education in the city's schools. At the same time, a report surfaced that Elissa Weindling, the gay/lesbian appointee to the curriculum revision group that developed the first grade curriculum, had not wanted the controversial books in question listed on the suggested readings and was surprised that they had been included.[32]

During that same week, Steven Myers, a *New York Times* reporter, tried to unravel how the situation had become so entangled. Myers noted the irony of a situation in which "a curriculum intended to foster tolerance has deeply divided the city and provoked vicious expressions of intolerance, including two threats on the Chancellor's life."[33] He went on to point out that the controversy over one small section of the curriculum had obscured completely what was actually in the curriculum.

The curriculum issue continued to be unresolved, and on February 10 the central board voted 4 to 3 not to renew Chancellor Fernandez's contract when it expired on June 30. The 5-hour meeting consisted of acrimonious debate and "testimony" for and against Fernandez's retention. Critics found fault with Fernandez for inattention to instructional issues, particularly basic skills, but also for focusing on "peripheral" issues such as condoms and tolerance. Several called him overly authoritarian and a micromanager.[34]

The arguments over the Rainbow Curriculum faded quietly with no real resolution. In May 1993, in a remarkably low voter turnout of less than 15%, many local school districts elected more conservative candidates. These results prompted one observer to note that "few teachers are likely to have the courage to teach the Rainbow Curriculum."[35]

In June 1994, the District 24 school board voted 7 to 2 to accept the new, revised Rainbow Curriculum with but five objections/suggestions; one suggested the elimination of three pages "on multiculturalism that mentioned homophobia as a 'form of bias' and included sexual orientation as well as culture and ethnicity as sources of diversity." The new president, Mary Crowley, stated that the board thought this was the right thing to do for the district's children. Mary Cummins and newly elected member Frank Borzellieri, who called multiculturalism anti-American, voted against approval.[36] In February 1999, a gay candidate for the District 24 Board of Education lost his contest; he received only 655 of the 1,650 votes needed for election.[37]

IS THIS A CURRICULAR STORY?

The controversy over the Rainbow Curriculum, to a large degree, was only remotely connected to the curriculum and to curricular issues. Josh Barbanel summed up the situation: "The fight over the Rainbow Curriculum has little to do with education and much to do with New York City politics, where race, ethnicity, and religion have always played big roles."[38]

THE MEDIA AND THE CONTROVERSY

The entire Rainbow Curriculum issue could not, indeed, would not, have become a national, or

even a city, issue without its almost constant coverage by the daily newspaper press (the national news magazines almost ignored the issue). Despite the seemingly neutral position of a free press, far more underlay the curricular issues of this period of time. Indeed, a tremendous battle for readership raged between the *New York Times,* the New York *Daily News,* and the New York *Post.* This economic fight pitted the latter two papers and the middle-class tabloid readers on whom they relied against each other. The *Times* readership remained relatively steady, but external factors plunged the *Daily News* and the *Post* into a death spiral that also brought in the Long Island daily, *Newsday.*

In the one-year period from March 1992 to February 1993, *Newsday* published more than 150 articles on the *Children of the Rainbow* curriculum, almost all from the Queens bureau. Without this dedicated commitment to publicizing every comment of Mary Cummins and the District 24 board, this story likely would have been far quieter.

The national press, too, gave unprecedented coverage to the Rainbow Curriculum, but with an agenda nearly identical to that of Mary Cummins and her colleagues at District 24. Early on, this issue spun out of control, leaving the curricular substance far behind the public specter of homosexuality.

Of course, the lack of control can be blamed somewhat on the chancellor and his aides. Central Board president McCall successfully pressured Fernandez, but too late, to replace the aides involved with the *Children of the Rainbow* curriculum. Fernandez himself also recognized the volatility and complexity of the issue far too late. When he was hired, unawareness of instructional issues was seen as his chief weakness. The Rainbow Curriculum controversy dramatically emphasized that flaw. Fernandez's efforts to bargain with District 24 from his position of power ultimately led to charges of authoritarianism and micromanagement. The chancellor's power eroded as he conceded that he had not read the entire curriculum and when he finally agreed in December 1992 to drop the demand that first graders deal with gays/lesbians in all curricular areas. At that time, he told area superintendents that they could postpone lessons about gay/lesbian families until the fifth or sixth grades.

In a spectacular display of poor timing, Fernandez's memoir appeared in 1993. As noted earlier, the book skewered a number of people on the central board. In New York City, Fernandez came off as arrogant and aloof. The book also contained a prescient comment on his tenure in the New York City Public Schools: "I don't expect to be running it [the school system] much longer because you can't separate politics and education in America, and the politics in New York are almost certain to bring me down sooner or later."[39]

So, the Rainbow Curriculum disappeared from the New York City schools. One would hope that its passing might have been accompanied by Judy Garland's rendition of "Over the Rainbow."

Discussion Questions

Nelson illustrates the relationship of curriculum and politics. After reading this case study, what are your feelings about the Rainbow Curriculum?

How will you deal with gay, lesbian, bisexual, and transgendered issues in your classroom when they arise?

Murry R. Nelson is a professor at Pennsylvania State University.

Article 29

A CONTEMPORARY CONTROVERSY IN AMERICAN EDUCATION

Including Intelligent Design in the Science Curriculum

VICKI D. JOHNSON

WHAT IS INTELLIGENT DESIGN?

Intelligent design has emerged as the most recent challenger to evolution. Proponents of this theory say that there are gaps in Darwin's theory—gaps that are best filled by recognizing the role of an intelligent agent in life's origin and development. According to Dembski and Ruse (2004, p. 3), "The claim is simply that there must be something more than ordinary natural causes or material mechanisms, and moreover, that something must be intelligent and capable of bringing about organisms." This definition of intelligent design is predicated on the writings of Behe (1996), who argued that some biological structures are so irreducibly complex that their existence cannot possibly be explained by the evolutionary biology of Darwin.

In an editorial opinion published in the *New York Times*, Behe (2005) stated that "design should not be overlooked" as a cause for irreducibly complex systems and that intelligent design is the most obvious explanation for the origin of these systems. He also asserted that "the theory of intelligent design is not a religiously based idea" and that "intelligent design itself says nothing about the religious concept of a creator." He added that intelligent design is an elegant theory that is overwhelmingly and sensibly embraced by the public.

The contemporary argument for intelligent design is based on physical evidence and a straightforward

SOURCE: Excerpted from Johnson, V. D. (2006). A contemporary controversy in American education: Including intelligent design in the science curriculum. *Educational Forum, 70*(3), 222–236. Reprinted by permission of Kappa Delta Pi.

application of logic. We can often recognize the effects of design in nature. For example, unintelligent physical forces like plate tectonics and erosion are sufficient to account for the origin of the Rocky Mountains. Yet they are not enough to explain Mount Rushmore.

Behe invoked the popularity of this idea as justification for its truthfulness. Because opinion polls (Newport, 2004) demonstrated that 45% of the American public believed in creationism and one-third were biblical literalists, Behe (2005) questioned the motivation of scientists who continue to promote the "messiness of evolution" as an explanation for life's complexities.

Opponents of intelligent design, the majority of scientists, and most scientific organizations, do not appreciate the logic of Behe's proposition. Many opponents view intelligent design as a new, pseudoscientific version of creationism, formulated in reaction to the Supreme Court's ruling in *Edwards v. Aguillard* 482 U.S. 578 (1987). In this case, the Court reviewed a Louisiana law requiring equal time for the teaching of creationism and evolution in school curricula. The Court ruled that creationism failed to meet the legal criteria for science and clearly represented a religious belief; therefore, the Louisiana law conflicted with the establishment clause of the U.S. Constitution (Alters & Alters, 2001; Moore, 2002; National Academy of Sciences, 1998). This defeat of creationism is viewed as a major impetus for the intelligent design movement.

WHO ARE THE PROPONENTS OF INTELLIGENT DESIGN?

In his book *Myths America Lives By* (2003), Hughes offered a historical account of the development of the myth of the Christian nation. This myth was born in the nationwide religious revival of the Second Great Awakening and fervently persists today as a powerful force in American society. Since the time that our nation's founders established America on Deist beliefs and the necessary principle of separation of church and state, Christian nation proponents have actively sought to demolish this framework and reconstruct American society according to their own religious viewpoints, making the tenets of American Protestantism central. Hughes explained:

> Some Christians were determined to fight the forces of the modern world, to resist the encroachment of secularity, and to preserve a Christian America against all odds. They typically identified Darwin's theory of evolution as the chief culprit, and they hammered that doctrine unmercifully. We know these Christians today as fundamentalists. (p. 85)

The chief proponents of intelligent design today are Christian fundamentalists and their conservative political organizations. One organization that is central to the intelligent design movement is the Center for Science and Culture, formerly known as the Center for the Renewal of Science and Culture (CRSC). Founded in 1996, the Center, which is affiliated with the conservative Christian think tank the Discovery Institute, authored a strategic plan entitled *The Wedge Strategy* (1999). This strategy was based on "The Wedge: A Strategy for Defining Truth," a chapter in *Defeating Darwinism by Opening Minds* (Johnson, 1997), in which two distinct definitions of science in society are argued: one devoted to unbiased research and the other devoted to explaining all phenomena that employ only natural or material causes (naturalism). Johnson (2000) argued that the philosophical school of naturalism is dominant in our society, not because of its merits but because of the ideology and paradigm prevalent in today's scientific community: Johnson (2000) asserted that for science to be vigorous and healthy, it also must include alternative theories, such as intelligent causes for the origin of life. The wedge of intelligent design, according to Johnson (2000), is that it reveals the inherent weaknesses of scientific naturalism and allows for a broader, more comprehensive view of the origins of the universe and life consistent with theistic views.

What Are the Goals of the of Intelligent Design?

The Wedge Strategy outlined a three-phased political action plan for promoting intelligent design as an alternative to evolutionary biology:

- Phase I—scientific research, writing, and publicity

- Phase II—publicity and opinion making

- Phase III—cultural confrontation and renewal

Each of these phases was designed to achieve two governing goals of the Discovery Institute: (a) to defeat scientific materialism and its destructive moral, cultural, and political legacies and (b) to replace materialistic explanations with the theistic understanding that nature and human beings are created by God. Ultimately, proponents of *The Wedge Strategy* aimed at "establishing intelligent design theory as the dominant perspective in science" and hoped "to see design theory permeate religious, cultural, moral, and political life." An interim goal was to ignite debates in education, life issues, and legal and personal responsibility and push these debates to the front of the national agenda.

OPPONENTS OF INTELLIGENT DESIGN

Opponents of intelligent design scoff at the notion that intelligent design is a new scientific theory. Some even refer to it as intelligent design creationism. They believe that intelligent design is merely a repackaged version of creationism or a contemporary revival of an old design argument proposed by theologian William Paley in 1803 (Nakhnikian, 2004). Intelligent design is characterized as a more nebulous form of creationism that is slickly marketed to appeal to a broad segment of Americans. According to Adler (2005), "The battle is being waged under a new banner—not the Book of Genesis, but 'intelligent design,' a critique of evolution couched in the language of science" (p. 46).

Eugenie C. Scott, director of the National Center for Science Education, has tracked the creationists' crusade for more than 30 years. She characterized intelligent design as the most highly evolved form of creationism to date. According to Scott (in Adler, 2005), "It's another way of saying God did it. It isn't a model; it isn't a theory that makes testable claims" (p. 50). According to Scott (in Ratliff, 2004), intelligent design advocates have been tremendously effective compared to traditional creationists; she described their strategy:

> To win in the court of public opinion, I'd needed only to cast reasonable doubt on evolution. Don't get involved in the details; don't get involved in fact claims. Forget about the age of Earth, forget about the flood, don't mention the Bible. Focus on the big idea that evolution is inadequate. Intelligent design doesn't really explain anything. It says that evolution can't explain things. Everything else is hand waving.

The current intelligent design controversy is merely an extension of the creationist controversy that erupted during the populist reform movement. As increasing numbers of teenagers attended secondary school in the 1920s, concern over evolutionary teaching turned into demands for legal action that continue today. Larson (1989) outlined the history of legal battles surrounding the creationist movement and summarized them as "efforts to reconcile publicly supported science teaching with popular opinion" (p. 4). When courts overturned bans on teaching evolution in high school, the creationist movement sought public support for granting equal time for competing scientific ideas. This same appeal to fairness is the tactic now employed by advocates of intelligent design. Because these advocates could not win equal time through the courtrooms, they have shifted the battle to the court of public opinion and to the school board (Larson, 1989).

School boards in 19 states and many more school districts are grappling with demands to include the teaching of intelligent design in science curricula (Slevins, 2005). Examples of contemporary conflicts in American education between the advocates of intelligent design and the defenders of evolution are presented.

DEBATES ABOUT ONE TEXTBOOK

For more than a decade, one high school–level biology textbook, *Of Pandas and People* (Davis and Kenyon, 1993), has been on the frontline of the intelligent design versus evolution battle. School boards from Montana to Alabama and from Texas to Idaho have been deluged with requests to adopt this book (Clark, 2004; Matsumura, 1995, 1999; Scott and Uno, 1989). *Bookwatch Reviews* (National Center for Science Education, 1989) provided multiple critiques (all negative) of this text, which challenges the adequacy of evolution theory and proposes intelligent design as a viable alternative. A storm of controversy among science teachers has ensued. Scott and Uno (1989) stated, "Although more slickly-produced than most creationist works, *Pandas* is similarly factually incorrect, and grossly mistakes evolutionary theory. This book has no potential to improve science education and student understanding of the natural world."

Despite science educators' criticism of the book, teachers such as Roger DeHart of Burlington, Washington, in 1999 sought approval of the school district's Instructional Materials Committee (IMC) to use *Of Pandas and People* in teaching his middle-school science class (Matsumura, 1999). When the IMC refused to grant permission to use the controversial text, DeHart succeeded in gaining approval from the school's principal to use portions of the book. The principal defended this action by stating that though DeHart could introduce the notion of irreducible complexity from the *Pandas* textbook, he also must teach a supporting theory of how evolution accounted for complex things (Matsumura, 1999). The school official's actions in negotiating this compromise acknowledged the intelligent design fairness strategy of giving equal consideration to opposing scientific theories.

Inherent in this compromise is an assumption that intelligent design represents a legitimate scientific challenge to evolution.

Two years earlier, George Gilchrist, a professor of zoology at the University of Washington, publicly criticized the textbook and the legitimacy of its scientific theory. In his critique, Gilchrist (1997) asked, "What sense would there be in presenting an idea as a scientific theory to high school students if the idea were not actually used by working scientists?" (p. 14). The professor conducted a review of more than 5,000 scientific publications to determine the frequency of scientists' use of intelligent design theory and evolution theory. His review of several hundred thousand scientific reports failed to reveal even one biological research study that used intelligent design theory. Evolution theory was used in 6,935 scientific research papers, and the keyword *evolution* was used in 46,749 articles (Gilchrist). Scientific research using intelligent design theory was glaringly absent. Gilchrist questioned,

> Why should we reserve a place in the science curriculum for science that apparently does not exist? Until intelligent design theory can be shown to have any status as a scientific theory of biological organization, it has no place in the biology curriculum. (p. 15)

Apparently, no real controversy exists among scientists about the theory of evolution.

Despite the negative reviews of *Pandas,* the book is now in its second edition and is vigorously promoted by its publisher.

Of Pandas and People also is being advanced by members of religiously oriented citizen pressure groups such as Concerned Women for America and Citizens for Excellence in Education. In Alabama, a petition to adopt the textbook was signed by more than 11,000 citizens (Scott and Uno, 1989). Lesson plans to accompany the *Pandas* textbook are readily available to teachers and parents online. In an appeal to parents who home-school their children, one Internet source of lesson plans, the Heart of Wisdom (2006), described its educational philosophy: "The Bible is the center of education, and all subordinate studies should be brought into the circle of light radiating from thence. Academics play an important part, but they are secondary." Meanwhile, state representative Cynthia Davis (R-MO) introduced a bill to the state legislature requiring biology textbook publishers who sell to school districts in Missouri to include at least one chapter with alternative theories to evolution. In defense of the bill, Davis (in Banerjee, 2004) explained:

> The bill reflects what people want. These are common sense, grass-roots ideas from the people I represent, and I'd be very surprised if the majority of legislators didn't feel they were the right solutions. It's like when the highjackers took over those four planes on September 11 and took people to a place where they didn't want to go. I think a lot of people feel that liberals have taken our country somewhere we don't want to go. I think a lot more people realize this is our country and we're going to take it back.

Not coincidentally, the contemporary arguments put forth by advocates for the inclusion of intelligent design in public school textbooks represent populist notions and conservative Christian ideology. These elements have been at the forefront of historic battles surrounding the inclusion of evolution in textbooks since Darwin's theory first gained support among scientists (Larson, 1989). Apparently, the skirmishes over the inclusion of intelligent design in textbooks are far from reaching an armistice.

The Debate Over Science Curriculum Standards in Ohio

During 2002, the Academic Content Standards for the State of Ohio were being revised, partially in response to accountability requirements in the No Child Left Behind Act of 2001 (Bilica and Skoog, 2004). The 2002 minutes of the State Board of Education (Ohio Department of Education [ODE], 2002a) do not accurately reflect the intensity of the debate that occurred over the writing, review, and approval of the

science standards. Public media, primarily Ohio and national newspapers and public radio broadcast transcripts, provided a more detailed and accurate portrayal of the hotly contested debate.

By law, the 19-member Board of Education was required to develop and adopt Academic Content Standards for grades K–12 by December 31, 2002. Writing the new science standards was the responsibility of a panel of 45 volunteers, mainly science educators, parents, employers, scientists, and leaders chosen by staff members of the ODE (Mangels and Stephens, 2002b). The Standards Committee of the State Board of Education oversaw the panel that wrote the revised standards.

On Sunday, January 13, 2002, the Standards Committee met to review the first draft of the new science standards. The draft called for teaching the evolution of life, which previously had been taught in Ohio under the more ambiguous title "change over time" ("Design on Ohio," 2001; Mangels and Stephens, 2002a). John Calvert, a Kansas City lawyer and cofounder of the Intelligent Design Network, was allowed to address the Standards Committee for 30 minutes. He described intelligent design as a groundbreaking paradigm and urged board members to permit Ohio school children to study this alternative origin theory. Scientists who attended the meeting were not allowed to present rebuttals (Mangels and Stephens, 2002a). During the meeting, five of the nine Standards Committee members expressed dissatisfaction that the new draft of the science standards did not include the teaching of intelligent design. One committee member claimed that the writing panel stacked the deck in favor of evolution, and another member called for immediate changes in the composition of the advisory group and the development of science standards with which Ohioans could be comfortable. She noted that Ohio could be on the cutting edge as the first state to include intelligent design in its curriculum (Associated Press, 2002a; Stephens and Mangels, 2002a). Only one Standards Committee member spoke against these proposals: "I can't go along with this. Somebody's dreamed up another way of expressing creationism, for heaven's sake." One board member was quoted as saying, "If a vote were held today, the intelligent design concept would get a thumbs up from the Board of Education" (Siegel, 2002).

Staff members of the ODE cautioned the board that presenting only one alternative to evolution could evoke lawsuits from groups whose views were not represented. Staffers also warned that the advisory panel probably would resign rather than write standards that contradicted their reasoned judgment and expert opinion of what students should be taught in science classes. Standards Committee cochair Joe Roman asked the committee to delay voting until the board's advisors could investigate the legal, political, and policy implications of these proposals (Mangels and Stephens, 2002a). One outcome of the meeting was that the Standards Committee would sponsor a debate, in a public forum open to all Ohioans, to examine only one alternative to evolution—intelligent design.

This public debate on evolution and intelligent design, held at the Franklin County Veterans Memorial Auditorium in downtown Columbus, Ohio, drew 1,500 attendees (Associated Press, 2002b; Fields, 2002). Seventeen of the 19 board members attended the debate and the press conference that followed. The debate placed two proponents of intelligent design, Stephen Meyer and Jonathon Wells from the Discovery Institute's Center for the Renewal of Science and Culture, against two intelligent design opponents, physicist Lawrence Krauss from Case Western Reserve University and biologist Kenneth Miller from Brown University.

During the debate, Meyer proposed that the State Board of Education create science guidelines that would allow teachers to discuss the controversy and permit students to learn about the scientific arguments for and against evolution (Fields). Meyer added that Ohio voters overwhelmingly favored this approach and that adopting intelligent design would be good politics (Feran, 2002). Krauss asserted that intelligent design does not provide a viable alternative to Darwin's theory of evolution because intelligent design offers no hypotheses to test and, therefore,

is not science (Fields). Krauss added that framing the debate in a two-on-two format may appear fair, but it gives intelligent design a credibility it doesn't deserve. Krauss (in Mangels, 2002) said, "A true representation of the ratio of support and evidence for evolution versus intelligent design would present 10,000 scientists on one side and one representative of the Discovery Institute on the other side." Miller stated that science deals only with natural processes, while intelligent design is merely a criticism of evolutionary theory leading to an inference. Miller and Krauss agreed that science cannot address the question of whether a divine intelligence is behind the creation of life (Feran).

Following the debate, an Associated Press survey (2002d) showed that Board of Education members remained split over the issue of teaching evolution and intelligent design. Seven members favored teaching evolution as an unproven theory and opening the door to other theories of the origin of life, another seven members supported the teaching of evolution only, and five remained neutral or refused to take a public stance on the issue (Sidoti, 2002b).

As the controversy received increased attention in the national news media, other stakeholders began to enter the debate. The presidents of Ohio's 13 public universities sent a letter to the Board of Education requesting that alternative ideas to evolution be excluded from the state science curriculum (Hottman, 2002; Ohlemacher, 2002). Governor Bob Taft, who appointed a majority of the members on the board, chose to stay neutral, while his opponent in the November 2002 elections, Tim Hagan, took a stand against intelligent design. Hagan stated that Ohio would be unable to attract members of the science community to high-tech jobs if the board adopted intelligent design into the science curriculum (Willard and Dyer, 2002).

Some Ohio legislators decided to take an active role in the controversy. Two bills, sponsored by Columbus Republican Linda Reidelbach (Zeleznik, 2002), were introduced into the state legislature's Education Committee. In her testimony during the first hearing of the bills, Reidelbach stated that the Board of Education refused to consider other scientifically proven origins theories. Her first bill mandated objectivity and academic rigor in the classroom by requiring teachers to explain that proving any of the theories presented is impossible and encouraging teachers to even-handedly teach other origins theories, such as intelligent design. The second bill required legislative approval before any of the new science standards were implemented.

Newspapers in Ohio's major cities contained numerous articles and editorials about the science curriculum standards debate. Most editorials strongly favored exclusion of intelligent design from the K–12 science curriculum, and many characterized the intelligent design initiative as a national embarrassment to Ohio.

The science curriculum writing team, apparently encouraged by the tenor of these news articles, incorporated an even stronger stance on teaching evolution into the second draft of the science curriculum standards, released on April 1, 2002. This draft also provided a new definition of science, worded to eliminate supernatural explanations of the origin of life by limiting scientific knowledge to natural explanations for natural phenomena (Mangels and Stephens, 2002b). Though some members of the writing team did not feel that a definition of science was necessary, others felt that a clear definition would keep nonscientific ideas, such as intelligent design, out of the classroom (Sidoti, 2002a). The writing team's actions were criticized by Board of Education member Deborah Owens-Fink (2002), who characterized the team as entrenched and unwilling to consider input from the public. She stated that she intended to make changes to the curriculum standards at the board level. The writing team claimed to have received 912 e-mails, letters, and petitions from scientists, the public, legislators, and educators; approximately half favored the teaching of evolution alone and the other half favored the inclusion of intelligent design. The writing team and advisors suggested that ultimately the science standards had to be based on the best consensus of scientific thinking, rather than on popular opinion (Associated Press, 2002c; Mangels and Stephens, 2002b). The Board of Education continued to post drafts of the new science standards on its Web site for public review and comment. The public and key stakeholders also reviewed the draft standards at 40 focus group meeting (ODE, 2002b).

The *Plain Dealer* sponsored a telephone opinion poll of 1,507 randomly selected Ohioans between May 28 and June 4, 2002. The poll ("Ohio issue poll," 2002) showed that 59% of the respondents supported teaching both evolution and intelligent design in public school. Ohioans indicated that they favored teaching intelligent design because it appealed to their sense of fairness. The poll also found that the public was not familiar with what intelligent design entails, nor were they very involved in the debate. Two-thirds of the respondents believed that God is the designer. In the poll, nearly a third of Ohioans described themselves as believers in the literal interpretation of Genesis—God created the universe and all life in 6 days, less than 10,000 years ago. The poll found that support for teaching intelligent design alongside evolution transcended geography, race, household income, and education levels. Most Ohioans, however, weren't completely at ease with challenging evolution in the science classroom. They preferred to have their children presented with evolution-conflicting beliefs in the home, religious institution, or in a class other than science. Proponents of intelligent design were encouraged by the results, while evolutionists like Eugenie C. Scott (in Stephens and Mangels, 2002b) said, "This tells me that science education has a long way to go." Following the opinion poll, proponents on both sides of the debate renewed their lobbying efforts toward those who would make the final decision.

On October 18, the Board of the American Association for the Advancement of Science (AAAS) (2002) published a resolution opposing teaching intelligent design in science classrooms. According to Pennock (2003), this resolution was intended to send a clear message to the State Board of Education:

> Intelligent design theory represents a challenge to the quality of science education; the ID movement has failed to offer credible scientific evidence, or a scientific means of testing its claims, and that the

lack of scientific warrant for so-called "intelligent design theory" makes it improper to include as part of science education; therefore AAAS urges citizens across the nation to oppose the establishment of policies that would permit the teaching of "intelligent design theory" as part of the science curriculum in public schools, and AAAS calls upon its members to assist those engaged in overseeing science education policy to understand the nature of science, the content of contemporary evolutionary, theory, and the inappropriateness of "intelligent design theory" as subject matter for science education.

On October 15, 2002, the Board of Education passed a resolution of intent to adopt the science standards, with changes. First, the following phrase was included in Benchmark H: "Describe how scientists continue to investigate and critically analyze aspects of evolutionary theory" (ODE, 2002b, 2002c). Second, a new definition of science was added: "Recognize that science is a systematic method of continuing investigation, based on observation, hypothesis testing, measurement, experimentation, and theory building, which leads to more adequate explanations of natural phenomena" (Science Excellence for All Ohioans, 2002). The AAAS predicted that these changes would undermine the teaching of evolution and open the door to teaching intelligent design in Ohio science classrooms. The Board of Education continued to solicit public comments about the science standards, and, as the state-level debate continued, one local school board passed a resolution to support the inclusion of intelligent design in classes in addition to other scientific theories.

Finally, on December 10, 2002, the Ohio Academic Content Standards for Science (K–12) were adopted, but with one significant amendment. The board added the phrase "The intent of this indicator does not mandate the teaching or testing of intelligent design to Benchmark H" (ODE, 2002c). During the meeting, Joe Roman characterized the standards as the best science standards to provide a foundation for what students need to know over the next 12–15 years. He justified the necessity of the amendment by stating that the board's actions in October had been misrepresented by adults who used them to fight their own battles. The motion was passed unanimously by all 19 members of the State Board of Education (ODE, 2002c).

Conclusion

While intelligent design has no place in the science classroom, it could be discussed in other forums. Public opinion polls have shown that teaching science in science class and teaching alternative origin theories in social studies or religious settings constitutes an acceptable solution for most Americans.

This issue eventually will reach the U.S. Supreme Court, and that court will find, as it did in *Edwards v. Aguillard,* that intelligent design constitutes a religious belief and does not warrant equal time in the science classroom. Still, such a decision will not end the debate. The preponderance of evidence suggests that the battles between intelligent design proponents and the defenders of evolution will continue unabated— a prime example of an enduring cultural conflict in American education.

Discussion Questions

Why is the issue of creationism versus evolution still such a major issue in the science curriculum?

After exploring this issue, what do you think should be included in the science curriculum? If not in science class, should intelligent design have another place in the curriculum?

Vicki D. Johnson is a professor at Cleveland State University.

Section VIII

How Does the Curriculum Meet the Needs of Diverse Populations?

There is no doubt that the demographics of the United States are changing. Schools are a reflection of those changes. As school populations become more diverse by ethnicity, race, economic status, and academic and physical abilities, teaching becomes more challenging. How can we meet the needs of all these children? The articles in this section of the reader try to address that question.

The Plains City Story is an excellent example of what happens in a school when the demographics of the community drastically change. Schools often cannot accommodate the changes because the majority community wants to ignore the new demographics.

Because the demographics of the United States are changing and the world is becoming more interdependent, educators are realizing the importance of making our curriculum more global. Andrew Smith shares with the readers the efforts we have made to globalize our curriculum.

Timothy Morse specifically addresses how students with disabilities need to be serviced in our urban schools. Today, there is a larger number of severely disabled urban students than there was 25 years ago. Thus, the curriculum they need must address the acquisition of basic academic skills as well as adaptive behaviors that will lead to independent functioning.

Teachers who work in inner city schools often assume that the students they teach cannot master the core curriculum offered at the school. Prime and Miranda specifically examine how teachers' beliefs about the abilities of their students affect what they teach in science.

One area of education frequently neglected in the preparation of teachers is the study of rural education. Yet there are hundreds of rural schools throughout our country. The question of what should be taught in these schools is a valid one. Aimee Howley reviews the history of rural education and highlights the pros and cons of using the "traditional" curriculum as the focus of education for rural students.

As you read these articles think about the following:

- How demographics have altered the makeup of your community and what that means for the schools in your community

- Scripted and "teacher proof" curricula. Do these curricula guarantee quality education?

- How the rapidly changing world affects how we function as a society and what we need to learn in order to preserve our society in a global environment

- Your teacher preparation and how confident you feel to work in inner-city or rural schools

- Why the curriculum of the inner city special needs population is critical to the social, economic, academic, and personal development of these students.

Article 30

THE PLAINS CITY STORY

MARCELA VAN OLPHEN

FRANCISCO RIOS

WILLIAM BERUBE

ROBIN DEXTER

ROBERT MCCARTHY

CASE NARRATIVE

The Setting

Plains City sits in a scenic valley just 12 miles from the historic Three Corners site where three plains states meet. Corn, potatoes, wheat, alfalfa, sunflowers, and cattle are all products of this rich and varied agricultural economy. Fresh, clean air and safe, quiet surroundings appeal to lovers of the outdoors no matter what their interests—fishing, hunting, hiking, boating, riding, biking, or bird watching. Plains City's municipal outdoor swimming pool, community golf course, lighted ballparks, tennis courts, museum, library, and recreation center offer many of the amenities commonly found in larger communities. Enhancing the services of the community are the new Plains City Community Hospital, education programs centered on Morgan Community College and Northeastern Junior College, the Plains City airport, 14 churches, restaurants, and motels, and bed-and-breakfasts.

 Plains City has a population of 2,160 (1.2% lower than in 2000), of which 89% of the population is White non-Hispanic, 10% is Hispanic, and the remaining 1% is American Indian and other ethnic groups. A billboard near the center of town welcomes people to "America's Hometown."

SOURCE: Excerpted from Van Olphen, M., Rios, F., Berube, W., Dexter, R., & McCarthy, R. (2006). The Plains City story. *Journal of Cases in Educational Leadership, 9*(6), 23–32. Reprinted by permission of Sage.

The School District

Arnold, Newman, Gaddy, and Dean (2005) stated, "Rural schools face a unique set of challenges, largely due to their geographic isolation" (p. 1). They also argued that professional isolation plays a detrimental role in the development of innovative practices. Plains City is not an exception and does not escape the challenges that plague rural communities. Like many rural school districts, Plains City's realities include (a) declining enrollment, (b) meeting the needs of each individual student with limited resources, (c) recruiting and retaining high-quality teachers, (d) updating and refining the skills of the teachers, and (e) involving parents and community members in the educational process.

In addition to the customary dilemmas faced by rural districts, the Plains City School District has just completed a reorganization of its schools and students with a neighboring town because of declining enrollment. The new district maintains high expectations and aims to continue in a tradition of educational excellence. The main goal of the district (and of many others in the era of No Child Left Behind) has been to have the students meet or exceed the 80% proficiency level on the Student Assessment Program test. While attempting to achieve this goal, the new superintendent had to address the tensions generated by the recent administrative change and reduce the friction caused by the needs of the increasing number of students who were English-language learners (ELL).

Origin of Demographic and Social Transformations

Beginning in the mid-1990s, large-scale pig farming was initiated just outside of Plains City. The introduction of this industry brought an essential improvement in the regional economy. As with any economic advancement, the Plains City pig industry generated an increased demand for workers. This industry attracted new workers and provided the basis for the economic boost in the region but resulting demographic changes led some Plains City residents to receive this economic development with mixed feelings. Many of the employees of the newly established industry were immigrants from Mexico. The threat of having alien workers take the extra (and mostly unwanted) jobs in Plains City raised this town's apprehension. These concerns were similar to those outlined in Hanson's (2003) book *Mexifornia.* Hanson, whose perspective is that of a California farmer who has experienced the influence of Mexican immigration, claimed, "The future of the state—and the nation too, as regards the matter of immigration—is entirely in the hands of its current residents" (p. xv). Plains City residents were neither ready to expand their multicultural horizons nor willing to accept the social and economic mesh.

The agricultural business interests did little to prepare the community (including the schools) for the changes that accompany the influx of newcomer families. Because multiculturalism involves more than "dealing just with diverse individuals versus a community, but particular cultural groups vis-à-vis the larger political community" (Burke, 2002, p. 7), Plains City residents were not ready to face the challenges that any social change can create in a community. The new situation was not seen or framed within the economic and sociocultural growth that could benefit Plains City and its residents. Neither was the economic impact of the new source of labor considered.

These Mexican workers, who we assume were undocumented because of their lack of access to social services and their earnings below minimum wages, were not alone. The workers brought their families with them. Most of these workers had two or three school-age children. Thus, the number of Mexican students in the Plains City school district increased significantly. By the 2002–2003 school year, 100 Mexican students out of 756 (13.2% of the district enrollment) were enrolled in the schools of the district. Despite the hardships that this increased educational burden would place on the residents of Plains City, the school district was required to provide newcomers with an education. As a result of the Supreme Court ruling in 1982 (*Plyer v. Doe;* for more information, visit http://www.law .cornell.edu), school districts are mandated to educate children regardless of their parents' immigration status. Another implication of this Supreme Court decision is that it is illegal to request students' Social Security numbers or to examine any immigration information. Many of these ELL were in the primary grades. Although they shared the same Mexican background, their literacy and linguistic competence varied widely. Some of the newcomers had adequate or limited formal schooling, whereas others were not literate in their first language. These issues constitute major barriers to student to success in school (Freeman & Freeman, 2003).

School and Community Climate

As we mentioned before, Plains City residents faced this new reality with trepidation. Their worries about sustaining a mainstream Anglo culture and identity led them to be less open. Because of the influx of Mexican families to the community, tensions began to arise in and outside school. Some community members did not welcome the Mexican families to Plains City and in fact were rude, racist, and discriminatory toward them in some situations.

Huntington's (2004) book *Who Are We?* serves us well to account for these reactions. In his work, Huntington expressed the concerns of the Anglo-Protestant culture and proposed that "Americans should recommit themselves to the Anglo-Protestant culture, traditions, and values that for three and a half centuries have been the source of liberty, unity, power, prosperity, and moral leadership as a force for good in the world" (p. xvii). Huntington also made a point of the value of bilingual and foreign language education. He argued, "Apart from the controversies over its impact on students' academic progress, bilingual education has clearly had a negative impact on the integration of Hispanic students into American society" (p. 312). Integration, as suggested in his work, conveys leaving behind or even eroding one's own cultural background.

In discussing the obligations that a community has with respect to newcomers, Díaz-Rico and Weed (2002) provided a counterargument: "When education is the only means of achieving social mobility for the children of immigrants, these young people must be given the tools necessary to participate in the community at large" (p. 158). Plains City school board views differed from this approach. Several contentious discussions took place at the school board meetings. During these meetings, residents vehemently discussed the allocation of their resources. Inclusion of newcomers in the agenda was not a popular idea. The Catholic priest was a main factor in holding the community together through some tough times. Specifically, he made continual attempts to present the multiple perspectives and to promote a climate of understanding and tolerance toward the newcomers. His efforts were chiefly intended to provide balance and to neutralize prejudice among residents and authorities. He worked arduously to serve as a peacemaker. Although there were individual efforts to make the Mexican students and families welcome in the schools, tensions escalated—teachers did not have an understanding or appreciation of the culture of the new community members, teachers did not feel prepared to adequately teach the non-English-speaking students, the schools did not know how to communicate with non-English-speaking parents, and in some cases, Hispanic parents did not feel welcome to visit the schools. Moreover, some teachers labeled the non-English-speaking attribute as a learning disability for the students, which seems to be a current practice for schools when confronted with the needs of culturally and linguistically diverse students (Klingner & Artiles, 2003).

Toward a Better Understanding: Some Actions to Promote Dialogue

The Plains City story unfortunately exemplifies the difficulties facing Latinos who now live in "new places where long-term residents have little experience with Latinos" (Worthan, Murillo, & Hamann, 2002, p. 1). Such unfamiliarity is difficult both for the Latinos and for the residents of these communities, including teachers who have lived their entire lives in stable White environments and find themselves unprepared to support differing concepts of family, culture, education, and belief systems. Nonetheless, despite implicit and explicit racism and social indifference, Latinos living outside their traditional homeland find ways to accommodate and resist their new lifestyles and surroundings with varying results (Worthan et al., 2002).

A major issue in Plains City was that some of the residents and teachers did not understand Mexican culture. According to Merrell (2003), culture is

> a complete form of life, a composite of the ways of living of an entire community. It includes values, beliefs, esthetic standards, linguistic expression, patterns of thinking, behavioral norms, and styles of communication which a group of people has developed to assure its survival in a particular physical and human environment. (p. 6)

Moreover, "culture is a participatory affair" (p. 24). Merrell, in his description of some "particular Mexican ways," stated that "a fondness for ceremony, formulas, and formalities . . . is the norm in Mexico." However,

> formalities are not usually rigorous and orderly. They do not follow the same set of procedures for all seasons and occasions. They evidence some constancy, yet there is always a degree of deviation from the norm, depending on the conditions that happen to present themselves. (p. 155)

As detailed in Merrell, anthropologist E. T. Hall (1969, 1976) described a continuum for both language-space and time use. Cultural conventions in terms of space rely on the use of context to complement linguistic communication. Mexicans are high-context oriented, whereas Americans, who rely more on linguistic meaning and less on the physical context, are low-context oriented. In terms of time, Hall proposed a temporal spectrum that places monochronic time (MC) at one end and polychronic time (PC) at the other. Time for MC cultures is mainly linear, whereas time for PC cultures has a nonlinear dimension. For example, the PC trait in Mexican culture can easily be observed when a group of people is holding what a Mexican would view as just a vivid conversation, whereas

to the American eye, the scene would present a chaotic and stressful situation because of the speakers' simultaneity. Some of these cross-cultural differences combined with the political views of some Plains City residents were the cause of many cross-cultural misunderstandings. The new superintendent considered these cross-cultural misunderstandings a major barrier to be overcome if he was to develop a plan to improve communication and to foster collaboration.

To alleviate rising tensions, the school district superintendent hired an interdisciplinary team of professors from the University of Wyoming. This team, which consisted of faculty from educational leadership, educational studies, and secondary education departments, designed professional development workshops along with some guiding principles to work with ELL to address the needs of the district. Both faculty and school district staff participated in these professional development sessions. Some of the issues that needed to be addressed were (a) cross-cultural awareness, (b) working with culturally and linguistically diverse students and their families, and (c) basic principles and foundations of second language acquisition.

The focus of the first session was to raise cultural awareness while providing school district members with an opportunity to voice their concerns and ask questions related to cross-cultural issues. Specifically, during this first session, participants addressed the values and beliefs of Mexican people; they defined terms such as *assumptions, biases, ethnicity, race,* and *stereotypes;* and they discussed the idea of "getting it" as defined in Merrell (2003). This was an interactive workshop, and school district members actively participated in generating ideas, sharing experiences, and reflecting on routes they were taking toward greater understanding and paths they could follow in the future. The workshop leader invited participants to work in small groups and to do collaborative work by asking questions throughout the session. One of the central questions raised was "What is culture?" Participants wrote down their ideas about culture and shared them within their small groups. The workshop leader composed a collective list of working definitions of culture (which were more important than the activity) and then presented the group with different working definitions that anthropologists have formulated. The two lists were compared and discussed. These discussions were framed within Plains City's realities. The next step was to find out what these participants knew and believed about Mexicans and Mexican culture. While working on this topic, participants began to become aware (through self-reflection) of how detrimental stereotypes and overgeneralizations about a given group can be. Some of the participants' views about Mexicans and Mexican culture were that (a) extended families live in the same home; (b) they have strong family ties; (c) religion—Catholicism—is part of daily life; (d) clothing is different, it is more showy and reveals more machismo; and (e) they are more laid-back—for example, they don't watch the clock closely.

Using these pieces as a springboard, the facilitator continued to work on stereotypes, inviting participants to identify the most common stereotypes about Mexicans and Mexican culture. Participants' reactions were diverse in nature and intensity. Plains City teachers discussed reasons for Mexicans to cross the border, perceived Mexican values and beliefs, and double messages sent by White society. Other topics such as verbal and nonverbal communication, conceptions of time, and ethnicity were also discussed.

A second faculty member, who has expertise on Mexican culture and English as a second language (ESL), conducted a second professional in-service training for the Plains City district. In a meeting before the session, an administrator was describing the challenges associated with laying off faculty and staff because of declining student enrollment. Despite concerns about the morale, the session was interactive and challenging. The facilitator worked to model a variety of strategies that affirm difference, employed multiple learning modalities, and focused on goals associated with teaching for diversity (i.e., multicultural education). Participants were actively involved and engaged.

The aim of both workshops was to open a forum to express school district members' concerns and questions to promote meaningful dialogue. Participants responded very well to the challenges posed by doing self-reflection and analyzing their own beliefs about stereotypes and prejudices. These processes gave participants the basis to outline tasks that would allow them to reach out and integrate parents (both White and Mexican) into the educational community.

Finally, as Burke (2002) put it,

> the challenge before us is to admit the intrinsic role that ethnic, linguistic, racial, and religious cultures play in political, economic, and social relationships and consider how the mixing rather than the extirpation of these cultures can lead to networks of collaboration, rather than of domination. (p. 27)

Discussion Questions

This case study confronts the changing demographics in many of our schools due to immigration. What kind of change to the curriculum was necessitated by the change in student population?

Should the curriculum be altered to meet the needs of students, or should students adapt to traditional school offerings?

Marcela van Olphen is an assistant professor at the University of South Florida.

Francisco Rios is a professor at the University of Wyoming.

William Berube is a professor at the University of Wyoming.

Robin Dexter is an assistant professor at the University of Wyoming.

Robert McCarthy is a senior lecturer at the University of Wyoming.

Article 31

HOW GLOBAL IS THE CURRICULUM?

ANDREW F. SMITH

G lobal illiteracy in the United States has many causes. For most of its history, the United States has been isolated behind oceans and not threatened by its neighbors. Until the second half of the 20th century, the United States was economically self-sufficient and had little political will to get involved in the affairs of other nations.

Rapid and widespread political, economic, and military changes after World War II gave rise to issues that were global in scope, and many people became aware of the impact that events outside U.S. borders had on domestic affairs. Yet the U.S. public education system remained largely unchanged.

During the mid-1970s, educators and policymakers began to raise concerns about how well U.S. schools were preparing students for this rapidly changing world, and global education began to take shape. Most advocates did not support teaching specific global education courses because they believed that all courses should incorporate global subject matter. Nonetheless, social studies and foreign languages were the courses most amenable to integrating global perspectives.

CURRICULUM SHIFTS

In 1979, U.S. president Jimmy Carter's President's Commission on Foreign Language and International Studies issued a report that set in motion four major curriculum shifts in K–12 global education.

Foreign Language Instruction

Only 8% of secondary school students enrolled in foreign language courses in 1979, but

---

SOURCE: Excerpted from Smith, A. F. (2002). How global is the curriculum? *Educational Leadership, 60*(2), 38–41. Reprinted by permission of ASCD.

today approximately 50% do. The rapid expansion of Spanish language programs has occurred at the expense of French and German programs; other language classes, such as Chinese and Japanese—languages commonly spoken but not commonly taught—have expanded slightly. An even more significant development is the increase in foreign language programs in elementary schools—from almost none in 1979 to thousands of programs today.

Despite this solid progress, foreign language programs in the United States do not come close to comparable instruction in other countries. Japan, for example, requires 4 years of English language instruction (many students take more) and offers other languages as electives. Executive director of the Joint National Committee for Languages J. David Edwards says that U.S. foreign language education during the past 20 years has moved from "scandalous to mediocre."

Geography

In 1979, geography was all but excluded from the K–12 curriculum. In 1988, the National Geographic Society established an education foundation to promote the teaching of geography. Since then, the Society has spent $110 million to support the National Geographic Bee, which this past year involved 5 million students, and to develop alliances of geography teachers and college professors concerned with improving instruction in geography from kindergarten through university; these alliances now exist in every state. In addition, four major geography organizations—the American Geographical Society, the Association of American Geographers, the National Council for Geographic Education, and the National Geographic Society—sponsored the development of national geography standards, and 48 states now have standards in geography. In 1994 and in 2002, the National Assessment of Educational Progress tested geographic knowledge and skills. The latest results showed unchanged average geography scores for

12th graders and low but improved scores for 4th and 8th graders.

World History

In 1979, few states required the study of world history in school. Those that did focused only on Western civilization. In the 1990s, the National Center for History in the Schools at the University of California at Los Angeles developed world history standards that include substantial global content. The World History Association, founded in 1982, has supported improved instruction of world history in the K–12 curriculum and helped schools develop world history courses. Two years ago, the World History Association, working with the Educational Testing Service, began summer training programs for an advanced placement course in world history, and the Educational Testing Service offered an advanced placement test in world history for the first time this year. More than 20,000 students took the exam, an all-time high for any new advanced placement subject. The National Assessment of Educational Progress will test world history within the next few years.

Public Schools With an International Focus

The fourth curriculum change has been the creation of public magnet schools with an international focus. Virtually no such schools existed in 1979, but today more than 100 have international programs, including, for example, the Bodine High School for International Affairs in Philadelphia. These schools typically require 4 years of instruction in foreign languages and 1 or 2 years of world history. Many specialize in extracurricular international experiences for students and teachers. The Center for Teaching International Relations at the University of Denver has helped improve instruction and promote communications among many of these schools. Similarly, the International Baccalaureate, which was rarely offered in U.S. schools 20 years ago, is now offered in 420 schools—the largest number of participating schools in any country.

OTHER OPPORTUNITIES

Extracurricular Activities

Independent of these formal curriculum shifts, many extracurricular activities have also strengthened U.S. students' understanding of global matters. These programs include student and teacher exchange programs, educational travel programs, Model United Nations, the Great Decisions programs sponsored by the Foreign Policy Association, and the Capitol Forum on America's Future sponsored by the Choices for the 21st Century Project at Brown University.

Technology

Many technological advances that were not even envisioned 20 years ago are now providing new opportunities for direct communication with students and teachers in other countries. Such groups as the International Education and Resource Network facilitate these contacts. Much of this communication does not take place in English, so U.S. students can practice their foreign language skills while they converse with people in other countries. In addition, many Web sites have global education materials and excellent global content for educators and students.

CHALLENGES

As impressive as the above programs are, they reach far too few students, teachers, and schools. Even current extracurricular global programs and courses in foreign language, geography, and world history do not develop global perspectives in a comprehensive manner.

The most serious problem is inadequate teacher knowledge of the subject. Many states license teachers in social studies or history without requiring coursework in geography or world history. In elementary schools, few teachers have had any such courses. Changes in teacher licensing and preparation will help those entering the teaching profession, and those currently teaching should have access to in-service programs.

Currently, about 50 global education projects offer in-service education programs that can serve as models for new efforts. For example, the American Forum for Global Education's New York and the World project offers programs for teachers in New York City; the Center for Teaching International Relations at the University of Denver works with teachers in Colorado; and the California International Studies Project, based at Stanford University, works with colleges and universities to conduct teacher education programs throughout the state.

Another challenge is the lack of research on global education, especially on the effectiveness of particular methodologies, the proper sequencing of global concepts and skills into the curriculum, and the effects of media and newspapers on student knowledge and understanding of the world. We need a national report card on global education to evaluate our successes and failures.

We can meet these challenges. It will take the political will to expend the money and effort to set new, important priorities in the U.S. education system.

State and local boards of education should make the teaching of global content and skills an important component of education for all students. The federal government has begun to take a leadership role by sponsoring International Education Week and Global Science and Technology Week; these events have involved thousands of students. The federal government should also fund model global education projects and assist state and local schools in the same way that the government fostered science and mathematics education after the Soviet Union launched *Sputnik* in 1957.

In the wake of September 11, we need to reaffirm the importance of a globally literate citizenry. A better educated citizenry would not have responded to the September 11 attacks with such unjust retaliations as vandalizing mosques, harassing innocent Muslim Americans, or attacking Sikhs because their turbans were confused with those worn by the Taliban. We must never again find ourselves in the position, as so many did after September 11, of being unable to answer students' challenging questions.

As educators, we have a responsibility to prepare our students to meet the challenges of our increasingly, sometimes dangerously, interconnected world. It is not likely that the United States will exert global leadership for long with a citizenry that is globally deaf, dumb, and blind.

Discussion Questions

What would a truly global curriculum need to include?

What do you believe students need to know about the world to become competent adults living in a democratic society?

Andrew F. Smith is president of the American Forum on Global Education.

Article 32

Designing Appropriate Curriculum for Special Education Students in Urban Schools

Timothy E. Morse

Much has been written in the past 25 years about appropriate placements for special education students (Edgar & Polloway, 1994). The Individuals With Disabilities Education Act Amendments of 1997 (IDEA), our nation's federal special education law, addresses this issue in its definition of the term *least restrictive environment*. In defining this term, the IDEA states that students with disabilities are to be educated in regular education classes to the maximum extent possible. Over the years, various terms have been used in the professional literature to describe the placement of special education students in regular education classes. Initially, the term *mainstreaming* was used to describe this placement but was recently replaced by the term *inclusion* (Simpson, 1996).

Efforts to include children with disabilities in regular education classes have been accompanied by controversial modifications to the curriculum that is presented in these settings. Lieberman (2001) argued that some educators, in their zeal to implement inclusion, have modified the regular education curriculum to the extent that the changes will enable some special education students to be included in regular education classes throughout their school careers. However, Lieberman noted that these students ultimately will be excluded from many community environments (e.g., competitive, paid employment

SOURCE: Excerpted from Morse, T. E. (2001). Designing appropriate curriculum for special education students in urban schools. *Education & Urban Society, 34*(1), 4. Reprinted by permission of Sage.

opportunities) during their adult years because they will not have acquired the skills they need to access these environments. Polloway, Patton, Epstein, and Smith (1989) supported Lieberman when they argued that the curriculum decisions educators make are paramount. Polloway et al. stated that, regardless of how effective educators' instructional strategies are, these strategies are of little use if the content that is taught to students is irrelevant.

Given these circumstances, it is appropriate to address the curriculum needs of special education students. More specifically, it is appropriate to address the curriculum needs of special education students in different settings, such as those who are attending urban schools versus rural schools. Cronin and Patton (1993) identified practical reasons why curriculum decisions should be local ones, such as the fact that students in some parts of our country need to be taught that the strip of land that separates roadways is called a median, but in other parts of our country students need to be taught that in their community this strip of land is called the neutral ground. However, four additional reasons support the need to examine the design of appropriate curriculum for urban special education students.

First, data suggest that special education programs in inner cities face unique challenges and differ from nationally representative data on special education students (U.S. Department of Education, 1996). Thus, any discussion about appropriate curriculum for special education students must, to some degree, acknowledge the uniqueness of urban special education students. McIntyre (1992) and Obiakor and Algozzine (1993) have argued that a shortcoming of some school reform efforts has been that they have failed to address the fundamental differences that exist between urban schools and their rural and suburban counterparts. These criticisms are germane to this discussion because it addresses curriculum reform for urban special education students.

A second reason why it is appropriate to discuss curriculum design for urban special education students is because data indicate that urban special education students differ from their similarly classified peers of 25 years ago. Specifically, today's urban special education students are more patently disabled than their similarly classified peers of 25 years ago. For example, some data indicate that students who are classified as "learning disabled" today would have been classified as "educable mentally retarded" 25 years ago (Gottlieb, Alter, Gottlieb, & Wishner, 1994). School personnel who are relying on the learning disabilities literature to guide them in their curriculum development efforts on behalf of these students may be honestly misguided in their work.

Third, the IDEA states that students with disabilities are to be educated in the general education curriculum. Yet, this law also states that these students are to be provided an appropriate education. This refers to an education that meets the student's presenting needs. The practical result of the IDEA's somewhat conflicting mandates is that some children with disabilities—such as the more patently disabled ones referred to above—will need to be placed in a modified general education curriculum or even an alternative curriculum (Clark, 1994; Knowlton, 1998; Weaver, Landers, & Adams, 1991). How these circumstances apply to urban special education students warrants discussion.

Fourth, some students' disabilities highlight the fact that the curriculum decisions school personnel make on their behalf are of utmost importance. Wolery, Ault, and Doyle (1992) stated that school personnel will always be able to identify more skills that need to be taught to students with severe disabilities than those personnel will be able to teach to these students. Again, how these circumstances apply to urban special education students warrants discussion.

IDEA AND THE MEANING OF THE TERM *CURRICULUM*

In the IDEA, special education is defined, in part, as specially designed instruction to meet the unique needs of a child with a disability. Specially designed instruction, in turn, refers to the content, methodology, and delivery of this instruction. According to these definitions, a student's placement in special education requires that the content of the student's school program, meaning his curriculum, be examined to insure that it is designed to meet the unique needs that result from the student's disability. Although many definitions for curriculum have been presented in the literature, for the purposes of this discussion, curriculum will refer to the skills, tasks, and behaviors that school personnel want their students to learn.

The U.S. Department of Education (1996) noted that the provision of appropriate special education services to urban youth rests in part on the school's ability to select an appropriate curriculum for these students. Because certain reform measures have been criticized for not examining the unique nature of urban schools, I will discuss the unique nature of urban schools and urban special education students before suggesting how curriculum should be designed for such students.

Urban Schools in America

Inner-city districts enroll 26% of all students in the United States (U.S. Department of Education, 1996) and, according to Gottlieb et al. (1994), the vast majority of these students are poor and members of minority groups. The U.S. Department of Education reported data indicating that 30% of all inner-city students live in poverty, compared to 18% of students living outside the inner city. Regarding minority group enrollment, data indicate that public schools in inner cities enroll almost twice as many African American and Hispanic students as do non-inner-city schools (U.S. Department of Education).

Urban districts in general and inner-city districts in particular enroll a greater percentage of limited English proficient students than do non-urban schools (U.S. Department of Education, 1996). Thus, one can see that a couple of the precursors that are associated with dropping out of school—poverty, lack of school success, single-parent families, and limited English proficiency—are prevalent in urban areas. In fact, dropout rates in urban areas range from 40% to 60% (McIntyre, 1992). In certain cities, dropout rates for some minority groups are as high as 75% to 80% (McIntyre). These data compare to a national dropout rate of 12% (Blumberg & Ferguson, 1999).

These disconcerting data are compounded by—and may even, to some extent, be the result of—the difficulties urban schools face in recruiting and maintaining qualified teachers. The number of teachers leaving teaching is markedly higher in urban schools, and inner-city schools reportedly have greater difficulty recruiting teachers than schools in other areas (Obiakor & Algozzine, 1993; Rousseau & Davenport, 1993). The lack of a trained, stable workforce could adversely affect the work these schools perform.

Special Education in Urban Schools

The U.S. Department of Education (1996) remarked that data pertaining to urban special education students and programs are scarce. However, the data that do exist suggest that special education programs in the inner cities face unique challenges and differ in some respects from nationally representative data on special education students, personnel, and services. Yet, the U.S. Department of Education also stated that there are some similarities between inner-city and suburban and rural districts. Each serves similar percentages of students with disabilities—10.4% and 10.8%, respectively—and the types of disabilities vary only slightly. Unfortunately, the ways in which these areas differ do not bode well for urban special education students.

Students with disabilities in urban areas are more likely to be exposed to risk factors that are associated with school failure, such as poverty, one-parent families, and families in which the parent does not have high school diploma.

Another risk factor associated with dropping out of school—limited English proficiency—is also more prevalent among urban special education students than their nonurban counterparts.

Not surprisingly, relatively high dropout rates for students with disabilities in urban areas have been reported in national studies and surveys conducted from 1985 to 1998. Similarly, high school graduation rates for urban special education students do not compare favorably to their nonurban peers.

Again, a possible contributing factor to the dropout and graduation data is the special education teacher shortages that are particularly severe in inner-city areas. Thirty-eight percent of all public schools had teaching vacancies in special education from 1990 to 1991, ranging from 42% in inner cities to 35% in rural communities. Not surprisingly, urban public school administrators have said that vacancies in special education were the most difficult to fill (U.S. Department of Education, 1996).

Given the fact that research consistently shows that high school graduation is an important predictor of postsecondary success for individuals with disabilities (U.S. Department of Education, 1996), the relevant data reported above are not very encouraging. In fact, postsecondary outcome data indicate that these individuals continue to struggle after exiting school.

Data indicate that individuals with disabilities are less likely to be employed than their peers in the years immediately after high school not employed and not looking for work 3 to 5 years after exiting high school.

Available data do not indicate that urban youth with disabilities are unemployed because they have opted to enroll in postsecondary education immediately after high school rather than enter the workforce. Only 14% of urban special education students who were out of secondary school for up to 2 years reported having taken any postsecondary coursework in the past year (U.S. Department of Education, 1996). Likewise, when they graduate from high school, urban special education students are less likely to attend any type of postsecondary school. Blumberg and Ferguson (1999) reported that 3 to 5 years after graduating from high school, 37% of these students had attended some type of postsecondary school compared to 68% of high school graduates in the general population.

These outcome data may be influenced by that fact that urban special education students are fundamentally different from their peers in other settings even though both sets of students share the same disability labels. In one study, Gottlieb et al. (1994) found that the mean IQ score of children labeled learning disabled in urban schools was 81.4 as compared to 102.8 for children labeled learning disabled in suburban schools. Thus, Gottlieb et al. have concluded that the textbook disability definitions, such as the one for learning disabled, may not apply to children identified as such in urban settings. Related literature, including discussions pertaining to appropriate curriculum for these students, may be equally inapplicable.

GENERAL DATA PERTAINING TO DISABLED YOUTH

Blumberg and Ferguson (1999) reported additional postschool adjustment data pertaining to individuals with disabilities that, even though they do not single out urban special education students, must be considered applicable to these individuals as they are applicable to all similarly situated persons.

APPROPRIATE CURRICULUM FOR URBAN SPECIAL EDUCATION STUDENTS

Gottlieb et al. (1994) stated that we must know who our students are before we can design appropriate programs for them. The information presented above addresses Gottlieb et al.'s concerns by providing educators insight regarding the curriculum needs of urban special education students. Hence, the six critical features of Polloway et al.'s (1989) comprehensive curriculum model can be applied to this information so that school personnel can design appropriate curriculum for urban special education students.

Comprehensive curriculum should be responsive to the needs of an individual student at the current time. Urban special education curriculum must account for the fact that, at present, the population of students who are being served in special education programs in urban settings (a) may not fit the textbook definitions of the disability classifications they have been assigned and (b) may be more patently disabled than their similarly identified peers just 25 years ago (Forness, 1985; Polloway, Epstein, Patton, Cullinan, & Luebke, 1986). Today, some urban special education students who have been identified as learning disabled are more characteristic of individuals who, in the recent past, would have been considered to have mild mental retardation (Gottlieb et al., 1994). Thus, an appropriate curriculum for these students should address both the acquisition of basic academic skills and adaptive behaviors (i.e., behaviors that lead to independent functioning, such as cooking and purchasing skills). If educators rely solely on the learning disabilities literature to determine the curriculum needs of urban learning disabled students, it is quite possible that these students would be offered an inappropriate curriculum that focused solely on remediating their academic deficits without addressing their adaptive behavior needs.

Furthermore, urban special education students who are presently labeled mentally retarded have average IQ scores (i.e., mean IQ = 54) that indicate they have moderate or more significant mental retardation (Gottlieb et al., 1994). This means that a functional curriculum—one that focuses primarily on teaching these students daily living skills rather than traditional academic skills—should be offered to them (Siegel-Causey & Allinder, 1998).

Comprehensive curriculum should be consistent with the objective of balancing maximum interaction with nondisabled peers against critical curricular needs. Data indicate that urban special education students are spending relatively more time in regular education classes than are their peers in suburban and rural settings (U.S. Department of Education, 1996). The placement of urban special education students in a regular education class for a relatively high amount of time may represent an effort on behalf of urban schools to (a) respond to the inclusion movement,

(b) address the data indicating that minority students tend to be placed into what are considered to be lower academic tracks that have the net effect of limiting their future options (Obiakor & Algozzine, 1993), and (c) respond to the special education teacher shortage these schools face.

Yet, given the extent of urban special education students' disabilities, one must question whether their curriculum needs are being met in these classes. The data presented above indicate a need to design curriculum for urban special education students that differs somewhat from the general education curriculum but still allows special education students opportunities to interact with their nondisabled peers.

These competing forces—designing an appropriate curriculum and maximizing interaction with nondisabled peers—can be addressed reasonably over the course of an urban special education student's academic career. First, because all students are working to acquire basic academic skills when they are in elementary school, urban special education students will have many appropriate opportunities to be educated in regular education classes during this time. When these students enter junior and senior high school, integration can be achieved through other means, such as community-based instruction (CBI) (Langone, Langone, & McLaughlin, 2000; Smith & Hilton, 1994). That is, when urban special education students receive needed life-skills instruction in the community, they will be integrated among nondisabled individuals. Even though CBI activities might be problematic in some urban neighborhoods (Dever & Knapczyk, 1997), they are one option that can be exercised to address integration concerns.

Comprehensive curriculum is integrally related to service delivery options (i.e., resource programs, self-contained classes, and modified models). Gottlieb et al. (1994) and others (MacMillan & Borthwick, 1980) have stated that, given the level of disability exhibited by urban special education students who have been classified as either learning disabled or mentally retarded, a self-contained special education classroom may be the least restrictive environment for these students. Thus, though much has been written about how students with these categories of disability can be kept in regular education classes through the use of consultative/collaborative service delivery models (e.g., see Zigmond & Sansone, 1986), this literature may not readily apply to urban special education students so labeled.

In fact, given the data presented above, one may question how applicable all of the placement literature is to urban special education programs. For example, the literature that exhorts the full inclusion of special education students in regular education classes acknowledges that additional resources, such as certified teachers, paraprofessionals, and planning time, will be needed when this service delivery model is used (Turnbull, Turnbull, Shank, & Leal, 1999). The data presented above indicate that providing these additional resources will be problematic for urban schools because, among other challenges, they experience difficulties retaining and recruiting qualified personnel.

This uninviting scenario does not mean that this feature of the comprehensive curriculum model cannot be addressed adequately. Urban educators can use available service delivery options and still allow for the integration of special education and non-disabled students by remaining mindful that the continuum of special education settings does not obviate every single opportunity for the inclusion of special education students in regular education classes. Even self-contained placements allow for some integration because, by definition, a self-contained placement means a student with a disability will be educated in a special education classroom for more than 60% of the school day. In other words, a student in this placement could be educated for approximately 40% of the school day in a regular education setting.

Comprehensive curriculum is delivered from a realistic appraisal of potential adult outcomes of individual students. Projecting potential adult outcomes for a student is a risky proposition for those who are making the projections. At the very least, any attempt at outcome projection should be based on available data rather than mere speculation. For example, Smith (1998) provided some guidance for individuals who are making projections on behalf of students with mental retardation. Smith stated that individuals with mild mental retardation have been shown to be capable of mastering elementary-school literacy skills and daily living skills, whereas students who are moderately mentally retarded can be expected to learn how to read basic sight words, master basic counting skills, and learn to perform some semi-independent living skills. This information is relevant to urban special education students because many who are presently classified as learning disabled are functioning like their mildly mentally retarded counterparts of 25 years ago, and those who are labeled mentally retarded are functioning as if they are moderately mentally retarded or more significantly disabled. Thus, the curriculum that is offered to these students should reflect an understanding of this adult outcome data.

When urban educators address this feature of the comprehensive curriculum model by taking into account the data just presented, they will also address several issues. For example, some data indicate that special education students achieve lower levels of independent living and experience social isolation as adults. Consequently, an appropriate curriculum for these students that includes the teaching of independent living skills would address these deficit areas (Polloway, Patton, Smith, & Roderique, 1991). Offering urban special education students this curriculum would also address the fact that their parents—approximately one-quarter of whom are not high school graduates—may not be as capable of teaching them daily living skills as are the parents of nondisabled students.

One caveat that school personnel must keep in mind is that the content in each special education student's individualized education program (IEP) must be based on the student's presenting needs and not his categorical label. The categorical label can provide some guidance for IEP development, but the student's individual needs should determine the precise content in the IEP (Beck, Broers, Hogue, Shipstead, & Knowlton, 1994).

Comprehensive curriculum is focused on transitional needs across the lifespan. The IDEA has, since 1990, emphasized the need to address special education students' transitions from high school to postsecondary environments (Halpern, Benz, & Lindstrom, 1992; Smith & Puccini, 1995). The data showing that urban special education students are achieving relatively low rates of employment and are not accessing postsecondary educational opportunities indicate a particular need to address the transitional needs of urban special education students across the lifespan. A lifespan focus in particular is appropriate given the fact that adulthood can cover a much longer period of time (e.g., 70 years) than a student's school career (Gerber, 1998).

Urban educators can address the employment needs of urban special education students by offering them a curriculum in which career preparation activities are included across each student's school career. Career awareness activities can be presented in elementary school, followed by career exploration and preparation activities in junior and senior high school (Moore, Agran, & McSweyn, 1990).

Increasing the postsecondary educational opportunities for these students will have to be addressed through collaborative efforts between the public schools and adult service agencies. An appropriate starting point would be for public schools to make known to adult service agencies the curriculum taught to urban special education students (Bruininks, Thurlow, & Ysseldyke, 1992). Adult service agencies can then design appropriate entry-level courses for these students as well as appropriate comprehensive adult curricula.

Comprehensive curriculum is sensitive to graduation goals and specific diploma track requirements. The relatively high dropout rates reported for both urban special education students and their nondisabled peers are cause for alarm. These dropout rates raise a number of questions, one being whether students in these settings are being presented a curriculum that, in their estimation, does not meet their needs and results in their decision to drop out of school (Smith &

Dowdy, 1992). This scenario is likely to emerge when a traditional college-preparatory curriculum is being offered to students who, for a number of reasons, simply do not belong in this curriculum.

The data presented in this article indicate that an alternative curriculum leading to the awarding of a high school diploma is certainly needed for today's urban special education students (Patton et al., 1996). This curriculum would focus on teaching these students basic, functional literacy skills and independent living skills that lead to securing a job, performing independent living tasks, interacting in the community, and being prepared to enroll in relevant postsecondary coursework.

CONCLUSION

Gottlieb et al. (1994) noted that there are no simple solutions to the issues that need to be addressed on behalf of urban special education students. Designing an appropriate curriculum for these students presents a complex challenge to the school personnel who must address this issue. This challenge will only be addressed adequately if these personnel possess a fundamental understanding of the unique circumstances that pertain to these students. This article is intended to be an initial attempt to provide school personnel with the relevant information they need to begin to adequately address the issue of designing an appropriate curriculum for these students.

Polloway et al. (1989) stated that there will always be a recurring need to develop innovative and relevant curriculum that addresses the six critical features of their comprehensive curriculum model. Consequently, urban school personnel can be assured that they will continually be challenged to create a comprehensive curriculum that meets the presenting needs of urban special education students. Because one-fourth of our nation's students are enrolled in inner-city schools, educators must ensure that this challenge is met.

As school personnel work to address the curriculum needs of urban special education students, these personnel must remain mindful of the IDEA's pronouncement that disabilities are a natural part of the human condition and that, after receiving an appropriate education, individuals with disabilities will be capable of becoming full participants in all facets of our society. By designing appropriate curriculum for urban special education students, school personnel bring this pronouncement into fruition.

Discussion Questions

What are your beliefs about tracking, mainstreaming, and inclusion?

What do the authors mean by "comprehensive curriculum"? Do you agree with their recommendations?

Timothy E. Morse is a visiting assistant professor at the University of Southern Mississippi–Gulf Coast.

Article 33

Urban Public High School Teachers' Beliefs About Science Learner Characteristics

Implications for Curriculum

Glenda M. Prime

Rommel J. Miranda

This study is premised on the view that student learning outcomes are determined in large measure by the nature of learning experiences. Thus, a study of the school and classroom experiences of urban children might hold the key to an understanding of the problems of underachievement that plague this population of students. This study probes one aspect of the classroom experiences of African American urban high school students. Specifically, the study looks at teachers' beliefs about these students' ability to succeed in science with a view to determining how these beliefs might be linked to the teachers' classroom practices.

Achievement gaps between African American and White students have been persistent. The poor standing in mathematics and science achievement of U.S. students relative to students

SOURCE: Excerpted from Prime, G. M., & Miranda, R. J. (2006). Urban public high school teachers' beliefs about science leader characteristics: Implications for curriculum. *Urban Education, 41*(5), 506–532. Reprinted by permission of Sage.

from other participating countries was widely publicized. Much less known is the fact that when the data are disaggregated, and Caucasian, African American, and Hispanic students from the United States are considered separately, White students were outperformed by only three nations, whereas African American students were outperformed by all others (Berliner, 2001). The reforms that have been initiated in response to America's low performance relative to the other countries include standards-based teaching, high-stakes testing, and increased school and teacher accountability. These, however, fail to address the specific reasons for underachievement of African Americans or other underrepresented groups.

Research into the causes of urban African American underachievement in science has typically looked at two groups of factors. On one hand, there is the cultural difference argument, which suggests that there is a mismatch between aspects of the culture of science and the culturally influenced understandings that students bring with them to their science learning. This argument encompasses the notion that traditional school science is Western science and is premised on a Western worldview, which is different from the worldview espoused by many underrepresented groups and may actually be alienating to students. Another aspect of the cultural difference explanation has to do with the alleged lack of relevance of the contexts in which science concepts are presented to the cultural contexts in which African American students live their lives. In another construction of the cultural difference argument, Norman, Ault, Bentz, and Meskimen (2001) have characterized urban science classrooms as "cultural interface zones" in which the culture of science as an intellectual discipline, the culture of the teachers, and that of the students might be in conflict (p. 1103). When the power imbalance inherent in such conflict is not satisfactorily negotiated, achievement suffers. In all of these arguments, the underachievement of African Americans is thought to be due in part to a failure on the part of science curricula to bridge the gap between the world of the student and the world of science. The other group of arguments about urban African American failure in science has to do with characteristics of the urban school learning environment. In a nutshell, these explanations suggest that the schools are underresourced, the teachers are underprepared, and this results in student underachievement.

This study is based on the conception of curriculum advanced by Schwab (1970). Schwab suggested that the enacted curriculum is the result of the interaction of the four commonplaces of curriculum: the teacher, the subject matter, the student, and the milieu. Changes in any one of these commonplaces, in effect, alter the received curriculum even when the manifest curriculum is the same. It is evident, then, that even within a single school district, children in different schools might be experiencing substantially different curricula.

The study makes the assumption that the reasons for the underachievement in science seen among urban African American high school students are to be found, at least in part, in the nature of their science curricular experiences. It further assumes that an understanding of the curricular experiences teachers provide for their students cannot be gained apart from an understanding of the beliefs that underpin teachers' instructional decision making.

THEORETICAL FRAMEWORK

This study is framed within a well-established body of literature that affirms the influence of various aspects of teacher thinking about students, and about teaching and learning, on classroom practice and learning outcomes (Braun, 1976; Brickhouse, 1990; Briscoe, 1991; Brophy & Good, 1970; Clark & Peterson, 1986; Cochran-Smith, 2000).

It is this relationship between belief and behavior that makes the study of teacher beliefs so critical to an understanding of educational outcomes.

This study makes no attempt to differentiate beliefs from the range of other closely related constructs but uses the term *beliefs about learner characteristics* to capture the range of dispositions about students that might be influencing teachers' classroom actions. For the purposes of this study, the notion of teachers' beliefs about learner characteristics encompasses such aspects of teacher thinking as expectations about student outcomes; beliefs about learner characteristics such as race, ethnicity, class, and gender; and beliefs about students' ability and performance in science. The article thus draws on relevant literature about a range of these constructs to establish the importance of teacher thinking to practice.

The body of research on teacher thinking demonstrates that teacher beliefs about teaching and learning affect many aspects of classroom practice, including lesson planning and the assessment of student learning (Pajares, 1992; Richardson, 1996; Taylor & Macpherson, 1992).

Teachers' beliefs about the characteristics of their students have not been as frequently investigated. Yet, it is possible that it is this class of teacher beliefs that has the most telling effect on student outcomes. Shepardson and Pizzini (1992) found that teachers held gender-biased perceptions of the scientific ability of their students that favored boys and posited the view that this might be a "potential explanation or cause for the differential educational treatment of girls in science, which results in performance discrepancies between girls and boys" (p. 148). Such biased perceptions might not only be gender based, but in urban schools where the majority of students belong to underrepresented groups, teachers' beliefs might be influenced by stereotypical views about their students' ability in mathematics and science. Braun (1976) suggests that race and socioeconomic status are an "apparently potent source of input into teachers' expectations of their students" (p. 193). Whether stereotypical or not, teachers' views about their students are likely to be powerful determinants of their instructional decisions and of the kinds of social climate they create in their classrooms. In addition, a growing body of research on the cultural aspects of science and science teaching suggests that teachers' cultural beliefs about the diverse student populations in the science

classrooms of urban schools influence their ability to provide varied and culturally responsive opportunities for such students to learn science (Atwater, 1995, 1999).

This study investigates urban science teachers' beliefs about the characteristics of their students in the context of the demands of the subject and explores teachers' reported curricular responses to those perceived student characteristics. It is recognized that investigations of beliefs pose methodological challenges. Interviews reveal only what teachers say they believe and are subject to some of the same problems of self-report instruments. Beliefs can also be inferred from teachers' descriptions of their practice and from observations of their actual practice. This study reports data gleaned by the first two methods.

Significance

The significance of this exploratory study of teachers' beliefs lies in its orientation toward praxis. It builds on the work of Lewis, Pitts, and Collins (2002) by exploring teachers' own accounts of how their beliefs about their students influence their instructional decisions. The study responds to the call by Bryan and Atwater (2002) for research that addresses high school mathematics and science teachers' "beliefs about issues of multiculturalism and its impact on science teaching and learning" (p. 834). Studies that link teachers' beliefs to their curricular practices are rare and are even more so for urban science education. It is proposed that the findings of this study, which probes teachers' accounts of their classroom practice, are followed by observational studies that examine the actual classroom practice of urban science teachers of African American students. Such studies will serve to illuminate the link between beliefs and practice. The study also has practical significance because of its potential to further illuminate the problem of the achievement gap between African American students and their majority counterparts. In addition, an understanding of teachers' beliefs about African

American students' ability to achieve in science is critical to the design of science teacher education programs that prepare teachers to be culturally responsive in their classroom practice.

METHOD . . . DATA COLLECTION

Eight teachers were purposefully selected from four schools in a large urban school district. Urban schools typically are located within or on the fringes of large cities; have large numbers of low-income students, many of whom are African American (Ennis, 1995); and have low levels of achievement. The schools selected for this study met all of these criteria. The percentage of African American students ranged from 70.0% to 96.9%. In none of the schools did the White population exceed 18%. The schools were selected to represent a range of achievement levels. Two were high-achieving schools and two were low-achieving schools, as evidenced by the state's school performance report achievement data (Maryland State Department of Education, 2002). Key contact in each of the schools solicited the participation of two science teachers. Selection of the eight participants was done so that all of the science disciplines were represented.

SEMISTRUCTURED INTERVIEW GUIDE

The purpose of the research was presented to the teachers as an investigation of factors related to student achievement in science. The interview was prefaced as follows:

> You are of course aware of the nationwide concern about student achievement in science. Several measures such as standards-based teaching have been instituted to address the problem of underachievement in science. We believe that the problem needs to be investigated from several angles and we are interested in looking at student and school characteristics as they relate to achievement. We would like to hear your views about student achievement in science.

Six preplanned questions were asked, but as is typical of interviewing techniques for qualitative research, probing questions were asked as needed to clarify participants' meanings, and where relevant, participants were asked for concrete examples to substantiate their espoused beliefs.

RESULTS

Conditions Necessary for High Achievement in Science

In addressing the question of the conditions for high science achievement, participants were prompted to focus on those conditions that derived from the nature of science as a school subject. The notion that science is a special subject that makes demands on learners that are different from the demands made by other subjects in the curriculum was a clear theme in all of the interviews. Science is more difficult; it demands different approaches to learning on the part of students and requires special learner characteristics.

In describing how science is different from other subjects, teachers referred to science as having a structure. It is made up of hierarchically organized concepts, and making connections between these concepts is important.

Teachers also spoke often about the relationship between science and mathematics and reading. Mathematics was seen as the "gatekeeper for science" (Karen). Given the beliefs that teachers had about the nature of school science, there are a number of characteristics that students need to possess to be successful in science. These can be categorized into four groups of student characteristics: qualities of mind, attitudes, prior experiences, and home and school factors.

Necessary qualities of mind. With respect to qualities of mind, it appears that teachers believed that some students come to high school with "a good mind for science."

> I feel like there are some kids I can look at and say, "Yeah, this kid has a good mind for science." They

have already acquired the mind for science, but I look at everybody else and say they need to acquire these skills, not that they can't—they just haven't yet. (Christa)

When prompted to explain what it means to have "a good mind for science," the teacher described such skills as the ability to formulate questions and the ability to find information. Like this teacher, every other participant elaborated a range of cognitive skills that he or she considered to be indispensable to success in science. The list includes a number of what are usually referred to as *science process skills*. Three of the eight teachers mentioned the skills of data interpretation and hypothesis development. These qualities of mind are, in effect, ways of thinking that science requires and that students need to have. It is interesting that Christa did not elaborate on the basis of her assessment about which students have a "good mind for science." It does not appear that it is based solely on objective criteria. The comment cited above suggests that the evaluation of whether the student has "a good mind for science" is based on external characteristics: "I feel that there are some kids I can look at and say, 'Yeah, this kid has a good mind for science.'" It would appear that some external markers, either physical or behavioral, are interpreted by this teacher as being indicative of ability to do science. Similarly, the judgment about those kids who do not possess the "good mind for science" is based on how those students look to the teacher.

Necessary attitudes. A range of attitudes was also identified as being necessary for success in science. Most frequently mentioned (by all eight teachers) was motivation.

Other attitudes that teachers mentioned were interest in science, personal discipline, inquisitiveness, open-mindedness, and flexibility to adapt to the demands of the subject and to the physical circumstances of school, which are often less than ideal. Students also need to be accepting of criticism and to take responsibility for their own learning.

Necessary prior experiences. The prior experiences that students need are, for the most part, the school experiences that develop reading and mathematical skills. Students need basic science concepts and the ability to communicate in science. One of the eight teachers expressed the view that everyday experiences with nature are necessary to provide a foundation of knowledge about the world on which school science learning could be built.

Necessary home and school factors. All teachers felt that the home environment was a contributing factor in science achievement. Parents need to provide discipline and a structured environment; they need to talk to their children about school, to support the teacher, and to check homework. Participants were divided on the question of the importance of parents' own educational level or knowledge of science. One teacher expressed the view that having parents who are knowledgeable about science is "helpful but not important" (Tina), whereas another observed that the children of better educated parents do better in science, although "she hated to admit it" (Christa). When the family's economic circumstances forced students to work, it was viewed as a disadvantage.

It is interesting that this group of teachers identified very few school factors as being necessary for success in science.

Beliefs About the Characteristics of Their Own Students

Teachers were asked to describe their own students with respect to those characteristics that they had identified as being necessary for high achievement. Without exception, the teachers were overwhelmingly negative in their beliefs about their students' preparedness to do well in science. It is important to note that the negative beliefs were, in most cases, not about their ability to do science but about their disposition to do it.

When queried about the need for intelligence in science relative to other areas of the curriculum, one teacher suggested that success in science is only partly due to "brightness." For most teachers, though, it was not that these urban students are incapable of doing well but that they lack a number of other characteristics needed to do well. Students were perceived as lacking the cognitive skills needed for science. They are constrained in their ability to grasp science concepts because they are concrete thinkers who are not able to engage in reflective thinking. This was mentioned by two teachers, including one from a high-achieving school, in the context of a discussion about laboratory work. Although laboratory work provides concrete experiences, it is still necessary for students to make the transition from the concrete experience to the abstract concept, and because these students are unable to do so, the benefit of the laboratory work is lost. Students were also thought to be deficient in problem-solving skills. They were seen as lacking in stamina and the ability to persevere at tasks, qualities that were thought to be needed in science more than in other disciplines. One teacher with 27 years of science teaching experience opined that there are many kids in urban schools with undiagnosed learning disabilities. In this teacher's view, increasing workplace demands that students stay in school longer exacerbates this problem.

Teachers viewed these students as having very poor attitudes that seriously undermine their achievement in science. The lack of motivation was a consistent theme in all these interviews. Students were described as "not interested," "not trying," and "not willing." It is surprising that even in the high-achieving schools, students were perceived either as unmotivated or as motivated by such extrinsic motivators as the fear of getting poor grades rather than by an interest in science.

Discipline problems were also consistently cited as being responsible for underachievement.

Another aspect of the perceived undiscipline is the students' preoccupation with having fun. Playing video games and talking on cell phones take precedence over schoolwork.

Specific reference to racial and ethnic factors was made by two teachers. One teacher observed that African American students do not think that it is "cool" to study and that their role models are basketball and football players who had become rich without succeeding in school. Another teacher, this one in a low-achieving school, saw her students as being without Black role models in science. Furthermore, the fact that they attend a school that is known to be low achieving and is populated predominantly by African American students makes them feel that they are stereotyped as low achievers. This is demotivating to these African American students. Another teacher made reference to the fact that students who live in urban communities do not have an interest in science because nothing in their out-of-school experiences "resonates" with the science that they learn in school (Jerry).

All of these teachers perceived their students as coming to high school with inadequate prior experiences. Their mathematics skills are poor as are their science process skills. They have no knowledge of experimental design and can not interpret data. Without exception, these eight teachers described their students as having had poor preparation in the middle school grades.

Teachers believed that parents were only minimally involved in their children's science learning. Seldom did parents communicate with teachers, and when they did, it was usually about custodial issues, such as student absences. With respect to school factors, these teachers felt that the schools were reasonably well resourced in spite of the fact that several of the teachers had used their own money to purchase materials for their classes. Extracurricular activities in science were seen as useful in promoting an interest in science, but the level of student engagement in these was low.

Curriculum Adaptation

It is clear that the teachers recognized the need to adapt the curriculum in response to the characteristics of their students as well as to the school conditions in which they worked. They were, however, constrained by issues of accountability. One teacher in a high-achieving school claimed that she started where the curriculum started, regardless of deficiencies in prior knowledge that her students might have on entry into high school.

We just start from the beginning. Whereas 9 years ago you could start at point A and move on, now you just have to start at the beginning. The students eventually fall into two groups: those who are motivated and those who aren't going to make it through this school. (Karen)

There was a clear tension between teachers' pedagogical knowledge and the accountability to the manifest curriculum to which they are held. Teachers were reluctant to say that they had departed in any way from the manifest curriculum and rejected the word *modified*: "not modified, but some things are deemphasized" (Jerry).

Analysis of teacher responses to this issue reveals that teachers modified the curriculum in response to two groups of factors. These were school conditions and learner characteristics. The school conditions that necessitated curriculum modifications were time and availability of resources. The learner characteristics were the deficiencies in prerequisite knowledge and the perceived lack of interest. In response to learner deficiencies, teachers reported slowing down the pace to ensure that students "got it," changing the sequence of topics so that more difficult topics were addressed first, spending more time on some topics than was suggested, reteaching topics that should have already been known, spending time teaching vocabulary, and increasing the number of activities done about a topic. Teachers reported attempting to reduce the level of difficulty of some topics. One physics teacher reported removing the difficult mathematics to ensure that the students' lack of mathematics skills did not hinder the learning of the science concepts.

Teachers made judgments about whether students were likely to use the science in the future and taught accordingly. If students were not science majors, then the depth of treatment of concepts was reduced and the "more technical stuff" was omitted.

When students were judged to be lacking in motivation or interest in science, teachers attempted to engage them by contextualizing the science in experiences that were familiar to them. Real-life application of the science concepts was the strategy used. One teacher reported helping the students to understand principles of heat transfer by referring to temperature differences between the basement and other parts of the house. Motivation was deemed by these teachers to be an important determinant of their students' success in science, and teachers sought to foster this by making the science more relevant.

Time was described as a major constraint for these teachers. A physics teacher complained that the physics curriculum needed three times as much time as was allotted to it. Teachers who adapted to their students' needs by slowing down the pace of teaching often ran out of time, and some topics were not taught. Teachers made judgments about what could be omitted and taught the more difficult or important topics first. When laboratory resources were in short supply or lacking, teachers reported using "informal labs and simulations."

Views about the curriculum varied depending on whether the teacher taught in a high- or low-achieving school. Teachers in the low-achieving schools felt that there was a mismatch between the prior experiences of their students and the demands of the high school science curriculum. Students' middle school science experiences had not prepared them for high school science, and their out-of-school experiences worked against high achievement in science. Teachers in the high-achieving schools, on the other hand, felt that the curriculum was not challenging and that unless the students received some enrichment, they would not be competitive in college. Furthermore, in that school system, there was no honors curriculum in at least one of the sciences. One teacher felt strongly that unless high school students were streamed by ability, "talent would never blossom" because the presence of so many ill-prepared or learning-disabled students in the classes only served to "dumb down" the curriculum (Karen).

DISCUSSION

The findings of this study could be useful for formulating questions to guide observational studies that could provide deeper understandings than we now have of the curricular experiences of urban science students.

A Deficit Model

It is clear that, for the most part, these teachers employed what has been described as a deficit model for understanding the problems that urban children face with respect to school achievement. These teachers viewed science as difficult, as more demanding than other subjects, and as requiring students with special characteristics. It is more difficult than other subjects, and only those who recognize that and who naturally have or acquire a good "science mind" can be successful. This leads one to wonder whether these teachers subscribe to a somewhat elitist view of science, which, although not necessarily motivated by an intention to be exclusive, might in fact function to exclude these students from full access to science.

The deficit model used to explain the low levels of school achievement of underrepresented groups absolves the school or the society of any complicity in the students' underachievement and places the blame on the students, their parents, and their communities. In this view, as is the case with the teachers in this study, the students are seen as not having what it takes to succeed. None of the teachers in this group applied any sociocultural lenses to their characterizations of their students' qualities or behaviors. Their characterizations reflected widely held stereotypes that charge African American students with a lack of interest in academics and low performance in school subjects, especially mathematics and science. Steele (1999) posited the notion of "stereotype threat," which suggests that members of stereotyped groups experience levels of anxiety that serve to depress their performance when they are placed in situations where the stereotype operates. The resulting underachievement serves to confirm the stereotype, creating a self-perpetuating cycle. Ogbu and Simmons's (1998) cultural-ecological theory is another sociocultural lens that provides for more insightful description of students' characteristics than the deficit model subscribed to by the teachers in this study. Ogbu and Simmons suggest that the apparent lack of interest in school and the poor work ethic that Black students are thought to display are responses to the sociohistorically

determined patterns of dominance in the wider society in which teachers and students live. The intersection of the cultural framework of a predominantly White teaching profession and that of Black students often mirrors the conflicts that exist in society due to differences in social positioning between majority and underrepresented groups. Through this lens, students' disengagement from academics might be construed not as the result of intellectual deficiency but as the result of feelings of alienation. Ennis and McCauley (2002) suggest that the lack of motivation, the failure to comply with school demands, and the lack of engagement with learning, all of which were described by teachers in this study, are evidence of a lack of trust in the educational system on the part of urban children. It is interesting to note that Atwater, Wiggins, and Gardner (1995) found that those urban African American middle school students who had negative attitudes to science had negative attitudes to science teachers, the science curriculum, the school climate, and the physical environment of the school.

With respect to teachers' beliefs about their students' parents, the deficit model was also apparent. Atwater et al. (1995) also noted the influence of parents' educational level on student achievement. In this study, the assertion by one teacher that student achievement in science correlates with parental educational level is supported by the work of Entwisle and Alexander (1988). It is possible that the lack of parental involvement in the academic lives of urban children, as perceived by the teachers in this study, might have more to do with feelings of disempowerment, engendered by parents' own poor educational backgrounds, than with a lack of interest in their children's education. It seems evident that the teachers in this study were unaware of other, more culturally sensitive, ways of viewing their students, and their beliefs about their students' characteristics seemed to reflect the racial stereotypes prevalent in the society. The literature on the impact of teacher beliefs on student outcomes suggests that these beliefs about students are likely to have a profound effect on teachers' instructional decisions.

CURRICULUM IMPLICATIONS

The tendency on the part of teachers to eliminate the more complex concepts, to deemphasize some topics because they did not believe their students would take another science class, and to reduce the depth of coverage of others might well be an indication that these students were being offered a "pedagogy of poverty" (Haberman, 1991). Indeed, if the students are seen as deficient, then reducing the complexity of the science content is the appropriate response. Like the pre-service teachers in the Lewis et al. (2002) study, these teachers did not appear to have any understanding of culturally relevant science teaching. They did not conceive of their students as possibly bringing to the science classroom a set of cultural meanings and understandings that might necessitate changes in pedagogy and that might indeed become a valued part of the interaction that is the essence of curriculum. Culturally relevant teaching is teaching that is based on the principle of leveraging the cultural frameworks that children bring to school to promote learning that is meaningful and that leaves them feeling valued and respected. It has implications for all aspects of schooling, including the organization of schools, classroom norms and values, the selection of content, and the design of learning experiences.

The fact that teachers were reluctant to report any adaptation at all suggests that they hold a view of curriculum as static and outside their control. This is in contrast to a view of the curriculum as dynamic interaction of which both teachers and students have ownership.

It is important to note that all of these teachers expressed deep concern about the academic progress of their students. They obviously cared about their welfare and wanted to be effective in teaching them science. It appears, however, that they had little understanding about how to teach science in ways that are culturally relevant. The implications for science teacher education programs, in both pre-service and professional development, are obvious. This spirit of caring for students is the capital on which effective professional development that sensitizes teachers to the principles and practices of culturally relevant teaching must be built. If teachers are to be able to make the change toward more culturally sensitive strategies, they must first understand the ways in which their teaching has been culturally insensitive and then confront the beliefs that underlie their practice.

Perhaps the most important finding of this study is that these urban students are perceived by their teachers as lacking the necessary qualities for high achievement in science and that these beliefs might be influencing the teachers' instructional decisions in ways that limit the students' opportunity to learn science. The fact that 95% of these students are African American, as is the case with many urban schools, suggests a possible reason for the persistent underachievement of urban students in science. The extent to which this is the case is best determined by observational studies that examine the curricular experiences of urban children and that explore more directly the link between teachers' beliefs and their classroom practice in science.

Discussion Questions

How do teacher beliefs change the formal curriculum into the taught (enacted) curriculum?

How do you feel about the science teacher's contention that science is different and more difficult than other subjects?

Glenda M. Prime is a science educator at Morgan State University.

Rommel J. Miranda is a professor at Columbia Union College.

Article 34

TRIED AND TRUE

The Rural School Curriculum in the Age of Accountability

AIMEE HOWLEY

Educators concerned about learning in rural schools recently have turned their attention to curriculum approaches that strive to complement the experiences of rural children and meet the needs of rural communities (Haas & Nachtigal, 1998; Theobald, 1997; Woodhouse & Knapp, 2000). Place-based pedagogy is one approach that focuses on curricula that "prepare people to live and work to sustain the cultural and ecological integrity of the places they inhabit" (Woodhouse & Knapp, p. 1). These curricula—grounded in local experience—are believed to offer greater "sense-making" opportunities than curricula narrowly construed to fit a business agenda for job preparation (Haas & Nachtigal).

Despite efforts to shift curricula toward local needs, most rural schools—like the majority of others throughout the United States—still rely on traditional curricula driven primarily by textbook content and standardized testing. As Haas and Nachtigal (1998; cf. Kliebard, 2002) argued,

> A national curriculum has existed since the introduction of *McGuffey's Reader*. Textbook publishing is big business. Textbooks are generically written to appeal to the largest possible market. They must be inoffensive and useable in all parts of the country, particularly in large states such as California and Texas, which adopt them statewide. Curriculum is bound by what is in these textbooks. Standardized tests form the third leg of the iron triangle of the national curriculum. (p. 1)

This essay explores the benefits and constraints of the traditional curriculum now used in most rural schools. Two important caveats must precede this analysis. First, literature pertaining to rural school

SOURCE: Excerpted from Howley, A. (2003). Tried and true: The rural school curriculum in the age of accountability. *Educational Forum, 68*(1), 14–23. Reprinted by permission of Kappa Delta Pi.

curriculum is sparse, and efforts to construct fine-grained pictures of that curriculum, such as the historical treatment offered by Kliebard (2002), necessarily focus on the way the curriculum evolved in a specific context. Given the lack of available evidence, it is unwise to place too much trust in generalizations made about the rural curriculum of the past or present. Second, despite efforts to remain dispassionate, my perspective is constructed from an idiosyncratic set of beliefs. I have argued elsewhere in favor of a liberal arts approach, which some may view as traditional. However, I also support progressive educational strategies, including the use of thematic units and contextualized learning experiences (Gibbs & Howley, 2000, Howley, Howley, & Pendarvis, 1995). I do object to the deployment of a fact-based curriculum that trains low-socioeconomic-status children in habits of compliance (Anyon, 1980) or sorts children into social categories based on background characteristics (Spring, 1989). My rural school experience suggests that this latter curriculum—what some call essentialist—represents the more frequently adopted traditional approach.

Nevertheless, schools can choose an essentialist curriculum without advancing the reproduction of social class divisions.

Origins of the Rural School Curriculum

Even before the United States became a nation, communities began to organize primary schools to provide instruction in basic skills such as reading and writing (Cremin, 1970). Though the initial impetus was to give children access to moral lessons in the Bible, these basic skills later were valued for their role in developing mental faculties and, even later, for their practical benefits (Gulliford, 1996; Kliebard, 2002; see, e.g., Woofter, 1917). Rural school curricula by the early 1800s included reading, grammar, spelling, and penmanship (Gulliford). Somewhat later in the century, other studies—typically arithmetic, civics, history, and health—were added but tended to receive less attention.

By the mid-1800s, city school enrollment began increasing rapidly, and school structures began to change. According to Kliebard (2002), the move to graded schools, first in cities and later in rural communities, reflected a major shift in schooling. With the development of grade-level cohorts, school terms were lengthened and regularized, group recitation began to replace individual recitation, and curriculum content and objectives began to be developed. A curriculum written by professional educators at the county or state level came to replace textbooks so that lessons could be structured for individual students in accordance with their abilities and needs.

Though a basic skills curriculum prevailed in primary schools across the nation, schools in different locales varied in the practical skills that were included. For example:

> Term lengths in rural schools were generally short, incorporating long breaks to accommodate agricultural needs in each region. Consequently, the amount of material covered in rural curricula varied across regions of the country and even districts within regions (Kliebard, 2002; Parkerson & Parkerson, 1998). Nevertheless, by 1860, the majority of school-aged children—at least those in northern states—were receiving a primary school education (Parkerson & Parkerson).

Widespread participation in secondary school education came about much later. By 1910, only 5.1% of enrolled students were attending secondary schools, increasing to 26% by 1940. With some variation, the number has remained in the 20% to 30% range ever since (U.S. Department of Education, 1996).

Like most secondary school curricula used throughout the country, rural curricula typically included traditional subjects such as English, math, history, and science (Barker, 1985a). This content was solidified during the early 1900s, after debates over the content of the "modern" curriculum settled down.

Contention during the late 19th century centered on the extent to which classical studies should be replaced by more practical studies emphasizing sciences and modern language

(Kliebard, 1992). A set of recommendations proposed by the National Education Association's Committee of Ten in 1893 introduced electives and multiple curriculum tracks into secondary schools, paving the way for early 20th-century "progressive" proposals supporting the inclusion of vocational options among the more traditional academic ones.

Progressive educators criticized the traditional curriculum for its over-reliance on discipline-based studies (Franklin, 1987). These educators advocated that problem-solving and critical thinking skills were more fully realized through interdisciplinary project-based approaches (Williams, 1998). In "Community Schools" of some rural locales, this progressive vision was put into practice in the 1930s and 1940s. The curriculum of a community school in Waialua, Hawaii, for example, included traditional subjects but also involved educators and students in efforts to improve community health, stimulate economic development, and foster community beautification (Midkiff, 1938).

Though progressive educators experimented with alternatives in some noteworthy cases, the traditional approach nevertheless prevailed in most rural communities (Cuban, 1993), where parents perhaps favored curriculum in the "basics" (Stockman & Powers, 1996). Even today, educators still may find that a traditional curriculum makes it easier to address the outcomes specified in the academic content standards increasingly being put forth by state education agencies (Brown, 1992; Romberg, Zarinnia, & Williams, 1998; Smith, 1991).

THE PRESENT STATE OF THE RURAL SCHOOL CURRICULUM

Very little survey research maps the landscape of rural school curriculum. The few existing studies examine only high school curricula and show that rural high schools typically offer academic curricula primarily comprised of required courses (Barker, 1985a, 1985b; Barker, Muse, & Smith, 1984; Monk & Haller, 1990). In some states, it appears that rural schools enroll a larger proportion of students in a general—as opposed to a college preparatory or vocational—curriculum track than do suburban and urban schools (McCracken & Barcina, 1991).

Although none of these studies examined the extent to which the curricula in rural schools are traditional or progressive, it seems reasonable to infer that such curricula are primarily traditional. Cuban (1993), for example, found that teachers mostly used traditional instructional methods, ultimately leading him to conclude that the impact of progressive education was not particularly robust. Since the 1930s, reported curricula innovations in rural schools have been positioned against a dominant (i.e., traditional) paradigm (Everett, 1938; Haas & Nachtigal, 1998). In addition, rural community members tend to value tradition, rejecting educational innovations they believe represent unnecessary "frills" (Allen & Dillman, 1994). Furthermore, state education agencies have taken an increasingly decisive role in assuring that all schools—irrespective of locale—offer uniform courses of study (Lambert, 1991).

TRADITIONAL CURRICULUM BENEFITS

With its focus on the basics—reading, writing, and math—and on discipline-based subject matter, the traditional curriculum promises significant benefits to rural students. First, it conveys skills needed for college or employment. Arguably, students who are competent readers and writers, and have mastered mathematics at least through algebra, will be able to perform well in a college program or an entry-level job. While the "facts" of science and the emphases of social studies are continually being revised, reading comprehension, mathematical knowledge, and good writing are less changeable. Given the exponential rate at which knowledge is increasing, no particular body of information can be said definitively to constitute the "knowledge of most worth" (Harding & Vining, 1997). Therefore, students who acquire basic skills and remain curious enough to read and research will, on their own, acquire a fund of general knowledge adequate to their roles as jobholders and citizens.

Second, most teachers are able to teach basic skills and subject matter. The fact that so few teachers have chosen to adopt the numerous curricular and instructional reforms directed toward them over the past 100 years suggests that they might not have had the ability to do so (cf. Cuban, 1993; Gitlin & Margonis, 1995). Certainly, the continual call for the professional development of teachers (Borko, Elliott, & Uchiyama, 2002; Smith & O'Day, 1991), in the face of the notable ineffectiveness of most professional development efforts (Sykes, 1996), offers some evidence that the sorts of instructional changes that reformers hope to see implemented actually exceed the capacity of most teachers. Furthermore, the relative effectiveness of "teacher proof" instructional programs such as "Success for All" (Borman & Hewes, 2001) and the relative ineffectiveness of constructivist approaches such as whole-language (Jeynes & Littell, 2000) perhaps also suggest that the practices associated with a traditional curriculum are easier to elicit from teachers.

Third, the traditional curriculum prepares students to perform mandated accountability measures, which clearly can impact a school's stability and survival. In a study of teachers in North Carolina, for example, more than half of the teachers surveyed indicated that they would attempt to transfer from a school whose ranking dropped to "low performing" (Jones et al., 1999). Many states also invoke sanctions against schools that fail to measure up on required accountability tests (Education Commission of the States, 2002). Among the more severe sanctions are state takeovers of schools and school closures. The recent reauthorization of the Elementary and Secondary Education Act (ESEA), dubbed "No Child Left Behind," incorporates measures designed to stimulate the development of private-sector alternatives to low-performing public schools.

Given these circumstances, many teachers, even those who claim to prefer more progressive approaches, default to a basic skills curriculum and traditional instructional methods (Brown, 1992; Cimbricz, 2002). These changes in instructional practice, moreover, do seem to be associated with modest increases in students' performance on state-mandated measures of achievement (Haney, 2000). Though many teachers express regret over the narrowing of the curriculum that takes place as a result of accountability testing, their schools are, nevertheless, performing better and are therefore rendered less vulnerable.

Finally, the traditional curriculum matches the expectations of rural parents and community members, who hold schools accountable in somewhat different ways, expressing resistance to practices they see as wasteful, frivolous, or incompatible with community values (Fikes, 1991; Keith, 1995; Kleinsasser, 1986; Page & Clelland, 1978). Though few studies examine the curriculum preferences of rural parents (cf. Stockman & Powers, 1996), anecdotal reports from school administrators suggest that parents prefer curricular options that are compatible with their own schooling experiences (cf. Hughes & Spence, 1971). In addition, rural community residents are often skeptical of the increasing costs of schooling—which may indicate their preference for basic, rather than more extensive or innovative, educational services.

TRADITIONAL CURRICULUM INADEQUACIES

Several scholars have argued that the traditional curriculum adopted by most rural schools serves the interests of county and state education agencies, which seek to standardize what schools teach (Haas & Nachtigal, 1998; Kliebard, 2002; Leo-Nyquist & Theobald, 1997; Moriarty, 1994). According to these scholars, standardization enabled bureaucrats to subvert the aims of rural schools, which originally assisted communities in sustaining a rural way of life. Increasingly through the 20th century, policymakers and professional educators instead directed rural schools to prepare workers for the nation's urban factories and, later, service industries. As Leo-Nyquist and Theobald (1997) noted,

> For most of this century, rural schools have been treated as a national "problem" that could best be solved by making them more like efficiently-managed large urban schools. From this perspective, the unique features of rural schools and communities are seen as liabilities to be overcome, rather than as potential strengths to be nurtured. (p. 2)

Arguably, these dynamics are still operant, perhaps even more intensely, in the current political environment. The focus on accountability, keyed to state and national standards, is prompting many rural districts to align curriculum with test specifications (Nilsen, 2000; Reichman & Rayford, 1988). Even advocates of place-based pedagogy are finding it necessary to show that the curricula they favor correspond closely to the outcomes specified in state curriculum frameworks (Jennings, 2000).

Arguments that support progressive—and oppose traditional—curriculum typically draw on three lines of reasoning. First, progressives maintain that, even when it includes substantive content, the traditional curriculum aims to prepare students for roles in the future (Leo-Nyquist, 2001). In contrast, a progressive curriculum supports students' development in the present, trusting that properly educated students will be able to make wise choices about their own futures. Next, attention can be drawn to the mismatch between the traditional curriculum and children's natural learning processes. These arguments suggest that an essentialist curriculum typically presents disembodied and decontextualized facts, which do not assist students in making sense of their lives. Lastly, those who believe education ought primarily to be aimed at liberation argue that traditional approaches sustain a "hidden curriculum" that reproduces social class divisions, preparing students from low-SES backgrounds for subordinate roles and those from high-SES backgrounds for managerial and professional roles (Anyon, 1980; Spring, 1989).

In rural schools, a curriculum that focuses on preparing students for future roles tends to devalue students' current circumstances. Because job prospects are far more prevalent in urban areas, such a curriculum encourages successful students to leave the countryside for more lucrative opportunities in cities. With roots in the pragmatism of the progressive education movement, vocational programs may help students imagine worthwhile futures within their local rural communities. Academic studies, particularly when presented in a traditional curriculum aimed toward job preparation, may condition students to believe that they must leave the rural locale to lead successful lives.

TWO PROGRESSIVE ALTERNATIVES

Whether or not a traditional curriculum is best is a question that may be impossible to answer definitively, but is definitely worth considering. Clearly the existence of rural educators using innovative teaching methods, rural support for progressive school programs, and a resistance to arbitrary mandates (Scott, 1999) suggest that alternatives are possible.

One progressive option, positioned to give rural adolescents reasons to stay in their local communities, places schools at the center of community economic development (Boethel, 2000; Wall & Luther, 1988). Schools function to some degree like small business incubators, providing a site for and brokering support for newly emerging local enterprises (Boethel). The curriculum sometimes is modified to focus particular attention on the skills needed to manage the locally operated business (Boethel). During their high school years, students become involved in these businesses, and some continue employment even after graduation.

Another progressive strategy, place-based pedagogy, focuses the curriculum on rural life experiences. Rather than viewing the school as the basis for a community's economic development, this approach considers the community to be the foundation for the schooling enterprise. The curriculum identifies the rural locale as the source of substantive content (Leo-Nyquist & Theobald, 1997). Using progressive methods, such as "thematic units" and "experiential learning," schools tie children's experiences in rural communities to academic content (Romano & Glascock, 2002).

This approach builds on children's natural learning processes, which tend to be both situated and adaptive (Lave & Wenger, 1991). The specific context provides a motive for learning, and it enables the learner to link newly acquired knowledge to a web of prior knowledge, some of which is personal, but much of which is shared widely among community members. Situated learning of this type enables a child to make sense of the world in ways that also make sense to members of his or her community. Such learning provides the basis for cultural stability, and it also enables the community to respond flexibly to pressures from the external environment.

Educators who advocate authentic curricula designed to promote deep and meaningful learning often justify this approach by arguing that it contributes to the self-determination of individuals and communities. By connecting progressive educational practices to liberatory aims, these educators are consciously setting out to offer an alternative to the social reproduction often attributed to an essentialist curriculum. To many rural educators, the benefits of freeing students from the vicious sorting that consigns them either to marginal social roles in rural places or to job-holding in cities seem obvious. These benefits may be less apparent to rural community members. In fact, many of the descriptions of initiatives to develop place-based curricula reveal that these efforts are primarily carried out by educators who are assisted by representatives of elite community groups (Wither, 2001).

RESPONDING TO CURRICULUM NEEDS OF RURAL SCHOOLS

Rural educators face challenges when they work to provide curriculum offerings that are academically rigorous yet responsive to students' and communities' interests and needs. In recent years, pressures associated with accountability have constituted an additional—and sometimes extraordinary—challenge.

Under most accountability provisions, the state develops academic content standards, which are used as the blueprint for achievement tests administered at specified grade levels to public school students. These test results can determine whether or not students will graduate from high school, whether a school will receive an award or a sanction, and whether a school district will remain self-governing or risk state takeover. Given these high stakes, the easiest—and perhaps most prudent—course of action is often to "align" curriculum with the state standards. While alignment may ensure that no essential content is overlooked, it certainly cannot help rural educators meet the interests and needs of their particular students and communities. What options are available to those with a stake in rural schools?

Rural schools can make judicious use of curriculum alignment, which does not typically involve replacing a local curriculum with one geared toward state standards. On most curriculum issues, states and communities likely will find that they agree more than they disagree. In a report of local curriculum development in a small city in Nebraska, Swidler and Hoffman (2000) explained that the standards created by a group of local citizens turned out to be comparable to, and in some cases more stringent than, those set by the state.

An extensive and inclusive discussion of rural curriculum ought to include parents and other community members as well as educators. Historically, rural communities played a decisive role in school governance; rural residents remember when citizens enjoyed direct involvement in the community school. More recently, however, school standardization and consolidation have eroded community engagement with school planning and evaluation.

In important ways, schools belong to the public (Mathews, 1996). Community members ought to participate actively in decision making about standards, and communities ought to hold schools accountable for providing educational services to best serve public interest. When such interests are defined by representative decision makers located at great distance from particular communities, specific local concerns may be overlooked or misconstrued. Matters of school curriculum, which at root concern fundamental values, ought to be decided closer to home.

Obviously, professional educators also play an important role in defining school curriculum. Their views, however, ought not necessarily to prevail. Considering the powerful voice they have in matters of school practice, professional educators owe communities careful explanations of their views concerning curriculum as well as the reasoning supporting those views.

Broad-based dialogue about curriculum matters eventually will lead educators and community members to the point of establishing accountability provisions that respond to local concerns. This is especially important in communities whose needs are not readily addressed by federal and state accountability provisions.

Considering these circumstances, curriculum reform in rural schools ought to be coupled with local accountability requirements that employ defensible measurement procedures and set challenging but attainable benchmarks. For example, the practice of comparing one cohort's performance with that of a different cohort is questionable. A better approach would be to use wide-range achievement tests to track the annual progress of each student. Testing should be avoided in subjects other than reading and math because instruments purported to measure knowledge of such subjects—science or social studies, for instance—usually are sensitive to (a) ability in reading comprehension and (b) knowledge of some body of facts and concepts not necessarily presented in the curriculum. Instead, assessment efforts in domains outside of reading and math might focus on progress portfolios that provide parents with evidence of their children's increasing competence. Though it may seem cumbersome to teachers and school leaders, a school report card that presents findings from locally developed assessment procedures can counter misleading generalizations inferred from the data disseminated via state report cards.

Finally, a school and community should adhere to the chosen assessment strategy, which is an important way to monitor trends. Using assessment results to guide reform efforts is critical to any accountability mechanism. By treating assessment results as an honest reckoning of performance, instead of a public relations issue, professional educators demonstrate their willingness to work *with* citizens to foster meaningful school improvement.

Discussion Questions

Given the standards movement and the discussion of national testing that appears in the news, should we design different curriculum for urban, rural, and suburban schools? (Keep in mind the concept of what is "fair.")

What does the author mean by "authentic" curriculum?

Aimee Howley is a professor at Ohio University.

Section IX

WHAT ARE CURRENT HOT-BUTTON ISSUES IN CURRICULUM?

Curriculum is a field of study that is fraught with a multitude of highly contentious topics. The nature of the topics changes according to the political climate of the country, the social issues of the times, and the special interest of parents and educators. Some topics are relegated to specific historical time periods (e.g., Progressive Education), and others cut across time periods, philosophical ideologies, and social constructs.

The articles in this section of the reader are a reflection of the current concerns within the curriculum strategies arena. They are precipitated by (a) the emphasis on high-stakes testing and accountability, (b) what employers expect of new hires, (c) the presumed moral decay of the country, (d) the increased violence in our society, (e) changing demographics, and (f) advances in technology. History will reveal that these issues have spawned curriculum inquiry in the past, but the intensity of these issues is what is driving the current concerns.

James Popham presents a beautiful case of the necessity for specialists in curriculum, instruction, and assessment to work collaboratively in order to make any headway in solving the many problems facing our schools.

"It's the Curriculum, Stupid," is an excellent argument for restructuring the curriculum so that it concentrates on specific skills needed by today's youth in order to be successful in a postsecondary environment.

James Banks is a world-renowned multicultural educator. He argues for the inclusion of knowledge, attitudes, and skills in the curriculum, which will allow diverse students to function not only in their community but also beyond their "cultural borders." He refers to this as the "development of a cosmopolitan citizen." Marginalized people cannot "endorse national values, become cosmopolitans, and work to make their communities, nation, and world more just and humane."

The increase in violence in our schools has been the stimulant for schools to adopt a zero-tolerance policy to control student behavior. Stinchcomb and her colleagues examine ways to address discipline infractions without relying on suspension and expulsion, which serve no educative value in schools. Their approach is referred to as restorative justice.

As you read this section think about the following:

- The appropriateness of what students are learning and being assessed on and its connection to the reality of the world they will face after high school

- What role the schools should play in the moral development of children

- The relationship between violence in our society and how it is treated, and violence in our schools

- The meaning of social justice and how schools can ensure that all students are treated equally and fairly in school

- The importance of service learning and how service learning can become an integral part of an emphasis on social justice

Article 35

Curriculum, Instruction, and Assessment

Amiable Allies or Phony Friends?

W. James Popham

Definitions and Bona Fides

Definition Time

Because in our field there are often different definitions lurking behind identical labels, I'd like to make sure you know what I'm referring to when I employ the terms *curriculum, instruction*, and *assessment*.

Curriculum, to me, consists of our educational aims—that is, the knowledge, skills, or affective changes in students we hope our educational efforts will produce. Curriculum, in short, consists of the ends that our educational system is intended to achieve for the students that we teach. When I entered the education profession eons ago, we described our curricular aims as "goals" or "objectives." These days, such aims are usually referred to as "content standards."

Instruction, on the other hand, consists of the means that educators employ in an attempt to achieve their curricular ends. Put more simply, instruction describes the things teachers do to help students learn what those students are supposed to learn. Instruction and teaching, to me, are synonymous.

Finally, *assessment* describes the measurement activities in which educators attempt to derive valid inferences about students' unseen knowledge, skills, or affect. For a variety of reasons, both curricular and instructional, educators need to assess students to determine what sorts of knowledge, skills, and affect those students actually possess. Such measurement endeavors

SOURCE: Excerpted from Popham, W. J. (2004). Curriculum, instruction, and assessment: Amiable allies or phony friends? *Teachers College Record, 106*(3), 417–428. Reprinted by permission.

are important, for example, when deciding (a) what curricular aims ought to be pursued, (b) how best to fashion instruction that will mesh with a student's current capabilities, and (c) whether an instructional sequence has been successful. When I first began teaching, we referred to assessment as "testing." But these days it seems that educators interchangeably use the labels *assessment, testing*, or *measurement.*

ALL TOO SEASONED

Now, just to get my qualifications on the table, I have personally worked in all three of these specializations—namely, curriculum, instruction, and assessment. I've written books about all three specializations. I've also taught graduate university courses in all three specializations. And I've directed many dissertations and supervised numerous research projects and development projects centered on curriculum, instruction, and assessment. Many of those projects took place in the real world—as opposed to the university. In short, I am no stranger to any of these specialties. To be completely accurate, although during my own graduate studies I emphasized curriculum and instruction, I've picked up what I know about assessment on my own—well after graduate school was a faint memory.

Throughout my career in education, now having hit the half-century mark, I have encountered heaps of first-rate professionals in each of these three specializations. And, although during the most recent past I have been primarily plucking and squashing grapes in the measurement vineyard, I still count as close friends a number of folks who specialize in either curriculum or instruction.

At different times in my career, then, I have spent substantial time in each of the three fields I'll be dealing with later in this analysis. I hope, therefore, that I will not be regarded as a measurement guy who's tossing stones at the curriculum and instruction crowd. Such, surely, is not my purpose.

ACCOUNTABILITY IN CONTROL

Okay, so much for foreplay. Let's get into the substance of this treatise. The genesis of my concern stems directly from the relentless escalation of accountability pressures under which our nation's educators have been operating for at least the past two decades. At the center of this accountability pressure is a pervasive demand for credible evidence that the nation's tax-supported educators have been doing a good job of operating our public schools. And this credible evidence almost always seems to take the form of students' test scores. In other words, assessment evidence is now being employed by both educators and noneducators to determine whether curriculum and instruction are effective. As never before, the testing tail has definitely been wagging the curriculum/instruction canine.

Educators, then, and even more so since the arrival of the No Child Left Behind Act, are being appraised on the basis of their ability to get students to sparkle on high-stakes achievement tests. If students' test scores fail to rise, then it is thought that teachers have definitely stumbled. If test scores do rise, however, teachers are not only applauded but, as was seen in California and a few other states, "successful" teachers receive some serious financial rewards. Test scores, it seems, trump everything that's available to be trumped.

Yet, even though assessment professionals appear to be holding most of the cards these days, we still see many instances in which the activities carried out by curriculum or instruction professionals can have a major impact—either positive or negative—on the work of assessment professionals. Indeed, specialists in any one of the three fields can make a difference in the activities carried out in either of the other two specializations. Let me illustrate with several real-world examples of these sorts of interrelationships:

- If a state-approved curriculum contains too many content standards, then the state's teachers will be unable to promote students' mastery of those content standards in the instructional time that's available.

- Similarly, if a state-approved curriculum contains too many content standards, then assessment personnel will be unable to accurately test students' mastery of those standards in the assessment time that's available.

- If an important assessment device focuses on only a modest number of important curricular targets, however, then teacher's instruction can be crafted to address those curriculum/assessment targets satisfactorily.

- If an important test has been deliberately developed, from its inception, so that what's measured can be effectively taught, teachers' instructional efforts will typically be more successful than if the test had been developed without attention to instruction.

- Instructionally insensitive high-stakes assessments will typically tend to make teachers reduce their curricular aspirations or degrade their classroom instructional practices or both.

All right, any sensible person who surveys American education these days will conclude that the fields of curriculum, instruction, and assessment are vitally interrelated. Why is it, then, that most professionals who function in those three fields seem oblivious of this powerful, implication-laden truth? But it's even worse than that. The bulk of today's curriculum specialists appear to be self-righteously content in their own content realms. Members of each of the three specializations not only display a form of other-field agnosticism, but they also seem to revel in that self-sired ignorance.

Earlier in my career, for a decade or so, I headed a group that developed high-stakes achievement tests for about a dozen states. In that role, I often found myself interacting with a given state department's curriculum, instruction, and assessment personnel. Typically, I encountered individuals who not only were totally happy to be working in their own special enclave but also were also quick to disparage the individuals in "those other fields." To be truthful, curriculum folks sometimes got along fairly well with instruction folks. But assessment personnel were, almost always, either feared or disdained by their curriculum or instruction colleagues. Assessment folks often regarded their curriculum or instruction counterparts as "soft heads." Curriculum or instruction personnel sometimes opined that their state department's assessment specialists must have been "cognitively damaged due to the computation of too many reliability coefficients." Interdisciplinary respect was rarely seen in those state departments of education.

Time and again, I would see a state's curriculum specialists, all by themselves, decide what their state's content standards ought to be. Time and again, I would see a state's assessment specialists, often abetted by their test contractor lackeys, decide on the specifics of a high-stakes test's items all by themselves. Time and again, after the state's curriculum had been decided and after the state's test had been built, I would see the state department's instruction specialists, all by themselves, try to come up with staff development activities intended to help the state's teachers do a better instructional job of promoting high test scores. Other than the occasional tokenistic inclusion of a few folks from one of the other two specialties, the state department of education specialists that I encountered functioned in almost total isolation.

This isolationism, of course, is all too understandable. Most of today's master's-level and doctoral-level professionals were trained by professors who were themselves, specialists. And those specialist-professors invariably operate in an academic reward structure that fosters specialization. Curriculum professors, especially those who want to advance academically, send their manuscripts to curriculum journals. Instruction professors fire off their manuscripts to instruction journals. And assessment professors send their manuscripts to assessment journals, or, if a given manuscript contains enough numbers and a few Greek letters, they send it to one of the higher-brow psychometric journals.

Similar specialization-focused activities are also seen when professors become active in their state and national professional associations. The widespread specialization currently seen in education's three chief content fields is far from surprising. It makes sense. But, today, it is flat-out folly. But, today, this sort of unrelenting specialization is harming our nation's students.

HYPERSPECIALIZATION'S HYPERHARM

A Personal Perspective

What I see going on all over the country is that, if the wrong kinds of high-stakes tests are adopted, classroom instruction suffers. My own children are no longer in school, but my grandchildren are. All four of my children experienced their entire education in public schools. Let me tell you honestly that, were my children in public schools today, I would be genuinely frightened about the caliber of schooling they'd most likely be receiving. I wouldn't be worried about too much accountability. No, I'd realize that our nation's current need for accountability evidence isn't going to be satisfied for quite some time. Moreover, I really don't think that educational accountability is an inherently evil thing. What I'd be chiefly worried about is the absence of any sort of constructive colloquy among the chief participants in the education profession—namely, the curriculum specialists, the instruction specialists, and the assessment specialists. I'd be concerned that the preoccupation of these professionals with their own specialties would, in an easily discernable fashion, erode the quality of education that my children would be likely to receive.

The reason almost all of us decided to go into the field of education is that we wanted children to be better educated. I know that there might have been other motives for some, but I believe the bulk of us who work in this field are dominantly concerned about what's best for children.

BIG-TIME BAD STUFF

Well, just look around at many of today's classrooms and you'll see blatant instances of curricular reductionism, excessive test preparation, and modeled dishonesty. First, *curricular reductionism*

takes place when teachers give little or no classroom attention to topics they believe aren't going to be assessed on a high-stakes test. Children are being curricularly shortchanged today as a consequence of their teachers' attention only to content the teachers think will be tested. Second, *excessive test preparation* arises when teachers, unable to determine what's going to be assessed on a high-stakes test, conclude that the only way they can realistically raise their students' scores is to drill those students relentlessly on testlike exercises. The cost of such excessive test preparation is that it jettisons the joy children ought to be experiencing in school. Finally, *modeled dishonesty* occurs when accountability-pressured teachers use unethical ploys to raise their students' test scores. For example, such teachers supply students, in advance of a high-stakes test, with copies of the actual items from that test—along with the correct answer key for those items. Later, during the administration of the high-stakes test itself, students realize that their teacher has been cheating just to raise test scores. What a terrible message to send students.

All these bad things happen because the wrong sorts of accountability tests have been employed. Those improper tests have often been installed, in my experience, chiefly because curriculum, instruction, and assessment specialists have functioned independently, not collaboratively. Grandiose, albeit unteachable and untestable curricular aims have been fashioned by curriculum specialists in isolation. Instructionally insensitive high-stakes tests have been installed—in isolation—by assessment specialists. Instructional specialists in isolation attempt to help teachers address too many curricular targets and design classroom instructional sequences to improve students' scores on instructionally insensitive tests.

I wouldn't really care all that much about this professional isolationism—if it didn't harm kids. But especially now, given the potential impact of the No Child Left Behind Act's significant accountability provisions, the potential for kid-harm is enormous. Professionals ought to be left to their own pursuits—as long as those pursuits are not damaging to the very individuals that those professionals are supposed to serve. And that's the sort of damage to children we see today. It occurs, in large part, because of our field's acceptance of excessive specialization. Such acceptance needs to be revoked.

What's to Be Done?

To remedy this situation, truly Herculean efforts are going to be required. That's because, to counter a specialist's proclivities to be special, a modification treatment must be provided that is every bit as robust as the one that produced the specialist's proclivities in the first place. Adolescent gangs arise for a reason, and they don't disappear merely because adults want them to go away. The same thing is true for professional specializations. However, given the educational mischief arising from today's excessive specialization in education, we clearly need to try something to remedy the situation. And, just as clearly, desperate measures are surely warranted. I wish to propose, therefore, both a short-term and a long-term solution strategy that might make at least a dent in education's isolationist armor plate.

Short Term: A State Department of Education Focus

Because we need to address the shortcomings of excessive specialization immediately, I believe that something can be done at the state level, the level at which many of the most influential decisions about children's education are being made these days. More specifically, I think that each of our chief state school officers can play a leadership role in significantly reducing the needless specialization so common throughout our nation's state departments of education.

There are, of course, exceptions to the too-specialized scenario that I have been ascribing to most state departments of education. If I had to guess, however, I'd bet there aren't more than a dozen states in which meaningful collaboration takes place among the state's curriculum, instruction, and assessment personnel. In such states, of course, little needs to be done.

However, in a typical state department—that is, one whose curriculum, instruction, and assessment workers function in sublime segregation—that state's chief ought to exert some powerful influence to get things changed. For example, a department policy could be promulgated calling for meaningful interaction among personnel from the department's curricular, instructional, and assessment camps. The chief could give subordinate leaders (e.g., the department's deputy commissioners or assistant superintendents) not only the responsibility to nurture such collaborative efforts on an ongoing basis but also a requirement to stringently monitor the degree to which such collaboration-engendering activities appear to be taking place. We need genuine collaboration among specialists, not pretend collaboration.

To support such interspecialist collaboration, special departmental seminars and colloquies could be set up specifically for key departmental representatives of the three groups. During any activities such as these, the rationale for interdepartmental collaboration could be cited along with a reiteration of the chief's commitment to the collaborative solving of curriculum-related, instruction-related, and assessment-related problems.

Another potentially useful procedure would be to encourage individuals from one specialization to actually learn something about the content of the other two specializations. For instance, each specialty group could be asked, collectively, to identify one book or one journal article that would be particularly informative to their coworkers in the other two specializations. Such readings could then be assigned. After a reasonable amount of time had been given to allow busy people to do their assigned reading, a group discussion of each of the chosen books/articles could take place. Clearly, the thrust of these sorts of activities would be to bolster the kind of genuine collaboration that, in the end, will turn out to benefit children.

Collaborative interspecialization activities, however, ought to deal with serious issues, not be carried out merely for the dubious dividends derivative from interdisciplinary collaboration per se. Thus, topics for potential collaboration should be selected by the chiefs and their subordinates with care. These days, of course, a state's approach to the implementation of the No Child Left Behind Act would surely yield a set of issues ideally addressable by the collaborative efforts of a state department's curriculum, instruction, and assessment personnel.

None of this would happen, of course, unless a state's chief state school officer believes in the value of having state department personnel from curriculum, instruction, and assessment work together. The chief's preferences in this situation will, and surely should, prevail. The chief's preferences, therefore, are pivotal.

If a chief state school officer really wants an increased level of departmental collaboration, one straightforward approach would be to appoint a small committee of staff members representing all three of the specializations under consideration here. Then the chief can simply charge the committee to come up with one or more sensible plans whereby the department's curriculum, instruction, and assessment personnel are obliged to work together more productively. The most promising of these committee-identified plans can then be implemented.

LONG TERM: A SCHOOL OF EDUCATION FOCUS

Over the long haul, however, we need to start much earlier with curriculum, instruction, and assessment personnel to foster the ability, and the inclination, for them to work together. I think we must start in graduate school. At the master's and, especially, the doctoral level, I believe we need to provide graduate programs that are deliberately designed to create cadres of educators who can work reasonably well in any of these three arenas—that is, in curriculum, instruction, and assessment. Most graduate students enrolled

in such collaboratively focused programs, of course, will end up emphasizing one of those three fields more than the other two. But I'm hoping that, in the future, we'll be able to produce a supply of master's and doctoral recipients who are truly comfortable when crossing curricular, instructional, and assessment boundaries.

How would such programs work? Well, because I've spent the majority of my life as a university faculty member, I know what a thoroughly intractable crowd any group of professors can be. However, I also know that professors are smart enough to put together an effective interspecialization program of the type I'm talking about if they want to do so. They'll also be more inclined to install such a program if a dean of education creates a set of reward contingencies so that it is in the personal best interest of a professor to participate in such an interdisciplinary program. Just as a chief state school officer's leadership is pivotal in state department settings, in higher education settings an education dean's support of the kind of collaborative effort I have been proposing is almost a sine qua non for any such program's success. These sorts of collaborative training programs might possibly occur even without deanly support, but they would be rare.

I have in mind a collaboratively staffed program in which there was a clear intention on the part of participating faculty to produce graduate students who could function effectively, and collaboratively, in curriculum, instruction, and assessment. To do so, a set of core courses in all three specializations would need to be identified, collaboratively—one would hope, by relevant faculty members. And collaboratively supervised theses and dissertations ought to deal with at least two of the three areas of specialization (and, preferably, with all three).

Moreover, because the promotion of students' dispositions to collaborate is every bit as important as students' actual mastery of the content in these three areas, there also should be ongoing collaboration-fostering activities—for instance, collaboratively staffed seminars, colloquies, and lectures provided for those students who aim to become more potent players in a tripartite educational-improvement game. Faculty should, insofar as their sometimes thin skins will allow, both endorse and, if possible, model the kind of interspecialization affective dispositions that the program ought to be promoting.

It should be apparent that I am not advocating the sort of sometimes mindless interdisciplinary proposals I have seen in the past, often presented by professors in search of fashionability. Some forms of interdisciplinary graduate education make sense. Many don't. What I am advocating here is a particular type of interdisciplinary graduate program, the need for which has been generated by today's increasing accountability pressures on educators. That interdisciplinary program must be unabashedly committed to the blending of students' studies in curriculum, instruction, and assessment.

One delightful dividend of such a three-pronged preparation program is that its graduates will have no trouble finding employment. Do you realize what a dearth now exists of educational professionals who can swim comfortably in our often choppy curricular, instructional, and assessment seas?

As indicated, however, an influential dean's endorsement is pivotal. I believe astute deans of education will recognize that their graduate programs could be producing students who, because of the acquisition of interspecialization expertise in curriculum, instruction, and assessment, can become big-time players in today's education arena. Such collaboratively prepared professionals can make a genuine difference in schooling. Moreover, I believe that if those deans are truly shrewd, they will see merit in my suggestions regarding how such a collaboration-focused graduate program might function. And be assured that if a key dean moves in the interdisciplinary direction I have suggested, it will follow—as night follows day or tenure follows refereed publication—that some faculty will surely wish to move in a similar direction.

As was true with state departments of education, one straightforward method of getting underway at the university level in the creation of graduate programs for multifield professionals is to rely on the time-honored appoint-a-committee ploy. A dean can ask a small group of seasoned professors (ideally those who have at least a nodding acquaintance with curriculum, instruction, and/or assessment) to come up with one or more proposals for a new interdisciplinary degree program aimed at producing multifield, make-a-difference professional educators. Having reviewed the committee's recommendations, the dean can then relay any meritorious proposals to the full faculty. As noted earlier, a dean's support of any such programs is imperative.

Discussion Questions

How does Popham define the danger of curriculum reductionism? Is he correct?

What relationship among curriculum, instruction, and assessment would be optimal and still hold teachers accountable for student learning?

W. James Popham is a professor emeritus at the University of California–Los Angeles.

Article 36

IT'S THE CURRICULUM, STUPID!

There's Something Wrong With It

DAVE F. BROWN

W hile waiting in Chicago for my connecting flight, I wandered over and picked up a *USA Today* to browse through the day's national events. I seldom get past the first section before I drop the paper and return to reading something more substantial. But this time a figure at the bottom of the "Money" section caught my eye.[1] The heading for the figure was "Are Schools Preparing Students to Meet Employers' Needs?" This survey of 450 business and political leaders, conducted by Duffey Communications, yielded the following results:

1. Seventy percent of those surveyed said, "No, schools are not preparing students to meet employers' needs."

2. Twenty percent said, "Yes, schools are preparing students to meet employers' needs."

3. The remaining 10% reported that schools are "somewhat" preparing students to meet employers' needs.

For the next hour, I began to reflect on many educational trends, issues, theories, and philosophies that could play a role in really answering that question. But I kept returning to two central questions: (a) What outcomes do employers want graduates to have achieved as a result of their years of schooling? and (b) If educators knew the answer to this question, how could they ensure that their students achieved those outcomes?

I realize that supposing educators want answers to these two questions assumes that at least one valued outcome of schooling is to provide an efficient workforce to ensure the continued success of capitalism. If teachers and

SOURCE: Excerpted from Brown, D. F. (2006). It's the curriculum, stupid! There's something wrong with it. *Phi Delta Kappan, 87*(10), 777–783. Reprinted by permission of David F. Brown. Dave F. Brown's latest book is *What every middle school teacher should know* (2nd ed., 2007) co-authored with Trudy Knowles.

parents, for argument's sake, genuinely believe that it is educators' responsibility to prepare students for a life of "meeting employers' needs," then we're going to have to better examine what it is that we choose to teach students. That is, what should be in the curriculum to ensure that students have the knowledge to prepare them for a life of employment?

To some extent, I fear I am treading on hallowed ground. James Beane summarized the challenge of questioning what is traditionally taught with his comment, "Changing the curriculum is like moving a graveyard; no one wants to disturb the dead."[2] Yet my recent research with the middle-level curriculum has led me to a renewed view both philosophical and practical—of how to create appropriate curricula for students, no matter what the desired outcomes.

Choosing Meaningful Outcomes

Educators and parents have what I consider to be a reasonable sense of what students should learn to prepare them for productive and successful lives. For four consecutive summers, I surveyed a sample of middle-level teachers to determine their views on the specific skills that students need prior to entering adult employment.[3] The prioritized list of their responses follows:

1. Critical-thinking skills
2. Problem-solving strategies and effective decision-making skills
3. Creative-thinking processes
4. Effective oral and written communication skills
5. Basic reading, mathematics, and writing abilities
6. Knowledge of when and how to use research to solve problems
7. Effective interpersonal skills
8. Technology skills
9. Knowledge of good health and hygiene habits
10. Acceptance and understanding of diverse cultures and ethnicities
11. Knowledge of how to effectively manage money
12. Willingness, strategies, and ability to continue learning.

Carol Smith noted that parents and teachers in Vermont who were asked to prioritize outcomes for students developed a similar list.[4] Kathy Emery and Susan Ohanian quote the words of "Car Talk" co-host Tom Magliozzi about what students should learn in school:

> Education really ought to help us understand the world we live in. This includes flora, fauna, cultures, governments, religions, money, advertising, buildings, cities, and especially people. Then it should help us cope with the world. And in the process, it would be nice if it helped us to become good, kind, empathetic people.[5]

Magliozzi's thoughts, coupled with the surveys of teachers and parents, provide educators with a range of outcomes that is better focused than the traditional curricula that students are subjected to each school year. Traditional curricular delivery systems suffer from trying to present too many facts in a completely isolated manner. Marion Brady described the problems with such an approach:

> The result is the perpetuation of an intellectually unmanageable, "mile wide and inch deep," artificially compartmentalized curriculum, a curriculum acceptable not because it is theoretically sound, nor because it is intellectually challenging, not because it meets individual societal needs, but because its familiarity blocks recognition of its fundamental inadequacy.[6]

Brady suggests that schools must design learning experiences that integrate all content areas in such a way as to encourage "a thorough understanding of the seamless, systematic nature of knowledge—and the ability to use that understanding to live life more fully and intelligently."[7]

I imagine that business leaders want the same general outcomes as parents and teachers, particularly since some parents *are* business leaders. However, Emery and Ohanian present evidence that the essential skills identified by teachers and parents may not be necessary or even valued because of the types of jobs available in the current economy. They cite data from the U.S. Bureau of Labor Statistics that indicate that between 1992 and 2005, "the largest increases in terms of numbers of jobs [were], in descending order: retail sales workers, registered nurses, cashiers, truck drivers, waiters and waitresses, nursing aides, janitors, food preparation workers, and systems analysts."[8] I insist, though, that anyone who has either worked these jobs or had contact with those who do might agree that such occupations require the same essential skills identified by parents and teachers.

Anyone who browses through the classified ads in a local newspaper would notice a match between the skills and qualities that employers are seeking and those that teachers and parents hope children will gain. One company promised the following to future employees: "This company . . . empowers you to innovate, to explore, and to make decisions as part of a global team. . . ." Another ad noted, "Requirements for this position include . . . leadership ability, team player, meeting tight deadlines, multitasking, technical writing and editing . . . ," and a third required "excellent writing skills, research and data analysis skills."[9] Donald Graves interviewed a businessman who provided this list of required traits: "They [employees] need to have initiative. I guess I'd call it drive. Next I want them to be creative, to come up with a different twist to solving problems. Finally, I need for them to be team players."[10]

These traits sound quite similar to those listed by the teachers I work with each summer. That list, however, certainly leads to more than mere preparation for working. I believe that, as teachers, we must be responsible for preparing young people for the types of critical thinking and decision making that have little to do with one's work and more to do with one's personal and civic lives. I prefer that schools prepare children to be social leaders, not blind followers; free, critical thinkers, not easily brainwashed dolts; creative thinkers, not rote assembly-line workers; and actively engaged members of a political community, not apathetic, apolitical

zombies. Those outcomes may be different from what the business and political leaders desire, though I hope not. As Gerald Bracey put it, "Schools should *not* prepare students for the world of work. . . . Schools should prepare children to live rich, generous lives in the hours they are freed from work."[11] I believe that schools can create empathetic and responsible critical thinkers who are also productive adults— in short, the kinds of people who meet the needs of all of society, not just those of employers.

But when I read those newspaper ads, I always ask myself, "Which part of the curricula in our high schools prepares students to engage in such advanced thinking, research, and teamwork?" I wish this question were on the minds of all those who ultimately decide what all students should learn in school.

And in fact some students don't believe they are ready for work as a result of their schooling. A recent survey of approximately 1,500 high school graduates revealed that 40% do not believe they are adequately prepared for the demands of work or college.[12] Many adolescents' perceptions of the significance of the curricula they are asked to study are also less than positive.

THE PROBLEM WITH CURRENT CURRICULAR DESIGN

It's no surprise to me that a small proportion of students choose to leave high school before graduating. Staying in school through 13 years requires considerable patience, in part because of the way students are so often "inactively engaged" cognitively with the material. Students tend to agree with this negative view of curricular offerings. One middle school student described the absurdity of his social studies curriculum:

> I don't think when we grow up anybody will come up on the street and say, "Excuse me, do you know who Constantine was?" We're learning about Constantine and his son, and his son's son, and his son's cousin. They didn't do anything in history, but we learned about it.[13]

Ceci Lewis, Scott Christian, and Eva Gold conducted extensive interviews with two high school seniors. When asked about curriculum, one of those students, Steve, remarked:

To clear up any confusion, the curriculum . . . for Buena High School in particular consists of classes, needed credits that are considered to make us the best possible student. . . . The curriculum they chose is teaching the students in the way they think could best help the student along into higher learning. . . . in some cases that's *not* so. My life is a perfect example.[14]

The other student interviewee, Amy, added:

Ever since kindergarten, I have become increasingly disappointed with the lessons taught within the classroom. Of course a certain amount of math, English, history, and science is necessary for later in life, but so is a certain amount of interaction with other people. My classroom education has fallen short of giving me the most vital skills needed to survive in the world today. It has failed to teach me how to communicate with others; in short, it has failed to teach me any type of social skills.[15]

Jeffrey Shultz and Alison Cook-Sather, in introducing the volume in which these students' comments appear, note that one of the central themes among the several students that they interviewed "is that students want school to be engaging. For these students, education isn't just about learning math, social studies, or science; it is also about being active partners in their own learning—contributing their ideas, being listened to, making choices, in their studies."[16]

If anyone doubts the meaninglessness of most secondary school curricula to most students, then please visit your local high school or middle school and observe the interactions among students—if you can find any. Better yet, ask high school graduates what they recall about their high school curricula. When I ask the question of my college students, they usually recall only those experiences that were highly interactive—that is, the times when the students were responsible for producing knowledge, conducting research, or engaging in meaningful problem

solving. In the aforementioned survey of almost 1,500 high school students, only 26% of those who went straight to college and 20% who went directly into the workforce say that they felt challenged during their high school careers.[17] Perhaps that finding might lead one to inquire, "What impact did the curricula you studied have on your feelings of being challenged?"

Of course, I know I'm generalizing about the passivity that exists in high school classrooms. Many high school and middle school teachers create a great deal of excitement and motivation through the strategies they use to engage students. But they do so despite a stifling curriculum. Even with the best of teachers, I suspect that most students find little in what they are asked to study that is connected to their lives. I believe that to be the primary problem with curricula: they are too disconnected from adolescents' lives to have meaning for them.

That leaves this significant question to be answered: What can be done to help students connect with the curricula? And the obvious follow-up question: Which curricula will actually encourage students to develop the essential skills and strategies that lead to productive adulthood?

CURRICULAR DECISIONS BELONG TO STUDENTS

Long ago, in what seems like a fantasyland compared to the current standards-driven mania that besets American education, John Dewey outlined the problems with the traditional top-down curriculum:

It imposes adult standards, subject matter, and methods upon those who are only growing slowly toward maturity. The gap is so great that the required subject matter [and] the methods of learning and of behaving are foreign to the existing capacity of the young. But the gulf between the mature or adult products and the experience and abilities of the young is so wide that the very situation forbids much active participation by pupils in the development of what is taught.[18]

Dewey spoke those words in 1938. Welcome to the past. Beane has addressed how to genuinely connect curricula to the needs and interests of our students.[19] He has described a curricular design that is invested in students' lives; it is known as "curriculum integration." Simply stated, it is this: Students and teachers build the curriculum each year based on students' questions.[20]

To begin with, each student is asked two questions: "What questions and concerns do you have about yourself?" and "What questions and concerns do you have about the world?" Students spend the first few weeks of the year working collaboratively to narrow each individual's lists of questions down to a small set of central questions to study during the academic year. By virtue of being organized "around significant problems and issues," the resultant curriculum, Beane notes, "enhance[s] the possibilities for personal and social integration."[21] A definitive difference between curriculum integration and all other so-called integrated curricula is that in curriculum integration no subject-area designations exist. These are not hypothetical themes contrived by teachers; instead, they are a set of genuine student-generated concerns.

When they engage in planning for curriculum integration, separate groups of students will often develop similar sets of themes to investigate. Among the most common are (a) environmental issues, (b) making and managing money, (c) questions about future technologies, (d) creating a peaceful world, (e) prejudice, (f) who has power and how it is managed, (g) crime and violence, and (h) what does the future hold for me?

I believe that the ultimate aim of much of traditional secondary schooling is for students to understand the significance of these same themes. The difference is that with traditional curricula the ideas do not seem to be as connected to students' lives as they are when students study these themes as a result of their own curiosity.

The way in which students dissect these general themes into specific topics of study during the year is determined through weekly small-group meetings. Within these groups, students are involved in deciding which specific questions they want to answer, how they will study a particular topic, how to collect information on the topic, and how they will present their findings to the rest of the class. Students are variously engaged in conducting their own research, finding guest speakers, planning field trips, collecting data, conducting surveys, and making presentations to the entire school or to public audiences.[22]

At many recent conferences of the National Middle School Association, Gert Nesin, Barbara Brodhagen, Carol Smith, and a few other middle-level teachers and researchers have conducted the first stage of curriculum integration with a group of middle-level students who have never been engaged in choosing the curriculum.[23] Each time this occurs, these students' classroom teachers are surprised by their own students' ability to ask such sophisticated questions. It's as if teachers don't believe that adolescents are capable of such independent thought, creativity, or curiosity. Yet, year after year in several schools across the United States, students engage in curriculum integration.[24]

WHAT ARE STUDENTS LEARNING?

For several reasons, curriculum integration is a good fit for a middle school or high school. If we examine the activities required in curriculum integration, it becomes clear that students are engaged in what David Hamburg described as the primary purposes of a middle-level curriculum: acquiring the strategies needed to construct their own knowledge, developing valuable questioning strategies, building on human relationships, and gaining a sense of belonging to a group.[25] Another valuable aspect of curriculum integration is that it meshes well with middle-schoolers' learning propensities. Cynthia Mee, in her interviews with 2,000 young adolescents, noted that they are extremely curious and enjoy asking questions.[26] And of course the very basis of curriculum integration is students' need to ask questions about significant issues that affect their lives.

Beane insists that the primary purpose of engaging students in curriculum integration is to provide them with a genuine democratic education.[27] Entrusting students with opportunities to ask meaningful questions, permitting them to work collaboratively with teachers and fellow students, and using their chosen themes as the foundation for a year of learning are all versions of the democratic actions that form the basis of the political culture of the United States. Curriculum integration involves students in genuine democratic activities that can yield solutions to practical problems they experience in their classrooms. What better method could there be for learning about democracy than living it in a classroom?

Curriculum integration provides daily opportunities for students to use thought processes as they plan, do research, and report on what they learn. Students engaged in curriculum integration think critically and creatively in evaluating sources of information, in choosing how to present research, and in evaluating their peers' and their own presentations. They participate in daily research processes to find information and design appropriate experiments to test their own hypotheses. And they solve problems ranging from determining how to present information to figuring out how to compromise with other team members.

Students who participate in curriculum integration work out their differences of opinion, choose research partners, learn how to negotiate, and practice reaching consensus—all vital social skills required in adult life. Curriculum integration teachers—more accurately called facilitators—don't worry about whether students are motivated by the curriculum. The motivation comes automatically with having chosen the questions. Classroom management problems seldom arise, perhaps primarily because of the high levels of engagement and motivation of students studying something of their own choosing.

DOES CURRICULUM INTEGRATION PREPARE STUDENTS FOR THE FUTURE?

I wanted to know whether students who engaged in curriculum integration thought they were better prepared for adult life than those who experienced a more traditional curriculum. Through extensive interviews that I conducted with 13 "graduates" of three separate years of an eighth-grade curriculum integration experience, I discovered that these students do indeed achieve meaningful outcomes.[28]

I asked students whether a curriculum integration experience was more motivating than a traditional classroom. All 13 agreed that curriculum integration is more motivating because of the opportunity to design the curricula themselves and the significance that involvement gives to the curricula. Seven students noted that the challenge of maintaining group cohesiveness and harmony also made the experience motivating.

I was particularly concerned with the growth in students' thought processes. I wondered whether they believed that curriculum integration had made them better thinkers than traditional curricula would have. All but one agreed that the curriculum integration experience had improved their abilities more than traditional curricula would have in the areas of creative thinking, critical thinking, decision making, and problem solving. They also believed that curriculum integration was better than traditional curricula in helping them improve their research abilities.

Since many adults value the development of students' social skills during their years in school, I asked the 13 students whether they thought that participating in curriculum integration had improved their ability to work with others, and 10 said that their overall social skills had improved as a result of the experience.

I also wondered if the curriculum integration experience had helped students maintain their growth in the traditional content areas of mathematics, writing, and reading. Students received their mathematics instruction in this particular school from traditional courses, since there was concern among the facilitators (i.e., teachers) that students would not be exposed to enough higher level mathematical principles if they chose the curricula themselves. All of the respondents, however, affirmed that the curriculum integration class had improved their writing skills because of the extensive journal and report writing involved. As part of the process, students received weekly feedback about their writing and were encouraged to revise papers until they were accurately written. Students were required to read a total of 25 books during the year. Some of those books were assigned reading while others were self-chosen or connected to research topics. Students were responsible for critiquing each book they had read. Once again, all 13 students agreed that this experience improved their reading skills more than work in a traditional classroom would have.

One distinct advantage of curriculum integration is that its flexibility with regard to time allows students to examine issues in depth. Extended learning time made possible longer engagement with challenging topics, and so genuine understanding became more likely. This in itself was probably an important factor in improving students' thinking.

THE RESULTS EVERYONE WANTS

So much of the focus of education policy recently has been on standardized testing. Many Americans, especially politicians, seem to be highly concerned with whether students' scores on these tests reach the level deemed "proficient." That specific and often unrealistic goal and the fact that standardized tests measure such limited skills and knowledge mean that public school teachers aren't able to effectively prepare students to live meaningful, productive future lives. The Association for Supervision and Curriculum Development recently reported that New York will be the first state to institute a test designed to measure high school seniors' preparedness for work.[29] The test, which will be voluntary, will measure students' knowledge of how to communicate, negotiate, and use decision-making skills. This is an assessment that has the potential to alter in a positive manner the method by which curricula are delivered.

Since the current culture of assessing students focuses only on basic skills, it is imperative to publicize the meaningful growth made by students who design their own curriculum. These students report that they have improved their skills and strategies in thinking critically and creatively, solving problems, working collaboratively with others, communicating well, writing more effectively, reading more analytically, and conducting research to solve problems. No traditional curricula, delivered as separate subjects, can provide students with the deep, diverse, and meaningful learning experiences that their own curriculum choices can lead to.

It's time that the public understood that no school can provide its students with "enough" curricula for life. It is foolish to believe that what one needs to know can be limited in such a way. Parents, educators, businesspeople, and political leaders should all be astute enough to recognize the fallacy of the arbitrarily established perfect spiral curriculum, accompanied by manufactured timelines for achieving each set of curricular content standards. I, like every other honest adult, can see through my own life experiences that basic traditional curricula did not prepare me well for life beyond the four walls of a school.

Educators have been talking about creating "life-long learners" for many years. But traditional curricula that are isolated and separately delivered do not engage learners with the principles needed to handle most of life's challenging circumstances. When students engage in curriculum integration, they can begin the process of becoming lifelong learners just when they are cognitively ready to move toward the advanced thinking that accompanies adulthood—during their middle and high school years. I did not have such an opportunity until I reached adulthood and began studying the world through my own trial-and-error experiences. Why should our children and grandchildren have to wait so long to be prepared for what counts in life? Educators can fix this now. But we must begin by admitting, "It's the curriculum, stupid! There's something wrong with it."

Discussion Questions

What do you believe the mission of the schools should be?

Would you feel comfortable allowing students in your classroom to design their curriculum? How would you accomplish this and how much freedom would you allow?

D. F. Brown is a professor of education at West Chester University, West Chester, PA.

Article 37

TEACHING FOR SOCIAL JUSTICE, DIVERSITY, AND CITIZENSHIP IN A GLOBAL WORLD

JAMES A. BANKS

The increasing ethnic, cultural, language, and religious diversity in nation-states throughout the world has raised new questions and possibilities about educating students for effective citizenship. Since World War II, nation-states throughout the Western world have become more diversified because of immigration and other factors. Ethnic and cultural diversity in the Western European nations such as the United Kingdom, France, Germany, and the Netherlands increased greatly after World War II. Groups from the former colonies of these nations in Asia, Africa, and the West Indies immigrated to Europe to satisfy labor needs and to improve their economic status (Banks & Lynch, 1986).

Although the United States has been diverse since its founding, the ethnic texture of the nation has changed dramatically since the Immigration Reform Act was enacted in 1965. Most of the immigrants to the United States came from nations in Europe between 1901 and 1910. Between 1991 and 1998, however, the majority of immigrants to the United States came from nations in Latin America and Asia. The U.S. Census Bureau (2000) projects that ethnic groups of color will make up 47% of the U.S. population in 2050. Students of color now make up 40% of the students in the nation's public schools.

CHALLENGES TO THE ASSIMILATIONIST NOTION OF CITIZENSHIP

An assimilationist conception of citizenship education existed in most of the Western democratic nation-states prior to the rise of the ethnic revitalization movements of the 1960s and 1970s. A major goal of citizenship education in these

SOURCE: Excerpted from Banks, J. A. (2004). Teaching for social justice, diversity, and citizenship in a global world. *Educational Forum*, 68(4), 296–305. Reprinted by permission of Kappa Delta Pi.

nations was to create nation-states in which all groups shared one dominant mainstream culture. It was assumed that ethnic and immigrant groups had to forsake their original cultures to fully participate in the nation-state (Patterson, 1977).

The ethnic revitalization movements of the 1960s and 1970s strongly challenged the assimilationist conception of citizenship education. These movements, triggered by the civil rights movement in the United States, echoed throughout the world. French and Indians in Canada, West Indians and Asians in Britain, Indonesians and Surinamese in the Netherlands, and Aborigines in Australia joined the series of ethnic movements, expressed their feelings of marginalization, and worked to make the institutions within their nation-states responsive to their economic, political, and cultural needs.

Indigenous peoples and ethnic groups within the various Western nations—such as American Indians in the United States, Aborigines in Australia, Maori in New Zealand, African Caribbeans in the United Kingdom, and Moluccans in the Netherlands—wanted their histories and cultures to be reflected in their national cultures and in school, college, and university curricula (Eldering & Kloprogge, 1989; Gillborn, 1990; Smith, 1999). Multicultural education was developed, in part, to respond to the concerns of ethnic, racial, and cultural groups that felt marginalized within their nation-states (Banks & Banks, 2004).

The right of ethnic and cultural minorities to maintain important aspects of their cultures and languages has been supported by philosophers and educators since the first decades of the 1900s. Julius Drachsler (1920) and Horace M. Kallen (1924)—of immigrant backgrounds themselves—argued that the southern, central, and eastern European immigrants who were entering the United States in large numbers had a right to retain parts of their cultures and languages while enjoying full citizenship rights. Cultural democracy, argued Drachsler, is an essential component of a political democracy.

In the first decades of the 1900s, Rachel Davis DuBois established school ethnic heritage programs for European immigrant groups. Leonard Covello was the principal of a community school that incorporated the culture of Italian American students (C. Banks, 2004). More recently, Will Kymlicka (1995), a Canadian political theorist, maintained that ethnic and immigrant groups should have the right to maintain their ethnic cultures and languages as well as participate fully in the civic cultures of democratic nation-states.

Balancing Unity and Diversity

Cultural, ethnic, racial, language, and religious diversity exists in most nations in the world. One of the challenges to diverse democratic nation-states is to provide opportunities for different groups to maintain aspects of their community cultures while building a nation in which these groups are structurally included and to which they feel allegiance. A delicate balance of diversity and unity should be an essential goal of democratic nation-states and of teaching and learning in democratic societies (Banks et al., 2001). Unity must be an important aim when nation-states are responding to diversity within their populations. They can protect the rights of minorities and enable diverse groups to participate only when they are unified around a set of democratic values such as justice and equality (Gutmann, 2004).

Citizenship education must be transformed in the 21st century because of the deepening racial, ethnic, cultural, language, and religious diversity in nation-states throughout the world. Citizens in a diverse democratic society should be able to maintain attachments to their cultural communities as well as participate effectively in the shared national culture. Unity without diversity results in cultural repression and hegemony. Diversity without unity leads to Balkanization and the fracturing of the nation-state. Diversity and unity should coexist in a delicate balance in democratic, multicultural nation-states.

Literacy, Social Justice, and Citizenship Education

Literacy as defined and codified in the high-stakes tests that are being implemented in most states in the United States is often interpreted as basic skills in reading, writing, and mathematics. I am very concerned about a conception of literacy that defines it only as basic skills and ignores citizenship participation in national and global contexts. Although it is essential that all students acquire basic skills in literacy, basic skills are necessary but not sufficient in our diverse and troubled world. Literate citizens in a diverse democratic society should be reflective, moral, and active citizens in an interconnected global world. They should have the knowledge, skills, and commitment needed to change the world to make it more just and democratic. The world's greatest problems do not result from people being unable to read and write. They result from people in the world—from different cultures, races, religions, and nations—being unable to get along and to work together to solve the world's intractable problems, such as global warming, the HIV/AIDS epidemic, poverty, racism, sexism, and war. Examples are the conflicts between the United States and Iraq, North Korea and its neighbors, and the Israelis and Palestinians.

In addition to mastering basic reading and writing skills, literate citizens in democratic multicultural societies such as the United States, Canada, and the United Kingdom should develop *multicultural literacy* (J. Banks, 2003). Multicultural literacy consists of the skills and abilities to identify the creators of knowledge and their interests (J. Banks, 1996), to uncover the assumptions of knowledge, to view knowledge from diverse ethnic and cultural perspectives, and to use knowledge to guide action that will create a humane and just world. When we teach students how to critique the injustice in the world, we should help them to formulate possibilities for action to change the world to make it more democratic and just. Critique without hope may leave students disillusioned and without agency (Freire, 1997).

The Bellagio Diversity and Citizenship Education Project

Citizenship education needs to be changed in significant ways because of the increasing diversity within nation-states throughout the world and the quests by racial, ethnic, cultural, and religious groups for cultural recognition and rights (J. Banks, 2004; Castles, 2004). The Center for Multicultural Education at the University of Washington has implemented a project to reform citizenship education so that it will advance democracy as well as be responsive to the needs of cultural, racial, ethnic, religious, and immigrant groups within multicultural nation-states. The first part of this project consisted of a conference, "Ethnic Diversity and Citizenship Education in Multicultural Nation-States," held at the Rockefeller Foundation's Study and Conference Center in Bellagio, Italy, June 17–21, 2002 (Bellagio Conference). The conference, which was supported by the Spencer and Rockefeller Foundations, included participants from 12 nations: Brazil, Canada, China, Germany, India, Israel, Japan, Palestine, Russia, South Africa, the United Kingdom, and the United States. The papers from this conference are published in *Diversity and Citizenship Education: Global Perspectives* (J. Banks, 2004).

One of the conclusions of the conference was that world migration and the political and economic aspects of globalization are challenging nation-states and national borders. At the same time, national borders remain tenacious; the number of nations in the world is increasing rather than decreasing. The number of United Nations member-states increased from 80 in 1950 to 191 in 2002 (Castles, 2004). Globalization and nationalism are contradictory but coexisting trends and forces in the world today. Consequently, educators throughout the world should rethink and redesign citizenship education courses and programs. Citizenship education should help students acquire the knowledge, attitudes, and skills needed to function in their nation-states as well as in a diverse world society that is experiencing rapid globalization and quests by ethnic, cultural, language, and religious groups for recognition and inclusion. It should also help them to develop a commitment to act to change the world to make it more just.

Another conclusion of the Bellagio Conference was that citizenship and citizenship education are defined and implemented differently in various nations and in different social, economic, and political contexts. It is also a contested idea in nation-states throughout the world. However, there are shared problems, concepts, and issues, such as the need to prepare students in various nations to function within, as well as across, national borders. An international group should identify these shared issues and problems and formulate guidelines for dealing with them. In response to this Bellagio Conference recommendation, the Center for Multicultural Education at the University of Washington created an international consensus panel that is developing principles and identifying concepts for educating citizens for democracy and diversity in a global age.

Increasing Diversity and Global Citizenship Education

Citizens in this century need the knowledge, attitudes, and skills to function in their cultural communities and beyond their cultural borders. They also should be able and willing to participate in the construction of a national civic culture that is a moral and just community. The national community should embody democratic ideals and values, such as those articulated in the Universal Declaration of Human Rights, the Declaration of Independence, the Constitution, and the Bill of Rights. Students also need to acquire the knowledge and skills required to become effective citizens in the global community.

The community cultures and languages of students from diverse groups were to be eradicated in the assimilationist conception of citizenship education that existed in the United States prior to the civil rights movement of the 1960s and 1970s. One consequence of assimilationist citizenship education was that many students lost their original cultures, languages, and ethnic identities. Some students also became alienated from family and community. Another consequence was that many students became socially and politically alienated within the national civic culture.

Members of identifiable racial groups often became marginalized in both their community cultures and in the national civic culture because they could function effectively in neither. When they acquired the language and culture of the Anglo mainstream, they often were denied structural inclusion and full participation into the civic culture because of their racial characteristics (Alba & Nee, 2003; Gordon, 1964).

The Development of Cultural, National, and Global Identifications

Assimilationist notions of citizenship are ineffective in this century because of the deepening diversity throughout the world and the quests by marginalized groups for cultural recognition and rights. *Multicultural citizenship* is essential for today's global age (Kymlicka, 1995). It recognizes and legitimizes the rights and needs of citizens to maintain commitments both to their cultural communities and to the national civic culture. Only when the national civic culture is transformed in ways that reflect and give voice to the diverse ethnic, racial, language, and religious communities that constitute it will it be viewed as legitimate by all of its citizens. Only then can citizens develop clarified commitments to the nation-state and its ideals.

Citizenship education should help students to develop thoughtful and clarified identifications with their cultural communities and their nation-states. It also should help them to develop clarified global identifications and deep understandings of their roles in the world community. Students need to understand how life in their cultural communities and nations influences other nations and the cogent influence that international events have on their daily lives. Global education's major goals should be to help students understand the interdependence among nations in the world today, to clarify attitudes toward other nations, and to develop reflective identifications with the world community.

Nonreflective and unexamined cultural attachments may prevent the development of a cohesive nation with clearly defined national goals and policies. Although we need to help students develop reflective and clarified cultural identifications, they also must be helped to clarify their identifications with their nation-states. Blind nationalism, however, will prevent students from developing reflective and positive global identifications. Nationalism and national attachments in most nations are strong and tenacious. An important aim of citizenship education should be to help students develop global identifications. They also must develop a deep understanding of the need to take action as citizens of the global community to help solve the world's difficult global problems. Cultural, national, and global experiences and identifications are interactive and interrelated in a dynamic way.

Students should develop a delicate balance of cultural, national, and global identifications. A nation-state that alienates and does not structurally include all cultural groups into the national culture runs the risk of creating alienation and causing groups to focus on specific concerns and issues rather than on the overarching goals and policies of the nation-state. To develop reflective cultural, national, and global identifications, students must acquire the knowledge, attitudes, and skills needed to function within and across diverse racial, ethnic, cultural, language, and religious groups.

The Continuing Importance of Cultural Identifications

I have argued that students should develop a delicate balance of cultural, national, and global identifications and allegiances. I conceptualize global identification similar to the way in which Nussbaum (2002) defined cosmopolitanism: people "whose allegiance is to the worldwide community of human beings" (p. 4). Nussbaum pointed out, however, that "to be a citizen of the world one does not need to give up local identifications, which can be a source of great richness in life" (p. 9).

I believe that cultural, national, and global identifications are interrelated in a developmental way, and that students cannot develop thoughtful and clarified national identifications until they have reflective and clarified cultural identifications, and that they cannot develop a global or cosmopolitan identification until they have acquired a reflective national identification. We cannot expect Mexican American students who do not value their own cultural identity and who have negative attitudes toward Mexican American culture to embrace and fully accept Anglo or African American students.

The Stages of Cultural Identity

Self-acceptance is a prerequisite to the acceptance and valuing of others. Students from racial, cultural, and language minority groups that have historically experienced institutionalized discrimination, racism, or other forms of marginalization often have a difficult time accepting and valuing their own ethnic and cultural heritages. Teachers should be aware of and sensitive to the stages of cultural development that all of their students—including mainstream students, students of color, and other marginalized groups of students—may be experiencing and facilitate their identity development.

Using my *Stages of Cultural Development Typology*, teachers can help students attain higher stages of cultural development and develop clarified cultural, national, and global identifications (J. Banks, 2001). I believe that students need to reach Stage 3 of this typology, "Cultural Identity Clarification," before we can expect them to embrace other cultural groups or attain thoughtful and clarified national or global identifications. The typology is an ideal-type concept. Consequently, it does not describe the actual identity development of any particular individual. Rather, it is a framework for thinking about and facilitating the identity development of students who approximate one of the stages.

During Stage 1, "Cultural Psychology Captivity," individuals internalize the negative stereotypes and beliefs about their cultural groups that are institutionalized within the larger society and may exemplify cultural self-rejection and low self-esteem. Cultural encapsulation and cultural exclusiveness, and the belief that their ethnic group is superior to others, characterize Stage 2, "Cultural Encapsulation." Individuals within this stage often have newly discovered their cultural consciousness and try to limit participation to their cultural group. They have ambivalent feelings about their cultural group and try to confirm, for themselves, that they are proud of it. In Stage 3, "Cultural Identity Clarification," individuals are able to clarify their personal attitudes and cultural identity and to develop clarified positive attitudes toward their cultural group. In this stage, cultural pride is genuine rather than contrived. Individuals within Stage 4, "Biculturalism," have a healthy sense of cultural identity and the psychological characteristics to participate successfully in their own cultural community as well as in another cultural community. They also have a strong desire to function effectively in two cultures.

Individuals in Stage 5, "Multiculturalism and Reflective Nationalism," have clarified, reflective, and positive personal, cultural, and national identifications and positive attitudes toward other racial, cultural, and ethnic groups. At Stage 6, "Globalism and Global Competency," individuals have reflective and clarified national and global identifications. They have the knowledge, skills, and attitudes needed to function effectively within their own cultural communities, within other cultures within their nation-state, in the civic culture of their nation, and in the global community. Individuals within Stage 6 exemplify cosmopolitanism and have a commitment to all human beings in the world community (Nussbaum, 2002). Gutmann (2004) argued that the primary commitment of these individuals is to justice, not to any human community.

Strong, positive, and clarified cultural identifications and attachments are a prerequisite to cosmopolitan beliefs, attitudes, and behaviors. It is not realistic to expect Puerto Rican students in New York City to have a strong allegiance to U.S. national values or deep feelings for dying people in Afghanistan if they feel marginalized and rejected within their community, their school, and in their nation-state. We must nurture, support, and affirm the identities of students from marginalized cultural, ethnic, and language groups if we expect them to endorse national values, become cosmopolitans, and work to make their local communities, the nation, and the world more just and humane.

Discussion Questions

Banks calls for balancing unity with diversity. How do you think the curriculum can accomplish this task?

What does Banks mean by the term "cosmopolitanism"? Do you agree with this as a curricular goal?

James A. Banks is a professor at the University of Washington, Seattle.

Article 38

BEYOND ZERO TOLERANCE

Restoring Justice in Secondary Schools

JEANNE B. STINCHCOMB

GORDON BAZEMORE

NANCY RIESTENBERG

As with contemporary responses to crime and violence in society overall, school-based reactions have primarily reflected perspectives that are grounded in a variety of general and specific deterrence-based strategies that have popularly become known as "zero tolerance." Although defined by some in purely retributionist terms (e.g., as "predetermined consequences" for certain offenses; Flaherty, 2001, p. 42), zero tolerance is perhaps more comprehensively viewed as a composite of perspectives related to deterrence, incapacitation, and retribution.

As secondary schools became the new front in the war on crime, some educational policymakers embraced the zero-tolerance concept with an enthusiasm similar to their counterparts in the criminal justice policymaking process.

Perhaps most important, the offenses for which various educational institutions declared their intolerance began to extend across a widely divergent spectrum of seriousness, ranging from transporting deadly weapons to school to talking back to teachers. Holding individuals accountable for their behavior through a punitive exclusionary response became the popular reaction to wrongdoing—regardless of age, background, situational factors, or other mitigating circumstances. But as the appropriateness of such reactions has recently come into question (Skiba & Peterson,

SOURCE: Excerpted from Stinchcomb, J., Bazemore, G., & Riestenberg, N. (2006). Beyond zero tolerance: Restoring justice in secondary schools. *Youth Violence and Juvenile Justice*, *4*(4), 123–147. Reprinted by permission of Sage.

1999), a search has emerged for alternative approaches.

In that regard, restorative justice has been identified by some policymakers, practitioners, and academicians as a potential theoretical framework within which to develop somewhat more balanced responses to occurrences of school-related misbehavior (Anderson, Gendler, & Riestenberg, 1998; Braithwaite, 2002; Karp & Breslin, 2001; Morrison, 2001; Riestenberg, 1999). In contrast to the punishment emphasis of zero tolerance, restorative approaches focus on repairing the harm that was caused, engaging victims and relevant community members in the decision-making process, holding offenders accountable, and preventing similar actions in the future (Bazemore, 1999; Van Ness & Strong, 2001).

In a restorative process, participants respond to offenses, conflict, and/or rule violations by bringing together the person who was harmed, the person who did the harm, and the community (bystanders, classmates, staff, family, and/or members of the wider community). Such strategies have been used in a number of criminal and juvenile justice contexts (Bazemore, 1999; Pranis, 1998) and in a variety of community settings (Karp & Breslin, 2001; Morrison, 2001; Riestenberg, 1999).

In primary and secondary schools, restorative justice has been used as a response to crime, bullying, and disciplinary violations, often providing an alternative to the use of more traditional processes (Ahmed, Harris, Braithwaite, & Braithwaite, 2001; Braithwaite, 2002; Karp & Breslin, 2001). In that context, restorative justice strategies convert the response to misbehavior from one of zero tolerance to interventions that accentuate accountability, fairness, and situational responses to unique events. Specifically, in contrast to the zero-tolerance emphasis on uniformity, isolation, and, often, expulsion or suspension, restorative approaches to discipline and school safety have been described as a "no tolerance" response (Riestenberg, 2003). As such, restorative justice is adamant about affirming the wrong that was done, acknowledging the harm that

resulted, and promoting acceptance of responsibility for the wrongdoing. Moreover, restorative justice is ultimately concerned with changing the behavior and conditions that caused it, incorporating consideration of both the circumstances of individual cases and a multiplicity of response options that focus on the spirit and intent, rather than the letter, of the law. Recognizing the seriousness of the offense, schools applying the no tolerance policies of restorative justice attempt to avoid being overly prescriptive in favor of a wider variety of approaches and consequences designed to hold students accountable for their behavior while also taking into account mitigating circumstances. The response is therefore more situational than absolute and, as Moore (1994) points out, potentially more authoritative than authoritarian.

Although there have been a number of efforts both internationally and within the United States to implement restorative approaches to school-related disciplinary issues, the state of Minnesota, through its Department of Children, Families, and Learning (DCFL), has perhaps progressed further in that direction than most jurisdictions. Beginning in 1995, DCFL began using restorative justice concepts and practices in schools to deal with incidents of serious and nonviolent misbehavior. In 1998, the Minnesota state legislature appropriated $300,000 for school districts to develop alternative disciplinary strategies in an effort to reduce suspensions and expulsions, increase attendance, and improve school climate (Riestenberg, 2003). Working in partnership with local juvenile justice agencies, the state Department of Corrections, and community volunteers, educational professionals involved in this initiative began using group conferencing and related processes in response to a variety of disciplinary problems in school districts.

The purpose of this article is to explore the potential for employing policies that are more consistent with a restorative justice approach in response to behavior that, without such options, would otherwise generate zero tolerance. In doing so, we draw on the Minnesota experience with restorative practices as a case study in alternative approaches to discipline and violence prevention in schools, with broader implications for more holistic educational reform (e.g., Gottfredson, 1990; Pearl & Knight, 1998). Although findings are preliminary and illustrative rather than inferential or summative, they are suggestive of promising future alternatives for addressing disciplinary infractions, student violence, and overall school climate without overreliance on suspension and expulsion.

Schools, Disruptive Behavior, and Disciplinary Alternatives

Policy Dimensions of Zero Tolerance

The origins of zero tolerance can he traced back to the 1990 Gun Free School Zone Act that prohibited possession of a firearm within 1,000 feet of a school, violation of which became a federal felony. Although that legislation was subsequently struck down in 1995 by the U.S. Supreme Court for exceeding congressional authority (*U.S. vs. Lopez*, 1995), it was quickly replaced by the Gun Free Schools Act (GFSA), which became effective in October 1995. This time Congress evaded direct involvement by passing demands for zero-tolerance legislative mandates on to the states in a more subtle carrot-and-stick approach.

With compliance tied directly to federal funding for secondary education, the GFSA requires all states to do the following:

- Pass legislation mandating a minimum 1-year expulsion of students bringing weapons to school (including firearms or bombs, but not knives—although that does not prevent a state or school district from encompassing knives or other less lethal weapons)

- Adopt a zero-tolerance policy requiring that anyone bringing a specified weapon to school be referred to either criminal or juvenile justice authorities (regardless of the nature of the

circumstances involved; Preventing Juvenile Gun Violence in Schools, 1996)

Under this legislation, every state receiving federal financial assistance under the Elementary and Secondary Education Act must therefore pass a law requiring expulsion (for not less than 1 year) of any student bringing a firearm to school.

Although a direct causal link with the federal GFSA legislation has yet to be empirically demonstrated, there is little doubt that zero-tolerance policies have expanded almost exponentially during the ensuing years. In a study designed to determine just what measures are being taken across the country to reduce school-related violence, findings indicate that the most frequent response—cited by 96% of the administrators surveyed—was automatic suspension for weapons violations (i.e., zero tolerance; Sheley, 2000, p. 48).

Nor are such disciplinary crackdowns limited to weapons-related offenses. As a result of policy-maker determination to demonstrate firm action in response to illicit or disruptive behavior, a widening variety of offenses has become subject to such mandates. For example, defining *zero tolerance* as "a school or district policy that mandates predetermined consequences or punishments for specific offenses," the National Center for Educational Statistics and the Bureau of Justice Statistics report that 94% of schools throughout the nation have such policies in place for firearms, along with 91% for weapons other than firearms, 87% for alcohol, 88% for drugs, 79% for tobacco, and 79% for violent behavior (Kaufman et al., 1999, p. 117). Moreover, these statistics represent only actions that have been subjected to mandatory, predetermined consequences by a sizable majority of schools nationwide. There are other locations where such policies regulate considerably less dangerous actions (Skiba & Peterson, 1999). In addition, schools maintain widely varying definitions of what constitutes violent behavior, as illustrated by a school district in Mississippi where authorities are required to report any "assaultive" behavior to the police, including something as innocuous as a "tussle on the playground" in which no injuries were sustained (Henault, 2001, p. 550).

In various school districts throughout the country, it would be possible to find zero-tolerance policies governing any number of disciplinary violations—ranging from cursing to carrying weapons. The message is clear and simple. The response is swift and steadfast. But the question is whether the results are satisfactory.

The Impact of Zero Tolerance on School Crime and Climate

Certainly, zero-tolerance policies have not abolished violence or weapons from U.S. public schools. But neither is the level of violence escalating, as the sporadic overdose of high-profile headlines following traumatic school-related incidents might lead us to believe. To the contrary, measures of violent victimizations of secondary school students have remained at consistently low levels during the past half dozen years (Kaufman et al., 1999, p. 3). Between 1993 and 2001, the percentage of students who reported carrying a weapon on school property during the previous 30 days declined from 12% to 6% (DeVoe et al., 2003, p. ix), and a 1997 study further indicated that only 2% of school administrators considered guns to be a "serious problem" on school grounds (Sheley & Wright, 1998, p. 2). In 1998, 29% of public school students reported that the level of violence in their school decreased in the past year, compared to only 8% who reported a decrease in 1993 (Binns & Markow, 1999, p. 7). Although no systematic attempt has been made to connect such data to the implementation of zero-tolerance policies, some would maintain that the correlation is intuitively apparent, especially in light of the widespread prevalence of zero tolerance toward firearms on school grounds.

Yet others dispute that notion, arguing against zero-tolerance policies as a result of either lack causal evidence of their effectiveness (Skiba & Peterson, 1999) or concern that such an approach ignores the underlying problem (Brendtro & Long, 1995). For example, in terms of effectiveness, a study by the National Center for Education Statistics found that after 4 years of zero tolerance, schools with such policies were still less safe than were those without them (Skiba & Peterson, 1999). As one high school principal observed, "We fixate on the weapon, when the problem is deeper" (Stinchcomb & Dobrin, 2000, p. 20). In addition, others are concerned with the fundamental lack of fairness that can result when a one-size-fits-all approach to punishment is employed with a no excuses consistency. For instance, Curwin and Mendler (1999) offer the following case to illustrate the painful reality of this drawback:

> A young high school student was expelled after bringing a gun to school. . . . That morning, his father, in a drunken rage, had put a gun down the youngster's throat and, before passing out, threatened to kill him and his younger brother. The student brought the gun to school to save their lives. Before he could give it to his principal, the gun was discovered. No amount of explaining helped because of zero tolerance. (p. 120)

As a result of arbitrary reactions to such behaviors, a new rallying cry has emerged for alternative approaches that contain greater potential for redirecting youthful misconduct rather than simply punishing its manifestations (without, in many cases, benefit of due process). In fact, the American Bar Association, in February 2001, voted to recommend ending zero-tolerance policies for school discipline (Henault, 2001). As one researcher on the topic has noted, "It is hard to think of any policy better calculated to increase crime than automatic expulsion from school" (Braithwaite & Drahos, 2002, p. 269), especially for minor offenses, with all of the stigma that involves.

Zero Tolerance as a Double-Edged Sword—Social and Fiscal Costs

Even if zero tolerance has played a role in curtailing the escalation of school violence (although no convincing empirical evidence to support such a conclusion has been presented to date), it may be functioning as a double-edged sword if the benefits achieved have incurred countervailing hidden costs. In that regard, recent commentary and research is beginning to suggest that the increasingly well-documented side effects of this remedy may be worse than the cure. For example, Costenbader and Markson (1998) summarized the empirically documented side effects of both in-school and out-of-school suspension as follows:

- An increase in maladaptive behaviors not addressed by the suspension

- Withdrawal or avoidance of school staff

- Negative impact on self-respect

- Stigma among peers

- Driving a school problem into the streets and community

- Disruption of educational progress

- Loss of state aid based on average daily attendance

In-school suspension has likewise been correlated with drug use, poor academic achievement, grade retention, and long-term disaffection and alienation, with research showing that "students who had been suspended were more likely to be involved with the legal system."

Alternative responses such as restorative justice are often resisted at least in part because of concerns that they may be more costly and time consuming than present practices. But despite greater investment of time in developing alternatives, some administrators are beginning to weigh these costs against the disadvantages of current disciplinary approaches, all of which entail their own fiscal downside.

Nevertheless, zero-tolerance policies have demonstrated a resiliency that seems to be almost self-justifying. Because they control the problem temporarily, such approaches are not dependent for their "success" on conventional outcomes such as avoiding recidivism or, in the case of educational policies, successful completion of schooling. Rather, like aggressive policing strategies whose proponents claim success

on the basis of "sweeping the streets of criminals" and managing (Harcourt, 2001), zero-tolerance policies may be viewed by some as successful simply because they provide a quick fix to problems that ultimately require more complex and long-term solutions.

On both a conceptual and an operational level, the nature of zero-tolerance policies in public schools appears to be generally equivalent to the determinate sentencing practices that have produced so many costly implications for the criminal justice system. Both represent a reaction to society's frustration with crime. Both emphasize holding offenders accountable for their behavior. Both impose mandated punishments based on policy guidelines governing the offense, with minimal (if any) consideration given to either the offender's characteristics or the circumstances involved. Both in effect exclude convicted violators from interaction with their law-abiding peers. In both cases, the social institution that has been victimized is seeking to rid itself of the victimizers.

Aside from being politically popular, zero tolerance is pragmatic, expedient, and fiscally advantageous, at least in the short term.

But long-term benefits of expulsion and suspension are considerably more difficult to identify. When students are expelled—regardless of the reason—they are essentially committed to a lifetime of struggle against the material and intellectual poverty that inevitably shadows those lacking a high school education (Lawrence, 1998). Although evidence linking zero-tolerance policies with high school dropout rates is not unequivocal, recent findings are pointing in the direction of an empirical connection. Especially for those who were already borderline students or who were contemplating leaving school voluntarily, a 1-year expulsion can become the catalyst for permanent withdrawal. In that regard, the U.S. Department of Education (1996) notes that "school districts across the country report experiencing significant increases in both the number of students expelled and the length of time they are excluded from their schools" (p. 65). Moreover, the report goes on to express concern that if educational counseling or behavior modification services are not provided to such students, they "generally return to school no better disciplined and no better able to manage their anger or peaceably resolve disputes" (p. 65). The question then becomes whether there are other alternatives that might achieve this objective and deal with disruptive behavior in school more effectively.

RESTORATIVE PRINCIPLES AND PRACTICES IN THE SCHOOLS

Restorative justice is best understood as a principle-based method of responding to crime or harmful behavior. It includes processes that seek to achieve justice by repairing the harm that crime causes (Bazemore & Walgrave, 1999; see Van Ness & Strong, 1997, 2001). As such, it is not a singular program or process but rather a fundamental concept that is based on core principles that provide a measure of how truly restorative a given response is.

Repairing the harm: Working toward healing victims, offenders, and communities that have been injured by crime.

Stakeholder involvement: Providing victims, offenders, and communities with the opportunity for active involvement in the justice process as early and as fully as possible.

Transforming the continuity–government relationship: Rethinking the relative roles and responsibilities of government and the community (Van Ness & Strong 1997, pp. 8–9)

These principles are interrelated and mutually reinforcing, but they also suggest somewhat independent goals and priorities. The first principle (repairing harm) establishes a set of outcomes for restorative practice, including making amends, rebuilding or strengthening relationships, and, in some situations, addressing past harms. To achieve this repair, it is important to

engage those affected by the crime in decision making about what needs to be done. The second principle (stakeholder involvement) therefore seeks to maximize participation of victim, offender, their supporters, and other community members in dialogue about the impact of the crime. This principle ultimately seeks to promote ownership of conflict and harm by those most affected by it (Christie, 1977). The third principle (transforming the community–government role and relationship) suggests a less directive role for the traditional justice system in favor of empowering community members and building community capacity to respond more effectively to harm and conflict.

On the basis of these principles, restorative justice tends to advocate informal resolutions that mobilize community control and support (Bazemore, 1999; Braithwaite, 2002; Christie, 1977). Such resolutions result from deliberations that occur in nonadversarial decision-making practices generically described as "restorative conferencing" approaches (Bazemore & Umbreit, 2001; Braithwaite, 2002) that seek to maximize the involvement and input of victims, offenders, and community members in a leadership role.

For better or worse, schools also share many characteristics of other communities where members live (at least in part) without choice. Like their institutional counterparts, schools are capable of operating in a fashion similar to the most secure prison, where residents may be protected from each other but have little opportunity for personal decision making or control of their own lives. Just as safe prisons often fail to prepare offenders for productive life in free society, even apparently safe schools may fail to teach students to live productively in peaceful interaction with others.

From this perspective, schools might also be viewed as mediating institutions. Like churches, small businesses, and community organizations, they play a vital role in socializing youth, establishing normative standards, and shaping character (Bellah, Madsen, Sullivan, Swidler, & Tipton, 1991, p. 40). Thus, schools can likewise operate as restorative environments where members take responsibility to repair harm when it occurs, hold each other accountable, and build skills in collective problem solving. In such an environment, collective values of prosocial behavior are learned primarily through modeling, conflict resolution, and mutual support.

Restorative Justice Practice and Research

Restorative practice is inclusive of a wide range of interventions that operationalize its three core principles (Van Ness & Strong, 1997). However, two general categories of practice are indispensable and mutually reinforcing in terms of achieving reparation of harm by empowering stakeholders and engaging them in a collaborative relationship with formal social control agents:

Restorative decision making or conferencing models: Designed to enable victims, offenders, their supporters, and affected community members to have input into a plan to repair harm, these processes can assume many variations within four general structural models: (a) family group conferences, (b) victim–offender mediation or dialogue, (c) neighborhood accountability boards, and (d) peacemaking circles (Bazemore & Umbreit, 2001), all of which share a focus on decision making that seeks to maximize stakeholder involvement.

Restorative sanctions or obligations: These include alternatives ranging from restitution to community service, apologies, victim service, behavioral agreements, and other efforts to make amends for harm caused by one's offense. Restorative obligations represent the concrete, behavioral aspect of righting the wrong that provides evidence to the community and victim that the offender has earned redemption (Bazemore, 1998; Maloney, Bazemore, & Hudson, 2001).

Research on restorative justice practices in criminal and juvenile justice settings has expanded in recent years, and findings are promising with regard to the impact on offenders and the participation of victims. (For summaries, see Bazemore, Nissen, & Dooley, 2000; Bazemore & Schiff, 2004; Bonta, Wallace-Capretta, Rooney, & Dooley, 2000; Braithwaite, 2002; Butts & Snyder, 1991; Nugent, Williams, & Umbreit, 2003; Schneider, 1986; Umbreit, Coates, & Vos, 2001.) We know very little, however, about how restorative justice is related to reoffending (Hayes, 2005), and empirical work on the impact of restorative practices in the school context is sparse.

Restorative Justice Experience in the Schools

The first documented use of restorative practices in schools began in the early 1990s with initiatives in Australia (Moore, 1994; Morrison, 2001). For various reasons relating to government leadership change, lack of resources, internal resistance, and funding cutbacks, most of these early implementation efforts were discontinued. Several new Australian projects have begun since 2000, with interest and commitment now more widespread, and other international applications have been reported in countries ranging from Canada and the United Kingdom to Japan, Brazil, and Indonesia.

In the United States, training and program implementation began in the late 1990s in several school districts in Minnesota, Colorado, Arizona, and New York and in private residential schools in states such as Pennsylvania (Karp & Breslin, 2001). Experimentation is also underway in several urban school districts, including Chicago, Denver, and Miami (Granaiery, 2002; Zamora, 2002), and a statewide effort was initiated to train school resource officers in restorative practices throughout New York (N. Tyler, director of New York Community Justice Initiative, personal communication, March 11, 1999). To date, however, little evaluation of these efforts has been attempted.

Undoubtedly, developing alternatives such as restorative justice demands an investment of time and effort, along with the disorientation associated with policy change that may be threatening and therefore provoke staff resistance (Morrison, 2001). Nevertheless, some administrators are beginning to weigh these costs against dissatisfaction with current disciplinary practices.

For example, as the principal of a high school in Arizona described it, getting staff trained and accustomed to participating in restorative group conferences (which, in the early months of implementation, are often held several times daily) took considerable time and personal investment. But with the initiation of conferencing as the first option for all disciplinary infractions, police calls to the school dropped from more than 300 in the previous year to 2 calls in the year following implementation (Bazemore & Schiff, 2004).

In addition to the success of conferencing as a tool for resolving disciplinary problems without resorting to suspension and expulsion, this Arizona school also experienced an impact on culture and climate that led to dramatic reductions in a wide range of behavioral problems. In the principal's view, this was a result of both an expansion of conflict resolution skills and a systemic commitment to minimize involvement of higher levels of authority.

CASE STUDY: MINNESOTA'S SCHOOL-BASED BEHAVIORAL INTERVENTIONS PILOT PROJECT

The most strategic commitment to school-based restorative justice in the United States has been through Minnesota's DCFL. By supporting small, relatively intensive pilot efforts with a very basic evaluation component attached to each program, the DCFL initiative provided important exploratory data pertinent to assessment of the immediate impact of restorative disciplinary responses. The following case study analysis describes these initiatives and their preliminary outcomes.

Background

Like many others throughout the country, Minnesota schools (K–12) have experienced high rates of suspensions, expulsions, dropping out, truancy, and behavioral infractions. In the

early 1990s, the Minnesota statewide expulsion rate increased from around 100 to more than 300 as an apparent result of the implementation of zero-tolerance policies by school districts. Consistent with what appear to be general trends, between the 1983–1984 and the 1998–1999 school years, incidents involving knives in Minnesota schools increased 83%, to the point that by 1998–1999, the primary reason for expulsion was carrying a knife (31.5%), followed by possessing a controlled substance (18.5%) and engaging in violence 17.2% (Riestenberg, 2003).

In an effort to decrease violence in schools and provide an alternative to expulsion and suspension for what were mostly nonviolent cases, the Minnesota DCFL in 1995 began promoting the use of restorative measures through publications such as *Restorative Measures: Respecting Everyone's Ability to Resolve Problems* (Anderson, 1997). Coupled with training programs, workshops, and funding opportunities (Riestenberg, 1999), these efforts appeared to signal a gradual shift in the school system's response to misconduct from punishment to problem solving.

Philosophical Vision, Theory, and Practice

Although restorative practices disapprove of the wrong done, they support the intrinsic worth of the individual engaged in the wrongful behavior. In that regard, DCLF developed a broad vision for the application of restorative practices in the state's schools:

A restorative philosophy emphasizes problem solving approaches to discipline, attends to the social or emotional and the physical or intellectual needs of students, recognizes the importance of the group to establish and practice agreed-upon norms and rules and emphasizes prevention and early restorative intervention to create safe learning environments. (Riestenberg, 2003, p. 10)

Schools interested in participating were exposed to a variety of restorative justice practices and were encouraged to be innovative in merging restorative principles into the curriculum and other aspects of the school experience.

Most of the participating schools eventually chose to focus on peacemaking circles as their primary restorative dialogue process. Derived from ancient practices, peacemaking circles bring together victims, offenders, their families and other supporters, and community stakeholders to determine the impact of the offense and what should be done about it (Bazemore & Umbreit, 2001). Anyone who feels that he or she was affected by the event is invited to participate (Stuart, 2001). By the end of the session, participants attempt to reach consensus about a rehabilitative and accountability plan for the offender and an approach to healing the victim and the community (Schiff & Bazemore, 2002).

In schools, circles have been applied in several ways—as a means of addressing a conflict situation, an alternative method for developing a disciplinary sanction, a forum for talking about the harm caused by an incident, or simply as a means of building interpersonal relationships. In addition to the focus on circles, program administrators also sought to encourage a broader effort to adapt traditional disciplinary practices to the overall restorative philosophy, including such approaches to classroom management as daily class meetings held as "community circles," peer mediation and conflict management, comprehensive antibullying efforts, and a greater emphasis on affective (social or emotional) curriculum development.

The Case Study—South St. Paul

Each of the participating school districts implemented a range of restorative practices and collected pre–post data measuring impact in five areas—suspensions, expulsions, attendance, academics, and school climate. Qualitative information based on observations, interviews, and focus groups was used to document implementation problems. Using these data sources, this article describes a formative case study focused on the South St. Paul district, selected largely as a result of its long-term experience, its comprehensive approach to implementing school-based restorative practices, and data gathering methodologies that enabled pre–post comparisons across several years. Although an experimental research design would obviously have been preferential, grant funding did not include resources for implementing control or comparison groups.

South St. Paul had actually begun its own restorative justice initiative in 1996 through a collaborative effort involving community members, government officials, school administrators, and other stakeholders, which formed the basis of what was then called the South Saint Paul Restorative Justice Council. In addition, South St. Paul was the most well funded and best supported of the pilot initiatives, with restorative justice planners located in each of its three schools—Kaposia Elementary, Lincoln Center Elementary, and South St. Paul Junior High (seventh and eighth grades). Throughout the 3 years of the pilot project (1998–2001), the planners conducted circles to repair harm, develop understanding in classrooms, and promote Make the Peace, a statewide campaign to promote alternatives to violence.

Teachers were also provided with technical assistance and a series of training programs during the 3 years of the pilot project. First, all school staff received basic training on restorative justice principles and practices. Staff in each school were then invited to attend more specific, intensive training on restorative practices and related school discipline issues. Because these schools were especially interested in the peacemaking circle model, most staff (60%–70%, along with a number of students) received one or more follow-up training sessions on circles. Training also included positive behavior support practices aimed at rewarding students who make an effort to resolve conflict as part of the statewide campaign, You're the One Who Can Make the Peace. In addition to resolving individual conflicts, this effort was targeted toward changing overall school culture.

Types of cases referred to restorative sessions in South St. Paul varied by school but included a variety of offenses and rule violations ranging from minor incidents of petty harassment to relatively severe offenses, including vandalism, serious sexual and racial harassment, assault, theft, and arson. Classroom incidents and physical violence (e.g., fighting) were generally the two largest categories of offenses handled.

For example, one case handled in the first quarter of 2000 involved an event in which a student showed a knife to a boy with whom he was in conflict and later brought it onto school grounds as a threatening gesture. Rather than referring the case to the county attorney for prosecution or suspending or expelling the student, a peacemaking circle, including the two youths involved, teachers, family members, and a police officer, was held. Following their circle experience, the two boys involved not only resolved their differences but were reported to be "nearly best friends" following a year-long conflict.

In another case, a student had stolen from two friends on separate occasions. An agreement was reached to address the harm, and the youths agreed that the boy who had stolen would shovel snow for a community member to earn the money to repay the victims. In addition to paying for the labor, the community member later voluntarily offered to buy the boy gloves and a heavier coat so he would be warm while shoveling. Overall, it is estimated that about half of the staff in participating schools used circles on a daily basis for a variety of purposes, ranging from checking in with students during homeroom to responding to rule violations or interpersonal conflicts.

That does not, however, mean that there were not also some less than successful outcomes, especially where implementation difficulties were encountered. As has also been the case with Australia's experience with introducing restorative justice in the schools, the process does not necessarily produce the most desirable results every time. Indeed, descriptions of individual cases that appear to have gone off track are becoming more common in the general restorative justice literature (Bazemore & Schiff, 2004; Braithwaite, 2002; Roche, 2003).

Outcome Measures

Although the qualitative anecdotes in this case study for the most part begin to point toward at least isolated evidence of promising results, it is the schoolwide quantitative data that are most encouraging.

At Lincoln Center Elementary, reported behavioral referrals for physical aggression were reduced from seven per day to fewer than two. Moreover, acts of physical aggression declined steadily, from 773 in 1997–1998 to 153 by 2000–2001. In-school suspensions dropped from 126 in 1999–2000 (the first year for which these data were available) to 42 in 2000–2001. Out-of-school suspensions likewise dropped from 30 in 1998–1999 to 11 in 2000–2001. At the elementary school level, expulsions were negligible or nonexistent in all years, but behavioral referrals dropped substantially, from 1,143 in 1998–1999 to 407 in 2000–2001 (despite the lack of change in either the student population or the mandatory reporting policy). Though perhaps less clearly linked to use of restorative processes, administrators were also pleased to note that average daily attendance likewise improved from 85.0% during 1997–1998 to 95.5% in 2000–2001.

In South St. Paul's other elementary school (Kaposia), however, in-school suspensions actually increased, although out-of-school suspensions decreased. The out-of-school suspension decrease was related to a policy change designed to keep students in an academic setting and working rather than giving them a "free day," and this policy was reinforced by the availability of circles as an alternative to out-of-school suspension. The increase of in-school suspensions in Kaposia was largely attributable to the fact that policy required removal from the classroom of those engaged in so-called bottom line behavior (i.e., menacing language, temper tantrums, possession of a weapon, and physical fighting), even for the lowest level and/or first infraction. In addition, teachers at this school did not develop sufficient trust for either the restorative justice staff or the process itself, and the principal suspended students without consideration of other options.

By contrast, the substantial drop in the Lincoln school seemed attributable to the fact that teachers there had the benefit of 6 months of prior experience, along with a separate room with a restorative justice planner who worked out alternative disciplinary plans that could be considered in the restorative conference. Despite the fact that these planners were themselves laid off because of budget cuts during this period, the culture of the school, and the level of commitment to restorative practice, was apparently strong enough to maintain focus.[1]

Finally, in the junior high, out-of-school suspensions decreased considerably—from 110 in 1998–1999 to 55 in 2000–2001 for both the seventh and eighth grades. This is especially notable in light of the fact that in-school suspension was not an option at South St. Paul Junior High. Thus, without maximizing the use of other available alternatives, there would, by default, presumably be more pressure to resort to out-of-school suspension. Although participants noted that use of circles to repair harm in the junior high school was not as regular as in the elementary locations (with teachers and administrators not always making restorative justice referrals), this reduction was believed to be because of the fact that having the option of a restorative circle helped to decrease the number of students sent out of school. In fact, it was not unusual for the students themselves to request a circle (or even establish one on their own initiative).

One related qualitative observation from other studies is that the need for conferences declines as people begin to apply the principles and logic of restorative justice in their routine responses to conflict and harm in a way that seeks to repair the harm without use of a full-blown conference (see Hines & Bazemore, 2003). In addition, the junior high students, who had had 1 to 3 years of experience in the elementary school with all forms of circles, were quick to initiate circles themselves by seeking out help with relationship issues, potential fights, and other conflicts.

Although the three schools in the South St. Paul district represent the focal point of this case study, it is also of interest to note similarly positive outcomes in other locations throughout the state.[2] Reviewing just two anecdotal examples:

- At Princeton High, an estimated 18 in-school suspension and 30 out-of-school suspension days were saved in 2000–2001 as a result of administrators sending students to a circle in an attempt to prevent a suspendable event—as one put it, "After screaming, but before a fight." Moreover, behavioral referrals declined substantially, from 1,940 in 1998–1999 to 1,478 in 2000–2001 (again, with no change in the baseline population).

- In the Minneapolis Public School System, both Nellie Stone Johnson Elementary and Ramsey International Fine Arts Center (K–8 schools) reported out-of-school suspension reductions of 63% and 45%, respectively, between the beginning of their circle training (2001–2002) and its full implementation. Both schools pursued a comprehensive approach in terms of encouraging employees to use circles, enjoyed positive administrative support, and benefited from strong staff leadership.

Experiential Accounts

To a large degree, the experience of Minnesota DCFL with restorative practice as an alternative to zero-tolerance policies cannot be captured in quantitative data alone. Each participating school, and many individual participants, had numerous examples of transformational experiences that occurred in the process of employing these approaches.

On one hand, some staff expressed concern about the time required to implement a restorative response to incidents formerly processed by traditional quick-fix methods. On the other hand, a number of student and teacher reactions have been quite positive, and small examples of cultural change in some schools provide hope for the future (e.g., many reports of former enemies resolving their differences and becoming friends).

However, that does not necessarily mean that restorative justice is a speedy solution—or that all problems are solved in the first attempt. To the contrary, a slow, patient, problem-solving attitude is essential, and sometimes several circles are actually needed before achieving resolution.

Nor does embracing a restorative approach negate the use of more punitive, deterrence-based measures. In fact, there is nothing to prevent both from being implemented simultaneously.

Implementation Challenges

Although both qualitative and quantitative results of Minnesota's experiment with restorative justice alternatives to zero tolerance appear, for the most part, to be quite promising, that is not to say that the process has been implemented without challenges. To the contrary, school districts throughout the state experienced difficulties with such issues as the following:

Providing training: Everyone involved needed an overview of restorative justice philosophy and practices. This required training, along with subsequent support from the principal and staff to encourage practicing the new capabilities.

Using restorative interventions in place of (or in conjunction with) traditional sanctions: The more serious the offense, the less likely this was—district policy sometimes superseded a restorative response. In other words, existing zero-tolerance policies often clashed with the intent of the new initiative.

Consistently applying the principles: Consistent application of a broad-based effort requires comprehensive endeavors, ranging from initial staff training and orientation to incorporating restorative options into daily classroom management.

Identifying and supporting advocates: Offering mentoring and support is essential to keep the momentum going. Many teachers have learned new ways of working with students that they like and find effective, but without on-going support, some have defaulted to the old ways of doing things. By identifying and supporting advocates, they in turn are more likely to inspire and support other staff.

Providing holistic approaches: When the majority of staff, teachers, and administrators are familiar with the same concepts, it is more likely that they will respond consistently. In addition, their shared experiences may well reinforce restorative justice principles and improve staff cohesion.

Offering reflective opportunities: Anything new will encounter success and failure and raise questions. Debriefing sessions help to continue the training after the trainers have left and enable staff to support and learn from each other.

Leadership: The overarching necessity of well-focused, visionary leadership cannot be overstated, not only to provide the encouragement for all stakeholders to embrace the restorative initiative but also to assure that time, resources, and effort are being used most effectively.

It is also noteworthy that there is an emerging body of literature on the latent spillover effects of restorative processes on organizational culture and the development of social capital and collective efficacy (Bazemore & Schiff, 2004). For example, peacemaking circles have been cited as having an impact on conflict resolution, problem solving, community building, and dialogue enhancement. But that is only likely to occur if these processes are applied as something more than an isolated program or technique—that is, as a way to deal with life in general rather than simply responding to some specific aspect of it (Boyes-Watson, 2004). In the school context and elsewhere, a more "communal" organizational culture (Payne, Gottfredson, & Gottfredson, 2003) and the replication of underlying principles rather than operational programs are the critical ingredients.

Notes

1. Although the culture of the school was not formally assessed in this project, the principal assumed a strong leadership role (in contrast to some of his colleagues in other schools), protecting the restorative project and encouraging (and allowing time for) the use of circles, especially in more complex cases. In fact, the principal himself participated in a number of these cases. This focus was therefore maintained despite the school's loss of the planner position.

2. Ideally, it would have been preferential to include data from matching schools that did not have a restorative justice program. However, because grant funding did not support such a research design, nonparticipating schools did not collect suspension and expulsion data in any systematic way. Including statistics from them would therefore be methodologically flawed, given the lack of consistency in the manner in which outcome variables were defined, reported, and coded. The authors realize that the additional accounts included here, while providing further anecdotal evidence, do not permit strong, empirically based, causal inferences.

Discussion Questions

How concerned are you about violence in your classroom and school?

What policies do you advocate so that all schools are safe places with students who are ready and willing to learn?

Jeanne B. Stinchcomb is an associate professor at Florida Atlantic University.

Gordon Bazemore is a professor at Florida Atlantic University.

Nancy Riestenberg is a violence prevention specialist for the Minnesota Department of Education.

Section X

WHERE ARE WE NOW?

The previous sections of the reader have provided you with a vast amount of information regarding the status of the curriculum field, its history, challenges, organization, and control. We organized the articles so that topics could be revisited in each section, albeit with a different perspective, much like Bruner's idea of a spiral curriculum. Curriculum study has many facets to it, and important to the understanding of the broad perspective of curriculum, it is imperative that you understand those facets. Hopefully these readings have given you sufficient knowledge to seriously engage in curriculum dialogue with yourself and your colleagues.

The bottom line in curriculum is that the teacher is the ultimate curriculum decision maker. As we approach the end of this reader, we have selected two articles that provide you with the opportunity to think about yourself as a curriculum creator.

In the environment of accountability and standardization, Maurice Holt cautions us to think about the long-term implications of a test-driven curriculum. How well prepared are our youth going to be able to face the complexity of the world they live in? How prepared will they be to handle the unpredictable problems of adulthood? How "educated" have they become?

The most important function schools can serve is what Liston calls the "lure of learning." The center of learning is the complex relationship between teacher, student, and content. Content, according to Liston, is the key to a well-educated person. Without content there is no teaching and therefore no interaction with students. To make content come alive for students, their teachers must have a love for their content and a love of learning. Teachers are central to making the curriculum exciting and meaningful to students. They are the magnets that attract students to a love for learning.

As you read these last two articles think about the following:

- How you can effectively engage students in their learning
- How you can make your content meaningful and exciting to the students
- How you can create greater depth in what students are learning
- How you can be a role model for constant learning
- How you can develop lifelong learners

Article 39

IT'S TIME TO START THE SLOW SCHOOL MOVEMENT

MAURICE HOLT

W hen the young Cole Porter left his elementary school in Indiana for a prep
school on the East Coast, his mother
gave his age as 12, although he was in fact
2 years older. She had always encouraged his
musical gifts and evidently decided that two
more years at home, practicing the piano and
entertaining passengers on the passing river-
boats, was a better way of fostering his song-
writing abilities.[1] We should all be grateful for
her foresight.

In today's school climate, Kate Porter's
deception appears both unlikely and unwise. The
pressure to proceed from one targeted standard to another as fast as possible, to absorb
and demonstrate specified knowledge with con-
veyor-belt precision, is an irresistible fact of
school life. Parents are encouraged to focus on
achievement, not self-realization. A present-day
Porter would soon be labeled a nerdy slow
learner if he flunked the math test and preferred

the keyboard to a baseball bat. It's curious that,
in an age when the right of adults to shape their
own lifestyle is taken for granted, the right of
children to an education that will help them
make something of themselves is more circumscribed than ever.

This curriculum straitjacket is the price
exacted for believing that education is about
assessed performance on specified content. The
march toward ruthless conformity began in the
1970s, as the Cold Warriors blamed schools for
the supposed deficiencies in American technology. It gained momentum in the 1960s, when, as
Arthur Levine has noted, the generation born
after World War II became young urban professionals, and "the education of their children
became the baby boomers' and the nation's preoccupation."[2] The 1983 Reagan-era report *A
Nation at Risk* set the agenda for all that has followed. Influenced on the one hand by the idea
that education is an atomistic, science-like activity,

SOURCE: Excerpted from Holt, M. (2002). It's time to start the slow school movement. *Phi Delta Kappan*, *84*(4), 264–271. Reprinted by permission of Maurice Holt.

and on the other by the output-led simplicities of supply-side economics, schools in America have been in the grip of some form of standard-based reform for nearly 20 years.

The current administration of George W. Bush has pushed through the idea of universal standards-based tests to be given each year in grades 3 through 8, a requirement that undermines the independence of the states and is widely thought to be unworkable. History may show, as is so often the case, that this ultimate adornment to the edifice of standards may mark the very moment when its foundations begin to crumble. The 33rd Phi Delta Kappa/Gallup poll shows a rising trend in favor of school-based assessment and of public schooling in general.[3] The results of state testing in English and mathematics, far from offering new insights, merely confirm that the chief determinants of performance are parental income and the level of school resources—in short, the affluence of the neighborhood. Conservative columnist George Will puts it more brutally: "The crucial predictor of a school's performance is the quality of the children's families."[4]

But this is not a law of nature: It reflects the tendencies of tests to reflect culturally embedded concepts of student "quality" and of school funding systems to offer least to those who need most. To excel in high-stakes tests, even schools in sleek suburbs are prepared to distort their curriculum, as Billie Stanton observes in a revealing report on the effects of standards-led reform in Colorado:

> Even parents in an affluent Boulder neighborhood . . . are questioning whether private school may not be preferable, since watching their fourth-graders return home dazed and drained from being drilled again and again in how to write a "power paragraph."[5]

In borderline schools, Stanton writes, there is "a narrowing of curriculum, a trend that sucks all enrichment and love of learning out of education while creating a 'drill and kill' focus on reading, writing, and math to the exclusion of everything else." Colorado rates schools on a bell curve, with the threat of intervention for those that "fail," creating a climate of fear that encourages recourse to dubious practices—not least by the state itself. Astonishingly, a state recommendation points out that a school can raise its rating and avoid humiliation merely by getting "three more kids to prove proficient on third-grade reading and five more on fifth-grade reading."[6] The pursuit of "tough standards" can corrupt everything it touches—not least, the results.

A FRESH PERSPECTIVE

There has to be a better way of understanding what schools should be about and how to improve them. For some, charter schools are the answer, but the recent RAND research offers little encouragement for this view, and privatized schools have fared no better.[7] We need to move away from mechanical models, where the ends are defined from above and the appropriate means are applied from below. We need to think instead about how people come together to examine and improve an activity that, like education, depends in its most realized form on the unexpected and the unpredictable. Learning and teaching are often at their richest when the moment gives rise to an expected insight, when what Dewey called the collateral experience can generate a new end and set in train new means to achieve it.

Something of this kind began to happen in 1986, when a McDonald's hamburger franchise opened its doors in the Piazza di Spagna in Rome. Carlo Petrini—then a journalist for a weekly magazine—made a joke that turned into a movement: "We said, there's fast food, so why not slow food?"[8] Now the International Slow Food Congress meets annually: There are American slow food convivia in New York, California, and North Carolina; and Italy has its first slow city. The founding manifesto declared: "A firm defense of quiet material pleasure is the only way to oppose the universal folly of Fast Life."

As the movement has grown, its main concerns have emerged: It is, "above all, a movement for cultural dignity," it is "a battle against a way of life based solely on speed and convenience," and it seeks to save "the cultural inheritance of humanity."[9] Preserving the variety of different kinds of food, challenging legislation that restricts small producers, and making good, cheap ingredients available to all have become particular issues, while of course encouraging ways of living that find time for agreeable meals and quiet reflection.

Some similarity is already evident with the ends of education, in which respect for our cultural inheritance and for a variety of ways of interpreting it goes hand in hand with an emphasis on the long-term implications of schooling rather than short-term rewards. We remember from our schooldays not the results of tests but those moments when a teacher's remark suddenly created a new perception. As Michael Oakeshott put in, "Not the cry, but the rising of the wild duck impels the flock to follow him in flight."[10] You are not a mere observer, a passive consumer—you become part of an experience, savoring the moment and benefiting from its intensity.

It is helpful to identify some aspects of the slow food movement that underpin its approach. First, it expresses a definite *philosophical position*—that life is about more than rushed meals. Second, it draws upon *tradition* and *character*—eating well means respecting culinary knowledge and recognizing that eating is a social activity that brings it own benefits. A respect for tradition also *honors complexity*—most sauces have familiar ingredients, but how they are combined and cooked vitally influences the result. And third, slow food is about *moral choices*—it is better to have laws that allow rare varieties of cheese to be produced, and it is better to take time to judge, to digest, and to reflect upon the nature of "quiet material pleasure" and how everyone can pursue it.

These attributes are not chosen at random; they are prominent in the writings of the curriculum theorist Joseph Schwab, and William Reid has suggested that they mark out what Schwab termed "the practical" approach to curriculum activity.[11] In "The Practical: A Language for Curriculum," Schwab argues that this view of social action itself embodies theoretical constructs such as tradition, character, and context and is fundamentally different from action conceived as "practice" and divorced from "theory."[12] The slow food movement is entirely concerned with the language of the practical; it is all about real people eating, arguing, and legislating in ways that take account of particular issues, informed by the three crucial elements of philosophical grounding, tradition and character, and moral choice.

The alternative view, which currently dominates the scene, draws a distinction between theory and practice. Because theory, Reid argues, tends to be seen in education as "abstract and refined in character," it follows that practice "is conceived as concrete and mundane." Practice then becomes "the deployment of knowledge and skills," such as management, presentation, and implementation.[13] By the same token, practice becomes value free: "Good practice is simply that which works. The idea of the practical, on the other hand, represents practice as deeply implicated with considerations of a social, cultural, and political nature that . . . confront problems of moral choice."[14] In sum, the prevailing view of practice is not philosophically grounded, is independent of tradition and character, and is unconcerned with moral issues.

DEVELOPING THE METAPHOR

I suggest that conventional fast food expresses this narrow conception of practice. There is no philosophy behind the concept of a hamburger—only the theory that a beef-filled bun is tasty and relieves hunger. Neither does its preparation draw upon tradition and character, as does, for example, the preparation of sole meunière or a Genoese sponge cake. Fast food involves only rudimentary skills, which can be taught to employees without any knowledge of the culinary arts.

The fact that virtually the same hamburger sells in Paris and Moscow demonstrates its supremely decontextualized nature. And the sourcing of its ingredients is not a matter of morality; in a hamburger, one kind of salt is as good as another.

There is assuredly a place for both fast food and slow food in the world. There is nothing intrinsically objectionable in hamburger practice. If one is in business to make hamburgers, the fast food model—theory and practice—makes perfect sense. It is wholly appropriate to the nature of the problem, which is uncomplicated and procedural. But this is not the case if one has in mind a meal that is at once eclectic, imaginative, and socially stimulating. Judgment, finesse, tradition, and ambience all have a part to play, since the taste of food on the palate is just as important as a full stomach. And indeed, it is possible to produce a quick meal within the slow food canon: An omelet takes less time to prepare than the average burger.

In the context of education, the form of schooling espoused under the banner of standards demonstrates the same deterministic thinking that governs the production of fast food. What is sought is a conception of educational practice that can be defined in terms of content and sequence and assessed in terms of agreed-upon ends capable of numerical expression. The engagement between teacher and learner should be as predictable as possible, and variation between one teacher and another can be offset by scripting the learning encounter and tightening the form of assessment. If the purpose of schooling is to deliver the knowledge and skills that business needs, this approach cuts costs, standardizes resources, and reduces teacher training to a school-base process. Above all, the efficacy of the operation can be measured and the results used to control it and its functionaries—the teachers.

But if schools exist to equip students with the capacity to address the unpredictable problems of adulthood and to establish themselves in a world of growing complexity, then crucial disadvantages emerge. Classroom practice becomes a boring routine, teachers feel de-skilled, and though what

is learned is measurable, its educative value is diminished. The "fast school" offers a static conception of education that has more in common with training. And how can this kind of practice be improved? Since it derives from an impoverished view of theory, distinct from practice, only practice itself can guide improvement. Hence the emphasis on defining "best practices" or "what works," based on the dubious assumption that practice is context free. But can it ever be?

Commitment to standards-led school reform means creating a system of schools geared solely to the product—test results—and not to the process of creating educative experiences. Gerald Bracey has offered a few of the personal attributes that standardized tests cannot measure—attributes crucial to the cultivation of the virtues and the formation of moral agents: "creativity, critical thinking, resilience, motivation, persistence, humor, reliability, enthusiasm, civic-mindedness, self-awareness, self-discipline, empathy, leadership, and compassion."[15] But these are as remote from the activity of fast schools as is gastronomic pleasure from fast food.

The result of creating fast schools is institutional indigestion, and signs of discomfort are now appearing. Even Advanced Placement courses in mathematics and science are not immune. A study commissioned by the National Science Foundation and the U.S. Department of Education's critical of "the curriculums that most of those courses cover and the way they are taught. . . . The courses crammed in too much material at the expense of understanding."[16]

Standards supporters have always claimed that if better tests are used, the quality of teaching will improve. The Maryland School Performance Assessment Program (MSPAP) is therefore of particular interest, since it has been rated "the best in the nation."[17] But the February 2002 MSPAP results were so misleading that the latest eighth-grade version has been "all but scrapped." What went wrong? It turns out that the MSPAP tests, devised to "emphasize critical thinking," were difficult to grade—"the process was rushed and subjective."[18] And in any case, all the state wanted was "content-based exams" and simple tests to match. The implication is clear: However much time is spent improving tests, the problem lies elsewhere—in the mistaken belief that tests and targets should drive the curriculum.

A school system based on testing content and basic proficiencies is better than none at all, and developing nations can afford to do little more. What is surprising is that the richest country in the world is hell-bent on doing exactly this.

It was certainly not meant to be so; the slow school requirement for philosophical grounding was very evident in the conclusions of the committee set up in 1918 by the National Education Association to develop the high school curriculum. Its members rejected continental models and decided to forge a uniquely American settlement. They took account of the earlier efforts of the Committee of Ten, of the writings of John Dewey, and of pressure from manufacturers who wanted school leavers to have the skills that would help them compete with European rivals. They took account of cultural tradition, too, and believed, like postrevolutionary France, that the success of the republic depended on schooling that was well conceived, free from sectarian bias, and equally accessible to all. But it was to be local rather than national. You went to high school to become an American, but you took a chance on what sort of Americans were running the school board.

The result in the United States was, and is, a system in which the language of the practical still lingers, but it is now in competition with an emphasis on deterministic doctrines that threaten to drive it underground. In part, this reflects the growing strength of the industrial lobby in American politics, but it also owes much to psychometric influences that, over the years, have persuaded Americans that numbers are everything: If you can't measure it, you can't manage it. Nothing, as W. Edwards Deming remarked, could be further from the truth: "The most important figures needed for management of any organization are unknown and unknowable."[19]

The system of local school boards was intended to frustrate federal interference, but the political prominence given to education since the 1960s has made such interference inevitable. Yet, unlike France, America has no tradition of education as a national construct. Indeed, the local character of the U.S. system was to be its strength. The current scenario could lead to the worst of both worlds: the individual character of schools undermined by national legislation based not on deliberation but on dogma. The more education is seen as a commodity, the less its power to animate the emotional attachment of students. The day may come when one goes to high school not to become an American but to acquire the technical skills of globalism.

The dissatisfaction of parents with fast schools is beginning to surface. One alternative is home schooling; another is to use a private school—some of which offer radical solutions. In Woodstock, New York, for example, a "Sudbury School" has opened, with no classrooms and no grades, based on the proposition that "there is no right way to learn, no time by which a student should have mastered a given skill."[20] A study of students attending a similar school in Massachusetts found that 87% went on to higher education, but much of the interest in the Woodstock enterprise "has come from middle-class children's parents,"[21] which is not irrelevant; these students are better able to cope with unstructured formats and benefit from family resources as well. But in the public sector, a slow school must have the practical underpinning to make it an enriching vehicle for students from all social and cultural backgrounds.

TOWARD THE SLOW SCHOOL

What would a slow school look like, and would parents make use of a school with such a counterintuitive name? How might Schwab's three principles of philosophical grounding, tradition and culture, and moral judgment play out in practice? The first point to make is that several American initiatives designed to reform public schools over the last two decades or so have much in common with the principled underpinnings of the slow school. And variety should be encouraged. There ought not to be a canonical slow school, any more than there can be standardized slow food. Commonality of approach does not imply uniformity of practice.

It's reasonable to suppose that Theodore Sizer's Horace would be happy to work in a slow school.[22] The idea that "less is more" fits exactly with an emphasis on intensive rather than extensive experience. Better to eat one portion of grilled halibut than three king-sized burgers. Better to examine in detail the reasons why Sir Thomas More chose martyrdom or why Alexander Hamilton argued for a strong federal government than to memorize the kings of England or the capitals of the states of the union. The slow school is a place where understanding matters more than coverage; one takes time to see what Newton's concepts of mass and force might imply, to appreciate their abstract nature and the intellectual leap they represent. Then the usual algorithms fall into place quickly and securely. The slow school offers the intellectual space for scrutiny, argument, and resolution.

These are all essential to practical inquiry, and it would seem that the Paideia schools established in Chattanooga demonstrate the value of such strategies, since they manage to incorporate Mortimer Adler's commitment to Socratic dialogue while satisfying Mammon's need for good test results.[23] Indeed, the supreme irony of the slow school is that precisely because it provides the intellectual nourishment students need and puts curriculum first, good test results follow. Success, like happiness, is best pursued obliquely.

Equally relevant is the work of Deborah Meier, who has shown how a school, given the autonomy to do so, can construct a demanding curriculum that engages students from widely varied environments and can carry them forward into higher education.[24] What all these schools have in common is the power to improve themselves, and this is the singular virtue of any school curriculum that uses the language of the practical. Because ends and means are allowed to interact, improvement stems naturally from the deliberation that arises from the interaction.

Improvement is not, as legislators have come to believe, a matter of extrinsic pressure; it is an intrinsic property of the school itself, precisely because the "practical" embodies theory within its practice.

Is this the time to start the slow school movement? I believe it is an idea whose time has come. At a stroke, the notion of the slow school destroys the idea that schooling is about cramming, testing, and standardizing experience. It legitimizes a range of admirable yet hitherto marginal strategies for schooling and brings them into the mainstream of argument, using a philosophical basis that is supple enough to accommodate a variety of reform programs, yet tough enough to resist the counterarguments of the standards movement.

The slow approach to food allows for discovery, for the development of connoisseurship. Slow food festivals feature new dishes and new ingredients. In the same way, slow schools give scope for invention and response to cultural change, while fast schools just turn out the same old burgers. If we think about the future of education, we assuredly want a more satisfying and stimulating approach than the present and state of affairs. Only slow schools hold out that kind of promise.

The putative Slow School Association would help parents, legislators, and administrators understand not only what a slow school is but also what it is not. It is important to establish the intellectual credential of the slow school, since it would be necessary to agree to certain preconditions with legislators and administrators. For example, frequent testing (as opposed to informal teacher monitoring) is inimical to the philosophy of the slow school. Once slow school students have demonstrated their ability to do well with fewer tests, the movement would acquire political clout and could help rein in the senseless overtesting that currently threatens schools and students.

One can suppose, for example, that a slow school would make use of computers as aids to learning, but without attributing to them the numinous educative powers that figure in the rhetoric of many politicians. Equally, the language of the practical, as the deliberative underpinning of curriculum thinking, has nothing to do with postmodernist flights of fancy of the kind espoused by some educational theorists, nor with the notion of basing a curriculum solely on practical work or students' transient needs and interests. Rather, the slow school philosophy, as expressed through the language of the practical, affirms an eclectic approach to schooling that addresses the question put by Robert Dearden: "Why should everything be judged by the standards appropriate to mathematics and science?"[25] The language of determinism, given brutal expression in the standards movement, obliges us to recall Aristotle's caution: "It is the mark of an educated man that in every subject he looks only for so much precision as its nature permits."[26] Between the precision of tests and the raw variety of classroom life lies a vast gulf.

Recent developments in Japan have a bearing on this issue. Starting in the 2002–2003 school year, Japan's public schools will pursue a radically different curriculum that offers students much more free time—a deliberate departure from the extreme formality and relentless drilling so admired a decade ago as the paradigmatic example of what American schools should be like if the United States were to regain its lead in the global economy. A senior official of the Japanese Ministry of Education, Ken Terawaki, has a convincing explanation:

Our current system, just telling kids to study, study, study, has been a failure. Endless study worked in the past, when . . . Japan was rebuilding. . . . But that is no longer the case . . . telling them to study more will no longer work. . . . We want to give them some time to think.[27]

There is concern "that an orderly and unimaginative school system excels at producing pliant, disciplined workers . . . but is failing to produce the problem solvers and innovators of the future."[28] By pursuing a punitive, outdated model of schooling rather than encouraging U.S. schools to individualize, innovate, and fulfill their historical purpose, America has become stuck in a time warp.

There is no reason why the phrase "slow school" should not acquire the cachet associated with "slow food." In many aspects of life, doing things slowly is associated with profound pleasure. Fast sunbathing is not regarded as particularly enjoyable. If we want to understand a striking baseball catch, we replay it in slow motion. Why try to absorb the treasures of Florence in a brief guided tour if you can spend a month appreciating them for yourself? If we want our children to apprehend the variety of human experience and learn how they can contribute to it, we must give them—and their teachers—the opportunity to do so. Let the slow times roll!

Discussion Questions

According to Holt, what are the underpinnings needed to have a slow schools movement?

What do you think the curricular differences would be between a slow school and the traditional public schools we are currently familiar with?

Maurice Holt is a professor emeritus at University of Colorado. He resides in England.

Article 40

THE LURE OF LEARNING IN TEACHING

DANIEL P. LISTON

At the center of the educational experience are teachers, students, and content; and the content, the curriculum, is key. Take away the teacher, and the student can be engaged with the material. Take away the student, and the teacher can be occupied with the subject matter. But take away the subject, and the center, the entire relationship, vanishes. Teaching, at its heart, is the creation of connections among teacher, student, and content so that educational experiences can be had. A love of learning, of inquiry, of coming to know is an essential ingredient in creating this web of interconnections.

Depicting this lure [of learning] will hopefully convey some of what the seduction of learning is all about. To accomplish this, I've constructed a "conversation" between Anne Carson and Annie Dillard. In *Eros the Bittersweet*, Carson explores the parallels between falling in love and coming to know, claiming that both experiences make her feel terribly alive.[1] In *An American Childhood*, Dillard offers some rather wonderful passages depicting what it's like to be lured into natural worlds.[2]

LOVE OF (AND) LEARNING

There would seem to be some resemblance between the way eros acts in the mind of a lover and the way knowing acts in the mind of a thinker. I would like to grasp why it is that those two activities, falling in love and coming to know, make me feel genuinely alive (*EB*, 70).

In *Eros the Bittersweet*, Anne Carson examines the dynamics of eros[3] and draws parallels to learning and "coming to know." In learning we

SOURCE: Excerpted from Liston, D. P. (2004). The lure of learning in teaching. *Teachers College Record*, *106*(3), 459–486. Reprinted by permission.

reach beyond ourselves to come into contact with the world and to connect with the grace of great things. Carson claims that falling in love and coming to know make her feel genuinely alive. Learning seems to have affected Annie Dillard in the same way. In her *An American Childhood*, she captures learning's attraction and the allure of the world around her. In fact Dillard seems to be responding to Carson's request to understand why loving and learning make her feel so alive. Dillard writes about her childhood love of coming to know when she recalls and conveys her seduction into the worlds of libraries, ponds, and streams; books and beds; and rocks and stones. She conveys how our love of learning connects us to the world, how it engages our minds and emotions, and how it illuminates the sensual and sacred.

LIBRARIES, PONDS, AND STREAMS

Growing up in Pittsburgh in the 1950s, Annie Dillard was one of four lively children in a family that did not appear to want for money or resources. Annie loved to read, and the closest library was the branch in Homewood. This branch was located in one of the Black sections of town. Because it was some distance from her house, Annie's mother would drive her there. Entering the Homewood Library (which had "Free To The People" engraved on its façade), a 12-year-old child with an adult card, Dillard recalls the large vaulted rooms; the high, leaded windows; and the quiet, cool floors. One day, during a visit in the adult room "in the cool darkness of a bottom shelf," she happened upon *The Field Book of Ponds and Streams*. It turned out to be a truly wonderful find, for in chapter 3 of the book Annie Dillard found what she had not known she was looking for. In this chapter the essential tools of the naturalist's trade were explained, field procedures elaborated, and the multiple worlds of water and insect life unveiled. This book outlined the accoutrements of the naturalist trade and in doing so fitted Annie Dillard for one of her most beloved adventures. She

learned that when a naturalist went out into the field she wore

> hip boots and perhaps a head net for mosquitoes. One carried in a "rucksack" half a dozen corked test tubes, a smattering of screw-type baby-food jars, a white enamel tray, assorted pipettes and eye droppers, an artillery of cheesecloth, . . . and [of course] *The Field Book of Ponds and Streams*. (*AC*, 81)

The *Field Book of Ponds and Streams* bowled Annie Dillard over. It was, as she recalls, a "shocker from beginning to end." And, she adds, the "greatest shock came at the end."

On the last page of each library book was the book's card, with the past borrowers' numbers inscribed, and the due-date sheet. Upon checking her beloved book out for a second time, she noticed that the book's card was almost full, with numbers on both sides:

> My hearty author and I were not alone in the world after all. With us, and sharing our enthusiasm for dragonfly larvae and single celled plants, were, apparently many Negro adults. . . . Who were these people? Had they, in Pittsburgh's Homewood section, found ponds? Had they found streams? At home I read the book again; I studied the drawings; I reread Chapter 3; then I settled in to study the due-date slip. People read this book in every season. Seven or eight people were reading this book every year, even during the war. . . . Often when I was in the library, I simply visited it. I sat on the marble floor and studied the book's card. There we all were. There was my number. There was the number of someone else who had checked it out more than once. Might I contact this person and cheer him up? For I assumed that, like me, he had found pickings pretty slim in Pittsburgh. (*AC*, 82–83)

Slowly, however, the reality of Homewood hit home. Many Homewood residents lived in visible poverty, yet it appeared from the number of checkouts that they too dreamed of ponds and streams.

Libraries open worlds, worlds otherwise not easily accessible, and in doing so they allow us all sorts of unimaginable pleasures. A library's holdings offer the possibility of immersion into other worlds, immersion into natural, unnatural, and human landscapes. These landscapes take us beyond ourselves into realms that seem to beckon our imagination and beg for further exploration. Dillard's discovery of *The Field Book of Ponds and Streams* did all this. It outfitted her in naturalist's gear and took her into the microscopic world of water insects. To the naked and untrained eye water is water, but with Ann Haven Morgan's field book in hand, hip boots secure, and collection jars ready, we can begin to plumb the depths of a pond. Once we have glimpsed the water pennies, dragonfly nymphs, and salamander larvae, other worlds exist beside(s) ours. The library's field book opened up worlds of water and, in doing so, illuminated connections within that natural world. When we explore these worlds, we create webs of connection with, and within those worlds. And having been introduced to these worlds, Annie Dillard wanted to know more.

Dillard wanted to take her understanding further, fill in the gaps and holes, and, hopefully, correct those troublesome conceptions that didn't fit with her ways of seeing the world. This seems to be a common experience. Coming upon new material we check it against what we already know and understand. We try to fit it into our current ways of understanding the world and ourselves, but all too often it just doesn't fit. If we are going to grow, and if we feel somewhat secure, we explore further these gaps and misconceptions. But if we are insecure and defensive, we may try to hide or ignore the poor fit of the new material. Coming to know seems to inevitably entail, at some point, a sense of insufficiency. As Anne Carson notes, the "activities of knowing and desiring . . . have at their core the same delight, that of reaching, and entail the same pain, that of falling short or being deficient" (*EB*, 71). Noisome cheesecloth and enamel trays don't quite fit. Is it a problem with me or the world? Dare I speak up and find out?

Dillard wanted to write to the author, to acknowledge the book's gift, and to connect with the author. But she did not write Ann Haven Morgan. She imagined the questions she might

pose, but did not address, to the author. Instead she sought out other readers.

Dillard's comfort in her company did not last long. She soon realized that while the library was open and free to all, access to these natural water-filled worlds was not. Her delight soured, the world around her became quite dry, and the library's marble floor turned chilly. Not all of us see so readily the connections between our delight and others' (and our own) sorrow. Dillard did. It seems that the natural worlds Dillard explored were filled with threads of connections. She brought those threads to her everyday world. She realized that the joys she had shared with others were constrained by something bigger than her and them. With her heart and mind she grasped, and found distasteful, the injustice.

LIFE IN ROCKS AND GEMS

It seems that soon after Dillard felt the chill of Homewood's marble floor she was bequeathed three rock-filled grocery bags. Mr. Downey, an old man who lived down the street from her grandparents, had passed on the rocks to the paperboy and then, 2 weeks later, passed away. The paperboy, in turn, gave them to Annie. The boy could not remember the rocks' names, and Dillard was sure they had names. Bent on knowing, on identifying these rocks, Annie went to the library and in the adult section got the true dope from various manuals and field guides. With the aid of these books, she performed all sorts of tests, the likes of which could only have originated from a world of people who knew and loved rocks. She performed scratch tests. She determined the rocks' hardness using Mohs' scale. She learned all sorts of ways to poke, prod, and test her treasures, to get the rocks to divulge their identity.

Rocks, it seems, not only have character but also have a complex life all their own. If we are fortunate enough to peer inside, we discover an intelligence that surprises and amazes. Pry open a rock and behold the precious beauty. Pry open a rock and glimpse elements of this other world.

Pry open a rock and see there reflected the dreams of your night before. Dillard hungered for an understanding of the rocks' world, their identity, and in honoring it she was invited in. Once in, she looked around and saw both this other world and herself.

Soon Dillard realized that rocks and ponds were not the only treasures in the world before her.

> I had been chipping at the world idly, and had by accident uncovered vast and labyrinth[ine] further worlds within it. I peered in one day and stepped in the next, and soon wandered in deep over my head. Month after month, year after year, the true and brilliant light, of the actual, historical, waking world invigorated me. Its vastness extended everywhere I looked, and precisely where I looked. . . . Everything in the world, every baby, city, tetanus shot, tennis ball, and pebble was an outcrop of some vast and hitherto concealed vein of knowledge, apparently, that had compelled people's emotions and engaged their minds in the minutest detail without anyone's having done with it. There must be enthusiasts for everything on earth— fanatics who shared a vocabulary, a batch of technical skills and equipment, and perhaps, a vision of some single slice of the beauty and mystery of things, of their complexity, fascination and unexpectedness. (*AC*, 157–159)

Attracted by the many worlds around her, Dillard was touched by a singular beauty and mystery they somehow all shared.

COMING TO KNOW OTHER WORLDS

I don't know if Annie Dillard and Anne Carson have ever met, but it seems to me they must talk to each other. It's as if Dillard responds lovingly to Carson's requests and Carson then replies, taking the conversation further. Carson asks what eros and coming to know have in common. Dillard responds: In coming to know we reach into other worlds with fascination, awe, and respect. Both eros and coming to know reach out and in the process, look back upon themselves

and see holes, gaps, insufficiencies. Both eros and coming to know leap into these worlds and ask others to come along to support and sanctify their loves.

Rocks or ponds, streams or gems, tennis balls or tetanus shots, Dillard tells us what it is like to reach out, to crack open a rock or delve into the depths of a pond. It is a movement from ourselves, to an other, and then back to ourselves. It is a movement that is motivated by a desire to know that other and a delight in seeing the other on its own terms. At times we are frustrated in our attempts to understand this otherness, and at times we sense our insufficiency next to it. When we do grasp it, a sense of awe can arise. We frequently look for others to travel with us. In coming to terms with the otherness, we seek companionship. We look to the last page of the book to see who else checked it out more than once.

Carson then takes us a bit further, telling us that

> we think by projecting sameness upon difference, by drawing things together in a relation or idea while at the same time maintaining the distinctions between them. A thinking mind is not swallowed up by what it comes to know. It reaches out to grasp something related to itself and to its present knowledge (and so knowable in some degree) but also separate from itself and from its present knowledge (not identical) with these. In any act of thinking, the mind must reach across this space between known and unknown, linking one to the other but also keeping visible their difference. It is an erotic space. To reach across it is tricky. . . . When the mind reaches out to know, the space of desire opens and a necessary fiction transpires. . . . for desire is a movement that carries yearning hearts from over here to over there, launching the mind on a story. (*EB*, 171–173)

In seeming response to Carson, Dillard details her mind thinking and bids us to go with her across that space between the known and unknown.

So what is this love's allure? What is it about coming to know that makes us feel so genuinely alive and wanting to share these pleasures by teaching others? This much I know: Coming to know engages me in a compelling, almost impelling way. I am enticed by learning. This enticement is something that seems to happen to me. I am drawn to topics that interest me. I am excited by the prospect that I will find another way to see into the world, glimpse its beauty, reconstruct it in a way not yet known to me. The rocks appeared at Annie Dillard's front doorstep. She could have deposited them in the back with the trash. She didn't. She seemed impelled to go to the library and join other rock hounds, name the rocks, and capture their mysteries.

There is an excitement that accompanies this engagement. Reaching across from the known to the unknown raises the possibility of discovering something new about the world and possibly ourselves. And it is humbling to glimpse our common frailties. (And it's even more humbling to acquiesce under the understanding that we may not understand, that there are limits to our knowing.)

Dillard captures not only learning's excitement, but she also evokes a sense of awe, a sense of the sacredness of the world around her. Dillard's rocks touched her with the grace of great things. In those rocks she envisioned an intelligence other than her own. There was something sacred about those rocks, something precious that set them apart, and Dillard felt and knew that. Part of learning's lure seems to be this recognition, this revelation of the special otherness of our world's worlds. For some this sense of reverence for other worlds may seem reserved for natural phenomena. But the grace of great things, while certainly found aplenty in the natural world, is also present in so many other realms. When I was an undergraduate at Earlham College, Gordon Thompson, my humanities professor, treated each novel and story as if they were worlds unto themselves. He taught us to look at a story with a careful, patient, and attentive eye. We didn't set these stories alight with a match or try to dissolve them with chemicals. Instead Gordon tried to give us the tools of literary analysis. I'm afraid I probably frustrated him. My skills always seemed to me, and I believe to him, a bit underdeveloped. But I can

recall the reverence and respect he reserved for the text. He could recall a minor character's eye color. I couldn't. He could recite the speech given in a pivotal scene while I struggled to make sense of its importance. He treated the text with an attitude and air that I, at age 19 years, had only seen reserved for close friends. He didn't succeed in educating me to become a literary analyst, but he did succeed in enabling me to see the otherness of a text.

And, inevitably, our engagement with learning invites frustration and self-doubt. To reach from the known to the unknown requires that we perform tasks for the first time. We are successful some of those times, but frequently we don't hit the initial mark. We have to try again, sometimes again, and ever so often again and again. At times this frustration can result in self-doubt. Is this obstacle a problem with me or the material I'm engaged with? Both? Neither? This self-doubt can build on earlier frustrations or begin anew. When we follow this lure of learning, of reaching across the divide between known and unknown, we frequently make a mark on the world, and by those marks we come to know ourselves. When my youngest son, Matthew (at age 8 years), practiced his cursive script, he found that he was good at some movements and not so good at others. It wouldn't surprise me if Dillard had discovered that she was a better scavenger of dragonfly larvae than geodes. The lure of learning holds forth success, failure, and other outcomes in between. Failure can be frustrating, and repeated failure can lead to self-doubt. But if the lure of learning always promised achievement, I doubt it would hold much attraction.

It seems to be one of the paradoxes of our love of learning that when reaching into the unknown, searching through the otherness of this world, we look for companionship and community. Perhaps we don't want to be alone. Or it could simply be that we want to share the pleasures of learning. But impelled as we are to leap into the unknown and explore other worlds, at some point we come back to something familiar. We seek companionship, we yearn for others who have or could share with us the intrigue and inroads of this learning. This seems to arise in a variety of ways. As learners, it is delightful to have other hungry learners around. In graduate school, I gained a great deal from my coursework, but in many ways it was the graduate student camaraderie that fueled and informed much of my graduate education. As I talk to middle and high school teachers, I hear that it is the absence of a community of meaningful discussion that deals a significant blow to their endurance as teachers. To endure as teachers they need to continue to learn. Without companionship in their love of learning, teaching feels quite isolated and can be difficult to sustain for a long period of time. It seems many teachers yearn for some sort of intellectual connection and companionship.

In seeking companionship, in asking others to come along and witness these worlds, Dillard also ran into injustice. The other worlds that were freely portrayed in her public library were not readily available to all in Pittsburgh. In Pittsburgh, if you were poor and Black, you could not easily venture off and explore the life-filled streams and ponds. The incongruity between the library's freedom and the real world's limitations struck Dillard as cold and unfair.

TEACHING WITH A LOVE OF LEARNING

What does teaching with a love of learning look and feel like? I know that, like the lure of learning and falling in love, teaching can make me feel genuinely alive. It can make my heart pound and my head throb, and I want to know why. I think I understand a bit of it. In falling in love and in coming to know, we reach beyond the boundaries of ourselves to something unknown yet promising. In teaching, we are trying to enable others to reach beyond themselves with the promise of achieving some understanding, some different way of seeing and being in the world. As teachers we are attempting to enable students to reach beyond their boundaries to something that has given us intrigue, understanding, or sustenance for our imagination. It is

an intellectual, emotional, and at times physical attraction that we want to share, so we invite students to be attracted by some "great thing." It is an invitation to become intellectually and emotionally engaged. It is an invitation to receive part of the human inheritance, to participate in some strand of the human conversation, to become educated. And this invitation is a heartfelt and resonant one. It is an invitation that comes from our depths, from who we are intellectually, emotionally, and, for some, spiritually.

THE INVITATION

I receive invitations all the time, but not all are educational. I'm invited to sign up for another credit card, take part in a university committee, or attend a breakfast as the school's representative. Generally these invitations have little or no educational purpose. They are neither motivated by a love of learning nor bid me to take part in the larger human inheritance. What makes an invitation potentially educational is that it holds out the possibility of participating in the human conversation and that the teacher, lured by her love of learning, is touched deeply by the material, offers this attraction to students, and communicates a respect for and faith in the students' ability to be attracted also. Before I detail these areas, a few preliminary considerations are important.

When I talk about teaching with a love of learning, I sense others envision something akin to a masterful dramatic performance. These teachers, the assumption seems to be, are the gifted, the unusual, the extremely talented ones. These are the ones whose personalities carry the day and, in the process, carry their students along. In these scenarios the educational invitation takes on rather grand dimensions and represents the achievements of only a capable few. But such expectations misconstrue the nature of the power and force of an invitation offered with a love of learning; such expectations place teaching with a love of learning within undue and unreasonable constraints. All sorts of teaching can be guided by this love, and the invitations can take innumerable and quite different forms. In elementary, secondary, and university classrooms, invitations can take the form of a teacher's story about a past experience, a reading of a portion of a text, the posing of a puzzling problem, a personal testimonial, or a brief experiential task. An invitation might occur on one day or persist throughout the year. They can be loud or quiet, showy or plain. What it seems to require is simply a measure of authenticity: The invitation has to be real, conveyed by the teacher, and felt by the students.

An Invitation to Receive the Human Inheritance and Join the Discussion

When my son Matthew practiced his cursive loops and curls, he seemed to believe that he was becoming part of the grown-up world. Moving from print to cursive is a seemingly minor but nevertheless important transition in our efforts to become part of the adult community, to inherit and participate in the human conversation. When invited to learn, it is possible to get glimpses of this rich human inheritance and with that, to feel the excitement of becoming a part of the human conversation this inheritance represents. Matthew's experience is not unique. Both Annie Dillard and Jane Tompkins mention this lure, the attraction knowledge and inquiry held for them. Jane Tompkins writes that when her high school geometry teacher, Mr. Bowler, asked students, in his deep-timbered voice, to talk about knowledge and understanding she realized that there were "untold reaches of mind, beyond plane geometry or the meaning of Thanksgiving, that knowledge and understanding would open to me."[4]

Matthew Liston, Annie Dillard, and Jane Tompkins felt the lure of those concealed veins of knowledge. They were lured by the worlds around them and heard the call of others who had been similarly intrigued. Dillard and Tompkins soon realized that many others had carried on conversations not only about the things they loved but all sorts of other "untold reaches." Informed

conversations exist about innumerable worlds. These conversations are, frequently, embedded in the intellectual disciplines, the organizing units of what we teach in schools. But our disciplines are neither the only container nor, at times, the most influential factors affecting our conversations. Our organized ways of inquiring into the world are both informed and deformed by the cultural and social forces of which they are a part. Communities of scholars—their inquiries—fuel (in part) our intellectual disciplines' movements, directions, and findings. Scholars inquire and they converse. But all of this occurs within a larger context that is integrally interwoven throughout these conversations. Understanding the complexities of those conversations is the chore that the sociology of knowledge has set for itself.[5] Learning is, in large part, learning to engage in, be critical of, and become a part of those conversations.

Many of these conversations, these strands of our human inheritance, exist outside of the academy. Popular culture, all sorts of craft-based endeavors (e.g., bee-keeping, mechanical trades, Web site designs, domestic efforts), distinct cultural (e.g., African American and Latino) understandings and practices, child-rearing endeavors and rebel causes all of these efforts contain a history of past understandings and interactions, and a sense of mastery and achievement. This is part of the inheritance. And these conversations, those within and outside of the academy, do not exist on an even playing field. All sorts of class, gendered, and cultural dynamics exist and are continually reinforced and contested to determine which conversations prevail, which understandings reach what kids, and which strands are obscured for some but not others. This occurs both in and outside of schools. Certainly many kids are more interested in the conversations and inheritances that exist outside of schools. It seems to be the teacher's (i.e., democratic public school teacher's) responsibility to illuminate shared and distinct, common and repressed, mainstream and even outlawed understandings. Selections among these various conversations will inevitably occur and our cultural selections will delineate what we value. It seems difficult to conceive of a defensible education that did not, at some point in an individual's development, encourage a critical inspection of our own shared and distinct beliefs and values.

To open our minds and hearts requires that we bequeath an inheritance that is varied, multifaceted, and multivoiced. Jane Roland Martin relates that the inheritance being offered by the traditionalists for today's schools is one that is much too narrowly focused.[6] It countenances a much too limited rather than enriching view. All too frequently our public educational inheritance is one that offers an already formed impression. It does not question or examine. It is neither multifaceted nor multidimensional. It is an impression that deforms rather than informs. When students are continually spoon-fed facts and told that these facts are true, when they are asked to accept material before them without engaging their minds, these seem to be deforming rather than informing invitations. They neither reach beyond nor invite a love of the grace of great things.

Teaching with a love of learning, inviting others to learn has to amount to more than simply offering a received view or delineating the facts, skills, and concepts to master. Certainly the realm of mastery is important. However, if we offer no more, if we don't teach with a love of learning, if we don't examine our culture's shared and distinct understandings then our invitation is bound to be rather flat and dull. It can't promise much beyond the assigned tasks or purported pragmatic payoffs. It will open neither mind nor heart.

AN INVITATION FROM THE DEPTHS

An invitation's authenticity issues from the source, and, in the case of teaching, a central source is the teacher's love. If this love of learning is real, it is inevitably conveyed. And if it is real, it taps and arises from the depths of the teacher's soul. Falling in love (with a text or another) is always an amazing experience. Its amazement derives from a variety of sources. When we fall in love with another human being,

we find ourselves confronted and comforted by another's significance. We find ourselves surprised by what this other person knows of us, by what we see ourselves. What we see, what is brought to the surface, are some of our elemental features.

Gasset's depiction of personal romantic love parallels the lure of coming to know and our love of learning in teaching. As Anne Carson reminds us, falling in love and coming to know have many shared features. Falling in love with the wet world of water insects and the formidable strength and resilience of the earth's rocks, Annie Dillard came to know more deeply the worlds around her and herself. She came to see the beauty and mystery therein. When she writes of these loves, she exposes features about the world and herself. In expressing her love she revealed her depths: Fears arose, desires multiplied, and concerns about others deepened. Teaching with a love of learning allows others to glimpse what we cherish, what is elementally us. It brings our depths out for others to see.

Jane Tompkins's geometry teacher, Mr. Bowler, was someone whose love of learning was broad and vigorous. The depths stirred by his love seemed to pave a clear path for others. Tompkins relates that Mr. Bowler was educated and trained as a historian. But the school where he worked needed a geometry, not history, teacher, so he taught himself geometry. It didn't come easily to him. He had to work hard to understand spatial axioms. Having worked extra hard, he knew what it was like to wrestle with the subject and so better understood others' struggles. And this extra effort didn't seem to obstruct, perhaps even enhanced, his appreciation and love for the beauty that geometry conveyed. He capably conveyed to Jane his love and his ability to see in geometry "beauty bare." And his interests were not parochial. History, geometry, in fact the entire arena of knowledge and understanding seemed to have an allure for Mr. Bowler. He invited his students along to experience this love. In Mr. Bowler's case, the depths illuminated by his love of geometry, knowledge, and understanding cleared the way for, rather than obstructed, his students' classroom involvement. Students did not have to stumble over Mr. Bowler to get to geometry, or knowledge, or understanding.

Certainly not all teaching is as clean and clear as Mr. Bowler's. Sometimes depths are illuminated that bespeak a conflicted, even while caring (though not always), self.

The interplay between a teacher's soulful depths her love of learning and her teaching are as complex and complicated as her kinship to the grace of great things. An interesting case can be found in Kathleen Hill's short story, "The Anointed."[7] In this rich account, Miss Hughes, a seventh-grade music teacher, teaches music appreciation to the narrator's class.

From the narrator's perspective, Miss Hughes neither cajoled nor wheedled her students. She treated them as her confidants.

Miss Hughes relates the story of a skiing accident in which she broke three fingers that never properly healed and thus ended her promising career as potential virtuoso. She woke the next day to a very dark morning. In inviting students to join her confidence, Miss Hughes exposed her depths. On this particular day she conveyed a time of crisis in her life, but on other days the lessons did not rely on relating her life's personal details. For Miss Hughes, music appreciation was intensely, but not irreducibly, personal. Music was an animating force in her life: It stirred her depths and seemed to be an avenue to and through other's souls. She seemed to connect the music with her students through her own love, sorrow, and joy. In inviting students to partake in the lure of music, she could not overlook the love and sorrows of her past, the fluid that connected her to the world around her. As she once related, "Some people's lives are affected by what happens to their person or their property; but for others fate is what happens to their feelings and their thought that and nothing more" (*TA*, 85). Miss Hughes didn't seem to fit into either category easily. Her injured hand and her musical love placed her in both. It seems she was able to employ her depths to illuminate the contours of classical musical expression and to connect them with features of her students' lives. Mr. Bowler and Miss Hughes seemed to be issuing invitations from their depths.

An Invitation to Experience the Allure

In music, Miss Hughes experienced, among other things, beauty. While auditioning, she found herself consumed by the music's fire and immersed in something larger than herself. It was this relationship, this immersion and what it allowed her, that she tried to convey to her students. In geometry class, Jane Tompkins found herself bathed in a cognitive realm of pure ether and bare beauty, where "only logic reigned." Mr. Bowler's invitation afforded her that place. And Annie Dillard pried open geodes, examined water droplets, and begged us to follow. All experienced beauty, and all wanted others to join them. Teaching with this love of learning, enjoining others to come along, is an invitation to experience something alluring. Now perhaps not all love of learning, and teaching with this love, are motivated by the lure of beauty (since beauty is not the only alluring thing). But it seems many teachers, when teaching with a love of learning, are offering to others something potentially magnificent to behold.

It's not that teaching with a love of learning encounters, with every stone uncovered or every page turned, something beautiful, something exquisite. It's not that we offer during each class session, every 50-minute period, each and every day something beautiful to behold. We can't promise gems marvelous to look upon or passages wondrous to regard. What we can promise is the distinct possibility that we might place ourselves closer to the grace of great things or create openings to some "truly precious things." As Simone Weil writes, "The truly precious things are those forming ladders reaching toward the beauty of the world, openings onto it."[8] Beauty. Truly precious things. Grace. The grace of great things. When we teach with a love of learning we invite students to come closer to those great things. To stand next to and to gaze on something beautiful is to be in the presence of grace. To enable others to be in the presence of beauty is to help others touch the grace of great things; it is to view teaching, and education, as capable of creating openings to "truly precious things." It is a wonderful invitation to receive. It promises much delight and wonder (and, at times, pain and anguish). It promises an invitation worth receiving.

Today beauty tends to be commercialized or deemphasized and only rarely placed alongside the sacred.[9] But it need not be that way. Dillard's geodes, an orchid blooming, or a breathtaking theatrical performance, all seem to evoke timeless beauty.

Beauty is not the only lure in our love of learning. When we teach with a love of learning, there are other lures, other attractions, we offer students. At times, we offer clarity through the fog of cognitive dissonance and confusion and the mastery of skills that might sustain that clarity. At other times, we hold out the possibility of coming to terms with, and maybe combating, present and past inhumanity, cruelty, and injustice. And still other times, it seems simple personal delight and pleasure bring us to the classroom doors. I'm tempted to say that even these lures engage us in something sacred, something unprecedented, and life affirming. But I think that might be stretching it too far. I can reasonably say that teaching with a love of learning promises the distinct possibility that we will enable others to find some openings to those truly precious things, precious understandings, to experiences of significance. And I can also say that an education without beauty, that teaching without the promise of some glimpse of beauty, is not worth having.

AN INVITATION THAT EXPRESSES FAITH, INSISTENCE AND RESPECT

In teaching with a love of learning, we hope, we believe, that our students will be lured by the object of our love. We have to have faith that they too will see our subject's power. It seems inconceivable, in teaching with a love of learning, to expect anything but a similar love. For if the lure of our subject is an allure that is sacred, unprecedented, and life affirming, then this faith seems well founded. It appears well placed. And yet this faith is also, like many other faiths, somewhat tenuous and continually tested. It is tenuous in the way that any human potential may or may not be fulfilled. Some students may, while others may not, catch glimpses of those precious things. It appears to be tested daily. When months go by without glimpses of anything significant, then boredom, apathy, and indifference can result. In these instances, it is the students who then test the teacher. But when the connection is made, a vibrant and quite special energy is present. Teaching with a love of learning, inviting students to come and share our loves, relies on a faith in students' capacity to be attracted by the lure of our loves. Without this faith, it is difficult to imagine how we can invite students to join us.

Faith is necessary in this invitation, but alone it is insufficient. We need to have faith that our students will see the precious things and stand in their grace, but faith alone does not do the trick. A large part of teaching, of inviting students to share in our loves, is spent finding ways to connect student with subject. At times, a kind of insistence is required. An insistent invitation is one that resolutely conveys to students the value of what is being offered and persists in looking for ways to connect students to the grace of these great things.

[Some who teach] elementary students in our poor urban centers spend a good portion of their academic year simply trying to get students to the point where they can hear the invitation to learn.[10] When our material needs are frustrated or our emotional needs not met, when we don't feel secure or comfortable in our surroundings, then it is difficult to see or feel the intrigue of the material at hand. And sometimes the kids are ready but the openings to these precious worlds are closed. When Dillard bemoaned that absence of ponds and streams in the all-Black Homewood section of Pittsburgh, she was pointing out how our societal conditions shut out some, but not all, individuals from the landscape of learning. Personal and societal conditions affect the degree to which our faith is tested or supported and the amount of effort it takes to insist on the value of our precious things. Acting on this faith and persisting in our insistence is a complicated effort, and much comes into play. However, if we don't insist on the value of what we teach, have faith in our students, and persist in our attempt to make the educational connections, then our invitation tends to have a shallow and probably false ring.

Our invitation will also have a shallow ring if we don't respect—that is, honor—our students' integrity. To honor a student's integrity is to see the student as more than a trainable product, more than a walking mind. It is to see the student as someone who yearns for meaning in his or her life, who asks questions and inquires, who thinks and feels.

Discussion Questions

What is the relationship between loving learning and the curriculum as explained by the illustration (Dillard) used by Liston?

How does Liston's invitation metaphor relate to the concept of curriculum as conversation?

Daniel P. Liston is a professor at the University of Colorado at Boulder.

REFERENCES AND ENDNOTES

Article 1 References

Arnold, M. (1986). Literature and science. In M. Allot & R. H. Super (Eds.), *Matthew Arnold*. Oxford, UK: Oxford University Press.

Bruer, J. (1997). Education and the brain: A bridge too far. *Educational Researcher, 26*(8), 4–16.

Donald, M. (1991). *Origins of the modern mind*. Cambridge, MA: Harvard University Press.

Egan, K. (1997). *The educated mind: How cognitive tools shape our understanding*. Chicago: University of Chicago Press.

Fodor, J. (1983). *The modularity of mind*. Cambridge: MIT Press.

Fodor, J. (1985). Précis of "The modularity of mind." *Behavioral and Brain Sciences, 8*, 1–42.

Havelock, E. A. (1963). *Preface to Plato*. Cambridge, MA: Harvard University Press.

Havelock, E. A. (1982). *The literate revolution in Greece and its cultural consequences*. Princeton, NJ: Princeton University Press.

Havelock, E. A. (1986). *The muse learns to write*. New Haven, CT: Yale University Press.

Reiber, R. W., & Carton, A. S. (Eds.). (1987). The collected works of L. S. Vygotsky. New York: Plenum.

Rousseau, J. J. (1762/1979). *Émile: Or, on education* (Allan Bloom, Trans.). New York: Basic.

Spencer, H. (1966). *Educational: Intellectual, moral, and physical* (*Works of Herbert Spencer*, vol. XVI).

Article 2 Endnotes

1. Pope, D. C. (1999). *Doing school: How we are creating a generation of stressed out, materialistic, and miseducated students*. New Haven: Yale University Press.
2. Tyack, D. (1974). *The one best system*. Cambridge, MA: Harvard University Press.
3. Goodlad, J. I., & Anderson, R. H. (1987). *The nongraded elementary school*. New York: Teachers College Press.
4. Polanyi, M. (1966). *The tacit dimension*. Garden City, NY: Doubleday.
5. Schwab, J. J. (1978). The practical: A language for curriculum. In I. Westbury & N. Wilkof (Eds.), *Joseph J. Schwab: Science, curriculum, and liberal education*. Chicago: University of Chicago Press.
6. Eisner, E. (2002). *The arts and the creation of mind*. New Haven: Yale University Press.
7. Atkin, M. (1992). Teaching as research: An essay. *Teaching and Teacher Education*, 8, 381–390.
8. Bruner, J. (1960). *The process of education*. Cambridge, MA: Harvard University Press.
9. Ravitch, D. (1994). *Left back: A century of failed school reform*. New York: Teachers College Press.
10. Bruner, op. cit.
11. Eisner, E. (2002). From episteme, to phronesis, to artistry in the practice of teaching. *Teaching and Teacher Education*, 18, 375–85; and Eisner, E. (2002, Fall). What education can learn from the arts about the practice of education. *Journal of Curriculum and Supervision*, 4–16.
12. Eisner, E. (1994). *Cognition and curriculum reconsidered*. New York: Teachers College Press.
13. Dewey, J. (1938). *Experience and education*. New York: Macmillan.
14. Langer, S. (1967). *Mind: An essay on human feeling*. Baltimore: Johns Hopkins University Press.
15. Arnheim, R. (1969). *Visual thinking*. Berkeley: University of California Press.

16. Eisner, "From Episteme, to Phronesis."
17. Tyack, D., & Cuban, L. (1995). *Tinkering toward utopia*. Cambridge, MA: Harvard University Press.

Article 3 Endnotes

1. Sarajevo students, teachers dodge war. (1993, September 9). *Orlando Sentinel,* p. A4.
2. United Nations International Children's Education Fund (UNICEF) (1993). *I dream of peace*. New York: HarperCollins.
3. UNICEF, p. 9.
4. All quotations are taken from *I Dream of Peace.*
5. First schools open in Rwanda. (1993, September 20). *Orlando Sentinel*, p. A3.
6. UNICEF, op. cit., p. 11.
7. Jonathan Kozol (1991). *Savage inequalities*. New York: Crown.
8. UNICEF, op. cit., p. 56.

Article 4 Endnotes

1. See Wraga, W. G. (1999, Fall). The educational and political implications of curriculum alignment and standards-based reform. *Journal of Curriculum and Supervision, 15,* 4–25.
2. McNeil, L. M. (1986). *Contradictions of Control*. New York: Routledge and Kegan Paul.
3. Glatthorn, A. A., & Fontana, J. (in press). *Coping with standards, tests, and accountability: Voices from the classroom.*
4. Kendall, J. S., & Marzano, R. J. (1997). *Content knowledge* (2nd ed.). Alexandria, VA: Association of Supervision and Curriculum Development.
5. Kendall & Marzano.
6. Kendall & Marzano.
7. Jackson, P. W. (1968). *Life in classrooms*. New York: Holt, Rinehart, and Winston.
8. Eisner, E. W. (1985). *The educational imagination*. New York: Macmillan.
9. Gehrke, N. J., Knapp, M. S., & Sirotnik, K. A. (1992). In search of the school curriculum. In G. Grant (Ed.), *Review of Research in Education 18*. Washington, DC: American Educational Research Association.
10. Gehrke, Knapp, & Sirotnik.
11. National Council of Teachers of Mathematics (1989). *Curriculum and evaluation standards for the teaching of school mathematics*. Reston, VA: Author.
12. Black, P., & Wiliam, D. (1998, October). Inside the black box. *Phi Delta Kappan, 80,* 139–148.
13. Allington, R. L., & McGill-Franzen, A. (1992, Spring). Does high-stakes testing improve school effectiveness? *ERS Spectrum, 10,* 3–12.
14. Saxe, D. W. (1998). *State history standards*. New York: Fordham Foundation.

Article 5 References

Blythe, T., & Associates. (1998). *The teaching for understanding guide*. San Francisco: Jossey-Bass.

Bransford, J. D., Franks, J. J., Vye, N. J., & Sherwood, R. D. (1989). New approaches to instruction: Because wisdom can't be told. In S. Vosniadou & A. Ortony (Eds.), *Similarity and analogical reasoning* (pp. 470–497). New York: Cambridge University Press.

Bransford, J. D., & Schwartz, D. I. (1999). Rethinking transfer: A simple proposal with interesting implications. In A. Iran-Nejad & P. D. Pearson (Eds.), *Review of research in education* (Vol. 24, pp. 61–101). Washington, DC: American Educational Research Association.

Detterman, D., & Sternberg, R. (Eds.). (1992). *Transfer on trial*. Norwood, NJ: Ablex.

Gardner, H. (1999). *The disciplined mind*. New York: Simon and Schuster.

Grotzer, T. A. (2000, April). *How conceptual leaps in understanding the nature of causality can limit learning: An example from electrical circuits.* Paper presented at the annual conference of the American Educational Research Association, New Orleans, LA.

Grotzer, T. A. (2003). Learning to understand the forms of causality implicit in scientific explanations. *Studies in Science Education, 39,* 1–74.

Housen, A., Yenawine, P., & Arenas, A. (1991). *Visual thinking curriculum.* (Unpublished but used for research purposes). New York: Museum of Modern Art.

Linn, M. (2002). *The role of customization of innovative science curricula: Implications for design, practice, and professional development.* Symposium at the annual meeting of the National Association for Research in Science Teaching. New Orleans, LA.

Perkins, D. N. (1992). *Smart schools: From training memories to educating minds.* New York: Free Press.

Perkins, D. N., & Blythe, T. (1994). Putting understanding up front. *Educational Leadership, 51*(5), 4–7.

Perkins, D. N., & Grotzer, T. A. (2000, April). *Models and moves: Focusing on dimensions of causal complexity to achieve deeper scientific understanding.* Paper presented at the annual conference of the American Educational Research Association. New Orleans, LA.

Perkins, D. N., & Salomon, G. (1988). Teaching for transfer. *Educational Leadership, 46*(1), 22–32.

Ritchhart, R. (2002). *Intellectual character: What it is, why it matters, and how to get it.* San Francisco: Jossey-Bass.

Tishman, S. (2002). Artful reasoning. In T. Grotzer, I. Howick, S. Tishman, & D. Wise, *Art works for schools.* Lincoln, MA: DeCordova Museum and Sculpture Park.

Tishman, S., Perkins, D. N., & Jay, E. (1995). *The thinking classroom.* Boston: Allyn and Bacon.

Wiske, M. S. (Ed.). (1998). *Teaching for understanding: Linking research with practice.* San Francisco: Jossey-Bass.

Article 6 References

Anyon, J. (1980) Social class and the hidden curriculum of work. *Journal of Education, 162*(1), 67–92.

Ayers, W. (2001). *To teach: The journey of a teacher.* New York: Teachers College Press.

Bobbitt, F. (1918). *The curriculum.* Boston: Houghton Mifflin.

Bobbitt, F. (1924). *How to make a curriculum.* Boston: Houghton Mifflin.

Dewey, J. (1916). Democracy and education. New York: Macmillan.

Freire, P. (1970). *Pedagogy of the oppressed.* New York: Continuum.

Highet, G. (1950). *The art of teaching.* New York: Knopf.

Hopkins, L. T. (1954). *The emerging self in school and home.* New York: Harper & Brothers (also 1970 reprint by Greenwood of Westport, CT).

Rehak, J. (1996). Go back and circle the verbs. In W. Ayers & P. Ford (Eds), *City kids, city teachers: Reports from the front row* (pp. 270–285). New York: The New Press.

Schubert, W. H. (1986/1997). *Curriculum: Perspective, paradigm, and possibility.* New York: Macmillan.

Schubert, W. H. (1997). Character education from four perspectives on curriculum. In Molnar, A. (Ed.), *The construction of children's character* (1997 NSSE Yearbook, Part II) (pp. 17–30). Chicago: University of Chicago Press and the National Society for the Study of Education.

Schubert, W. H., & Lopez, A. L. (1980). *Curriculum books: The first eighty years.* Lanham, MD: University Press of America.

Schubert, W. H., & Lopez, A. L. (1993). Teacher lore as a basis for in-service education of teachers. *Teaching and Teachers' Work, 1*(4), 1–8.

Schubert, W. H., Lopez, A. L., Thomas, T. P., & Carroll, W. M. (2002). *Curriculum books: The first hundred years.* New York: Peter Lang.

Tyler, R. W. (1949). *Basic principles of curriculum and instruction.* Chicago: University of Chicago Press.

Article 7 References

Alexander, H. A. (1986). Eisner's aesthetic theory of evaluation. *Educational Theory, 36*(3): 259–70.

Alexander, H. A. (1989). Liberal education and open society: Absolutism and relativism in curriculum theory. *Curriculum Inquiry, 19*(1): 11–32.

Alexander, H. A. (2001). *Reclaiming goodness: Education and the spiritual quest.* Notre Dame, IN: University of Notre Dame Press.

Alexander, H. A. (2003). The Frankfort school and post-Zionist thought. In S. Sharan (Ed.), *Israel and the post Zionists* (pp. 71–86). Brighton: Sussex Academic Press.

Apple, M. W. (1979). *Ideology and Curriculum.* London: Routledge and Kegan Paul.

Aristotle (2001). *The basic works of Aristotle.* New York: Modern Library Classics.

Bernstein, R. J. (1983). *Beyond objectivism and relativism: Science, hermeneutics, and praxis.* Philadelphia: University of Pennsylvania Press.

Bobbitt, F. (1924). *How to make a curriculum.* Boston: Houghton Mifflin.

Bode, B. (1927). *Modern educational theories.* New York: Macmillan.

Charters, W. W. (1923). *Curriculum construction.* New York: Macmillan.

Counts, G. (1978). *Dare the schools build a new social order.* Carbondale: University of Southern Illinois Press.

Eisner, E. W. (1997). *The enlightened eye: Qualitative inquiry and the enhancement of educational practice.* New York: Macmillan.

Eisner, E. W. (2001). *The educational imagination: On the design and evaluation of school programs* (3rd ed). Saddle River, NJ: Prentice-Hall.

Ennis, R. H. (1996). *Critical thinking.* Upper Saddle River, NJ: Prentice-Hall.

Frankfurt, H. (1971). Freedom of will and the concept of a person. *Journal of Philosophy, 67*(1), 5–20.

Garrison, J. (1997). *Dewey and eros: Wisdom and desire in the art of teaching.* New York: Teachers College Press.

Goodman, N. (1978). *Ways of worldmaking.* Hassocks, UK: Harvest Press.

Gur-Zeev, I. (2003). *Destroying the other's collective memory.* New York: Peter Lang.

Hirst, P. H. (1974). *Knowledge and the curriculum.* London: Routledge and Kegan Paul.

Hirst, P. H., & Peters, R. S. (1970). *The logic of education.* London: Routledge and Kegan Paul.

Horkheimer, M., & Adorno, T. W. (1972). *Dialectic of Enlightenment.* New York: Herder and Herder.

Hume, D. (1953). *An enquiry concerning the principles of morals.* La Salle, IL: Open Court.

Kliebard, H. (1975). The Tyler rationale. In W. Pinar (Ed.), *Curriculum theorizing* (pp. 70–83). Berkeley, CA: McCutchan.

Langer, S. K. (1957). *Problems of art.* New York: Scribners.

Marx, K., & Engels, F. (1947). *The German ideology.* New York: International.

McLaren, P. (1989). *Life in schools: An introduction to critical pedagogy in the foundations of education.* New York: Longman.

McPeck, J. E. (1990). *Teaching critical thinking: Dialogue and dialectic.* New York: Routledge.

Moore, G. E. (1993). *Principa ethica.* Cambridge, UK: Cambridge University Press.

Murdoch, I. (1970). *The sovereignty of good.* London: Routledge and Kegan Paul.

Norris, S. P. (1992). *The generalizability of critical thinking.* New York: Teachers College Press.

Paul, R. (1994). *Critical thinking: What every person needs to survive in a rapidly changing world.* Rhonert Park, CA: Center for Critical Thinking and Moral Critique.

Peters, R. S. (1965). *Education as initiation.* London: Evans.

Phenix, P. H. (1971). Transcendence and the curriculum. *Teachers College Record, 73*(2).

Phillips, D. C., & Burbules, N. C. (2000). *Postpositivism and educational research.* New York: Rowman and Littlefield.

Plato (1987). *The republic.* London: Penguin.

Schwab, J. (1982). *Science, curriculum, and liberal education.* Chicago: University of Chicago Press.

Shulman, L., & Keisler, E. R. (Eds.). (1968). *Learning by discovery: A critical appraisal.* Chicago: Rand McNally.

Siegel, H. (1988). *Educating reason.* New York: Routledge.

Smith, N. (2002). *Charles Taylor: Meaning, morals, and modernity.* Cambridge, UK: Polity.

Spencer, H. (1945). *Education: Intellectual, moral, physical.* London: Watts.

Taylor, C. (1964). *The explanation of behaviour.* London: Routledge and Kegan Paul.

Taylor, C. (1989). *Sources of the self.* Cambridge, MA: Harvard University Press.

Taylor, C. (1991). *The ethics of authenticity.* Cambridge, MA: Harvard University Press.

Tyler, R. (1949). *Basic principles of curriculum and instruction.* Chicago: University of Chicago Press.

Walzer, M. (1994). *Thick and thin: Moral argument at home and abroad.* Notre Dame, IN: University of Notre Dame Press.

Watt, J. (1994). *Ideology, objectivity, and education.* New York: Teachers College Press.

Article 8 References

Aikin, W. M. (1942). *The story of the Eight-Year Study: With conclusions and recommendations.* New York: Harper & Brothers.

Alberty, H. B. (1937, April). The social philosophy of the school. *Thirty Schools Bulletin, 1,* 6–11.

Bestor, A. E. (1953). *Educational wastelands: The retreat from learning in our public schools.* Urbana: University of Illinois Press.

Bode, B. H. (1937). Democracy as a way of life. New York: Macmillan.

Bode, B. H. (1938a). *Progressive education at the crossroads*. New York: Newson and Company.

Bode, B. H. (1938b). The concept of needs in education. *Progressive Education, 15*(1), 7–9.

Bode, B. H. (1940). Needs and the curriculum. *Progressive Education, 17*(8), 532–537.

Commission on Secondary School Curriculum (CSSC) (1935). *Minutes, General Education Board, Rockefeller Foundation, New York, May 11–12*.

Commission on Secondary School Curriculum (CSSC) (1936). *Preliminary report of the Science Committee to the Commission on Secondary School Curriculum of the Progressive Education Association, General Education Board*. Rockefeller Foundation, New York.

Commission on Secondary School Curriculum (CSSC) (1938). *Science in general education: Suggestions for science teachers in secondary schools and in lower divisions of colleges, report of the committee on the function of science in general education*. New York: D. Appleton-Century.

Commission on Secondary School Curriculum (CSSC) (1940a). *Language in general education: Report of the Committee on the function of English in general education*. New York: D. Appleton-Century.

Commission on Secondary School Curriculum (CSSC) (1940b). *Mathematics in general Education: Report of the Committee on the function of mathematics in general education*. New York: D. Appleton-Century.

Commission on Secondary School Curriculum (CSSC) (1940c). *The social studies in general education: Report of the Committee on the function of the social studies in general education*. New York: D. Appleton-Century.

Commission on Secondary School Curriculum (CSSC) (1940d). *The visual arts in general education: Report of the Committee on the function of art in general education*. New York: D. Appleton-Century.

Davis, M. (1936) *The lost generation: A portrait of American youth today*. New York: Macmillan.

Douglass, H. R. (Ed.). (1950). *Education for life adjustment: Its meaning and implementation*. New York: Ronald Press.

Gillis, J. R. (1974). *Youth and history: Tradition and change in European age relations 1770–present*. New York: Academic Press.

Hollingworth, L. S. (1928). *The psychology of the adolescent*. New York: D. Appleton-Century.

Kliebard, H. M. (1986). *The struggle for the American curriculum, 1893–1958*. Boston: Routledge & Kegan Paul.

Kridel, C., & Bullough, Jr., R. B. (2002). What was the Eight-Year Study? Misperceptions and misconceptions. *Journal of Curriculum and Supervision, 18*(1), 63–82.

Lagemann, E. C. (2000). *An elusive science: The troubling history of education research*. Chicago: University of Chicago Press.

Meek, L. H. (1943). *The personal–social development of boys and girls with implications for secondary education*. New York: Committee on Workshops, Progressive Education Association.

National Education Association, Commission on the Reorganization of Secondary Education (1918). *The cardinal principles of secondary education* (Bulletin No. 35). Washington, DC: U.S. Bureau of Education.

Taba, H. (1962). *Curriculum development: Theory and practice*. New York: Harcourt, Brace and World.

Tanner, D., & Tanner, L. (1975). *Curriculum development theory into practice*. New York: Macmillan.

Thayer, V. T. (1940). V. T. Thayer replies. *Progressive Education, 17*(8), 437–540.

Thayer, V. T., Zachry, C. B., & Kotinsky, R. (1939). *Reorganizing secondary education*. New York: D. Appleton-Century.

Tyler, R. W. (1950). *Basic principles of curriculum and instruction: Syllabus for education 360*. Chicago: University of Chicago Press.

Zachry, C. B. (1937). *Seminar report, January 14*. New York: Rockefeller Foundation, General Education Board.

Zachry, C. B. (1940). *Emotion and conduct in adolescence: For the commission on secondary school curriculum*. New York: D. Appleton-Century.

Zepper, J. T. (1970). V. T. Thayer: Progressive educator. *Educational Forum, 34*(4), 495–504.

Article 9 References

Apple, M. W., & Beane, J. A. (Eds.). (1995). *Democratic schools*. Alexandria, VA: Association for Supervision and Curriculum Development.

Bode, B. H. (1935). Education and social reconstruction. *Social Frontier, 1*(4), 18–22.

Cremin, L. A. (1961). *The transformation of the school: Progressivism in American education, 1876–1957*. New York: Knopf.

Csikszentmihalyi, M. (1996). *Creativity: Flow and the psychology of discovery and invention*. New York: HarperCollins.

Cuban, L. (1995). Foreward in D. Tanner and L.N. Tanner (eds.) *Curriculum Development: Theory into Practice,* 3rd Ed. Upper Saddle Creek, NJ: Simon and Schuster.

Dewey, J. (1987). Education and social change. In J. A. Boydston (Ed.), *The later works of John Dewey, 1925–1953* (Vol. 12, pp. 408–417). Carbondale and Edwardsville: Southern Illinois University Press). (Originally published in 1937.)

Faulkner, W. (1966). *Requiem for a Nun*. New York: Random House.

Foshay, W. (1975). Foreword. In D. Tanner & L. N. Tanner (Eds.), *Curriculum development: Theory into practice* (p. vii). New York: Macmillan.

Hargreaves, A., & Moore, S. (2000). Curriculum integration and classroom relevance: A study of teachers' practice. *Journal of Curriculum and Supervision, 15*(2), 89–112.

Hlebowitsh, P. S. (1992). Amid behavioral and behaviouristic objectives: Reappraising appraisals of the Tyler Rational. *Journal of Curriculum Studies, 24*(6), 533–547.

Hlebowitsh, P. S. (1993). *Radical curriculum theory reconsidered: A historical approach*. New York: Teachers College Press.

Hlebowitsh, P. S., & Wraga, W. G. (1995). Social class analysis in the early progressive tradition. *Curriculum Inquiry, 25*(1), 7–21.

Kuhn, T. S. (1970). *The structure of scientific revolutions* (2nd ed.). Chicago: University of Chicago Press.

Lincoln, Y. S. (1992). Curriculum studies and the traditions of inquiry: The humanistic tradition. In P. W. Jackson (Ed.), *Handbook of research on curriculum* (pp. 79–97). New York: Macmillan.

Marshall, J. D., Sears, J.T., & Schubert, W. H. (2000). *Turning points in curriculum: A contemporary American memoir*. Upper Saddle River, NJ: Merrill.

Milburn, G. (2000). Understanding curriculum [Review of the book *Understanding curriculum: An introduction to the study of historical and contemporary curriculum discourses*]. *Journal of Curriculum Studies, 32*(3), 445–452.

Myrdall, G. (1944). Appendix 2: A methodological note on facts and valuations in social science. In G. Myrdal (Ed.), *The America dilemma: The Negro problem and modern democracy* (pp. 1035–1064). New York: Harper & Brothers.

Pinar, W. F. (1988). The reconceptualization of curriculum studies, 1987: A personal retrospective. *Journal of Curriculum and Supervision, 3*(2), 157–167.

Pinar, W. F. (1992). "Dreamt into existence by others": Curriculum theory and school reform. *Theory Into Practice, 31*(3), 228–235.

Pinar, W. F. (Ed.). (1998). *Curriculum: Toward new identities*. New York: Garland.

Pinar, W. F., Reynolds, W. M., Slattery, P. and Taubman, P. M. (1995). *Understanding curriculum: An introduction to the study of historical and contemporary curriculum discourses*. New York: Peter Lang.

Porter, L. (1998). *John Coltrane: His life and music*. Ann Arbor: University of Michigan Press.

Reid, W. A. (1992). The state of curriculum inquiry [Review of the book *Forms of curriculum inquiry*]. *Journal of Curriculum Studies, 24*(2), 165–177.

Rorty, R. (1998). *Achieving our country: Leftist thought in twentieth-century America*. Cambridge, MA: Harvard University Press.

Schwab, J. J. (1969). The practical: A language for curriculum. *School Review, 78*(1), 1–23.

Slattery, P. (1995). *Curriculum development in the postmodern era*. New York: Garland.

Tanner, D., & Tanner, L. N. (1990). *History of the school curriculum*. New York: Macmillan.

Whipple, G. H. (Ed.). (1926). *The foundations of curriculum-making,* 26th Yearbook, Part 2, of the National Society for the Study of Education. Bloomington, IL: Public School Publishing.

Wraga, W. G. (1996). Toward a curriculum theory for the new century [Review of the book *Curriculum development in the postmodern era*]. *Journal of Curriculum Studies, 28*(4), 463–474.

Wraga, W. G. (1998). "Interesting, if true": Historical perspectives on the "reconceptualization" of curriculum studies. *Journal of Curriculum and Supervision, 14*(1), 5–28.

Wraga, W. G. (1999a). "Extracting sun-beams out of cucumber": The retreat from practice in reconceptualized curriculum studies. *Educational Researcher, 28*(1), 4–13.

Wraga, W. G. (1999b). The continuing arrogation of the curriculum field: A rejoinder to Pinar. *Educational Researcher, 28*(1), 16.

Wright, H. K. (2000). Nailing Jell-O to the wall: Pinpointing aspects of state-of-the-art curriculum theorizing. *Educational Researcher, 29*(5), 4–13.

Article 11 References

Board of Education Minutes (1922). Columbus, OH.

Board of Education Minutes (1937). Columbus, OH.

Boris, J. J. (1928). *Who's who in colored America: A biographical dictionary of notable living persons of African descent in America. Second edition, 1928–1929*. New York: Who's Who in Colored America Corporation.

Butchart, R. E. (1988). Outthinking and outflanking the owners of the world: A historiography of the African American struggle for education. *History of Education Quarterly, 28*(3), 333–366.

Champion guide. (1947). Columbus, OH: Author.

Champion middle school: Hall of champions. (1977). Columbus, OH: Designs Etcetera.

Clark , L. (1997, June 15). Interview with author.

Cole, J. (1993). *Conversations: Straight talk with America's sister president*. New York: Doubleday.

Cook, R. C. (1934). *Who's who in American education*. New York: Burckel & Associates.

Dawson, D. J. (1984). Community participation in urban schooling. A critical assessment. *Urban Review, 16*(3), 177–186.

Dempsey, V., & Noblit, C. (1993). The demise of caring in an African-American community: One consequence of school deseg-regation. *Urban Review, 25*(1), 47–61.

Dilworth, M. (1988). Black teachers: A vanishing tradition. *Urban League Review, 11*(2), 54–58.

Franklin, V. P. (1979). *The education of Black Philadelphia: The social and educational history of a minority community, 1900–1950*. New York: Lawrence Hill Books.

Franklin, V. P. (1990). "They rose and fell together": African American educators and community leadership, 1795–1954. *Journal of Education, 172*(3), 39–64.

Frontiers of America. (1954). Advancement. Columbus, OH: Chapter of the Frontiers of America, Inc.

Futrell, M. H. (1985). *The Black teacher as a leader: Working paper*. Presented at the annual meeting of the National Alliance of Black School Educators, New York, NY.

Gaines, K. K. (1996). *Uplifting the race: Black leadership, politics, and culture in the twentieth century*. Chapel Hill: University of North Carolina Press.

Gatewood, W. B. (1990). *Aristocrats of color: The Black elite, 1880–1920*. Bloomington: Indiana University Press.

Giddings, P. (1984*). When and where I enter: The impact of Black women on race and sex in America*. New York: Bantam Books.

Guy-Sheftall, B. (1990). *Daughters of sorrow: Attitudes toward Black women, 1880–1920*. New York: Carlson.

Hale, J. (1986). Black children: Their roots, culture and learning styles. Baltimore, MD: Johns Hopkins University Press.

Hale, J. (1994). *Unbank the fire: Visions for the education of African American children*. Baltimore, MD: Johns Hopkins University Press.

Hale, J. (2001). Learning while Black: Creating educational excellence for African-American children. Baltimore, MD: Johns Hopkins University Press.

Irvine, J. J. (1989). Beyond role models: An examination of cultural influences on the pedagogical perspectives of Black teachers. *Peabody Journal of Education, 66*(4), 51–63.

Jones, F. C. (1981). *A traditional model of educational excellence: Dunbar High School of Little Rock, Arkansas*. Washington, DC: Howard University Press.

Kliebard, H. M. (1987). *The struggle for the Amen can curriculum: 1893–1958*. New York: Routledge

Laney, L. C. (1899, September). The burden of the educated colored woman. *Southern Workman,* 341–346.

Lightfoot, S. L. (1983). *The good high school: Portraits of character and culture*. New York: Basic Books.

Lomotey, K. (1989). *African American principals: School leadership and success*. Westport, CT: Greenwood Press.

McCluskey, A. T. (1989). *We specialize in the wholly impossible: African American women school founders and their mission*. Paper presented at the Women Studies Program, Indiana University, Bloomington, IN. Martin, O. (1998, May 20). Interview with author.

Mitchell, J. A. (1924). The problems of the Negro child of school age in the light of mental tests. *Educational Research Bulletin,* 322–330.

Moody, C. D., & Moody, C. D. (1988). Elements of effective Black schools. *Urban League Review, 11*(2), 176–186.

Orfield, G., & Eaton, S. E. (1996). Dismantling desegregation: The quiet reversal of *Brown v. Board of Education*. New York: Basic Books.

Pearson, R. (1998, May 19). Interview with author.

Perkins, L. M. (1987). *Fannie Jackson Coppin and the Institute for Colored Youth, 1865–1902*. New York: Garland.

Perkins, L. M. (1989). The history of Blacks in teaching: Growth and decline within the profession. In D. Warren (Ed.), *American teachers: Histories of a profession at work* (pp. 344–369). New York: Macmillan.

Philipsen, M. (1994). The second promise of *Brown. Urban Review, 26*(4), 257–272.

Pitts, W. E. (2003). *A victory of sorts: Desegregation in a southern community*. Lanham, MD: University Press of America.

Saunders, J. (1992, January 20). Interview with author.

Siddle Walker, V. (1996). *Their highest potential: An African American school community in the segregated South*. Chapel Hill: University of North Carolina Press.

Smith, W. D., & Chunn, E. W. (1989). *Black education: A quest for equity and excellence*. New Brunswick, NJ: Transaction Publishers.

Sowell, T. (1976). Patterns of Black excellence. *Public Interest, 43*, 26–58.

Stewart, J., Meier, K. J., & England, R. E. (1989). In quest of role models: Change in Black teacher representation in urban school districts. *Journal of Negro Education, 58*(2), 140–152.

Stringfield, S. (1997). Research on effective instruction for at-risk students: Implications for the St. Louis public schools. *Journal of Negro Education, 66*(3), 259–288.

Trent, W. T. (1997a). Outcomes of school desegregation: Findings from longitudinal research. *Journal of Negro Education, 66*(3), 255–257.

Trent, W. T. (1997b). Why the gap between Black and White performance in school?: A report on the effects of race on student achievement in the St. Louis public schools. *Journal of Negro Education, 66*(3), 320–329.

Walker, E. (1996, May 9). Interview with author.

Ward Randolph, A. (1996). *A historical analysis of an urban school: A case study of a northern de facto segregated school. Champion avenue school: 1910–1996.* Doctoral dissertation, The Ohio State University.

Watkins, W. H. (1993). Black curriculum orientations: A preliminary inquiry. *Harvard Educational Review, 63,* 321–338.

White, R. Y. (1936). We too built Columbus (1st ed.). Columbus, OH: Stoneman Press.

Wright, L. (1996, May 13). Interview with author.

Yenser, T. (1932). *Who's who in colored America: A biographical dictionary of notable living persons of African descent in America. Third edition, 1930–1932.* New York: Burckel & Associates.

Article 12 References

Adelman, C. (2006). *The toolbox revisited: Paths to degree completion from high school through college.* Washington, DC: U.S. Department of Education.

Carter, H. M. (2004). *A case study of the Middle College High School, 1972–2003: An effort to improve the persistence of at risk students in high school and facilitate their access to college.* Doctoral dissertation, New York University.

Cohen, A. M., & Brawer, F. B. (2003). *The American community college* (4th ed.). San Francisco: Jossey-Bass.

Cohen, M. (2001). *Transforming the American high school: New directions for state and local policy.* Washington, DC: The Aspen Institute, Program on Education in a Changing Society.

Eby, F. (1928). The four-year junior college and the advent of the 6-4-4 plan. *Educational Administration and Supervision, 14,* 536–542.

Eby, F. (1929). Should the junior college be united with the senior high school? *Nation's Schools, 3,* 33–38.

Eby, F. (1932). The four-year junior college. *Junior College Journal, 2*(8), 471–489.

Eells, W. C. (1931). *The junior college.* Boston: Houghton Mifflin.

Four-School Study Commission. (1970). *16–20: The liberal education of an age group.* New York: College Entrance Examination Board.

Goldberger, S., & Haynes, L. (2005). *Designing and financing an integrated program of college study: Lessons for the California Academy of Liberal Studies.* Boston: Jobs for the Future. Available from http://www.earlycolleges.org/Downloads/calsechs.pdf

Goodwin, G. L. (1976). The nature and the nurture of the community college movement. *Community College Frontiers, 4*(3), 5–13.

Hoffman, H., & Vargas, J. (2005). *Integrating grades 9–14. State policies to support and sustain early college high schools.* Boston: Jobs for the Future. Available from http://www.earlycolleges.org/Downloads/Integrating9t014.pdf

Huebner, T. A., & Corbett, G. C. (2004). *Rethinking high school: Five profiles of innovative models for student success.* Seattle, WA: Bill and Melinda Gates Foundation. Available from http://www.earlycolleges.org/Downloads/RethinkingHigh School_WestEd.pdf

Hughes, K. L., Karp, M. M., Fermin, B. J., & Bailey, T. R. (2005). *Pathways to college access and success.* Washington, DC: U.S. Department of Education, Office of Vocational and Adult Education.

Jacobson, J. (2005, March 11). The early-college experiment. *Chronicle of Higher Education, 51*(27), A36.

Jobs for the Future. (2004). *The early college high school initiative at a glance.* Boston: Author. Available from http://www .earlycolleges.org/Downloads/ECHSIAtAGlance120204.pdf

Jobs for the Future. (2005). *Early college high school initiative by the numbers.* Boston: Author. Available from http://www .earlycolleges.org/Downloads/ECHSIByNumbersLong.pdf

Jobs for the Future. (n.d.). *Early college high school initiative: Core principles.* Boston: Author. Available from http://www .earlycolleges.org/Downloads/CorePrinciples.pdf

Kisker, C. B. (n.d.). *Integrating high school and community college: A historical policy analysis.* Doctoral dissertation in preparation, University of California, Los Angeles.

Koos, L. V. (1925). *The junior college movement.* Boston: Ginn and Company.

Koos, L. V. (1946). *Integrating high school and college: The six-four-four plan at work.* New York: Harper and Brothers.

Krugg, E. A. (1972). Robert J. Havighurst: Pursuit of excellence. In H. Walberg & A. T. Kopan (Eds.), *Rethinking urban education* (pp. 317–324). San Francisco: Jossey-Bass.

Lieberman, J. E. (Ed.). (1988). *Collaborating with high schools* (New Directions for Community Colleges No. 63). San Francisco: Jossey-Bass.

Lieberman, J. (2004). *The early college high school concept: Requisites for success.* Boston: Jobs for the Future. Available from http://www.earlycolleges.org/Downloads/ECHSConcept.pdf

New York Department of Education. (2003). *Annual school report: Middle College High School.* Albany, NY: Author.

Orrill, B. (n.d.). *Grades 11–14: The heartland or wasteland of American education?* Washington, DC: National Council on Education and the Disciplines. Available from http://www.earlyeolleges.org/Downloads/Heartland.pdf

Pasadena City College. (2003). *Pasadena City College history.* Pasadena, CA: Author. Available from http://www.pasadena.edu/about/history

Pedersen, R. P. (2000). *The origins and development of the early public junior colleges: 1900–1940.* Doctoral dissertation, Columbia University, New York.

Pennington, H. (2002, February 15–18). Better and faster: Accelerating advancement in school and work. Paper prepared for the Aspen Institute Congressional Seminar, Aspen, CO.

President's Commission on Higher Education. (1947). *Higher education for American democracy* (6 vols.). New York: Harper & Brothers.

Riesman D. (1956). *The academic procession: Constraint and variety in American higher education.* Lincoln: University of Nebraska Press.

Stoel, C. F. (1988). History of the high school connection. In J. E. Lieberman (Ed.), *Collaborating with high schools* (New Directions for Community Colleges No. 63, pp. 13–33). San Francisco: Jossey-Bass.

U.S. Department of Education. (1998). *New American high schools: Profiles of the nation's leading edge schools.* Washington, DC: Author.

Venezia, A., Callan, P. M., Finney, J. E., Kirst, M. W., & Usdan, M. D. (2005). *The governance divide: A report on a four-state study on improving college readiness and success.* San Jose, CA: Institute for Educational Leadership, National Center for Public Policy and Higher Education, and the Stanford Institute for Higher Education Research.

Webb, M. (2004). *What is the cost of planning and implementing early college high school?* Boston: Jobs for the Future. Available from http://www.earlycolleges.org/Downloads/FinanceReport.pdf

Wechsler, H. S. (2001). *Access to success in the urban high school: The middle college movement.* New York: Teachers College Press.

Wolk, R. A. (2005). *It's kind of different: Student experiences in two early college high schools.* Boston: Jobs for the Future. Available from http://www.earlycolleges.org/Downloads/KindOfDifferent.pdf

Article 13 References

Abelmann, C., Elmore, R., Even, J., Kenyon, S., & Marshall, J. (1999). *When accountability knocks, will anyone answer?* (Research Report No. RR-42). Philadelphia, PA: Consortium for Policy Research in Education.

Buechler, M. (1996, January). *Charter schools: Legislation and results after four years* (Policy Report No. PR-B13). Bloomington: Indiana Education Policy Center.

Caldwell. B. J. (1996, September). *Factors associated with improved learning outcomes in the local management of schools: Early findings from Victoria's schools of the future.* Paper presented at the Annual Conference of the British Educational Management and Administration Society, Coventry, England.

Center for Education Reform. (2000). Information available at http//www.edreform.com

David, J. L. (1996). The who, what, and why of site-based management. *Educational Leadership, 52*(4), 4–9.

Education Week (1999, January 11). School accountability in 50 states. *Quality counts: Rewarding results, punishing failure* (Special Issue), *28*(17), 81–101.

Elmore, R. F. (1995). Structural reform and educational practice. *Educational Researcher, 24*(9), 23–26.

Finn, C. E., Jr., Manno, B. V., & Bierlein, L. (1996) *Charter schools in action: What have we learned?* Indianapolis: Hudson Institute Educational Excellence Network.

Gusky, T. R., & Peterson, K. D. (1996). The road to classroom change. *Educational Leadership, 53*(4), 10–14.

Kelley, C. (1997). Teacher compensation and organization. *Educational Evaluation and Policy Analysis, 19*(1), 15–28.

Kelley, C., & Odden, A. (1995, September). *Reinventing teacher compensation systems* (Finance Brief no. 6). Madison, WI: Consortium for Policy Research in Education.

Kirst, M. (1990). *Accountability: Implications for state and local policy-makers*. Washington, DC: U.S. Department of Education, Office of Educational Research and Improvement, Information Services.

Levacic, R. (1995). *Local management of schools: Analysis and practice*. Buckingham, England: Open University Press.

Lindle, J. C. (1996). Lessons from Kentucky about school-based decision-making. *Educational Leadership, 53*(4), 20–23.

Louis, K. S., & Kruse, S. D. (1995). *Professionalism and community: Perspectives on reforming urban schools*. Newbury Park, CA: Corwin Press.

Louis, K. S., Marks, H. M., & Kruse, S. (1996). Teachers' professional community in restructuring schools. *American Educational Research Journal, 33*(4), 757–798.

Murphy, J., & Beck, L. (1995). *School-based management as school reform: Taking stock*. Thousand Oaks, CA: Corwin Press.

Murphy, J., & Louis, K. S. (Eds.). (1994). *Reshaping the principalship: Insights from transformational reform efforts*. Newbury Park, CA: Corwin Press.

Nathan, J. (1996). *Charter schools: Creating hope and opportunity for American education*. San Francisco: Jossey-Bass.

Newmann, F. M., King, M. B., & Rigdon, M. (1997). Accountability and school performance: Implications from restructuring schools. *Harvard Educational Review, 67*(1), 41–74.

Newmann, F. M., & Wehlange, G. G. (1995). *Successful school restructuring: A report to the public educators*. Madison: University of Wisconsin–Madison, Center on the Organization and Restructuring of Schools.

Odden, A., & Odden, E. (1994). *School-based management: The view from down under* (Brief no. 62). Madison: Center on the Organization and Restructuring of Schools, University of Wisconsin–Madison.

Robertson, P., Wohlstetter, P., & Mohrman, S. A. (1995). Generating curriculum and instructional changes through school-based management. *Educational Administration Quarterly, 31*, 375–404.

RPP International. (1998). *A national study of charter schools: Second year report*. Washington, DC: Department of Education, Office of Educational Research and Improvement.

Slavin, R. E., Madden, N. A., Dolan, L. J., Wasik, B. A., Ross, S., Smith, L., & Dianda, M. (1996). Success for all: A summary of research. *Journal of Education for Students Placed at Risk, 1*(1), 41–76.

Wohlstetter, P. I., & Anderson, L. (1994). What can U.S. charter schools learn from England's grant-maintained schools? *Phi Delta Kappan, 75*, 486–491.

Wohlstetter, P. I., & Briggs, K. (1994). The principal's role in school-based management. *Principal, 74*, 14–17.

Wohlstetter, P. I., Mohrman, S. A., & Robertson, P. J. (1997). Successful school-based management: A lesson for restructuring urban schools. In D. Ravitch, & J. J. Viteritti (Eds.), *New schools for a new century: The redesign of urban education*. New Haven, CT: Yale University Press.

Wohlstetter, P., Smyer, R., & Mohrman, S. A. (1994). New boundaries for school-based management: The high involvement model. *Educational Evaluation and Policy Analysis, 16*, 268–286.

Article 14 Endnotes

1. See Hrycauk, M. (2002). A safety net for second-grade students. *Journal of Staff Development, 23*, 55–58; and Joyce, B., Hrycauk, M., & Calhoun, E. (2001, March). A second chance for struggling readers,. *Educational Leadership,* 42–47.

2. Calhoun, E. (1998). *Literacy for the primary grades*. Saint Simons Island, GA: Phoenix Alliance.

3. Juel, C. (1988). Learning to read and write. *Journal of Educational Psychology, 80*, 437–447.

4. In a long-term study of students who had experienced formal reading instruction in kindergarten, Ralph Hanson and Donna Farrell followed students through their high school years and found that the effects could be detected even as they graduated. See Hanson, R., & Farrell, D. (1995). The Long-term effects on high school seniors of learning to read in kindergarten. *Reading Research Quarterly, 30*, 908–933. Delores Durkin's work on the positive effects of learning to read early is well known but has not changed the minds of the large number of experts on early childhood education who are more worried about damage than about benefits. See Durkin, D., (1966). *Children who read early*. New York: Teachers College Press.

5. See, for example, Nagy, W., Herman, P., & Anderson, R. (1985). Learning words from context. *Reading Research Quarterly, 19*, 304–330.

6. A crisp general review can be found in Duke, N., & Pearson, P. D. (2002). Effective practices for developing reading comprehension. In A. Farstrup & J. Samuels (Eds.), *What research has to say about reading instruction* (3rd ed.) (pp. 205–242). Newark, DE: International Reading Association.

7. Students need to learn to inquire into word patterns and build word-identification skills around concepts about word structures. A fine summary is provided by Ehri, L. *Phases of acquisition in learning to read words and instructional implications.* Paper presented at the annual meeting of the American Educational Research Association, Montreal, 1999.

8. The connection of early writing to beginning reading is growing clearer. See Englart, C., et al. (1991). Making strategies and self-talk visible. *American Educational Research Journal, 28*, 337–372.

9. Several lines of research are gradually discovering a great deal about comprehension strategies and how to develop them. See Garner, R. (1987). *Metacognition and reading comprehension.* Norwood, NJ: Ablex; and Pressley, M., et al. (1995). *Cognitive strategy instruction that really improves student performance.* Cambridge, MA: Brookline.

10. The Picture Word Inductive Model provides a set of ways to track student progress. Some variables (such as vocabulary development) are tracked weekly or more often. Others are tracked a little less frequently. See Calhoun, E. (1999). *Teaching beginning reading and writing with the Picture Word Inductive Model.* Alexandria, VA: Association for Supervision and Curriculum Development; and Joyce, B., & Showers, B. (2002). *Student achievement through staff development.* Alexandria, VA: Association for Supervision and Curriculum Development.

11. Stauffer, R. (1970). *The language-experience approach to the teaching of reading.* New York: Harper & Row.

12. Joyce & Showers, op. cit.

13. Gunning, T. (1968). *Best books for beginning reader*s. Boston: Allyn and Bacon.

14. Wiederholt, J. L., & Bryant, B. (2001). *Gray Oral Reading Tests.* Austin, TX: Pro-Ed.

Article 15 References

Bauman, J. F. (1984). Implications for reading instruction from research on teacher and school effectiveness. *Journal of Reading, 28,* 109–115.

Bean, T. (1997). Preservice teachers' selection and use of content area literacy strategies. *Journal of Educational Research, 90*(3), 154–163.

Beane, J. (1993). Problems and possibilities for an integrative curriculum. *Middle School Journal, 25*(1), 18–29.

Binkley, M. R., & Williams, T. (1996). *Reading literacy in the United States: Findings from the IEA Reading Literacy Study.* Washington, DC: National Center for Educational Statistics.

Curran, C. E. (1997). Analyzing story characteristics: Facilitating higher level comprehension skills in students. *Intervention in School and Clinic, 32*(5), 312–315.

Donahue, P. L., Voelkl, K. E., Campbell, J. R., & Mazzeo, J. (1999). *NAEP 1998 reading report card for the nation and the states.* Washington, DC: U.S. Department of Education, Office of Educational Research and Improvement. Available online at: http://nces.ed.gov/pubsearch/pubsinfo.asp?pubid=1999500

Farr, R., & Tone, B. (1998). *Portfolio and performance assessment: Helping students evaluate their progress as readers and writers* (2nd ed.). New York: Harcourt Brace.

Georgia Department of Education. (2001). *1999–2000 Georgia public education report card: Chatham County schools – 625.* Retrieved July, 29, 2002, from http://accountability.doe.k12.ga.us/report2000/Educ/625.pdf

Georgia Department of Education. (2002). *2000–2001 Georgia public education report card: Chatham County schools–625.* Retrieved July, 29, 2002, from http://accountability.doe.k12.ga.us/report2001/Educ/625.pdf

Goodlad, J. I. (1984). *A place called school: Prospects for the future.* New York: McGraw-Hill.

Hoffman, J. V., Assaf, L. C., & Paris, S. G. (2001). High-stakes testing in reading: Today in Texas, tomorrow? *Reading Teacher, 54*(5), 482–492.

Horkay, N. (Ed.). (1999). *The NAEP guide.* Washington, DC: National Center for Education Statistics, U.S. Department of Education.

Jensen, L. C., Strauser, E. B., & Worley, M. T. (2001). *Learning together: Connecting the college and community in an adult literacy program.* Presented at the 12th Annual Conference on College Teaching and Learning, Jacksonville, FL.

Ormrod, J. E. (1999). *Human learning* (3rd ed.). Upper Saddle River, NJ: Prentice Hall.

Pfordresher, J. (1991). *Trends and issues report: The commission on literature.* Presented to the National Council of Teachers of English, Urbana, IL.

Shannon, P. (1991). *Trends and issues report: The commission on reading.* Presented to the National Council of Teachers of English, Urbana, IL.

Shepard, L. (1987). *The assessment of readiness for schools: Psychometric and other considerations.* Presented to the National Center for Educational Statistics, Washington, DC.

Stevenson, C., & Carr, J. (Eds.). (1993). *Integrated studies in middle grades: "Dancing through walls."* Williston, VT: Teachers College Press.

U.S. Census Bureau. (2002). *State and county quick facts: Georgia, Chatham County.* Retrieved July, 29, 2002, from http://quickfacts.census.gov/qfd/states/13/13051.html

Whitin, P. (1996). Exploring visual responses to literature. *Research in the Teaching of English, 30*(1), 114–140.

Article 16 References

Baker, F. (2004). State standards. *Media literacy clearinghouse.* Retrieved February 24, 2004, from http://www .med.sc.edu:1081/statelit.htm

Carnes, M. C. (Ed.). (1995). *Past imperfect: History according to the movies.* New York: Henry Holt.

Hobbs, R. (1997). Expanding the concept of literacy. In R. Kubey (Ed.), *Media literacy in the information age* (pp. 163–183). New Brunswick, NJ: Transaction.

Hobbs, R. (2000). *Assignment: Media literacy.* Bethesda, MD: Discovery Communications.

Kubey, R., & Baker, F. (2000, Spring). Has media literacy found a curricular foothold? *Telemedium, The Journal of Media Literacy, 46*, 8–9, 30.

Scheibe, C., & Rogow, F. (2004). *12 basic principles for incorporating media literacy and critical thinking into any curriculum* (2nd ed.). Ithaca, NY: Project Look Sharp—Ithaca College.

Sperry, C. (2003). *Media construction of war: A critical reading of history.* Ithaca, NY: Project Look Sharp—Ithaca College.

Thoman, E. (1999, February). Skills and strategies for media education. *Educational Leadership, 46*, 50–54.

Article 17 Endnotes

1. See *The civic mission of schools.* New York: Carnegie Corporation and Center for Information and Research in Civic Learning, 2003).

2. For an overview of positions on critical thinking, see Bailin, S., & Siegel, H. (2003). Critical thinking. In Nigel Blake et al. (Eds.), *The Blackwell guide to the philosophy of education* (pp. 181–193). Oxford: Blackwell.

3. Swofford, A. (2003). *Jarhead* (pp. 6–7). New York: Scribner.

4. See the accounts in Le Shan, L. (1992). *The psychology of war.* Chicago: Nobel Press.

5. Two WWI novels that might be helpful here: Hemingway, E. (1929). *A farewell to arms.* New York: Scribner; and Remarque, E. M. (1929). *All quiet on the western front.* London: Putnam's. A book of WWI poetry is also useful: Macdonald, L. (Ed.). (2000). *Anthem for doomed youth.* London: Folio Society. Students familiar with Tony Hillerman's Navajo mystery novels might enjoy his 2001 account of service in WWII (*Seldom disappointed.* New York: HarperCollins).

6. See Moskos, C. C., & Whiteclay Chambers II, J. (1993). *The new conscientious objection.* Oxford: Oxford University Press; see also True, M. (1995). *An energy field more intense than war.* Syracuse, NY: Syracuse University Press.

7. Hedges, C. (2002, Winter). War is a force that gives us meaning. *Amnesty Now,* p. 10; see also idem, *War is a force that gives us meaning* (New York: Public Affairs, 2002).

8. James, W. (1929). *The varieties of religious experience* (Reprint) (p. 359). New York: Modern Library.

9. See, for example, Brock-Utne, B. (1985). *Educating for peace: A feminist perspective.* New York: Pergamon Press; and Reardon, B. A. (1985). *Sexism and the war system.* New York: Teachers College Press.

10. See Kimmel, M. S. (1993). "Clarence, William, Iron Mike, Tailhook, Senator Packwood, Spur Posse, Magic, . . . and us," in E. Buchward, P. R. Fletcher, & M. Roth (Eds.), *Transforming a rape culture* (pp. 121–138). Minneapolis: Milkweed Editions.

11. Klein, J., & Chancer, L. S. (2000). "Masculinity matters: The omission of gender from high-profile school violence cases. In S. Urso Spina (Ed.), *Smoke and mirrors* (pp. 129–162). Lanham, MD: Rowman & Littlefield.

12. See Ruddick, S. (1989). *Maternal thinking: Toward a politics of peace.* Boston: Beacon Press.

13. See Reardon, op. cit.; and Early, F. H. (1997). *A world without war.* Syracuse, NY: Syracuse University Press.

14. Ruddick, p. 154. On women's support of war, see also Elshtain, J. B. (1987). *Women and war.* New York: Basic Books.

15. Quoted in Ruddick, p. 154.

16. See Woolf, V. (1966). *Three Guineas* (Reprint). New York: Harcourt Brace; and Sontag, S. (2003). *Regarding the pain of others.* New York: Farrar, Straus & Giroux.

17. Sontag, pp. 14–15.

18. Ibid., p. 41.

19. For a lengthier discussion of educating students on the processes of socialization, see Noddings, N. (2002). *Starting at home: Caring and social policy.* Berkeley: University of California Press.

20. Postman, N., & Weingartner, C. (1969). *Teaching as a subversive activity.* New York: Delta. Postman and Weingartner borrow the term "crap detecting" from Ernest Hemingway.

21. See the discussion of pedagogical neutrality in Noddings, N. (1993). *Educating for intelligent belief or unbelief.* New York: Teachers College Press.

22. It would be useful here to draw on the poetry of Rudyard Kipling, especially his "Tommy." See *The Works of Kipling* (Roslyn, NY: Black's Readers Service, n.d.). See also Jones, J. (1996). *From here to eternity.* New York: Bantam Books.

23. Glover, J. (2000). *Humanity: A moral history of the 20th century* (p. 7). New Haven, CT: Yale University Press.

24. Ibid., p. 168.

25. Ibid., p. 16.

26. Nishida, K. (1990). *An inquiry into the good* (M. Abe & C. Ives, Trans.) (Reprint). New Haven, CT: Yale University Press.

27. For the classic argument against reason as a motivating force, see Hume, D. (1983). *An enquiry concerning the principles of morals* (Reprint). Indianapolis: Hackett; for a powerful recent argument, see Roland Martin, J. (1992). Critical thinking for a humane world. In S. P. Norris (Ed.), *The generalizability of critical thinking* (pp. 163–180). New York: Teachers College Press.

28. *The Iliad* (1900) (A. Lang, W. Leaf, & E. Myers, Trans.) (p. 419). London: Macmillan.

29. Weil, S. (1977). The poem of might. In G. A. Panichas (Ed.), *Simone Weil reader* (pp. 153–183). Mt. Kisco, NY: Moyer Bell.

30. Ibid., p. 153.

31. Ibid., p. 157.

32. Ibid., p. 158.

33. Ibid., p. 183.

34. Remarque, E. M. (1952). *Spark of life* (p. 182). New York: Appleton-Century-Crofts.

35. Levi, P. (1988). *The drowned and the saved* (Raymond Rosenthal, Trans.) (p. 202). New York: Vintage.

36. For more on this, see Noddings, N. (2002). Coping with violence. *Educational Theory, 52,* 241–55.

37. See Naimark, N. M. (2002). *Fires of hatred: Ethnic cleansing in twentieth-century Europe.* Cambridge, MA: Harvard University Press.

38. See Sebald, W. G. (2003). *On the natural history of destruction* (Anthea Bell, Trans.). New York: Random House.

39. See Grass, G. (2002). *Crabwalk* (Krishna Winston, Trans.). Orlando, FL: Harcourt. For a set of resources on the Wilhelm Gustloff, see www.click2disasters.com/stories/gustloff/wilhelm_gustloff_ch1.htm.

40. Grass, p. 234.

Article 18 References

Apple, M. (1992). Do the standards go far enough? Power, policy, and practice in mathematics education. *Journal for Research in Mathematics Education, 23*(5), 412–431.

ARC Center. (2003). *Full report of the Tri-State Student Achievement Study.* Retrieved from http://www.comap.com/elementary/projects/arc/tri-state%achievement%20full%20report.htm

Becker, J., & Jacob, B. (2000). The politics of California school mathematics: The anti-reform of 1997–99. *Phi Delta Kappan, 81*(7), 527–539.

California Department of Education. (1985). *Mathematics framework for California public schools, kindergarten through grade 12.* Sacramento: Author.

California Department of Education. (1992). *Mathematics framework for California public schools, kindergarten through grade 12.* Sacramento: Author.

Conference Board of the Mathematical Sciences. (2001). *The mathematical education of teachers.* Washington, DC: Author.

Daro, P. (2003). *Math wars peace treaty.* Manuscript in preparation.

Jacob, B. (1999). Instructional material for K–8 mathematics classrooms: The California adoption, 1997. In E. Gavosto, S. Krantz, & W. McCallum (Eds.), *Contemporary issues in mathematics education* (Mathematical Sciences Research Institute Publications 36, pp. 109–122). Cambridge, UK: Cambridge University Press.

Jacob, B. (2001). Implementing standards: the California mathematics textbook debacle. *Phi Delta Kappan, 83*(3), 264–272. Also available from http://www.pdkintl.org/kappan/k0111jac.htm

Jacob, B., & Akers, J. (2003). Research-based mathematics education policy: The case of California 1995–1998. *International Journal for Mathematics and Learning.* Retrieved June 27, 2003, from the Centre for Innovation in Mathematics Teaching, University of Exeter, UK, http://www.intermep.org

Klein, D. (1998, May 3). The state's invisible math standards: California adopts a set of world-class guidelines for public schools—And the power that be promptly try to make them disappear. *Los Angeles Times,* p. 15.

Klein, D. (2003). A brief history of American K–12 mathematics education in the 20th century. Retrieved July 1, 2003, from http://www.csun.edu/~vcmth00m/AHistory.html

Kozol, J. (1992). *Savage inequalities.* New York: Harper Perennial.

Lappan, G. (1997, October). *Lessons from the Sputnik era in mathematics education.* Paper presented at the National Academy of Sciences symposium titled Reflecting on Sputnik: Linking the past, present and future of educational reform. Retrieved March 7, 2003, from http://www.nas.edu/sputnik/index.htm.

Madison, B. L., & Hart, T. A. (1990). *A challenge of numbers: People in the mathematical sciences.* Washington, DC: National Academy Press.

McKnight, C., Crosswhite, J., Dossey, J., Kifer, E., Swafford, J. Travers, K., et al. (1987). *The underachieving curriculum: Assessing U.S. mathematics from an international perspective.* Champaign, IL: Stipes.

McKnight, C., Travers, K., Crosswhite, J., & Swafford, J. (1985). Eighth grade mathematics in the secondary schools: A report from the Second International Mathematics Study. *Arithmetic Teacher, 32*(8), 20–26.

McKnight, C., Travers, K., & Dossey, J. (1985). Twelfth grade mathematics in U.S. high schools: A report from the Second International Mathematics Study. *Mathematics Teacher, 78*(4), 292–300.

National Action Committee for Minorities in Engineering. (1997). *Engineering and affirmative actions: Crisis in the making.* New York: Author.

National Commission on Excellence in Education. (1983). A nation at risk: The imperative for educational reform. Washington, DC: Government Printing Office. Available from http://www.ed.gov/pubs/NatAtRisk/risk.html

National Council of Teachers of Mathematics. (1980). *An agenda for action: Recommendations for school mathematics of the 1980s.* Reston, VA: Author.

National Council of Teachers of Mathematics. (1989). *Curriculum and evaluation standards for school mathematics.* Reston, VA: Author.

National Council of Teachers of Mathematics. (2000). *Principles and standards for school mathematics.* Reston, VA: Author.

National Research Council. (1989). *Everybody counts: A report to the nation on the future of mathematics education.* Washington, DC: National Academy Press.

National Research Council. (2001). *Adding it up: Helping children learn mathematics.* Washington, DC: National Academy Press.

National Science Foundation. (2000). *Science and engineering indicators.* Washington, DC: Author.

No Child Left Behind Act of 2001, Pub. L. No. 017–110. Available from http://www.ed.gov/policy/elsec/leg/esea02/index.html

Pearson, P. D. (2004). The reading wars. *Educational Policy, 18,* 216–253.

Riley, R. E. (1998). The state of mathematics education: Building a strong foundation for the 21st century. *Notices of the American Mathematics Society, 45*(4), 487–491. Also available from http://www.ams.org/notices/199804/riley.pdf

Rosen, L. (2000). *Calculating concerns: The politics of representation in California's "math wars."* Unpublished doctoral dissertation. University of California, San Diego.

Saunders, D. (1995a, March 13). New-new math: Boot licking 101. *San Francisco Chronicle.* Retrieved from http://sfgate .com/cgi-bin/article.cgi?file=/chronicle/archive/1995/03/13/ED41966.DTL

Saunders, D. (1995b, September 20). Creatures from the new-new math lagoon. *San Francisco Chronicle.* Retrieved from http://sfgate.com/cgi-bin/article.cgi?file=/chronicle/archive/1995/09/20/ED51431.DTL

Senk, S., & Thompson, D. (Eds.). (2003). *Standards-oriented school mathematics curricula: What does the research say about student outcomes?* Mahwah, NJ: Lawrence Erlbaum.

Shermer, M. (2002). *Why people believe weird things? Pseudoscience, superstition, and other confusions of our time* (Rev. ed.). New York: Holt, Rinehart & Winston.

Stanic, G. M. A. (1987). Mathematics education in the United States at the beginning of the twentieth century. In Thomas S. Popkewitz (Ed.), *The formation of school subjects: The struggle for creating an American institution* (pp. 147–183). New York: Falmer.

Article 19 References

American Association of Physics Teachers (2002). *AAPT Announcer, 32,* 11.

Conant, J. B. (1959). *The American high school today: A first report to interested citizens.* New York: McGraw-Hill.

Efron, A. (1937). *The teaching of physical sciences in the secondary schools of the United States, France and Soviet Russia.* Unpublished Ph.D. thesis. Teachers College, Columbia University.

Fay, P. J. (1931). *Journal of Chemical Education, 8,* 1533–1562.

Glasoe, P. M. (1938). *Journal of Chemical Education, 15,* 364–367.

Gordon, N. E. (1924). *Journal of Chemical Education, 1,* 33–34, 87–99.

Gold, M. (1988). *Journal of Chemical Education, 65,* 780–781.

Haber-Schaim, U. (1984). *Physics Teacher, 22,* 300–332.

Hale, H. (1932). *Journal of Chemical Education, 9,* 729–744.

Harvard Committee (1945). *General education in a free society.* Cambridge, MA: Harvard University Press.

Hoag, J. B. (1945). *Journal of Chemical Education, 22,* 152–154.

Hunter, G. W. (1910). *School Science and Mathematics, 10,* 103–111.

Hunter, G. W. (1925). *School Review, 33,* 370–381, 453–466.

Hunter, G. W. (1931). *Science Education, 16,* 103–115. *a.* p. 108; *b.* p. 113.

Hunter, G. W. (1934). *Science teaching: At junior and senior high school levels.* New York: American Book Company.

Hunter, G. W., & Spore, L. (1942). *Science Educator, 25,* 359–370.

Hunter, G. W., & Spore, L. (1942). *Science. Education, 26,* 66–77.

Key state education policies on K–12 education 2002. Retrieved January 2005 from *http://www.ccsso.org/Publications/Download.cfm?Filename=KeyState2002.pdf*

Lederman, L. M. (2001). *Physics Today, 54,* 11–12.

Meyers, F. R. (1987). *Physics Teacher, 25,* 78–81.

Nappi, C. R. (1990). *Physics Today, 43,* 77.

National Center for Education Statistics (2002). *Digest of Education Statistics* (Table 141). Washington, DC: U.S. Government Printing Office.

National Center for Education Statistics. *Digest of educational statistics.* Retrieved January 2005 from *http://nces.ed.gov/*

National Commission on Excellence in Education (1983). *A nation at risk: The imperative for educational reform.* Washington, DC: U.S. Government Printing Office.

National Educational Association (1893). *Report of the Committee on Secondary School Studies.* Washington, DC: Government Printing Office. *a.* p. 119; *b.* p. 42; *c.* p. 48.

National Educational Association. Report on the Committee on College Entrance Requirements (1899). *Journal of Proceedings and Addresses of the Thirty-Eighth Annual Meeting.* Chicago: National Educational Association.

National Education Association (1920). *Reorganization of science in secondary schools: A Report of the Commission on the Reorganization of Secondary Education* (Bulletin No. 26). Washington, DC: U.S. Bureau of Education.

National Society for the Study of Education (1932). *A program for teaching science: thirty-first yearbook of the NSSE.* Chicago: University of Chicago Press.

Newell, L. C. (1976). *Journal of Chemical Education, 53,* 402–404.

Osborn, G. (1960). *School Science and Mathematics, 60,* 621–625.

Palombi, J. (1971). *Physics Teacher, 9,* 39–40.

Pauley, P. J. (1991). *ISIS, 82,* 662–688.

Physics-First Web site. Retrieved January 2005 from *http://members.aol.com/physicsfirst/*

Powers, S. R. (1926). *Journal of Chemical Education, 24,* 498–503.

Reeves, E. T. (1940). *Journal of Chemical. Education, 17,* 442.

Robinson, J. T. (1960). *School Science and Mathematics, 60,* 685–692.

Rosen, S. (1956). *Journal of Chemical Education, 33,* 627–633.

Rowe, M. B. (1982). *Journal of Chemical Education, 60,* 954–956.

Sheppard, K., & Robbins, D. M. (2002). *Physics Teacher, 40,* 426–431.

Smith, A., & Hall, E. (1902). *The teaching of chemistry and physics in the secondary school* (pp. 42–44). New York: Longmans, Green.

Stout, J. E. (1921). *The development of high school curricula in the north central states from 1860 to 1918.* Educational Monograph No. 15. Chicago: University of Chicago.

Webb, H. A. (1959). *School Science and Mathematics, 59,* 421–430.

Woodhull, J. F. (1918). *The teaching of science* (p. 223). New York: The Macmillan Company.

Article 21 References

Barber, B. L., Eccles, J. S., & Stone, M. R. (2001). Whatever happened to the "Jock," the "Brain," and the "Princess"?: Young adult pathways linked to adolescent activity involvement and social identity. *Journal of Adolescent Research, 16,* 429–455.

Barber, B. L., Jacobson, K. C., Horn, M. C., & Jacobs, S. L. (1997, August). *Social and individual factors that predict adolescents' school attachment during high school.* Paper presented at the seventh EARLI conference, Athens, Greece.

Barber, B. L., Stone, M. R., Hunt, J., & Eccles, J. S. (2005). How do activities link to benefits: Identity and peer work synergy. In J. L. Mahoney, J. S. Eccles, & R. W. Larson (Eds.), *Organized activities as contexts of development: Extracurricular activities, after-school and community programs.* Mahwah, NJ: Lawrence Erlbaum.

Brown, B. B., Mory, MS., & Kinney, D. (1994). Casting adolescent crowds in a relational perspective: Caricature, channel, and context. In R. Montemayer, G. R. Adams, & T. P. Gulotta (Eds.), *Advances in adolescent development: Vol. 5, Personal relationships during adolescence* (pp. 123–167). Newbury Park, CA: Sage.

Cooper, C. R., Denner, J., & Lopez, E. M. (1999). Cultural brokers: Helping Latino children on pathways toward success. *Future of Children, 9*(2), 5 1–57.

Dishion, T. I., McCord, J., & Poulin, F. (1999). When interventions harm: Peer groups and problem behavior. *American Psychologist, 54*(9), 755–764.

Duda, J. L., & Ntoumanis, N. (2005). After-school sport for children: Implications of a task-involving motivational climate. In J. L. Mahoney, J. S. Eccles, & R. W. Larson (Eds.), *Organized activities as contexts of development: Extracurricular activities, after school and community programs.* Mahwah, NJ: Lawrence Erlbaum.

Eccles, J. S. (1987). Gender roles and women's achievement-related decisions. *Psychology of Women Quarterly, 11*, 135–172.

Eccles, J. S., & Barber, B. L. (1999). Student council, volunteering, basketball, or marching band: What kind of extracurricular involvement matters? *Journal of Adolescent Research, 14*, 10–43.

Eccles, J. S., & Gootman, J. A. (Eds.). (2002). *Community programs to promote youth development.* Washington, DC: National Academy Press.

Eccles, J. S., & Templeton, J. (2002). Extracurricular and other after-school activities for youth. *Review of Research in Education, 26*, 113–180.

Eckert, P. (1989). *Jocks and burnouts: Social categories and identity in the high school.* New York: Teacher College Press.

Elder, G. H., Jr., & Conger, R. D. (2000). *Children of the land: Adversity and success in rural America.* Chicago: University of Chicago Press.

Erikson, E. H. (1963). *Childhood and society.* New York: Norton.

Erikson, E. H. (1968). *Identity, youth and crisis.* New York: Norton.

Fine, G. A. (1987). *With the boys: Little league baseball and preadolescent culture.* Chicago: University of Chicago Press.

Glancy, M., Willits, F. K., & Farrell, P. (1986). Adolescent activities and adult success and happiness: Twenty-four years later. *Sociology and Social Research, 70*, 242–250.

Gould, D., & Weiss, M. R. (Eds.). (1987). *Advances in pediatric sport sciences, Vol. 2: Behavioral issues.* Champaign, IL: Human Kinetics.

Hansen, D. M., Larson, R. W., & Dworkin, J. B. (2003). What adolescents learn in organized youth activities. *Journal of Research on Adolescence, 13*(1), 25–55.

Hunt, J. E. (2002). *High school sports as a protective factor: What happens to athletes who stop playing.* Unpublished master's thesis, University of Arizona, Tucson.

Larson, R. W. (2000). Toward a psychology of positive youth development. *American Psychologist, 55*(1), 170–183.

Larson, R. W., & Kleiber, D. (1993). Daily experience of adolescents. In *Handbook of clinical research and practice with adolescents: Wiley series on personality processes* (pp. 125–145). New York: John Wiley & Camp.

Larson, R. W., & Verma, S. (1999). How children and adolescents spend time across the world: Work, play, and developmental opportunities. *Psychological Bulletin, 125*(6), 701–736.

Lemer, R. M., & Galambos, N. L. (1998). Adolescent development: Challenges and opportunities for research, programs, and policies. *Annual Review of Psychology, 49*, 413–446.

Mahoney, J. L. (2000). School extracurricular activity participation as a moderator in the development of antisocial patterns. *Child Development, 71*(2), 502–516.

Mahoney, J. L., & Cairns, R. B., (1997). Do extracurricular activities protect against early school dropout? *Developmental Psychology, 33*(2), 241–253.

Mahoney, J. L., Larson, R. W., & Eccles, J. S. (Eds.). (2005). *Organized activities as contexts of development: Extracurricular activities, after-school and community programs.* Mahwah, NJ: Lawrence Erlbaum and Associates.

Marsh, H. W. (1992). Extracurricular activities: Beneficial extension of the traditional curriculum or subversion of academic goals? *Journal of Educational Psychology, 84*(4), 553–562.

Marsh, H. W. (1993). Relations between global and specific domains of self: The importance of individual importance, certainty, and ideals. *Journals of Personality & Social Psychology, 65*(5), 975–992.

Marsh, H. W., & Kleitman, S. (2002). Extracurricular school activities: The good, the bad, and the non-linear. *Harvard Educational Review, 72*(4), 464–514.

Marsh, H. W., & Kleitman, S. (2003). School athletic participation: Mostly gain with little pain. *Journal of Sport and Exercise Psychology, 25*, 205–228.

McNeal, R. B. (1995). Extracurricular activities and high school dropouts. *Sociology of Education, 68*, 62–81.

Pedersen, S., & Seidman, E. (2005). Extracurricular participation among low-income urban adolescents. In J. L. Mahoney, J. S. Eccles, & R. W. Larson (Eds.), *Organized activities as contexts of development: Extracurricular activities, after-school and community programs.* Mahwah, NJ: Lawrence Erlbaum and Associates.

Pittman, K., Tolman, J., & Yohalem, N. (2005). Developing a comprehensive agenda for the out-of- school hours: Lessons and challenges across cities. In I. L. Mahoney, J. S. Eccles, & R. W. Larson (Eds.), *Organized activities as contexts of development: Extracurricular activities, after-school and community programs.* Mahwah, NJ: Lawrence Erlbaum.

Psychological Corporation (1981). *Differential Aptitude Test, 4th Edition, Form VNW.* San Antonio, TX: Harcourt-Brace & Company.

Rehberg, R. A. (1969). Behavioral and attitudinal consequences of high school interscholastic sports: A speculative consideration: *Adolescence, 4,* 69–88.

Roberts, G. C., & Treasure, D. C. (1992). Children in sport. *Sport Science Review, 1*(2), 46–64.

Scales, P. C. (1999). Increasing service-learning's impact on middle school students. *Middle School Journal, 30,* 40–44.

Smoll, F. L., Smith, R. E., Barnett, N. P., & Everett, J. J. (1993). Enhancement of children's self-esteem through social support training for youth sport coaches. *Journal of Applied Psychology, 78*(4), 602–610.

Stattin, H., Kerr, M., Mahoney, J., Persson, A., & Magnusson, D. (2005). Explaining why a leisure context is bad for some girls and not for others. In J. L. Mahoney, J. S. Eccles, & R. W. Larson (Eds.), *Organized activities as contexts of development: Extracurricular activities, after-school and community programs.* Mahwah, NJ: Lawrence Erlbaum.

Youniss, J., McLellan, J. A., Su, Y., & Yates, M. (1999). The role of community service in identity development: Normative, unconventional, and deviant orientations. *Journal of Adolescent Research, 14*(2), 248–261.

Youniss, J., McLellan, J. A., & Yates, M. (1999). Religion, community service, and identity in American youth. *Journal of Adolescence, 22*(2), 243–253.

Youniss, J., & Yates, M. (1997). *Community service and social responsibility in youth.* Chicago: University of Chicago Press.

Article 22 References

After-School Corporation. Policy Studies Associates (2000a). *Increasing and improving after-school opportunities, evaluation of results from the TASC after-school program's first year.* New York: TASC.

After-School Corporation. Policy Studies Associates (2000b). *Increasing and improving after-school opportunities* (Parent survey). New York: TASC.

Lake Snell Perry & Associates & The Tarrance Group (2001). *Mott Foundation/JCPenney nationwide survey on after-school programs.* Washington, DC: Afterschool Alliance.

National Commission on Time and Learning (NCTL) (1994). *Prisoners of time.* Washington, DC: NCTL.

Newman, S., Fox, J. A.,, Flynn, E. A., & Christeson, W. (2000). *America's after-school choice: The prime time for juvenile crime, or youth enrichment and achievement.* Washington, DC: Fight Crime: Invest in Kids.

Owings, W. A., & Kaplan L. S. (2001). *Alternatives to retention and social promotion. Fastback 481.* Bloomington, IN: Phi Delta Kappan.

Superintendents' Task Force (1999). *Service learning linking classrooms and communities.* Sacramento: California Department of Education.

U.S. Department of Education (2000a). *21st Century Community Learning Centers: Providing quality after-school learning opportunities for America's families.* Washington, DC: Author.

U.S. Department of Education (2000b). *Working for children and families: Safe and smart after-school programs.* Washington, DC: Author.

U.S. Department of Education (2001, June). *Summary of 21st Century Community Learning Centers grantee reports.* Adriana De Kanter speech at the Mott Foundation Afterschool Evaluation Forum. Flint, MI: C. S. Mott Foundation.

University of California at Irvine, Department of Education (2001). *Evaluation of California's after-school learning and safe neighborhoods partnerships program: Preliminary report.* Irvine: Author.

Article 23 References

Ballantine, R. J. (1981). *What the research says: About the correlation between athletic participation and academic achievement.* (ERIC Document Reproduction Service No. ED 233994).

Braddock, J. H., II, Royster, D. A., Winfield, L. F., & Hawkins, R. (1991). Bouncing back: Sports and academic resilience among African American males. *Education and Urban Society, 24*(1), 113–131.

Buhrmann, H. G. (1972). Scholarship and athletics in junior high school. *International Review of Sport Sociology, 7*(72), 119–131.

Durbin, B. B. (1986). High school athletics: A valuable educational experience. *NASSP Bulletin, 70*(492), 32–34.

Gerber, S. B. (1996). Extracurricular activities and academic achievement. *Journal of Research and Development in Education, 30*(1), 42–50.

Gholson, R. E. (1985). Student achievement and cocurricular participation. *NASSP Bulletin, 69*(483), 17–20.

Goldberg, A. D., & Chandler, T. J. L. (1992). Academics and athletics in the social world of junior high school students. *School Counselor, 40*(1), 40–45.

Joekel, R. G. (1985). Student activities and academic eligibility requirements. *NASSP Bulletin, 69*(483), 3–9.

Lederman, D. (1989, August 16). Female basketball players outperform their counterparts in the classroom. *Chronicle of Higher Education,* pp. 1, A33.

Mihoces, G. (1996). Athletes adept at getting jump on their studies. *USA Today,* May 16, pp. 1c, 2c.

Silliker, S. A., & Quirk, J. T. (1997). The effect of extracurricular activity participation on the academic performance of male and female high school students. *School Counselor, 44*(4), 288–293.

Soltz, D. F. (1986). Athletics and academic achievement: What is the relationship? *NASSP Bulletin, 70*(492), 20–24.

Stegman, M., & Stephens, L. J. (2000). Athletics and academics: Are they compatible? *High School, 7*(6), 36–39.

Article 24 Endnotes

1. Berman, N. (2004). *Purple hearts: Back from Iraq.* New York: Trolley.
2. Dobie, D. (2005, March). AWOL in America. *Harper's,* 35.
3. Goodman, D. (2002, January/February). Recruiting the Class of 2005. *Mother Jones,* 1–8. All information in this paragraph comes from Goodman.
4. Goodman, p. 1.
5. Wedekind, J. (2005, June 20). The children's crusade. *In These Times,* 6–7.
6. Goodman, p. 3.
7. Reed, C. L. (2005, July 5). Military finally gives Hispanic war dead proper recognition. *Chicago Sun Times,* pp. A-18–A-19.
8. Herbert, B. (2005, June 16). Uncle Sam really wants you. *New York Times,* p. A-29.
9. Dobie, p. 40.
10. All quotes in this paragraph are from Dobie, pp. 34–35.
11. Kilian, M., & Horan, D. (2005, March 31). Enlistment drought spurs new strategies. *Chicago Tribune,* p. 1.
12. Cave, D. (2005, June 3). Growing problem for military recruiters: Parents. *New York Times,* p. B-6.
13. Cave, p. A-1.
14. Herbert, op. cit.
15. Hedges, C. (2003). *What every person should know about war* (pp. 1, 3, 7, 115.s). New York: Free Press.
16. Hedges, p. 8.
17. Bigelow, B. (2005, Spring). The recruitment minefield. *Rethinking Schools,* 46.

Article 26 References

Allardyce, J. (2002). Youthful outlook: Tapping into the teen market. *Rural Telecommunications, 21*(5), 54–56.

Angrisani, C. (2003, April 21). Giant Eagle tours teach kids good nutrition, prevent obesity. *Supermarket News,* p. 74.

Applebaum, M. (2003, March 10). Don't spare the brand. *Brandweek.*

Associated Press. (2002, November 4). Pepsi pours cold water on girl's project. *Seattle Times,* p. B2.

Auchmutey, J. (2002, November 17). America's craving for all things sweet expands bite by supersize bite. *Atlanta Journal-Constitution,* p. 1A.

Brady, S. (2002, September 9). The new cable in the classroom. *Cable World,* p. 33.

Bruce, A. L., (2002, August 9). Charleston schools go Pepsi only. *Post and Courier* (Charleston, South Carolina), p. 1A.

Council for Corporate and School Partnerships. (2002, September 25). *Council led by former U.S. education secretaries provides guidelines for model school business relationships* [Press release distributed by PR Newswire].

Critics balk, but schools say student fundraising needed to boost budget (2002, December 2). Associated Press.

Dunnewind, S. (2002, August 31). Beyond bake sales. *Seattle Times,* p. E1.

Fromm, E. (2003, March 17). PMA Reggie Awards 2003. *Brandweek.*

Gendar, A., & Feiden, D. (2002, December 22). Schoolbooks flubbing facts. *Daily News* (New York), p. 4.

Grannan, C. (2003, May 12). Industry claims kids don't drink much soda [Press release distributed by Parents Advocating School Accountability, quoting the *Atlanta Journal-Constitution* (2003, April 6)].

Karlin, R. (2003, April 14). Even fundraisers cut calories. *Times Union* (Albany, New York), p. B1.

Kelly, R. (2003, March 21). Punishment undeserved. *Fort Pierce Tribune* (Fort Pierce, Florida), p. A10.

Kim, R. (2003, February 7). Corporate sponsorship of classroom proposed. *San Francisco Chronicle,* p. A21.

LaScala, R. (2002, September 27). Helping kids chart their path. *Business Journal* (Research Triangle, North Carolina).

Macmillan, C. (2002, September 1). Readin', writin', and sellin'. *Promo,* 10.

McGraw, P. B. (2002, October 4). Vernon Hills ready to christen new stadium tonight. *Chicago Daily Herald,* Sports Extra, p. 3.

McNeal, J. U. (1992). *Kids as customers.* New York: Lexington Books.

Miller, R. (2002, October 28). Minority students targeted. *Dallas Morning News,* p. 2D.

Q1 2003 General Mills earnings conference call (2002, September 18). Transcript distributed by Fair Disclosure Wire.

Rawlings, M. (2002, October 8). Testimony before the Subcommittee on Education Reform. House Committee on Education and the Workforce Federal Document Clearing House.

St. John, K. (2003, May 22). Parents try to cover schools' budget gap. *San Francisco Chronicle,* p. A1.

Article 27 References

American Psychological Association (2002, September). What exactly is "scientifically based research"? *APA Monitor, 33*(8), 53.

Banks, J. A. (1997). *Educating citizens in a multicultural society.* New York: Teachers College Press.

Bennett, W. J. (Ed.). (1993). *The book of virtues.* New York: Simon & Schuster.

Berkowitz, M. W. (2000). Civics and moral education. In R. Moon, S. Brown, & M. Ben-Peretz (Eds.), *Routledge international companion to education* (pp. 897–909). London: Routledge Kegan Paul.

Berkowitz, M. W. (2002). The science of character education. In W. Damon (Ed.), *Bringing in a new era in character education* (pp. 43–63). Stanford, CA: Hoover Institution Press.

Berman, S. (1997). *Children's social consciousness.* Ithaca, NY: SUNY Press.

Bhaerman, R., Cordell, K., & Gomez, B. (1998). *The role of service-learning in educational reform.* Needham Heights, MA: Simon & Schuster.

Billig, S. H., & Waterman, A. S. (2002). *Studying service-learning innovations in education research methodology.* Mahwah, NJ: Lawrence Erlbaum.

Bowles, S., & Gintis, H. (1976). *Schooling in capitalist America: Educational reform and the contradictions of economic life.* New York: Basic Books.

Bush, G. W. (2002, June 19). *President speaks at White House conference on character and community.* Washington, DC: White House, Office of the Press Secretary. Retrieved May 3, 2003, from http://www.whitehouse.gov/news/releases/2002/06/print/20020619-22.html

de Tocqueville, A. (2000). *Democracy in America.* Chicago: University of Chicago Press. (Original work published 1835)

Dewey, J. (1966). *Democracy and education.* New York: Free Press. (Original work published 1916)

Dewey, J. (1975). *Moral principles in education.* Carbondale: Southern Illinois University Press. (Original work published 1909)

Education Commission of the States (1999). *State examples of policies concerning character education.* Denver, CO: Author.

Education Commission of the States (2001). *Service-learning and character education: One plus one is more than two.* Denver, CO: Author. Retrieved April 24, 2003, from http://www.ecs.org/clearinghouse/24/81/2481.htm

Elias, M. J., Zins, J. E., & Weissberg, R. P (1997). *Promoting social and emotional learning: Guidelines for educators.* Alexandria, VA: Association for Supervision and Curriculum Development.

Engle v. Vitale, 370 U.S. 421 (1962).

Ennett, S. T., Tobler, N .S., Ringwalt, C. L. . & Flewelling, R. L. (1994). How effective is Drug Abuse Resistance Education? A meta-analysis of Project DARE outcome evaluations. *American Journal of Public Health, 84*(9), 1394–1401.

Eyler, J., & Giles, D. (1999). *Where's the learning in service-learning?* San Francisco: Jossey-Bass.

Goodlad, J. I., & McMannon, T. J. (Eds.). (1997). *The public purpose of education and schooling.* San Francisco: Jossey-Bass.

Goodlad, J. I., Soder, R., & Sirotnik, K. (Eds.). (1990). *The moral dimensions of teaching.* San Francisco: Jossey-Bass.

Grillo, R. D. (1998) *Pluralism and the politics of difference: State, culture, and ethnicity in comparative perspective.* Oxford, UK: Oxford University Press.

Habermas, J. (1990). *Moral consciousness and communicative action.* Cambridge, MA: MIT Press.

Hartshorne, H. & May, M. A. (1928). *Studies in the nature of character: Vol. I: Studies in deceit.* New York: Macmillan.

Hartshorne, H., May, M. A., & Mailer. J. B. (1929). *Studies in the nature of character Vol. II: Studies in self-control.* New York: Macmillan.

Hartshorne, H., May, M. A., & Shuttleworth, F. K. (1930). *Studies in the nature of character: Vol. III: Studies in the organization of character.* New York: Macmillan.

Haynes, C. C., & Thomas, O. (Eds.). (1998). *Finding common ground: A first amendment guide to religion and public education.* Nashville: First Amendment Center/Freedom Forum.

Josephson Institute (2001). *The six pillars of character.* Retrieved May 24, 2003, from http://www.character counts.org/defsix.htm

Josephson Institute (2002). *Making ethical decisions: The six pillars.* Retrieved May 24, 2003, from http://www.josephsoninstitute .org/MED/MED-2sixpillars.htm

Kahne, J., & Westheimer, J. (2003). Teaching democracy: What schools need to do. *Phi Delta Kappan, 85*(1), 34–40, 57–66.

Kielsmeier, J. (Ed.). (2000). Service-learning. *Phi Delta Kappan, 81*(9), 652–680.

Kilpatrick, W. (1992). *Why Johnny can't tell right from wrong: Moral illiteracy and the case for character education.* New York: Simon & Schuster.

Kirschenbaum, H. (1995). *100 ways to enhance values and morality in schools and youth settings.* Needham Heights, MA: Longwood.

Kohlberg, L. (1981). *Essays on moral development. Vol. I: The philosophy of moral development.* San Francisco: Harper & Row.

Kohlberg, L. (1984). *Essays on moral development. Vol. II: The psychology of moral development.* San Francisco: Harper & Row.

Lickona, T. (1989). *Educating for character: How our schools can teach respect and responsibility.* New York: Bantam.

McClellan, B. E. (1999). *Moral education in America: Schools and the shaping of character from colonial times to the present.* New York: Teachers College Press.

National Center for Education Statistics (2003). *Digest of education statistics, 2002.* Washington, DC: United States Department of Education.

No Child Left Behind Act of 2001, Pub L. No. 107–110 (2002).

Noddings, N. (2002a). *Educating moral people: A caring alternative to character education.* New York: Teachers College Press.

Noddings, N. (2002b). *Starting at home: Caring and social policy.* Berkeley: University of California Press.

Nord, W. A. (1995). *Religion and American education: Rethinking a national dilemma.* Chapel Hill: University of North Carolina Press.

Nord, W. A., & Haynes, C. C. (1998). *Taking religion seriously across the curriculum.* Alexandria, VA: Association for Supervision and Curriculum Development and First Amendment Center.

Parker, W. C. (1996). "Advanced" ideas about democracy: Toward a pluralist conception of citizen education. *Teachers College Record, 98*(1), 104–125.

Parker, W. C. (Ed.) (2002). *Education for democracy: Contexts, curricula, assessments.* Greenwich, CT: Information Age Publishing.

Parker, W. C. (2003). *Teaching democracy: Unity and diversity in public life.* New York: Teachers College Press.

Piaget, J. (1965). *The moral judgment of the child.* New York: Free Press. (Original work published 1932)

Power, F. C., Higgins, A., & Kohlberg, L. (1989). *Lawrence Kohlberg's approach to moral education.* New York: Columbia University Press.

Putnam, R. (2000). *Bowling alone: The collapse and revival of American community.* New York: Simon & Schuster.

Raths, L., Harmin, M., & Simon, S. (1966). *Values and teaching.* Columbus, OH: Merrill.

Reed, D. R. C. (1997). *Following Kohlberg: Liberalism and the practices of democratic community.* Notre Dame, IN: University of Notre Dame Press.

Reimer, J., Paolitto, D. F., & Hersh, R. H. (1990). *Promoting moral growth: From Piaget to Kohlberg* (2nd ed.). Prospect Heights, IL: Waveland Press. (Original work published 1983)

Ryan K., & Bohlin, K. (1999). *Building character in schools: Practical ways to bring moral instruction to life.* San Francisco: Jossey-Bass.

Scheffler, I. (1974). *Four pragmatists: A critical introduction to Pierce, James, Mead, and Dewey.* London: Routledge Kegan Paul.

Shweder, R. (1982). [Review of the book *Essays on moral development. Vol. I: The philosophy of moral development*]. *Contemporary Psychology, 27*(2), 421–424.

Simon, S., Howe, L., & Kirschenbaum, H. (1972). *Values clarification.* New York: Hart.

Simpson, E. L. (1974) Moral development research: A case study of cultural bias. *Human Development, 17,* 81–106.

Sizer, T. R. & Sizer, N. F. (2000). *The students are watching: Schools and the moral contract.* Boston: Beacon.

Soder, R. (2001). Education for democracy: The foundation for democratic character. In R. Soder, J. I. Goodlad, & T. J. McMannon (Eds.), *Developing democratic character in the young* (pp. 182–205). San Francisco: Jossey Bass.

Sullivan, E. V. (1977). A study of Kohlberg's structural theory of moral development: A critique of liberal social science ideology. *Human Development, 20,* 231–242.

U.S. Department of Education (2003, September 29). *$16.7 million in character education grants go to states and school districts.* Washington, DC: Author. Retrieved October 20, 2003, from http://www.ed.gov/news/pressreleases/2003/09/09292003.html

U.S. Department of Education, Office of the Deputy Secretary, Strategic Accountability Service (2003). *FY 2004 annual plan.* Washington, DC: Author.

U.S. Department of Education (n.d.-a). *Awards—The Partnerships in Character Education Project Program.* Washington, DC: Author. Retrieved October 27, 2003, from http://www.ed.gov/programs/charactered/awards.html?exp=0ed

U.S. Department of Education (n.d.-b). *Awards—The Partnerships in Character Education Project Program: 2002 state educational agencies character education projects.* Washington, DC: Author. Retrieved October 27, 2003, from http://www.ed.gov/programs/charactered/sea.html

U.S. General Accounting Office (2003, January 15). *Youth illicit drug use prevention* (GAO-03-172R). Washington, DC: Author.

Values, depoliticized [Editorial] (2001, August 16). *Christian Science Monitor.* Retrieved August 16, 2001, from http://www.csmonitor.com/2001/0816/p8s1-comv.html

Voting for character ed.: So light, tasty & flakey (Editorial). (2000, January 18). *Seattle Times.* Retrieved January 18, 2000, from http://wwwseattletime.com/news/editorial/htm198/chared-2000018.html

Wade, R. C. (Ed.). (1997). *Community service learning: A guide to including service in the public school curriculum.* New York: SUNY Press.

Wade, R. C. (Ed.). (2000). *Building bridges: Connecting classroom and community through service-learning in social studies.* Washington, DC: National Council for the Social Studies.

Westbrook, R. B. (1991). *John Dewey and American democracy.* Ithaca, NY: Cornell University Press.

Wilmsen, E. N., & McAllister, P. (Eds.). (1996). *The politics of difference: Ethnic premises in a world of power.* Chicago. University of Chicago Press.

Young, I. M. (1990). *Justice and the politics of difference.* Princeton, NJ: Princeton University Press.

Zimmerman, J., & Brown, C. (2003, April). Let them eat more than phonics. *Phi Delta Kappan, 84*(8), 603–605.

Article 28 Endnotes

1. Willen, E. (1992, April 23). School furor—Queens board nixes guide mentioning homosexuality. *Newsday,* City Section, p. 3.
2. Belluck, P. (1995, November 7). Mix and match, live and learn. *New York Times,* p. B1.
3. Fernandez, J., with Underwood, J. (1993). *Tales out of school.* Boston: Little, Brown.
4. New York City Public Schools (1990). *Children of the Rainbow—Implementing a multicultural kindergarten curriculum* (p. iii). New York: Author.
5. New York City Public Schools (1990).
6. New York City Public Schools (1990), p. vii.
7. New York City Public Schools (1990), p. 3.
8. New York City Public Schools (1990), p. 267.
9. New York City Public Schools (1991). *Children of the Rainbow—First grade* (*Ninos del Arco Iris—Primer grado*). New York: Author.
10. New York City Public Schools (1991), p. viii.
11. New York City Public Schools (1991).
12. New York City Public Schools (1991), p. 137.
13. New York City Public Schools (1991).
14. New York City Public Schools (1991), p. 138.
15. New York City Public Schools (1991).
16. New York City Public Schools (1991), p. 145.
17. Newman, L. (1989). *Heather has two mommies.* Boston: Alyson Wonderland; Newman, L. (1991). *Gloria goes to gay pride.* Boston: Alyson Wonderland; Willhoite, M. (1990). *Daddy's roommate.* Boston: Alyson Wonderland.
18. Ravitch, D. (1974). *The great school wars* (p. 397). New York: Basic Books.
19. Cuban, L. (1984). *How teachers taught* (p. 161). New York: Longman.
20. Willen, op. cit., p. 3.
21. Willen, p. 3.
22. Negron E., & Willen, L. (1992, December 1). Board: We won't crawl; District 24 defies orders to appear. *Newsday,* City Section, p. 4.
23. D. Ravitch, op. cit., p. 259.
24. Fernandez, with Underwood, op. cit., p. 209.
25. Willen, L. (1992, June 21). First grade to learn respect for gays—Schools ordered to address issue. *Newsday,* City Section, p. 21.

26. Fernandez, with Underwood, op. cit., p. 188.

27. Leo, J. (1992, August 1). Respecting diversity is not the same thing as endorsing it. *Seattle Times,* sec. A, p. 9; Heather has a message (1992, August 17). *U.S. News and World Report,* p. 16.

28. Leo, J. (1992, September 27). Teaching about gays and tolerance [Editorial]. *New York Times,* sec. 4, p. 16.

29. Leo, J. (1992, December 1). Get the aspirin [Editorial]. *Newsday,* p. 36.

30. Negron & L. Willen, op. cit., p. 4.

31. Berger, J. (1992, December 16). Queens board rejects Fernandez's offer to talk. *New York Times,* sec. p. B2.

32. Berger, J. (1992, December 18). Board chief assails aides to Fernandez. *New York Times,* p. B1.

33. Myers, S. (1992, December 13). How a rainbow curriculum turned into fighting words. *New York Times,* sec. 4, p. 6.

34. Randolph, E. (1993, February 11). New York City's controversial schools chancellor ousted. *Washington Post,* p. A3.

35. Dillard, S. (1993, May 19). "Light" New York vote was really the heaviest ever. *New York Times,* p. A1.

36. Kim, R. (1994, June 11). Nearing the Rainbow. *Newsday,* p. A16.

37. Gendar, A. (1999, February 18). Gays v. anti-Rainbow school board out to crack conservative stronghold. *New York Daily News,* Suburban Section, p. 4.

38. Barbanel, J. (1992, December 27). Under "Rainbow," a war: When politics, morals and learning mix. *New York Times,* sec. 1, p. 34.

39. Fernandez, with Underwood, op. cit., p. 13.

Article 29 References

Adler, J. (2005, February 7). Doubting Darwin. *Newsweek,* 44–50.

Alters, B. J., & Alters, S. M. (2001). *Defending evolution: A guide to the creation/evolution controversy.* Boston: Jones and Bartlett.

American Association for the Advancement of Science (2002). *AAAS Board resolution on intelligent design theory.* Available at www.aaas.org/news/releases/2002/1106id2.shtml

Associated Press (2002a, January 16). Board reviews science standard. *Cincinnati Post.*

Associated Press (2002b, March 9). "Intelligent design" debate to draw crowd, 3,920 seat hall reserved for state school board meeting on Monday. *Akron Beacon Journal.*

Associated Press (2002c, April 2). Science teaching debate escalates. *Cincinnati Post.*

Associated Press (2002d, June 10). Poll finds support for intelligent design, 59 percent of Ohioans favor teaching theory alongside evolution in public schools, paper says. *Akron Beacon Journal.*

Banerjee, N. (2004, December 13). Christian conservatives press issues in statehouses. *New York Times.*

Behe, M. J. (1996). *Darwin's black box: The biochemical challenge to evolution.* New York: Free Press.

Behe, M. J. (2005, February 7). Design for living. *New York Times.*

Bilica, K., and Skoog, G. (2004). Ohio teachers on teaching evolution and counter-evolutionary concepts in biology classrooms. *Reports of the National Center for Science Education, 24*(1). Available at www.ncseweb.org/resources/rncse_content/v0124/8949_ohio_teachers_on_teaching_evol_12_30_1849.asp

Clark, V. (2004). Shall we let our children think? *Reports of the National Center of Science Education, 24*(2). Available at www.nsceweb.org/resources/rncse_content/v24/5568_shall-we-let-our-children-think-evol 2–4568.asp

Center for the Renewal of Science and Culture (1999). *The wedge strategy.* Available at www.antievolution.org/features/wedge.html.

Davis, P., & Kenyon, D. H. (1993). *Of pandas, and people. The central question of biological origins* (2nd ed.). Richardson, TX: Foundation for Thought and Ethics.

Dembski, W. A., & Ruse, M. (Eds.). (2004). Debating design. *From Darwin to DN*A. Cambridge, UK: Cambridge University Press.

Design on Ohio, A scheme of "controversy," compromise, and curriculum [Editorial] (2001, March 13). *Akron Beacon Journal.*

Edwards v. Aguillard, 482 U.S. 578 (1987).

Feran, T. 2002, (March 12). Human origin debate hasn't evolved much. *Plain Dealer.*

Fields, R. (2002, March 12). Educators debate how life began. Discussion on evolution "design" theories heats up. *Akron Beacon Journal.*

Gilchrist, G. W. (1997). The elusive scientific basis of intelligent design theory. *Report of the National Center for Science Education, 17*(3), 14–15. Available at www.natcseted.org/resources/article-/2083_the__elusive_scientific_basis_v_3_1b_2001.asp

Heart of Wisdom (2006). *Heart of wisdom. Teaching approach.* Available at http://www.heartofwisdom.com/artman/publish/cat_index_39_html

Hottman, S. (2002, March 14). A governor's position evolves. *Akron Beacon Journal.*

Hughes. R. T. (2003). *Myths America lives by.* Chicago: University of Illinois Press.

Johnson. P. E. (1997). *Defeating Darwinism by opening minds.* Downers Grove, IL: InterVarsity Press.

Johnson. P. E. (2000). *The wedge of truth. Splitting the foundations of naturalism.* Downers Grove, IL: InterVarsity Press.

Larson. E. I. 1(989). *Trial and error. The American controversy over creation and evolution.* New York: Oxford University Press.

Mangels, J. (2002, March 12). Darwin, "Design" face off at hearing. *Plain Dealer.*

Mangels, J., & Stephens, S. (2002a, January 15). Evolution targeted in curriculum study: Ohio's guidelines may be rewritten. *Plain Dealer.*

Mangels, J., & Stephens, S. (2002b, March 16). Curriculum team backs evolution. *Plain Dealer.*

Matsumura. M. (1995). Texas: No pandas for Plano. *Reports of the National Center for Science Education, 15*(1), 7. Available at www.ncseweb.org/resources/articles/b190_40_matsumura_1995_texts_11_24_2004.alsp

Matsumura, M. (1999). A new tactic for getting "creation science" into classrooms. *Reports for the National Center for Science Education, 19*(3). 24–26. Available at www.ncseweb.org/resources/ncse_content/Vol19/5108_a_new_tactic_for_getting_crea_12_30_1899.asp

Moore. J. A. (2002). *From genesis to genetics. The case of evolution and creationism.* Berkeley: University of California Press.

Nakhnikian, G. (2004). It ain't necessarily so. An essay review of intelligent design creationism and its critics: Philosophical, theological, and scientific perspectives. *Philosophy of Science, 71*(4): 593–604.

National Academy of Sciences (1998). *Teaching about evolution and the creation of science.* Washington, DC: National Academy Press.

National Center for Science Education. [Reviews of the book *Of panda and people*]. *Bookwatch Reviews, 2*(11). Available at www.nationscedorg.article.asp/category_21

Newport. F. (2004). *Third of Americans say evidence has supported Darwin's evolution theory* [Gallup poll]. Princeton, NJ: The Gallup Organization. Available at http://poll.gallup.com/content/default.aspx?ci=1410

Ohio Department of Education (2002a). *State Board of Education minutes, March 10–12.* Available at www.ode.state.oh.us/board/meetings/march02/minutes.asp

Ohio Department of Education (2002b). *Science academic content standards.* Available at www.ode.state.oh.us/academic_content_standards/arsscience.asp

Ohio Department of Education (2002c). *State Board adopts academic content standards for science and social studies.* Available at www.ode.state.oh.us/board/meetings/December02

Ohio issue poll (2002, June 9). *Plain Dealer.*

Ohlemacher, S. (2002, March 13). Legislators keep "intelligent design" at arm's length. Issue left with state school board. *Plain Dealer.*

Owens-Fink, D. (2002, March 22). Columnist sows confusion on evolution. *Plain Dealer.*

Pennock. R. T. (2003, September). Creationism and intelligent design. *Annual Review of Genomics and Human Genetics, 4,* 143–163.

Ratliff, E. (2004). The crusade against evolution. *Wired, 12*(10). Available at www.wired.com/wired/archive/12.10/evolution.html

Science Excellence for All Ohioans (2002). *Adoption of Ohio science standards.* Available at www.stohio.org/sbc1015.htm

Scott, E. C., & Uno, G. E. L. (1989). Introduction to NCSE [Reviews of the book *Of pandas and people*]. *Bookwatch Reviews, 2*(11). Available at www.ncseorg/resource/articles/5403_20_scott_uno_1989_ intro_11_24_2004.asp

Sidoti, L. (2002a, March 16). Evolution debate rages in Ohio. Second draft of standards includes definition of science that limits "intelligent design" teaching. *Akron Beacon Journal.*

Sidoti, L. (2002b, March 25). Ohio school board split on evolution. Survey of 19 members finds no clear majority for intelligent design. *Akron Beacon Journal.*

Siegel. R. (2002, March 12). Ohio's intelligent design forum. *All things considered* [Radio series]. National Public Radio.

Slevins, P. (2005, March 14). Battle on teaching evolution sharpens. *Washington Post.*

Stephens, S., & Mangels, J. (2002a, January 16). Education panel to get some tutoring: Experts to explain evolution, creationism. *Plain Dealer.*

Stephens, S., & Mangels, J. (2002b, June 9). Poll: Teach more than evolution: A majority of those surveyed want evolution, intelligent design to get equal time in school. *Plain Dealer.*

Willard, D. J., & Dyer, S. (2002, March 12). Opponent feels Taft should be clear on science issue, Governor says he's watching classroom biology issue closely, Hagan says he should take a stand. *Akron Beacon Journal.*

Zeleznik, J. (2002, March 6). Bill would encourage other origin theories in classrooms. *Dayton Daily News.*

Article 30 References

Arnold, M. L., Newman, J. H., Gaddy, B. B., & Dean, C. B. (2005). A look at the condition of rural education research: Setting a direction for future research. *Journal of Research in Rural Education, 20*(6). Retrieved from http://www .umaine.edu/jrre/20–6.pdf

Burke, J. F. (2002). *Mestizo democracy: The politics of crossing borders.* College Station: Texas A&M University Press.

Díaz-Rico, L. T., & Weed, K. Z. (2002). *The cross-cultural, language, and academic development handbook* (2nd ed.). Boston: Allyn & Bacon.

Freeman, Y., & Freeman, D. (2003). Struggling English language learners: Keys for academic success. *TESOL Journal, 12*(3), 5–10.

Hall, E. T. (1969). *The hidden dimension.* Garden City, NY: Doubleday.

Hall, E. T. (1976). *Beyond culture.* New York: Anchor.

Hanson, V. D. (2003). *Mexifornia: A state of be coming.* San Francisco: Encounter Books.

Huntington, S. P. (2004). *Who are we? The challenges to America's identity.* New York: Simon & Schuster.

Klingner, J. K., & Artiles, A. J. (2003). When should bilingual students be in special education? *Educational Leadership, 61*(2), 66–71.

Merrell, F. (2003). *The Mexicans: A sense of culture.* Boulder, CO: Westview.

Worthan, S. E., Murillo, E. G., Jr., & Hamann, E. T. (2002). *Education in the new Latino diaspora: Policy and the politics of identity.* Norwood, NJ: Ablex.

Article 32 References

Beck, J., Broers, J., Hogue, E., Shipstead, J., & Knowlton, E. (1994). Strategies for functional community-based instruction and inclusion for children with mental retardation. *Teaching Exceptional Children, 26*(2), 44–48.

Blumberg, R., & Ferguson, P. M. (1999). *Brief discussions of critical issues in urban education: On point . . . on transition services for youth with disabilities.* (ERIC Document Reproduction Service No. ED 437 472)

Bruininks, R., Thurlow, M. L., & Ysseldyke, J. E. (1992). Assessing the right outcomes: Prospects for improving education of youth with disabilities. *Education and Training in Mental Retardation, 27,* 93–100.

Clark, G.M. (1994). Is a functional curriculum approach compatible with an inclusive education model? *Teaching Exceptional Children, 26*(2), 36–39.

Cronin, M. E., & Patton, J. R. (1993). *Life skills instruction for all students with special needs: A practical guide for integrating real-life content into the curriculum.* Austin, TX: Pro-Ed.

Dever, R. B., & Knapczyk, D. R. (1997). *Teaching persons with menial retardation: A model for curriculum development and teaching.* Boston: McGraw-Hill.

Edgar, E., & Polloway, E. A. (1994). Education for adolescents with disabilities: Curriculum and placement issues. *Journal of Special Education, 27,* 438–452.

Forness, S. R. (1985). Effects of public policy at the state level: California's impact on MR, LD, and ED categories. *Remedial and Special Education, 6*(3), 36–43.

Gerber, P. J. (1998). *Characteristics of adults with specific learning disabilities* [Online]. Available http://www.ldonhine.org/ ld_indepth/adult/characteristics.html

Gottlieb, J., Alter, M., Gottlieb, B. W., & Wishner, J. (1994). Special education in urban America: It's not justifiable for many. *Journal of Special Education, 27,* 453–465.

Halpern, A. S., Benz, M. R., & Lindstrom, L. E. (1992). A systems change approach to improving secondary special education and transition programs at the community level. *Career Development for Exceptional Individuals, 15,* 109–120.

Knowlton, E. (1998). Considerations in the design of personalized curricular supports for students with developmental disabilities. *Education and Training in Mental Retardation and Developmental Disabilities, 33,* 95–107.

Langone, J., Langone, C. A., & McLaughlin, P. J. (2000). Analyzing special educators' views on community-based instruction for students with mental retardation and developmental disabilities: Implications for teacher education. *Journal of Developmental and Physical Disabilities, 12,* 17–34.

Lieberman, L. M. (2001, January 17). The death of special education: Having the right to fail in regular education is no entitlement. *Education Week, 20,* 60–61.

MacMillan, D. L., & Borthwick, S. (1980). The new educable mentally retarded population: Can they be mainstreamed? *Mental Retardation, 18,* 155–158.

McIntyre, T. (1992). The impact of reform recommendations on urban special education. *Preventing School Failure, 36*(4), 6–10.

Moore, S.C., Agran, M., & McSweyn, C. A. (1990). Career education: Are we starting early enough? *Career Development for Exceptional Individuals, 13,* 129–134.

Obiakor, F. E., & Algozzine, B. (1993). Urban education, the general education initiative, and service delivery to African-American students. *Urban Education, 28,* 313–327.

Patton, J. R., Polloway, E. A., Smith, T.E.C., Edgar, E., Clark, G. M., & Lee, S. (1996). Individuals with mild mental retardation: Postsecondary outcomes and implications for educational policy. *Education and Training in Mental Retardation and Developmental Disabilities, 31,* 75–85.

Polloway, E. A., Epstein, M. H., Patton, J. R., Cullinan, D., & Luebke, J. (1986). Demographic, social, and behavioral characteristics of students with educable mental retardation. *Education and Training of the Mentally Retarded, 21,* 27–34.

Polloway, E. A., Patton, J. R., Epstein, M. H., & Smith, T.E.C. (1989). Comprehensive curriculum for students with mild handicaps. *Focus on Exceptional Children, 21*(8), 1–12.

Polloway, E. A., Patton, J. R., Smith, J. D., & Roderique, T. W. (1991). Issues in program design for elementary students with mild retardation: Emphasis on curriculum development. *Education and Training in Mental Retardation, 26,* 142–150.

Rousseau, M. K., & Davenport, R. (1993). Special education in urban and correctional education in the year 2000: A response to Ludlow and Lombardi. *Education and Treatment of Children, 16,* 90–95.

Siegel-Causey, F., & Allinder, R. M. (1998). Using alternative assessment for students with severe disabilities: Alignment with best practices. *Education and Training in Mental Retardation and Developmental Disabilities, 33,* 168–178.

Simpson, R. L. (1996). *Working with parents and families of exceptional children and youth: Techniques for successful conferencing and collaboration* (3rd ed.). Austin, TX: Pro-Ed.

Smith, J. D. (1998). Defining mental retardation: The natural history of a concept. In A. Hilton & R. Ringlaben (Eds.), *Best and promising practices in developmental disabilities* (pp. 15–21). Austin, TX: Pro-Ed.

Smith, T.E.C., & Dowdy, C. (1992). Future-based assessment and intervention for students with mental retardation. *Education and Training in Mental Retardation, 27,* 255–260.

Smith, T.E.C., & Hilton, A. (1994). Program design for students with mental retardation. *Education and Training in Mental Retardation and Developmental Disabilities, 29,* 3–8.

Smith, T.E.C., & Puccini, I. K. (1995). Position statement: Secondary curricula and policy issues for students with mental retardation. *Education and Training in Mental Retardation and Developmental Disabilities, 30,* 275–282.

Turnbull, A., Turnbull, R., Shank, M., & Leal, D. (1999). *Exceptional lives: Special education in today's schools* (2nd ed.). Upper Saddle River, NJ: Merrill.

U.S. Department of Education. (1996). *To assure the free appropriate public education of all children with disabilities: 18th annual report to Congress on the implementation of the Individuals With Disabilities Education Act.* Washington, DC: Author.

Weaver, R., Landers, M. F., & Adams, S. (1991). Making curriculum functional: Special education and beyond. *Intervention in School and Clinic, 26,* 284–287.

Wolery, M., Ault, M. J., & Doyle, P. M. (1992). *Teaching students with moderate to severe disabilities: Use of response-prompting strategies.* New York: Longman.

Zigmond, N., & Sansone, J. (1986). Designing a program for the learning disabled adolescent. *Remedial and Special Education, 7*(5), 13–17.

Article 33 References

Atwater, M. (1995). The multicultural science classroom, part III: Preparing science teachers to meet the challenges of education. *Science Teacher, 62*(5), 26–30.

Atwater, M. (1999). Inclusive reform: Including all students in the science reform movement. *Science Teacher, 66*(3), 44–48.

Atwater, M., Wiggins, J., & Gardner, C. (1995). A study of urban middle school students with high and low attitudes toward science. *Journal of Research in Science Teaching, 32,* 665–677.

Berliner, D. (2001, January 28). Our schools vs. theirs: Averages that hide the true extremes. *Washington Post,* p. 3.

Braun, C. (1976). Teacher expectations: Sociopsychological dynamics. *Review of Educational Research, 46,* 185–213.

Brickhouse, N. (1990). Teacher beliefs about the nature of science and their relationship to classroom practice. *Journal of Teacher Education, 41,* 53–62.

Briscoe, C. (1991). The dynamic interactions among beliefs, role metaphors, and teaching practices: A case study of teacher change. *Science Education, 75,* 185–199.

Brophy, J., & Good, T. (1970). Teachers' communication of differential expectations for children's classroom performance. *Journal of Educational Psychology, 61,* 365–374.

Bryan, L., & Atwater, M. (2002). Teacher beliefs and cultural models: A challenge for science teacher education programs. *Science Education, 86,* 821–839.

Clark, C., & Peterson, P. (1986). *Teachers' thought processes.* New York: Macmillan.

Cochran-Smith, M. (2000). Blind vision: Unlearning racism in teacher education. *Harvard Educational Review, 70,* 157–190.

Ennis, C. (1995). Teachers' responses to noncompliant students: The realities and consequences of a negotiated curriculum. *Teaching and Teacher Education, 11,* 445–460.

Ennis, C., & McCauley, M. (2002). Creating urban classroom communities worthy of trust. *Journal of Curriculum Studies, 34,* 149–172.

Entwisle, D., & Alexander, K. (1988). Factors affecting achievement test scores and marks of Black and White first graders. *Elementary School Journal, 88,* 449–471.

Haberman, M. (1991). The pedagogy of poverty versus good teaching. *Phi Delta Kappan, 73,* 290–294.

Lewis, B. F., Pitts, V. R., & Collins, A. C. (2002). A descriptive study of pre-service teachers' perceptions of African American students' ability to achieve in mathematics and science. *Negro Educational Review, 53,* 31–42.

Maryland State Department of Education. (2002). *Maryland school performance 2002 report.* Baltimore: Author.

Norman, O., Ault, C., Bentz, B., & Meskimen, L. (2001). The Black–White "achievement gap" as a perennial challenge of urban science education: A sociocultural and historical overview with implications for research and practice. *Journal of Research in Science Teaching, 38,* 1101–1114.

Ogbu, J., & Simmons, H. (1998). Voluntary and involuntary minorities: A cultural-ecological theory of school performance with some implications for education. *Anthropology and Education Quarterly, 29,* 155–188.

Pajares, M. (1992). Teachers' beliefs and educational research: Cleaning up a messy construct. *Review of Educational Research, 62,* 307–322.

Richardson, V. (1996). The role of attitudes and beliefs in learning to teach. In J. Sikula, T. Buttery, & E. Guyton (Eds.), *Handbook of research on teacher education* (2nd ed., pp. 102–119). New York: Macmillan.

Schwab, J. (1970). *The practical: A language for curriculum.* Washington, DC: National Education Association.

Shepardson, D. P., & Pizzini, E. L. (1992). Gender bias in female elementary teachers' perceptions of the scientific ability of students. *Science Education, 76,* 147–153.

Steele, C. (1999, August). "Stereotype threat" and Black college students. *Atlantic Monthly,* 44–54.

Taylor, N., & Macpherson, C. (1992). Primary science in Fiji: Some reflections on activity-based lessons. *Journal of Science and Mathematics Education in Southeast Asia, 15,* 40–44.

Article 34 References

Allen, J. C., & Dillman, D. A. (1994). *Against all odds: Rural community in the information age.* Boulder, CO: Westview.

Anyon, J. (1980). Social class and the hidden curriculum of work. *Journal of Education 162*(1), 67–92.

Barker, B. (1985a). Curricular offerings in small and large high schools: How broad is the disparity? *Research in Rural Education, 3*(1), 35–38.

Barker, B. (1985b). *Attitudes of principals concerning curriculum needs in small high schools.* Lubbock: Texas Tech University. (ERIC ED 260 876)

Barker, B., Muse, I, & Smith, R. (1984). Curriculum characteristics of rural school districts in thirteen selected states. *Research in Rural Education, 2*(3), 91–94.

Boethel, M. (2000). *Rural student entrepreneurs: Linking commerce and community (Benefits)[Squared]: The exponential results of linking school improvement and community development.* Austin, TX: Southwest Educational Development Lab. (ERIC ED 440 805)

Borko, H., Elliott, R., & Uchiyama, K. (2002). Professional development: A key to Kentucky's educational reform effort. *Teaching and Teacher Education, 18*(8), 969–87.

Borman, G. D., & Hewes, C. M. (2001). The long-term effects and cost-effectiveness of Success for All. Baltimore: Center for Research on the Education of Students Placed at Risk. (ERIC ED 460 217)

Brown, D. F. (1992). *Altering curricula through state-mandated testing: Perceptions of teachers and principals.* Paper presented at the annual meeting of the American Educational Research Association, April, 20–24 San Francisco, CA.

Cimbricz, S. (2002). State-mandated testing and teachers' beliefs and practices. *Educational Policy Analysis Archives, 10*(2), 1–13. Available at http://epaa.asu.edu/epaa/v10n2.html

Cremin, L. A. (1970). *American education: The colonial experience, 1607–1783.* New York: Harper & Row.

Cuban, L. (1993). *How teachers taught: Constancy and change in American classrooms, 1890–1990* (2nd ed.). New York: Teachers College Press.

Education Commission of the States (2002). *Recent state policies/activities: Accountability—sanctions/interventions.* Available at www.ecs.org

Everett, S. (Ed.). (1938). *The community school.* New York: D. Appleton-Century.

Fikes, R., Jr. (1991). Book censorship, social dynamics, and the education-library establishment's response to the Kanawha County textbook controversy. (ERIC ED 338 251)

Franklin, B. (1987). Education for an urban America: Ralph Tyler and the curriculum field. In I. Goodson (Ed.), *International perspectives in curriculum history* (pp. 277–296). London: Croom Helm.

Gibbs, T. J., & Howley, A. (2000). *"World-class standards" and local pedagogies: Can we do both?* Charleston, WV: ERIC Clearinghouse on Rural Education and Small Schools. (ERIC ED 448 014)

Gitlin, A., & Margonis, F. (1995). The political aspect of reform: Teacher resistance as good sense. *American Journal of Education, 103*(4), 377–405.

Gulliford, A. 1996. *America's country schools* (3d ed.). Niwot: University Press of Colorado.

Haas, T., and Nachtigal, P. (1998). *Place value: An educator's guide to good literature on rural lifeways, environments, and purposes of education.* Charleston, WV: ERIC Clearinghouse on Rural Education and Small Schools. (ERIC ED 420 461)

Haney, W. (2000). The myth of the Texas miracle in education. *Educational Policy Analysis Archives, 8*(41). Available at http://epaa.asu.edu/epaa/v8n41html

Harding, P. A., & Vining, L. C. (1997). The impact of the knowledge explosion on science education. *Journal of Research in Science Teaching, 34*(10), 969–75.

Howley, C. B., Howley, A., & Pendarvis, E. P. (1995). *Out of our minds: Anti-intellectualism and talent development in American schooling.* New York: Teachers College Press.

Hughes, L. W., Spence, D. L. (1971). *Attitudes and orientations of rural groups and effects on educational decision-making and innovation in rural school districts: A synthesis of research.* Las Cruces, NM: ERIC Clearinghouse on Rural Education and Small Schools. (ERIC ED 054 892)

Jennings, N. E. (2000). Standards and local curriculum: A zero sum game? *Journal of Research in Rural Education, 16*(3), 193–201.

Jeynes, W. H., & Littell, S. W. (2000). A meta-analysis of studies examining the effect of whole language instruction on the literacy of low-SES students. *Elementary School Journal, 101*(1), 21–33.

Jones, M. G., Jones, B. D., Hardin, B., Chapman, L., Yarbrough, T., & Davis, M. (1999). The impact of high-stakes testing on teachers and students in North Carolina. *Phi Delta Kappan, 81*(3), 199–203.

Keith, J. (1995). Country people in the new south: Tennessee's Upper Cumberland studies in rural culture. Chapel Hill: University of North Carolina Press. (ERIC ED 409 143)

Kleinsasser, A. M. (1986). *Exploration of an ambiguous culture: Conflicts facing gifted females in rural environments.* Paper presented at the annual conference of the National Rural and Small Schools Consortium, October 9, Bellingham, WA. (ERIC ED 278 522)

Kliebard, H. M. (1992). *Forging the American curriculum: Essays in curriculum history and theory.* New York: Routledge.

Kliebard, H. M. (2002). *Changing course: American curriculum reform in the 20th century.* New York: Teachers College Press.

Lambert, R., P. (1991). Broad policies, local schools: Re-thinking rural education in an age of reform. In M. H. Lee (Ed.), *Reaching our potential: Rural education in the 90s* (Conference proceedings). Rural Education Symposium, March 17–20, Nashville. (ERIC ED 342 533)

Lave, J., & Wenger. E. (1991). *Situated learning: Legitimate peripheral participation.* New York: Cambridge University Press.

Leo-Nyquist, D. (2001). Recovering a tradition of rural progressivism in American public education. *Journal of Research in Rural Education, 17*(1), 27–40.

Leo-Nyquist, D., & Theobald, P. (1997). *Toward a pedagogy of place: Finding common ground for rural researchers, teacher educators, and practitioners.* Paper presented at the annual meeting of the American Educational Research Association, March 24–28, Chicago. (ERIC ED 432 416)

Mathews, F. D. (1996). *Is there a public for public schools?* Dayton, OH: Kettering Foundation Press.

McCracken, J. D., & Barcina, J. D. T. (1991). High school and student characteristics in rural and urban areas of Ohio. In *School and community influences on occupational and educational plans of rural youth* (pp. 43–50). Ohio Agricultural Research and Development Center. (ERIC ED 338 456)

Midkiff, F. E. (1938). Community schools in Waialua, Hawaii. In S. Everett (Ed.), *The community school* (pp. 298–339). New York: D. Appleton-Century.

Monk, D. H., & Haller, E. J. (1990). *High school size and course offerings: Evidence from high school and beyond.* (ERIC ED 325 298)

Moriarty, T. E. (1964). *State educational policies and the mission of rural community schools.* Paper presented at the annual Northern Rocky Mountain Educational Research Association Meeting, October 4–6, Jackson Hole, WY. (ERIC ED 252 334)

Nilsen, K. L. (2000). *Implementing the aligned and balanced curriculum (ABC): Building capacity for continuous school improvement.* Paper presented at the annual meeting of the American Educational Research Association, April 24–29, New Orleans. (ERIC ED 450 994)

Page, A. L., Clelland, D. A. (1978). The Kanawha County textbook controversy: A study of the politics of lifestyle concern. *Social Forces, 57*(1), 265–81.

Parkerson, D. H., & Parkerson, J. A. (1998). *The emergence of the common school in the U.S. countryside.* Lewiston, NY: E. Mellen Press.

Reichman, S. L., & Rayford, L. (1988*). Using test results for curriculum alignment: An approach to program evaluation and improvement.* Paper presented at the annual meeting of the American Educational Research Association, April 5–9, New Orleans. (ERIC ED 299 327)

Romano, R. M., & Glascock, C. H. (Eds.). (2002). *Hungry minds in hard times: Educating for complexity for students of poverty.* New York: P. Lang.

Romberg, T. A., Zarinnia, L. A., & Williams, S. R. (1988). *The influence of mandated testing on mathematics instruction: Grade 8 teachers' perceptions.* Madison: University of Wisconsin, Center for Educational Research, School of Education, and Office of Educational Research, and Improvement of the U.S. Department of Education.

Scott, B. D. (1999). Standing up for community and school: Rural people tell their stories. Randolph, VT: Rural Challenge Policy Program. (ERIC ED 440 788)

Smith, M. L. (1991). Put to the test: The effects of external testing on teachers. *Educational Researcher, 20*(5), 8–11.

Smith, M. S., & O'Day, J. (1991). Systemic school reform. In S. H. Fuhrman & B. Malen (Eds.), *The politics of curriculum and testing: The 1990 yearbook of the Politics of Education Association* (pp. 233–267). New York: Falmer Press.

Spring, J. H. (1989). *The sorting machine revisited: National educational policy since 1945* (Updated ed.). New York: Longman.

Stockman, C., & Powers, P. J. (1996). *Analysis of differences between educator and parent perceptions of rural elementary school priorities.* Paper presented at the annual meeting of the Northern Rocky Mountain Educational Research Association, October 5, Detroit Lakes, MN. (ERIC ED4OI 072)

Swidler, S. A., & Hoffman, J. L. (2000). *Anticipating state standards: Nebraska City schools.* Paper presented at the annual meeting of the American Educational Research Association, April 24–28, New Orleans. (ERIC ED 450 975)

Sykes, G. (1996). Reform of and as professional development. *Phi Delta Kappan, 77*(7), 464–467.

Theobald, P. (1997). *Teaching the commons: Place, pride, and the renewal of community.* Boulder, CO: Westview Press.

U.S. Department of Education. 1996. *Digest of education statistics.* Washington, DC: U.S. Government Printing Office.

Wall, M., & Luther, V. (1988). Schools as entrepreneurs: Helping small towns survive. Lincoln, NE: Heartland Center for Leadership Development. (ERIC ED 312 097)

Williams, B. (1998). The genius of place. In V. Perrone (Ed.) *Toward place and community,* (pp. 62–78). Granby, CO: Annenberg Rural Challenge. (ERIC ED 444 793)

Wither, S. E. (2001). *Local curriculum development: A case study.* Paper presented at the annual meeting of the American Educational Research Association, April 10–14, Seattle. (ERIC ED 456 022)

Woodhouse, J. L, & Knapp, C. E. (2000). *Place-based curriculum and instruction: Outdoor and environmental education approaches.* Charleston, WV: ERIC Clearinghouse on Rural Education and Small Schools. (ERIC ED 448 012)

Woofter, T. J. (1917). *Teaching in rural schools.* Boston: Houghton Mifflin.

Article 36 Endnotes

1. Snapshots (2004, December 28). *USA Today,* p. 1-B.
2. Beane, J. (2004). *No progressive idea left alone: A middle school curriculum ten years later.* Paper presented at the annual meeting of the National Middle School Association, Minneapolis, November 2004.
3. Brown, D. F. (2000–2003). *Informal assessment of middle-level teachers' perceptions of prioritized learning outcomes.* Unpublished raw data, West Chester University.
4. Smith, C. (2002, November). *Conversation on Vermont's learning outcomes.*
5. Emery, K., & Ohanian, S. (2004). *Why is corporate America bashing our public schools?* (p. 19). Portsmouth, NH: Heinemann .
6. Brady, M. (2004, December). Thinking big: A conceptual framework for the study of everything. *Phi Delta Kappan,* 281.
7. Brady.
8. Emery & Ohanian, p. 20.
9. *Philadelphia Inquirer,* January 9, 2005, pp. G-4–G-5.
10. Graves, D. H. (2002). Testing is not teaching: *What should count in education* (p. 63). Portsmouth, NH: Heinemann.
11. Bracey, G. W. (2003). *On the death of childhood and the destruction of public schools* (p. 39). Portsmouth, NH: Heinemann,.
12. Mezzacappa, D. (2005, February). Survey: Many grads of high school say they're not prepared. *Philadelphia Inquirer,* p. A-16

13. Knowles, T., & Brown, D. E. (2000). *What every middle school teacher should know* (p. 84). Portsmouth, NH, and Westerville, OH: Heinemann and National Middle School Association.

14. Lewis, C., Christian, S., & Gold, E. (2001). An education for what? Reflections of two high school seniors. In J. Shultz & A. Cook-Sather (Eds.), *In our own words: Students' perspectives on school* (p. 93). Lanham, MD: Rowman & Littlefield.

15. Lewis et al., p. 98.

16. Lewis et al., pp. 4–5.

17. Mezzacappa, op. cit.

18. A Kappa Delta Pi lecture by John Dewey, cited in Parkay, F. W., & Hass, G. (2000). *Curriculum planning: A contemporary approach* (7th ed.) (p. 34). Needham Heights, MA: Allyn & Bacon.

19. Beane, J. A. (1997). *Curriculum integration: Designing the core of democratic dducation.* New York: Teachers College Press.

20. Beane, J. A. (1993). *A middle school curriculum: From rhetoric to reality* (2nd ed.) (pp. x–xi). Columbus, OH: National Middle School Association .

21. Beane, J. A., p. xi.

22. See Brown, D. F. (2002, September). Self-directed learning in an eighth-grade classroom. *Educational Leadership, 54–58.*

23. Nesin, G., Brodhagen, B., & Smith, C. (2005). *Middle grades curriculum: Planning with students—Part 1.* Paper presented at the annual meeting of the National Middle School Association, Minneapolis, November 2005. Similar sessions have been held at each NMSA meeting for the past decade.

24. A number of schools throughout the U.S. that have been engaged in curriculum integration with middle-schoolers for several years are noted in Knowles & Brown, p. 94.

25. Hamburg, D. A. (1993). The opportunities of early adolescence. *Teachers College Record, 93,* 466–71.

26. Mee, C. (1997). *2,000 voices: Young adolescents' perceptions and curriculum implications.* Westerville, OH: National Middle School Association.

27. Beane, *Curriculum Integration.*

28. Brown, D. F., & Morgan, J. L. (2003). *Students' perceptions of the impact of a curriculum integration experience on their learning.* Paper presented at the annual meeting of the American Educational Research Association, Chicago, April 2003.

29. New York may institute job readiness test. *Smart Brief.* Association for Supervision and Curriculum Development, January 31, 2005.

Article 37 References

Alba, R. D., & Nee, V. (2003). *Remaking the American mainstream: Assimilation and contemporary immigration.* Cambridge, MA: Harvard University Press.

Banks, C. A. M. (2004). *Improving multicultural education: Lessons from the intergroup education movement.* New York: Teachers College Press.

Banks, J. A. (Ed.). (1996). *Multicultural education, transformative knowledge, and action: Historical and contemporary perspectives.* New York: Teachers College Press.

Banks, J. A. (2001). *Cultural diversity and education: Foundations, curriculum, and teaching* (4th ed.). Boston: Allyn and Bacon.

Banks, J. A. (2003). *Teaching strategies for ethnic studies* (7th ed.). Boston: Allyn and Bacon.

Banks, J. A. (Ed.). (2004). *Diversity and citizenship education: Global perspectives.* San Francisco: Jossey-Bass.

Banks, J. A., & Banks, C. A. M. (Eds.). (2004). *Handbook of research on multicultural education* (2nd ed.). San Francisco: Jossey-Bass.

Banks, J. A., & Lynch, J. (Eds.) (1986). *Multicultural education in Western societies.* London: Holt.

Banks, J. A., Cookson, P., Gay, C., Hawley, W. D., Irvine, J. J., Nieto, S., Schofield, J. W., & Stephan, W. G. (2001). *Diversity within unity: Essential principles for teaching and learning in a multicultural society.* Seattle: Center for Multicultural Education, University of Washington.

Banks, J. A., Banks, C. A. M., Cortés, C. E., Hahn, C., Merryfield, M., Moodley, K., Osler, A., Murphy-Shigematsu, S., & Parker, W. C. (2005). *Democracy and diversity: Principles and concepts for educating citizens in a global age.* Seattle: Center for Multicultural Education, University of Washington. [AU: HAS THIS BEEN PUBLISHED? UPDATE ENTRY?]

Castles, S. (2004). Migration, citizenship, and education. In J. A. Banks (Ed.), *Diversity and citizenship education: Global perspectives* (pp. 17–48). San Francisco: Jossey-Bass.

Drachsler, J. (1920). *Democracy and assimilation: The blending of immigrant heritages in America.* New York: Macmillan.

Eldering, L, & Kloprogge, J. (1989). *Different cultures, same school: Ethnic minority children in Europe.* Amsterdam: Swets and Zeitlinger.

Freire, P. (1997). Pedagogy of the oppressed (20th anniv. ed.) (M. B. Ramos, Trans.). New York: Continuum.

Gillborn, D. (1990). *Race, ethnicity, and education: Teaching and learning in multi-ethnic schools.* London: Unwin Hyman/Routledge.

Gordon, M. M. (1964). *Assimilation in American life: The role of race, religion, and national origins.* New York: Oxford University Press.

Gutmann, A. (1987). *Democratic education.* Princeton, NJ: Princeton University Press.

Gutmann, A. (2004). Unity and diversity in democratic multicultural education: Creative and destructive tensions. In Banks, J. A. (Ed.), *Diversity and citizenship education: Global perspectives* (pp. 71–96). San Francisco: Jossey-Bass.

Kallen, H. M. (1924). *Culture and democracy in the United States.* New York: Boni and Liveright.

Kymlicka, W. (1995). *Multicultural citizenship: A liberal theory of minority rights.* New York: Oxford University Press.

Nussbaum, M. (2002). Patriotism and cosmopolitanism. In J. Cohen (Ed.), *For love of country* (pp. 2–17). Boston: Beacon Press.

Patterson, O. (1977). *Ethnic chauvinism: The reactionary impulse.* New York: Stein and Day.

Smith, L T. (1999). *Decolonizing methodologies: Research and indigenous peoples.* New York: Zed Books.

U.S. Census Bureau (2000). *Statistical abstract of the United States: 2000* (120th ed.). Washington, DC: U.S. Government Printing Office.

Article 38 References

Ahmed, F., Harris, N., Braithwaite, J., & Braithwaite, V. (2001) *Shame management through reintegration.* Cambridge, UK: Cambridge University Press.

Anderson, C. (1997). *Restorative measures: Respecting everyone's ability to resolve problems* [Monograph]. Roseville: Minnesota Department of Children, Families, and Learning.

Anderson, C., Gendler, G., & Riestenberg, N. (1998). *Restorative measures: Respecting everyone's ability to resolve problems.* Roseville: Minnesota Department of Children, Families, and Learning.

Bazemore, G. (1998). Restorative justice and earned redemption: Communities, victims and offender reintegration. *American Behavioral Scientist, 41,* 768–8 13.

Bazemore, G. (1999). The fork in the road to juvenile court reform. *Annals of the American Academy of Political Social Science, 564*(7), 81–108.

Bazemore, G., Nissen, L., & Dooley, M. (2000). Mobilizing social support and building relationships: Broadening correctional and rehabilitative agendas. *Corrections Management Quarterly, 4*(4), 10–21.

Bazemore, G., & Schiff, M. (2004). *Juvenile justice reform and restorative justice: Building theory and policy from practice.* Cullompton, UK: Willan.

Bazemore, G., & Umbreit, M. (2001). *Comparison of four restorative conferencing models.* Washington, DC: Office of Juvenile Justice and Delinquency Prevention, Office of Justice Programs, U.S. Department of Justice.

Bazemore, G., & Walgrave, L. (1999). Restorative juvenile justice: In search of fundamentals and an outline for systemic reform. In G. Bazemore & L. Walgrave (Eds.), *Restorative juvenile justice: Repairing the harm of youth crime* (pp. 45–62). Monsey, NY: Criminal Justice Press.

Bellah, R., Madsen, R., Sullivan, W., Swidler, A., & Tipton, S. (1991*). The good society.* Berkeley: University of California Press.

Binns, K., & Markow, D. (1999). *The Metropolitan Life survey of the American teacher, 1999: Violence in America's public schools—Five years later.* New York: Metropolitan Life Insurance Company.

Bonta, J., Wallace-Capretta, S., Rooney, J., & Mackanoy, K. (2002). An outcome evaluation of a restorative justice alternative to incarceration. *Contemporary Justice Review, 5,* 319–338.

Boyes-Watson, C. (2004). What are the implications of growing state involvement in restorative justice? In H. Zehr & B. Toews-Shenk (Eds.), *Critical issues in restorative justice* (pp. 215–226). Monsey, NY: Criminal Justice Press.

Braithwaite, J. (2002). *Restorative justice and responsive regulation.* New York: Oxford University Press.

Braithwaite, J., & Drahos, P. (2002). Zero tolerance, naming and shaming: Is there a case for it with crimes of the powerful? *Australian and New Zealand Journal of Criminology, 35,* 269–288.

Brendtro, L., & Long, N. (1995). Breaking the cycle of conflict. *Educational Leadership, 52*(5), 52–56.

Butts, J., & Snyder, H. (1991). *Restitution and juvenile recidivism.* Pittsburgh, PA: National Center for Juvenile Justice.

Christie, N. (1977). Conflict as property. *British Journal of Criminology, 17*(1), 1–15.

Costenbader, V., & Markson, S. (1998). School suspension: A study with secondary school students. *Journal of School Psychology, 36*(1), 59–82.

Curwin, R, & Mendler, A. (1999). Zero tolerance for zero tolerance. *Phi Delta Kappan, 81*(1), 119–120.

DeVoe, J. F., Peter, K., Kaufman, P., Ruddy, S. A., Miller, A. K., Planty, M., et al. (2003). *Indicators of school crime and safety: 2003.* Washington, DC: U.S. Department of Education, U.S. Department of Justice.

Flaherty, L. (2001). School violence and the school environment. In Shafii, M., & Shafii, S. L. (Eds.), *School violence: Assessment, management, prevention* (pp. 25–52). Washington, DC: American Psychiatric Publishing.

Gottfredson, D. C. (1990). Changing school structures to benefit high-risk youths. In P. E. Leone (Ed.), *Understanding troubled and troubling youth.* Newbury Park, CA: Sage.

Granaiery, L. E. (2002). *A record of accomplishment: Interim evaluation of school peer jury pilot program in 21 Chicago public schools.* Chicago: Chicago Public Schools.

Harcourt, B. E. (2001). *Illusion of order: The false promise of broken window policing.* Cambridge, MA: Harvard University Press.

Hayes, H. (2005). Assessing reoffending in restorative justice conferences. *Australian and New Zealand Journal of Criminology, 38*(1), 77–102.

Henault, C. (2001). Chalk talk. *Journal of Law and Education, 30,* 547–553.

Hines, D., & Bazemore, B. (2003). Restorative policing, conferencing and community building. *Police Practice and Research: An International Journal, 4,* 441–427.

Karp, D., & Breslin, B. (2001). Restorative justice in school communities. *Youth & Society, 33,* 249–272.

Kaufman, P., Chen, X., Choy, S. P., Peter, K., Ruddy, S. A., Miller, A. K., et.al. (1999). *Indicators of school crime and safety, 1999.* Washington, DC: U.S. Department of Education, U.S. Department of Justice.

Lawrence, R. (1998). *School crime and juvenile justice.* New York: Oxford University Press.

Maloney, D., Bazemore, G., & Hudson, J. (2001, Summer). The end of probation and the beginning of community Justice. *Perspectives,* pp. 23–30.

Moore, D. (1994). *Illegal action-official reaction.* Canberra: Australian Institute of Criminology.

Morrison, B. (2001). The school system: Developing its capacity in the regulation of a civilized society. In J. Braithwaite & H. Strang (Eds.), *Restorative justice arid civil society* (pp. 195–224). Cambridge, UK: Cambridge University Press.

Nugent, W., Williams, M., & Umbreit, M. S. (2003). Participation in victim-offender mediation and the prevalence of subsequent delinquent behavior: A meta-analysis. *Utah Law Review,* 137–166.

Payne, A., Gottfredson, D., & Gottfredson, G. (2003). Schools as communities: The relationships among communal school organization, student bonding, and school disorder. *Criminology, 41,* 749–777.

Pearl, A., & Knight, T. (1998). *The democratic classroom.* Cresskill, NJ: Hampton Press.

Pranis, K. (1998). *Restorative justice: Principles, practices and implementation, section 6, building community. National Institute of Corrections curriculum.* Washington, DC: U.S. Department of Justice, Federal Bureau of Prisons, National Institute of Corrections.

Preventing Juvenile Gun Violence in Schools. (1996). In *Creating safe and drug-free schools: An action guide* (pp. 21–30). Washington, DC: U.S. Department of Justice, U.S. Department of Education.

Riestenberg, N. (1999). *In-school behavior intervention grants: A three year evaluation of alternative approaches to suspensions and expulsions.* Roseville: Minnesota Department of Children, Families, and Learning.

Riestenberg, N. (2003). *Zero and no: Some definitions.* Roseville: Minnesota Department of Education.

Roche, D. (2003). *Accountability in restorative justice.* New York: Oxford University Press.

Schiff, M., & Bazemore, G. (2002). *Final report on understanding the community role in restorative conferencing for youthful offenders.* Princeton, NJ: Robert Wood Johnson Foundation.

Schneider, A. (1986). Restitution and recidivism rates of juvenile offenders: Results from four experimental studies. *Criminology, 24,* 533–552.

Sheley, J. (2000). Controlling violence: What schools are doing. In S. G. Kellam, R. Prinz, & J. F. Sheley (Eds.), *Preventing school violence: Plenary papers of the 1999 Conference on Criminal Justice Research and Evaluation—Enhancing policy and practice through research* (Vol. 2, pp. 37–57). Washington, DC: National Institute of Justice.

Sheley, J., & Wright, J. (1998). *High school youths, weapons, and violence: A national survey.* Washington, DC: National Institute of Justice.

Skiba, R., & Peterson, R. (1999). Zap zero tolerance. *Education Digest, 64*(8), 24–31.

Stinchcomb, J., & Dobrin, A. (2000). *A study of firearms-related incidents and related issues in the city of Ft. Lauderdale, Phase II report: School related data, interviews, and school safety issues.* Unpublished manuscript, Florida Atlantic University, Fort Lauderdale.

Stuart, B. (2001). Guiding principles for designing peacemaking circles. In G. Bazemore & M. Schiff (Eds.), *Restorative and community justice: Repairing harm and transforming communities* (pp. 219–241). Cincinnati, OH: Anderson.

Umbreit, M., Coates, R., & Vos, B. (2001). Victim impact of meeting with young offenders: Two decades of victim offender mediation practice and research. In A. Morris & G. Maxwell (Eds.), *Restorative justice for juveniles: Conferencing, mediation and circles* (pp. 121–143). Oxford, UK: Hart.

U.S. Department of Education. (1996). *Creating safe and drug-free schools.* Washington, DC: Office of Juvenile Justice and Delinquency Prevention. Office of Elementary and Secondary Education.

U.S. vs. Lopez, 514 U.S. 549 (1995).

Van Ness, D., & Strong, K. H. (1997). *Restoring justice.* Cincinnati, OH: Anderson.

Van Ness, D., & Strong, K. H. (2001). *Restoring justice* (2nd ed.). Cincinnati, OH: Anderson.

Zamora, P. (2002). *Chicago public school peer jury program: Initial report program implementation, July 2001–February 2002.* Chicago: Alternatives, Inc.

Article 39 Endnotes

1. McBrien, W. (1998). *Cole Porter* (p. 18). New York: HarperCollins.
2. Levine, A. (2001, December 12). An endgame for school reform. *Education Week,* 52.
3. Rose, L. C., & Gallup, A. M. (2001, September). The 33rd annual Phi Delta Kappan/Gallup poll of the public's attitudes toward the public schools. *Phi Delta Kappan,* 44, 54.
4. Will, G. F. (2002, January 7). "Fixing" education. *Boston Globe,* p. A-15.
5. Stanton, B. (2001, November). Education reform causes major fallout. *Denver Post,* p. 12.
6. Stanton, p. 12.
7. Gill, B., et al. (2002). *Rhetoric versus reality: What we know and what we need to know about vouchers and charter schools* (chap. 2). Santa Monica, CA: RAND Corporation.
8. Auerbach, D. (1998, February/March). Carlo Petrini's digestive system. *Civilization,* 27.
9. Auerbach, p. 27.
10. Oakeshott, M. (1989). Teaching and learning. In T. Fuller (Ed.), *Michael Oakeshott on education* (p. 62). New Haven, CT: Yale University Press.
11. Reid, W. A. (1999). *Curriculum as institution and practice* (p. 8). Mahwah, NJ: Erlbaum.
12. Schwab, J. J. (1978). The practical: A language for curriculum. In I. Westbury & N. Wilkof (Eds.), *Joseph J. Schwab: Science, curriculum, and liberal education* (pp. 287–321). Chicago: University of Chicago Press.
13. Reid, p. 8.
14. Reid, p. 8.
15. Bracey, G. W. (2001, October). The 11th Bracey Report on the condition of public education. *Phi Delta Kappan,* 158.
16. Arenson, K. W. (2002, February 15). Study faults advanced-placement courses. *New York Times,* p. 15.
17. Aizenman, N. C. (2002, March 11). Once-lauded MSPAP undermined by format. *Washington Post,* p. B-1.
18. Aizenman.
19. Quoted in Neave, H. (1990). *The Deming dimension* (p. 151). Knoxville, TN: SPC Press.
20. Rowe, C. (2002, February 20). "In Woodstock, a nonschool with nonteachers. *New York Times,* p. 16.
21. Rowe, p. 16.
22. Sizer, T. (1992). *Horace's school.* Boston: Houghton Mifflin.
23. Wheelock, A. (1994). Chattanooga's Paideia schools: A single track for all—And it's working. *Journal of Negro Education,* 63, 77–92.
24. Meier, D. (1996, September). The big benefits of smallness. *Educational Leadership,* 12.
25. Dearden, R. (1968). *The philosophy of primary education* (p. 68). London: Routledge.
26. Dearden, p. 68.
27. Quoted in French, H. W. (2001, February 25). More sunshine for Japan's overworked students. *New York Times,* p. 18.
28. French, p. 18.

Article 40 Endnotes

1. Carson, A. (1986). *Eros the bittersweet.* Princeton: Princeton University Press. This book will be cited as *EB* in the text for all subsequent references.
2. Dillard, A. (1987). *An American childhood.* New York: Harper and Row. This book will be cited as *AC* in the text for all subsequent references.

3. It is difficult to capture or succinctly define Carson's use of *eros*. Her work, *Eros the Bittersweet*, is an exploration and attempt to gain a clearer understanding of eros. An appropriate but perhaps potentially misleading shorthand definition would be the following: Eros is the paradoxical desire that motivates and inhabits romantic yearning. Others—for example, Birch—write of eros more broadly as yearning and desire. In Carson's work, however, the context is one of romantic love and yearning.

4. Thompkins, J. (1996). *A life in school* (p. 56). Redding, MA: Addison-Wesley. This book will be cited as *LS* in the text for all subsequent references.

5. The last two decades of the last century were an active time for this effort. See Ladwig, J. (1996). *Academic distinctions.* New York: Routledge.

6. Martin, J. R. (1992). *Schoolhome*. Cambridge: Harvard University Press.

7. Hill, K. (1999, Fall).The anointed. *Doubletake,* 79–89. This short story will be cited as *TA* in the text for all subsequent references.

8. Weil, S. (1951). *Waiting for God* (p. 180). New York: G. Putnam's Sons.

9. Iris Murdoch writes tellingly about the connections among beauty, the sacred, and the good. See Murdoch, I. (1973). *The sovereignty of good*. New York: Schocken Books. Another work attempting to discern connections among beauty, truths, and the good is by Wendy Farley. See Farley, W. (1996). *Eros for the other*. University Park: Pennsylvania State University Press.

10. Kidder, T. (1990). *Among schoolchildren*. New York: Avon Books.

INTERNET RESOURCES

General Resources

ASCD (Association of Supervision and Curriculum Development)   www.ascd.org
ASCD offers a multitude of publications and resources of interest to curriculum practitioners.

Journal of Curriculum Studies   www.edu.uwo.ca/jcs
The site will give additional articles on curriculum definition, theorizing, and issues.

Kappa Delta Pi   www.kdp.org
An honor society for educators, this site has links to the Educational Forum archives for additional articles of interest to curriculum studies.

Phi Delta Kappa   www.pdkintl.org
An honor society for educators, this site has links to the Phi Delta Kappan archives for additional articles of interest to curriculum studies.

Teachers College Record   www.tcrecord.org
The site will give additional articles on curriculum definition, theorizing, and issues.

Curriculum Theory

AATC (American Association of Teaching and Curriculum)   http://aatchome.org
The AATC homepage contains information on past and present conferences and links to publications.

American Association for the Advancement of Curriculum Studies
http://calvin.ednet.lsu.edu/~aaacs/index.html
The AAACS homepage contains information on past and present conferences and links to publications.

Curriculum Theory and Practice   www.infed.org/biblio/b-curric.htm
This Web site offers some basic definitions of curriculum.

John Dewey Society   http://johndeweysociety.org
The John Dewey Society is an organization dedicated to the study of Dewey's philosophical beliefs in relation to schools.

Curriculum Definitions/Types and Concepts

Curriculum Alignment   http://pdonline.ascd.org/pd_demo/lesson.cfm?SID=41

Curriculum Blog on What Is Curriculum   http://curricublog.org/2006/10/22/curriclum-what/

Integrated Curriculum   www.nwrel.org/scpd/sirs/8/c016.html;
http://vocserve.berkeley.edu/ST2.1/TowardanIntegrated.html
These Web sites define and illustrate the concept of integrated curriculum.

Types of Curriculum   www.uwsp.edu/education/lwilson/curric/curtyp.htm

Charter/Magnet/School Organization

Block Scheduling   http://killeenroos.com/link/block.htm
This Web site offers models of organizing schools around block schedules.

Charter Schools   www.uscharterschools.org
A Web site discussing charter schools in the United States.

Coalition of Essential Schools   www.essentialschools.org
Ted Sizer's movement to reorganize and restructure schools.

Bill and Melinda Gates Foundation–Education
www.gatesfoundation.org/UnitedStates/Education
The Gates Foundation is dedicating significant funds to school reform, particularly high school reform in the United States.

Magnet Schools   www.magnet.edu/modules/news
This Web site offers information about magnet school programs.

NEA Charter Schools   www.nea.org/charter/index.html
The National Education Association Charter School homepage.

Rethinking Schools   www.rethinkingschools.org
This Web site offers information and links to publications of interest to people interested in school reform.

Small Schools Project   www.smallschoolsproject.org
An offshoot of the Gates ideas, the Small Schools Project promotes small schools as a solution for problems in education.

What Is a Magnet School?   www.publicschoolreview.com/magnet-schools.php
Definitions of magnet schools and their operations.

Character/Moral Education/Peace Education

Association for Moral Education (AME)   www.amenetwork.org

Character Counts   www.charactercounts.org

Character Education Partnership   www.character.org

Education for Global Citizenship   www.oxfam.org.uk/coolplanet/teachers/globciti/index.htm

National Paideia Center   www.paideia.org

PeaceJam Curricula   www.peacejam.org/curricula.htm

Project Wisdom   www.projectwisdom.com

Studies in Moral Education and Development   http://tigger.uic.edu/~lnucci/MoralEd/index.html

Professional Organizations

American Federation of Teachers   www.aft.org

International Society for Technology in Education   www.iste.org

National Association for Multicultural Education   www.nameorg.org

National Association for Music Education   www.menc.org

National Council of Teachers of English   www.ncte.org

National Council of Teachers of Mathematics   www.nctm.org

National Council for the Social Studies   http://socialstudies.org

National Education Association   www.nea.org

National Institute for Urban School Improvement   www.urbanschools.org

National Middle School Association   www.nmsa.org

National Rural Education Association   www.nrea.net

National Science Teachers Association   www.nsta.org

Curriculum Reports

Cardinal Principals of Secondary Education 1918   www.ux1.eiu.edu/~cfrnb/cardprin.html
This report contains curriculum objectives for secondary education.

Goals 2000   www.ncrel.org/sdrs/areas/issues/envrnmnt/stw/sw0goals.htm
Summary of the Goals 2000 Educate America Act.

National Education Technology Standards (NETS)   http://cnets.iste.org
The NETS page offers not only the current technology standards but links to curriculum integration ideas for teachers and curriculum developers.

NCLB (No Child Left Behind)   www.ed.gov/policy/elsec/leg/esea02/index.html
This is the U.S. Department of Education Web site containing the legislation on No Child Left Behind (Elementary and Secondary Act 2001).

SCANS Report   http://wdr.doleta.gov/SCANS
The Secretary's Commission on Achieving Necessary Skills for the workforce report. U.S. Department of Labor. 1992.

Special Education Legislation   www.ed.gov/policy/speced/leg/edpicks.jhtml?src=rt
This U.S. Department of Education Web site contains the legislation for special education, including the IDEA (Individuals with Disabilities Education Act) guidelines.

A Test of Leadership: Charting the Future of U.S. Higher Education (Sept. 2006)
www.ed.gov/about/bdscomm/list/hiedfuture/reports/final-report.pdf
Embedded in this report are recommendations for reforming high school curriculum to meet the needs of postsecondary education.

U.S. Department of Education   www.ed.gov
This Web site can be searched for reports and discussions on school progress and school reform as monitored by the U.S. government.

Curriculum Politics and Issues

The Arts Edge (Kennedy Center) K–12 Standards for Arts Education
http://artsedge.kennedy-center.org/teach/standards.cfm

Arts in Education: New Horizons for Learning
www.newhorizons.org/strategies/arts/front_arts.htm

Center for Civic Education   www.civiced.org

Committee for Children   www.secondstep.org
This Web site contains information on school violence curricula, including antibullying, anti-touching, etc.

Core Curriculum Comes to Clarksville   www.asbj.com/achievement/ci/ci11.html

Council for Global Education   www.globaleducation.org

Creation and Evolution in the Public Schools
http://en.wikipedia.org/wiki/Creation_and_evolution_in_public_education

Global Education: The UN Global Teaching and Learning Project   www.un.org/cyberschoolbus

The Harvard Civil Rights Project (Segregated Schools)
www.civilrightsproject.harvard.edu/research/deseg/separate_schools01.php

Immigration and Education   www.ncela.gwu.edu/resabout/immigration/pathfinder

Keep Schools Safe   www.keepschoolssafe.org

Multicultural Curriculum Suggestions   http://education.byu.edu/diversity/curriculum.html

National Association for Single Sex Public Education   www.singlesexschools.org

Sex Education Curriculum   www.avert.org/sexedu.htm
www.advocatesforyouth.org/sexeducation.htm
www.kff.org/kaiserpolls/pomr0129040th.cfm

Teaching Controversial Issues   www.esrnational.org/sp/we/uw/controversialissues.htm

Teaching Tolerance   www.tolerance.org

Extra- and Co-Curriculum

Answers.com on extracurricular activity definitions, research, etc.
www.answers.com/topic/extracurricular-activity-3

Learn and Serve America   www.learnandserve.org   *This Web site is operated by the YMCA.*

National Athletic Testing System
www.nats.us/?KEY=&DB_OEM_ID=9300&DB_LANG=&IN_SUBSCRIBER_CONTENT=
A Web site detailing a program of standards and tests for high school athletes.

National Federation of High Schools   www.nfhs.org
Excellent links to issues surrounding extracurricular athletics, clubs, and other co-curricular topics.

National High School Coaches Organization   www.hscoaches.org

National Service Learning Clearinghouse   www.servicelearning.org

INDEX

AAAS. *See* American Association for the Advancement of Science

Abuse, curriculum and, 23–26

Academic achievement, sports participation and, 189–193

Academic clubs, adolescent development and, 175–176

Academic ideal, 5–7

Academic year, 12

Accelerated coursework, 92

Accelerated Schools Network, 104

Accountability:
  in charter schools, 106–109
  market/client, 108
  pressures for, 284–286

Activities, adolescent development and, 171–182

Activity analysis, 45

Adler, J., 237

Adler, Mortimer, 326

Adolescence, social development and, 60–61

Adolescent development, and extracurricular activities, 171–182

Adolescent needs, curriculum and, 59–67

Afghanistan, war atrocities in, 139

African-American schools. *See* All-black schools

After-school programs, educational development and, 183–188

Age grading, 13

Agenda for Action, An (NCTM), 144

Aikin, Wilford, 60

Alberty, Harold, 61, 62, 65

Alexander, K., 270

Algozzine, B., 256

All-black schools, 83–90

Allen, Frederick, 196

Alm, John, 211

American Association for the Advancement of Science (AAAS), 241, 242

American Association of School Administrators, 92

American Association of University Professors, 217

American Childhood, An (Dillard), 329, 330

American music, 163–168

Amin, Idi, 138

Anointed, The (Hill), 337

Antz (movie), 129, 130

Anyon, Jean, 46

Apple, Michael, 55, 148

Aristotle, 15, 52, 79

Arnold, Matthew, 6

Arnold, M. L., 246

Art, socialization and, 137–138

Artistry, in teaching, 16–17

ASCD. *See* Association for Supervision and Curriculum Development

Assessment, curriculum and instruction, 283–289

Assignment: Media Literacy, 133

Association for Supervision and Curriculum Development (ASCD), 31, 297

Atrocities, of war, 138–139

Atwater, M., 265, 270

Ault, C., 264

Ault, M. J., 256

Baker, Frank, 133

Baker, Maud C., 84

Baldwin, Steve, 150

Bannot de Condillac, Etienne, 7

Banzhaf, John, 211

Barbanel, Josh, 233

Barber, B. L., 179

Barzun, Jacques, 79
Basic Principles of Curriculum and Instruction (Tyler), 60
Bass, Hyman, 151
Beane, James, 292, 295, 296
Beatles, The, 167
Behavioral intervention pilot project, 312
    case study, 313–314
    experiential accounts, 315–316
    implementation challenges, 316
    outcome measures, 314–315
Behe, M. J., 235, 236
Bell, T. H., 145
Bellagio Diversity and Citizenship Education Project, 301–302
Bentz, B., 264
Berman, Nina, 195
Berry, Chuck, 166, 168
Bestor, A. E., 66
Bigelow, Bill, 199, 200
Black schools, 83–90
Blackwell, Otis, 167
Blumberg, R., 258
Bobbitt, Franklin, 45, 50
Bode, Boyd, 50, 60–61, 64, 66, 67, 73–74
Book It!, 211
Bookwatch Reviews (National Center for Science Education), 238
Borzellieri, Frank, 233
Box Tops for Education, 213
Boyes, Andrea, 209
Boy Scouts, 216
Bracey, Gerald, 324
Braddock, J. H. H., 191
Brady, Marion, 292
Braun, C., 265
Bridges Program, 185
Brodhagen, Barbara, 295
Brown, Roy, 167
Brown (1954 court decision), 83, 89–90
Bruner, Jerome, 15
Bryan, L, 265
Buhrmann, H. G., 190
Burke, J. F., 249
Bush, George W., 195, 221, 222, 322

Cable in the Classroom, 212
California Academy of Liberal Studies, 98
California Achievement Test (CAT), 191, 192
California Department of Education, 149

California Learning Assessment System, 150
Calvert, John, 239
Cardinal Principles of Secondary Education, The (NEA), 65
Carnegie Units, 158
Carson, Anne, 329, 331, 332, 336
CAT. *See* California Achievement Test
CCER. *See* Committee on College Entrance Requirements (CCER)
Center for Multicultural Education, 302
Center for Science and Culture, 236
Center for the Renewal of Science and Culture (CRSC), 236
CERU. *See* Commercialism in Education Research Unit
Challenge of Numbers, A (National Research Council), 147
Champion Avenue School, 84
Chancer, Lynn, 137
Chandler, T.J.L., 192
Character, teaching of, 215–216
Character Counts, 219, 223
Character education, politics of, 215–224
Charter, W. W., 50
Charter schools, 81–82,101–111
Chemistry, as central science, 155–162
"Child centeredness," 8
Children of the Rainbow, 225–234
Christian, Scott, 294
Citizenship:
    assimilationist notion of, 299–300
    education, 300–302
City University of New York, 95
Clark, Kenneth, 89
Clark, Larry, 88
Coalition of Essential Schools, 104
Cognition, 18
Cole, Johnetta, 86
Collicott, J. G., 86
Collins, A. C., 265
Collins, Judy, 24
Coltrane, John, 72
Columbus Board of Education, 84
Commercialism in Education Research Unit (CERU), 209, 210, 213
Commission on the Relation of School and College, 60, 61
Commission on the Secondary School Curriculum (CSSC), 60, 61, 62, 64
Committee of Ten (CoT), 156–159, 161, 275, 325

Committee on College Entrance Requirements (CCER), 158
Committee on Curriculum-Making, 73
Communities of Character, 222
Community, schools and, 81–82
Community colleges, integration with high schools, 91–99
Community of Caring, 223
Community Oriented Policy (COP) program, 187
Competition, among schools, 16
Concept formation, 18
Content:
    in schools, 17
    standards, 203
Contexts, identity formation, 178–180
Cook-Sather, Alison, 294
Cooper, William J., 93
COP. *See* Community Oriented Policy program
Copernicus, 79
Coppin, Fannie Jackson, 84
Cosmopolitanism, 303
Costenbader, V., 309
CoT. *See* Committee of Ten
Coursework:
    accelerated, 92
    flexible, 92
Covello, Leonard, 300
Crabwalk (Grass), 141
Creative coping, 28–29
Critical pedagogy, 55–56
Critical reconstructionist, 42, 46
Critical thinking, 135–141
Cronin, M. E., 256
Crowley, Mary, 233
CRSC. *See* Center for the Renewal of Science and Culture
Crudup, Arthur (Big Boy), 167
CSSC. *See* Commission on the Secondary School Curriculum
CSSC Committee on Adolescents, 61
Cuban, Larry, 230, 275
Cultural history, 167–168
Cultural identification:
    developing, 302–303
    stages of, 303–304
Culture of learning, 36–37
Cummins, Mary, 230, 231, 233–234
Curricular decisions, students and, 294–295
Curricular design, 291–297

Curricular reductionism, 286
Curricular understandings, psychological prejudices and, 62–63
Curriculum:
    adaptation, 268–269
    adolescent needs and, 59–67
    aims of, 205–206
    alignment of, 27–32
    in an all-Black school, 87–89
    analysis of, 28
    assessments and, 204
    in charter schools, 103–106
    clarity of documentation, 204
    content standards and assessments, 206
    control of, 21–22
    design, 255–262, 291–297
    development of, 69–74
    enrichment, 28
    excluded, 29, 31
    field, 69–74
    future directions of, 206–207
    global nature of, 251–254
    hidden, 29, 30–31
    human agency and, 49–58
    ideology in, 72–74
    importance of, 203–207
    Individuals with Disabilities Education Act Amendments of 1997 (IDEA) and, 256–257
    instruction and assessment, 283–289
    integration, 295–297
    interactions of, 30
    in kindergarten, 117–118
    learned, 30, 31
    mastery, 28–29
    mathematics in, 114
    meaning of, 21–22
    media literacy in, 132–133
    multicultural, 225–234
    organic, 28
    organization of, 15–16, 81–82
    practice, 74
    problems with, 291–297
    radical, 55–56
    reading in, 113–114
    recommended, 29, 31
    reform, 113–114
    relevance of, 23–26
    renaissance in, 69–74
    in rural schools, 273–279

school reform and, 19
science in, 114, 235–242, 271
second, 37
shifts, 251–254
supported, 29, 31
taught, 30–31
technology in, 50–52, 113–114
tested, 29, 31
theory, 39–40, 69–74
thinking skills in, 114
types of, 29–30
written, 28, 29, 31
Curriculum and Evaluation Standards for School
    Mathematics. See Standards (NCTM)
"Curriculum as experience," 25
Curriculum Books: The First Eighty Years
    (Schubert), 42
Curriculum-curriculum, 41–47
Curwin, R., 308

Daddy's Roommate, 230, 232
Dark Ghetto (Clark), 89
Daro, Phil, 153
Darwin, Charles, 235, 236
DAT. *See* Differential Aptitude Test
Davis, Cynthia, 239
Davis, M., 61
Dayton Early College Academy (DECA), 98
DCFL. *See* Department of Children, Families,
    and Learning
Dean, C. B., 246
Dearden, Robert, 327
DECA. *See* Dayton Early College Academy
Defeating Darwinism by Opening Minds (Johnson), 236
DeHart, Roger, 238
Dembski, W. A., 235
Deming, W. Edwards, 325
Demographic transformations:
    origins of, 246–247
    Plains City, 245–249
    promoting dialogue, 247–248
Department of Children, Families, and Learning
    (DCFL), 306, 312, 315
de Tocqueville, Alexis, 220
Development:
    ideal of, 7–8
    social, 60–61
Dewey, John, 17, 43, 73, 217, 294–295, 322, 325
Díaz-Rico, L. T., 247
Dickens, Charles, 197

Differential Aptitude Test (DAT), 174, 175
Dillard, Annie, 329–338
DiMarco, Maureen, 150
Discovery Institute, 236, 237
Dishion, T. I., 176
Diversity, teaching for, 299–304
Dobie, Kathy, 196, 197
Domino, Fats, 166
Dossey, John, 147
Douglass, Frederick, 89
Doyle, P. M., 256
Drachsler, Julius, 300
DuBois, Rachel Davis, 300
Dunbar High School, 88
Durbin, B. B., 190
Durkin, Delores, 116
Dylan, Bob, 166

Early college high schools, 97–99
Eastin, Delaine, 150
Eby, F., 97
Eccles, J. S., 178, 179
Eckert, P., 177
Edison Project, 104
Educated Mind, The (Egan), 10
Education:
    assumptions of, 1
    contentiousness of, 3–10
    indoctrination vs., 5
    in-service, 41
    K–14, 91–99
    liberal, 93
    progressive, 39–40
    reform, 16
    segregated, 83–90
    special, 255–262
Educational ideas/ideals:
    language development, 3–5
    literacy invention, 5–7
    natural development, 7–8
Edwards, J. David, 252
Edwards v. Aguillard, 236, 242
Eells, Walter Crosby, 94–95, 96
Egan, Kieran, 10
Eight-Year Study, 59–67
Einstein, Albert, 42–43, 79
Eisner, Elliot, 44, 53–55
Elementary and Secondary Education Act (ESEA).
    See No Child Left Behind (NCLB) Act of 2001
Emery, Kathy, 292

Engle v. Vitale, 218
Enlightenment, 7
Ennis, C., 270
Enrichment curriculum, 28
Entwisle, D., 270
Epstein, M. H., 256
Erikson, E. H., 178
Eros the Bittersweet (Carson), 329
Esthetic humanism, 53–55
Ethics, human agency and, 49–50
E.T. (movie), 78
Evaluation practices, school reform and, 19.
    See also Tests
Everybody Counts (National Research Council), 147, 148
Excluded curriculum, 29, 31
Experientialist, 42, 46–47
Extracurricular activities, adolescent development
    and, 171–182

Fallibility, 57–58
"False consciousness," 55
Farr, Roger, 207
Ferguson, P. M., 258
Field Book of Ponds and Streams, The, 330, 331
Field Trip Factory, 212
Fine, G. A., 176
Flexible coursework, 92
Fodor, Jerry, 4
Foreign language instruction, 251–252
Frank, Anne, 24
Freed, Alan, 167
Free will, 56–57
Freud, Sigmund, 79
Friedrich, Ernst, 138
Funding, private sources for schools, 209–214
Futures for Kids, 212

Gaddy, B. B., 246
Galileo, 79
Gardner, C., 270
Gender, connection with violence, 137
General education, science in, 61–62
Geography, instruction in, 252
Georgia Public Education Report Card, 124
Gerber, S. B., 191
GFSA. *See* Gun Free Schools Act
Gholson, R. E., 190
Ghost of Tom Joad, The (Springsteen), 166
Gilchrist, George, 238
Global citizenship, teaching for, 299–304

Global identifications, 302–303
Global Science and Technology Week, 253
Gloria Goes to Gay Pride, 230
Glover, Jonathan, 139
Gold, Eva, 294
Goldberg, A. D., 192
Gore, Al, 222
Gottlieb, J., 258, 261
Grading, age, 13
Grant, James P., 24
Grapes of Wrath, The (Steinbeck), 166
Grass, Günter, 141
Graves, Donald, 293
Gray Oral Reading Test, 121
Greeks, educational beliefs of, 14
Grotzer, Tina, 35–36
Gun Free Schools Act (GFSA), 307
Gun Free School Zone Act, 307
Gunning, Thomas, 118, 120
Guthrie, Woody, 166
Gutmann, A., 304

Haas, T., 273
Hagen, Tim, 240
Hale, Janice, 88
Hall, E. T., 248
Hall, G. Stanley, 93, 95
Hamburg, David, 295
Hamilton, Alexander, 326
Harlem Renaissance, 166
Hart, T. A., 147
Hartshorne, H., 217, 218
Harvard Graduate School of Education, 35
Havel, Vaclav, 78
Havelock, Eric, 5
Havighurst, Robert, 61
Hawkins, R., 191
Hayes, William, 85
Healy, Timothy, 95
Heart of Wisdon, 238
Heather Has Two Mommies, 230, 232
Hedges, Chris, 136, 199
Hegel, G.W.F., 50
Herbert, Bob, 197, 198
Hetland, Lois, 36
Hidden curriculum, 29, 30–31
High schools:
    integration with community colleges, 91–99
    military recruitment in, 195–200
    science sequence in, 155–162

Hill, Kathleen, 337
Hippie Day, 167
Hirsch, E. D., 104, 151, 152
History:
    cultural, 167–168
    world, 252
Hitler, Adolf, 78, 138
Hoffman, J. L., 278
Hollingworth, L. S., 60–61
Holly, Buddy, 167
Hopkins, L. Thomas, 41
Hughes, R. T., 236
Hull, J. Dan, 65
Human agency, curriculum and, 49–58
Humanism, esthetic, 53–55
Hume, David, 50
Hunger, curriculum and, 23–26
Hunter, G. W., 159, 160
Hunter-gatherers, 3–5
Huntsman What Quarry (Millay), 75
Hussein, Saddam, 138
Hutchins, Robert M., 93

Ibsen, Henrik, 79
IDEA. *See* Individuals with Disabilities
    Education Act (IDEA) Amendments
    of 1977
Identity:
    formation, 178–180
    politics, 220
Ideology, in curriculum, 72–74
I Dream of Peace (UNICEF), 24
IEP. *See* Individualized education program
Iliad, The, 139
Immigration Reform Act, 299
*Implementing a Multicultural Kindergarten
    Curriculum,* 226
Inclusion, 255
Individualized education program (IEP), 260
Individuals with Disabilities Education Act (IDEA)
    Amendments of 1977 (IDEA),
    255–257, 261, 262
Indoctrination, vs. education, 5
Information age, 75–79
Information overload, 75–79
In-service education, 41
Instruction:
    curriculum and assessment, 283–289
    foreign language, 251–252
    geography, 252

world history, 252
See also Curriculum
Intellectual traditionalist, 42, 45
Intelligent Design, 235–242
International Education Week, 253
International Slow Food Congress, 322
Iraq, invasion of, 136
Ithaca College, 129

Jacob, Bill, 151
James, William, 136
Jobs for the Future, 94, 97
Joekel, R. G., 190
John Burroughs School, 60
Johnson, P. E., 236
Johnson, Tyson, III, 196
Jones, Faustine, 88
Jordan, David Starr, 93
Joseph, Marion, 151
Joyce, Bruce, 118
JROTC. *See* Junior Reserve Officers' Training Corps
Juel, Connie, 116
Junior Reserve Officers' Training Corps (JROTC),
    196, 197
Just Communities, 219
Justice, in secondary schools, 305–317

Kaczynski, Theodore, 218
Kahne, J., 220
Kalibala, Evelyn, 232
Kallen, Horace M., 300
Kant, Immanuel, 49
Kids as Customers (McNeal), 214
Kindergarten, reading in, 115–122
Klein, David, 150, 152
Klein, Jessie, 137
Kliebard, Hebert, 51–52, 59
Kliebard, H. M., 274
Knowledge:
    definition of, 14
    teaching of, 33–37
    theoretical, 52
Knowledge arts, 33–37
Kohlberg, Lawrence, 217, 219
Koos, Leonard, 91–92, 94–95, 96
Kozol, Jonathan, 24
Krauss, Lawrence, 240
Krieg dem Kriege! (Friedrich), 138
Kymlicka, Will, 300
K–14 education, 91–99

LaGuardia Community College, 91, 93, 94–97
la Momposina, Toto, 165
Langer, Suzanne, 53–54
Language, development of, 3–5
Larson, E. I., 237
Larson, Yvonne, 150
Learned curriculum, 30, 31
Learners, life-long, 297
Learning:
    culture of, 36–37
    in teaching, 329–339
    love of, 329–330
Lederman, D., 190
Lenin, Vladimir, 78
Leo, John, 231, 232
Leo-nyquist, D., 277
LeShan, Lawrence, 136
Levi, Primo, 140
Levine, Arthur, 321–327
Lewis, B. F., 265, 271
Lewis, Ceci, 294
Lewis, Jermaine, 195, 196, 200
Lewis, Jerry Lee, 167
Liberal education, 93
Lickona, Thomas, 216
Lieberman, Janet, 93, 95–96
Lieberman, L. M., 255, 256
Life-long learners, 297
Linn, Marcia, 34–35
Literacy, 14
    education, in secondary schools, 123–127
    invention of, 5–7
    media, 129–134
    skills, in kindergarten, 115–122
Little Richard, 167
Locke, John, 7, 79
Luddites, 77
Lyman, Frankie, 167

MACOS. See Man: A Course of Study
Madison, B. L., 147
Magliozzi, Tom, 292
Mahoney, J. L., 172, 173
Mainstreaming, 255
Make the Peace, 313
Man: A Course of Study (MACOS), 145, 146
Market/client accountability, 108
Markson, S., 309
Marsalis, Wynton, 164
Martin, Jane Roland, 336

Martin, Octavia, 86, 87
Marx, Karl, 55, 78
Maryland School Performance Assessment Program
    (MSPAP), 324
Mastery curriculum, 28–29
*Mathematical Framework for California Public
    Schools, Kindergarten through Grade 12*
    (California Department of Education), 149
Mathematical Science Education Board, 147
Mathematics curriculum, 114
Math wars, 143–154
May, M. A., 217, 218
MC. *See* Monochronic time
McCall, H. Carl, 232
McCauley, M., 270
McClellan, B. E., 217, 218
McGuffey's Reader, 273
MCHS. *See* Middle-College High School
McIntyre, T., 256
McNeal, James, 214
Measurement, accountability and, 284–286
*Media Construction of War: A Critical Reading of
    History*, 133
Media literacy, 129–134
Media Literacy Clearinghouse (Web site), 133
Mee, Cunthia, 295
Meek, L. H., 66
Megginson, Robert, 152
Meier, Deborah, 326
Mendler, A., 308
Merrell, F., 248
Meskimen, L., 264
Mexifornia (Hanson), 246
Meyer, Stephen, 240
Michigan Study of Adolescent Life Transitions
    (MSALT), 173–174, 179, 180
Middle-College High School (MCHS), 91–92, 93, 94–97
Middle-School Cadet Corps (MSCC), 196, 197
Military recruitment, in high schools, 195–200
Millay, Edna St. Vincent, 75–76
Miller, Kenneth, 240
Ming, Yao, 211
Mitchell, John Arnett, 84–86, 87
Modeled dishonesty, 286
Mohs' scale, 331
Monochronic time (MC), 248
Monroe, Bill, 167
Montaigne, Michel de, 6
Moore, D., 306
Moore, G. E., 50

Moral intelligence, 50, 57
More, Thomas, 326
Morgan, Ann Haven, 331
Mosner, Joseph, 196
Mott Foundation, 183
MSALT. *See* Michigan Study of Adolescent Life
    Transitions
MSCC. *See* Middle School Cadet Corps
MSPAP. *See* Maryland School Performance
    Assessment Program
Multicultural citizenship, 302
Multicultural curriculum, 225–234
Multicultural education, 300
Multicultural literacy, 301
Multilogue, 42
Music, American, 163–168
Myers, Steven, 232
Myths America Lives By (Hughes), 236

NAACP. *See* National Association for the
    Advancement of Colored People
Nachtigal, P., 273
NAEP. *See* National Assessment of Educational
    Progress
Nakkula, Michael, 98
Narratives, for school organization, 79
National Assessment of Educational Progress
    (NAEP), 124, 126
National Association for the Advancement of
    Colored People (NAACP), 217
National Center for Educational Statistics
    (NCES), 190
National Center for Science Education, 237
National Commission on Excellence in Education,
    145, 160, 321
National Council of Teachers of Mathematics
    (NCTM), 30, 144, 147, 153
National Education Association (NEA), 92, 325
National Education Longitudinal Study
    (NELS), 180, 190, 191
National Geographic Society, 252
National identifications, developing, 302–303
National Research Council (NRC), 116, 147
National Science Foundation (NSF), 69, 144
Nation at Risk, A (National Commission on
    Excellence in Education), 145, 160, 321
Natural development, 7–8
Nazis, war atrocities committed by, 140
NCES. *See* National Center for Educational
    Statistics

NCTM. *See* National Council of Teachers of
    Mathematics
NEA. *See* National Education Association
Needs:
    classification of, 63
    concept of, 64
NELS. *See* National Education Longitudinal Study
Neo-Marxist analysis, 55–56
Nesin, Gert, 295
Newcomers High School, 226
New Deal, 166
Newman, J. H., 246
Newton, Isaac, 79, 326
Nishida, Kitaro, 139
No Child Left Behind (NCLB) Act of 2001,
    114, 198, 204–207, 222, 239, 246, 284, 286, 288
Noddings, N., 220
No Gods to Serve (Postman), 79
Norman, O., 264
Northern Lights School District, 115–116
November, Alan, 133
NRC. *See* National Research Council
NSF. *See* National Science Foundation
Numeracy, 14
Nussbaum, M., 303

Oakeshott, Michael, 323
Obiakor, F. E., 256
Office of Juvenile Justice and Delinquency
    Prevention, 185
Of Pandas and People (Davis and Kenyon), 238
Ogbu, J., 270
Ohanian, Susan, 292
Olson, Josh, 195
Organic curriculum, 28
Outcomes:
    meaningful, 292–293
    measuring, 13
Owens-Fink, Deborah, 241

Paley, William, 237
Paris Peace Conference, 137
Parker, W. C., 220
Parks, Rosa, 220
Partnership for Family Involvement in
    Education, 185
Pasadena High School, 95
Pasadena Junior College, 95
Past Imperfect: History According to the Movies, 133
Patton, J. R., 256

PC. *See* Polychronic time

PEA. *See* Progressive Education Association

Pearson, Ruthene, 87–88

Pedagogy:
  critical, 55–56
  of poverty, 271
  school reform and, 19

Peer contexts, activities as, 177–178

Peers:
  academic, 178
  risky, 178

Pennock, R. T., 241

Performance rewards, in charter schools, 108–109

Peters, Richard, 49, 52

Phantom Tollbooth, The, 37

Philipsen, Maike, 89–90

Phronesis, 15

Piaget, Jean, 8, 217

Picture Word Inductive Model, 117, 119, 120, 121

Pieters, Charles E., 86

Pinar, W. F., 70

Pitts, V. R., 265

Pizzini, E. L., 265

Plains City (school case study), 245–249

Plato, 5–8, 49, 54

Plyer v. Doe, 246

Polanyi, Michael, 14

Politics, of character education, 215–224

Polloway, E. A., 256, 258, 261

Pol Pot, 138

Polychronic time (PC), 248

Postman, Neil, 138

Poverty, curriculum and, 23–26

Powell, Colin, 196

Practical, The (Schwab), 323

Practical wisdom, 52

Practice, in curriculum, 74

Practitioners, scientific knowledge and, 15

Prejudices, psychological, 62–63

Presley, Elvis, 167

President's Commission on Higher Education, 92, 96

Preventing Reading Difficulties in Young Children (National Research Council), 116

Principles and Standards for School Mathematics (National Council of Teachers of Mathematics), 153

Professional development, teachers and, 105–106

Progressive education, 39–40

Progressive Education Association (PEA), 60, 61, 66

Progressive Education at the Crossroads (Bode), 65

Progressivism, 7–8

Project Look Sharp, 129–134

Project Zero, 35

Psychological prejudices, curricular understandings and, 62–63

Ptolemy, 79

Public schools, with instructional focus, 252–253

Purple Hearts (Berman), 195, 200

Purposeful reading, 207

Quirk, J. T., 190

Race, in American music, 164–166

Radical curriculum, 55–56

Rage Against the Machine, 166

Rainbow Curriculum, 202, 232–234

Ravitch, Diane, 230

Reading:
  curriculum, 113–114
  in kindergarten, 115–122
  programs, in secondary schools, 123–127

Recommended curriculum, 29, 31

Reform, school, 16, 18–19

Rehberg, R. A., 176

Reid, William, 323

Reidelbach, Linda, 240

Remarque, Erich Maria, 140

Reorganizing Secondary Education (Thayer, Zachry, and Kotinsky), 64

Restorative justice, 306, 309, 311–312

Rewards, for performance, 108–109

Rhapsodies in Black: Music and Words from the Harlem Renaissance (records), 166

Riesman, D., 97

Riley, Richard, 152

Rockefeller, Nelson, 230

Roman, Joe, 240, 242

Romberg, Thomas, 147

Rosen, L., 149

Rousseau, Jean-Jacques, 6, 7–8

Royster, D. A., 191

Ruddick, Sara, 137

Rural schools, 273–279

Ruse, M., 235

Rwanda, schools in, 24

Sarajevo, education in, 23–24

Saunders, Debra, 150

Savage Inequities (Kozol), 24

Savannah-Chatham County School District, 124

SBM. *See* School-based management
Schmidt, William, 151
School-based management (SBM), 105–106, 111
"School Day" (song), 168
Schooling:
    assumptions about, 11–19
    knowledge arts in, 34–35
School Recruiting Program Handbook
    (U.S. Army), 198
Schools:
    aims of, 18–19
    all-Black, 83–90
    charter, 81–82, 101–111
    commercialization of, 210–214
    community and, 81–82
    competition among, 16
    content in, 17
    disruptive behavior and disciplinary alternatives,
        307–310
    organization of, 79
    private funding sources and, 209–214
    reform of, 16, 18–19
    restorative principles and practices in, 310–312
    rural, 273–279
    test scores and, 17
    urban, 83–90, 255–262
    zero tolerance in, 307–310, 312
    See also Secondary schools
Schwab, Joseph, 14–15, 52–54, 70–71, 264, 323, 325
Science:
    classes, and the Committee of Ten, 159–161
    curriculum, 114, 235–242, 271
    general education and, 61–62
    high school sequence, 155–162
    learner characteristics, 263–271
Science in General Education, 61, 63
Scientific knowledge:
    application of, 14–15
    of teaching practices, 16–17
Scott, Eugene C., 237, 238, 241
Sebald, W. G., 140–141
Secondary schools:
    chemistry in, 156
    justice in, 305–317
    literacy education in, 123–127
Second curriculum, 37
Second Great Awakening, 236
Second International Mathematics Study, 145
Segregated education, 83–90

Self-determination. *See* Free will
Self-evaluation. *See* Fallibility
Self-expression. *See* Moral intelligence
Self-understanding, through critical thinking,
    135–141
Service learning, 221
Shakespeare, William, 79
Shenker, Joseph, 93, 95
Shepardson, D. P., 265
Sherner, Michael, 152
Showers, Beverly, 118
Shultz, Jeffrey, 294
Shweder, R., 219
Silliker, S. A., 190
Simmons, H., 270
Simpson, E. L., 219
Simpson, O. J., 78
Singer, Susan, 212
6-4-4 plan, 91–99
Sizer, Theodore, 326
Slow School Association, 326
Slow school movement, 321–327
Smith, Carol, 292, 295
Smith, J. D., 260
Smith, T. E. C., 256
Smoll, F. L., 180
Soble, Joan, 36
Social behaviorist, 42, 45
Social democracy, 67
Social development, adolescence and, 60–61
Socialization, 3–5, 137–138
Social justice, teaching for, 299–304
Social transformations, in Plains City case, 245–249
Soltz, D. F., 190
Sontag, Susan, 137–138
Soviets, war atrocities committed by, 139
Special education, 255–262
Specialization, problems with, 287–289
Spencer, Herbert, 6, 23
Spielberg, Steven, 78, 79
Sports participation, academic achievement
    and, 189–193
Springsteen, Bruce, 166
Sputnik, 69, 144, 253
Stages of Cultural Development Typology, 303
Stalin, Joseph, 138
Standardized tests, in charter schools, 107
Standards (NCTM), 147–153
Stanton, Billie, 322

Stattin, H., 176
Steele, C., 270
Stegman, M., 190, 191
Stephens, L. J., 190, 191
Stone, Albert, 88
"Structure of the disciplines" movement, 52–53
Students:
    curricular decisions and, 294–295
    learning content, 295–296
    sports participation by, 190–191
"Subject centeredness," 8
Subjects, affective and cognitive, 18
"Success for All," 276
Sullivan, E. V., 219
Supervisors, role of, 16
Supported curriculum, 29, 31
Swidler, S. A., 278
Swofford, Anthony, 136, 138

Taft, Bob, 240
Taught curriculum, 30–31
Taught/learned gap, 31–32
Taylor, Charles, 49–50
Teachers:
    in an all-Black school, 86–87
    beliefs of, 263–271
    content and, 17
    professional development of, 105–106
    role of, 21–22
    time with students, 12–13
Teaching:
    artistry in, 16–17
    for social justice, global citizenship, and
        diversity, 299–304
    goal of, 14–15
"Teaching for Understanding" framework, 36
Team sports, in adolescent development, 175
Technology curriculum, 113–114
Terawaki, Ken, 327
Tested curriculum, 29, 31
Tests:
    as measurements, 13, 17
    preparation for, 286
    standardized, 107
    See also Evaluation practices
Thayer, V. T., 60–67
Theobald, John P., 231, 277
Theoretical knowledge, 52
Theory, in curriculum, 74

Thinking skills, 114
Thompson, Gordon, 333
Thompson, William Oxley, 84, 87
Tishman, Shari, 35
Tompkins, Jane, 335, 336, 337
Tuner, Joe, 166–167
Twenty-First Century Community Learning
    Centers, 184
Tyler, Ralph, 50–52, 53, 93
Tyler rationale, 50–52

Unabomber, 218
UNICEF, 24
University of Chicago, 52
Uno, G.E.L., 238
Urban League, 85
Urban schools, 83–90, 255–262
U.S. Department of Education, 96, 190, 257
U.S. Office of Education, 65

Vallas, Paul, 184
Values clarification movement, 218, 219
Vietnam, war atrocities in, 139
Vygotsky, L. S., 10

Waldorf schools, 12–13
Walker, Eugene, 85
War:
    attractions of, 136–137
    critical thinking about, 135–141
    curriculum and, 23–26
    reality of, 198–200
Watkins, William, 87
Wechsler, H. S., 96–97
Wedge Strategy, The, 236, 237
Weed, K. Z., 247
Weil, Simone, 139, 337
Weindling, Elissa, 232
Weingartner, Charles, 138
Wells, Jonathon, 240
Westheimer, J., 220
Who Are We? (Huntington), 247
Wiggins, J., 270
Wilhelm Gustloff, 141
Will, George, 232, 322
Wills, Bob, 166
Wilson, Pete, 150, 151
Winfield, L. F., 191
Wisdom, practical, 52

Wittchen, Ed, 116
Wolery, M., 256
Women, peace movements by, 137
Women's International League for Peace and
    Freedom, 137
Woodhull, J. F., 159
Woodward, N. Jeanne, 88
Woolf, Virginia, 137
Wright, Lucien, 85

Written curriculum, 29, 31
WWII, war atrocities in, 139–140

Yates, M., 178
Youniss, J., 178

Zachry, Caroline, 61–66
Zaremba, Adam, 196
Zero tolerance, in schools, 307–310, 312

About the Editors

Marcella L. Kysilka, Professor Emerita in the College of Education at the University of Central Florida, received her bachelor's degree from Ohio State University, her master's from Kent State University, and her Ph.D. in curriculum and instruction from the University of Texas at Austin. Dr. Kysilka has held many leadership roles in professional organizations. She has been president of Kappa Delta Pi, editor of the *Educational Forum*, and associate editor of the *Journal for Curriculum and Supervision*. She has also served on the board of directors and Leadership Council of the Association for Supervision and Curriculum Development and as president of Florida Association for Supervision and Curriculum Development, president of the International Study Association for Teachers and teaching factotum for professors of curriculum, and executive secretary of the American Association for Curriculum and Teaching. Dr. Kysilka currently serves as editor of the *Florida Educational Leadership* journal. Dr. Kysilka has published over 60 journal articles and eight books. While at the University of Central Florida, Dr. Kysilka served as a full professor in the Educational Studies Department, as associate dean of academic affairs, director of educational research, assistant chair to the Educational Studies Department, and as coordinator of the Curriculum and Instruction Doctoral Program. She currently is a consultant with the P.A.C.E. High School in Cincinnati, Ohio, a school for underachieving inner-city students.

Barbara Slater Stern is an associate professor at James Madison University. She received her bachelor's degree from the University of Rhode Island, her master's degree from the University of Louisville, and her doctoral degree in curriculum and instruction from the University of Central Florida. Dr. Stern teaches courses in curriculum, middle and secondary curriculum and co-curriculum, and methods of teaching middle and secondary social studies. She is a member of several professional organizations, including the American Association of Teaching and Curriculum, Professors of Curriculum, the American Educational Research Association, the College and University Faculty Assembly, and the National Council for the Social Studies. Her research interests include the history of the curriculum field, the history of teaching history/social studies, and the integration of technology into the curriculum in general and social studies in particular. She is the author of *Social Studies: Standards, Meaning and Understanding* (2002). She serves on the editorial board of the Kappa Delta Pi *Forum*. Dr. Stern is currently serving as editor of *Curriculum and Teaching Dialogue*, the journal of the American Association of Teaching and Curriculum.